The
A+
Cram Sheet

This Cram Sheet contains the distilled key facts about A+. As the last thing you do before you enter the testing room, review this information, paying special attention to those areas you feel you need to remember the most. You can transfer any of these facts from your head onto a blank sheet of paper when you enter the test room.

MOTHERBOARDS

1. The ATX motherboard was an open standard and introduced built-in, double-high I/O connectors. The CPU was relocated toward the back of the board, near the cooling fan, for better cooling and accessibility.

2. The two basic expansion card types are the Industry Standard Architecture (ISA), used on XT, AT, and ATX boards, and the PCI bus. ISA is used less and less these days.

3. XT boards use an 8-bit ISA bus. AT and ATX boards use a two-part 8-bit/16-bit ISA bus, together with a PCI bus (typically, four slots).

4. 16-bit ISA bus slots are usually long and in two parts, and tend to be near one edge of a motherboard. If a slot is shorter and in one piece, it's probably an 8-bit ISA slot. Toward the middle of the board, it's PCI.

5. A PCI bus is a 32-bit/64-bit bus specification with smaller slots, generally nearer the center of a motherboard. PCI slots can sometimes be interwoven between the ISA slots: ISA, then PCI, then ISA again, and so forth.

6. CMOS is a battery-backed chip that contains system settings, configured from a hot-key combination at boot-up. CMOS stores passwords. The best way to recover from a forgotten CMOS password is to disconnect the chip's power supply, thereby clearing all settings. A badly configured CMOS (where the hardware attached is set with the wrong name) usually means a device mismatch error.

7. Jumpers are used to set motherboard clock speeds. 1 hertz (Hz) is one cycle per second, or one clock tick. 1 megahertz (MHz) is one million cycles (clock ticks) per second. Motherboard speeds should match the fastest CPU speed. Jumpers can also configure a master/slave IDE or EIDE drive. ATA is a specification.

8. The power supply takes in 110 volts (AC) and typically puts out 12 and 5 volts (DC). Sometimes jumpers can set a voltage regulator module (VRM) on the system board to provide other voltages. Many processors continue to use 3.3 volts.

PROCESSORS/MEMORY

9. Real Mode originates with the 8086 processor, when the chip could address only 1MB of real memory addresses. The first 1MB of physical memory is called *conventional memory* and can be split into low memory (IRQ tables), application memory (640KB), and upper and high memory (around 370KB).

7. ERU.EXE is used to back up the system registration (Registry). SCANREGW.EXE is used to check the Registry for structural integrity. LOGVIEW.EXE opens Windows 9x startup logs. BOOTLOG.TXT contains startup error conditions. SYSEDIT.EXE opens startup configuration files.

48. The five main Registry handles are:
- HKEY_LOCAL_MACHINE
- HKEY_CLASSES_ROOT
- HKEY_CURRENT_CONFIG
- HKEY_CURRENT_USER
- HKEY_USERS

49. Safe Mode loads VGA drivers and keyboard drivers, but no network drivers. F8 interrupts the startup and presents a text Startup menu.

50. Windows 2000 and Windows NT use NTLDR.COM to control the boot process. Other files are BOOT.INI, NTDETECT.COM, NTOSKRNL.EXE, HAL.DLL, SYSTEM.INI, SMSS.EXE, WINLOGON.EXE, and LSASS.EXE.

NETWORKING

51. Ethernet is a bus network that can be wired in a *star* or *bus* configuration. Token ring networks can be wired in a *ring* or *star* topology. Star topology uses hubs.

52. Network interface cards (NICs) usually include a link-status light indicating whether they're working or not.

53. Bridges *segment* a congested network. Routers *direct traffic* between networks. PING tests a connection.

54. Ethernet cables are 10Base2, 10Base5, and 10BaseT. The "2" and 5" are 200- and 500-meter limits. The "T" stands for twisted-pair wire.

55. An email address (**a-plus@jamesgjones.com**) requires a *user* name (a-plus) and a *domain* name (jamesgjones.com). Email uses the Internet TCP/IP networking protocol.

56. An IP address consists of many numbers and periods. A Domain Name System (DNS) server converts the IP address to a readable name.

27. USB supports Plug and Play external peripherals. Devices can be changed without turning off the power (hot swapping). ESD is electrostatic discharge. EMI is electromagnetic interference.

28. If a keyed connector doesn't have a physical notch, the red stripe refers to Pin 1.

29. Interlaced monitors scan odd lines and then even lines in a two-step process. Noninterlaced monitors scan every line in one pass.

30. There are 8 DMA channels and 16 IRQ lines.

31. A good circuit (e.g., working fuse) shows 0 ohms on a multimeter. Capacitors store an electrical charge and are used in power supplies.

32. Dots per inch is written as dpi (printers and scanners). Pixels measure graphics resolutions. Standard VGA is 640×480×16 colors. SVGA is *Super* VGA and provides resolutions up to 1600×1200×16 million colors.

DOS

33. FDISK.EXE is used to create partitions. FORMAT.COM is used to create logical drives (volumes). **FORMAT C: /S** transfers system files to drive C:, making that drive bootable.

34. **SYS C:** (SYS.COM) is used to transfer system files to a corrupted drive C: that shows a "Missing or bad system files" error.

35. An operating system is a command line, a command interpreter (COMMAND.COM), and a user interface. The three critical DOS (system) files are IO.SYS, MSDOS.SYS, and COMMAND.COM, in that order.

36. The DOS load order is ROM BIOS, POST, IO.SYS, CONFIG.SYS, MSDOS.SYS, COMMAND.COM, AUTOEXEC.BAT, in that order. Beep codes are POST-level error codes, using the internal speaker.

37. CONFIG.SYS loads Real Mode device drivers (**DEVICE=**). AUTOEXEC.BAT executes commands at startup. Device drivers usually have a .SYS extension. **LASTDRIVE=** tells the system how many logical drive letters have been assigned and is a directive in CONFIG.SYS. The default is five drives.

38. Wild cards are * and ?. The * finds any number of characters to the right, and ? finds only one character per question mark. **DIR *.DLL** will find all DLL files in a folder. **DIR *.DLL /S** will search all subfolders.

39. ATTRIB.EXE is used to set file attributes such as Hidden, Read-only, System, and Archive. The Hidden and System attributes prevent DOS from showing a file with the **DIR** command.

40. DEFRAG.EXE is a way to move parts of files (clusters) next to each other and to speed up access times on a hard drive. SCANDISK.EXE checks a disk for bad sectors and file allocation problems.

WINDOWS

41. SMARTDRV.EXE is a software cache for reading hard drives. Windows 9x removes SMARTDRV from a CONFIG.SYS file by placing a **REM** (remark) at the beginning of the line. The semicolon (;) remarks out lines in an INI file.

42. EMS is expanded memory. XMS is extended memory. EMM386.EXE is never used in Windows 9x (it's commented out if found). HIMEM.SYS loads from MSDOS.SYS (Windows 9x) and is a required extended memory manager in Windows 9x.

43. Core files for Windows 3.x are USER.EXE, GDI.EXE, and KRNL386.EXE. GDI is the acronym for graphics device interface. The global heap is all the memory Windows can use.

44. WIN.COM starts Windows. SYSTEM.INI contains device drivers and program configurations. WIN.INI holds user options and environment configurations. WIN.INI is not necessary, but it is created if it doesn't exist.

45. Windows 9x loads IO.SYS, CONFIG.SYS, and MSDOS.SYS. HIMEM.SYS must load from MSDOS.SYS, or Windows 9x won't start. All versions of Windows may use an optional CONFIG and AUTOEXEC file.

46. Registry files for Windows 9x are SYSTEM.DAT and USER.DAT. Windows 9x uses the REGEDIT.EXE editor. Windows NT and Windows 2000 use the REGEDT32.EXE editor.

10. Windows 9x creates a Real Mode virtual machine (VM) to run 16-bit applications and device drivers. Windows NT and Windows 2000 use the hardware abstraction layer (HAL) to control devices.

11. Enhanced Mode (386 Enhanced Mode, 32-bit Protected Mode) originated with the 80386 chip. Modern processors use Enhanced Mode. The 32-bit 80386 was the first chip to switch between Real Mode and Protected Mode without requiring a system reset.

12. Parity tests RAM chips (on SIMMs and DIMMs) for structural integrity. Thermal changes can affect the RAM chips and can cause parity errors. The POST routine cannot uncover heat-related problems because everything on the board is cool. Heat problems usually cause software problems and are uncovered using software utilities.

13. First generation Pentium chips generally run between 66MHz and 200MHz. Pentium Pro chips were sold in two speeds: 180MHz and 200MHz. Intel makes Pentium chips. AMD makes Athlon and Duron chips. Rambus makes RDRAM, but the generic copy is DDR DRAM or DDR SDRAM.

14. L-1 cache (Level 1) is between 8KB and 64KB, and it is internal to the CPU. L-2 cache (Level 2) is usually an external chip or near the CPU on the chip die, and it works best at between 256KB and 512KB.

15. Slot 1, Slot 2, Socket 7, and Socket 370 chip-mounting technologies are used by Intel processors. Slot A and Socket A are technologies used by AMD Athlon and Duron processors.

INPUT/OUTPUT

16. One IEEE-1394 (i.Link or FireWire) controller can support speeds up to 400Mbps and 63 daisy-chained devices. USB supports speeds up to 12Mbps. One USB controller can support 127 devices, and it uses hubs in a tiered-star topology.

17. Parallel cables usually have a DB25 male connector on one end and a 36-pin male Centronics connector at the other end. The parallel port on the back panel of the PC is usually a 25-pin female socket.

18. Serial cables connect to the back panel with a 9-pin connector. Video cables use a 15-pin connector. A PS/2 connector is a small 6-pin circular connector. AT DIN connectors (older keyboards) are larger than PS/2 connectors and have a 5-pin circular plug. A USB connector looks like a rectangle.

19. SCSI cables are usually 50-pin ribbon cables. SCSI chains almost always have 1 host adapter and can have up to 7 additional devices. The cable must be terminated at both ends. IDE controllers can have up to 2 devices. SCSI and USB are usually used for external devices like CD-ROM drives and scanners.

20. COM1 and COM3 are logically joined, and COM2 and COM4 are logically joined. COM1 and 3 use IRQ 4, and COM2 and 4 use IRQ 3.

21. COM port addresses include com1=03F8; com3=03E8; com2=02F8; and com4=02E8.

22. LPT1 uses IRQ 7, and LPT2 uses IRQ 5.

23. IRQ 14 is the primary (first) drive controller. IRQ 15 is the secondary drive controller. Floppy controllers use IRQ 6. IRQ 2 cannot be used when it *cascades* to IRQ 9.

24. Laser printers use a *primary corona wire* to charge the EP drum. The drum is cleaned, charged, and written to. The image develops (by the corona charge) and pulls toner to the drum. Paper is charged and pulls toner from the drum, where it's fused by the *fuser rollers*. If the heat sensor on the fuser rollers shuts down, the toner will fail to stick to the paper. Paper jams are usually caused by a bad separator pad.

25. Sectors are 512 bytes. Clusters grow to fit the size of the logical drive, depending on the formatting system. FAT16 is 16KB and uses 16-bit addressing. The Master Boot Record (MBR) is in Sector 0, Track 0, Head 0, Cylinder 0 of the active, primary partition. FAT32 uses smaller clusters and can address more than the FAT16 2GB drive limit. NTFS is the Windows NT File System.

26. Physical disks can have a maximum of 24 logical drives (A: and B: are floppies). When a drive C: has been partitioned, the largest extended partition can have 23 drive letters.

A+

Second Edition

James G. Jones
Craig Landes

A+® Exam Cram, Second Edition

Limits of Liability and Disclaimer of Warranty

The author and publisher of this book have used their best efforts in preparing the book and the programs contained in it. These efforts include the development, research, and testing of the theories and programs to determine their effectiveness. The author and publisher make no warranty of any kind, expressed or implied, with regard to these programs or the documentation contained in this book.

The author and publisher shall not be liable in the event of incidental or consequential damages in connection with, or arising out of, the furnishing, performance, or use of the programs, associated instructions, and/or claims of productivity gains.

Trademarks

Trademarked names appear throughout this book. Rather than list the names and entities that own the trademarks or insert a trademark symbol with each mention of the trademarked name, the publisher states that it is using the names for editorial purposes only and to the benefit of the trademark owner, with no intention of infringing upon that trademark.

The Coriolis Group, LLC
14455 N. Hayden Road
Suite 220
Scottsdale, Arizona 85260

(480)483-0192
FAX (480)483-0193
www.coriolis.com

Library of Congress Cataloging-in-Publication Data
Jones, James G.
    A+ exam cram / by James G. Jones and Craig Landes.-- 2nd ed.
        p.   cm.
    Includes index.
    ISBN 1-57610-695-0
    1. Electronic data processing personnel--Certification.   2. Computer technicians--Certification--Study guides.   I. Landes, Craig.
QA76.3 .J68   2001
004.16--dc21   2001028146
                                                         CIP

President and CEO
Keith Weiskamp

Publisher
Steve Sayre

Acquisitions Editor
Shari Jo Hehr

Product Marketing Manager
Brett Woolley

Project Editor
Meredith Brittain

Technical Reviewers
Michelle Roudebush
Jeffrey Dowdy

Production Coordinator
Todd Halvorsen

Cover Designer
Laura Wellander

Layout Designer
April Nielsen

Printed in the United States of America
10 9 8 7 6 5 4 3 2 1

CORIOLIS™

The Coriolis Group, LLC • 14455 North Hayden Road, Suite 220 • Scottsdale, Arizona 85260

ExamCram.com *Connects You to the Ultimate Study Center!*

Our goal has always been to provide you with the best study tools on the planet to help you achieve your certification in record time. Time is so valuable these days that none of us can afford to waste a second of it, especially when it comes to exam preparation.

Over the past few years, we've created an extensive line of *Exam Cram* and *Exam Prep* study guides, practice exams, and interactive training. To help you study even better, we have now created an e-learning and certification destination called **ExamCram.com**. (You can access the site at **www.examcram.com**.) Now, with every study product you purchase from us, you'll be connected to a large community of people like yourself who are actively studying for their certifications, developing their careers, seeking advice, and sharing their insights and stories.

I believe that the future is all about collaborative learning. Our **ExamCram.com** destination is our approach to creating a highly interactive, easily accessible collaborative environment, where you can take practice exams and discuss your experiences with others, sign up for features like "Questions of the Day," plan your certifications using our interactive planners, create your own personal study pages, and keep up with all of the latest study tips and techniques.

I hope that whatever study products you purchase from us—*Exam Cram* or *Exam Prep* study guides, *Personal Trainers*, *Personal Test Centers*, or one of our interactive Web courses—will make your studying fun and productive. Our commitment is to build the kind of learning tools that will allow you to study the way you want to, whenever you want to.

Visit ExamCram.com now to enhance your study program.

Help us continue to provide the very best certification study materials possible. Write us or email us at **learn@examcram.com** and let us know how our study products have helped you study. Tell us about new features that you'd like us to add. Send us a story about how we've helped you. We're listening!

Good luck with your certification exam and your career. Thank you for allowing us to help you achieve your goals.

Keith Weiskamp

Keith Weiskamp
President and CEO

Look for these other products from The Coriolis Group:

A+ Exam Prep, 3rd Edition
by Scott Reeves, Kalinda Reeves, Stephen Weese, and Christopher S. Geyer

A+ Exam Cram Personal Test Center
by Brad Grandorff

A+ Exam Cram, 2nd Edition Personal Trainer
by James G. Jones and Craig Landes

Network+ Exam Cram
by Scott Reeves and Kalinda Reeves

Network+ Exam Prep
by Melissa Craft, Mark A. Poplar, David V. Watts, and Will Willis

Network+ Exam Cram Personal Test Center
by Brad Grandorff

Network+ Exam Cram Personal Trainer
by Scott Reeves and Kalinda Reeves

i-Net+ Exam Cram
by Emmett Dulaney and Martin Weiss

i-Net+ Exam Prep
by Tcat Houser, Laurel Ann Spivey Dumas, and Matt Simmons

i-Net+ Exam Cram Personal Trainer
by Emmett Dulaney and Martin Weiss

Server+ Exam Cram
by CIP Author Team

Server+ Exam Prep
by Drew Bird and Mike Harwood

About the Authors

James G. Jones has more than 30 years of experience in the IT industry. He has held positions ranging from System Engineer and Sales Manager to Senior Vice President of a Fortune 500 multinational. He is currently the president of an international consulting firm and regularly performs as a guest speaker and consultant to some of the industry's largest corporations. In addition to a BS in Education and an MBA in Information Technology, Jim has earned numerous technical certifications, including A+, MCSE, and CNE.

Craig Landes has more than 10 years of experience in the IT field. He has held numerous positions, from Database Programmer to Manager of Information Systems in the field of health care. Craig regularly helps some of today's largest consulting firms develop technical programs for clients and employees at all levels. He is currently heading the development of The National Association of Personal Systems Administrators (NAPSA), a professional organization of technology specialists servicing the more than 46 million home and small business computer users.

Table of Contents

Introduction

Welcome to *A+ Exam Cram, Second Edition*! This introduction is very much like the "Quick Setup" reference section for a software application, and we use it to give you some important insights into the exam. The purpose of this book is to get you ready to take—and pass—both modules of the 2001 CompTIA A+ certification exam. In the following pages, we've outlined the CompTIA A+ certification in general, and we talk about how this *Exam Cram* can optimize your knowledge of PCs and help you focus on critical exam topics.

New job listings often require applicants to be A+ certified, and many individuals who complete the program qualify for increases in pay and/or responsibility. If the job requirements don't require an existing A+ certification, many corporations require that you complete the certification process within 90 days of being hired.

This book is aimed strictly at exam preparation and review. It will *not* teach you everything you need to know about a topic. Instead, it will present and dissect the question topics that you're probably going to see on the exam. We've drawn on material from CompTIA's own listing of requirements, from other preparation guides, and from the exams themselves. We've also drawn from a battery of third-party test preparation tools and from our own experience with microcomputers, going all the way back to the Altair. Our aim is to bring together as much information as possible about the revised A+ certification exams.

Our explicit purpose in writing this book is to stuff as many facts and technical answers about computers as possible into your brain before you begin the test. The A+ exam makes a basic assumption that you already have a *very* strong background of experience with PCs, hardware, and Windows operating systems. On the other hand, we think that microcomputers are changing so fast that no one can be a total expert. We think this book is the most up-to-date analysis of the 2001 A+ exam on the market.

Depending on your experience with PCs, we recommend that you begin your studies with some classroom training or that you visit the CompTIA Web site (www.comptia.org) for a definition of what it means to be A+ certified. We *strongly* recommend that you install, configure, and generally "fool around" with the DOS and Windows operating environment that you'll be tested on. Nothing beats hands-on experience and familiarity when it comes to understanding the questions you're likely to encounter. Book learning is essential, but hands-on experience is the best teacher of all!

Perhaps a quick way for you to decide where you stand in relation to the current certification process is to turn to the end of the book and examine the Sample Test (Chapter 15). This is a highly accurate representation of both the test format and the types of questions you will encounter.

The New A+ Certification Program

The A+ Certification Program has been extensively revised as of March 2001. You must pass both the Core Hardware module and the Operating System Technologies module to receive your A+ certification.

Many people feel that the two exams are so closely related that they should be combined into one. Regardless of whether they're eventually combined, we recommend that you treat the two components as one exam. In fact, we have organized this book as if they were one exam, and we urge you to sign up for *both* exams at the same time.

The Core Hardware exam tests your knowledge of microcomputer hardware, including motherboards, processors, memory, peripherals, IRQs, electronics, and buses. The Operating System Technologies exam tests your knowledge of Windows in all of its versions (9x, ME, NT, 2000)—and do not forget DOS commands, because they are still needed in troubleshooting.

Taking a Certification Exam

Unfortunately, testing isn't free. You'll be charged $132 for each test you take, whether you pass or fail. You can either take both exams at the same time or take them at different times. If you take both tests together, there is a break between the Core Hardware and Operating System Technologies exams.

The United States and Canadian tests are administered by either Prometric or VUE. Prometric can be reached at 1-800-776-4276 or **www.2test.com**. VUE can be reached at 1-952-995-8800 or **www.vue.com**.

To schedule an exam, you must call at least one day in advance. To cancel or reschedule an exam, you must call at least 12 hours before the scheduled test time (or you may be charged). When calling either service, please have the following information ready for the sales representative who handles your call:

➤ Your name, organization, and mailing address

➤ The name of the exam(s) you wish to take (Core Hardware and/or Operating System Technologies)

➤ A method of payment

The most convenient payment method is to provide a valid credit card number with sufficient available credit. Otherwise, payments by check, money order, or purchase order (PO) must be *received* before a test can be scheduled. If you choose one of these latter methods, ask your sales representative for more details.

Keep in mind that if you choose to pay for your exam by a method that involves the postal service and banking system (i.e., check, PO, and so on), you'll have to call to schedule your exam much earlier than one day in advance.

Arriving at the Exam Site

On the day of your exam, try to arrive at least 15 minutes before the scheduled time slot. You must bring *two* forms of identification, one of which *must* be a photo ID. Typically, a driver's license and credit card are valid forms of identification. Insurance cards, birth certificates, state ID cards, employee identification cards, or any other legal identification can also be used. If you're not sure whether your identification is acceptable, ask the person you schedule your exam with.

You will be given a user ID code as an identification number for your test, which you enter in the computer at the time you begin your exam(s). The exam is fully computer based, and it is all multiple choice. Ordinarily, your ID number is the same as your Social Security number, though it may be different. Your ID number will be used to track your session.

In the Exam Room

All exams are completely closed-book. In fact, you will not be permitted to take anything with you into the testing area other than a blank sheet of paper and a pencil provided by the exam proctors. We suggest that you *immediately write down the most critical information* about the test you're taking on the blank sheet of paper you're given. *Exam Cram* books provide a brief reference that lists essential information from the book in distilled form. This reference is The Cram Sheet, a tear-out card located in the front of the book. You need to master this information (by brute force, if necessary) so you can dump the information out of your head onto a piece of paper before answering any exam questions. You need to remember the information only long enough to write it down when you walk into the test room. You might even want to look at The Cram Sheet in the car or in the lobby of the testing center just before you walk in to take the exam.

Each question offers you an opportunity to mark that question for review. We strongly suggest that you mark any questions about which you have any shade of doubt. Each exam gives you an ample amount of time to complete the questions, and by marking questions for review, you can go back without the pressure of worrying whether you'll have time to complete the whole exam.

Note: When the A+ test goes adaptive (expected the third quarter of 2001), you will no longer be able to mark questions for review.

How long you take to answer each question is not factored into scoring your test. Your answers can be changed at any time before you terminate the session, and the review option is not tracked for scoring. Many terms and words are easy to mix up, so take time to review your work.

When you complete the exam, the software will tell you whether you've passed or failed. Even if you fail, we suggest that you ask for (and keep) the detailed report that the test administrator prints out for you. You can use the report to help you prepare for another go-round, if necessary. If you need to retake an exam, you must call one of the testing services, schedule a new test date, and pay another $132 per exam.

Certification

When you've passed the Core Hardware and Operating System Technologies exams, you will be A+ certified. It's a good idea to save the test results you are given at the conclusion of the test, because they are your immediate proof. Official certification normally takes anywhere from four to six weeks, so don't expect to get your credentials overnight. When the package arrives, it will include a Welcome Kit, a certificate (suitable for framing), and an identification lapel pin.

As an official recognition of hard work and broad-based knowledge, A+ certification is also a badge of honor. Many organizations view certification as a necessary foundation for a career in the information technology (IT) industry.

How to Prepare for an Exam

A+ certification requires an extensive range of knowledge about the entire field of microcomputers. Preparing for network certification, aerobics certification, or even driving certification (driver's license) is somewhat simpler. In these cases, the area you're being certified in is a limited subset of everything in that field. A+ certification, on the other hand, has no boundary limitations. Anything at all about a PC is a valid subject for testing!

By using this book in your preparation efforts, you'll be able to concentrate your efforts on the areas considered to be the most important in understanding PCs. We've "been there, done that," so to speak, and we'll point you in the right direction for your studies.

At a minimum, preparing for the A+ exams requires a good test guide (this book) and detailed reference materials addressing the information covered on the exams.

We've attempted to make no assumptions whatsoever about your current knowledge and to cram between the covers of the book as much information as possible about PCs. However, our main focus is to get you through the exam. Using the self-study method, you might consider us as virtual tutors, coming to your site at your convenience and stuffing the facts between your ears.

In the past, candidates have used many individual reference books that, taken together, cover most of the required material on the exam. A good professional should always have a solid reference library as a matter of course. See the "Need to Know More?" sections at the end of each chapter for our lists of recommended references.

If you like a little more structure, there are several good programs available in both a self-paced and classroom format. However, you must be sure the program you select has been developed for the revised A+ requirements. Consider too that the cost of structured class instruction is significantly higher than the price of this book.

The A+ certification exam is constantly being updated to reflect the ever-evolving developments in the microcomputer industry. The best source of current exam information is CompTIA's Web site: **www.comptia.org**. If you don't have access to the Internet, you can call or write CompTIA directly at:

Computing Technology Industry Association
450 East 22nd Street, Suite 230
Lombard, IL 60134-6158
Phone: (630) 268-1818

In addition, you'll probably find any or all of the following materials useful in your quest for A+ expertise:

➤ *Study guides*—The Coriolis Group certification series includes the following:

   ➤ *The Exam Cram series*—These books give you information about the material you need to know to pass the tests.

   ➤ *The Exam Prep series*—These books provide a greater level of detail than the *Exam Cram* books and are designed to teach you everything you need to know from an exam perspective. Each book comes with a CD that contains interactive practice exams in a variety of testing formats.

   Together, the two series make a perfect pair.

➤ *Multimedia*—These Coriolis Group materials are designed to support learners of all types—whether you learn best by reading or doing:

   ➤ *The Exam Cram Personal Trainer*—Offers a unique, personalized self-paced training course based on the exam.

➤ *The Exam Cram Personal Test Center*—Features multiple test options that simulate the actual exam, including Fixed-Length, Random, Review, and Test All. Explanations of correct and incorrect answers reinforce concepts learned.

About This Book

Each *Exam Cram* chapter follows a regular structure, along with graphical cues about especially important or useful material. The structure of a typical chapter includes:

➤ *Opening hotlists*—Each chapter begins with lists of the terms you'll need to understand and the concepts you'll need to master before you can be fully conversant with the chapter's subject matter. We follow the hotlists with a few introductory paragraphs to set the stage for the rest of the chapter.

➤ *Topical coverage*—After the opening hotlists, each chapter covers a series of topics related to the chapter's subject title. Throughout this section, we highlight topics or concepts likely to appear on the exam by using a special Exam Alert layout that looks like this:

 This is what an Exam Alert looks like. An Exam Alert stresses concepts, terms, software, or activities that will most likely appear in one or more certification exam questions. For that reason, we think any information found offset in Exam Alert format is worthy of unusual attentiveness on your part.

Even if material isn't flagged as an Exam Alert, *all* the content in this book is associated in some way to something test related. The book is focused on high-speed test preparation; you'll find that what appears in the meat of each chapter is critical knowledge.

➤ *Sidebars*—When we discuss an exam topic that may be based on common knowledge among people in the IT industry, we've tried to explicitly describe the underlying assumptions of the discussion. You may have many years of experience with PCs, or you may be just starting out. Your certification shouldn't depend on "secret knowledge" that you're supposed to "just know" somehow.

Something You May Not Know

A sidebar like this is a way to step outside the flow of the discussion to provide you with "insider" information that you may not have heard before. A sidebar is a way to increase the saturation level of your knowledge and apply some "fixative" to help keep topical facts from slipping out of your ears.

➤ *Notes*—Notes throughout the text dip into nearly every aspect of working with and configuring PCs. Where a body of knowledge is far deeper than the scope of the book, we use Notes to indicate areas of concern or specialty training.

Note: Cramming for an exam will get you through a test, but it won't make you a competent IT professional. Although you can memorize just the facts you need to become certified, your daily work in the IT field will rapidly put you in water over your head if you don't know the underlying principles of computers.

➤ *Tips*—We provide tips that will help you build a solid foundation of knowledge. Although the information may not be on the exam, it is highly relevant and will help you become a better test-taker.

 This is how tips are formatted. Here's an example of a tip: You should always choose the Custom or Advanced option, if the setup routine offers one. In every case we've ever seen, there is a default setting for any steps in the program where you're given a choice. In situations where you don't know what you're looking at, you can choose the default. However, in places where you do know what you're looking at, you may often disagree with what some faraway programmer has decided to do to your system.

➤ *Practice questions*—This section presents a series of mock test questions and explanations of both correct and incorrect answers. Each chapter has a number of practice questions that highlight the areas we found to be most important on the exam.

➤ *Details and resources*—Every chapter ends with a section titled "Need to Know More?" This section provides direct pointers to resources that offer further details on the chapter's subject matter. In addition, this section tries to rate the quality and thoroughness of each topic's coverage. If you find a resource you like in this collection, use it, but don't feel compelled to use all these resources. On the other hand, we recommend only resources that we have used on a regular basis, so none of the recommendations will be a waste of your time or money.

The bulk of the book follows this chapter structure, but there are a few other elements that we would like to point out:

➤ *Sample Test and Answer Key*—A very close approximation of the 2001 A exam is found in Chapter 15. Chapter 16 presents the answers to the sample test, as well as explanations of the correct and incorrect answers.

➤ *Acronym Glossary*—An extensive glossary of acronyms.

➤ *The Cram Sheet*—A tear-away card inside the front cover of this *Exam Cram* book, this is a valuable tool that represents a condensed and compiled collection of facts and numbers that we think you should memorize before taking the test.

Using This Book

If you're preparing for the A+ certification exam for the first time, we've structured the topics in this book to build upon one another. Therefore, the topics covered in later chapters will make more sense after you've read earlier chapters. In our opinion, many computer manuals and reference books are essentially a list of facts. Rather than simply list raw facts about each topic on the exam, we've tried to paint an integrated landscape in your imagination, where each topic and exam fact takes on a landmark status.

We suggest you read this book from front to back for your initial test preparation. You won't be wasting your time, because everything we've written pertains to the exam. If you need to brush up on a topic or you have to bone up for a second try, use the index or table of contents to go straight to the topics and questions that you need to study. After taking the tests, we think you'll find this book useful as a tightly focused reference and an essential foundation of microcomputer knowledge.

We've tried to create a real-world tool that you can use to prepare for and pass both modules of the A+ exam. We are definitely interested in any feedback you would care to share about the book, especially if you have ideas about how we can improve it for future test-takers.

We would like to know if you found this book to be helpful in your preparation efforts. We'd also like to know how you felt about your chances of passing the exam *before* you read the book and then *after* you read the book. Of course, we'd love to hear that you passed the exam, and even if you just want to share your triumph, we'd be happy to hear from you.

Send your questions or comments to Coriolis at **learn@examcram.com**. Please remember to include the title of the book in your message. Also, be sure to check out the Web pages at **www.examcram.com**, where you'll find information updates, commentary, and certification information.

Thanks for choosing us as your personal trainers, and enjoy the book!

Self-Assessment

The reason we included a Self-Assessment in this *Exam Cram* book is to help you evaluate your readiness to tackle A+ certification. But before you tackle this Self-Assessment, let's talk about concerns you may face when pursuing A+ certification and what an ideal candidate might look like.

CompTIA Certified Computer Technicians in the Real World

In the next section, we describe an ideal A+-certified candidate. Many people will take the two modules of the A+ certification exam in order to serve in the PC hardware and software repair field. Others may see these tests as a great starting point for gaining the basic PC knowledge that can be used in many other fields.

Many people are already certified, so it's obviously an attainable goal. You can get all the real-world motivation you need from knowing that many others have gone before, so you'll be able to follow in their footsteps. If you're willing to tackle the process seriously and do what it takes to obtain the necessary experience and knowledge, you can take—and pass—the certification modules involved in obtaining A+ certification. In fact, *Exam Crams*, and the companion *Exam Preps*, are designed to make it as easy as possible for you to prepare for certification exams. But prepare you must!

The same, of course, is true for other CompTIA certifications, including the following:

➤ CompTIA's Certified Document Imaging Architech (CDIA) certification is a nationally recognized credential acknowledging competency and professionalism in the document imaging industry. CDIA candidates possess critical knowledge of all major areas and technologies used to plan, design, and specify an imaging system.

➤ Network+ certifies the knowledge of networking technicians with 18 to 24 months of experience in the IT industry.

➤ i-Net+ certification is designed specifically for any individual interested in demonstrating baseline technical knowledge that would allow him or her to pursue a variety of Internet-related careers.

Put Yourself to the Test

The following series of questions and observations is designed to help you figure out how much work you must do to pursue A+ certification and what kinds of resources you may consult on your quest. Be absolutely honest in your answers; otherwise, you'll end up wasting money on exams you're not yet ready to take. There are no right or wrong answers, only steps along the path to certification. Only you can decide where you really belong in the broad spectrum of aspiring candidates.

Two things should be clear from the outset, however:

➤ Even a modest background in computer science will be helpful.

➤ Hands-on experience with personal computers is an essential ingredient of certification success.

Educational Background

1. Have you ever taken any computer-related classes? [Yes or No]

   If Yes, proceed to question 2; if No, proceed to question 4.

2. Have you taken any classes on computer operating systems? [Yes or No]

   If Yes, you'll probably be able to handle operating system architecture and system component discussions. If you're rusty, brush up on basic operating system concepts, especially virtual memory, multitasking regimes, user-mode versus kernel-mode operation, and general computer security topics.

   If No, consider some basic reading in this area. We strongly recommend a good general operating systems book, such as *Operating System Concepts*, by Abraham Silberschatz and Peter Baer Galvin (Addison-Wesley, 1997, ISBN 0-201-59113-8). If this title doesn't appeal to you, check out reviews for other, similar titles at your favorite online bookstore.

3. Have you taken any networking concepts or technologies classes? [Yes or No]

   If Yes, you'll probably be able to handle the A+ certification networking terminology, concepts, and technologies. If you're rusty, *A+ Exam Prep, Third Edition*, by Scott Reeves et al. (The Coriolis Group, 2001, ISBN 1-57610-699-3) will help you brush up on basic networking concepts and terminology, especially networking media, transmission types, the OSI Reference Model, and networking technologies such as Ethernet, Token Ring, FDDI, and WAN links.

If No, you might want to supplement the material available in this book with other good works. The three best books that we know of are *Computer Networks, 3rd Edition*, by Andrew S. Tanenbaum (Prentice-Hall, 1996, ISBN 0-133-49945-6), *Computer Networks and Internets*, by Douglas E. Comer (Prentice-Hall, 1997, ISBN 0-132-39070-1), and *Encyclopedia of Networking*, by Tom Sheldon (Osborne/McGraw-Hill, 1998, ISBN 0-07-882333-1).

Skip to the next section, "Hands-on Experience."

4. Have you done any reading on operating systems or networks? [Yes or No]

If Yes, review the requirements stated in the first paragraphs after questions 2 and 3. If you meet those requirements, move on to the next section, "Hands-on Experience." If No, you'll find the real-world projects of *A+ Exam Prep, Third Edition* to be most helpful.

Hands-on Experience

The most important key to success on all the CompTIA tests is hands-on experience, especially with basic computer hardware, as well as Windows 95, Windows 98, Windows NT Workstation, Windows 2000 Professional, and, to a lesser degree, MS-DOS. If we leave you with only one realization after taking this Self-Assessment, it should be that there's no substitute for time spent installing, configuring, and using PC hardware and software.

Before you even think about taking any exam, make sure you've spent enough time with the related hardware and software to understand how it may be installed and configured, how to maintain such an installation, and how to troubleshoot when things go wrong. This will help you in the exam, and in real life.

Testing Your Exam-Readiness

Whether you attend a formal class on a specific topic to get ready for an exam or use written materials to study on your own, some preparation for the A+ certification exams is essential. At $128 or $78 a try—pass or fail—you want to do everything you can to pass on your first try. That's where studying comes in.

For any given subject, consider taking a class if you've tackled self-study materials, taken the test, and failed anyway. The opportunity to interact with an instructor and fellow students can make all the difference in the world, if you can afford that privilege. For information about CompTIA classes, visit the CompTIA Web site at **www.comptia.org** (follow the Certification link to find training).

If you can't afford to take a class, visit the Web page anyway, because it also includes a detailed breakdown of the objectives for both modules of the A+ certification exam. This will serve as a good roadmap for your studies. Even if you can't afford to spend much at all, you should still invest in some low-cost practice exams from commercial vendors, because they can help you assess your readiness to pass a test better than any other tool. The CompTIA Web site lists sources for additional study material.

5. Have you taken a practice exam on your chosen test subject? [Yes or No]

If Yes, and you scored 75 percent or better, you're probably ready to tackle the real thing. If your score isn't above that crucial threshold, keep at it until you break that barrier.

If No, obtain all the free and low-budget practice tests you can find and get to work. Keep at it until you can break the passing threshold comfortably.

 When it comes to assessing your test readiness, there's no better way than to take a good-quality practice exam and pass with a score of 75 percent or better. When we're preparing ourselves, we shoot for 80-plus percent, just to leave room for the "weirdness factor" that sometimes shows up on exams.

One last note: We can't stress enough the importance of hands-on experience in the context of both modules of the A+ certification exam. As you review the material, you'll realize that hands-on experience with basic PC hardware, operating system commands, tools, and utilities is invaluable.

Onward, through the Fog!

Once you've assessed your readiness, undertaken the right background studies, obtained the hands-on experience that will help you understand the products and technologies at work, and reviewed the many sources of information to help you prepare for a test, you'll be ready to take a round of practice tests. When your scores come back positive enough to get you through the exam, you're ready to go after the real thing. If you follow our assessment regime, you'll know what you need to study, as well as when you're ready to make a test date at Prometric or VUE. Good luck!

A+ Certification Exams

Terms you'll need to understand:

✓ Exhibit

✓ Multiple-choice question formats

✓ Traditional versus adaptive testing

✓ Careful reading

✓ Strategy

Concepts you'll need to master:

✓ Preparing to take a certification exam

✓ Budgeting your time

✓ Marking for review

✓ Using one question to figure out another question

✓ Analyzing responses logically

✓ Guessing (as a last resort)

As experiences go, test-taking isn't something most people anticipate eagerly, no matter how well they're prepared. In most cases, familiarity reduces exam anxiety. In other words, you probably wouldn't be as nervous if you had to take a second A+ certification exam as you will be taking your first one. We've taken a lot of exams, and this book is partly about helping you to reduce your test-taking anxiety. This chapter explains what you can expect to see in the exam room itself.

Whether it's your first or your tenth exam, understanding the exam particulars (how much time to spend on questions, the setting you'll be in, and so on) and the testing software will help you concentrate on the material rather than on the environment. Likewise, mastering a few basic test-taking skills should help you recognize—and perhaps even outfox—some of the tricks and "gotchas" you're bound to find in A+ exam questions.

The Test Site

When you arrive at your scheduled testing center, you'll be required to sign in with a test coordinator. He or she will ask you to produce two forms of identification, one of which must be a photo ID. After you've signed in and your time slot arrives, you'll be asked to deposit any books, bags, or other items you brought with you, and then you'll be escorted into a closed room.

Typically, the testing room will be furnished with anywhere from one to six computers. Each workstation will be separated from the others by dividers designed to keep you from seeing what's happening on someone else's computer.

When you sign in with the exam administrators, you'll be furnished with a pen or pencil and a blank sheet of paper, or, in some cases, an erasable plastic sheet and an erasable felt-tip pen. You're allowed to write down any information you want on both sides of this sheet. As mentioned in the Introduction, you should memorize as much of the material that appears on The Cram Sheet (inside the front cover of this book) as you can and then write down that information on the blank sheet as soon as you are seated in front of the computer. You can refer to your rendition of The Cram Sheet anytime you like during the test, but you'll have to surrender the sheet when you leave the room. Keep in mind that if you've registered for both exams, you can take a break between the Core Hardware and Operating System Technologies specialty exams, or you can proceed directly into the second exam. If you do take a break, you may have to turn in your notes and start over fresh on the second exam.

Most exam rooms feature a wall with a large picture window. This is to permit the test coordinator to monitor the room and to observe anything out of the ordinary that might go on, and also to prevent test-takers from talking to one another. The exam coordinator will have preloaded the A+ certification test, and you'll be permitted to start as soon as you're seated in front of the computer.

All A+ certification exams are designed to be taken within a 90-minute period, and there's a countdown timer on the screen showing you the time remaining. In our opinion, the amount of time is fair and generous, and it offers ample time for reviewing your responses.

A+ certification exams are computer generated and use a multiple-choice format. Although this may sound easy, the questions are constructed to check your mastery of basic facts and figures, as well as to test your ability to evaluate one or more sets of circumstances or requirements.

You might be asked to select the best or most effective solution to a problem from a range of choices, all of which technically are correct. You might be asked to select the best choice from a graphic image. You might also find questions where a series of blanks represent a list of terms used to complete a sentence. All in all, it's quite an adventure, and it involves real thinking. This book shows you what to expect and how to deal with the problems, puzzles, and predicaments you're likely to find on the test.

The sample test in Chapter 15 is a very close approximation of the combined exams. As you'll see, we've included a sample of every type of question, as well as mimicked the phrasing style of the overall exam. (You can find detailed answers to these questions in Chapter 16.)

In the final analysis, knowledge breeds confidence, and confidence breeds success. If you study the materials in this book carefully, review the practice questions at the end of each chapter, and take the sample test in Chapter 15, you should be aware of all the areas where additional studying is required.

Test Layout and Design

As mentioned earlier, the questions on A+ exams are multiple-choice. CompTIA has announced that the A+ certification exam will be moving to an adaptive testing format, expected the third quarter of 2001.

Note: Adaptive tests work by evaluating the test-taker's most recent answer. A correct answer leads to a more difficult question (and the test software's estimate of the test-taker's knowledge and ability level is raised). An incorrect answer leads to a less difficult question (and the test software's estimate of the test-taker's knowledge and ability level is lowered). This process continues until the test targets the test-taker's true ability level.

Some questions will provide the information in paragraph format, and others will provide an exhibit (line drawing) and ask you to identify specific components. *Paying careful attention* is the key to success! Be prepared to toggle between a picture and a question as you work. Often, both are complex enough that you might not be able to remember all of either one.

Each question stands alone in a windowed page. The text of the question displays near the top of the screen, and the response choices are listed below the question. Each response appears next to a typical Windows radio button, where clicking on the appropriate circle turns it black. You can change your selection at any time from within the question window. Some questions indicate that more than one answer is correct, in which case you should chose the number of answers specified. The time you take to respond and the number of times you change a response are not factored into the scoring process. When a question includes a graphic exhibit, an additional button displays and links to the graphic. Along the top of the screen is the countdown timer.

Review Responses

When you complete the last question of the exam and press the Next button, you will find that, if you take the traditional test format before the conversion to an all adaptive format, a final screen will offer you the option to review your responses and any questions that you specifically marked for review. A listing of all the question numbers, along with your chosen response letter, shows on the screen, and the marked questions have a graphic indicator. When you highlight a marked question and choose Review, the software displays the selected question.

When you review a question, you'll see a window displaying the original question and your response. You can use the window to change or verify your answer. When you're satisfied with your response, you can unmark the question by clicking on the Mark For Review checkbox, or you can proceed to the next review question. At the bottom of the screen, you'll see a Review Next button, which will take you to your next marked question (bypassing unmarked questions). The number of questions you choose to review is not factored into the scoring process.

Take Your Test Seriously

The most important advice we can give you about taking any test is this: *Read each question carefully!* Some questions are deliberately ambiguous, offering several responses that could be correct, depending on your reading of the question. Other questions use terminology in very precise ways. We use exam alerts and tips throughout this book to point out where you might run into these types of questions.

We've taken numerous practice and real tests, and in nearly every case, we've missed at least one question because we didn't read it closely or carefully enough. For example, the use of the word *requires* commonly causes test-takers to answer incorrectly. Consider the following sample question.

Sample Question 1

> Windows 95 requires the WIN.INI and SYSTEM.INI files during the startup process in order to load device drivers and user options.
>
> ○ a. True
>
> ○ b. False

Answer b, false, is correct because the WIN.INI file isn't *required*.

Here are some suggestions for dealing with the tendency to select an answer too quickly:

➤ Read every word in the question! If you find yourself jumping ahead impatiently, go back and start over.

➤ Schedule your exam on a day when you don't have a lot of other appointments and errands. This should help you feel a little more relaxed.

➤ As you read, try to rephrase the question in your own terms.

➤ When returning to a question after your initial read-through, reread every word again—otherwise, you might fall into a rut. Sometimes, seeing a question fresh after turning your attention elsewhere enables you to catch something you missed earlier. This is where the review option comes in handy.

➤ If you return to a question more than twice, try to explain to yourself what you don't understand about the question, why the answers don't appear to make sense, or what appears to be missing. If you ponder the subject for a while, your subconscious might provide the details you're looking for, or you might notice a "trick" that will point to the right answer.

Finally, try to deal with each question by thinking through what you know about hardware and software systems. By reviewing what you know (and what you've written down on your Cram Sheet), you'll often recall or understand concepts sufficiently to determine the correct answer.

Question-Handling Strategies

Based on the tests we've taken, we've noticed a couple of interesting trends in exam question responses. Usually, some responses will be obviously incorrect, and two of the remaining answers will be plausible. Remember that only one response can be correct. If the answer leaps out at you, reread the question to look for a trick—just in case.

Unfamiliar Terms

Our best advice regarding guessing is to rely on your intuition. None of the exam topics should come as a surprise to you if you've read this book and taken the sample test. If you see a response that's totally unfamiliar, chances are good that it's a made-up word. Recognizing unfamiliar terms can help narrow down the possible correct answers for a question. For example, the following sample question shows how you can use the process of eliminating unfamiliar terms to arrive at the correct answer.

Sample Question 2

Which is the most useful tool for checking a circuit?

○ a. Differentiometer

○ b. Benchmark analyzer

○ c. Multimeter

○ d. Integrity meter

Answer c is correct. Chances are that you've at least heard of a *multimeter* before, thereby enabling you to take an educated guess at this question.

Last-Minute Guesses

As you work your way through the test, the traditional exam format indicates the number of questions completed and questions outstanding. Under the adaptive format model, you will not be given information on how many questions are left. It will be up to the adaptive testing engine to determine when you are through. If you are taking the traditional format test, budget your time by making sure that you've completed one-fourth of the questions one-quarter of the way through the test period. Check again three-quarters of the way through. If you're not finished with the test at the five-minute mark, use the last five minutes to *guess* your way through the remaining questions.

Guesses are more valuable than blank answers, because blanks are *always* wrong. A guess has a 25 percent (one in four) chance of being right. If you don't have a clue regarding the remaining questions, pick answers at random, or choose all a's, b's, and so on. The important thing is to submit a test for scoring that has *an answer for every question*.

Additional Resources

By far, the best source of information about A+ certification tests comes from CompTIA. Because products and technologies—and the tests that go with them—change frequently, the best resource for obtaining exam-related information is the Internet. If you haven't already visited the CompTIA Web site, do so at **www.comptia.org**. You can also find A+ exam information at **www.examcram.com**.

There's *always* a way to find what you want on the Web, if you're willing to invest some time and energy. As long as you can get to the CompTIA site (and we're pretty sure that it will stay at **www.comptia.org** for a long while yet), you have a good jump on finding what you need.

Motherboards

Terms you'll need to understand:

✓ Motherboard form factors

✓ Megahertz (MHz)

✓ Pin grid array (PGA) and staggered pin grid array (SPGA)

✓ Alternating current (AC) and direct current (DC)

✓ Cards and integrated circuit (IC) boards

✓ Bus types (ISA, EISA, VESA, MCA, PCI, and PC card)

✓ Data flow

Concepts you'll need to master:

✓ Connectivity

✓ System components

✓ Slots and sockets

✓ Throughput

✓ Process and data flow

The motherboard, sometimes called the system board or *planar* board, is the basic foundation of a computer and connects all the components of the system. Most PCs today have consolidated almost all the electronic components onto the motherboard. Besides containing the central processing unit (CPU) and the supporting chip set, the motherboard holds the expansion bus, Input/Output (I/O), interfaces, drive controllers, and random access memory (RAM).

The system board provides *connectivity* for all system components. Essentially, it is the hardware foundation to which all the connecting parts involved in the computer are attached. The motherboard does the following:

➤ Distributes power from the power supply

➤ Provides data paths for control signals and data

➤ Offers various sockets and pads for mounting components

System Boards: A Brief History

All motherboards are affected by three basic factors: the *form factor*, which determines the actual physical dimensions of the board; the *chip set*, which specifies what supporting chips will be placed on the board to control the flow of information; and lastly, the *bus structure*, which determines the actual design of the circuit traces on the board and the electrical signals that flow across those circuit traces.

In 1981, International Business Machines (IBM) released the original personal computer (PC). This original PC's motherboard had five expansion slots that were configured much like today's Industry Standard Architecture (ISA) slots. The data path for those five expansion slots was 8 bits wide, meaning the bus structure could handle only 8 bits of information at a time. Likewise, the main board could support memory between 64KB (kilobytes) and 256KB. The back of the board had two connectors: a keyboard connector and a cassette tape connector. At the time, the floppy disk was too expensive to include in most of these machines, so many of them were programmed using a cassette tape.

The eXtended Technology (XT) computer was released in 1983, with three additional slots for expansion added to the motherboard. Although the keyboard connector became standard on all later motherboards, the cassette connector quickly gave way to floppy drives and the newly released hard drives. The primary memory capability was increased to 640KB. We will be discussing primary memory, RAM, and other types of memory in Chapter 4.

Finally, in 1984, the PC began to catch on, and one of the most influential changes occurred when IBM released the advanced technology (AT) form factor. The AT used a 16-bit data path, allowing information to travel across the motherboard 16 bits at a time. The ISA slots were modified to handle the increase and became predominantly 16-bit slots, although one or two slots were kept to an 8-bit configuration for backward compatibility.

A second slot was added to the original 8-bit slot, which gave the 16-bit ISA technology backward compatibility. The second slot had a sort of extension to the original 8-bit slot, and the expansion cards had additional edge connectors. The card itself acted as a sort of bridge across the two slots on the motherboard. Figure 2.1 shows an ISA network interface card (NIC) that is often found in a modern PC.

Another important change was the introduction of ROM BIOS and CMOS. Essentially, these are two types of memory used for configuring the basic elements of a computer. The use of a memory chip to hold configuration information moved computers away from having to use dual inline package (DIP) switches and jumpers. Additionally, BIOS and CMOS eliminated the need for the special configuration diskette—a boot-up disk or system disk—that earlier PCs used. (We discuss BIOS in further detail in Chapter 4.)

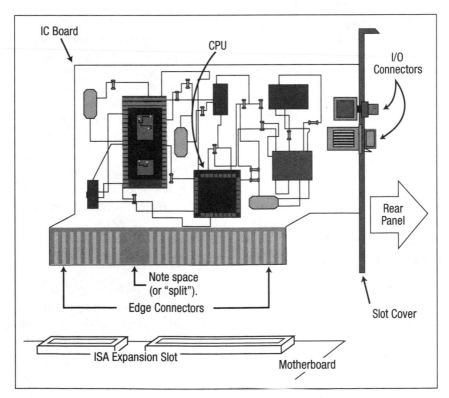

Figure 2.1   A typical 16-bit ISA expansion card.

CMOS

Complementary metal oxide semiconductor (CMOS) RAM is a small, battery-backed memory bank that stores configuration settings. XT motherboards were relatively simple, so basic configuration changes were done manually through jumpers and switches. The AT form factor has many more configuration options, and CMOS allows many of these settings to be configured through the keyboard.

CMOS settings are maintained for as long as any electrical current is available. Even when the PC is disconnected from a wall outlet, a small battery on the motherboard provides enough current to maintain the CMOS settings. In the event that those settings become corrupted, or if someone changes the settings, a common way to reset the CMOS is to remove the battery and wait a few minutes.

Advanced Technology (AT)

The IBM AT form factor made the motherboard much larger than the XT boards, requiring a larger case to hold all the parts. Additionally, the common manufacturing process placed the bus slots flat on the motherboards, with expansion cards inserted perpendicular to the main board, standing straight up. Later motherboards introduced a riser card, which allowed the expansion cards to be inserted parallel to the board; this made the outer casing smaller.

By this time, other companies were getting into the computer market and were producing machines that were exactly compatible with IBM machines. These PCs were called *clones*, and whenever IBM came up with a new idea, the clone manufacturers produced a copy. The 16-bit expansion cards could still fit on a cloned XT board, but those companies didn't want to market old technology. Instead, they retrofitted the new cards to the smaller motherboards and called them *Baby AT* boards. In the process, they accidentally produced a smaller, more streamlined PC that used less desktop space.

Components of the Motherboard

Figure 2.2 is a stylized diagram (not a schematic) of a typical AT motherboard. The diagram is for your general reference, showing an outlined representation of the motherboard's components. Although ATX and NLX boards (discussed later in this chapter) can be laid out quite differently, the relative size and shapes of the various components is easier to see on an AT board.

One of the important changes in the ATX family of motherboards is the relocation of the CPU to the back of the board near a single cooling fan. Figure 2.3 demonstrates this change, and it's important that you remember it.

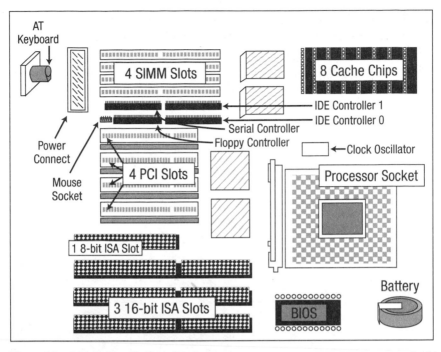

Figure 2.2   A basic AT motherboard.

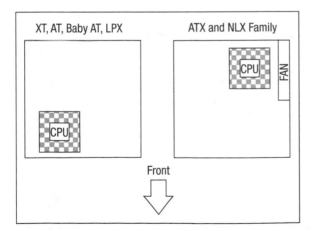

Figure 2.3   CPU moves to the back near the cooling fan on ATX and NLX boards.

Low Profile Extensions (LPX)

When Lotus released the 1-2-3 spreadsheet, it quickly became a "must-have" application. Corporate America began buying personal computers in very large quantities, and desk space became a problem. Therefore, in 1987, Western Digital Corporation released an even smaller form factor. This was the Low Profile

Extensions (LPX) design, which introduced the bus riser card. The riser card was mounted in the center of the motherboard and was narrower than a typical expansion card. By installing the expansion cards parallel to the motherboard, the LPX form factor significantly lowered the overall height of the outer casing. (This "low profile" is signified by the LP in LPX.) We'll discuss the NLX boards in a moment, but Figure 2.4 shows how the form factor reflects the movement of the riser card.

Typically, when you look at the back of an AT or Baby AT computer, you'll see that the slot covers are in a vertical (up-and-down) orientation. However, on the

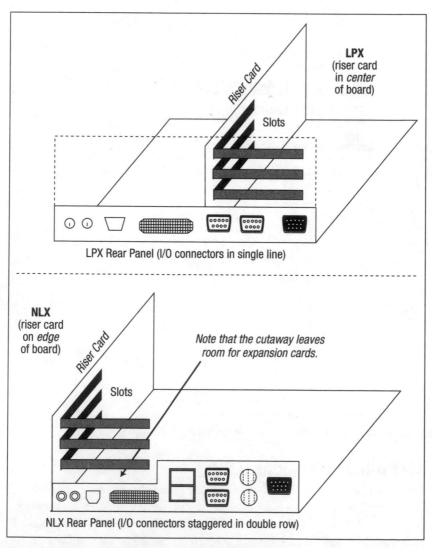

Figure 2.4   Riser card location in LPX and NLX motherboards.

back of an LPX machine, the slot covers are in a horizontal (left-right) orientation. Within the past few years, the AT, Baby AT, and LPX form factors have largely been replaced by the ATX family of motherboards.

 The design of a computer's case is engineered to provide an even flow of air around the inside of the machine. Keeping unused expansion slots covered maintains this flow of air. Therefore, an expansion slot should either have an expansion card installed in it, or the slot cover should be in place.

Clock Speed and Megahertz

Clock speed is a frequency measurement that refers to cycles per second. It is frequently written in megahertz (MHz), where 1MHz refers to 1 million cycles per second. The motherboard has an oscillator, or electronic clock, which is configured through jumpers to yield a specific frequency. This oscillator is the foundation for all the timing cycles used by other components.

The motherboard design matches the speed of the oscillator, and the processor chip must be matched to the motherboard clock speed. The frequency of the motherboard determines the processor chip's running speed. Placing a 100MHz processor chip on a 166MHz motherboard can overheat the chip, lead to random lockups and glitches, and destroy the chip.

 Newer motherboards are designed to run at multiple clock speeds that can be manually configured. All components on the motherboard should be rated to run at the maximum speed rating for the motherboard.

ATX Boards

It wasn't long before IBM lost its dominance in the PC industry. Compaq was one of the first clone manufacturers, leading to the microprocessor revolution that swept across the world in the 1990s. With motherboards directly related to processor chips, the leading chip manufacturer didn't take long to get involved with the design of boards. In 1995, Intel released its specifications for the ATX form factor, calling for an open standard in the design of future motherboards. An *open standard* means that anyone can use the design freely. Apple Computer chose to use a *proprietary standard*, meaning that anyone who wanted to build an Apple-compatible computer or device had to pay a licensing fee to Apple Computer.

The ATX specification called for several important improvements. One of the changes was a built-in, double-high, external I/O connector panel shown in Figure 2.5. Along with the changes in the connector panel, the locations of the connectors were moved to allow for shorter cables between devices, such as hard

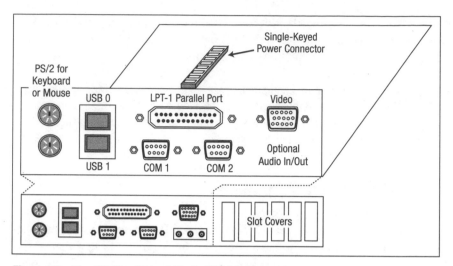

Figure 2.5 The ATX form factor (with double-high I/O panel).

drives and floppy drives. Another change was the standardization of single-keyed power connectors. The CPU and memory banks were relocated to allow for easier accessibility and cooling.

The ATX form factor features I/O ports built right into the board (as opposed to just their connectors being built-in on AT boards), and there is an integrated PS/2 mouse connector rather than the AT DIN connector. The board is rotated 90 degrees for access to the entire board, and better cooling circulation reduces heat. Air blows into rather than out of the case, and the CPU is placed closer to the power supply with its cooling fan.

The ATX uses a single-keyed, 20-pin power supply connector. A so-called keyed connector means that it can be connected to its opposite connection in only one direction. Usually, this is done by a molded notch or groove in the plastic connector casing or by color coding the ribbon cable attached to the connector. Keying a connector means designing the plug and the socket with matching notches. If the notches don't line up, the plug can't fit into the socket.

These changes in form factor were designed to reduce the cost of manufacturing and to provide for faster and easier maintenance. However, competition in the processor manufacturing sector was heating up as Advanced Micro Devices (AMD) and Cyrix began selling their own brands of processor chips. When the original ATX specification was released by Intel, the AMD K-5 and K-6 CPUs were plug compatible. However, AMD later released its own open standard, which was different from Intel's and required a corresponding chip set.

The original ATX form factor was smaller than previous designs, but it wasn't long before Intel released a second standard for an even smaller board, which allowed for smaller cases (profiles). This smaller board was called a Mini ATX form factor. Later, even smaller designs were released, including the Micro ATX and Flex ATX. Regardless of the type, all system boards in the ATX family use the same mounting system. ATX boards are installed in most of today's computers.

NLX

In 1996, when Intel updated the LPX form factor to the NLX form factor (see Figure 2.4), the new design moved the riser card to the outer edge of the motherboard. This provided more room on the board for expansion slots, along with greater accessibility to system components. Both the LPX and NLX retain the parallel (horizontal) slot orientation, with the NLX having a sort of L-shaped profile where the riser card sits on the edge of the motherboard.

An easily recognizable feature of the NLX board is that it has a sort of step shape to the back panel, as shown in Figure 2.6. Some of the connectors are in a single line, and others are one above the other in a double line. The step shape leaves room for expansion cards.

Slots and Sockets

Most processors today are mounted on the motherboard with either a *socket* or a *slot* arrangement. With increasing competition in the motherboard and micro-processor manufacturing market, Intel and AMD have created variations on these two ways a CPU can be installed on a motherboard.

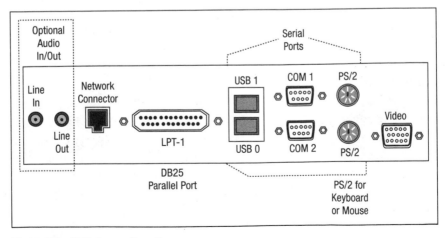

Figure 2.6   NLX step configuration.

Socket 7

A socket is designed for what's called pin grid array (PGA) chip packaging. Typically, this is a rectangular type of chip with hundreds of tiny pins on the bottom side. The chip plugs directly into the socket itself, which is usually a Zero Insertion Force (ZIF) socket. A ZIF socket commonly has a lever along one side, making it look much like the handle of a typical paper cutter. Raising or lowering the lever handle moves the chip mechanically in or out of the socket with zero force, eliminating bent or broken pins.

Another common form of the standard pin grid array, is the staggered pin grid array (SPGA). This is where the pins at the bottom of the chip are staggered, decreasing the overall size of the chip and allowing for more pins. Sockets are sometimes referred to as *flat technology*.

The most popular socket was Socket 7, which used a voltage regulator module (VRM) that was either in the circuitry of the motherboard itself, or in a module that could be mounted on the motherboard. This allowed the socket to provide the different voltages required for the many different chips that were designed for the socket. These voltages include 5 volts (V), 3.3V, 3.2V, 2.9V 2.4V, and all the way down to 1.8V.

The design of the Pentium Pro, using a built-in L-2 cache, was much larger than previous Pentiums and led to Socket 8. The complexity of this socket led to its being replaced by Socket 370 (370 pins in PGA), which has become popular with the Celeron processor series.

AMD created its own socket for the Athlon and Duron chips using a standard pin grid array and called it Socket A. Socket A used 462 pins and 11 plugs, with the same physical layout as a Socket 370, but with different locations for the pins. Each socket is specific to the chips designed for it, and neither socket will accept both types of chips.

Indexing

Socket architecture (sometimes called *flat architecture*) calls for some way to know the correct way to install the chip. This system, called *indexing*, has changed through the years. Prior to the Pentium family of chips, it was very difficult to find the index marker. Often, a single (very small) pin was square rather than round. However, modern chips are a bit easier to index, as shown in Figure 2.7, because they use a missing pin on the one side of the chip, with a corresponding indicator (or index marker) on the top of the chip.

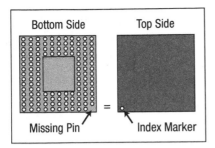

Figure 2.7   Using a missing pin for indexing a chip.

Slot Technology

A second method of mounting a chip is with a slot that uses what's called either Single Edge Connector (SEC) or Single Edge Processor (SEP) packaging. Pentium II, Pentium III, the Celeron, and AMD's Athlon chip are all provided in SEC or SEP packaging. Rather than needing hundreds of pins, the processor is mounted on its own integrated circuit (IC) board, or "cartridge," using the board's contacts to connect to the motherboard. As you can see from Figure 2.8, these slots look very much like an expansion card.

In Slot 1 or Slot A, the IC board is keyed so that it fits into the slot in only one way. Using a slot (and miniature IC board) is more expensive than a simple horizontal, flat socket. For that reason, and the fact that a Celeron chip is a less expensive version of the Pentium II and III, the Celeron can be purchased in either a socket or a slot configuration.

The slot looks much like a standard Peripheral Component Interconnect (PCI) slot, but it is usually mounted towards the rear of the motherboard, away from

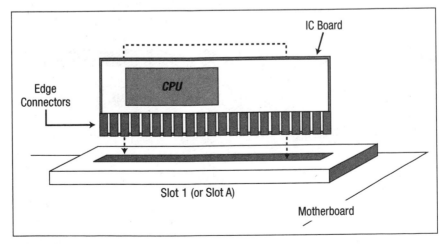

Figure 2.8   Vertical CPU slot technology.

the bus (we discuss PCI later in this chapter). A common feature of slots is their use of a brace, or bracket, as part of the motherboard, which ensures that once the cartridge is inserted into the slot, it won't move or come free.

Note: The IC board may sometimes be referred to as a daughterboard, or cartridge.

Slot 1 is designed for mounting a 242-pin, single-edged chip cartridge. It looks a lot like a very large SIMM (discussed in Chapter 4). Slot 2 was designed for the Pentium II and III Xenon processors, using 330 pins with a vertical architecture like Slot 1. Once again, AMD created Slot A to compete with Intel. Slot A was used for the Athlon and Duron processors, and was incompatible with Slot 1 or 2. Table 2.1 shows the differences among the various sockets and slots.

A few so-called conversion boards use a Socket 370 mounted on a vertical board, where the board will fit into a Slot 1 environment. This allows processors designed for flat technology to be plugged into the conversion board, which can then be plugged into a Slot 1.

Finally, in 1999, Intel developed flip chip pin grid array (FC-PGA), where the chip die was mounted upside down. This allowed for a reduction in manufacturing costs that couldn't be achieved with standard slot technology. The Pentium III, Pentium IV, and later chips will most likely be this configuration.

Power Supply

The power supply converts *alternating* current (AC) to *direct* current (DC) at the voltages required by the system components. Computer components usually require direct current at 24V, 12V, 5V, and 3V, whereas in the United States, typical wall outlets provide alternating current at 110V. Although technically not a component of the motherboard, the power supply is physically attached to the computer case and connects to the motherboard through either a single, keyed

Table 2.1 Sockets and slots.			
Name	**Pins**	**Layout**	**Chips**
Socket 7	321	SPGA	Pentium 75-266+, MMX, OD, x86, K-5, K-6
Socket 8	387	Dual-pattern SPGA	Pentium Pro
Socket 370 (PGA 370)	370	SPGA	Celeron PGA, Pentium III PGA
Socket A (Socket 462)	462	PGA socket	Duron, Athlon PGA
Slot 1 (SC242)	242	Edge connector	Pentium II, Celeron SEP, Pentium III SEC
Slot A	242	Edge connector	Athlon SEC
Slot 2 (SC330)	330	Edge connector	Pentium II Xeon, Pentium III Xeon

connector or a set of two connectors. The single, keyed connector was developed to eliminate the possibility of destroying a motherboard by reversing the connectors.

 Keying a connector means designing the plug and the socket with matching notches. If the notches don't line up, the plug can't fit into the socket. Note that connectors are keyed, but chips are indexed.

The motherboard distributes power to all its system components, except for high-current components such as the fan or disk drives, which connect directly to the power supply. Today's power supplies are usually rated at more than 200 watts (W) and are capable of powering almost any configuration of system components. Older computers, such as the early XTs, had power supplies rated at less than 100W and often failed to meet the demand of additional components.

 The power supply is a swap-out, or exchange component, rather than a repair item. Voltage and current levels within a power supply can be lethal. Furthermore, computer-grade capacitors can hold a charge even after the supply is unplugged. Always treat a power supply with respect and replace it if defective. Do not repair it!

Expansion Bus Architecture

New peripheral devices, such as printers, drives, monitors, and so forth, are being developed every day. For a system to take advantage of these new developments, there has to be a common way of connecting them to the motherboard. This common connection point is the *expansion bus*, sometimes called an *I/O bus*.

A *bus* is simply a way to move electrical signals from one place to another on a circuit board. In this case, the circuit board we're talking about is the motherboard. The bus structure provides long, narrow connection slots so that integrated circuit (IC) boards—often called cards—can be pushed into them edgewise. We often refer to these connections by their architecture, such as an ISA slot or a PCI slot. Expansion cards are designed to work with specific bus structures, and have become known as ISA cards, PCI cards, and so forth, following the convention of including the bus architecture.

The expansion bus is a set of standardized connectors (slots), located on the motherboard, which provide connectivity to the data path. You can think of the expansion bus as a toll plaza on a highway. With eight tollbooths on an eight-lane highway, traffic moves fairly smoothly. This is analogous to an 8-bit bus with an 8-bit processor. However, with a 16-lane highway and only 8 tollbooths, traffic jams will occur as the traffic is funneled down from 16 lanes to 8 lanes. This is what happens when a 16-bit processor is connected to an 8-bit bus.

Note: Although the expansion bus provides exceptional flexibility, it can also be a bottleneck as processor speed increases. The design of the expansion bus has changed almost as fast as processors in the need to improve performance.

PCs use a processor bus, a memory bus, an address bus, and an expansion bus. The first three, which relate to moving data in or out of various chips, are discussed further in Chapter 4. We'll talk about expansion buses here. An expansion bus is usually a visible slot on the motherboard that is used to hold add-on cards (e.g., sound card or internal modem). You need to be able to distinguish the various expansion buses on the basis of their names, shapes, and general locations on the board.

Remember that a bus is a way to move information around a circuit board. A *signal trace* is the piece of circuitry that allows for the flow of electricity. If we use eight pulses of electricity in a combination, we can call that an 8-bit piece of information. Therefore, if we want to move an 8-bit piece of information, we need eight signal traces—an 8-bit bus.

Bus configurations can be 8-bit, 16-bit, 32-bit, 64-bit, and so on. The more bits of information that can be processed simultaneously, the faster the *throughput* for a given clock speed. Remember that we spoke about the earliest personal computers using an 8-bit signal track, and that a fundamental change in the AT boards was the use of a 16-bit bus. This allowed the AT motherboards to move far more complex information across the system. *Throughput* is essentially the amount of data that can move through a bus.

Although we say a bus is so many bits, that doesn't mean that there are only 8, or 16, or some other number of connectors on the bus. A bus has additional connectors used for such things as addressing, interrupts, or other functions within the bus itself. However, we always refer to the size of the bus in terms of how many bits of data can move across that bus—the *data path*.

Most of today's motherboards have at least three different buses, and often a fourth bus. These buses include:

➤ *ISA bus*—This bus is typically a 16-bit bus for compatibility with older machines using legacy cards.

➤ *PCI bus*—This bus provides a bridge between the processor and slower ISA bus.

➤ *Accelerated Graphics Ports (AGP) bus*—This bus is dedicated to high-speed processing for video.

➤ *L-2 cache processor bus*—This bus, discussed in Chapter 4, uses a high-speed memory management technique.

Industry Standard Architecture (ISA)

The original ISA 8-bit bus was designed to use the edge of an IC card (an edge connector), with 62 contacts. It provided 8 data lines and 20 address lines. This allowed every card installed in the system to be addressed within the first megabyte of memory. Because the original 8086 and 8088 processors could address only 1MB of memory, this was fine.

We can also measure the time it takes for information to move across a bus, much like we measure the speed of a microprocessor. We'll talk about clock speed in a moment, but for now it's useful to know that, although the CPU in earlier machines ran at various clock speeds, the original ISA buses ran at only 4.77MHz.

As processor speeds increased, new devices and applications were developed that required moving more information through the buses. At 4.77MHz, the original throughput for an ISA bus was 39 megabits (Mb)—not megabytes (MB)—per second.

Bits and Bytes

Everyone throws around terms like bits, bytes, megabits, megabytes, and ever larger numbers referring to larger amounts of storage. You need to know that a 1MB file isn't exactly 1,000 bytes, but 1,024 bytes. To avoid any possibility of confusion, Table 2.2 lists the exact number of bytes and bits in single units of each category. In abbreviations, note that a bit uses a lowercase "b," whereas a byte uses an uppercase "B."

Table 2.2 Standard terminology for bits and bytes.	
Term	Number of Bits
bit	Single 0 or 1
kilobit (Kb)	1 bit×1,024—1,024 bits
megabit (Mb)	1 bit×1,024^2 (or 1,024×1,024)—1,048,576 bits (millions)
gigabit (Gb)	1 bit×1,024^3—1,073,741,824 bits (billions)
terabit (Tb)	1 bit×1,024^4—1,099,511,627,776 bits (trillions)
Byte	8 bits
Kilobyte (KB)	1 byte×1,024-—1,024 bytes (8,192 bits, or 1,024×8)
Megabyte (MB)	1 byte×1,024^2—1,048,576 bytes (millions)
Gigabyte (GB)	1 byte×1,024^3—1,073,741,824 bytes (billions)
Terabyte (TB)	1 byte×1,024^4—1,099,511,627,776 bytes (trillions)

Faster throughput means larger buses, so the AT form factor began to use the 16-bit bus. Originally, the 16-bit buses ran at 6MHz. Not long after, they sped up to 8MHz, and the industry soon decided a standard speed should be used. The 16-bit ISA bus speed was eventually set to 8.33MHz, allowing for a throughput of 128MB per second—much faster than the previous buses.

The 16-bit bus continued to be the standard far beyond the introduction of 32-bit microprocessors. As is typical of the computer industry, no new standard was set for changing technology, so standards for a new bus didn't exist. To take advantage of the faster processors, many companies began using proprietary (not open) technology in their own buses. At that time, many different types of expansion cards were coming out, but they had to match the particular bus technology on the motherboard. Areas impacted by bus technology were memory cards and video cards.

MCA and EISA

In trying to standardize a 32-bit bus, IBM came out with the Micro Channel Architecture (MCA) bus. MCA took full advantage of 32-bit processing, providing a much faster data path. However, the MCA bus wasn't backward compatible with the ISA bus. If you had a device—for instance, a tape backup unit—that used a 16-bit bus, you couldn't use it in a new IBM machine. Instead, you'd have to buy a whole new card connector, and often you'd have to buy a new backup machine to go along with it. Additionally, IBM required a license fee from any manufacturer that wanted to install the bus on its motherboards, and the clone manufacturers didn't want to do that. Because of the incompatibility, licensing fee, and the rapidly expanding clone machine market, the MCA bus never caught on and died a quiet death.

Meanwhile, the clone manufacturers, spearheaded by Compaq, came up with their own standard, calling it the Extended Industry Standard Architecture (EISA) bus. The EISA bus added 90 new connections and 55 new signal traces, making the slot and card much larger. However, rather than a single row of connectors (like the ISA cards), the EISA cards used two lines of connectors running along both sides of the card's edge. This allowed an ISA card to fit in an EISA connector, and the ISA card would work just fine. However, you couldn't put an EISA card into an older ISA connector. The connector had to have contact points on both sides, and older ISA bus connectors did not.

Note: This idea of using both sides of an edge connector inspired the change in architecture between a SIMM and a DIMM, memory modules that we'll discuss in Chapter 4.

Although the EISA bus ran at 8.33MHz, the transfer rate was increased to 32 bits of information, making for a maximum theoretical throughput of 33.32MB per second. Both MCA and EISA were superior technologies, but the EISA bus was significantly more expensive and never really caught on for anything other than network servers and high-end PCs. The EISA bus and the VESA bus, discussed next, were eventually replaced by the PCI bus, which is in use today.

VESA Local-Bus—32-Bit

As you can imagine, there was a real gap as processors got faster and faster, but the 16-bit ISA bus continued to limit throughput, causing a bottleneck. To fix the problem, an organization called the Video Electronics Standard Association (VESA) developed a new type of local bus. It was called a *local* bus because it attached directly to the processor itself through what's called the *local processor bus*. This meant that data didn't have to go through the slow ISA bus, but could come right out of the 32-bit processor and move off to whatever device it was targeted for. These devices usually were memory cards and graphics cards.

Windows, designed to take advantage of 32-bit processing, was hitting the market in 1992. The new graphical user interface (GUI) moved a tremendous amount of information, and the local bus was very useful for speeding up the video monitor and graphics processing. The VESA Local-Bus (VL-Bus) was actually an extension of the 80486 processor bus. As a result, although it connected with newer chip sets and was inexpensive to produce, the VL-Bus didn't interface well in terms of speed. The VL-Bus had numerous glitches when it connected to other chips, along with timing problems.

The VL-Bus was an important step in the development of graphics accelerator cards, along with inspiring the idea of offloading graphics processing from the CPU and moving it to the video card. Because of the intermittent problems, the VL-Bus quickly lost favor when the PCI bus was developed. The PCI bus also came out in 1992, promoted initially by Intel. Once again, the power of the world's leading chip manufacturer brought a lot of influence to bear, along with the advantages of better technology and some basic standardization.

Peripheral Component Interconnect (PCI)

Prior to the VESA bus, a video card would have to be inserted into one of the slots on the motherboard's main expansion bus. This led to competition with other cards for the CPU's attention, so the VESA specification created a new bus, separate from the main bus and dedicated exclusively to the CPU. The VESA bus became the PCI specification, and as it's used in today's motherboards, PCI places an additional bus between the CPU and the ISA bus. The PCI bus doesn't tie directly to the processor bus, but through the use of bridges it avoids the timing issues of the VESA bus.

The main difference between a PCI bus and a VL-Bus is that the PCI bus is a specifically designed, high-speed main expansion bus to be shared by multiple devices. The VL-Bus was a separate bus dedicated to a single device.

 A PCI bus runs at 33MHz, which makes it much faster than the older ISA bus. Many of today's computers have both a PCI and an ISA bus available on the motherboard. However, the ISA bus is gradually falling into disuse.

North Bridge and South Bridge

Keeping in mind that the PCI bus is a sort of bridge between the processor and ISA bus, we should point out that there are really two units involved: the *North bridge* and the *South bridge*. The North bridge is generally used for high-speed interface cards, such as video accelerators and high-speed memory. The South bridge is generally used for slower cards such as USB ports, IDE drives, and ISA slots. As you can see in Figure 2.9, data flows from the CPU to the North bridge and then out of that to the South bridge in a sort of daisy chain.

The South bridge works in conjunction with what's called a Super I/O chip. Originally, the COMmunications (COM) ports, as well as the Line Printer Terminal (LPT) ports, were all separate I/O connections on the motherboard. The Super I/O chip brought them all together onto one chip, reducing the space required. Usually, a manufacturer orders the Super I/O chip from a third-party manufacturer, and so many people don't consider it part of the chip set.

 Pentium machines, in particular, reference the North bridge and South bridge of a PCI bus. Remember that the North bridge is connected to the CPU for high-speed components. Coming out of the North bridge, data passes through to the South bridge, which is used for "S"lower components.

North bridge components are usually Accelerated Graphics Ports (AGPs), SRAM, and other memory chips. South bridge components are usually the Universal Serial Buses (USBs), Integrated Drive Electronics (IDE) drives, ISA slots, and the Super I/O chip with COM1, COM2, LPT1, and the floppy drives (A: and B:).

Chip Sets

The chip set is the foundation of the motherboard. It supports every function of the main processor, or CPU, including the processor interface, memory controllers, bus controllers, I/O controllers, and more. The chip set determines the way that the main processor connects to everything else. As such, the chip set determines what type of processor you can have; how fast it will run; how fast the

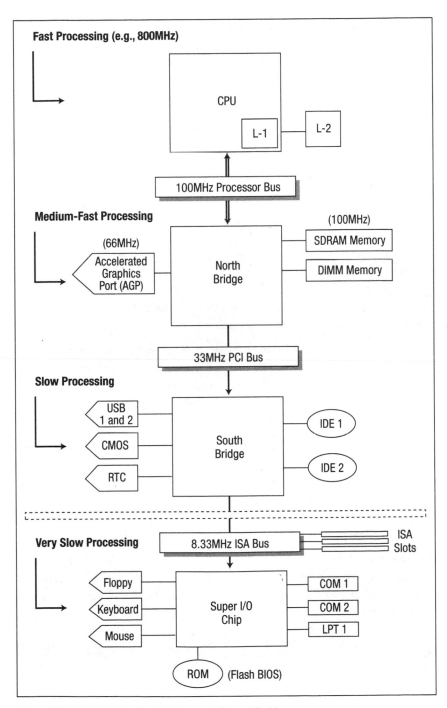

Figure 2.9   North bridge, South bridge, and Super I/O chip.

buses will run; and the speed, type, and amount of memory you can have. Anyone knowledgeable in computers usually refers to both the main processor and the chip set, because the motherboard chip set determines so much about how the CPU will run.

IBM originally designed PCs to use individual microprocessor chips for each individual need. This included the main processor, eventually working with a math coprocessor, or floating-point unit (FPU); clock generators; bus controllers; system timers; interrupt request (IRQ) controllers; direct memory access (DMA) controllers; CMOS; BIOS; RAM; and a number of other chips involved in the motherboard circuit.

The XT boards used six discrete chips, but the AT boards used nine. Then, in 1986, a company called Chips and Technologies released an integrated chip that combined most of the functions of the AT chip set. They used other chips that acted as buffers and minor controllers, making an entire AT motherboard with only five chips. With that, many different companies started combining different chips until Intel entered the market with its own motherboards and chip sets to go along with its processors.

By 1994, Intel established a dominant market position for integrated chip sets, processors, and motherboards. The Intel design, which is also becoming a standard for non-Intel boards, is built around a three-tier architecture using the North bridge, South bridge, and Super I/O chip. Table 2.3 provides a listing of the various chip sets.

An 800 series chip set was released in 1999. The main difference with this chip set is that it does not use the North bridge and South bridge architecture, but uses a hub architecture composed of three basic components: the Graphics and Memory Controller Hub (GMCH), the I/O Controller Hub (IOCH), and the Firmware Hub (FH). Figure 2.10 shows how a hub sits between the CPU and the various buses in modern, high-speed architecture.

The lowest speed bus in hub architecture is a 33MHz PCI bus. In the bridge architecture, the slowest bus is the 8.33MHz ISA bus. Because processing throughput is often set to the slowest speed bus, hub architecture provides great flexibility in connecting newer high-speed devices.

Table 2.3   Chip sets.

Chip Set	Processor Supported
420	80486
430	P5 Pentium
440	P6 (Pentium Pro, Pentium II, Pentium III)
450	P6-Server (Pro, II, III) and Xeon in multiprocessor format

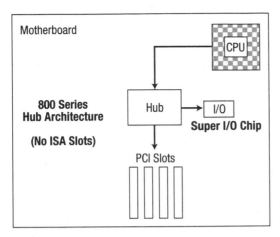

Figure 2.10   The 800 series chip set with hub.

What's important to remember about North bridge-South bridge technology is that it is used in all chip sets prior to the 800 series, which we discuss in a moment.

AMD Chip Sets

Intel is clearly the dominant factor in today's microprocessor manufacturing. However, AMD has continued to be a significant competitor. The AMD 640 chip set is designed to compete with Intel's Pentium processors using the AMD K-5 and K-6 series processors. With the release of the Athlon and Duron processors, which are not compatible with Intel's specifications, AMD also produced the 750 chip set.

The AMD K-6 series processor will plug into Socket 7 architecture used for Intel's Pentium processors. However, the AMD Athlon and Duron are not pin compatible with Intel's Pentium II, Pentium III, and Celeron chip sockets. Therefore, the AMD chips will not work with Intel chip sets and motherboards.

Accelerated Graphics Port (AGP)

The AGP, a local bus that was developed at around the same time as the PCI bus, is similar to a PCI bus, with additional features that center around high-speed video (graphics) processing. With the heavy demands of Windows and computer games, moving the video processing into its own channel dramatically speeds up how fast a computer appears to be running. The AGP connects to the North bridge of the three-tier chip set architecture in most of today's computers.

PC Card (PCMCIA)

The Personal Computer Memory Card Industry Association (PCMCIA) card was introduced in 1990 to give laptop and notebook computers an expansion capability similar to that of desktop computers. Originally, the PC card was designed to store memory on a card, but many manufacturers of peripherals came to realize the implications of this for I/O devices. Because no one could remember the acronym PCMCIA, it became known as the PC card (and the way to remember the acronym is now "people can't memorize computer industry acronyms"). These credit card-size expansion boards have the following features:

➤ Currently exist in four types: Types I, II, III, and IV.

➤ Are differentiated into types according to card thickness in millimeters: Type I, 3.3 mm; Type II, 5 mm; Type III, 10.5 mm; and Type IV, thicker than 10.5 mm, but not yet standardized.

➤ Are included in the Plug-and-Play specification.

➤ Introduced the concept of combining the device and its I/O card on the card (e.g., tiny hard drives, fax modems, network cards, and memory expansion).

Practice Questions

Question 1

> Motherboards are designed to fit one of two basic form factors.
>
> ○ a. True
>
> ○ b. False

Answer b, false, is correct. Motherboards were originally divided into two, somewhat artificially categorized, types: the XT and the AT. Modern specifications now include the LPX, NLX, and ATX form factors.

Question 2

> Many system boards can support multiple clock speeds, which are set with the DOS **Time** command.
>
> ○ a. True
>
> ○ b. False

Answer b, false, is correct. Motherboards use an oscillator to define the overall timing for components. Although many boards do support multiple clock speeds, those speeds are usually set through jumpers that synchronize the system board speed to the processor speed. The DOS **Time** command is used to set or display the time of day, and that time is also derived from the motherboard clock.

Question 3

> The power supply (usually mounted to the case) performs what function?
>
> ○ a. Provides consistent 110V AC to the system board.
>
> ○ b. Converts AC to DC at the voltage required by the system board and system components.
>
> ○ c. Protects the system components from power outages.
>
> ○ d. Boosts power coming from the power utility to acceptable AC voltages for system components.

Answer b is correct. Computers require direct current (DC) at several voltages, including 5V+, 5V-, 12V+, and 12V-. Standard wall outlets in the United States provide 110V alternating current (AC). The power supply's main purpose is to convert that AC to DC at the voltages required by the computer.

Question 4

What type of expansion bus is included on most current system boards? [Choose the two best answers]

- ❑ a. MCA
- ❑ b. ISA
- ❑ c. PCI
- ❑ d. EISA
- ❑ e. VESA

Answers b and c are correct. Most system boards include both the PCI bus and the ISA bus for compatibility, although this is changing. The MCA bus, developed by IBM, never really caught on. VL-Buses were predominantly used for video controllers prior to the adoption of the PCI bus. The EISA bus became primarily a network file server niche-market bus.

Question 5

Which of the following components are usually connected to the South bridge of a 440 series chip set? [Choose the two best answers]

- ❑ a. L-P2 cache
- ❑ b. SDRAM
- ❑ c. USB 0
- ❑ d. Master IDE drive
- ❑ e. AGP

Answers c and d are correct. The North bridge is for high-speed devices such as SDRAM memory chips and an Applied Graphics Port (AGP). The South bridge connects lower speed devices like the USB ports, IDE drive controllers, and CMOS. The Super I/O chip is for very slow COM and LPT ports. The L-2 cache is usually part of the chip die, very close to the CPU.

Question 6

> Which of the following is true of Socket 7?
>
> ○ a. It provides a key connector for expansion bus sockets.
>
> ○ b. It uses a ZIF lever to remove SIMMs.
>
> ○ c. It installs a CPU using flat technology.
>
> ○ d. It works with Slot 1 to increase the CPU clock speed.

Answer c is correct. Socket 7 is typically a horizontal, flat socket design using a particular type of CPU architecture. Key connectors are mostly found on cables of some kind, whereas a Zero Insertion Force (ZIF) socket is designed for CPUs. Slot 1 technology is designed for vertical architecture CPUs and has nothing whatsoever to do with setting clock speeds.

Need to Know More?

 Freedman, Alan. *Computer Desktop Encyclopedia, 2nd Edition*. AMACOM, 1999. ISBN 0-814-479-855. Great for a fast look-up or refresher.

 Messmer, Hans-Peter. *The Indispensable PC Hardware Book, 3rd Edition*. Reading, MA: Addison-Wesley Publishing Company; May 2000. ISBN 0-201-403-994. This is a comprehensive, up-to-date reference book that covers far more than you will need to know for the exam.

 Minasi, Mark. *The Complete PC Upgrade and Maintenance Guide, 11th Edition.* San Francisco, CA: Sybex Network Press, 2000. ISBN 0-782-128-009. This is considered one of the best reference books available. In fact, Minasi's book was instrumental in the formulation of the first A+ exam.

 Muller, Scott. *Upgrading and Repairing PCs, 12th Edition*. Indianapolis, IN: Que, 2000. ISBN 0-7897-2303-4. This is one of our favorites! If you are going to have only one reference book, give this one serious consideration.

 Reeves, Scott, Kalinda Reeves, Stephen Weese, and Christopher S. Geyer. *A+ Exam Prep, 3rd Edition*. Scottsdale, AZ: The Coriolis Group, 2001. ISBN 1-57610-699-3. This is a good reference that concentrates on providing exam-required information.

 Rosch, Winn. *Hardware Bible, 5th Edition*. Indianapolis, IN: Sams Publishing, 1999. ISBN 0-789-717-433. This is a well-organized reference book that covers software issues as well as hardware.

Processors

Terms you'll need to understand:

✓ Microprocessor, processor, chip

✓ Slot cartridge, socket

✓ Electrostatic discharge (ESD), electromagnetic interference (EMI)

✓ Megahertz (MHz)

✓ Chip die, chip package

✓ Throughput

✓ Level 1 (L-1) and Level 2 (L-2) caches

Concepts you'll need to master:

✓ On-die versus external central processing unit (CPU) functions (internal and external bus)

✓ Bus speed

✓ Clock speed, clock cycle, or clock tick

✓ How a cache works

✓ Clock multiplier and overclocking

At the heart of every personal computer (PC) is the central processing unit (CPU), often referred to as a *chip* or *processor*. Traditionally, processors are referred to by their clock speed in megahertz (MHz). Intel is the market leader in chip manufacturing, but several other companies, such as Advanced Micro Devices (AMD) and Cyrix, also manufacture chips. International Business Machines (IBM) also manufactured chips and originally worked in cooperation with Intel to develop a PC that would take advantage of microprocessors. Today, AMD is Intel's strongest competitor.

Central Processing Unit (CPU)

The CPU is where most of the software instructions, math, and logic calculations are performed. Early CPUs added a *math coprocessor*, or *floating-point unit* (FPU), where some of the more complex mathematical calculations were offloaded to improve performance. Beginning with the 80486 family of processors, the math coprocessor began to become an integral part of the CPU.

When you open up a PC and look at the motherboard, the CPU is usually the largest chip on the board. On many motherboards, the CPU is inserted into a plastic holder, or *socket*, making it easy to spot. Modern motherboards tend to have the CPU standing vertically in a slot, which isn't as easy to spot. We'll discuss sockets and slots later in this chapter. If the CPU is in a large, square socket, it often has its own cooling fan directly above it, hiding the actual chip from view. In a vertical configuration, you'll often see what looks like a very deep comb, or a vertical piece of metal with many small ledges coming out at right angles.

Most of today's sockets have what's called a Zero Insertion Force (ZIF) design. *ZIF design* means that you don't need a chip extractor to remove the chip, which reduces the chance of breaking the connector pins. It takes about 100 pounds of insertion force to install a chip into a standard machine socket. ZIF goes a long way toward reducing damaged sockets, chips, and pins.

Electrostatic Discharge (ESD) and ESD Kits

Your body routinely builds up static electricity that discharges to the ground when you touch something conductive. This discharge is known as *electrostatic discharge (ESD)*.

Before you touch any component inside a computer, you should ground yourself by touching a metal part of the chassis (e.g., the power supply casing or the metal frames of the chassis). A better way to ground yourself is to have an ESD kit, which consists of a wrist strap with a ground wire and a specially made floor mat that also has a ground wire.

Some people think the static charge is removed by touching the metal in the chassis. This isn't true; the charge is merely equalized. An ESD kit with floor mat is the only way to move the charge to the ground, thus fully removing the charge.

Perhaps you have heard someone suggest that you should place circuit boards, system boards, and loose chips on a piece of aluminum foil. This is not a good idea. Placing these pieces on aluminum foil can result in a small explosion because many motherboards, expansion cards, and other boards have built-in lithium or nickel cadmium (Nicad) batteries. If these batteries become short circuited, they can overheat and react violently by exploding and throwing off pieces of their metal casings.

 Never place a circuit board of any kind onto conductive surfaces, such as metal foil. Remember the ESD is electrostatic discharge. On the other hand, EMI is electromagnetic interference (when several wires are placed in close proximity).

Processor Speed

Starting with the original 8088 processor, CPUs were referred to by their clock speed. This continued through the 80486 family of chips (486 machines) and even into the early Pentium chips. Today, companies try to use a name that can be trademarked, so most CPUs are referred to by a name instead of a number.

Clock Speed

A processor always processes instructions internally at its rated speed (133MHz, 200MHz, 550MHz, and so forth). After the internal processing is completed, the CPU stores the results in memory. Although that memory is often the *main*, or *system* memory, which is called random access memory (RAM), it can also be in a separate area of memory called *cache memory*. The rate at which the CPU transfers information to main memory is controlled by the motherboard's oscillator. This oscillator vibrates very quickly, acting like a tiny clock, which gives rise to the term "clock speed." A "clock tick" is when the oscillator makes 1 vibration, much like a tiny metronome needle swinging back and forth.

The 486-DX2/Overdrive chip ran internally at twice the clock speed of the motherboard. A DX4 could be configured to run at two or three times the motherboard clock speed. However, even though the internal processing took place at double, triple, or quadruple the speed of the original chip, the transfer rate of the results of all that processing was still the original motherboard clock speed.

Bus Speed

Although processors are often identified by their speed, measured in megahertz (MHz), another important aspect is the width of several closely related buses. The processor speed is fairly straightforward, but "width" includes several variables, such as the processor bus, data input/output (I/O) buses, and memory address buses. For instance, the internal address bus may be one size, but the external bus may be a different size.

Internal vs. External Buses

When we speak of a chip's *internal* bus, we mean that the bus is cast right on the manufacturing die (like an L-1 cache, covered in a later section). A *die*, sometimes called the *chip package*, is essentially the foundation for the multitude of circuit traces making up a microprocessor, along with the many transistors, diodes, and a host of other electrical components. A manufacturing *mask* is the photographic blueprint for the given chip. It is used to etch the complex circuitry into a piece (chip) of silicon.

Conversely, an *external* bus indicates that information moves out of the CPU, across a bus to another destination (e.g., an L-2 cache, discussed in a later section). Because *bus width* is typically measured by the number of bits that the bus can process at one time, we can have an 8-, 16-, 32-, and 64-bit bus, all of which have different widths. This width generally depends upon where the processor is directing information.

Advanced technology (AT) boards run at either 33MHz or 66MHz, and we call this speed the *motherboard bus speed*. The 80486-DX2, followed by the Pentium family of processors, introduced running speeds that have gone far beyond the motherboards. To that end, we now have differing bus speeds in different locations on the motherboard.

Processor Families

When IBM introduced the first PC, it contained an Intel 8088 processor chip. Although the 8086 was the first CPU in existence, the 8088 was actually the first chip to be released on the market. IBM used the 8088 in its eXtended Technology (XT) computers. Features of the 8088 included the following:

➤ A clock speed of 4.77MHz, or 4,770,000 cycles (ticks) per second. Each cycle represents the execution of one instruction or part of one instruction. Later, it was designed to run at 8MHz, which is close to double the speed of the original.

➤ An 8-bit external bus that could move 8 bits of information into memory at one time.

➤ A 16-bit internal bus.

The 8088 chip was designed with a 20-bit address bus that enabled it to access 1 megabyte (MB) of random access memory (RAM). This was considered far more than adequate for any expected application. However, the introduction of graphical user interfaces (GUIs) and Windows quickly demonstrated the need for a chip that could address far more memory. RAM and memory are discussed at length in Chapter 4.

The 8086 chip, produced prior to the 8088, was a somewhat faster chip. The 8086 was a true 16-bit chip that used 16 bits for both the internal and the external bus. However, at the time IBM felt that people would be unwilling to pay a premium price for this capability, and it adopted the less expensive 8088 for the first PCs. The 8086 had approximately 20 percent faster *throughput* than the 8088 because of its ability to communicate at 16 bits with the other system components. For the moment, understand that throughput is basically how much data can travel across a bus in a given time segment. Both the bus speed and bus width impact the throughput. We discuss throughput more thoroughly in Chapter 8.

IBM could say that the 8MHz 8086 PS/2-30 was two and a half times faster than the 4.77MHz 8088 PC/XT because of the change in the external bus from 8 bits to 16 bits. This was one of the first indications that performance could be increased by making the data path larger.

IBM

Because IBM had a specific license to produce Intel-designed chips, the IBM processors are somewhat different than the AMD and Cyrix chips in that they use the official masks and microcode developed by Intel. A manufacturing *mask* is the photographic blueprint for the given chip that is used to etch the complex circuitry into a piece (chip) of silicon. IBM chips also have additional features and capabilities, although the "Intel Inside" marketing campaign has successfully limited IBM's chip usage. One of the chips offered by IBM was the Blue Lightning, a 32-bit chip comparable to the Intel 486-DX.

AMD and Cyrix

While Intel continues to dominate the chip-manufacturing business, other manufacturing companies are making inroads into the microprocessor market. Two of the better-known chip makers are AMD and Cyrix. An interesting lawsuit came about when Intel tried to trademark the numbers 80386, 80486, and so on, only to discover that it wasn't legal to do so. That's why Intel created the Pentium name; a name can be trademarked.

Real Mode and the Virtual Machine (VM)

Beginning with the 80286 chip, reference to Real Mode means that the newer chips could imitate the original 8088 chip. Put another way, the chip addresses the first 1,024 bytes of *conventional memory* by assigning "real" addresses to "real" locations in memory. Even in today's Windows machines, running a DOS application initiates a virtual 8088 PC called a virtual machine (VM). (We discuss VM sessions in the latter half of this book, when we discuss operating systems.)

With its 20-bit address bus, the 8088 could directly assign memory addresses to 1MB of memory. A CPU operating in Real Mode addresses memory in the original 1MB range that the 8088 used. The 286 could address a total of 16MB of memory, but it had to maintain backward compatibility with the many PCs and applications already on the market. Many of the applications had to be re-written to take advantage of any memory beyond the first 1MB of conventional memory.

 Virtual Real Mode (or Virtual 86 Mode) allows several Real Mode sessions to run concurrently in what's called a virtual machine.

Breaking the 1MB Limit

Although the 8088/86 CPU could address 1MB of memory, software applications and the operating system rapidly took over the entire megabyte and demanded more. Unfortunately, a number of engineering decisions had been made that would affect the PC industry for the next 10 years. As a result, Intel developed the 80286 CPU, which was a fundamental turning point in how chips accessed memory. The release of the 286 coincided with the new AT motherboard design.

The 80286 was used in the new IBM AT, along with the original PS/2 models. Later PS/2 models began using the 80386 chip. Windows 2.0 was starting to catch on, and in an effort to reduce the boxy size of computers, IBM also moved away from the standard five-pin Deutsche Institut für Normung (DIN) connector. A smaller connector—known as a PS/2 connector—lives on today as one of the standard keyboard and mouse connectors.

The increasing market for PCs led to the emergence of many new companies that manufactured computers. These computers came to be known as *IBM clones*, which were referred to as *AT-compatible* or *AT-class* computers, leading to the standardization of the AT-type motherboard.

Real Mode vs. Protected Mode

The 286 chip, which could address 16MB of memory, introduced the concept of Real Mode along with Protected Mode. In Real Mode, the 286 acted essentially the same as the 8088/86 chips and could run older software with no modifications. Once again, Real Mode means that the chip addresses the first 1,024 bytes of *conventional memory* by assigning "real" addresses to "real" locations in memory.

As software began requiring more memory, the 286 introduced a way for software to access 1 gigabyte (GB) of memory. This was called *virtual memory*, and it was done by "swapping" code held in RAM to a disk. This enabled the software to use the freed-up actual memory, and to think that it could use up to 1GB of RAM while remaining unaware of the swapping.

With an appropriate operating system and software, the chip could run multiple programs at once, using the 286 Protected Mode feature. This sparked the development of OS/2, and later, the Windows 3.0 Standard Mode. As we've said, we discuss operating systems later in this book, but consider that even today, DOS applications running in Windows and the way that Windows manages virtual memory can be traced all the way back to the 80286 microprocessor.

Switching from Protected Mode to Real Mode

Both the operating system and the CPU control *virtual memory*, or information being swapped out of RAM to a disk. 286 Protected Mode introduced this capability, but software development was slow to catch up. The 286 was unable to switch from Protected Mode to Real Mode without resetting (warm rebooting) the computer. However, it could go the other way and switch from Real Mode to Protected Mode without resetting.

The next generation of chips, the 386, allowed switching to either mode without a system reset. This inability to come back from Protected Mode without a warm reboot changed history when IBM continued to develop OS/2 for the 80286 and began to fall behind in relation to Microsoft's desire for a multitasking operating system. Microsoft built the Windows GUI into New Technology (NT), and OS/2 became an also-ran.

The 80386 Processor

The introduction of the 80386 represented another fundamental change in the world of PCs. At that time, the PC was catching on and bringing major changes to the business world. The graphic interface of Windows was demanding lots of processing power, and Intel was beginning to dominate the chip market. The constant demand for more speed and more power was pushing development efforts, and new chips were coming out every year.

Applications were becoming larger, requiring more memory to hold their code and data, and customers were prepared to spend more money for RAM if it would make their machines faster. The PC had hit a critical acceptance point, and the expanding market was bringing software that could work with as much memory as a chip could address. The 80386 opened the door to that memory, and finally provided enough speed for the new multitasking operating systems and programs.

The 386 chips had a full 32-bit processor (32-bit internal registers, 32-bit internal data bus, and 32-bit external bus), a 32-bit memory address bus, and clock speeds from 16 to 33MHz. Manufacturers other than Intel offered chips up to 40MHz, but all 386s had the ability to address 4GB (4 billion bytes) of physical memory. The main difference from the 286 was that the 80386 had the ability to switch between Protected Mode and Real Mode through software control, and didn't have to reset the system. This made multitasking (more properly called "task switching") more practical.

With built-in memory management, the 386-DX enabled software to access 64 terabytes (TB) of memory, or about 1 trillion bytes, so software written for the 386 chip could access 64 trillion bytes of memory. (Current estimates of the space requirements of the human mind suggest that a complete lifetime of memories can be stored in about 15TB.)

SX Versions

Market forces and the dramatic increase in consumer interest led Intel to develop a chip for people who wanted 386 capability at a price closer to that of the older 286 chips. This budget-conscious buying is essentially what led to an entire line of derivative chips—the SX chips—being developed. Later, with the same market forces at work, but with the names of CPUs moving away from clock speeds, Intel and AMD continued the practice of releasing less expensive chips with reduced capabilities (e.g., Celeron and Duron).

The 386-SX ended the reign of the 286 because of its better memory management unit (MMU) and the new Virtual Real Mode feature. The 386-DX and the 386-SX could both run Windows 3.x in Enhanced Mode (formally called 386 Enhanced Mode). Enhanced Mode allowed Windows software to take advantage of the 80386 chip's ability to continually switch between Real Mode and Protected Mode.

Along with the increased market for PCs, both in business and at home, people wanted portability and a general reduction in the space that their computers were taking up. Portable computers were introduced, but didn't really excite the market the way that laptop computers did.

Laptop computers came about with the development of liquid crystal display (LCD) panel technology, and they began driving the research into size reduction and lower power consumption. To meet those needs, yet another line of chips—the SL line—introduced lower power consumption and something called System Management Interrupts (SMI), with power management features for battery conservation, including several sleep modes.

Coprocessors

Starting with the Intel 80386, another major marketing push began stressing the performance advantages of adding a *math coprocessor*, or *floating-point unit (FPU)*. Models were differentiated by changing the last digit of the main CPU's number to a seven, but the "87" chips were always the same speed as the primary "86" chip. For example, the 33MHz 80386 was paired with an optional 33MHz 80387. These math coprocessors had been available as far back as the 8086, but at that time they affected only arithmetic calculations (add, subtract, multiply, and divide). Therefore, they greatly speeded up spreadsheet applications, but did not necessarily speed up all applications.

This marketing campaign was so effective that when the 486 chips internalized the floating-point unit, it was simply disabled in the SX line and a separate—so-called 487—math coprocessor was offered (for an additional fee). This coprocessor was actually a fully functional 486 CPU, and when inserted in its special socket, it disabled the preexisting 486.

 Remember that a math coprocessor is a floating-point unit (FPU) and affects only applications that do a lot of arithmetic. Such a processor greatly speeds up spreadsheet applications, but not necessarily other applications.

The 80486 Processor

With the introduction of the 386 AT-class machines and Windows 3.0, more and more businesses began to move to computers, and a PC on every desktop became typical. This led to bigger, more feature-packed software that demanded faster computers, more memory, and increasing storage capacity. The GUIs of Windows and OS/2—along with huge spreadsheets, databases, and computer-aided design (CAD)—increased the demand for intense mathematical calculation and higher clock speeds.

The 486 processor, about twice as fast as the 386 chip, had 32-bit internal, external, and memory address buses. It could execute one instruction at two cycles (clock ticks) rather than the 4.5 cycles of the 386, and it introduced an internal Level 1 (L-1) cache (with a typical hit ratio of 90 to 95 percent). The 486 also used something called *Burst Mode*, and used a built-in synchronous math coprocessor in some versions.

Caches, Synchronous Mode, and Pipeline Burst Mode

A *cache* (pronounced "cash") is a small area of memory that is set aside to store data that the CPU expects to call for in the immediate future. Caches can be located in RAM, on disk, or in dedicated chips. If the cache is in a separate, dedicated chip, the speed of the cache memory can be disassociated from the motherboard clock speed. This allows cache memory chips to process instructions faster than main memory in many instances.

When the CPU executes instructions, the speed that it processes those instructions is the *processing speed*. Processing takes place inside microprocessors only. After the instructions have been executed, the results have to be stored in some kind of memory—dynamic RAM (DRAM), static RAM (SRAM), or virtual memory. If the processor moves the results to main system memory, the timing of that movement is tied to the speed of the motherboard. Disassociating a *Burst Mode* cache from the motherboard allows the transfer between the microprocessor and the cache memory to take place at the optimal speed of the chips, rather than the speed of the motherboard.

Some cache chips have their own internal clock, making something called *Synchronous Burst Mode* possible. Ordinarily, the CPU sends a memory address, followed by data to fill that address. This happens again and again until the cache is full. Then, the process goes back to the beginning, and the CPU overwrites previously used addresses. Synchronous Burst Mode means that the CPU needs to send only one address for a given stream of data (a *burst*). The clock on the cache chip increments the address with each new byte of data until the burst is complete.

Pipeline Burst Mode replaces the internal clock on a cache chip with a less expensive *register* (an internal storage area) that holds the next piece of data to be used. You might think of this as a cache for the cache.

With the advent of the 486, and because it was nearly twice as fast as the 386, the graphical user interface finally came into its own. Market acceptance of the Windows GUI prompted the sale of more expensive hardware, larger hard drives, and faster video cards. This ultimately began the price competition that has brought the prices of PCs down and driven their capability continually upward.

The 486 primarily differs from the 386 and 286 in its integration and upgradability. *Integration* refers to the number of components that have been moved onto the chip. *Upgradability* means that the CPU can be taken off of the motherboard and replaced with a better (faster or feature-enhanced) chip.

L-1 and L-2 Caches

Cache memory is covered as memory in Chapter 4. However, the two onboard caches we discuss here are part of the CPU as well. An *internal cache* means that the area of memory being used by the CPU to store results of processing is separated from the main, system RAM. This separate memory is inside, is part of the CPU, and is not limited to the motherboard's clock speed. The storage capacity of internal cache memory is usually anywhere from 8KB to 64KB. Keep in mind that the main, system RAM in modern computers is often 64MB or more.

By caching data in fast cache memory, you speed up system performance. Level 1 cache, also called L-1, or *primary* cache, is very fast, and is integrated into the CPU chip on the chip's manufacturing die. On the other hand, L-1 cache memory is not very large (typically 16KB). Although it is useful for storing some data, it usually relies on a secondary, *external* (L-2, or Level 2) cache for an all-around boost in system performance.

Each family of chips, from the original 8086 through the current Pentiums, has represented a breakthrough in technology. The 286 introduced Protected Mode, and the 386 improved on that as it moved to 32-bit processing. The 486 family began pulling together various speed-enhancing components and building them right into the chip.

Although L-2 caches can be more than 512KB, increases in performance are minimal beyond 512KB. The CPU is already caching the probable-next data in an internal cache. We discuss how a cache works in Chapter 4. However, if the data is predictable but can't fit into the small L-1 cache, having that data handy in very fast (nine nanosecond) L-2 SRAM allows the CPU to continue processing without waiting for transfers from system RAM.

Pentium Processors

The Pentium, introduced in 1992, was entirely compatible with previous processors from Intel but added a fundamental difference: superscalar technology. *Superscalar technology* is based on a twin data pipeline, meaning that the Pentium can execute two instructions at the same time. All previous chips executed one instruction at a time.

Superscalar technology allows the Pentium to execute two instructions per cycle (1 hertz [Hz] clock tick), which moved the chip's execution factor beyond the single clock-tick barrier for the first time. Another way of looking at this is that the Pentium performs one instruction in 0.5Hz (half of one cycle).

After improving processor speed, Intel turned its attention to increasing the bus width. Like the 80386-DX and 80486 processors, Pentiums have a 32-bit-wide address bus, allowing them to address up to 4GB of memory.

Although the memory address bus was 32 bits wide, the Pentium's data bus was expanded to 64 bits, meaning that data could be moved around the system almost twice as fast as previous chips allowed. For this reason, first-series Pentiums also required two 32-bit-wide single inline memory modules (SIMMs) for each data bank on the motherboard. Initially, these memory chips had to be mounted in pairs, as opposed to modern Pentiums, which can use a single 64-bit-wide SIMM.

First Series

When Intel discovered it couldn't trademark a number, the company began releasing each new CPU with its own registered name. Most people were used to calling a CPU a 286, a 386, or a 486 and understood that a bigger number meant a faster CPU. Even though the Pentium name was owned by Intel, other manufacturers (and many consumers) carried on the tradition of using a number. *Fifth generation* chips refer to the 586 line of CPUs, just as fourth generation refers to the variations of a 486 processor.

The Pentium comes in three basic *series* with variations within each series. The first series (of fifth generation) Pentiums began to phase out the tradition of differentiating a chip primarily by speed. They were available in both 60MHz and 66MHz, used a 273 pin grid array (PGA) form factor, and ran on approximately 5 volts (V). Because the processor ran at about the same speed as the motherboard, the chips were said to have a "1X clock speed," referring to the 1:1 relationship between the processor speed and the motherboard's clock speed.

Note: The 66MHz Pentium required 16 watts (W) of power and drew 3.2 amps, making it a very "hot" processor. For the first time, designers had to come up with ways to cool the chip. This led to chip-cooling fans and heat sinks, and eventually helped change the overall design of motherboards.

Second Series

In 1994, Intel released the second series of Pentiums, with variations running at 75MHz, 90MHz, or 100MHz. Soon after, the speed was increased to 120MHz, 133MHz, 150MHz, 166MHz, and 200MHz. This second series of processors used a different manufacturing technique, allowing for a significantly smaller die and a current requirement of 3.3V (running somewhat cooler than the 5V series). The chips used a 296 staggered pin grid array (SPGA) form factor and were physically incompatible with the first series chips. One of the improvements to the second series Pentiums included a program interrupt controller (PIC) and a dual-processor interface that allowed two processors to be installed on a single motherboard.

Third Series: MultiMedia eXtensions (MMX) Instruction Set

In late 1996, in an effort to capitalize on the expanding market for multimedia applications, Intel introduced the third series Pentium processors, or Series 3 Pentiums (not to be confused with a Pentium III), with MultiMedia eXtensions (MMX) capabilities. MMX technology is a set of basic, general-purpose, integer instructions that can be applied to a wide variety of multimedia and communications applications. MMX introduces 57 new instructions for accelerating calculations typical of audio, two-dimensional (2D) and three-dimensional (3D) graphics, video, speech synthesis, and voice recognition. Acceleration can be as much as eight times faster than without MMX. This should provide an apparent 50 to 100 percent performance improvement in multimedia programs.

 MMX is a hardware technology in which the instructions are built into the system. To take advantage of MMX, software must be written specifically for these enhancements.

Many of these newer chips ran on 2.8V, lower than the previous generation of chips, and were designed for installation on 66MHz motherboards. The speed for these third series Pentiums climbed from 166MHz to 200MHz or 233MHz.

Note: A Pentium mobile chip, running at 266MHz, was used in laptops.

Clock Multiplier

Pentium motherboards come with one of three basic, or "core" speed settings: 50MHz, 60MHz, or 66MHz. Even at their introductory speed of 120MHz, the second series Pentiums ran much faster than the motherboards on which they were installed. When we compare the speed of the motherboard to the speed of the CPU's bus width, we refer to that comparison as the *core-to-bus frequency ratio*, or the *clock multiplier*.

Originally, pins BF1 or BF2 on the chip were used to synchronize the processor to the motherboard. Even today, there are still either jumpers or switches on many motherboards, which allow you to control the BF pins, and subsequently, the clock multiplier ratio.

Overclocking

Pentium chips can be set to run faster than their design specification. This is called *overclocking*. For example, a 75MHz Pentium can be set on the motherboard (using jumpers) to run at 133MHz. Due to conservative estimates on the part of the manufacturers, this overclocked chip may continue to function quite well in the short term. However, as time passes, the chip will likely begin to perform unreliably.

It is important to check that the speed setting on the motherboard is at the design specification for the installed Pentium chip. In some cases, unscrupulous third-party distributors will re-mark the speed setting on the chip, making it very difficult to correctly identify the optimum performance configuration.

The P6 Family: Sixth Generation

In November 1995, Intel released the Pentium Pro, the first of the sixth generation chips. With the P6 family, Intel finally broke away from using chip speeds anywhere in the popular name of the CPU. Even so, the "6" in P6 refers to the traditional 686 number. Members of the P6 family include Pentium Pro, Pentium II, Pentium III, and Celeron. The Pentium Pro was designed to run at different speeds, depending on the motherboard on which it was installed:

➤ On a 60MHz motherboard, the Pentium Pro ran at 150MHz or 180MHz.

➤ On a 66MHz motherboard, the Pentium Pro ran at 166MHz or 200MHz.

Up until the introduction of the P6, motherboards used a single motherboard *host processor bus*, which sometimes created bottlenecks in the data path. The way around this was to create a *backside processor bus* that would run at the processor speed. This bus went around the back door of the motherboard processor bus and connected the processor directly to an L-2 cache.

The main feature change in the Pentium Pro was moving the previously external L-2 cache onto the chip die itself and giving it a dedicated bus.

Note: Some of the earlier Pentium Pros had an L-2 cache built directly into the chip. However, the cost of manufacturing was so high that most Pentium Pros were later released with a separate L-2 cache that was accessed through the backside processor bus running at full, core speed.

Pentium II

Pentium Pro chips could not be installed in a Socket 7, which brought about the development of Socket 8 technology, with 387 pins. These very large sockets cost a lot to manufacture, and they brought about the relatively quick replacement of the Pentium Pro by the Pentium II in 1997.

Pentium II processors moved away from the socket and chip design, and they introduced Slot 1 and 2 architecture (see Chapter 2). Once again, the L-2 cache was moved onto the integrated circuit (IC) board (often called a cartridge), maintaining its close proximity to the central processing unit. These sixth generation Pentiums all ran at different voltages. However, instead of having the motherboard set that voltage with jumpers or dual inline package (DIP) switches and a voltage regulator module (VRM), the voltage could now be set automatically by some-

Table 3.1	Pentium II speeds in relation to clock multipliers.	
Motherboard	**Clock Multiplier**	**Speed**
66MHz	3.5	233MHz
66MHz	4	266MHz
66MHz	4.5	300MHz
66MHz	5	333MHz
100MHz	3.5	350MHz
100MHz	4	400MHz
100MHz	4.5	450MHz

thing called the *voltage identification (VID)* pins. These four special voltage identification pins are located directly on the processor cartridge itself. Table 3.1 shows
the wide variety of processor speeds, depending on the variation in motherboard
bus speed and clock multiplier.

Pentium III

The Pentium III was released in 1999, using both flip chip pin grid array (FC-
PGA) Socket 370 and Single Edge Contact (SEC) Slot 1 packaging. The primary difference between the Pentium III and the earlier Pentium II was the
addition of 70 new instructions that dramatically improved the chip's performance in advanced imaging, 3D graphics, streaming audio, video, and speech
recognition.

Another important (and somewhat controversial) feature of the Pentium III was
a self-reportable processor serial number. Although this was introduced originally for security, it was possible to use the serial number for managing corporate
inventories of computers (asset tracking). However, some people felt the feature
might be used as an invasion of privacy if the serial number could be reported out
(stolen by the site developers) during a visit to an Internet site.

*Note: The Pentium III has a locked clock multiplier, which is designed in such a way
that it cannot be reset. However, unscrupulous dealers have been known to actually
disassemble the chip itself, making the necessary modifications to overclock the chip,
and they then reassemble the chip with different markings. Be careful at flea markets
and other places where the price seems "too good to be true," and remember Robert
Heinlein's TANSTAAFL (There ain't no such thing as a free lunch!).*

The Pentium III had many different speeds, depending on which motherboard it
was installed on, and the clock multiplier being used. As we saw in Table 3.1, both
the motherboard and clock multiplier work together to generate an advertised processor speed, so perhaps the best way to think of the Pentium III is as follows:

➤ Pentium III chips were installed on motherboards with an original clock speed of either 100MHz or 133MHz.

➤ The clock multipliers could be 4 (133MHz only), 4.5, 5, 5.5, 6, 6.5, 7, 7.5, 8, or 8.5.

➤ On a 100MHz motherboard, chip speeds became 450MHz, 500MHz, 550MHz, 600MHz, 650MHz, 700MHz, 750MHz, 800MHz, and 850MHz.

➤ On a 133MHz motherboard, chip speeds became 533MHz (multiplier 4), 600MHz, 667MHz, 733MHz, 800MHz, 866MHz, 933MHz, and finally broke the 1 gigahertz (GHz) ceiling.

Celeron

With the need for faster computers at lower costs, Intel developed the Celeron processor in much the same way that the old 386 and 486 chips came out in DX and SX versions. Although the older chips lowered prices by adding or removing the FPU, or math coprocessor, the Celeron's core processor is actually either a Pentium II or a Pentium III, depending on its version.

Celeron processor packaging is generally found in one of two formats: a PGA 370 socket (Socket 370) or FC-PGA. Both packaging formats are less expensive to manufacture than a PII or PIII, with the Socket 370 being similar to the typical flat installation of an older 486 or Pentium. The FC-PGA package looks similar to the vertical architecture of the Pentium II and III, but the Celeron uses a less expensive cartridge that can be placed in a Slot 1. In terms of speed, the Celeron was configured as follows:

➤ Celeron chips were only installed on 66MHz motherboards.

➤ The multipliers ranged from 4 through 9, generating chip speeds of 266MHz, 300MHz, 333MHz, 366MHz, 400MHz, 433MHz, 466MHz, 500MHz, 533MHz, 566MHz, and 600MHz.

Pentium Xeon

Certain applications, often referred to as high-end applications, require extremely sophisticated processing. An example of this kind of throughput demand would be a file server in a network (networking is discussed further in Chapter 8). The Pentium Xeon package is much larger than a Pentium II, Pentium III, or Celeron. The L-2 cache typically begins at 512KB, but can hold all the way up to 2MB of memory. All the cache chips in a Xeon run at the same, core speed of the processor itself, making the cache very expensive (often more expensive than the processor itself).

AMD Processors

Most of the questions on the exam will refer to Intel microprocessors, but you may encounter a few questions on the different Advanced Micro Devices (AMD) chips. AMD, the second largest manufacturer of processors (with Cyrix being the third), has designed several chips to compete directly with the Pentium line. The company named the first of these the K-6, but soon found that they too would have to match the market demand for variations of chips. Taking a lesson from Intel, AMD created the Athlon and Duron chips.

The K-6, which performed somewhere between a Series 1 Pentium and a Pentium II, was designed to fit into a Socket 7. It had a higher performing L-1 cache, helping the K-6 to get around limitations of the Socket 7 architecture. Remember that an L-1 cache is internal to the processor, and though competitive Pentium chips generally used 32KB of L-1 cache, AMD increased K-6 cache to 64KB. Because of this, the K-6 could sometimes perform on a par with the Pentium II, and even sometimes match a Pentium III.

Note: K-6 processors were found on motherboards that ran at 66MHz, 95MHz, and 100MHz, generating chip speeds from 166MHz to 450MHz.

Athlon and Duron

When the K-6 was replaced by the Athlon chip, the manufacturing process led to a completely different design process. The Athlon, similar to the Pentium II, mounted vertically on a cartridge using a single edge connector. It had a large (512KB) external L-2 cache mounted on the cartridge, which used a separate bus for direct access by the CPU (like the Pentium II and III). With the introduction of the Athlon processor (and its subsequent Slot A architecture), AMD chips could no longer be installed on Pentium motherboards.

In June 2000, AMD released the Duron processor as a competitor to Intel's Celeron with its less expensive Socket 370 packaging. The Duron used similar packaging to the Celeron, which AMD called Socket A. It used the same core as the Athlon, but it moved the L-2 cache internal to the chip, reducing the cache size to 64KB. Both the Athlon and Duron could be released in either a Slot A or Socket A package design.

All motherboards designed for the Athlon and Duron ran at 100MHz, using an unusual method of increasing throughput. This method, called an EV6 bus, worked by doubling the data transfer rate per clock cycle. However, the chips were clocked at the original motherboard speed (100MHz) using varying clock multipliers, depending on which chip was installed.

Although the overall vertical form is similar in shape to the Pentium chips, the Athlon uses a different pinout from the Pentiums, thereby requiring AMD's Slot A design, as opposed to Intel's Slot 1 design. This pin incompatibility means that AMD uses Slot A ("A" like in AMD), but Pentium uses Slot 1.

A good way to remember this is that both Socket A and Slot A have the AMD "A" in their name, and the "A" from Athlon. Everything else is the Intel specification.

Also, remember that sockets are cheap, but slots are expensive— just like *socks* are cheap, but a *slot* for your boat at the marina is expensive!

Note: We refer back to this concept of clock-doubling through the use of voltage conditions when we discuss the Universal Serial Bus (USB) in Chapter 8.

Using Slot A, the Athlon processor ranged in speed from 500MHz to 1GHz. On the other hand, using Socket A, the chips ran at 650MHz to 1GHz. If you noticed the higher speeds in what was supposedly older technology (Socket A), you can understand why today's chips are tending to go back to flat technology. Regardless of whether it was installed in a Slot A or a Socket A, the Duron ran in speeds ranging from 550MHz to 700MHz.

So what new developments can we expect in processors? Well, it shouldn't be any surprise that the release of the Pentium IV (not included on the test) has announced clock speeds in excess of 1GHz, with system bus speeds of 400MHz and a new 850 chip set. The chip set is optimized for the Pentium IV and Rambus dynamic RAM (RDRAM) memory (discussed in Chapter 4), allowing throughput of 3.2GB per second. That would be 3,200,000,000 bytes every second!

Practice Questions

Question 1

The floating-point unit or coprocessor was internally integrated into which Intel microprocessor?

- ○ a. Intel 8088
- ○ b. Intel 8086
- ○ c. Intel 80286
- ○ d. Intel 80386
- ○ e. Intel 80486

Answer e is correct. The floating-point unit (FPU) or coprocessor was first integrated into the Intel 80486. The unit was disabled in the Intel 80486-SX for marketing reasons, but it was still present.

Question 2

Which was the first Intel microprocessor to be able to address more than one 1 megabyte (MB) of memory ?

- ○ a. Intel 8086
- ○ b. Intel 80286
- ○ c. Intel 80486
- ○ d. Intel 80386

Answer b is correct. The Intel 80286 could address 16MB of memory and was the first Intel microprocessor to break the 1MB limit.

Question 3

Two common causes of electrical trouble in a PC are _____ and _____.

○ a. ESD, EMM

○ b. EMI, DMA

○ c. EMI, ESD

○ d. EDS, AMD

Answer c is correct. EMI, or electromagnetic interference, is caused by multiple cables running too closely together. ESD, or electrostatic discharge, occurs when static electricity build-up in a technician's body is accidentally passed to the computer system, possibly destroying the circuitry. EMM is an expanded memory manager, DMA is direct memory access, AMD is a chip-manufacturing company, and EDS doesn't stand for anything.

Question 4

Flat CPUs use _____, and vertical CPUs work with _____ technology. [Choose the three best answers]

❑ a. ZIF, Slot

❑ b. Socket 7, Slot A

❑ c. Socket 8, Slot 1

❑ d. Slot B, Socket 7

Answers a, b, and c are correct. Socket 7 and Socket 8 are both referred to as flat technologies, and the sockets mostly are Zero Insertion Force (ZIF) sockets. Vertical processors can use Slot 1 or Slot A, depending on whether they are Intel or AMD chips. Answer d is backwards in the use of "slot" and "socket," and there's no such thing as Slot B.

Question 5

MMX enhancements refer to _____.

- O a. Video accelerator cards
- O b. L-1 and L-2 cache improvements
- O c. Memory Management eXtensions
- O d. MultiMedia eXtensions

Answer d is correct. MMX, or MultiMedia eXtensions, is a set of instructions on a CPU that helps speed up such things as video, audio, and speech recognition. Modern PCs have an Accelerated Graphics Port (AGP). There's no such thing as "Memory Management eXtensions," and neither the Level 1 nor Level 2 cache has any sort of improvement enhancements.

Question 6

Level 1 (L-1) and Level 2 (L-2) caches were provided to speed CPU operation by reducing the need of the processor to access system RAM. The difference between the two types is that the L-1 cache is internal to the processor and the L-2 cache is external to the processor.

- O a. True
- O b. False

Answer a, true, is correct. The internal L-1 cache provided 8KB to 16KB of fast memory to the processor, but the external L-2 cache provided 256KB or more of memory.

Need to Know More?

 Freedman, Alan. *Computer Desktop Encyclopedia, 2nd Edition.* AMACOM, 1999. ISBN 0-814-479-855. This is great for a fast look-up or refresher.

 Messmer, Hans-Peter. *The Indispensable PC Hardware Book, 3rd Edition.* Reading, MA: Addison-Wesley Publishing Company, 2000. ISBN 0-201-403-994. This is a comprehensive, up-to-date reference book that covers far more than you will need to know for the exam.

 Minasi, Mark. *The Complete PC Upgrade and Maintenance Guide, 11th Edition.* San Francisco, CA: Sybex Network Press, 2000. ISBN 0-782-128-009. This is considered one of the best reference books available. In fact, Minasi's book was instrumental in the formulation of the first A+ exam.

 Muller, Scott. *Upgrading and Repairing PCs, 12th Edition.* Indianapolis, IN: Que, 2000. ISBN 0-7897-2303-4. This is one of our favorites. If you are only going to have one reference book, give this one serious consideration.

 Reeves, Scott, Kalinda Reeves, Stephen Weese, and Christopher S. Geyer. *A+ Exam Prep, 3rd Edition.* Scottsdale, AZ: The Coriolis Group, 2001. ISBN 1-57610-699-3. This is a good reference that concentrates on providing exam-required information.

 Rosch, Winn. *Hardware Bible, 5th Edition.* Indianapolis, IN: Sam's Publishing, 1999. ISBN 0-789-717-433. This is a well-organized reference book that covers software issues as well as hardware.

 www.amd.com—This is the corporate Web site for Advanced Micro Devices. When you are looking for the most up-to-date information relating to software or hardware, the manufacturer's Web site is usually the best place to find it.

 www.intel.com—This is the corporate Web site for Intel.

Memory

Terms you'll need to understand:

✓ Memory controller

✓ Read-only memory (ROM), erasable programmable ROM (EPROM), and electrically erasable programmable ROM (EEPROM)

✓ Capacitor

✓ Bus

✓ RAM, DRAM, SRAM, SDRAM, VRAM, RDRAM

✓ DIP, SIMM, DIMM, RIMM

Concepts you'll need to master:

✓ Volatile versus nonvolatile memory

✓ Megahertz (MHz) and nanoseconds (ns.)

✓ Memory address

✓ Synchronization to clock cycle (clock tick)

✓ Memory module versus memory chip

✓ Odd and even parity checking

Computers use many different microchips and processors, with perhaps the most familiar being the CPU and the main memory. Memory is just a temporary place to store information until the CPU can get to it. This information can be program instructions, data, or both. A typical instruction might be a request to store a number or an event somewhere, and another might be to retrieve that information from a particular place—an *address*. Volatile memory can only hold information when a normal electrical current is present. Nonvolatile memory can hold information without *any* electrical current.

 Volatile, from the Latin "to fly," means that information "flies away" when there's no electricity to keep it in place. Television reporters often refer to an explosive situation as a volatile situation, meaning that it could change at any second. Nonvolatile memory, because it is not volatile, stays the same without any need for electricity.

Conceptual Overview

Memory is fairly easy to understand after you've grasped the basic concepts. In a nutshell, a CPU moves bits of data across a memory bus into registers (addresses) on a chip. It does this with the help of a memory controller. Most memory began as dynamic random access memory (DRAM), and the main changes have been to either speed up the memory to match the CPU, or to speed up the CPU to match the memory. *Synchronizing* these two chips is what much of the history of memory development has involved.

We measure memory speed in *nanoseconds* (billionths of a second). On the other hand, we measure CPU speed in megahertz (millions of cycles per second). Blending the two, we come up with *million instructions per second* (*MIPS*). Disk speed is measured in milliseconds (thousandths of a second), and a hard disk typically reads information at around 100 *reads* per second—not to be confused with *revolutions per minute* (*rpm*). A floppy disk generally performs 10 reads per second, while RAM can make a billion reads per second. So moving data in and out of RAM is extremely fast—much faster than moving it to and from a disk.

Memory involves several basic concepts, the first of which is a grid or *matrix*. Because of this, we're going to put Table 4.1 to a slightly different use, making it a sort of "mind map." If you can see the way the overall concepts break down on a grid, then perhaps they'll be easier to remember.

Note: A matrix is nothing more than a grid of columns and rows, like a spreadsheet or an Etch-a-Sketch. Columns go across the page, and rows go down the page. Cells going left to right (horizontally) have an X coordinate. Cells going up and down (vertically) have a Y coordinate. Combining both the X and Y coordinates gives us an address in the grid, like a cell address in a spreadsheet.

Table 4.1	Mind map of basic memory concepts.	
Data Storage–Nonvolatile		
Disks Temporary swap files		
ROM–Nonvolatile BIOS		

Programmable ROM
    CMOS–volatile (trickle charge)
    Flash BIOS–Nonvolatile		

RAM–Volatile	**Types of RAM**	**Types of Packaging**
Main memory	DRAM SRAM SDRAM RDRAM VRAM (DDR SDRAM)	DIP SIMM DIMM RIMM
Cache memory	L-1 and L-2	Card modules

Read-Only Memory (ROM)

Every computer uses both random access and read-only memory. *RAM* is read/write memory, whereas *ROM* is read-only memory. In other words, information can be temporarily stored in RAM, and then a moment later, it can be taken out, and new information can be written to the same place (address). When information is placed in memory, we say that we are "writing to" a memory address. When information is retrieved out of memory, we "read from" that memory.

ROM can have information written into it only one time. From that point on, we can only read the information. No electrical current is required for the information to remain stored—it's nonvolatile. ROM is mostly used for BIOS.

In some instances, ROM can be changed through the use of certain tools. Flash ROM is nonvolatile memory that occasionally can be changed, such as when a BIOS chip must be updated.

Picture a bulletin board under glass at the back of a classroom. One way to think of ROM is that it's like the hard-copy notes placed under the glass. At the end of the day, they remain unchanged, and the next day, the notes are exactly the way they were the day before. We were able to only read them.

RAM, on the other hand, would be like a blackboard. It starts out blank, and during the day, information is written on it, read from it, and maybe even erased.

New information is then written in the same place. If a lot of writing and erasing takes place, a chalk buildup forms on the blackboard. This buildup is similar to *memory fragments*, which can cause computer lockups. When you go home at the end of the day, you turn off the lights, wash the blackboard clean, and whatever data was on the blackboard goes away forever.

 A single letter can really mess you up on the exam if you don't pay close attention. We've seen questions similar to, "RAM BIOS is used to permanently store instructions for a hardware device: True or False?" (The answer is false.) Keep your eyes peeled, and remember that RAM sounds like RANdom. RAM is never used in BIOS. Because the BIOS instructions are permanent, they almost always use ROM.

Basic Input/Output System (BIOS)

When you turn on a PC, the processor first looks at the system basic input/output system (BIOS) to determine the system's fundamental configuration and environment. This information, which is stored in a ROM BIOS chip, largely determines what peripherals the system can support. BIOS instructions are updated regularly by the manufacturer, and if the chip is made to be updated (reprogrammed) by the end user, it is sometimes called *Flash BIOS*. These programmable chips are often referred to as EEPROM chips, which we discuss later in this chapter.

CMOS Setup Program

Although a basic motherboard can be pretty standard, the system can vary in components like hard drives; floppy, CD, or DVD drives; memory; and so forth. The complementary metal oxide semiconductor (CMOS) is a small memory chip that stores the optional system settings (e.g., hard drive specifications, amount of memory, and so forth). Because these settings are held in CMOS memory with a small electrical charge, CMOS is volatile. However, this *trickle charge* comes from a battery installed on the motherboard, so even when the main power is turned off, the charge continues. If the battery power fails, all CMOS information vanishes.

Note: Technically, CMOS is different from ROM BIOS in that the CMOS settings require some source of electrical power. Nonvolatile memory doesn't require electricity at all.

Older computers, such as some IBM PS/2 models and the original IBM AT, required a setup program stored on a special floppy disk. When you ran the program, a setup screen allowed you to configure the machine. These configurations were stored in special files on the hard drive. Compaq continued the idea of putting a setup program on a disk. Typically, CMOS like this was held on a dedicated 3MB to 4MB, non-DOS partition on the hard drive, but it could also be run from a floppy.

 Today, most computers use a keystroke combination such as Ctrl+Del, or a function key such as F1 or F2, to access the CMOS. The keys are pressed at startup before the BIOS transfers control to the operating system. (This is not the same as accessing Windows Safe Mode.)

Flash BIOS

Advancing technology led to an easier way to change the BIOS rather than pulling out the ROM chip and replacing it with an updated one. To that end, most BIOS chips became Flash EEPROM (electrically erasable programmable ROM). This allowed upgrades to be downloaded through the Internet or a bulletin board service (BBS) without the need for pulling apart hardware. Instead, a small software installation program makes the change.

 BIOS determines compatibility. Modern BIOS is often stored in the CMOS, whereas older BIOS was stored in nonvolatile ROM, often soldered into the motherboard. Remember that the CMOS is almost always where the computer's configuration is stored. BIOS is where the software instructions for the basic input/output (I/O) operations are stored (e.g., COM and LPT ports, expansion bus, and so forth).

Programmable ROM

Another common use for one-time, read-only memory is on a CD-ROM. In the same way that rewriteable CDs (CD-RWs) changed the way that we use the disks, programmable ROM chips changed the way BIOS was stored. The formal name for a chip that cannot be modified is *mask ROM* (from the manufacturing mask). ROM chips have a varying capacity for change, named in the following manner:

➤ *Programmable ROM (PROM)*—Requires a special type of machine called a PROM programmer or PROM burner (like a CD burner) and can only be changed one time. The original chip is blank, and the programmer burns in specific instructions. From that point, it can't be changed.

➤ *Erasable programmable ROM (EPROM)*—Uses the PROM burner, but can be erased by shining ultraviolet (UV) light through a window in the top of the chip. Normal room light contains very little UV light.

➤ *Electrically erasable programmable ROM (EEPROM)*—Can be erased by an electrical charge and then written to by using slightly higher-than-normal voltage. EEPROM can be erased one byte at a time, rather than erasing the entire chip with UV light. Because these chips can be changed without opening a casing, they are often used to store programmable instructions in devices, such as printers and other peripherals.

Flash ROM

This type of chip is sometimes called *Flash RAM* or *Flash memory* and stores data much like the EEPROM. It uses a super-voltage charge to erase a block of data (rather than a byte). Flash ROM and EEPROM can perform read/write operations, but can only be erased a certain number of times. Flash BIOS relies on this ability to change the program instructions in a ROM chip.

A RAM Game

Before we get into the types and packaging of RAM chips—that is, single inline memory modules (SIMMs) and dual inline memory modules (DIMMs)—we're going to talk about how memory works. To help you understand how memory concepts are interrelated, we've made up a cool game called Bop. Imagine a very small planet called System-X (motherboard), where the CPU is like some weird genius living on a hill and spending most of its time concentrating on matters of important problem solving. Away from this hill live a bunch of furry rodents—sort of like that gopher in the movie "Caddy Shack"—called gopher bits (data bits).

The CPU lives on these bits, and has a Controller in charge of caring for them (memory controller). Gopher bits live in a grid of underground burrows nicely laid out in rows and columns (matrix). Most of the time the rodents are docile and well-behaved, but every once in a while, they pop up out of their burrows and the Controller has to run over and bop them on the head to keep them underground—hence the name Bop (not a technical term).

In some cases, a gopher pops out of a hole and tries to get completely away. The Controller then has to grab the bit (or go back to the CPU for a copy of the bit) and shove it back into the correct hole (memory refresh). Sometimes, the Controller has to ask the CPU if it has a bit in the right hole—the correct address.

In the dynamic RAM (DRAM) era, when life was first developing on System-X, the CPU had to tell the Controller to run around shoving gopher bits into whatever hole it could find, hoping the bits would stay there. However, as soon as the Controllers turned their backs, the bits would pop up out of their hole and run away. The gopher holes are actually *capacitors* (see Chapter 5 for more on capacitors), which have either a charge (1) or no charge (0). If the capacitor has a gopher bit stuck in it (a charge), it holds a data bit. If the capacitor's gopher bit gets away (leaks or loses its charge), it has no data bit, which is a nice binary environment.

On System-X, life is controlled by the motherboard clock, a sort of biorhythm. Each tick is like a bell that goes off every so often (cycles per second). At the sound of the tick, the CPU pauses to sniff the air and waits for a moment. In DRAM, the memory controller had no idea what was going on with the clock, and it would barge in on the CPU—interrupt, INT, or interrupt request (IRQ) line—whenever it needed to talk. Then, it would have to wait around (wait states) until the CPU paused on the clock tick before they could have a conversation.

At the same time, those old CPUs would sometimes hear a clock tick and send the Controller zooming out to grab dinner, only to discover that Controller was in the middle of bopping a bunch of gopher bits over the head (refresh)! Therefore, the CPU would have to wait until the Controller was done before it could grab a data bit.

A *wait state* is the time that a CPU has to wait for RAM to complete a storage or refresh sequence. CPUs run faster than both the motherboard (based on a clock multiplier) and older RAM chips (up to four wait states). Newer RAM often can run as fast as the CPU.

Because the Controller keeps track of where each gopher bit lives, it has to keep checking with the CPU every time it bops a gopher bit over the head to make sure that the bit was in the right place. That leads to an awful lot of interruptions: some to check addresses, some to shove new bits into holes, some to grab existing bits for dinner—a lot of confusion.

An interesting thing about eating gopher bits is that the CPU will often eat whole families (a *page*) or four at a time (a *burst*). Because of peculiar reasons of zoology, four related families will often live nearby in a sort of *range*. The Controller will often swoop down and grab them right out of their row (when it's not bopping them over the head with a refresh rate).

One day SRAM (Synchronous RAM) came along, and the Controllers evolved to where they, too, could hear the clock. They didn't hear it quite the same way as the CPU did, but at least they had an idea of when to check in for a talk. The Controller still had to interrupt the CPU, but now it knew when it was a good time.

This concept of using the motherboard clock cycle to time the interrupts coming from the memory controller, is the general basis for many of the changes to memory chips. SRAM chips have a clock synchronizer built onto the chip to synchronize them to the motherboard clock. This is why they're called Synchronous RAM.

It takes a lot of time for the CPU to tell the Controller every single address for every single column and row of data bits. With the development of Fast Page Mode (FPM) memory, the memory controller got smart enough so that the CPU could tell it a range name and the Controller could go get a whole set of go-phers—a byte to eat, so to speak. It wasn't long before the Controller started assuming that if the CPU wanted one particular *page*, it would "probably" want the pages next to it—*caching*.

Finally, with RDRAM, the CPU evolved a clock on its own processor bus, and the memory controller started hearing that clock rather than the motherboard clock. We'll talk more about the actualities as we develop the chapter, but these are the main concepts.

Cache Memory

Cache memory is a type of high-speed memory designed to speed up processing. *Cache* (pronounced "cash") is derived from the French word *cacher*, meaning "to hide." A cache attempts to predict which information is about to be used, using an algorithm (logical formula) based on probabilities and proximity. Cache memory is usually much faster than main memory, and because it contains only *pointers* to the probable-next information, it's much smaller than main memory. Typically, a memory cache is a separate SRAM chip, running much faster than DRAM (both types of memory chips are discussed later in this chapter).

The *cache memory controller* stores the algorithms that predict what instructions the CPU will be needing next. Generally, the next instruction is the adjacent one, and the controller gets it and places it in cache memory. When the CPU looks for the next instruction, the chances are good that it will find it faster in small cache memory rather than in large main memory.

The Memory Hierarchy and Caches

A cache is like an expectation. If you expect to see a piece of information and it's right beside you, you can access that information much faster than if you had to go look for it. When you open a book and look at page 22, you'll look at the top of the page, then at the middle of the page, then at the bottom of the page, and then at the top of page 23. That's how computer caching operates.

Because memory size is always increasing, more time is needed to decode increasingly wider addresses and to find the information stored in the ever-increasing size of the storage device. The strategy used to remedy this problem is called *memory hierarchy*. Memory hierarchy works because of the way that memory is stored in addresses. *Proximity* means how close one instruction or data byte is to the next instruction or data byte.

A hierarchical memory structure contains many levels of memory, usually defined by access speed. A small amount of very fast SRAM is usually installed adjacent to the CPU, matching up with the speed and *memory bus* of the CPU. As the distance from the CPU increases, the performance and size requirements for the memory are relaxed. Parts of the memory hierarchy include registers, caches, main memory, and disks.

When a memory reference is made, the processor looks in the memory at the top of the hierarchy. If the data is there, it wins. Otherwise, a so-called miss occurs, at which time the requested information must be brought up from a lower level of hierarchy.

A miss in the cache (that is, the desired data isn't in the cache memory) is called a *cache miss*. A miss in the main memory is called a *page fault*. When a miss occurs, the whole block of memory containing the requested missing information is brought in from the lower, slower hierarchical level. Eventually, the information is looked for on the hard disk—the slowest storage media. If the current memory hierarchy level is full when a miss occurs, some existing blocks or pages must be removed for a new one to be brought in.

SMARTDRV.SYS and SMARTDRV.EXE are DOS program utilities that provide disk caching. The efficiency of a cache is reported as its *hit ratio*. To send an efficiency report to the screen, issue the command **SMARTDRV /S** from a DOS command prompt.

L-1 and L-2 Cache Memory

We've seen how technology moves toward consolidating components, for speed and cost efficiencies. The Super I/O chips combined different adapters into a single package, and central processors soon moved in the same direction. Although caches were originally outside the chip die, new developments paved the way to move them inside the chip. Today, we have *internal* caches (inside the CPU housing) and *external* caches (outside the die).

The Intel 486 and early Pentium chips had a small, built-in 16KB cache on the CPU called a Level 1 (L-1), or *primary cache*. Another cache is the Level 2 (L-2), or *secondary cache*. The L-2 cache is usually a separate memory chip that is one step slower than the L-1 cache, and it almost always uses a dedicated *memory bus*.

You should remember that the primary (L-1) cache is internal to the processor chip itself, and the secondary (L-2) cache is almost always external. Up until the 486 family of chips, the CPU had no internal cache, so any external cache was designated as the "primary" memory cache. The 80486 introduced a 16KB internal L-1 cache. The Pentium family added a 256KB or 512KB external L-2 cache.

Memory Pages

Typically, memory is divided into chunks (or blocks). At the cache level, a chunk is called a *cache block* or a *cache line*. At the main level, a chunk is referred to as a *memory page*. A *register* is 8 bits wide, and a *cell* is one of the bits in a register. Technically, only a CPU has registers. Memory chips have capacitors and transistors. The memory controller keeps track of the *state* and location of the charges held on a memory chip—addresses. The charges relate to the original byte transmissions from the CPU's registers. The CPU can empty its registers for more calculations.

DRAM is usually accessed through *paging*. A page is a related group of bytes (with their bits), similar to a range on a spreadsheet. It can be from 512 bits to several kilobytes, depending on the way the operating system is set up. Changes in memory chips and controllers are similar to how flat, one-page spreadsheets developed the concept of *named ranges*.

Originally, a formula included every single cell in a spreadsheet (e.g., A1+B1+C1 and so forth). By selecting a group of cells and giving them a name, the formula has to list only the range name, and the spreadsheet figures out which specific cell addresses to use. This is analogous to the memory controller giving a unique name (address) to a range of charges, so it doesn't have to go looking for every single capacitor or transistor.

Fast Page Mode (FPM)

In Fast Page Mode (FPM), the controller makes an assumption that the data read/write following a CPU request will be in the next three ranges (pages), very much like a cache. The controller doesn't have to waste time looking for a range address for at least three more times.

Note: When the controller passes through the memory chip, it turns off something called a data output driver when it reads the page it just read or wrote to. This process takes approximately 10 nanoseconds. (Fast Page Mode memory can also be called Fast Page Memory.)

A 60-nanosecond DRAM might run in what's called *5-3-3-3 Burst Mode* timing. The first access—using one particular page—requires 5 cycles (on a 66MHz system), or about 75 ns. The next three accesses would take only 3 cycles, because they didn't need to look up the ranges. That equates to about 45 ns, with a 90-nanosecond (about 40 percent) savings in time. Regular old page mode would be *5-5-5-5 Burst Mode*.

RAM and Speeds

Back when system clocks ran between 5 and 66MHz, and CPUs ran at 5 to 200MHz, we had Fast Page Mode or Extended Data Output (EDO) RAM. When motherboards stabilized at 66MHz with the release of the Pentium Pro, CPU speeds climbed from 200 to 660MHz. RAM became PC-66 SDRAM running synchronized at 66MHz, and it was installed as the typical memory on most motherboards.

Let's say a motherboard is running at 66MHz with a clock multiplier of 2. Therefore, the CPU is running at 133MHz. If an SRAM chip is synched to the board (66MHz), the memory controller has to wait two clock ticks for an interruption (133 divided by 66), unless it accidentally happens to catch the CPU at exactly the right time.

When motherboards increased to 100MHz, CPUs went beyond 500MHz, and that's where PC-100 SDRAM came in. These memory chips were synchronized at 100MHz. Modern 133MHz boards have CPUs running at well over 600MHz, with PC-133 SDRAM synchronized at 133 MHz. PC-800 RDRAM is part of the new 800 series chip set, runs at 800MHz, and is synched to the CPU and the board.

Extended Data Output (EDO) RAM

This is sometimes referred to as hyper-page mode, and it's a modification of Fast Page Mode. Extended Data Output (EDO) memory is a specially manufactured chip that allows a *timing overlap* between successive read/writes. In this case, unlike FPM, the data output drivers are not turned off when the memory controller reads a page at the beginning of the next cycle. This allows an overlap in the process, no longer requiring the 10 ns. per cycle delay we noted above.

EDO RAM became popular for a time with a typical burst cycle of 5-2-2-2, yielding about a 22 percent savings in time over Fast Page Mode memory. However, SDRAM developed a burst cycle of 5-1-1-1, which is even faster than EDO RAM, so SDRAM became the most popular type of memory toward the end of the 1990s.

Types of RAM

RAM is a sort of universal name for memory, and each category within RAM refers more to the mode of operation than an actual type of memory. The "D" in DRAM refers to the dynamic access. The "S" in SRAM and SDRAM refers to synchronizing the chip to the motherboard. EDO RAM refers to the extended data output, whereby the column address isn't turned off after a read.

Dynamic RAM (DRAM)

First of all, *dynamic* means moving or always changing. In dynamic RAM, electricity has to be kept moving through the chip so as to keep refreshing the memory. DRAM is the basic type of memory chip, and everything that came later was mainly a way to get address information faster. Dynamic also means that data can be moved into or out of memory, over and over again, for as long as power is available.

Data in a DRAM chip is stored in very compact form, with each bit using only its own capacitor and accompanying transistor. Once again, if the capacitor has a charge, the computer reads that as a 1. If it does not have a charge, it's a 0. Capacitors have a tendency to leak their charge fairly quickly. For that reason, they often have to be refreshed. The controller refreshes the DRAM sequentially during any given operation (much like bopping gopher bits one after the other, down the columns in a sequence, to refer back to our analogy).

Synchronous RAM (SRAM)

SRAM uses an internal clock on the memory chip, which synchronizes the chip to the motherboard speed. SRAM chips aren't as dense as DRAM because they use a matrix of six transistors and no capacitors. The transistors don't require power to prevent leakage, so SRAM does not have to be refreshed. In other words, the memory stays charged without a refresh cycle, and data changes only when a register changes. Eliminating the refresh makes it a lot faster than DRAM, and it's why faster machines began selling SRAM as the primary memory.

Note: Some people refer to SRAM as being static RAM because the data doesn't need to be refreshed. Technically, SRAM stands for Synchronous RAM because of the internalized clock.

Because of the extra space in the matrix, SRAM uses more chips than DRAM for the same amount of storage space. Manufacturing costs are very high, so although DRAM is slower, the higher density and lower cost still make it very popular in modern machines. Combining the best of both quickly led to the SDRAM chip.

L-2 memory caches are usually on SRAM, which is extremely fast (as fast as 7 to 9 ns., and 2 to 5 ns. for *ultrafast* SRAM). Level 2 cache is usually installed in sizes of 256KB or 512KB.

SRAM is also used for CMOS configuration setups and requires a small amount of electricity, provided by a backup battery on the system board, to keep its data. It comes on credit-card-sized memory cards, is available in 128KB, 256KB, 512KB, 1MB, 2MB, and 4MB sizes, and has a battery life of 10 or more years.

Synchronous DRAM (SDRAM)

When the concept of synchronizing a memory chip to the motherboard proved successful, the idea was retrofitted to DRAM chips. Synchronous DRAM synchronizes the interrupt requests to the motherboard and works just like SRAM, only with the higher density (and lower cost) of the DRAM chip. Most SDRAM controllers are built into the North bridge of the motherboard chip set.

Video RAM (VRAM)

VRAM chips have a different design in that they have two access paths to the same memory address. It's as if VRAM is a café that has two doors (ports), one in the front and one in the back. Information can come in one "entrance" at the same time that other information is flowing out the other "exit." Because manipulating graphics is so processing-intensive, this ability to push data out of the chip at the same time as it receives new data helps give the appearance of continuity to an image.

When the video controller reads the memory for information, it accesses an address with one of the paths. When the CPU writes data to that memory, it accesses the address using the other path. This extra circuitry requires more physical space, so VRAM chips are about 20 percent larger than DRAM chips. Although they are more expensive to make, VRAM chips can boost video performance by up to 60 percent.

VRAM and AGP

AGP stands for Accelerated Graphics Port. Modern computers are often sold with this accelerated port, which is part of the I/O system. An AGP is not the same thing as a video accelerator card, which uses the expansion bus. Nor is the AGP the same thing as VRAM.

To say that a computer has "AGP memory" or "comes with AGP" can be confusing at best. At worst, it can demonstrate a faulty knowledge of the distinction between video memory and I/O subsystems.

Windows RAM (WRAM)

We'll take a moment to speak about additional types of video memory that are being developed out of a need for faster video processing and photographic quality resolutions on video monitors. High resolution is particularly important in document imaging systems, where people would like to store legal contracts as electronic images. We've all heard that we should read the fine print on a contract, but the resolutions needed for that fine print often surpass 1024×768 with 24-bit color.

A typical page of information with 1024×768 resolution uses approximately 4MB of VRAM memory with older video memory cards. Additionally, memory chips have certain speed limits at the moment, and the best areas where we can speed up data transfers are in either how much information can be moved, or how quickly it can be accessed. VRAM uses separate input and output *ports* (entry and exit places) to speed up access to information. In this type of *dual port* system, information flowing into memory doesn't have to wait for space while information flows out to the monitor.

Windows RAM (WRAM) has nothing whatsoever to do with Microsoft Windows; rather, it is a type of memory that increases the bandwidth (transfer rate) of the two ports in the memory cards. WRAM can move larger blocks (windows) of data in and out of memory by supporting larger memory addresses. (There's no particular reason why these large blocks are called *windows* rather than page frames.)

Note: We discuss bandwidth in the "Throughput and Bandwidth" section of Chapter 8, and the concepts of memory paging in the "Page Frame Memory and Page Swapping" section of Chapter 11. WRAM ports offer approximately 25 percent more bandwidth than VRAM, leading to a 50 percent performance increase with an approximately 20 percent reduction in costs.

Synchronous Graphic RAM (SGRAM)

We've said that video information is written to and read from a frame buffer, and if we can increase the movement of that information through the two ports, we can speed up the video memory. WRAM can support 24-bit color images at resolutions of 1600×1200 by moving information faster than the memory can become filled.

SGRAM is another type of memory used on video adapters and graphics accelerators. SGRAM, like Synchronous RAM (SRAM), uses a synchronizing clock to move information across a video bus at 100MHz. Like WRAM, SGRAM provides increased bandwidth for graphics-intensive functions, but unlike WRAM, SGRAM is a single port system. In order to get a comparative transfer rate, SGRAM opens up two memory pages at the same time.

Multibank DRAM (MDRAM)

MDRAM uses yet another technology for moving information in and out of video memory. Whereas VRAM has the two ports and WRAM increases the bandwidth of the ports, SGRAM has only one port but opens up two frames at once. MDRAM uses an interleaving (woven together) process to set up an array of 32KB DRAM memory banks. Each bank connects to an internal bus, and data can be moved into or out of multiple banks simultaneously. We've said that video memory typically requires 4MB of space to produce a 24-bit color image at 1024×768. MDRAM allows the memory to be set up in such a way that the same image can be processed in 2.5MB of memory.

Rambus DRAM (RDRAM)

All the memory systems that we've talked about are known as *wide channel* systems because the memory channel is equal to the width of the processor data bus. RDRAM is known as a *narrow channel* system because data is transferred only 2 bytes (16 bits) at a time. This might seem small, but those 2 bytes move extremely fast. Up until RDRAM, the fastest chips had a throughput of 100MHz, which means those chips moved 800MB of data per second (100MHz times 8 bytes). RDRAM chips running at 800MHz move 1,600MB per second (800 times 2 bytes), which translates to 1.66 gigabytes (GB) or a billion bytes per second—about twice as fast as SDRAM.

RDRAM comes out of technology developed originally for the Nintendo 64 gaming system. It's not that new, but it seems new because Intel is starting to use it in its Pentium IV processors, with the 800 series chip set. Earlier Pentiums have a data bus up to 64 bits wide. The memory module is also 64 bits wide, which means data can be moved across the memory bus in 64-bit chunks, or 8 bytes. Remember that a byte is equal to 8 bits at a time, and in this case, the time is 1 second.

RDRAM also improves something called *latency*, meaning that all the RDRAM chips are synchronized to the processor's memory bus (not the motherboard clock). Therefore, the processor won't request something at mid tick (the reverse of an interrupt). Typically, the CPU is synchronized to the motherboard (which is fairly slow), but the memory chip is not. In SRAM and SDRAM, both the CPU and the memory are synched to the motherboard. In RDRAM, the synchronization is no longer tied to a slow motherboard, but synched to the memory bus. The memory bus clock is derived from the processor, but it still uses a multiplier of the motherboard clock.

Double Data Rate SDRAM (DDR SDRAM)

DDR SDRAM probably won't be on the exam, but we'll mention that it came about as a response to the creation of RDRAM specifications by Intel and Rambus. Intel eventually bought Rambus and began licensing the technology for a fee. In much the way that IBM created Micro Channel Architecture (MCA) and charged a fee, both situations led to the development of separate consortiums for a different standard. DDR comes from a consortium of non-Intel manufacturers.

In our discussion of motherboards in Chapter 3, we mentioned that AMD developed faster processing by using a double-speed bus. Instead of using a full clock tick to run an event, they use a "half-tick" cycle, which is the voltage *change* during a clock cycle. In other words, as the clock begins a tick, the voltage goes up and an event takes place. When the clock ends the tick, the voltage goes down and a second event takes place. Therefore, every single clock cycle can have two memory cycle events. The AMD Athlon and Duron use the DDR specification with the double-speed bus.

Packaging Modules

We've discussed how memory chips work on the inside, but you'll need to know how these chips are installed on a motherboard. Once again, most of the changes came about either to make maintenance easier or to avoid bad connections. Keep in mind that installing a combined "unit" or module of some kind is less expensive than having many individual units to install.

Dual Inline Package (DIP)

Originally, DRAM came in individual chips called *dual inline packages (DIPs)*. XT and AT systems had 36 sockets on the motherboard, each with one DIP per socket. Later, a number of DIPs were mounted on a memory board that plugged into an expansion slot. It was very time-consuming to change memory, and there were problems with *chip creep* (thermal cycling), where the chips would work their way out of the sockets as the PC turned on and off. Heat expanded and contracted the sockets, and you'd have to push the chips back in with your fingers.

To solve this problem, manufacturers finally soldered the first 640 kilobytes of memory onto the board. That helped, but the soldering led to a problem when anyone tried to replace a bad chip. Finally, chips went onto their own card, called a *single inline memory module* or *SIMM*. On a SIMM, each individual chip is soldered onto a small circuit board with an edge connector (Holy Pentium II architecture, Batman!).

Connectors: Gold vs. Tin

SIMMs and DIMMs come with either tin (silver-colored) or gold edge connectors. Although you may assume that gold is always better, that's not true. You want to match the metal of the edge connectors to the metal in the board's socket. If the motherboard uses gold sockets, use a gold SIMM. Tin sockets (or slots) should use tin edge connectors. The cost difference is minimal, but matching the metal type is critical.

Although it's true that gold won't corrode, a gold SIMM in a tin connector will produce much faster corrosion in the tin connectors. This quickly leads to random glitches and problems, so look at the board and match the color of the metal.

It's important to note, too, that each module is rated for the number of installations, or *insertions*. Each insertion causes scratches, and the more metal that is scratched off, the worse the connection becomes. In flea market exchanges and corporate environments, modules are subjected to constant wear and tear, and nobody is looking at the rated number of insertions.

Single Inline Memory Modules (SIMMs)

When DRAM chips were placed in a line on their own circuit board, it gave rise to the term *inline* memory. Once the chips were formed into a *module*, the entire module would fit into a socket on the board. These modules and sockets are referred to as *memory banks*. Depending on how the chips are connected on their own little circuit board, the module is called either a single or dual inline memory module (SIMM or DIMM).

The memory bus grew from 8 bits to 16 bits and then from 32 bits to 64 bits wide. The 32-bit bus coincided with the development of a SIMM, which meant that the 32-bit-wide data bus could connect directly to 1 SIMM (4 sets of 8 bits). However, when the bus widened to 64 bits, rather than making one gigantic SIMM, we started using two SIMMs in a paired memory *bank*. The development of the 64-bit-wide DIMM superseded the SIMMs and used only one module per socket again.

 SIMMs and DIMMs are sometimes referred to as chips, but they are really series of chips (modules). DRAM itself is a chip, and DRAM chips are grouped together to form SIMMs and DIMMs. SIMMs can come with a varying number of pins, including 30-pin and 72-pin. (Even though the 72-pin module could have chips on both sides, it was still a SIMM.)

Be careful when you read a question on the exam that you don't accidentally agree that a SIMM is a memory chip. A good way to keep alert is that the actual chips almost always have the letters RAM in their name.

Dual Inline Memory Modules (DIMMs)

Dual inline memory modules (DIMMs) are very similar to SIMMs in that they install vertically into sockets on the system board. DIMMs are also a line of DRAM chips combined on a circuit board to form a module. The main difference is that a DIMM has two different *signal pins*, one on each side of the module. This is why they are *dual* inline modules.

The differences between SIMMs and DIMMs are as follows:

➤ DIMMs have opposing pins on either side of their board. The pins remain electrically isolated to form two separate contacts—a dual set of electrical contacts.

➤ SIMMs also have opposing pins on either side of the board. However, the pins are connected, tying them together. The connection forms a single electrical contact.

DIMMs began to be used in computers that supported a 64-bit or wider memory bus. Pentium MMX, Pentium Pro, and Pentium II boards use 168-pin modules. They are 1 inch longer than 72-pin SIMMs, with a secondary *keying notch* so they'll fit into their slots in only one way.

Don't Mix Different Types of Memory

Mixing different types of SIMMs or DIMMs within the same memory bank prevents the CPU from accurately detecting how much memory it has. In this case, the system will either fail to boot, or will boot and fail to recognize or use some of the memory.

You can, however, substitute a SIMM with a different speed within the same memory bank, but only if the replacement is equal to or faster than the replaced module.

All memory taken together (from all memory banks) will be set to the speed of the slowest SIMM.

Rambus Inline Memory Modules (RIMMs)

Rambus inline memory modules (RIMMs)—as opposed to dual inline DIMMs— use Rambus dyamic RAM (RDRAM) chips. Previously, on a standard bidirectional bus, data traveled down the bus in one direction, and then returning data traveled back up the same bus in the opposite direction. It did this for each bank of memory, with each module being addressed separately. A wait occurred until the bus was ready for either the send or reverse.

RIMMs use a *looped* system, where everything is going in one direction (unidirectional). In a looped system, data moves forward from chip to chip and module to module. Data goes down the line, and then the *results* data continues forward on the wire in the same direction. The results data doesn't have to wait for downstream data to finish being sent.

These chips are set on their modules contiguously (next to each other in a chain) and are connected to each other in a series. This means that if an empty memory bank socket is in between two RIMM chips, you must install a *continuity module*, which is a low-cost circuit board that looks like a RIMM, but that doesn't have any chips. All it does is allows the current to move through the chain of RDRAM chips. It's like Christmas tree lights wired in series, where one bulb is missing.

Note: Latency is a combination of two things: Bus turnaround time and the cycle time. RDRAM cycles are a fast 800MHz, so you don't have to wait very long for the next cycle. Using RDRAM chips, signals go from one module to the next in a linear (serial) flow, eliminating bus turnaround. Throughput is triple that of 100MHz SDRAM, and you can also use two to four RDRAM channels (narrow channel memory) at the same time. This can further increase throughput to either 3.2GB or 6.4GB.

Memory Diagnostics—Parity

When a PC runs through the POST (power-on self test), commonly called a *cold boot*, memory integrity is one of the first things tested. *Parity* is the state of either oddness or evenness assigned to a given byte (not bit) of data. *Parity checking* is the way that the computer uses a special set of logical rules and chips to make decisions based on the parity (state) of a particular byte. This checking is designed to verify the accuracy (integrity) of the bits contained in memory, and it happens after every read/write operation.

 Remember that computers think in binary bits and bytes. The binary computer language uses "words" composed of 1s and 0s.

Even and Odd Parity

Parity can be set to odd, even, or off. The *parity circuit* works by adding one bit to every byte of data, resulting in 9 bits. (Remember that a byte is already 8 bits.) The value of any given bit (1 or 0) is determined at the time that data is written to memory. Then, a 1 or 0 is assigned to the parity bit, depending on whether the overall byte is made up of an odd or even number of 1s. Figure 4.1 shows various bytes of data with their additional parity bit.

 SIMMs come in both 30-pin and 72-pin versions. The 30-pin module is an 8-bit chip, with 1 optional *parity* bit. The 72-pin SIMM is a 32-bit chip, with 4 optional parity bits.

In plain odd and even parity, every byte gets 1 parity bit attached, making a combined 9-bit byte. Therefore, a 16-bit byte has 2 parity bits, a 32-bit byte has 4 parity bits, and so forth. This produces extra pins on the memory module, and

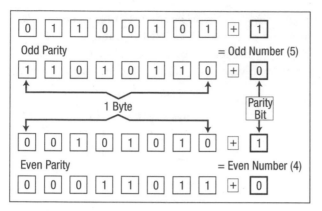

Figure 4.1 Odd and even parity.

that's why different types of DIMMs and SIMMs have different numbers of pins. The number depends on the parity.

The parity circuit tells the computer how to remember what it sent, by comparing the byte to what it reads. The combined process puts a byte into memory along with its parity bit, then reads the byte from memory. If the byte plus the parity bit matches what was sent, the memory is okay. Otherwise, we have a *parity error*. Until recently, parity checking has been the most common way to check the ability of memory cells to accurately hold data.

Fake or Disabled Parity

Some computer manufacturers install a less expensive "fake" parity chip that simply sends a 1 or a 0 to the parity circuit to supply parity on the basis of which parity state is expected. Regardless of whether the parity is valid, the computer is fooled into thinking that everything is valid. This method means no connection whatsoever exists between the parity bit being sent and the associated byte of data.

A more common way for manufacturers to reduce the cost of SIMMs is to simply disable the parity completely, or to build a computer without any parity checking capability installed. Some of today's PCs are being shipped this way, and they make no reference to the disabled or missing parity. The purchaser must ensure that the SIMMs have parity capabilities and must configure the motherboard to turn parity on.

As we saw in Figure 4.1, *even* parity checking is where the total of all the 1 bits in a byte must equal an even number. If five of the bits are set to 1, the parity bit will also be set to 1 to total six (an even number). If 6 bits were set to 1, the parity bit would be set to 0 to maintain the even number six.

In even parity, the overall number of 1s must come out to an even number.

Odd parity works in the reverse of even parity, but the concept is the same. The total number of 1s in any given byte must come out to an odd number. Once again, this is done by using either a 1 or a 0 for the parity bit, as you can see in Figure 4.1.

You'll receive a *parity error* if the parity is odd and the parity circuit gets an even number, or if the parity is even and the parity circuit gets an odd number. The circuit can't correct the error, but it can detect that the data is wrong.

Error Correction Code (ECC)

Parity checking is limited in the sense that it can only detect an error—it can't repair or correct the error. This is because the circuit can't tell which one of the eight bits is invalid. Additionally, if multiple bits are wrong but the result according to the parity is correct, the circuit will pass the invalid data as okay.

Error correction code (ECC) uses a special algorithm to work with the memory controller, and it adds an *error correction code bit* to each data bit when it's sent to memory. When the CPU calls for data, the memory controller decodes each error correction bit and determines the validity of its attached data bit.

The system requires twice the number of bits, but the benefit is that ECC can correct a single-bit error. Because approximately 90 percent of data errors are single-bit errors, ECC does a very good job. On the other hand, ECC costs a lot more, due to the additional number of bits.

Remember that ECC can correct only single-bit errors, but it can also detect multibit errors. Parity checking understands only that the overall byte coming out of memory doesn't match what was sent into memory. Parity checking cannot correct *anything*.

Usually, whoever is buying the computer will decide which type of data integrity checking they want, depending mainly on cost benefits. They can choose ECC, parity checking, or nothing. High-end computers (e.g., file servers) typically use an ECC-capable memory controller. Midrange desktop business computers typically are configured with parity checking. Low-cost home computers often have nonparity memory (no parity checking or "fake" parity).

Why Memory Becomes Corrupted

Most DRAM chips in SIMMs or DIMMs require a parity bit because memory can be corrupted in the following two ways: Alpha particles can disturb memory cells with ionizing radiation, resulting in lost data, or electromagnetic interference (EMI) can change the stored information.

A DRAM cell (transistor) shares its storage charge with the bit line. This creates a small voltage differential, which can be sensed during read access. The differential can be influenced by other nearby bit line voltages. This, along with other electrical noise, can corrupt the electrical charge in the memory cell.

Practice Questions

Question 1

> Part of a computer's RAM chip is dedicated to storing key system settings required for boot-up.
>
> ○ a. True
>
> ○ b. False

Answer b, false, is correct. Random access memory (RAM) is volatile and loses all of its data without a source of power. RAM comes in modules and is almost never referred to as a chip. System boards commonly use nonvolatile CMOS to store system settings. CMOS memory uses very little current (a trickle charge) and continues to be powered for extended periods of inactivity by a small battery on the system board.

Question 2

> Over-clocking allows a microprocessor to run considerably faster than motherboard components. What type of memory structure was developed to minimize the delay of accessing RAM on the motherboard?
>
> ○ a. Processor resident pipeline
>
> ○ b. L-2 cache
>
> ○ c. CMOS memory
>
> ○ d. Duplex memory

Answer b is correct. Intel 486 and Pentium processors have a small amount of memory integrated in the chip called an L-1 cache. However, as processor speeds increased, additional high-speed memory was needed. This second block of memory was called an L-2 cache and was typically located outside of the CPU on a special high-speed bus. Note that the question refers to a connection between the processor and the motherboard, indicating something between the CPU and the motherboard. An L-1 cache is typically internal to the CPU. Later, some designs included an L-2 cache on the processor cartridge or the die itself. Answer c is incorrect because CMOS is used to store configuration settings for the PC. Duplex memory and a processor resident pipeline do not exist.

Question 3

DIMMs and SIMMs are interchangeable, provided speed and capacity requirements are observed.

○ a. True

○ b. False

Answer b, false, is correct. SIMMs and DIMMs look similar, and both use edge connectors. However, DIMMs use both sides of the connector to support a 64-bit or wider memory bus, and they have two separate connector pins, one on each side of the module board.

Question 4

Which of the following is not a type of memory?

○ a. SDRAM

○ b. VRAM

○ c. ECC RAM

○ d. RDRAM

Answer c is correct. ECC is a form of parity using error correction code; it is not a type of memory. Answer a is incorrect because SDRAM is a synchronous DRAM chip. Answer b is incorrect because video RAM is a type of memory used on graphics accelerator cards. Answer d is incorrect because RDRAM is the Rambus DRAM chip often found on a motherboard using the 800 series chip set.

Question 5

Which of the following choices best describes what is meant by cache memory?

- ○ a. A place where instructions are stored about the operations of a device or application
- ○ b. Extended memory that can be made accessible with the **SMARTDRV /ON** command
- ○ c. Memory that holds applications and data that the CPU isn't running
- ○ d. Memory that holds data that the CPU will search first

Answer d is correct. The CPU will look in cache memory first. If it fails to find the necessary data, it will look in main memory. If it fails to find what it needs in main memory, the CPU will look on the disk. Answer a is incorrect because ROM is where device instructions are stored, and applications use the Help menu to store instructions. Answer b is incorrect because cache memory and extended memory are two distinct types of memory. Answer c is incorrect because suspended applications and the data being held in memory aren't running at the moment, and caching is a method of speeding up immediate access by the CPU to data.

Question 6

Which of the following features make SRAM and SDRAM faster than DRAM? [Choose the two best answers]

- ❑ a. Lower density
- ❑ b. Reduced refresh rate
- ❑ c. Internal clock
- ❑ d. Serialized data transfers

Answers b and c are correct. Both Synchronous RAM and SDRAM store data in transistors rather than capacitors, meaning that data does not leak out and does not need to be refreshed. Both types of memory use an internal clock to synchronize with the motherboard clock and reduce wait states. Answer a is incorrect because although SRAM and SDRAM chips have a lower density than DRAM chips, this is a cost benefit and not a speed benefit. Answer d is incorrect because the (borderline) term applies to the unidirectional movement of data along a bus.

Need to Know More?

Freedman, Alan. *Computer Desktop Encyclopedia, 2nd Edition.* AMACOM, 1999. ISBN 0-814-479-855. This is great for a fast look-up or refresher.

Messmer, Hans-Peter. *The Indispensable PC Hardware Book, 3rd Edition.* Reading, MA: Addison-Wesley Publishing Company, 2000. ISBN 0-201-403-994. This is a comprehensive, up-to-date reference book that covers far more than you will need to know for the exam.

Minasi, Mark. *The Complete PC Upgrade and Maintenance Guide, 11th Edition.* San Francisco, CA: Sybex Network Press, 2000. ISBN 0-782-128-009. This is considered one of the best reference books available. In fact, Minasi's book was instrumental in the formulation of the first A+ exam.

Muller, Scott. *Upgrading and Repairing PCs, 12th Edition.* Indianapolis, IN: Que, 2000. ISBN 0-7897-2303-4. This is one of our favorites. If you are only going to have one reference book, give this one serious consideration.

Reeves, Scott, Kalinda Reeves, Stephen Weese, and Christopher S. Geyer. *A+ Exam Prep, 3rd Edition.* Scottsdale, AZ: The Coriolis Group, 2001. ISBN 1-57610-699-3. This is a good reference that concentrates on providing exam-required information.

Rosch, Winn. *Hardware Bible, 5th Edition.* Indianapolis, IN: Sams Publishing, 1999. ISBN 0-789-717-433. This is a well-organized reference book that covers software issues as well as hardware.

5

Peripherals: Input Devices

Terms you'll need to understand:

✓ Resistor, capacitor, ohms, potentiometer (pot)

✓ Pixels, charge-coupled device (CCD), and dots per inch (dpi)

Concepts you'll need to master:

✓ Interrupt request (IRQ) lines and direct memory access (DMA) channels

✓ Binary and hexadecimal numbering

✓ Electricity and circuits

✓ Image resolution versus optical resolution

Human beings understand information through written and spoken language, but machines communicate and process in binary machine language. The results of machine processing, or *digital* information, must be turned into something that people can understand—*analog* information.

On one side of the human/machine communication equation are the ways that people talk to a machine. This requires *input devices,* such as keyboards, mice, scanners, and modems. The other side of the equation is the way that machines talk to people. This requires *output devices,* such as printers, video displays, modems, and speakers. The motherboard and associated chips make up the basic computer, and anything else is a *peripheral device* of some kind.

Finally, because random access memory (RAM) doesn't retain information when the power is turned off, there must be some way to keep the applications (ways of getting work done), and the work that the applications produce, from disappearing at the end of a session. This requires *storage devices.*

For our purposes, we're going to call the motherboard, the central processing unit (CPU), and the processing events the core system. Any device that makes a connection to the CPU through the motherboard will be a peripheral device. People mostly define peripherals as devices that aren't critical to the operations of a computer. However, even though a monitor, keyboard, and mouse are considered critical elements, for the sake of this discussion, we'll address them as peripheral devices.

Before we discuss these devices, we want to take a moment to review interrupt requests (IRQs), direct memory accesses (DMAs), and how computers use a base-16 numbering system (hexadecimal).

Interrupt Requests (IRQs)

We've seen that, when the CPU is busy with a process, any new request for processing must *interrupt* the process already in progress. The specific instructions for these interruptions are provided by the ROM BIOS on both the motherboard and on many devices. The operating system also understands interrupts, and uses part of low memory to store something called the *interrupt vector table.*

If you think of the CPU as the Wizard of Oz, then an IRQ line is like an 8- or a 16-lane yellow brick road. An IRQ is a signal from a piece of hardware (e.g., a mouse) indicating that it needs the CPU to do something. To take pressure off the CPU, International Business Machines (IBM) created a chip called an *interrupt controller*, which is analogous to that weird gatekeeper to the Emerald City.

When a piece of hardware sends a demand to the busy CPU, it tries to interrupt the processing by sending an IRQ down its own IRQ line. The IRQ signals (Dorothy and pals) run along the IRQ lines (yellow brick road) to an interrupt controller (that bizarre gatekeeper), which assigns *priorities* to incoming IRQs (puts them in the waiting room) and then delivers them to the CPU (the wizard).

Because the interrupt controller (different from the memory controller) expects signals from only one hardware device per IRQ line, an *IRQ conflict* occurs when two devices try to use the same IRQ line, much like two cars using the same lane at the same time. When that happens, computers usually crash. The gatekeeper loses his mind, and you're left in the poppy fields! This is why assigning IRQs to new hardware as you install it is so important—and why it can be such a pain when it goes wrong. A technical term for this pain is major aggravation. This is also why so much effort went into developing Plug and Play, which helps the computer and new devices figure out all the IRQs on their own.

IRQ 2 Cascades to IRQ 9

The original XT interrupt controller chip could handle only eight IRQs at once. Starting with the AT and continuing with the ATX, PCs began using two interrupt line controllers, each able to handle eight lines (0 through 7 and 8 through 15). To get the two controllers working together, IRQ 2 on the first controller is set aside to pass certain requests to IRQ 9 on the second controller. This is known as *cascading*.

By daisy-chaining the two chips (see Chapter 8 for more on chaining), the AT motherboard could handle 16 IRQs at the same time. ATX motherboards continue the precedent set by the AT boards, so all in all, there are 16 IRQ lines— IRQ 0 through IRQ 15.

 The AT controllers began using interrupts 8 through 15 and left the original XT lines 0 through 7. Because of this, the old IRQ 2 is often borrowed by the new IRQ 9 using something called "cascading." Be sure to know the term *cascading* for the exam.

Hexadecimal Numbering

We just presented a concept that may be difficult to understand. We said that AT boards had 16 IRQs, and we then made the highest number 15. The decimal, hexadecimal, and binary numbering systems all start with zero. Our habit is to think of the "first" of something as being number 1, but in the world of computers and technology, you need to become accustomed to the first thing being numbered 0.

Never forget that in computer technology, the "first" of something is numbered with a 0 (zero). For instance, the primary hard drive is drive 0.

If you remember your high school math, the number of digits that can fit into the units (ones) column is called the *base*. The word "decimal," from the Latin "ten," allows 10 digits in the ones column (0 through 9). Decimal numbering is also called *base-10*. In base-10 numbering, when you have more than 10 digits, you cross over to the tens column.

In regular counting, we start with a one and go to a nine. When we add one more number, we put a 0 in the ones column, a 1 in the tens column, and make a "10." In computer math, we start with zero! When we get to the end of the allowed numbers in the ones column, we go back to the beginning, put down a zero, and move a one to the tens column.

Binary Numbers—Base-2

Binary refers to base-2 numbers, in that only two units are used before you begin using the tens column. In base-2 numbering, you can have only a zero and a one in the ones column. There is no "two," and you have to go to the tens column instead. You put a 1 to the left of the zero after two digits (binary), just as you do after 10 digits in base-10 numbers (decimal).

There's actually no "10" symbol in decimal numbering. The word "ten" actually describes only a one in the tens column and a zero in the ones column. Ten is the same word in any base of numbering, but we get to that 10 by a different number of units in the ones column. In base-3 numbers we would count zero, one, two...ten.

Binary (base-2) counting would be: zero, one, ten, eleven, one hundred, one hundred and one, one hundred and ten, one hundred and eleven, one thousand. The same sequence in symbols would be 0, 1, 10, 11, 100, 101, 110, 111, and 1000. Because binary has only ones and zeros, there's no such thing as a "two." The two is replaced by what we think of as a 10. Confusing? Of course! That's what computers are all about. The exam probably won't have any binary or hexadecimal math, but you need to know the concept.

The largest eight-bit binary number is 11111111, which is made up of eight "ones," and converts to 255 in decimal. By an amazing coincidence, the last character in the American Standard Code for Information Interchange (ASCII) keyboard character translation table is 255, which is a blank space. On the other hand, decimal/binary zero is also a space, so maybe it's not that incredible.

Hexadecimal Numbers—Base-16

Hexadecimal is *base-16* numbering, where numbers in the ones column must go beyond 10 digits, all the way to 16 digits. For that, we need to use letters, because decimal numbering (base-10) has only ten available digits—0, 1, 2, 3, 4, 5, 6, 7, 8, 9—before we make a 10. Hexadecimal (often abbreviated as Hex, H, or h) adds A, B, C, D, E, and F.

Counting a full, hexadecimal sequence would be: 0, 1, 2, 3, 4, 5, 6, 7, 8, 9, A (no ten), B (11), C (12), D (13), E (14), and F (15). Note how the A replaces the 10. The F represents the tens column crossover point, just like the nine does in decimal numbers. In this case, 15 (the F) is the sixteenth digit and the last that can fit in the ones column. Don't forget that zero was the first digit.

Following F (in base-16) would come a "tens unit," so the next number is 10. The sequence continues as 11, 12, 13, 14, 15, 16, 17, 18, 19, 1A, 1B, 1C, 1D, 1E, 1F, and then another tens unit, making 20.

Hexadecimal numbering allows for cramming more information into a smaller space. For example, the decimal 255 is three bits—two, five, five. However, it becomes FFh (two bits) in Hex. Observe the small "h" following the number. This identifies the number as a hexadecimal number.

Be sure to remember that computer memory addresses are usually written in hexadecimal notation. Hex notation can appear as 10h, 10H, &H10, or &h10, but the first two formats are the most common. Therefore, decimal 255 is typically written as FFh in hexadecimal format.

Direct Memory Access (DMA) Channels

A number of semi-intelligent chips work together with the CPU. The interrupt controller, which handles IRQs, is one of these chips. Another peripheral chip is the direct memory access (DMA) controller. Like IRQ lines, DMA channels are limited in number, and you can allocate only one channel to one device. There are eight DMA channels.

No matter how fast the CPU runs, it can easily be loaded down if it wants to send data to something like a very slow (relative to the CPU) hard drive, and then it has to wait around for the drive to report back. This movement of data from slow disk to fast memory used to have to pass through some very small memory registers in the CPU. The DMA controller was developed to offload this sort of drudgework and to avoid bottlenecks in processing.

The DMA controller is like a highway bypass. It bypasses the CPU registers and moves information directly into and out of RAM. In another astounding coincidence, this is why it's called "*direct* memory" access! The DMA controller chip is capable of taking over control of the system, but must first request control from the microprocessor. When this happens, the CPU makes itself appear as though it has been removed from the circuit.

When the hard drive needs to access RAM for addresses or instructions, those interrupt requests don't have to interrupt the CPU. Fewer interruptions leads to more work getting done (just like in real life) and better system performance.

 Originally, a motherboard had only one DMA controller. The system worked so well that a second DMA controller was added. Each controller allows four channels, so today we have eight DMA channels available on most systems.

IRQs, DMA, and I/O Ports

The certification exam has a number of questions about IRQs, COMmunications (COM) and Line Printer Terminal (LPT) port addresses, and DMA channels. Remember that an IRQ is the way in which a device interrupts the CPU. A DMA channel is a shortcut around the main expansion bus that allows a device to access RAM directly.

DMA channels and IRQ lines interconnect the components (devices), CPU, and memory. You should document the current devices and their IRQs and DMA settings before you install and configure a new device. Table 5.1 lists IRQ lines and their default device services. MSD.EXE includes a report under IRQ Status that shows which IRQs are being used on a specific PC.

 Remember that 16 IRQs are available to devices. Because the IRQs are numbered in the hexadecimal technical format, the first IRQ is 0. The upper limit is IRQ 15. There are 16 IRQs to conform with hex memory addressing (base-16) and the 16 segments of conventional memory.

IRQ 14 is set aside for the primary Integrated Drive Electronics (IDE), or advanced technology (AT), drive controller. However, terminology might refer to a master drive, the primary hard drive, or the first hard disk. An IDE or Enhanced IDE (EIDE) controller can have two devices chained to it, and a second hard drive is the slave. IRQ 15 (the last IRQ) is typically set aside for the secondary IDE drive controller, *not a second drive*.

Ordinarily, a second disk is chained to the IDE controller. Remember that IDE controllers allow for a daisy chain of two devices, so the master and slave usually connect to a single controller.

Table 5.1 A typical MSD.EXE report of IRQ usage.		
Device	**IRQ**	**Handler**
Timer output	0	WIN386.EXE
Keyboard	1	Block device
Cascade from IRQ 9	2	BIOS
COM2, COM4 (serial ports)	3	BIOS
COM1, COM3 (serial ports)	4	BIOS
LPT2 (parallel port, XT drive)	5	BIOS
Floppy disk controller	6	Default handler
LPT1 (parallel port)	7	System
Realtime clock	8	Default handler
Redirected IRQ 2 (video, network)	9	BIOS
(Reserved)	10	BIOS
(Reserved)	11	BIOS
(Reserved), built-in mouse	12	Default handler
Math coprocessor	13	BIOS
Primary fixed disk controller (IDE)	14	BIOS
Secondary fixed disk controller	15	Default handler

Remember that the default IRQ 14 is used for the primary hard disk IDE controller. IRQ 15 most likely is used for a *third* physical disk. Typically, two physical disks use the primary controller on IRQ 14. Adding a third disk requires using a second IDE controller, which then uses IRQ 15.

Be sure you don't get confused by a response on the exam that refers to IRQ 16. There isn't a number 16. If you can remember that hex (Latin for *6,* e.g., *hex*agon) numbering uses 16 numbers starting at 0, at least the numbers assigned to the last IRQs make sense; 14 is primary, and 15 is secondary for the disk controllers.

As we mentioned earlier in this chapter, the original XT BIOS provided for eight IRQ lines (0 through 7). The AT BIOS adds eight more (8 through 15). Instructions for controllers designed to work on an AT motherboard are usually located at IRQ 9. However, these instructions typically are *redirected,* or *cascaded,* to IRQ 2.

Make a note that if IRQ 2 is being used by BIOS instructions, IRQ 9 is also being used. IRQ 9 is *cascading, vectoring,* or *redirecting* to IRQ 2. All three words refer to the same process of pointing to somewhere else. When source information is *redirected* to a destination, the destination receives *cascaded* information from that source.

Input/Output (I/O) Addresses

We know that a PC has a number of input/output (I/O) devices connected to the motherboard. Each device requires a unique I/O hardware address. Programs and the operating system send instructions to, and read instructions from, the hardware by calling to the I/O addresses. The first megabyte (MB) of conventional memory has room for 1 million *real* addresses used by data (Real Mode). Extended memory allows for many millions more data addresses. Usually, only about 800 addresses can be used as hardware addresses.

Some memory addresses are reserved for system use, and a typical device uses 4, 8, or 32 bytes of address information. Some of the hardware addresses have been predefined as available for use by the most common devices (although they might not always be used for that purpose).

We did see questions having to do with the origin of a hardware address. During the power-on self-test (POST), the basic input/output system (BIOS) checks the complementary metal oxide semiconductor (CMOS) tables for the existence of an I/O port interface. If this port exists, the CPU assigns a hardware memory address and stores the address in memory for the length of the running session. The main I/O ports (e.g., COM ports) have common default settings.

After the device has a hardware memory address (from the CPU), the operating system uses the low-memory IRQ vector table to point to this address when moving instructions back and forth between the device and the software.

User-configurable devices store configuration settings that tell the device to use a particular port and an I/O address. Often, the I/O address is described in either the CONFIG.SYS or the AUTOEXEC.BAT file.

COM and LPT IRQs

Most modern computers have two serial interfaces built into the motherboard. The two physical interfaces are broken up into four logical COM ports. Each logical port has its own default address. COM1 and COM3 go together with the first serial interface. COM2 and COM4 go together with the extra serial interface.

In the real world, you're able to research memory addresses, such as those of the COM ports on a given PC. Even on an old DOS machine, MSD.EXE prints out whether a device is attached to either of the serial ports and which address the device is using. For the purposes of the exam, Table 5.2 lists the default memory addresses assigned to each COM port.

Table 5.2	Default COM port addresses and IRQs.		
I/O Serial Interface	Port	Address (Hexadecimal)	IRQ
Controller 1	COM 1	03F8	4
Controller 1	COM 3	03E8	4
Controller 2	COM 2	02F8	3
Controller 2	COM 4	02E8	3

Here's a mnemonic that might help you build COM addresses during the exam. Observe that the only changing address values are "2-3" and "F-E." All four default addresses begin with 0 and end with 8. The only IRQ choices are 4 and 3.

It might help to think of COM3 and COM4 as "Extra," with an "E" hex address. COM1 and COM2 are "First," with an "F" hex address. The exam is multiple choice, so you won't really need to remember the 0 or the 8.

Using an odd/even trick, COM1 and COM3 use the "3" (odd address) and COM2 and COM4 use the "2" (even address), or, in other words:

➤ Port 1 (odd), COM1 and COM3, use odd "03".

➤ Port 2 (even), COM2 and COM4, use even "02".

➤ First (Ph)ysical interfaces 1 and 2 use "F" for First.

➤ Extra logical interfaces 3 and 4 use an "E" for Extra.

➤ The only place the rule reverses is IRQs 3 and 4 (odd port/even IRQ 4, even port/odd IRQ 3).

Aside from the COM ports, the default printer (LPT) ports and their IRQs are also considered testable knowledge. The good news is that although the default COM port memory addresses are considered common knowledge, the LPT addresses aren't. LPT ports have a range of addresses, although they commonly try for a default address. Table 5.3 lists the two LPT ports and their default IRQs.

LPT2 is rarely used these days, except on network print servers (PCs under the control of a network operating system and dedicated to managing a shared printer). IRQ 5 is usually assigned to a sound card on standalone systems. In fact, IRQ 5

Table 5.3	LPT2 and LPT1 and their default IRQ lines.
Parallel Interface	IRQ
LPT2 (parallel port)	5
LPT1 (parallel port)	7

is the default for Sound Blaster cards, with LPT1 going to IRQ 7. If LPT2 is being used, it is usually assigned to IRQ 5 and 278h.

Note: LPT2 comes first because IRQ 5 was originally the XT hard drive controller's IRQ. Later PCs have a normal configuration of two parallel ports, so LPT2 took over from the obsolete XT controller.

 We've tried to come up with some ways to help you remember the proper order of the LPT ports and their default IRQs. Here are some suggestions, although you might have your own method:

➤ You have 2 hands with 5 fingers (LPT2-IRQ 5).

➤ "There's only 1 God and only 1 heaven, and LPT1 uses IRQ 7."

DMA Channels

Modern (AT-class) PCs have two DMA controllers, each of which provides four channels for Fast DMA. Again, a device can use a DMA channel to bypass the CPU and directly access main memory, allowing for faster performance.

The original 8088/86 (8-bit/16-bit) processors provided four DMA channels that were capable of supporting both 8- and 16-bit cards. The 80286 added four more 16-bit-only channels. Table 5.4 lists the DMA channels and the most common devices configured to use them.

It's very good policy to follow the instructions recommended by the manufacturer for setting IRQs, DMA channels, and I/O ports, especially with sound cards and scanners. Install the sound card first and then let it find the IRQ and DMA channel it needs. Install everything else next. Install the sound card before CD-ROM drives as well, and then let the CD take whatever DMA channel is open.

Table 5.4	DMA channels and associated devices.	
DMA Channel	**Bus Width (Bits)**	**Common Device**
1	8 or 16	Sound cards
2	8 or 16	Sound cards; network (LAN)
3	8 or 16	Floppy drive
4	8 or 16	ECP or EPP parallel port
5	16	Cascade channel
6	16	Not assigned
7	16	Not assigned
8	16	ISA IDE hard drive controller

Basic Electronics

Before we move into keyboards, this is a good place to review some of the essential elements of electricity. The exam has some questions relating to basic electronic concepts like AC, DC, voltage, multimeters, ohms, and basic electricity, so you should know something about the terms. You won't need to be overly concerned with the definition of electrical measurements, but you do need to be familiar with the terms.

Electricity

Electricity is actually a flow of electrons. The electrons can be flowing in one direction (direct current, DC), or they can change direction, going back and forth sort of like a bidirectional bus (alternating current, AC).

Voltage (often called *potential voltage*) is a measure of the pressure pushing electrons through a medium such as a wire, and is often called "potential." *Current*, on the other hand, is the actual number of electrons moving through wire, and we measure it in *amps*. *Watts* are what you get when you multiply volts (V) by amps, and are often called a "measure of work."

Electrons repel each other, which is why a device or substance holding a whole lot of electrons will *discharge* to something with fewer electrons. For example, when you rub your feet across a wool carpet, you can build up a charge of electrons in yourself that will discharge to a doorknob when you touch it.

If you see a spark, the discharge was more than 650V, which brings up two important facts. First, as little as 35V can destroy the semiconductors used in computers! That's right. You wouldn't even feel the spark that destroyed a $200 CPU. This is why electrostatic discharge (ESD) must be prevented while handling components. Secondly, current—as measured in amps—is more dangerous to life forms (that's you) than voltage. You can zap the doorknob all day long with static electricity at 650V from your finger, but, if you short out a 12V car battery with your body, you may not get up! That is why old electricians say, "Volts jolt, mills [milliamps] kill."

ESD means electrostatic discharge. EMI means electromagnetic interference. When many electrical wires are placed near or next to each other, you can have EMI. Fluorescent lights (with their ballast) can also cause EMI. However, rubbing a cat's fur the wrong way or walking on a carpet when you work on a computer can generate ESD.

All electrical circuits have an influence on the atomic structure of their surrounding environment. To fire the gases contained in a fluorescent lighting tube, a device called a *ballast* generates a powerful spark. The power required by the ballast is sufficient to radiate interference quite a distance from the unit itself.

When electricity modifies a surrounding area, we call it (simplistically) an *electromagnetic field*. Electricity flowing through a conductor is one thing. However, the modifying effect of that flow of current to the surrounding area is a *field effect*. Small currents, such as those in parallel or video cables, have a lesser impact than large currents. Bundling cables next to each other, where the current is moving in similar directions, can increase their EMI.

All technicians know they should ground themselves while working on computers. Many ESD kits provide safe, efficient grounding. However, to avoid the cost of an ESD kit, some young technicians have been known to ground themselves with a metal strap, which is a bad idea. ESD kits have a *resistor* in the grounding strap, which limits current flow in the event of a short circuit. A metal strap is a perfect conductor, and in the event of a short, your body is part of the conduction path.

ESD is electrostatic discharge. An ESD kit is designed to prevent static electricity from accidentally destroying the innards of a computer. Rubber-handled pliers can sometimes prevent static discharge, but an ESD kit is better. EMI is electromagnetic interference.

Basic Electrical Components

Of the hundreds of basic electrical components, two are especially important to know: *resistors* and *capacitors*. Keep in mind that when you connect a number of electrical components together and move electrical current through them, you have a *circuit*.

Resistance and Ohms

Resistors "resist" (hold back) the flow of electricity, and we measure that resistance in *ohms*. Some resistors, called *potentiometers* (or "pots"), can change the amount of resistance. A good example of a potentiometer is the volume control on a radio. When you turn the volume control, you vary the resistance. This directly affects the current flowing to the speakers, and as such, controls the volume.

Capacitors

Technically, a capacitor is an electrical component, usually formed by separating two conductive plates with an insulating material. A capacitor stores energy in an electric field. The strength of this field is referred to as *capacitance* and is measured in *farads* (farads are not on the exam). One of the variables that affects capacitance is the distance between the two plates. Keyboards use this attribute in *capacitive switches* (discussed in the "Keyboards" section later in this chapter).

When capacitors are used in computer memory chips, they are part of the chip itself and are extremely small. Although capacitors do hold a charge (quantity of electrons), that charge slowly leaks away and must be refreshed periodically. This is the *memory refresh* we spoke about in Chapter 4, and the number of times it happens in a set of cycles, is the *refresh rate*.

 Capacitors *store* electricity. Resistors *impede* (slow the progress of) electricity. Impedance is measured in *ohms*. A failing power supply may have some bad capacitors, although that isn't necessarily the only cause of the problem.

Capacitors store a charge for a short period of time. Large capacitors, such as those used in power supplies, can store a huge charge, and are capable of delivering a nasty shock even when the power cord has been disconnected. We've seen the tip of a screwdriver vaporized by accidentally shorting the terminals of a capacitor! Replace the word "screwdriver" with "finger," and you can see why power supplies are given a great deal of respect.

HAZMAT and MSD Sheets

Keep in mind that power supplies and integrated circuit (IC) boards can be classified as *Hazardous Material (HAZMAT)*, which may require special disposal considerations. Whenever hazardous materials are present in the workplace, U.S. law requires that a readily accessible Material Safety Data (MSD) sheet be on-site and in a known location. These sheets, usually in a looseleaf binder, provide the details of that material and how to handle it properly.

Disposing of power supplies and IC boards may be subject to federal laws and/or local ordinances.

Multimeters

At one time, individual meters were used to measure different electrical values; voltmeters measured electrical potential, ohmmeters measured resistance, and so on. Often, one instrument was used for direct current and a different one for alternating current. Today, most of these instruments have been combined into one instrument called a *multimeter*. Most multimeters are small and portable, and they can measure ohms, volts, and amps for both DC and AC. They are simply the most versatile test instruments you can have.

 When you use a multimeter to check a circuit, remember that a complete circuit has no resistance. A complete circuit has a reading of 0 ohms.

Keyboards

Arguably, the most important peripheral component is the keyboard. A keyboard has a set of keys with language symbols for a human operator. When you press a key, it generates an electrical signal, and a microprocessor in the keyboard changes the signal to a digital code—a *scan code*. It then sends the scan code to the computer. Most PCs check to see whether a keyboard is attached during the power-on self test (POST) process, and they generate a keyboard error message if a keyboard can't be found. We discuss the POST at length in Chapter 11.

Switch Technology: Mechanical

Depending on how an electronic signal is generated by the key, there are two basic types of keyboards: *switches* and *capacitive*. Switch technology tries to solve two problems: how to produce an electrical contact, and how to get the keycap back up after it's been pressed. The four basic switches are:

➤ *Pure mechanical*—Metal contacts and a spring, providing audible feedback with a "click," along with resistance feedback for touch typists. They are durable and usually self-cleaning, and they last around 20 million keystrokes.

➤ *Foam element*—Like a plunger, but using foam, metal foil, and a spring. Compressible foam attaches to a stem, with a foil contact attached under the foam. Circuit board contacts are closed when the foil bridges them. The spring pushes the key back up after it's pressed. Foil gets dirty with corrosion, leading to intermittent key strikes. The foam reduces bounce, but at the same time, it gives the keyboard a "mushy" feel. Because the lack of audible feedback tends to hinder touch typists, they sometimes resort to sending a clicking sound to the PC speaker to provide audible feedback.

➤ *Rubber dome*—A rubber dome, similar to half of a handball with a carbon button contact on the underside of the dome, which resists corrosion better than the foil of the foam switch. On a key press, the dome begins to collapse and then "snaps through" like the handball, which is good tactile feedback. Key release allows the rubber to re-form, pushing the key back up. This type of keyboard is sealed, protecting the contacts from dust and dirt, and has few moving parts, making it reliable and inexpensive. However, it doesn't provide enough tactile feedback for the touch typist.

➤ *Membrane sheet*—A simplified version of the rubber dome, placing all keys together on what looks like a single-sheet rubber dome. This limits key travel, making membrane switches impractical for touch typists. Because the keys and membrane are sealed together, the keyboard is practically spill- and dust-proof. This type is often used in commercial and industrial environments for simple data entry (e.g., cash registers).

Debouncing

In mechanical and dome-type switches, most keys bounce somewhat when you press them, leading to several high-speed contacts. Keyboards also generate some amount of electrical noise whenever you press a key, which the CPU could interpret as something you meant to do. To clean up the noise, and to help the keyboard processor determine real key presses from noise, the processor constantly scans the keyboard, looking at the state (condition and status) of every key. This constant scanning is why you should never plug in or unplug a keyboard while the power is on.

Typically, *debouncing* waits for two scans before deciding that a key is legitimately depressed. Usually, key bounce is far faster than a human being can press a key twice.

Capacitive Technology: Nonmechanical

Capacitive switches are the most expensive keyboards. They last longer, resist dust and dirt even better than rubber dome keyboards, and are the only *nonmechanical* keyboards currently in use. Additionally, they offer the highest level of tactile feedback of any switch.

A capacitive switch puts two conductive plates inside a switch housing designed to sense changes in the *capacitance* of a circuit. The upper plate connects to the key plunger (stem), and as the key moves downward, the distance between the two plates changes the capacitance. This change is detected by the keyboard's circuitry.

Usually, a mechanism provides tactile feedback, and a strong click when the upper plate crosses a center point makes these keyboards exceptionally well-suited for touch typists. Because of the enclosed housing and the lack of metal contacts, the capacitive switch is essentially corrosion free and immune to dust and dirt. The switch is highly resistant to bounce because not a single strike is produced by closing a contact. These keyboards are expensive, but they are the most durable type, rated at around 25 million or more keystrokes.

Mice and Trackballs

Although people might think that Apple Computer invented the mouse, it was actually invented in 1964 by scientists at Stanford University. Then, Xerox applied it to an experimental computer system called the Alto. The story of how Xerox pretty much gave away most of its modern computer industry technology, including the original laser-printer technology, is legendary: Xerox didn't think much money could be made from a so-called X-Y position indicator, but Apple

Computer did, so in 1979, Apple Computer bought the mouse technology and lured away most of the innovative scientists from the now-famous Palo Alto Research Center.

How a Mouse Works

Two thin rollers are set at a right angle to each other inside a mouse or trackball. The rollers are attached to a notched wheel mechanism called an *encoder*. The rollers touch the rubberized ball as the ball moves, and the friction turns the rollers, which moves the encoder.

The encoder wheels have very small notches on their edges, with fine contact points where they touch the wall of the mouse. By calculating the number of times a contact is made from both encoders, the system can calculate where to put the pointer (or cursor) on the screen. This is the X-Y matrix again.

Mice come in many shapes and sizes, but a mouse is essentially a case with a rolling rubber ball underneath it. Turning the mouse upside down and putting a plastic ball on top makes it into a *trackball*. For convenience we use the term *mouse*, but the following discussion applies to trackballs as well. With the mouse, the case moves the ball against a mouse pad. With the trackball, the case stays in one place and your fingers move the ball.

Generally, a mouse requires some sort of software program (a device driver) to tell either the operating system or an application how to relate the physical movement to an on-screen pointer. Either the device driver is loaded (installed) with special software, or it is built into an operating system such as OS/2, Windows 9x, Windows NT, and so forth.

Types of Mice

The different ways that a mouse tracks the movement of the ball distinguish the types of mice. A basic mouse is mechanical because the encoder wheel and contacts are metal and make physical movements.

Optical Mouse

An *optical* mouse has no moving parts and works in conjunction with a reflective mouse pad. As the mouse moves, a beam of light bounces from the inside of the casing to the reflective pad, then back onto a sensor inside the mouse. The sensor calculates the changes in the light beam to define the X-Y coordinates of the screen cursor.

Some mice are called *optomechanical* devices. These are hybrids of mechanical and optical mice; they use a rubber ball, but they replace the encoder contacts with a *photo-interrupter* disk. The X-Y calculations are performed by counting the interruptions to a beam of light, rather than by making contacts with a mechanical wire.

Wireless Infrared

Although the way a mouse develops X-Y information is almost always the same, the way that it sends (outputs) the information to the computer can vary. A new and sometimes most convenient way is through the use of wireless infrared technology. This technology is discussed more in Chapter 9, but it essentially uses a specific frequency of infrared light, much like the remote control of a television or video cassette recorder (VCR).

Modems

It isn't easy to decide whether a modem should be categorized as an input device, used for *downloading* information to the local machine, or an output device, used for *uploading* information to another computer. We'll include the basics of dial-up modems here, before we go any further, because the exam may ask you about a few of the basic modem commands. In Chapter 8, we examine other types of online connectivity.

Modems come in many types and varieties, including dial-up modems, cable modems, digital subscriber line (DSL) modems, and wireless modems, to name just a few. On the A+ exam, the word "modem" usually refers to those used with analog telephone lines—dial-up modems.

The word "modem" is really an acronym for MODulator DEModulator, which is the way analog signals are converted to digital signals and then back again. Computers work with digital information, whereas phone lines work mainly in analog mode. However, telephone systems are gradually being converted to all-digital signaling technology.

Universal Asynchronous Receiver Transmitter (UART) Chips

Modems can either be internal or external. An internal modem is usually installed as an expansion card, using an IRQ to configure it through the operating system and/or a setup program. An external modem is easier to install because it connects to one of the COM (serial) ports, which the computer already understands. Serial and parallel transfer is discussed further in Chapter 9.

Because a computer works with bytes (8 bits), and the serial port transfers 1 bit at a time in *series*, we needed a device to break apart each byte into its component bits and then remember how to fit them back together. That device is the Universal Asynchronous Receiver Transmitter (UART) chip.

Three Types of UARTs

Most of today's PCs have a 16550A UART chip installed. The difference among the three types of UARTs is primarily how fast they can transfer information. The UARTs are as follows:

➤ *8250*—The original chip in XTs and PC-AT, with a 1-byte buffer.

➤ *16450*—Introduced with the AT, with a 2-byte buffer.

➤ *16550A*—Popular in 486 and Pentium computers; adds 16-byte *first in, first out (FIFO)* buffering to eliminate data overrun when a port receives data faster than it can process that data (needed for speeds faster than 15.5 kilobytes per second [KB/s]). Comes in two types: 16550AN and 16550AFN.

16550AN vs. 16550AFN

The original 16550AN had some problems limiting the buffer. This was fixed by the 16550AFN replacement chip.

The 8250 and 16450 UARTs send one interrupt to the CPU after each character is received. Adding the 16-byte buffer to the 16550A accumulates more characters without losing some of them (*buffering*). Another feature of the 16550A is that it uses only one interrupt to handle all the characters in the buffer. The buffer stores characters, waits for the CPU to be available, and interrupts only once at that time. This is a significant improvement in reliability with high-speed communication rates.

Windows 3.x couldn't take advantage of the 16550A's buffering, but Windows 9x can.

Basic Modem Commands

These days, you almost never have to remember simple modem commands; however, you may find some questions on the exam relating to them. Some simple terminal emulators are still buried in among the many accessories that come with most operating systems. One of the original companies to develop low-cost modems for PCs was Hayes. As a result, many of today's commands originate from those first modems, leading to what is often referred to as a "Hayes-compatible" modem.

Table 5.5 lists the typical commands for manually controlling a modem, using their generic syntax (typed structure). Usually, the operating system or online service's installation routine performs this drudgework. These commands may not work on all modems, so consult the particular modem's reference manual for the exact commands. Most commands begin with an **AT** statement, with the exception of a few that begin with a +++ statement.

Table 5.5	Basic modem commands.
Command	**Translation**
+++	Escape (for configuration or hang-up)
A/	Repeat
ATA	Answer incoming call
ATD [*string*]	Dial, or attention. **[*string*]** might be a phone number.
P	Pulse dialing, as in ATDP
T	Tone dialing, as in ATDT
, (comma)	Pause 2 seconds, as in ATDT 9, 123-4567 for an outside line
!	Flash (depress the hook and then release)
W	Wait for dial tone, as in ATDT 9 W 123-4567
H	Hang up, as in AT H
O	Online (often used after working in **+++** mode), as in ATO
Z*n*	Reset the modem to defaults, where *n* is usually 0 or 1, as in AT Z0
ATE	Echo to host (show command information on screen)
ATF*n*	Select transmission mode or speed, where *n* is a number
ATZ	Reset the modem (e.g., AOL uses **ATZHO^M** for fast disconnect)
AT&F*n*	Return to factory defaults (if any)
ATI	Show product identification (e.g., diagnostics and who made the modem)
ATL*n*	Speaker volume, where *n* is number 0, 1, 2, or 3
ATM*n*	Turn off the modem sound, as in AT M0 (*n* = 0, 1, 2, or 3)
AT&C	Carrier detect
XON or XOF	Software flow control

Scanners

By now, you should be thinking of input as anything that sends or helps you send information to the CPU. Output, in our breakdown, is anything that receives information from the CPU. We sometimes think of input devices as being only mice or keyboards, but suppose you want to send a picture to the hard drive? To do this, information must be sent to the CPU through an adapter interface. The DMA controller will probably perform some of the details of transferring data to the disk because it's good at that sort of thing.

Simply stated, a scanner is a device that *converts* an analog image—a pattern—into digital information. On the other hand, a photocopier or a camera *transfers* an analog image to paper or to film, keeping it in analog form. An image can be a graphic, an alpha character, a bar code, a fingerprint, a retina, or any other

Analog vs. Digital

The difference between the analog world of the brain and the digital world of computers is comparable to the difference between physical matter and symbols and is directly connected to the issue of measurement.

Analog information has a potentially infinite number of settings—states, conditions, or values—that can't be stored in a profile and recalled. Digital values, on the other hand, are either on or off—one or zero, yes or no. Analog information (the world of perceptions) varies with respect to time, and we can't encode all the different analog values as digital—only some of them. The digital process can arbitrarily *approximate* the analog, and because of this variability, whatever digital value is assigned represents only that specific state at that specific moment.

In physical reality, the analog concept of "up" can mean many things, with infinite increments of direction and distance relative to gravity. In the digital world, an immediate question is "How far up?" From a digital perspective, an immediate problem is that the initial starting point (or state) varies constantly and has a significant effect on the next, or ending state.

Because analog is essentially infinite, it includes the presence of noise: random information from random sources. Digital information never varies, has no noise, and always has an exact initial and ending state.

An example of analog versus digital is the concept of two, or "two-ness." The human, analog mind understands the abstract concept of two, and can apply it to sets of two apples, two people, two fingers, and so forth. The digital computer understands only a specific two, in a specific situation, in a specific context, and in a specific state.

A computer can assign a value of two when it's told to, but it can't hold the infinite values of all potentialities in the set of two. This is a complex point of research in artificial intelligence, pattern recognition, robotics, and graphics resolution. Experiments designed to develop an analog computer "mind" seem to be having better results in robotics than in the digital paradigm.

An analog brain interprets a newspaper image as a pattern with shades of gray. Magnifying the image shows the underlying digital format of the same image composed of only black dots on a white field. The separation values of the dots, along with their sizes and even the yes/no value of a dot's existence, are exact values and can be considered digital information.

pattern stored on a solid material. Naturally, a digital camera is like a scanner, only it converts real-life analog patterns to digital information.

Scanners capture an image optically by using a light source and capturing the reflection. Some scanners, such as Magnetic Ink Character Recognition (MICR), capture a magnetic pattern. Other specialized scanners capture transparencies using a light source, but they don't capture reflections. A slide-transparency scanner works this way.

Although the scanner is not directly connected to the motherboard, but uses an interface to bring data into the system, a scanner is a peripheral input device. Scanners require either some sort of expansion card, often a SCSI interface, or they work with an existing parallel or USB port. Using a port often means a reduction in the speed of scanning. We discuss interface ports, connectors, and cables in Chapter 9.

Charge-Coupled Devices (CCDs) and Resolution

A typical scanner or digital camera uses a series of photosensitive cells called charge-coupled devices (CCDs), which are mounted in a fixed row. Each CCD registers whether light is present. The point (or spot) of light being registered by one CCD is roughly equivalent to a dot on a piece of paper. The smaller the physical size of the CCD, the more *dots per inch (dpi)* of image it can acquire. For more information on dots and resolution, see Chapter 7.

Scanners are usually measured in terms of resolution in *optical* dpi. This means the actual number of dots the scanner can discern, based on how many CCDs are built into it. Any image or pattern can be broken down into a number of discrete areas, or *pixels* (picture units). The smaller the area, the more pixels that area contains, and the finer the resolution. A CCD is often said to roughly correspond to one picture unit; however, this isn't technically accurate. A CCD is composed of many small *diodes*, and a decision process defines how many diodes will generate a pixel. Today's digital cameras use fewer diodes on a CCD to capture a "unit of picture." This allows other diodes to capture other pieces of the picture, generating many more pixels—the so-called *megapixel* resolutions.

The *optical resolution* of a scanner is the one-to-one ratio of a physical CCD with a single dot. Software enhancement (*interpolation*) is a way to add pixels beyond a scanner's capability to scan a picture area. When software is used to change the image clarity, we refer to software resolution, interpolated resolution, or enhanced resolution.

Horizontal resolution depends on how close together the CCDs are placed in a single row. The smaller the CCDs and the closer they can fit together, the higher the number of pixels in a row.

Vertical resolution depends on how slowly the light source and mirror mechanism move from the top to the bottom of the image. A slower speed means smaller incremental steps. Again, the smaller the increments, the finer the resolution.

In the rating of 300×600 optical dpi, the first number applies to horizontal placement—in this case, 300 CCDs in a row. The second number (600) refers to vertical movement. Today, most scanners have an optical resolution of 300×600, 600×600, or 1200×1200 dpi. However, the amount of memory and storage space a 1200 dpi image requires is more than a typical person is willing to work with. In addition, no matter how high a resolution an image has, the resolution of the output device limits the resolution that can be displayed. Monitors generally have a 96 dpi resolution, with many printers being capable of at least a 750 dpi resolution.

Scanner Connections

The primary difference between the parallel port and a SCSI adapter card, is the *data transfer rate*. A parallel port moves 8 bits of information at a time, whereas an internal interface card transfers at bus speeds. Therefore, parallel ports are slower than internal card adapters. We discuss transfer rates more in Chapter 9.

Some sheet-fed scanners are built into a keyboard, interfacing with an internal keyboard processor in the casing. The scanner borrows the keyboard cable to transfer data. On the other hand, handheld scanners are very small and portable, often connecting through their own interface cable, which also provides power to the scanner.

Note: This concept of borrowing a cable for power became a problem when many devices began using a single cable. USB technology (discussed in Chapter 8) had to deal with the problem, so it introduced powered hubs.

Installing an internal SCSI adapter is another exercise in IRQ/DMA conflicts. Also, some inexpensive scanners don't provide Advanced SCSI Programming Interface (ASPI) support, which is necessary if you want to run the scanner on the same SCSI bus as other peripherals (see the "SCSI Interface" section in Chapter 8). Scanners and sound cards are legendary for their installation and configuration difficulties, creating a strong market for the Plug-and-Play specifications.

Practice Questions

Question 1

> Modems that interface with analog telephone lines require parallel trans-
> mission paths, and because of this, are almost always connected to the
> parallel port of the computer.
>
> ○ a. True
>
> ○ b. False

Answer b, false, is correct. Modems transmit data 1 bit at a time and, as such, are
serial devices. The parallel port transfers 8 bits at a time.

Question 2

> What kind of keyboard is considered mechanical? [Choose the three best
> answers]
>
> ❑ a. Foam element
>
> ❑ b. Capacitive
>
> ❑ c. Membrane
>
> ❑ d. Rubber dome

Answers a, c, and d are correct. Foam element, capacitive, and rubber dome keyboards are considered mechanical. Answer b is incorrect because the capacitive
switch (c) doesn't rely on metal contacts, but instead puts two plastic plates inside
a switch housing designed to sense changes in capacitance of a circuit.

Question 3

> Why is an optical mouse different from other types of mice?
>
> ○ a. Optical mice do not require a cable connecting them to the PC.
>
> ○ b. Optical mice have no moving parts.
>
> ○ c. Optical mice do not require the use of a mouse pad.
>
> ○ d. The friction ball in an optical mouse rarely requires cleaning.

Answer b is correct. An optical mouse has no moving parts and works in conjunction with a reflective mouse pad. As the mouse moves, a beam of light from the inside of the casing hits the reflective pad, then bounces back onto a sensor inside the mouse. The sensor calculates the changes in the light beam and defines the X-Y coordinates of the screen cursor.

Question 4

Most optical scanners use photosensitive devices called _____ to convert the scanned image into a machine-readable format.

○ a. Quartz tube emitters

○ b. Light-emitting diodes

○ c. Electro-optical couplers

○ d. Charge-coupled devices

Answer d is correct. Charge-coupled devices (CCDs) are photosensitive cells mounted in a fixed row. Each CCD registers whether there is light or no light—on or off. The point or spot of light being registered by one CCD is equivalent to a dot on a piece of paper. A light-emitting diode (LED) is used as a light transmitter, not a light sensor. There's no such thing as a "quartz tube emitter," nor is there an "electro-optical coupler."

Question 5

What basic electrical component can store a charge for a short period of time?

○ a. Resistor

○ b. Transistor

○ c. Capacitor

○ d. Diode

Answer c is correct. Capacitors store a quantity of electrons for a short period of time. Large capacitors can store a huge charge and are capable of delivering a shock even after the power cord has been disconnected. Resistors impede the movement of electrical current and are measured in ohms. A diode does not store current, and a transistor is a small switching device.

Question 6

How many IRQ lines are on a typical, modern-day motherboard, and which line is used for cascading various requests?

○ a. 15, 2

○ b. 16, 9

○ c. 15, 9

○ d. 16, 2

Answer d is correct. IRQs 0 through 7 were the original interrupt lines, and the AT boards added IRQs 8 through 15, making a total of 16. IRQ 2 is often used to pass requests to IRQ 9, which is called cascading.

Question 7

Which command does a dial-up modem use to connect to the Internet?

○ a. **ATD**

○ b. **ATA**

○ c. **ATX**

○ d. **AOL**

Answer a is correct. A dial-up modem uses the **ATD** (AT[tention] Dial) command to connect to the Internet. Answer b is incorrect because the **ATA** command answers an incoming call. Answer c, refers to the ATX form factor for a motherboard. Answer d is the acronym for America Online.

Question 8

What is the default address of COM2?

○ a. 02E8

○ b. 03E8

○ c. 03F8

○ d. 02F8

Answer d is correct. The default address of COM2 is 02F8. 02E8 is used for COM4, 03E8 is used for COM3, and 03F8 is used for COM1.

Question 9

What is the default IRQ for LPT1?

○ a. 5

○ b. 7

○ c. 3

○ d. 2

Answer b is correct. The default IRQ for LPT1 is 7. IRQ 5 is used for LPT2, but because many people do not have a second printer, it is often available for use; in many cases, a sound card will choose this as its default IRQ. IRQ 3 is used by COM2 and COM4. IRQ 2 is the cascade IRQ to IRQ 9.

Need to Know More?

Freedman, Alan. *Computer Desktop Encyclopedia, 2nd Edition*. AMACOM, 1999. ISBN 0-814-479-855. This is great for a fast lookup or refresher.

Messmer, Hans-Peter. *The Indispensable PC Hardware Book, 3rd Edition*. Reading, MA: Addison-Wesley Publishing Company, 2000. ISBN 0-201-403-994. This is a comprehensive, up-to-date reference book that covers far more than you will need to know for the exam.

Minasi, Mark. *The Complete PC Upgrade and Maintenance Guide, 11th Edition*. San Francisco, CA: Sybex Network Press, 2000. ISBN 0-782-128-009. This is considered one of the best reference books available. In fact, Minasi's book was instrumental in the formulation of the first A+ exam.

Muller, Scott. *Upgrading and Repairing PCs, 12th Edition*. Indianapolis, IN: Que, 2000. ISBN 0-7897-2303-4. This is one of our favorites. If you are only going to have one reference book, give this one serious consideration.

Reeves, Scott, Kalinda Reeves, Stephen Weese, Stephen, and Christopher S. Geyer. *A+ Exam Prep, 3rd Edition*. Scottsdale, AZ: The Coriolis Group, 2001. ISBN 1-57610-699-3. This is a good reference that concentrates on providing exam-required information.

Rosch, Winn. *Hardware Bible, 5th Edition*. Indianapolis, IN: Sams Publishing, 1999. ISBN 0-789-717-433. This is a well-organized reference book that covers software issues as well as hardware.

Peripherals:
Storage Devices

Terms you'll need to understand:

✓ Disk, storage

✓ Floppy drive, hard drive, revolutions per minute (rpm)

✓ Clusters and sectors

✓ Integrated Drive Electronics (IDE) and Enhanced Integrated Drive Electronics (EIDE)

✓ Advanced technology attachment (ATA) and Peripheral Component Interconnect (PCI)

✓ Removable disk

Concepts you'll need to master:

✓ Data transfer rates

✓ Master/slave configurations for physical drives

✓ Controller and bus specification

✓ Small Computer System Interface (SCSI) chains

If we want to keep the results of our input, we need a place to put everything after the power is shut down. Remember that without a steady power supply, RAM loses whatever it was holding. Software applications, work, and new information we've created, all have to be stored somewhere for continuity, sharing, and output. The most common way to store information and data is on a disk of some type (although this is changing). The original floppy disks were inexpensive, easy to use, and could be shared among computers. Today, we have hard disks, CD-ROMs, floppy disks, tape drives, removable hard disks, flash memory cards, and network file servers.

We've chosen the original floppy disk and drive as our entry point into the various components making up storage technology. Obviously, a hard drive is far more complex than a floppy disk, but for the most part, it uses the same essential concepts and basic technology as a hard drive. We believe that focusing on these essential concepts will help you better retain the many details involved in the exam.

Floppy Disks

The floppy disk drive was developed by Alan Shugart of Shugart Associates, who also developed the Shugart Associates Systems Interface (SASI). Later, SASI was renamed Small Computer System Interface (SCSI) when the American National Standards Institute (ANSI) committee approved the interface in 1986. *Floppy disk* refers to a round, flimsy, bendable piece of Mylar coated with magnetic material and in a protective jacket. The first *minifloppy* disk, which we know as the 5¼-inch disk, followed the original 8-inch disks used prior to 1974. The protective jacket was changed from somewhat floppy on 5¼-inch disks, to rigid on 3½-inch disks.

Shugart created the floppy disk, hard disk, SCSI drive, and controller interfaces that are still used in most PCs today. The Shugart Technology, Inc. (ST)-506/412 interface was the accepted standard for all PC hard disks and stood as the basis for the Enhanced Small Device Interface (ESDI) and Integrated Drive Electronics (IDE) interfaces. Because Shugart left his company right before the market release of the 5¼-inch floppy drive, he never profited fully from his inventions. In 1979, he resurfaced and formed a partnership with Finis Conner. They created Seagate Technology, Inc., and developed the now-obsolete 5¼-inch hard drive.

Floppy disks are available in different densities, using one (single) or two (dual) sides of the disk. *Density*, in this case, means that floppy disks originally used eight tracks and then changed to nine tracks. The original disks used only one side for data storage and were referred to as *single-sided, single density*. Almost any floppy disks you find today use both sides for data storage and therefore are called *double-sided, double density*.

Density

We spoke about the concept of density in Chapter 4 when we described the capacitors and transistors used on memory chips. Magnetic disks use tracks and sectors, which are also measured in density. Keep in mind that the amount of space a given number of bits takes up, regardless of what the space is made of or how the bits are formed, is called density.

The density of a newspaper graphic could be defined in terms of how many dots can fit into a given square inch on a matrix. We generally think of the matrix as having X-Y coordinates and being in two dimensions. The more dots in a square inch, the higher the resolution, hence "dpi" (dots per inch). DVDs use a third dimension—depth. This requires a so-called Z coordinate, generating X-Y-Z addresses. This isn't any different than measuring a box or a cube. Using all three coordinates, we can find a single point anywhere within the volume of the cube.

The number of sides used on a floppy disk, along with its density, are still referred to as: double-sided (DS), low density (LD), and high density (HD). The four typical floppy disk sizes and densities are named as follows:

➤ *DS,DD*—360KB 5¼-inch double-sided, dual density

➤ *DS,HD*—1.2MB 5¼-inch double-sided, high density

➤ *DS,DD*—720KB 3½-inch double-sided, double density

➤ *DS,HD*—1.44MB 3½-inch double-sided, high density

Note: The IBM 2.9MB floppy disk developed for OS/2 distribution is referred to as "extra" density. Microsoft also has a proprietary disk-formatting process for storing 1.7MB on a typical floppy. Microsoft disks are referred to as Distributed Media Format (DMF). Windows 9x and above can read all normal sizes, along with the extra sizes, but neither the 2.8MB nor 1.7MB formats are supported by DOS.

Floppy Drive Components

The inside of a floppy drive uses many of the same general components as a hard drive. Remember your hexadecimal numbering, and the fact that the first cylinder and track on a disk are numbered *cylinder 0, track 0.* The exam sometimes uses the informal term *head* in place of the technical term *cylinder*. The boot sector could also be said to be on head 0, track 0.

Note: For the remainder of this book, we will relate the boot sector to head 0 and track 0. That being said, due to the low-level nature of cylinders, heads, and actuator arms, this isn't an absolute fact in all instances. However, the level of detail for a total explanation of head 0 goes far beyond the scope of this discussion, as well as being relative only to an engineering perspective. This book is intended to help you pass the exam by understanding the normal use of the concepts.

Read-Write Heads

Most floppy drives have two *read-write heads,* which is why disks can be made dual-sided. The first head (head 0) is actually the bottom one, and the second head (head 1) is the top one. Read-write heads are the hardware pieces that actually change the magnetic *state* of the disk surface. When the magnetic state is changed by the head, it *writes* to the disk. When the existing state is sent back to the CPU, the head *reads* from the disk.

The two heads are spring loaded and physically touch the surface of the disk to read or write data. A 3½-inch floppy disk spins at 300 revolutions per minute (rpm). The original 5¼-inch high-density drives spun at 360 rpm.

Each head is actually a combination read-write head. The separate heads are each centered within a pair of *tunnel erase heads.* In other words, each tunnel erase head contains both a read and a write head, and they move together. The heads are made of soft iron materials with electromagnetic coils.

When a track of information is produced, the trailing tunnel erase heads erase the outer edge of the track, making the data stand out cleanly on the disk. This forces the data to be confined in a narrow "tunnel" in the middle of the track, and prevents peripheral magnetic interference from nearby tracks of data. The process also removes fading magnetic changes trailing off to the sides of the written data, which could lead to some confusion during reading.

State, Status, and Condition

We first brought up the concept of "state" when we talked about how AMD uses the changing state of voltage on a motherboard clock oscillator. Anything that is "either/or" can be translated into a 1 or 0—a binary bit. If voltage always is either 4V or 2V, we can assign a 1 or 0 to either voltage.

If voltage is "steady" or "not steady," we can also assign a bit-status condition to either of those two states. Think of a voice-activated answering machine. If someone talks, the machine records. If the person pauses too long, the machine stops. If noise is present, the machine is on, but when noise ceases, the machine turns off. Continuous/Broken, Regular/Irregular, Quiet/Loud, Yes/No, and On/Off are all binary conditions that can be assigned a 1 or 0.

Head Actuator

Moving the read-write heads is done by a stepper motor called a *head actuator*. This motor moves the heads back and forth over the disk (or platters on a hard disk). The heads go from edge to center and back again, moving over *tracks* that were created by *low-level formatting* (usually performed by the manufacturer).

Note: Computer disks are not like the old vinyl music records (disks). On an old record player, a rotating platter would spin the disk while a needle picked up analog information from one very long groove on each side of the disk. You had to physically turn the disk over to use the second side.

The head actuator motor is also controlled by a *disk controller*. The disk controller works with the operating system and ROM BIOS so that the PC can move the read-write heads to specific locations on a disk to find data (files).

Spindle Motor

To get a disk spinning at 300 rpm, the spindle motor works very much like the old record players. Older floppy drives used a belt-driven system with inconsistent speeds, making them unreliable. The belts would wear and slip over time, making them even more unreliable. Just as record players evolved from belt driven to direct drive, so did computer floppy drives. The direct-drive motor doesn't have any belts, so the spindle doesn't slip, making for very consistent speed.

Newer disk drives use automatic torque compensation to provide greater spin force, and have very little slippage. Therefore, these drives rarely need adjustment, unlike older drives. However, with a typical 3½-inch drive costing around $30, it's often simpler and cheaper to replace the drive.

Note: Observe how the operating system takes control of the head actuator through the drive controller. CD-ROMs and DVDs use the way information is stored to take control of the spindle motor and further guarantee a consistent speed. (We discuss optical disks in the "Optical Storage" section later in this chapter.)

Logic Board

The drive mechanism is attached to one or more *logic boards* (printed circuit boards) located underneath the main housing. This board contains the controls for the head actuator, spindle motor, disk sensors, and any other drive components. A CMOS setting may need to be changed, depending on the installation context (e.g., switching the A: and B: drives).

Floppy Drive Configuration

Installing a floppy drive or a hard drive may require configuring some jumper settings. One difference between the drives is whereas floppy drives are designated either A: or B:, hard drives are either a *master* or a *slave*. The *drive select jumper* defines the unique drive number, and in the overall scheme of drives and controllers, every drive must have its own drive number! The drive select jumper defines a floppy drive as either drive 0 or drive 1.

Drive 0 does not necessarily correspond to drive A: drive, just as drive 1 does not necessarily correspond to drive B:. This is because IBM wired its system to make installing preconfigured drives as easy as possible. Assigning a letter to a disk drive is part of the operating system's logical formatting, and we cover this in the "Logical Formatting and Partitions: FDISK" section of Chapter 10.

One of the fundamental things you must remember for the exam is that IBM (and all clone makers) designed drive A: and drive B: into every system. This affects your understanding of *partitioning* because all PCs continue to set aside two drives (A: and B:) for the basic floppy drives. The C: drive is always drive 3. Any additional drives take on whatever is the next consecutive letter of the alphabet.

Media Sensor Jumper

Have you ever noticed the small hole in the upper right corner of a 3½-inch disk? That hole is for the *media sensor*. If a beam of light (media sensor light) can pass through the hole and make contact with a photo sensor, the system knows that a high-capacity 1.44MB disk is in the drive. Extended-capacity 2.8MB disks have a different hole on the disk jacket, so a multi-capacity floppy drive actually has two media sensors: one for 1.44MB and one for 2.8MB disks. (A 1.7MB disk uses 21 sectors per track, rather than 18, and doesn't require a special media sensor.)

Low-density 720KB disks have no hole in the media sensor position, so the media sensor light fails to make contact with the photo sensor. This led to an interesting scheme in which a special hole-punch tool was marketed for converting cheaper 720KB disks to 1.44MB disks. The reformatted disk eventually becomes unstable because of the density of the magnetic structure of low-density disks. This leads to a rapid degradation of the format, with a catastrophic loss of data. (On the other hand, placing a piece of tape over the media sensor hole on a 1.44MB disk fools the drive into thinking that it has a 720KB disk that can be formatted with no data loss.)

Write Protect

Looking at the back (or bottom) of a high-density disk, notice that there's a hole in the upper *left* corner with a place for a sliding piece of plastic. When this hole is covered, it locks the disk and prevents any writing to it, making it write protected.

Note: Write protection makes it physically impossible to write data to the disk. This is a way to guarantee that a virus program can't be placed on the disk. There's no way to write-protect RAM, but a virus in memory won't be able to transfer to a write-protected disk.

Change Line Jumper

The AT system uses pin 34 to carry a signal called the *diskette change line*. This signal is used to tell the system whether a disk in the drive is still the same disk since the last time a disk access was requested. This control signal is a pulse sent to the controller (to a status register) that changes one time on insertion and one time on ejection.

When the drive responds with information that the heads have moved, the system knows whether a disk has been inserted. If a change signal isn't received between accesses, the controller assumes that the same disk is in the drive. This allows information that is stored in RAM (having been read from the floppy) to be used without rereading the disk.

Controllers

Most PCs have some amount of peripheral control right on the motherboard. To distinguish this rudimentary control from the more sophisticated I/O control of later PCs, we refer to various *controllers*. A controller is a component containing additional microprocessors and logic, and works through a connection with the motherboard BIOS. Depending on the age of the computer, controllers take on more or less of the actual management of their specific type of peripheral. A SCSI drive controller, for instance, can work directly with a multitasking operating system, bypassing the CPU and allowing for faster access to the disk.

Note: Controllers don't usually have a ROM BIOS chip. The motherboard BIOS contains instructions for working with different types of controllers. The peripherals that the controller manages may have their own BIOS chips. Peripherals can be Plug and Play. Controllers are part of the motherboard system platform and aren't referred to as PnP controllers.

Different peripherals have different controllers. A typical PC can have a keyboard controller, floppy drive controller, and hard disk controllers. There are also memory, IRQ, DMA, and video controllers. With all these controllers working around the CPU, you can imagine the number of instructions flying around the motherboard circuitry. The places where those instructions often cross over to other devices are the buses.

You might think of a controller as a traffic cop working at a busy intersection. Traffic laws (software instructions) define the way that the traffic flows through the intersection. At certain times, traffic (processing) is so heavy that it speeds things up to have a human being in the intersection who can override the standard laws with individual decisions. Peripheral controllers take on localized processing management and help speed up overall performance.

Modern systems have a floppy disk controller and a hard disk controller built into the motherboard. AT computers often had an adapter card with both controllers attached to it. Drive controllers use interrupts, the same way that serial and parallel ports do. Because almost every PC has a hard disk, the ROM BIOS includes a default IRQ (14) for the master (primary) hard disk controller, along with default IRQs for the floppy drives and other basic ports.

Remember that IRQ 14 is usually assigned to the primary disk controller. IRQ 15 is assigned by default to any secondary disk controller. The obsolete XT used IRQ 5 for its disk controller, so modern PCs tend to assign a secondary parallel port (LPT2) to IRQ 5 instead.

Fixed Disks/Hard Drives

Because hard disks cost so little these days, the preferred storage device is an internal, non-removable storage media, or *hard disk*. Tape storage may be cheaper, but its use of sequential access makes it much slower. The hard disk is actually called a *fixed disk drive* because you don't remove it except to permanently replace it. (Presumably, once it's replaced, it's fixed.) Many people call it a *hard drive* because the platters aren't flexible and floppy, and in fact you can replace it like any other drive. The technical name given by the IBM PC Institute is a direct access storage device (DASD).

Note: When we speak of high-capacity removable storage media, we refer to them as removable drives. These include the Iomega Zip and Jaz drives, which are designed to be quickly disconnected. Removable drives offer the advantage of a removable disk with storage capacity similar to a fixed disk, where the entire drive bay can be unplugged and carried to another machine.

Although the disk, drive mechanisms, drive controller, and cable/interface subsystem are separate components, familiar language joins them together as the "hard drive" or simply "the drive"—terms that we will use in the following discussion. Many disks are partitioned with a single, primary, active partition making them drive C:. Drive C: and the fixed disk are often referred to as the same thing, even though this leads to a great deal of confusion when it comes to understanding logical drives as opposed to physical disks. FDISK.EXE, FORMAT.COM, and logical drives are covered explicitly in Chapter 10.

 Be very careful that you don't confuse a physical disk and a logical drive. Although many people call the fixed disk a hard drive, the physical disk can contain anywhere from 1 to 24 logical drives. Additionally, a system can have more than one physical disk, where each disk can have many logical drives. Be sure to remember that a fixed disk can contain up to 24 drives. (See Chapter 10 for more information on FDISK and partitions.)

A hard drive has many internal components, consisting mainly of several plates of highly electroconductive metal spaced extremely close together. These plates are called *platters*. A spindle motor, connected to the plates at their centers, spins the platters. Each side of each platter has a read-write head. The heads are attached to an actuator arm under each platter to move the heads back and forth over the disk.

Note: Assigning the boot sector to head 0, cylinder 0, track 0, sector 0 explicitly points to the first platter and first cylinder. In common usage, either the head 0 or cylinder 0 may be dropped.

Hard disks spin at thousands of revolutions per minute (e.g., 5,200 rpm), making them dramatically faster than floppy disks. The disk drive also has a circuit board and connectors to transfer data and to supply power to the drive. Although we speak of a single disk, you can see in Figure 6.1 that, technically, a hard drive has a number of physical disks.

When the CPU requests data from the disk, the platters rotate, and the heads move back and forth over them. The back-and-forth movement allows for *random access* of the data rather than the sequential data reads of a tape cassette. *Sequential reading* means that if you have a file stored somewhere on a tape, the tape machine must spin through the entire length of tape before it gets to the beginning of that file. A hard drive, on the other hand, skips over whole platters and tracks, going directly to the first *cluster* of a file. (We discuss sectors and clusters in Chapter 10.)

Figure 6.1 A typical hard drive, showing the platters and spindle.

Random access means that if an area (cluster) of a platter is near a read-write head and is available for storage, the head can begin storing a file immediately. A tape must have enough room to store the complete file from beginning to end. If a tape doesn't have space for a complete file, we either have to wait for it to spin all the way through to the end of used space, or we must use a new tape. A hard drive can also store pieces of a file in many different sections.

Tracks and Sectors

All disks, including floppy disks, are divided into *tracks* and *sectors* by the manufacturer, and *clusters* by a formatting process defined by the operating system. Initially, a fixed disk is magnetized (physical, or low-level formatting) by creating magnetic tracks and cylinders on the plates of the disk. If you were to take an apple corer and smash it down on a hard drive (not recommended), it would cut through one cylinder. The edge of the corer would be like the width of one track. Tracks and cylinders are characterized by the following:

➤ *Tracks*—Concentric, circular paths placed on both sides of the platter. They are identified by number, starting with track 0.

➤ *Cylinders*—A set of all the tracks on all sides of all the platters located the same distance from the center of the stack of platters.

Each track is subdivided into sectors that store a fixed amount of data. Sectors are usually formatted to store 512 bytes of data. Binary data is stored in the sectors using various combinations of zeros and ones. The ones are magnetized areas, and the zeros are not.

 A way to remember the difference between sectors and clusters is that the formatting process adjusts the size of file clusters. Perhaps files can clutter up a disk, and clutter sounds like cluster. Sectors never change size, and the word sounds a little like secure—never changing. The exam always uses 512 bytes for a sector size.

Over time, the magnetic coating of the platters begins to deteriorate, preventing them from holding a magnetic pattern. When this happens, the heads can't read or write data from a sector. Reformatting the disk or using certain software programs, such as SCANDISK or Norton Disk Doctor, labels the sector as a *bad sector*. Even with modern engineering, most brand new disks have some number of bad sectors that are marked as unusable by the manufacturer during physical formatting.

Note: After physical formatting, the operating system performs logical formatting, which we cover in the discussion of FDISK.EXE in Chapter 10.

Hard Drive Controllers

Hard drives have such a huge responsibility in a PC that a lot of attention has been focused on how to make the drive controllers more intelligent. We've seen that controllers can take over a lot of the management for a particular type of device, and hard drive controllers are in constant development. Hard drive controllers include:

➤ IDE (Integrated Drive Electronics), EIDE (Enhanced IDE), and XT IDE (eXtended Technology IDE)

➤ SCSI (Small Computer System Interface)

➤ ESDI (Enhanced Small Device Interface)

➤ ST-506/412 (Shugart Technologies 506/412. Remember the story of Alan Shugart of floppy fame? Don't worry, the story isn't an exam topic.)

Part of what makes understanding drive controllers difficult is that each controller *interface* has even more acronyms and descriptive words used for different features. Some of these acronyms include:

➤ ATA IDE (AT attachment IDE)

➤ MCA IDE (Micro Channel Architecture IDE)

➤ Fast, Wide, Ultra, and Ultra-wide SCSI

 The exam covers the IDE, EIDE, and SCSI interfaces for the most part. The ATA IDE bus and the PCI bus show up as well. Remember that ATA is a specification, but IDE is an interface architecture. The IDE controller is built into the drive.

ATA Interface

You'll find an IDE controller in most of today's computers. Strictly speaking, IDE refers to *any* drive that has a built-in controller. The actual *interface bus* uses the AT attachment (ATA) specification, which refers back to AT-class motherboards. The specification was "attached" to the AT form factor. Until recently, an IDE controller was typically a 16-bit ISA motherboard interface. Keep this in mind, because new computers are dropping the ISA bus completely in favor of hub architecture or the North-South bridge technology.

The ATA IDE combination was first developed by Compaq, Control Data Corporation (CDC), and Western Digital Corporation, who decided to use a 40-pin keyed connector with a 5 1/4-inch form factor. As we've said, the keyed connector is designed to be plugged in only one way (plugging in a drive backward can damage both the drive and its related circuits). These original drives were physically large, and could hold only 40MB of data.

IDE and EIDE controllers work with a 40-pin keyed connector.

The drive and built-in controller plug into a bus connector on either the motherboard or an expansion card. Because the controller is on the drive unit, these drives are easy to install and require a minimum amount of cabling. Fewer parts are involved, so signal paths are shorter, which improves the reliability of the drive.

Shorter Data Paths Improve Data Reliability

Because of the physical properties of wire, especially cheap ribbon cable wires, signals traveling along a piece of wire are subject to various types of degradation. Electromagnetic interference and structural resistance (not to mention signals bouncing back from improperly terminated cables) make a trip from the CPU to the drive heads a risky business for any given byte of data. The shorter the path, the more likely the data byte will arrive safely.

Another advantage of the integrated controller is that the manufacturer doesn't need to worry about compatibility issues with the drive. This makes the overall hard drive unit easier and cheaper to build, and cheaper to sell, which is partly why IDE drives are so common.

Make a note that an ATA IDE cable should be a maximum of 18 inches long. The drives use a 40-pin keyed connector, with a cable 40 wires wide that carries all signals to and from the controller. SCSI connectors are generally 50-pin connectors. Some connectors don't use a physical notch for keying, in which case the ribbon cables have matching colored stripes to indicate the correct orientation.

The ATA Specification

A controller works with the ROM BIOS on a motherboard. In 1989, ATA IDE was accepted as the ANSI standard, ending many compatibility issues. ATA is an ongoing set of specifications, with each development aimed at increasing the access speed between the software, the operating system, the CPU, and the drive.

Because ATA is a specification, it defines, for example, a standard for the signals on the 40-pin connector, the functions and timing of signals, and cable specifications. The ATA specification does the following:

➤ Provides a way for two separate drives (each with its own controller) to interface with the same bus

➤ Creates the master drive (drive 0) and secondary (slave) drive (drive 1) hierarchy

Remember that autoconfiguration in a CMOS file is different than Plug and Play. PnP uses a combination of system BIOS, operating system, and device BIOS. Autoconfiguration applies only to CMOS.

Think back for a moment to the intersection with the traffic cop. Also recall that a bus is like a toll plaza where traffic moves through the tollbooths and back onto the highway. The PCI specification is really a way to connect various types of processor chips together. If you think of different types of roads being developed for cars, trucks, pedestrians, or bikes, then the PCI specification isn't really a specific road, so much as the rules for how to build all roads. After a device takes on the PCI specification, it can work with roads designed for it. In other words, a PCI bus can work with an old ISA card and slow down, or it can work with an ATA-2 EIDE controller and go very fast.

Like the IDE and ATA specifications, the PCI specification allows developers and manufacturers to follow a set of rules for connecting their devices. Rather than having to rebuild a device, hoping it will be compatible with everything in the market, PCI takes care of the compatibility as long as the new device follows the PCI rules.

PCI cards come in two lengths: full-sized and short. The full-sized card is about 12.2 inches long, and the short card is about 6.8 inches long. The cards can have varying numbers of pins, but the physical bus connector is a 32-bit, 124-pin slot.

EIDE (ATA-2)

The ATA-2 specification is the same thing as EIDE. ATA was extended to add Programmed Input/Output (PIO) modes, along with DMA transfer support. The PIO mode determines how fast data can be transferred to and from the drive. PIO is available in five modes. 0 through 2 are the ATA-1 specification, and 3 and 4 are the ATA-2 specification. Let's pause for a second and take another look at this alphabet soup:

➤ The underlying device that we're talking about is the IDE drive controller. IDE is a type of hard drive with a built-in controller. Ordinarily, a controller is separate from the disk and tells the drive system how to operate. IDE puts the controller right in the housing, along with the read-write heads and the platters.

➤ Instructions get from the controller to the drive by crossing over a bus—an interface. Data transfers from the drive back to RAM across a bus. The amount of data that can move from the disk to memory is measured in MB/s, or how many megabytes can move in one second.

➤ Different drives require different ways of communicating with the motherboard's BIOS. ATA specifies a standard for that communication. Part of the specification means that IDE drives and their controllers have to be made a certain way.

➤ The first ATA specification defined most of the manufacturing process and included a way to hook two drives to a single controller.

➤ ATA and ATA-1 changed as the sophistication for controlling the hard drive increased. ATA was one set of rules, and ATA-1 was the next set of rules. ATA-2 is the third set of rules, and each set builds on the previous set of rules.

➤ ATA-2 allows even more complicated instructions to go between the controller and the hard drive. Along with the new instructions, the controller can take charge of other ways that the system moves data into memory, such as PIO.

➤ One of the ways ATA-2 speeds things up is with PIO, which comes in five modes. Another way the controller speeds things up is by using direct memory access (DMA).

We're still talking about a hard drive with *Integrated Drive Electronics*, but the description and capabilities keep changing. The actual performance of the disk gets better, and the disk can store more data. However, the connection between the IDE disk and the rest of the system has to improve as well. That improvement is described with the letters ATA.

➤ ATA is a specification—a set of rules for doing things.

➤ In order for PIO and DMA to work correctly, a different kind of connection has to be made for the controller—a different type of bus. The PCI bus is a new type of bus that lets the ATA-2 controller work at its best.

➤ ATA-2 changed the original IDE controller so much, that the industry began calling the new version an enhanced version—the *Enhanced* IDE (EIDE)— with transfer rates from 3.3MB/s to 8.3MB/s.

PIO Modes 3 and 4

ATA-2 added PIO modes 3 (11.1MB/s) and 4 (16.6MB/s). However, to run in these modes, the IDE port on the motherboard must be on either a VESA local (VL) bus or a PCI bus. Some motherboards have two IDE controllers, but only the first one is connected to the PCI bus. The second controller is connected to an ISA bus and limited to PIO mode 2. The manufacturers claim that the ISA connection is required because slower devices, such as CD-ROM drives, don't need the higher speed of the PCI bus. As we've said, many new systems don't even come with any ISA slots.

Note: Mixing fast and slow devices (such as hard disk and CD-ROM drives) on the primary controller can cause slower data transfer for the hard disk. Typically, all transfers travel at the speed of the slower device. Connect only hard disks to the primary controller, and make the faster of two disks the master.

Fast ATA

ATA-2 did a number of things to speed up data transfer. It provided support for drives larger than 504MB, and the PIO 3 and 4 modes allowed for faster data transfers. The inclusion of a new ATA Packet Interface (ATAPI) allowed extra drives (e.g., tape drives or CD-ROM drives) to connect to the ATA connector.

EIDE used PIO modes 3 and 4, along with the DMA channels on the motherboard. The additional PIO modes were referred to as *Fast ATA*, and they required upgraded device drivers, along with an enhanced BIOS. Fast ATA used a burst transfer rate of 16.7MB/s.

Ultra ATA

In October 1996, Quantum introduced a way to double the data transfers from IDE hard disks, calling it Ultra ATA. Intel backed the technology and included support for the process in its new chip sets. The rest of the industry and disk manufacturers followed suit, and Ultra ATA became the current standard. EIDE drives are now a direct competitor to SCSI drives, in terms of speed. Ultra ATA doubles the existing performance with burst transfer rates of 33MB/s, and it is fully backward compatible with Fast ATA.

Hard drive controllers have a small, built-in memory buffer due to the difference in how fast the drive heads can move information, relative to how fast the timing strobe, cables, and DMA channels can transfer information to the CPU. At the drive itself, small bursts of data, such as reading or writing small files and portions of a file, are transferred in *bursts*—the *burst transfer rate*.

For longer file transfers, such as during the boot process or when a very large application begins to load, data is transferred in a long, continuous, *sequential* mode. The *sequential transfer rate* for earlier ATA controllers would often fall to just above 10MB/s as the buffer filled up. One reason the buffer fills up is that the time it takes for a host machine to send 4KB commands to the controller is longer than the time it takes for the hard drive to act on that command.

Command Turnaround Time and Overhead

When a 4KB command comes from the host machine to save a file, it takes approximately 400 microseconds for the drive controller to read the command data into its buffer. Fast ATA, with a burst transfer rate of 16.7 MB/s, had a sustained sequential data rate of 10.2 MB/s. The buffer emptied 4KB in about 250 microseconds, leaving 150 microseconds of *overhead* between commands to keep the filling and the emptying of the buffer in balance. A typical desktop PC has a command turnaround time of around 275 microseconds and takes approximately 525 microseconds to empty the buffer. This reduces the effective transfer rate of Fast ATA to approximately 7.8MB/s (4,096 bytes divided by 525). Keep in mind that the drive has a burst transfer rate of 16.7MB/s.

7.8MB/s is 75 percent of the drive's 10.2 MB/s sequential data rate. What this means is that for every 3 bytes being sent to the host, 1 byte accumulates in the buffer. A typical buffer holds 64KB worth of data, and 1 buffer's worth of data is accumulated for every 3 buffers of data being sent to the host. At that point, the drive "slips a rev (revolution)", meaning that before the host can drain the buffer, the system has to wait until a requested sector rotates past the head a second time. The buffer typically holds 64KB, which means 1 slipped rev occurs for every 256KB of data being transferred.

The *effective* data transfer rate of the bus equals the burst transfer rate minus the command turnaround time. By doubling the rate at which the buffer is emptied, Ultra ATA compensates for command turnaround overhead. Ultra ATA's 33MB/s burst transfer rate allows a 4KB data block to transfer in 125 microseconds (half the time of Fast ATA), leaving 275 microseconds for overhead. 125 plus 275 equals 400 microseconds (the buffer fill rate), and as a result, the buffer doesn't accumulate data and can avoid slipped revs.

Another reason a drive controller buffer fills up is that a command has to wait for a timing signal from the controller. The signal is somewhat like a motherboard clock tick in that it uses a timing strobe with an "up" (positive) and a "down" (negative) transition cycle. Fast ATA used only the positive cycle to send data, but Ultra ATA uses both the positive and negative transition of the timing signal. Using both transitions doubles the frequency of data transfers, so data can be sent twice as fast without doubling the speed of the timing strobe.

Fast ATA specified that the drive had to wait for the strobe from the host (propagation delay) before responding by putting data into the buffer (data turnaround delay). The timing signal was a two-way (bidirectional) event between the host (computer) and the drive. Ultra ATA, much like *double data rate (DDR)* DRAM, doubles the data transfer rate by making the drive the single source for both the timing strobe and the data transfer—a unidirectional process. Both the strobe signal and data signal travel simultaneously down the cable in the same direction, eliminating the propagation delay where the drive is waiting for signals coming from the opposite direction.

Note: Ultra ATA uses something called a Cyclical Redundancy Check (CRC) as a way of verifying data (somewhat like parity checking). The CRC, which is calculated for each burst of data by both the host and the drive, is stored in CRC registers on both the host and the drive. After each burst, the host sends the contents of its CRC register back to the drive, which compares it against its own register's contents. Matching CRCs indicate that the data sent was the same as the data received. This provides better data integrity, making an Ultra ATA drive more accurate as well as faster.

Ultra DMA (UDMA or UDMA/33)

Ultra ATA essentially brings the transfer process from the controller to the CPU more in line with the internal transfer rates of fast disks. To keep the process synchronized from the read/write heads of the drive all the way through to the CPU, the technology of direct memory access (DMA) channels had to be upgraded. Quantum first improved the way DMA works by doubling the transfer rate to 33MB/s, then applying those improvements to the ATA specification. Ultra DMA/33 refers to the 33MB/s transfer rate through the UDMA channels. In order to use an Ultra ATA drive, the motherboard chip set must also have UDMA/33.

Hard Drive Configuration

After you've installed an IDE, EIDE, or SCSI drive (SCSI is discussed in Chapter 8), the drive still won't be ready to run without going back to the motherboard. The BIOS must properly recognize the drive. IDE drives are usually autoconfigured (in CMOS), and today, almost any BIOS can query an IDE drive for its settings.

Note: As we've stated, SCSI manufacturers have opted for their own closed architectures, so almost every adapter is different. The immediate problem that this presents is the lack of autoconfiguration. Be sure to keep the reference manual for any SCSI device, because this is the only place to find which BIOS settings are required by the device.

Although people say that SCSI drives are faster than IDE drives, that's just not true. SCSI—like PCI and USB—is a bus, not a controller. Hard drive speed is partly related to the interface, but is mostly related to average seek time. Other parts of the drive also contribute to overall speed.

A hard drive can often move data into a *command buffer* at just over 10MB/s on a sustained basis. With a transfer rate of 16.7MB/s, you would think that Fast ATA would be capable of keeping the buffer from becoming full. The reason that it can't has to do with the turnaround time that the PC takes between the commands it issues to the drive. This command turnaround time is what causes most of the slowdown in overall performance.

Command turnaround time delays come from the number of commands a PC makes to a drive, depending upon the size of the command requests. The requests are typically 4KB in size and are equivalent to the page size supported by a virtual memory operating system like Windows. It takes approximately 4 milliseconds for a drive to read a 4KB instruction command.

Most PCs use the IDE interface because it's inexpensive and performs reliably. Many manufacturers sell the same drive in both the IDE and the SCSI models, and put an extra chip on the SCSI circuit board. In that case, the extra chip is a SCSI adapter. Because this extra chip requires data to go through an extra step, the IDE model performs slightly better.

One of those extra steps is the command buffering, whereby up to 256 commands can be sent by the system and rearranged by the SCSI adapter. On a system using multitasking, where several programs are running at once, the extra intelligence of the SCSI adapter boosts system performance. A couple of hundred microseconds here and there, and pretty soon you're talking about real time!

Another advantage of the SCSI interface is that if bad sectors develop on the disk, a SCSI system can mark the sector as bad and can avoid crashing on a disk read. IDE systems require either reformatting the disk or running a disk repair utility.

SCSI devices can communicate independently of the CPU and can operate at the same time. IDE devices have individual controllers that can operate only one at a time. Similar to DMA transfer, this allows SCSI devices to run a bypass around the CPU for simple device-related tasks. This bypass keeps the CPU from bogging down.

Removable Media and Drives

Many years ago, a very inexpensive notebook appeared on the market that used a stylus-based operating system. It was available in various sizes, stored data in character recognition and graphic format, offered many color styles, and cost about one dollar at the local stationery supply store. The stylus cost about 29 cents. The main thing about these spiral bound notebooks (SBNs), as they were called, was that the stored data could be easily transported. You ripped a sheet of paper out of the notebook and jammed it in your pants pocket.

Portability and extra storage have always been issues for computer customers, which is why 3½-inch floppies lasted so long. If you needed to mail a file to someone, drop a copy of a file off at a service bureau, or even make backups of your hard drive, you had to use either floppy disks or a tape drive. Email changed all that, of course, but who wants to email a 100MB attachment?

Tape and Digital Audio Tape (DAT)

Dating back to the IBM mainframes, which used magnetic tape for data storage, auxiliary tape machines have stored data as *backups*. Prior to removable hard drives and write-enabled CD-RW drives, backups often involved 10MB to 50MB of a PC's hard disk. Tape drives usually interface with a SCSI connection and an internal expansion card.

The basic tape cartridge used in most home-market tape machines was the *quarter-inch cartridge* (QIC) analog tape format. QIC was replaced by *digital audio tape (DAT)* storage, which is a competitive technology to the CD-ROM and DVD optical storage, discussed shortly. Tape transfer on a high-end tape system ranges from 1MB/s to 3MB/s.

Tape storage has both high capacity and low cost. Current cartridges can store more than 7GB of information, and both the tape and the backup software use a high degree of error correction. The error checking results in very reliable data backup, and many networks continue to use either analog or DAT tape systems for archiving data.

The introduction of DVDs, CD carousels (multiple CDs available in a single drive), and optical read-write technology, is having a strong effect on the consumer market for tape. Redundant Arrays of Inexpensive Disks (RAID), the multigigabyte capacity of removable drive cartridges, Iomega's Zip and Jaz drives, along with the downward trend in costs, may make the last remaining advantage of tape systems their complex error checking. However, that checking comes at a cost in terms of time, and consumers may be willing to sacrifice error-free backups for convenience and speed.

Flash Memory

We saw how the CCD brought about the development of scanners, and how these charge-coupled devices could be used to capture analog images. Naturally, the chips were almost immediately put to work in photographic equipment. The CCDs could be used to convert an image to digital information, but cameras still required film to store the image. Disk storage was physically still too large to help in that department.

The laptop and notebook computer market have been driving development efforts toward smaller-sized components. Smaller size means less weight, easier transportation, and perhaps most important, less power consumption. Flash memory, which comes out of the desire for small storage devices, migrated first to the digital camera market and now to the general storage market. Ongoing sophistication in CCDs has joined with memory "cards" to produce a new demand for digital still cameras and video cameras, and the recent Motion Picture Experts Group, Audio Layer 3 (MP3) compression format has carried flash memory into the music industry.

Flash memory is divided into *blocks*, as opposed to the bytes of conventional memory. Because it is nonvolatile memory, it requires a way to both write and erase information. The cards use a very small amount of voltage to change the blocks, and they operate very quickly. This makes flash memory fast, with very low voltage requirements and very compact in size. Four types of flash memory are succeeding in the market at the moment: CompactFlash, SmartMedia, ATA Data Flash, and Sony's MemoryStick. Table 6.1 shows the way that these memory cards interface with a device, as well as their varying amounts of storage memory.

CompactFlash emulates (imitates) a disk drive to the degree that once the card has been formatted, it can be plugged into a PC and acts like any other disk drive. The cards are about an inch-and-a-half long and include an interface adapter. They can be plugged directly into a camera or into an adapter that plugs into a PC card. The adapter can then be inserted into a laptop. The other three types of cards require a proprietary adapter to install in a device.

SmartMedia was originally called a Solid State Floppy Disk Card (SSFDC) and is actually a NAND-type EEPROM "chip," about the size of a postage stamp. What makes these cards so interesting is that unlike an integrated circuit board, a SmartMedia card is made up of only *logic gates*. As technology shrinks the size of the gates, more of them can be put on a standard-size card. Toshiba has already announced a 512MB die, with a proposed 1GB card coming next.

The simplicity of a SmartMedia card makes it compatible with a wide variety of devices. Although the cards were initially used in the digital camera market, so-called *card readers* are becoming widely available for anything that requires storage. These readers attach to a system with a USB cable and make the flash memory look like another disk drive. (USB is covered in Chapter 8.)

The ATA-compliant PC card, which was used for everything from game adapt-

Table 6.1 Flash memory types and storage.		
Card Name	**Interface**	**Storage**
CompactFlash	Proprietary	8–128MB
SmartMedia	Proprietary	2–64MB
ATA DataFlash	PC card, type II	8–512MB
Sony MemoryStick	Proprietary	4–32MB

Note: Memory capacities continue to increase, and the numbers given are as of 2001.

Logic Gates

Have you ever wondered how a microprocessor actually thinks? How does it know something is true or false? How does it distinguish between AND and OR, TRUE and FALSE? Microprocessors have an area on their die that's taken up by *logic gates*. These gates are extremely small electronic components that are somewhat like transistors. The fundamental unit of a digital circuit, a logic gate usually has two input terminals and one output terminal, along with a single evaluation instruction for the comparative voltage levels at the input terminals. If the voltage is the same, the output sends a signal. If the voltage is different, the output sends a different signal. The output signals can represent a 1 or a 0.

The seven basic logic gates are: AND, OR, XOR, NOT, NAND, NOR, and XNOR. SmartMedia cards use NAND gates, but other EEPROM chips can be NOR-type chips. NAND technology has a speed advantage in storage processes, making NAND-type chips ideal for nonvolatile storage. NOR-type chips have an advantage in terms of random byte access but are slower when storing information.

---

ers to modems to SCSI interface cards, was originally designed as ATA-compliant memory. These memory cards also act like a disk, and they use the ATA specification much like an IDE and EIDE drive.

The main difference with a Sony MemoryStick is an erase-protection switch and the rectangular shape. Like the CompactFlash and SmartMedia, the Sony cards use a proprietary interface, but a memory stick is about five inches wide and four inches long.

Optical Storage

Since the introduction of the compact disk (CD), both the music industry and the computer industry have been coming together in the way they use optical storage technology. At the moment, there are no real standards, and we can only generalize about the main concepts relative to CDs and digital versatile disks (DVDs). That being said, we can break the optical storage disk into four broad categories:

➤ *CD-ROM*—Information is written by a manufacturer and becomes *read-only memory*.

➤ *CD-R*—Information can be written only once by a consumer, making these disks *Recordable*. CD-R disks are technically called Write Once, Read Many (WORM).

➤ *CD-RW*—Information can be written to and erased from 1 to approximately 25 times, making these disks *rewritable*. These are significantly more expensive than other CDs, and do have a limit as to the number of rewrites.

➤ *DVD*—These disks have a much higher storage capacity than a CD and a different storing process.

CDs

CDs started out as a layer of highly reflective aluminum foil sandwiched between layers of transparent plastic. These original disks used a writing laser beam to etch microscopic marks, or *pits*, in the foil. A reading laser beam then bounced the reflections from nonpitted (flat) areas of the foil back to a *photo sensor*. The combination of the pits and the flat areas (*lands*) results in the binary 1s and 0s of digital information. A standard CD can hold up to 640MB of information (approximately 74 minutes of music).

Optical disks, unlike hard disks, return to the old, vinyl record method of writing in a long, single track. The track spirals from the outer edge of the disk to the center. *Tracking* is where the laser maintains a specified *optical path* to read correct information. The reading laser tracks the spiral, reading a 1 for *reflective* surfaces, or a 0 for *nonreflective* surfaces.

Note: A track on a magnetic disk is one of many independent and concentric circles. The track on an optical disk is a single spiral that begins at the outer edge and terminates at the center. "Laying down tracks" in a recording studio means recording a song. For a time, there were magneto-optical drives that worked like typical floppies and hard drives. They used a track and sector system in concentric rings around the center of the disk.

A problem with audio CDs is that the surface at the outer edge is moving faster than the surface near the center, making music sound slower and slower as the laser reads data closer and closer to the spindle motor. To overcome this, audio CDs use a process called *Constant Linear Velocity (CLV)*. As the reading laser moves inward, the revolutions per minute of the spindle motor increase. A mechanical feedback system works to sustain an exact velocity (speed) as the reading laser moves closer or farther from the center. Unfortunately, this is an expensive manufacturing process.

Data disks, originally distinguished as CD-ROMs, developed a different method of handling velocity. *Constant Angular Velocity (CAV)* uses a small buffer to vary the data stream through a microprocessor. In other words, it doesn't matter how slow or fast data enters the buffer (from variable surface velocity) because the data coming out of the buffer is adjusted for speed.

A feature of the CAV process is that information regarding the mechanical environment is included with the data being stored. This means that the CD-ROM is constantly correcting itself for speed and signal strength, resulting in extremely reliable data reads. With the CLV CD, the spindle motor uses a mechanical process to adjust the head mechanism as it moves closer or farther from the center, keeping speed constant.

 The two methods used with CDs for handling variable surface velocity are CLV, where the speed of the spindle motor is controlled, and CAV, where processing adjusts the data stream.

The distinguishing feature of a data CD is that it reads information in segments that can be located anywhere on the disk. This is much like the random access of a hard drive. Audio CDs are more like the sequential reads of a tape backup unit. The *seek*, or *access* time, is how fast the reading laser can be repositioned at the start of a requested segment of data. Repositioning doesn't matter on an audio CD, but on a typical data CD, the average access time is approximately 95 msec. on a 24X drive. A typical hard drive has an average seek time of 4 to 10 msec.

Note: Increasing the spin velocity and size of the buffer in a CAV CD drive multiplies the throughput from the original (1X) buffer speed of 150KB per second (KB/s). Various multiples led to the designation of 2X, 4X, 16X, and so on. Audio CDs slow down the buffer for music, but data CDs favor faster throughput. A so-called 100X CD actually copies data to the hard drive before reading it.

CD-R

The original CD-ROM worked with actual pits that were "burned" into the surface of a piece of foil by the manufacturer. To give consumers the ability to write their own CDs without putting someone's eye out, CD-Rs use a type of organic dye (not to be confused with a chip die, or engraved stamp). The dye is layered into the plastic of the disk, and heat from the laser as it passes by changes the reflective properties of the dye.

After the dye particle changes, it stays that way. Once again, reflection equates to 0 and less reflection equates to 1. Different colors of dye have different properties. Gold-green has a rated life of 10 years. Silver-blue has a rated life of 100 years. Reading a disk is one simple sweep over a disk, but in order to write a disk, the laser has to generate a certain temperature to change the dye, which takes time. Original 1X CD-Rs could take up to 90 minutes to write an entire disk. Current drives are at 4X.

Note: If the stream of data to be written to a CD-R isn't uniform, any interruption in the data flow destroys the CD. Writing or "burning" software uses either a series of buffers to ensure data continuity, or creates an image of the data as it will appear on the disk. It then reads out the image in a steady, continuous stream.

DVD

CD-ROMs, CD-Rs, and CD-RWs are gradually being replaced by digital *versatile* disks. Because these DVDs were initially developed for the movie industry, the "V" is sometimes thought to stand for "video," but be sure to call them digital versatile disks. A DVD uses the same diameter as a CD-ROM, but varies somewhat in thickness.

The Motion Picture Experts Group (MPEG) is another bunch of people who set standards. MPEG files, MOV files, and AVI files are all specifications for storage and/or compression, and MPEG-2 (second version) allows for 135 minutes of video, with 3 channels of digital audio and 4 channels of subtitles. By only using 1 audio channel, a DVD can store more than 160 minutes of video.

Once again, the technology quickly migrated to PCs, and we ended up with DVD and DVD-ROM. Both types of disks are read-only, and a video disk is differentiated from a data disk in much the same way that the "ROM" in CD-ROM distinguishes a computer disk from a music disk. An audio CD player can't use the data tracks from a CD-ROM, but a computer can read the data tracks and also play music. The same principle applies to DVDs and DVD-ROMs; a video DVD player is designed to work only with a video or audio installation.

For the moment, there aren't any real standards in DVD technology. DVD Recordable (DVD-R) disks are entering the market, but they're currently very expensive. Typical DVDs can either use one or both sides, and can have a single or dual layers, not unlike the division of floppy disks. The four current types of DVDs at the moment are:

➤ *Single-sided, single-layer (SS/SL)*—Holds 4.7GB

➤ *Single-sided, dual-layer (SS/DL)*—Holds 8.5GB

➤ *Dual-sided, single-layer (DS/SL)*—Holds 9.4GB

➤ *Dual-sided, dual-layer (DS/DL)*—Holds 17GB

The reason storage is higher on a DVD than a CD is that the data markings on a DVD are much smaller and closer together. Therefore, the *pit length* is shorter and the optical path is much narrower, requiring a reading laser with a shorter wavelength to read the pits and lands. Some combination units actually have two reading lasers: one for DVDs and one for standard CDs.

A dual-layer DVD uses two layers of media. One layer is set deep in the plastic, and one layer is shallow. The focal length of the laser is set up so that it can read both layers even though one is behind the other.

The photo sensor connects to a digital-to-analog converter for music and video. For computer data, as in the case of CD-ROM data disks, the information continues straight through in digital format. DVDs use an IDE/ATAPI (see the "Fast ATA" and "Ultra ATA" sections earlier in this chapter) interface, with a dual-connector 40-pin cable, and they require configuration as either a master or slave (primary or secondary) drive.

All DVDs require bus mastering, which means that they connect to a PCI bus, not an ISA bus. If the drive is used to play video, it also requires an MPEG decoder. The decoder, usually a hardware device, also requires a slot in the bus. To conserve slots, many decoders are now integrated onto a video expansion card.

Beginning with Windows 95, the software drivers (instructions) for all DVDs are part of the PnP specification. Older systems require manual installation of the drive, using the generic MicroSoft CD EXtensions (MSCDEX.EXE) program, and the specific ATAPI driver for the DVD device.

Note: Although dust is the main problem in optical drives, a can of compressed air can usually keep them clean. However, because optical disks use transparent plastic around a data layer, a smudge, scratch, or anything that impairs the optical transparency generates read errors. A good nonabrasive plastic polish, such as those found in automotive stores, can sometimes buff out minor scratches. There are also small machines (e.g., Disk Doctor) that work well for minor repairs.

Practice Questions

Question 1

> Which 3½-inch floppy disk format is the most common?
>
> ○ a. DS,SD 1.44MB
>
> ○ b. DS,SD 720KB
>
> ○ c. DS,DD 1.44MB
>
> ○ d. DS,DD 1.7MB

Answer c is correct. 3½-inch floppy disks are usually double-sided, double-density (DS,DD) and hold 1.44MB of information. Double-sided, single-density (DS,SD) 720KB disks are almost obsolete. Certain 3½-inch floppy disks can be formatted in 1.7MB (Microsoft distribution format), and 2.8MB (super disk) densities are rare.

Question 2

> The read-write heads for a platter are all that are necessary to read and write data to the disk.
>
> ○ a. True
>
> ○ b. False

Answer b, false, is correct. Unless data is erased, a disk will run out of room. Each read-write head is contained within a tunnel erase head.

Question 3

> On a typical IDE or EIDE controller, drive 0 is called the _____ drive, with a default IRQ of _____.
>
> ○ a. master, 14
>
> ○ b. slave, 14
>
> ○ c. master, 15
>
> ○ d. master, 14

Answer d is correct. When two drives are connected, one must be configured as the primary, or master (drive 0). The second must be configured as the secondary or slave (drive 1). IRQ 14 is set aside as the default for a primary hard drive controller.

Question 4

> The organization of a platter in a hard drive is described using which of the following pairs of terms? [Choose the two best answers]
>
> ❑ a. Cylinders and tracks
>
> ❑ b. Sections and FAT
>
> ❑ c. Segments and clusters
>
> ❑ d. Sectors and clusters

Answers a and d are correct. Tracks are concentric, circular paths placed on both sides of the platter. They are identified by numbers, starting with track 0. Tracks in the same position on multiple platters are called cylinders. Tracks are divided into sectors during formatting, and the operating system stores data in clusters. A hard drive does not use sections or segments. The file allocation table (FAT) is used by the operating system to locate files.

Question 5

> An IDE hard drive controller connection on a motherboard can operate up to how many disk drives?
>
> ○ a. One
>
> ○ b. Two
>
> ○ c. Four
>
> ○ d. Seven

Answer b is correct. Many motherboards have two IDE controllers, each of which can run two drives. The drives are not limited to only IDE hard drives. The system can run a total of four drives, using both controllers; however, the question asks about a single controller.

Question 6

> Which of the following statements is true?
>
> ○ a. An ATA drive uses an IDE controller.
>
> ○ b. An IDE controller uses an ATA bus.
>
> ○ c. An IDE drive uses an ATA controller.
>
> ○ d. An ATA bus uses an IDE controller.

Answer b is correct. An IDE controller uses an ATA bus. Any drive with a built-in controller is technically called an IDE drive. However, the question makes a distinction among a drive, a controller, and a bus. ATA is a specification for an interface bus. ATA is never a controller or a drive. Answers b and c have the correct use of IDE, but answer c includes an ATA controller.

Need to Know More?

 Freedman, Alan. *Computer Desktop Encyclopedia, 2nd Edition.* AMACOM, 1999. ISBN 0-814-479-855. This is great for a fast look-up or refresher.

 Messmer, Hans-Peter. *The Indispensable PC Hardware Book, 3rd Edition.* Reading, MA: Addison-Wesley Publishing Company, 2000. ISBN 0-201-403-994. This is a comprehensive, up-to-date reference book that covers far more than you will need to know for the exam.

 Minasi, Mark. *The Complete PC Upgrade and Maintenance Guide, 11th Edition.* San Francisco, CA: Sybex Network Press, 2000. ISBN 0-782-128-009. This is considered one of the best reference books available. In fact, Minasi's book was instrumental in the formulation of the first A+ exam.

 Muller, Scott. *Upgrading and Repairing PCs, 12th Edition.* Indianapolis, IN: Que, 2000. ISBN 0-7897-2303-4. This is one of our favorites. If you are only going to have one reference book, give this one serious consideration.

 Reeves, Scott, Kalinda Reeves, Stephen Weese, and Christopher S. Geyer. *A+ Exam Prep, 3rd Edition.* Scottsdale, AZ: The Coriolis Group, 2001. ISBN 1-57610-699-3. This is a good reference that concentrates on providing exam-required information.

 Rosch, Winn. *Hardware Bible, 5th Edition.* Indianapolis, IN: Sam's Publishing, 1999. ISBN 0-789-717-433. This is a well-organized reference book that covers software issues as well as hardware.

Peripherals:
Output Devices

Terms you'll need to understand:

✓ Video Display Terminal (VDT), cathode ray tube (CRT), liquid crystal display (LCD)

✓ Red, green, and blue (RGB); cyan, magenta, and yellow (CMY)

✓ Pixel, dots per inch (dpi)

✓ Triad (triangular color units)

✓ Dot matrix, ink jet, and laser printers

Concepts you'll need to master:

✓ Display resolutions

✓ Interlaced versus noninterlaced screen refresh

✓ Resolution versus dpi

✓ Electrophotographic (EP) drum and relative negative electrostatic charge

✓ Laser printing process steps

Chapters 5 and 6 looked at getting data into the system and then storing that data when the power is turned off. The third part of the equation is getting data back out of the system—the *output*. If everything goes well, the information coming out of the computer makes sense to a human being. On the other hand, output can just as easily be meaningless garbage or noise. An *output device* is the thing that produces the output, and the display screen is usually the standard output device.

Whenever we connect something to a motherboard for the purpose of input, storage, or output, we refer to that thing as a *device*. When a device is outside the computer's main case, we generally call it a *peripheral device*. "Peripheral" means on the edge or outside of an area. Standard devices include keyboards, floppy and hard drives, monitors, and mice. Peripheral devices include scanners, printers, modems, CD-ROM or digital versatile disc (DVD) drives, and sound cards, to name a few.

Transient vs. Final Output

Output relates to time, in the sense that you can have transient output and final output. *Transient output* is the stream of data being sent somewhere for fleeting observation or temporary storage. *Final output* is data that moves away from the system completely and stays fixed in time. "Transient" is a fancy way of saying "just passing through."

An example of transient output is pressing a key on the keyboard or inputting a scan code to the system. The code exists only long enough to be picked up by the CPU. Additionally, you have no way to verify which code you sent because you have no way to see a translation of that code. The CPU accepts the code and then sends it on to the video subsystem, which is in charge of outputting a representation of that code to the screen—a letter or a number. The screen displays the output only long enough for you to act on it.

Another example of transient output is when an application is holding too much information for the installed RAM and sends part of that information to the hard disk for temporary storage. This is called a *swap file*. After the data in the swap file has been used, it's erased by new temporary (transient) data. A swap file is somewhat similar to a *buffer*. We discuss Windows swap files in Chapter 11.

Final output is just that: final. After you've completed inputting and the system has finished its calculating, the result (you hope) is something useful (e.g., a report, spreadsheet, or database) and something that stays put. When you save a file and copy it to a disk, you're creating output from both an application (the file) and from the overall system (the copy on the disk). Sounds from a speaker coming from a sound card can also be considered output.

Buffers

Imagine a faucet, a sink, and a drain at the bottom of the sink. If the water from the faucet is coming out slowly, then it goes right down the drain. The water is like a data stream coming to a modem (the drain). If the water starts pouring out of the faucet faster than it can drain, the sink begins to fill up. The sink is a buffer, and can only hold so much water (data). When the sink becomes full, water pours over the edge onto the floor. In a buffer, data is thrown away. If the data source and the buffer are intelligent, meaning that some sort of software logic is being used by the devices, the speed of the data stream can be adjusted so that no data will be lost. Making a bigger drain is like widening a bus or increasing the processing speed of the device.

The video monitor is the standard output device for working with a computer. The printer is the most common peripheral for creating final output. Characters on a screen are transient and change from moment to moment. A *screen capture* of a particular set of characters at a particular moment in time can be sent to the printer. The paper with the image of what was on the screen, is the final output.

Video Displays

The most important output device in a computer system is the monitor. Monitors have been called cathode ray tubes (CRTs); Video Display Terminals (VDTs); CONsole (CON), which is the DOS device name; or simply the screen. In this section, we refer to display monitors generically as monitors.

The two main categories of monitors are CRT and liquid crystal display (LCD). A CRT is a vacuum tube with a layer of phosphor dots at the viewing end and an electron gun at the other. The gun shoots a beam of electrons at the phosphor, making the electrons glow. When we look at the glass face of the monitor, we're seeing through the glass to the backside of the phosphor layer.

Color monitors have a separate electron beam for the three primary colors in the pixel *triads* (discussed in the "Pixel Resolution" section later in this chapter), and they can create a color effect by making different phosphorescent dots glow. We can create every color of *light* by using three primary colors: red, green, and blue (RGB). However, for *solids*, we have to use cyan (bluish), magenta (pinkish red), and yellow (CMY). Monitors work with light, and we use an RGB designation. Color-separation printing works with solids, and for that, we use a CMY abbreviation.

Note: CMY is also used in LCD panels. Solid materials reflect light and react differently than glowing light does when the materials are blended together.

Display Technology

Displaying data involves a number of *subsystems*, all of which work together to bring a visual pattern to the human eye. We saw that a typical motherboard has a video interface connector as part of the system board. We also saw that monitors often make use of an expansion slot in the I/O bus for a graphics accelerator card, or an Accelerated Graphics Port (AGP). The basic display subsystems are a monitor, a video adapter (controller), and a graphics card.

Pixel Resolution

A *pixel* is a fancy name for a dot. A pixel is loosely defined as a "picture unit," which is a term invented by Microsoft. Depending on how closely pixels can be bunched together per inch, we can say that a monitor has a *resolution* measurement. The word "resolution," in the context of computer video, should technically be replaced with "pixel addressability." We're really discussing how many pixels can be addressed in something called the video frame buffer, but you won't need to worry about the frame buffer for the exam.

True resolution should refer to the smallest object capable of being displayed on the screen, and therefore would be more related to *dot pitch*. A neurotically correct definition of resolution is "the degree of detail visible on a monitor, and therefore it is related to the size of the electron beams, the degree of focus in their alignment, the arrangement of the pixel triads, and video bandwidth." But who's neurotic?

Scanners and monitors both define *optical resolution* by the number of pixels per inch. The only difference is that scanners use one charge-coupled device (CCD) per pixel, and the resolution is limited by the physical size of the CCD. An RGB monitor uses lighted dots, each of which is one pixel. LCD panels use a molecular crystal as a pixel device, and gas-plasma screens use a pinpoint flash of heated gas to describe a pixel.

Regardless of how resolution is defined, if we follow common terminology, the smallest piece of light or darkness that a screen can physically display is the resolution of that screen. The Super Video Graphics Array (SVGA) standard of today's monitors is typically 1,280 by 1,024 pixels or 1,600 by 1,200 pixels. Typically, this is written on a specification sheet (spec sheet) as 1280×1024 or 1600×1200.

A standard VGA monitor has 640 pixels in a horizontal axis (line), and 480 pixels vertically. We use the × to mean the word "by," so the measurement is commonly written as 640×480. (To remember that the horizontal measurement comes first, just remember that "H" is before "V" in the alphabet). Because different graphics modes can also have varying numbers of colors, a third number refers to the number of *colors* associated with pixel resolution. A monitor resolution of 640×480×256 means that the monitor uses 640 pixels horizontally by 480 pixels vertically and has 256 colors to display information.

HHH × VVV × CCC

You've probably heard carpenters and builders talk about two-by-fours. They're referring to a piece of wood two inches in width by four inches in height. That means measuring one pair of sides produces two inches, and measuring the other pair (at right angles) produces four inches. In a computer matrix, the horizontal (left to right) measurement and the vertical (top to bottom) measurement become dots, pixels, addresses, and so on.

Standard VGA

Following the Color Graphics Adapter (CGA) and Enhanced Graphics Adapter (EGA) monitors, a new technology was developed called Video Graphics Array (VGA). Actually a superset of EGA, VGA was developed by IBM to provide higher pixel resolution and graphics capabilities.

The VGA system didn't really support any processing, so the CPU still had to manage all the new calculations and logic. This made VGA very dependent on processor speed and linked it directly to the computer's processor in terms of speed comparisons. Installing the same model VGA monitor on either a 386 system or a 486 system, gave the appearance of making the monitor on the 486 faster, cleaner, and sharper. This was one of the first examples of apparent speed, as opposed to actual speed generated by technical specifications.

 Safe Mode, in Windows, is when the monitor resolution goes to 640×480×16 (colors) as the original and default VGA standard. Windows will set the monitor to standard VGA mode, regardless of what higher resolution was last set during normal operation.

Frame Buffers

Any image being sent to a monitor begins as a series of instructions programmed into an application. The application may be a drawing program, or it may be a mouse driver asking the computer to display a pointer picture (cursor) on the screen. The image on the monitor takes up the whole screen, and every part of it is placed on the screen in a specific location. All this is done by software working with the CPU.

You probably know that a strip of movie film contains a number of still pictures. As the film moves across the light source, the eye perceives movement. Each still picture on the strip is called a *frame*. The same term applies to the single picture being shown on a monitor at any given time. The difference is that some parts of the picture stay still while other parts of the picture change. For example, a menu and toolbar stay constant while a new cursor position and new characters are formed during typing.

The CPU keeps an area of memory—a buffer—where it stores the information being displayed on a screen at any given time. When it's ready, the CPU lets data out of the buffer. The keyboard has a small buffer that allows you to press keys faster than the system can process the presses. If you hold down a key, you'll eventually fill the buffer, in which case the CPU sends an alert tone to the PC's speaker. Likewise, the video system uses a buffer for image data, and the whole amount of data that goes to the screen is called the *frame buffer*.

SVGA and high-resolution monitors that take advantage of video RAM (VRAM) include a more complex set of graphics instructions than VGA does. These instructions, working together outside of main memory, allow for faster data transfers between the CPU and the screen. The older VGA instructions were not sophisticated enough for independent intelligence between the monitor and CPU.

Early VGA circuitry was integrated onto the motherboard in a very large-scale integration (VLSI) chip, and IBM developed the PS/2 *display adapter* to use the chip's functions. This adapter, which is just like the early VGA card, used an 8-bit expansion slot. Clone makers jumped on the bandwagon and produced many third-party VGA cards.

Note: VLSI is the process of placing thousands (or hundreds of thousands) of electronic components on a single chip. Modern chips are almost always VLSI or Ultra Large-Scale Integration (ULSI) chips. There is no specific dividing point between VLSI and ULSI.

8514/A and XGA

The 8514/A and the eXtended Graphics Array (XGA) standards were developed by IBM in its quest for ever-increasing resolution and the need for speed in graphic interfaces. The 8514/A adapter was developed to work with the proprietary MCA bus and provided three new graphics modes. Like the VLSI controller, it required a VGA controller. Built on rudimentary graphic commands that began with VGA, the 8514/A could perform a few video memory transfers, draw a few lines, and calculate rectangular areas in a display image.

The XGA followed on the heels of the 8514/A and was the first IBM video adapter to use VRAM. The XGA specification could include an additional 500KB or 1MB of video memory, and it supported resolutions from 640×480 to 1024×768 for graphics and 1056×400 for text, with a color palette of up to 65,535 colors (640×480 mode with additional memory installed).

SVGA and UVGA

Super VGA (SVGA) and Ultimate VGA (UVGA) aren't standards, and they mean different things to different manufacturers. "Ultimate," in particular, seems a bit optimistic, given statements from IBM like "10MB of hard disk is all anyone will ever need." IBM, like so many corporations involved with PCs, has a history of making failed assumptions about the market. Many of those assumptions led to the complex series of patches and bug fixes we deal with every day in modern computers. However, the common ground for standardization seems to be the VESA VGA BIOS extensions, sometimes (improperly) called VESA SVGA. These VESA extensions at least allow programmers to try and provide a common software interface. Most monitors come with software drivers designed specifically to optimize their performance.

Advantages of SVGA include the following:

➤ SVGA can produce millions of colors at a number of different resolutions, depending on the card and the manufacturer.

➤ The VESA resolution standards range from 6405400 to 128051024, with 256 colors.

 Remember "15-pin video" and "9-pin COM". Modern monitors use a 15-pin connector, where the back panel of the PC has a *female* connector and the cable has a male connector (also 15-pin). Serial (COM) connectors are usually 9-pin connectors. (See Chapter 8.)

Screen Size

After resolution, the next most popular way of differentiating monitors is by screen size. Monitors have borrowed from the television industry by measuring screen size diagonally. Any monitor larger than 16 inches is called a *full-page monitor* because it can display a full page in a one-to-one (1:1) ratio. A monitor that is wider than it is tall is called a *landscape monitor* and can usually display two pages side by side. A monitor that is taller than it is wide is called a *portrait monitor*.

Portrait vs. Landscape

Silly as it may seem (and computer jargon is often downright goofy), the orientation of a page or monitor is called *portrait* or *landscape* because of the way painters turn their canvases. A painter who was painting a person usually did the head, shoulders, and upper torso, which created a taller, narrow painting—a portrait of that person.

On the other hand, to capture the expanse of an outdoor scene, a painter would turn the canvas sideways to achieve a wide view—a landscape view of the scene.

To this day, when the paper is tall and narrow (e.g., a letter), it is said to have a portrait orientation. When the paper is wide and short (e.g., a spreadsheet), it is called landscape orientation.

The box that holds the cathode ray or the LCD panel has a physical diagonal dimension. The actual tube or panel has another size. The actual image being displayed is somewhat smaller than the physical edges of the tube or panel against the casing.

Image Size

The actual area used to display the image is called the *raster*. The raster varies according to the resolution of the monitor and the internal physics of the screen. VGA at 640×480 on a 15-inch screen displays differently than SVGA at 1024×768. Television monitors usually *over scan* the image, putting the actual edge out beyond the physical edge of the screen. However, because a computer image contains information up to the edge and often beyond the raster edge, PC monitor images are designed to be smaller than the physical edges.

Many video cards have logic to automatically resize the raster, depending on the brand name and model of the monitor. On the outside of the monitor are a number of physical controls that can manually adjust the raster, along with the brightness, contrast, centering position, and so on.

Ordinarily, if a true black border appears around the image, then either the monitor is failing, or the image controls need to be adjusted. However, if the resolution of a monitor is changed from lower to higher, it can shrink all the images on the screen. Normally, this would not produce a black band around the entire image.

On an LCD panel, an image resolution change could potentially cause a black band to appear around the edge of the panel. Because the display is designed to match the number of pixels in an image, the LCD process turns crystals on and off, based on usage. If the resolution is set too low for the panel, the images would be too small to go all the way to the edges of the panel.

Color Triads

In a CRT monitor, an electron gun shoots a stream of electrons at a wall of phosphorous chemicals. Phosphors happen to glow for a short time after being struck by an electron beam; however, the glow quickly fades away (kind of like a capacitor). The electron beam must continually restrike the chemicals to refresh the level of light. In monochrome monitors, the phosphors glow in green or amber.

When three different phosphors are arranged in a triangle of dots, they become a *triad*. The video card can manipulate the electrons to change how each dot glows. By combining red, blue, and green glowing light, we can fool the eye into thinking that it sees all sorts of colors in between. One triad in an RGB monitor makes up one pixel.

Technically, *dot pitch* is the diagonal measurement between the centers of two neighboring triads. Because the triangles are all arranged in the same way, this works out to be the same measurement from the center of any two dots of the same color.

Note: Dot pitch is the space between each pixel triad, measured in millimeters. Generally, the smaller the dot pitch, the sharper the images, though a very small dot pitch can result in a loss of brightness and contrast. Typically, a good dot pitch ranges from .28 mm to .25 mm.

These triads are very small, so the inside of the CRT has a lot of them next to each other in a horizontal line. There are also many vertical lines running down the inside face of the tube, forming a large matrix of triads. Take a look at the lower-right corner of Figure 7.1, where you can see how a pixel is made up of three-dot triads.

Scan Cycle and Refresh Rate

Because the electron gun is a kind of mechanical device, it can blast electrons onto only one triad at a time. It takes a certain amount of time for the beam to sweep from the top left to the bottom right of the screen (as we face it). This time is one *scan cycle*.

Figure 7.1   Smaller pixels mean sharper resolution.

The video card tells the monitor how to time the scan cycle by sending a *scan frequency* to the monitor. Recall from our discussion of motherboards that frequency is measured in cycles per second, hertz (Hz) and megahertz (MHz). The electron beam must synchronize with the scan frequency to redraw the screen. A *redraw* is simply a technical term for blasting those phosphor triads with electrons a second time to make them glow again.

When the beam of electrons reaches the lowest-right set of dots, it starts over again at the top left. If the image hasn't changed at all, it does the whole thing over again, refreshing the image. The entire cycle, from top to bottom then back to top, is called the *refresh rate*.

If you've ever watched an old movie shown on an old projector, you know that the flicker is caused by the spaces between the frames passing the projector's beam of light. The refresh rate includes the momentary pause during which the upper lines of triads are starting to fade and the electron gun is swinging into action to light them up again. We see this as a flicker.

Note: You can see the actual interlacing process if you stand in front of, and a bit off to the side of, a video monitor in a typical office environment. Florescent light flickers as the ballast triggers the explosive gases in the lighting tubes. The rate of flicker in the light is different than the refresh rate of the monitor, causing a so-called beat wave every half second or so. Another way to see interlacing is by videotaping a television set.

The faster the electrons can refresh the phosphors, the faster the refresh rate is and the less flicker the human eye perceives. For minimum flicker, the refresh rate should be at least 70 times per second (70Hz).

Noninterlaced and Interlaced

When the electron beam sweeps across the pixels from top to bottom and left to right, all in one pass, we call it the *noninterlaced* mode. This involves sweeping past every pixel triad, one after the other, covering the entire screen once and then beginning over again.

Interlaced mode, on the other hand, means that the beam sweeps from top to bottom in *two* passes. First it refreshes the odd lines, and then the even lines—like weaving, or lacing shoes half a side at a time. Figure 7.2 shows an interlaced monitor in the process of redrawing a screen. Every other row of pixels is glowing, and each row in between is black (the phosphor has lost its glow).

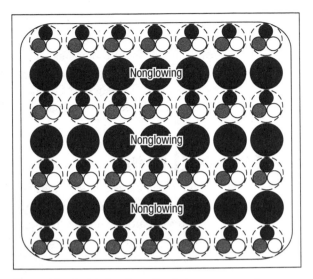

Figure 7.2 An interlaced monitor during a screen redraw.

Be sure to understand that noninterlaced means a big wad (technical term) of glowing chemicals, but that interlacing is weaving two things together. (The prefix "inter" means between, among, or in the midst of.) You can count on this being on the exam! Noninterlaced is a one-time pass by the electron gun. Interlaced is a two-time pass. You might even remember that "non" is very close to "one," which could stand for one pass over the screen.

Be sure to take your time on a question involving interlacing. Stop, think, and remember that interlacing is like weaving your shoelaces together. Remember that just as you wear two shoes, it takes two passes to interlace a monitor.

Both modes take the same amount of time. However, given the same refresh rate, interlaced mode provides a more stable image and less flicker to the human eye. The problem is that manufacturers slow the refresh rate in interlaced monitors, and this slower rate allows for cheaper manufacturing and therefore cheaper monitors. The ideal would be to have an interlaced monitor with the *same* refresh rate as a noninterlaced monitor.

Let's say a single-pass noninterlaced process means the gun has to sweep across the whole screen 2 times per minute, taking 30 seconds to go from top to bottom. The gun hits the starting point at the top 2 times in that minute, but in the 30 seconds it takes to travel down the back of the screen, the upper phosphors begin to fade. By the time the ray hits the bottom of the screen, the top phosphors have faded and the ones in the middle of the screen are on their way out. At the 30-second point, we notice the upper half of the screen has gone black.

In a two-pass, interlaced example, the ray gun hits the top of the monitor four times every minute. Granted, it actually hits the very top odd row (row 1) twice and the even row (row 2) twice, but our eyes can't distinguish that small a distance (the width of 1 row). In 15 seconds, all the odd rows light up as the gun skips the even rows and goes to the bottom of the screen. The physics of the delay time for the phosphors to start fading means that we can't tell they're fading in that short a time.

Liquid Crystal Displays (LCDs)

Whereas a CRT produces a beam of light, liquid crystal technology relies on another source of light to pass through crystals. If light can pass through the crystal, our eye can see it. When the crystal is turned off, it won't let light pass and we see an area of black. Each crystal can be either on or off, much like binary computer numbers can be either 0 (off) or 1 (on).

LCD technology allows for a much thinner screen than the bulky CRT, which gives rise to a group of monitors called *flat-panel displays*. Because a CRT monitor uses a vacuum tube to contain the beam of electrons, physics mandates that the tube be a certain depth. Flat-panel technology is most often thought of as an LCD monitor, but other displays can be categorized as flat panel—e.g., LCD panels, gas-plasma panels (or Plasma Display Panels [PDPs]), and electroluminescent display (ELD) monitors.

Note: A flat technology monitor (FTM) is not the same as a flat-panel display. A flat technology monitor is technically a CRT that uses a flat screen to reduce glare. Flat-panel displays are the typical screens used in laptops and notebooks. FTMs are still tubes.

Plasma Display Panels (PDPs)

A *Plasma Display Panel (PDP)* is a type of flat-panel display. Instead of sandwiching liquid crystals, an ionized gas is placed between the panels. One panel has wires going across in rows, and the other panel has wires going up and down in columns. By combining a specific horizontal and a specific vertical wire on the two panels, a charge can be sent through the gas, making it glow as a dot of light. The type of gas determines the color of the glow.

Plasma displays are monochrome only, and most use neon gas and glow orange. Although advances are being made in colorizing gases, current technology makes these panels very expensive and provides no grayscale capability. However, the panels can be scaled to very large sizes and provide excellent brightness and contrast, making them an attractive technology for signs and public information displays.

Until recently, LCD panels were almost always found on laptop or notebook computers. As color technology and the use of *active matrix* advances, full-size LCD monitors are arriving on the market. Flat panel technology is also advancing rapidly in television and high definition television (HDTV). The ability to control the size of the crystals (and therefore the size of the pixels) allows for ways to produce very high resolutions. Potentially, LCD technology could replace cathode ray technology and bring film-quality video capability to the market.

Liquid Crystals

A fascinating property of liquid crystals is that they exist in either a solid or a near-liquid state, depending on electrical conditions. In their near-liquid state, the crystals can pass light. Another interesting feature is that the crystals have a tendency to be straight (like rods) in their natural state, but they twist into a right angle under electrical stimulation. This ability to pass light when they're straight, or to turn at right angles and block light, gave rise to the LCD panel.

Polarization

Have you ever used polarized sunglasses? The science used in making these glasses works on the principle that most light tends to be polarized (lined up) according to its wavelength. It's somewhat like iron molecules facing the same direction around a magnet. The molecules in lenses of polarized glasses are constructed so they line up in rows leaning over at an angle. The molecules of regular glass don't line up this way. Because polarized sunglasses have this alignment property, the lenses allow only light waves traveling at the correct angle to pass, which is only a fraction of the entire spectrum of sunlight.

If you hold a polarized lens in front of another polarized lens and rotate the first lens, all the light will gradually be blocked, and the background will turn black. When the polar alignment of one lens is 90 degrees (at right angles) against the other, no light passes.

LCD Panel Construction

An LCD panel is made of two polarized planes of glass placed at right angles to each other. Sandwiched between the panes of glass is a layer of liquid crystals (with that weird bending quality). Behind the back panel is a fluorescent light source that tries to get through the two misaligned panels of glass. In the default state, the light is blocked, and the panels appear black.

Each liquid crystal is in a matrix, with very thin wires leading to a set of switches along the top and side edges of the glass panels. When electrical current is sent to a specific X-Y location on the grid, the crystal at that point goes into its act, bending 90 degrees and turning almost transparent.

What's so cool about this process is this: Let's say the light coming in from the back is vertically aligned (straight up and down). The crystal is also up and down, but the front pane of glass is horizontally aligned (left and right). When the liquid crystal becomes transparent and twists over on its side, it carries the light over sideways and passes it through the front pane. (Let there be light!) We can envision all these little liquid crystals doing the Macarena dance, and when they bend down, they form images.

In any event, forming an image pattern always involves making a series of dots. If you can create a dot of light against a background of black, you've met the basic criterion for making an image. Depending on how often a crystal is turned on in relation to the crystals next to it, the human eye can be fooled into thinking that it sees about 16 shades of gray.

Color and Light

Eventually, liquid crystals were developed that could cut out all colors of light except one. Using the cyan, magenta, yellow process, the number of crystals in the matrix was tripled. Once again, triads of three crystals (each able to pass only one primary color) were put together in the matrix, and the switches were tripled to access each subcrystal. By turning one of the three crystals in each triad on or off, the same effect was produced as with an electron beam and phosphor triads.

Twisted Nematic

LCD panels have a limited angle of viewing because of the physics of polarization and light transmission. Therefore, the types of crystals have been modified to allow light to branch off to the sides. Without getting into scientific jargon, we can see three modifications to the crystals:

➤ Super-twisted nematic (also known as super-twisted nematic display [STND])

➤ Double super-twisted nematic

➤ Triple super-twisted nematic

The first two modifications allow a wider viewing angle and a brighter contrast in the panels. The third kind, triple super-twisted nematic, allows for the color subtraction method of CMY along with added brightness and side viewing.

Because the crystals are only acting like a very tiny camera shutter, they can't produce light on their own. On the other hand, a fluorescent light doesn't need the space of an electron gun and beam. LCD panels can have very thin light sources behind them, making the entire panel far thinner than a CRT, which is perfect for notebook and laptop computers.

Passive Matrix

As we just mentioned, LCD panels have a matrix of wires. VGA resolution is 640×480 pixels in a matrix. Therefore, a VGA liquid crystal display panel requires 640 transistor switches along the sides, and 480 along the top and bottom to produce 640×480 dots of light. As in a CRT, the rows are activated sequentially, moving from top to bottom, resulting in a refresh rate and limited contrast. The fundamental difference between passive and active matrix is the number of switches. Passive matrix has only one switch per column, whereas active matrix has at least three times that many.

Dual Scan

Some LCD panels divide the screen into a top half and a bottom half, allowing a *simultaneous* refresh of two rows, one in each half, which is similar to interlacing. On the one hand, this dual scanning process decreases the contrast, making the screen less bright. On the other hand, it consumes less power than panels that use a single refresh rate.

Either way, the response time of LCD panels is slow. It takes from 40 milliseconds (msec.) to 200 msec. to move the crystal through its twist-and-relax cycle. This explains why earlier LCD panels showed a shadowy trail when the cursor moved, and why the expected position of the cursor seemed to take a moment to catch up with an actual picture of a cursor.

Active Matrix

In Chapter 5, we discussed how a capacitance field allows a charge to be sent to a specific part of a wire, somewhere between two transistors. Using capacitance, an active matrix gives every liquid crystal its own switch address.

Oddly enough, in reverse of Burst Mode memory (see Chapter 4), giving every crystal in the matrix a separate address increases the speed of pinpointing a specific X-Y coordinate. In an LCD matrix, this allows each crystal to be turned on and off more quickly and provides better control over how long a crystal stays on in relation to its neighboring crystals. Individual addressing also provides better control over each crystal in a triad at a grid point. Active matrix LCD panels are basically huge integrated circuits, much like microprocessors.

The number of components in an active matrix LCD is at least three times the number in a passive matrix panel. Although active matrix panels are much more expensive to manufacture, they have far better contrast and response time than the passive matrix models.

Printers

Printer output is by far the most common way to share information among people. The driving forces in printer technology have been speed and resolution. Printer resolution is measured in dots per inch (dpi). Think of a newspaper picture composed of black and white dots. The more dots in a given area, the darker the area. The smaller the dots, the sharper the edges of the area.

When they hear the term "output," most people think of a printer. A printer is a way to capture information on paper, film, transparencies, or anything else (sometimes, even thin cloth) that can be handled by the roller mechanism and that won't get stuck in the printer. In Chapter 14, we'll examine some of the problems with printers, but for now, we'll focus on the basic differences among the types of printers and how they work:

➤ *Impact printers*—Includes the daisy wheel and dot matrix

➤ *Direct thermal printers*—Includes some fax machines and inexpensive and high-portability printers

➤ *Thermal ink/color printers*—Includes ink jet and bubble jet

➤ *Laser printers*

For the exam, remember that the most common printer cable is a 25-pin male DB25 connector on one end, and a 36-pin male Centronics connector on the other. Serial interfaces (ports) use a male 9-pin connector on the back panel of the PC's chassis.

Typically, printers connect to the CPU by either a serial interface or a parallel interface. You must remember the difference between a 9-pin serial cable and a 25-pin parallel cable. The confusing part is that there's also a 25-pin *serial* printer cable.

Dots per Inch (dpi)

If you've ever used a graphics program that allows you to zoom in on an image (making an area incrementally larger or smaller), imagine zooming in on the pupil of a person's eye in a photograph. At low resolution, zooming in to a certain pixel level shows that all the pixels are square. You'll discover that only seven or eight squares were used to form the pupil, making the pupil look like a mix between a rectangle and a cross.

If you scan that same photograph again with, say, a 1,200 dpi optical scanner, and then zoom in to the same pixel level, you'll discover a couple of differences. First, you need to click the zoom button a few more times to get down to the pixel squares. Second, the pupil is now made up of perhaps 25 or more pixels. The pixel squares are much smaller than those in the first image.

We've seen that the smaller a series of dots used on a monitor, the sharper the resolution is. This principle applies exactly the same way with printing dots. Under a microscope, the dots in printer resolution are actually round. The phosphorus spots on the back face of a CRT are generally also round. Pixels in a graphic image are square.

 Remember that printed images resolve with dots per inch (dpi), but displayed images resolve with picture units (pixels).

Ink Pixels and Resolution

Advances in ink jet technology allow for the controlled breakup of a single dot into even smaller parts, guaranteeing the size and spread of pieces. These pieces of an ink drop are how ink jet printers can improve on the resolution of a laser printer. However, the slight amount of drying time it takes for the ink to be absorbed into the paper allows a microscopic amount of *capillary bleeding* (spreading out into paper threads) into the paper. This reduces the original resolution. With newer, glossy papers and appropriate drying time, a modern ink jet printer can reproduce photographic-quality resolution.

Ink Bubbles

Print heads in an ink jet printer have extremely tiny nozzles (orifices) for spewing out the dots of ink. A hole can be engineered to be much smaller than the rods used by a dot matrix printer, because the hole doesn't require the structural strength to withstand being smashed into a ribbon hundreds of times per minute.

Not only can the dot of ink be much finer than the diameter of a pin, but multiple cartridges can contain the four typical colors of ink (CMY plus black). Depending on the color required, any or all of the cartridges can be told to put a drop of ink on a specific spot on the paper.

Ink is held in a containing well in the print head until the CPU sends a control signal for that color of ink. The control signal generates a rapid heat increase in a *thermal resistor*, heating the ink and causing it to expand to form a bubble under the ink in the well. The bubble expands just enough to force a tiny drop of ink from the orifice and onto the paper.

Ink/Bubble Jet vs. Piezoelectric

The problem with ink bubbles is that the resulting dot is a single size when it leaves the orifice, and it has a tiny amount of splatter when it hits the paper—much like a raindrop hitting the ground. Another problem is that we can only guess at the size of the original bubble. Incremental differences from one bubble to the next are extremely small, but they do exist.

To solve these problems, the bubble-forming process changed from a thermal resistor to a *piezoelectric crystal*. These crystals have the unusual attribute of changing size when an electrical charge is sent through them. This change is exactly related to the amount of charge and the size of the crystal. By sending an exactly increasing charge across a crystal, the crystal contracts and pulls an exact amount of ink down from the well above it. When the charge ends, the crystal returns to its original size, forcing the drop of ink out of the orifice.

We can use electronic frequencies to "bend" a drop across a cutting edge as it emerges from the orifice. With a specific frequency and a drop of a specific size, we can cut exact subdrops with a controlled "splatter pattern." This allows for resolutions of greater than 1,440 dpi (some printers currently have a resolution of 2880×720 dpi).

Ink jet technology is faster than impact-pin printing because the jet of ink has only a single mechanical step: the movement of bubbling. Also, blowing liquid ink drops is a lot quieter than ramming a metal pin against a piece of paper and a *platen* (the big roller behind the paper that backs the paper and ribbon).

Form Feed

Printers almost always require a piece of paper—a *form*—that must be moved at the front end of the printing process and then out of the printer. The old printing press used human labor as a paper-feed mechanism. A human being inserted paper into the press and used a letterpress to lay down a series of aligned letters on the paper. The letterpress was then raised, and the human laborer reached in and lifted off the sheet of paper. Very few people use human labor for printing anymore, and this printing process has become nearly obsolete. (However, we still see it in the $1.95 laptop notebook systems being sold on the market these days, where the printer is integrated into the system. In these instances, the integrated printer is called your hand.)

Feeding a form—a *form feed*—involves pulling a piece of paper into a printer, aligning it in front of a printing mechanism, and moving it back out of the printer. If only one piece of paper (a single form) is moved through the printer at a time, the printer is commonly called a *sheet feed printer*. If the pieces of paper are connected into one long sheet and move through the printer continuously, the printer is called a *continuous feed printer*.

Dot Matrix

Impact printers will have a place in society as long as there are multipart forms. A typical environment for a dot matrix printer is in medical offices, where Medicare reimbursement forms use carbon copies attached to a front sheet. Laser printers might print faster and sharper, but because they use a heat-transfer process, printing works on only one sheet of paper at a time. Thermal color printers can also work only on single sheets of paper, which leaves impact printers alone in the field of multi-sheet forms.

Thermal Paper and Thermal Printers

Thermal paper is a type of paper used mainly in small calculators, inexpensive fax machines, and some very small thermal printers designed for cash registers and laptop computers. This paper is chemically treated so that a print head can heat it in the typical dotted patterns. The print head is essentially the same as a dot matrix print head, but it uses heated pins to form a mark on the thermal paper rather than pressure on an ink ribbon.

Thermal paper is somewhat expensive, and it is very sensitive to ultraviolet (UV) light (i.e., sunlight), which can fade the images on the paper to the point of being illegible.

The term *impact* applies to dot matrix printers because a mechanical device is driven forward in space and rams into the surface of the ink ribbon with great impact. Think about the process of impact printing with a pin-based dot matrix printer. A rod of metal—the pin—must be held in a ready position within the print head. This is done with an electromagnet that pulls the base of the pin back against a coiled spring. A control signal from the CPU turns off the power to the magnet, and the spring gathers momentum to push the pin forward. Gradually, the pin gathers speed until it slams into the ribbon, driving the ribbon backward into the paper and stopping.

Ink is forcibly thrown from the back of the ribbon, splattering all over the paper, with the paper crushed between the pin, the ribbon, and the roller platen behind the paper. The ribbon and the pin exchange phone numbers and insurance information, and then the CPU calls the electromagnet to turn on the magnetism again. The pin is hauled away by the magnetic tow truck and returned to its housing in the print head. The paper is left to recover in the hospital. The piece of ribbon moves away from the scene with only a few scratches.

All this happens very quickly from a human perspective, but at a microcosmic level, it takes a lot of time. No matter how strong the spring is, it must be very small. It has to overcome inertia in the pin, and then the electromagnet has to overcome the resistance when it pulls the pin back into the head. In addition, the pins themselves must be able to withstand the carnage and "pinslaughter" of being smashed into the paper again and again, at least a few million times. Let's take a moment of silence to remember those heroic pins that have paved the way to the modern day ink jet and laser printer.

A dot matrix printer uses a *print head* housing a number of very small pins. The print head moves back and forth along a *guide rail*. As each line is printed, the paper moves up one line. The pins in the print head are pushed toward the ribbon and paper in various combinations to form letters. The number of pins defines the quality of the letter, just as the number of dots defines printer resolution.

With only nine pins, there's a limit to how many pins can form the curve at the top of, for example, the number 9. However, with 24 pins, the pins are much smaller, so more of them can be used to form the curve at the top of the number 9, resulting in a sharper-looking character.

 Make a note that dot matrix printers are distinguished by how many pins the print head uses. Common varieties are 9-pin, 18-pin, and 24-pin print heads.

Home Position

Dot matrix and many ink jet printers require the print head to start in an exact location—the *home* position. Some printers use a system of counting a series of pulses sent by the printer's motor. When the correct number of pulses has been counted, the print head is in the home position. Other printers use an optical sensing device to locate the print head in the home position.

Typically, when power is supplied to a printer at startup, part of the initialization procedure is to set the print head to its home location. When the print head is aligned, many printers sound two beeps to let you know the printer is ready to accept print jobs.

Printer Problems

Problems with printers are so common and, in many cases, so complicated that many corporations have a dedicated information systems person assigned to working with printers. The only questions we saw on the certification exam dealing with printer problems related to cleaning, paper jams, and the printing process.

Cleaning

Electronic components made of plastic usually come with a reference manual of some kind. Somewhere in the beginning of these manuals is a short statement about cleaning the components with a damp cloth and mild detergent. This instruction applies to computer parts and external printer parts as well.

Paint and lacquer thinners are designed to take paint and grease off metal or wood that you're about to paint. Electronic components are *delicate,* so use some common sense when answering questions dealing with how to clean devices such as printers. If the component is delicate, you don't use hydrochloric acid to clean it!

Paper Jams

A likely cause of paper jams in printers is either the wrong type of paper (ink jet) or too many sheets of paper trying to get into the printer (laser). A laser printer uses a paper pick-up roller and registration rollers to grab a piece of paper from the paper bin. A *rubber separation pad* prevents more than one sheet of paper from entering the printer at a time.

 Remember that laser printers tend to develop paper jams if the separation pad fails to prevent more than one sheet of paper at a time from being pulled into the printer.

Continuous/Tractor Fed

Continuous-form paper is a very long, single sheet of paper with a perforated divider line every 11 (U.S. letter) or 14 (legal) inches, and with a series of holes along both sides. The perforations allow individual sheets to be separated after the print job; the holes along the sides fit over a pair of *form tractors* or a *sprocket* that rotates and then pulls the paper forward (or backward) into the printer. Today, most continuous-form paper is several sheets thick and can be preprinted and multipart, containing blanks to be filled in with variable data.

The difference between a form tractor and a sprocket is that a form tractor is a belt that has knobs protruding from the outer surface. A *sprocket-feed* (also called a *pin-feed*) printer uses a less expensive plastic wheel with molded pins protruding around the edge of the wheel. Again, the pins align with the holes on the edge of the paper. Because a tractor belt has more knobs per inch than a sprocket, tractor-feed printers can work with smaller increments of movement, so line spacing can be smaller. However, the tractor belt has a tendency to slip with usage, whereas the sprocket wheel is usually glued onto a kind of axle.

Friction Feed

One of the original single-sheet, friction-feed printers was a *typewriter.* This device, which used a biochemical software application called the human typist to produce output, pulled a single sheet of paper through the printer with friction and rollers. Friction-feed devices rely on the friction of a *pinch roller* to catch the leading edge of a piece of paper and then draw it forward into the printer. The leading edge is the first edge (though not always the top edge) that goes into the printer. A roller mechanism then presses down on the surface of the paper, rolling it along a *paper path*. These rollers continue to turn, moving the paper along the paper path until there's no more paper to work against—usually when the paper has reached the *output tray* and the print job is complete.

Although oil is beneficial in places where constant mechanical movement can wear down a part, it becomes a detriment where friction is required. Common areas of a printer that depend on friction are: pinch rollers, platens, tractor belts and sprockets, and paper separation wheels.

Consumer products have followed a trend over the years of reducing as much as possible the amount of maintenance necessary. Because many of today's printers use replaceable components, the only task the consumer must attend to is general cleaning, which doesn't require much mechanical know-how. When a part is used up (consumed) and then thrown away, we call it a *consumable*. The cost of a printer is a one-time expense. However, the overall cost of operating a printer depends on how expensive the various consumables are. Typical consumables are paper, ink cartridges, and toner cartridges.

 We saw some questions on the exam that had to do with lubricating parts of a printer. Aside from possibly using some light oil on a bidirectional print-head rail, most printers don't provide for this type of general maintenance.

Print rollers are designed to rub against a piece of paper and pull it through a printer. Print rollers need friction to work, so they're often made of rubber. Rubber against paper tends to produce a lot of friction. Grease on rubber is like wax on a ski. The more grease buildup, the less friction the rubber has.

When oil or grease begins to build up on surfaces that require a lot of friction, the most common way to clean them is with rubbing alcohol. Alcohol is a liquid solvent that evaporates, leaving almost no residue of any kind. Rubber wheels used in various rollers, areas under tractor belts, and sometimes the platen roller behind the paper on a dot matrix printer can benefit from cleaning with alcohol.

The solvent properties of alcohol break down oils, grease from fingers, and ink residues for removal, then evaporates cleanly, leaving a clean surface. Electrical circuits should be as clean as possible to minimize an accidental connection between two lines (short circuit) in the wrong place. Use alcohol on parts that need to retain their friction. Use alcohol on any parts that can't have any liquid residue on them (electronic or electrical conducting parts).

Special cleaning kits are available that include a cleaning solvent that leaves no residue, rubber restorers for cleaning roller wheels, and pressure dusters. A blast of compressed air can blow dust out of keyboards and printers without allowing pieces of a physical duster to fall into a delicate mechanism. In addition, you should always check the instructions on rubber-cleaning chemicals. Some chemicals are destructive to various types of rubber. Check the printer's reference manual as well before using solvents.

Note: Always be sure that you've disconnected components from all electrical power sources before cleaning them with liquids. Liquids tend to conduct electricity and can lead to electrocution.

Dot Matrix

Remember that dot matrix printers use either a tractor-feed or pressure roller (friction) method of pulling paper through the printer. The pressure rollers press down on a piece of paper and hold it tight against the platen. When the print head pushes the pins into the ribbon and paper, the platen takes the pounding. Once the line of characters has been printed, the platen turns, as do the tractor gears on the sides of the platen. As the gears turn, they pull the paper forward one line.

The platen has no real effect on moving the paper, so it doesn't need to be cleaned. However, the tractor gears don't always turn at the same speed, so if the paper isn't lined up exactly and the tractor wheels don't turn at the same speed, the paper begins to develop a slant as it moves through the printer and eventually will jam.

Cleaning a dot-matrix printer is usually a preventative maintenance measure. Vacuuming out dust and debris periodically, or using a can of compressed air to blow out dust, is a simple process. The internal tractor belts and the rubber parts of the pressure rollers can often be cleaned with a proper chemical rubber-cleaning compound. Keeping torn pieces of paper out of the internal drive mechanism is another periodic cleaning task.

Fonts

The words *font* and *typeface* are used to describe two ways of looking at a letter. A font is the overall way a set of characters looks. A typeface refers to whether the font characters are bolded, italicized, or plain (regular). In the days of hot-metal type, three different character sets had to be created to produce the three changes in the typeface of a single font.

Without going deeply into the process of mathematically creating lines, points, and curves on a computer screen, we can say that software can produce graphics in two different ways: by vector calculations and by pixel points. Remember that a pixel (picture element) is the smallest dot that can be represented on a graphic display.

DOS uses a grid and Basic to fill in sets of squares created by intersections of columns and rows (a matrix). Windows converts information being sent to the screen to a graphic—the GUI. Rather than working with the fixed character spacing of the DOS rows and columns, Windows uses pixels to draw everything, including letters.

Raster vs. Bitmap Fonts

Imagine a blue square with black lines making up the outline of the square. You can draw that square in two different ways. One way is called a *vector drawing*. You send a mathematical point coordinate to the computer, which puts the point on the screen and virtually extends a line for a specified length in a specified direction. From the end of that line, the computer can extend the line in a different direction. Each time you click the mouse one time and move in a new direction, you tell the computer to remember the new length and direction.

When it comes time to print, the printer prints the line(s). Because the computer knows where every intersection for each part of the line is located, it can fill in any area enclosed by that line with some color. This fill color is a single color (in this example, blue) that is surrounded by the connecting line points, and it exists virtually until the printer converts it to ink.

In other words, you're telling the computer to keep track of when you click in an area, and how far you moved the mouse pointer before you clicked. The computer only remembers numbers and doesn't care what kind of shape you're drawing. When you use a coloring book to connect numbered dots and make a picture to color, the dots and their numbers are similar to the data the computer stores about a vector graphic.

Another way to draw the square is with dots (pixels). Starting at a certain point, the computer draws small dots to the left or to the right as you move the mouse along. The next line in the drawing begins at a new point, and does the same thing all over again with some number of dots. The dots are pixels when they're created on a monitor, and dots per inch (dpi) when they're created by a printer. These types of images are called *bitmaps*, because every single bit (dot) of the image just created is stored by the computer. If you draw lines and then color them in, every dot used for every line and every part of the coloring is a separate piece of data to be stored.

In summary, raster images are mathematically created by a vector-drawing process. Microsoft calls vector-based fonts *vector fonts*. You might also hear them called *raster fonts*. Bitmap images are grids of pixels; a grid position either has a dot of some color or is blank (containing the background color).

To change the size of a vector image, you simply tell the computer to change the image's stored numbers and recalculate the lengths of the virtual lines. To change the size of a bitmap image, the computer has to change the size of every one of the image's dots and recalculate the overall image.

True Type Fonts (TTF Files)

We've seen that dot matrix and thermal ink technology printers place dots of ink on paper. Because of this ability to reduce anything to a series of dots, an application can create a font in memory, break down each letter to a dot, and send it to the printer as a bitmap graphic image. It takes a lot of time to create a grid for every letter and to determine which squares in the grid will be dots.

Another problem with bitmaps involves the size of the dots. If you create a square using 16 dots, where each dot is one inch in diameter, you would have a nice four-inch square. But suppose you wanted to enlarge that square to 16 inches? The original dots are only one inch wide, so the bigger square would look fuzzy because of the spaces between the one-inch dots.

Adobe's Postscript font description language provides a way to tell a computer how to draw a letter from a mathematical description (vector drawing). The advantage of this is that regardless of how large or small the letter is, the computer sees it as only a series of mathematical line segments. The virtual lines and the places where they change directions can be as long or as short as you choose, making for very little degradation at the edges and therefore a sharper-looking font. The color of the font can be changed on the fly by telling the computer which fill color to use.

Microsoft and Adobe had an argument over how much it would cost Microsoft to license the Adobe process. Eventually, Microsoft figured out a way to make its own raster fonts and named the process TrueType. The original invention wasn't perfect, so Microsoft worked on it and released a second version that fixed the problems in the first version.

TrueType and TrueType II fonts are vector-based raster fonts. TrueType fonts can be *scaled* (enlarged or shrunk), in increments of 1 point, by the computer from the minimum display capabilities of a printer or monitor, to as large as 999 points. A point is $1/72$ of an inch, making a 72-point letter 1 inch tall.

Note: Modern laser printers can often allow a font to be scaled in increments of less than 1 point.

Windows 3.x includes three vector-based fonts stored in files that use a .FON extension as well as a number of TrueType fonts, in a TTF file and a companion FOT file for each typeface. When a laser printer contains the stored calculations for a vector font, those fonts are called internal fonts. Windows added a feature whereby it could work with printers to convert its TrueType fonts to graphics, and the printer would print what Windows was showing on the screen even if there were no matching internal fonts.

Laser Printers

Around 1980, a new technology was being moved forward from the famous Xerox Palo Alto Research Center (PARC) labs. It was called electrophotographic (EP) printing, better known as the laser printer. Dot matrix and ink jet printers put dots on paper in blocks, from 7 to 64 dots at a time, depending on the number of pins or ink nozzles being used.

A laser printer still puts dots on a piece of paper, but these dots are made up of tiny pieces of plastic toner, heated until it bonds with the paper. Regardless of how small those pieces of plastic are, they're still solid matter and probably can't be made smaller than a liquid dot of ink. For this reason, current ink jet printers can attain resolutions of 1,400 dpi or higher, but current laser printers are limited to around 600 dpi.

Laser printer toner is a near-microscopic combination of plastic resin and some organic compounds bonded to iron particles. Remember that toner powder is a combination of plastic, metal (iron), and organic compounds.

The Laser Printing Components

A laser printer is a complex grouping of subsystems, all of which interact exactly to move a blank piece of paper from the input side to the output side. In between, information is stored to the paper. The components of a laser printer are as follows:

➤ *AC/DC power supply*—The main power supply takes in AC from the wall. The DC power supply converts the AC to the DC voltages typically used in a computer system.

➤ *High-voltage power supply*—Electrophotography requires around 1,000 volts or more to create a static electricity charge that moves the toner particles into position.

➤ *Fusing assembly*—Heat and pressure are required to fuse the plastic toner particles to the paper.

➤ *Erase lamp assembly*—The laser beam writes a preliminary, or *latent,* image to the photosensitive drum before transferring the image to paper. To clear the latent image, an erase lamp resets the drum to clear.

➤ *Writing mechanism*—The image in RAM must be initially written as the latent image on the drum. A laser beam is moved across the photosensitive material by the writing mechanism.

➤ *Main motor*—A number of small motors drive various rollers, the drum, and mechanical processes. The main motor provides the mechanical energy needed by the submotors.

➤ *Scanner motor assembly*—To move the laser beam across the photosensitive drum, a mirror and motor direct the reflected light beam.

➤ *Paper control assembly*—This includes the entire process and all the mechanics of grabbing the leading edge of a piece of paper and moving it through the paper path to the output tray.

➤ *Main logic assembly*—Sometimes called the electronic control package (ECP), this includes all the circuitry for communicating with the CPU, the control panel, and the internal memory of the printer.

➤ *Toner cartridge*—Technically, this is the EP cartridge. The cartridge includes a number of subassemblies for cleaning, developing, and moving toner particles.

➤ *Control panel assembly*—This is the user interface where the printer control codes can be entered for configuration or manual paper operations. The control panel is also where the printer communicates various internal problems to the user.

A camera uses reflected light from an object to influence the molecular structure of a piece of film and to capture an image. A scanner also uses reflected light, but it's bounced onto a CCD and transferred to a file for storage. A laser printer is called a *laser* printer because it uses a laser beam to draw a sort of photograph of an image onto a photosensitive drum.

The Laser Printing Process

The A+ exam devotes a number of questions to the specific mechanics of printing with a laser printer. We suggest that you take the time to understand the step-by-step movement of paper through the printer. Although the technical science behind the electrostatic and electrophotographic (EP) process may seem obscure, we found that by knowing the process, we could usually puzzle out a correct response to these questions.

Remember that EP is short for electrophotographic. The EP drum in a toner cartridge is where images are created and developed.

In a laser printer, a page of information is formed in RAM first, and then is transferred as a whole unit to the paper (similar to how a photocopier works). This speeds up the process of printing. On the other hand, the process requires a heating time to *fuse* (set) the image on the paper permanently.

Ink: How Long Will It Last?

Remember that an ink jet printer puts ink on paper. The ink soaks into the fibers of the paper itself. A high-quality ink is designed to be resistant to ultraviolet light and won't fade or otherwise degrade. Because the ink is literally a part of the paper, it usually will last as long as the paper lasts.

Laser printing uses bits of plastic that effectively are melted onto the surface of the paper. Although the plastic is also impervious to UV light and its fading effects, the bond between the paper and the plastic is degradable. At the moment, laser-printed information hasn't been around long enough to really test its longevity against embedded ink. However, for historical and archival documents, it's worth keeping in mind that the fused bond between the paper and the plastic is an area of weakness.

Non-laser printers mainly use a single system to put a tiny part of a pattern onto paper, one part at a time. Laser printers depend on a whole group of systems and processes to get an image from memory onto paper. The heart of the Image Formation System (IFS) is the photosensitive EP drum.

This drum is an extruded aluminum cylinder coated with a nontoxic organic compound that reacts to light in an unusual way: It turns light into electricity, a process called *photoconductivity*. When light touches the compound, it generates a bit of electricity that is conducted (moved) through the compound.

Figure 7.3 is a stylized representation of the various parts involved in the printing process. We didn't see any questions on the exam asking you to identify parts by letters, but we feel it may help you to keep the steps in their right order if you can visualize them. A good starting point is with the EP drum covered in toner. It has a neutral charge in its photoconductive surface. Creating an image creates an electrical charge.

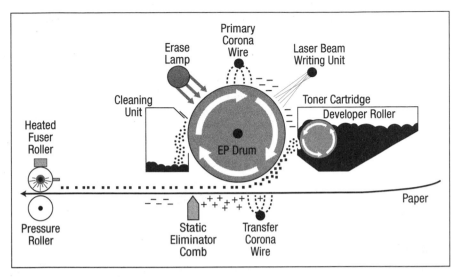

Figure 7.3 The main parts of a laser printing cycle.

Cleaning

Latent images are like a memory of a picture. If a drum simply accumulated images and printed them, it wouldn't take very long before we'd have a piece of paper covered in black. All the remembered images would build up, one on top of the other. (Take 5 or 10 photographic slides, put them on top of each other, and then try to look through them.)

To get the drum ready to accept a new image, it has to be cleaned and erased. No matter how high the quality of the drum and toner, one way or another, a microscopic amount of residue will stay on the drum from the previous image transfer.

The printer uses a rubber *cleaning blade* to gently scrape the drum clean of any residual toner. This residue drops into a debris cavity on the side of the cartridge, down below the cleaning blade. Some cartridges allow the residual toner to be returned to the main toner supply.

 The EP drum must be clean to take on a new image. (This is one of the cases where, if you think about it logically, you can almost work out the details in your mind when you're facing a question.)

Erasing

As soon as the laser beam touches a point on the drum, it changes that point to a "less negatively" charged spot. This creates a relatively positive point that stands out from the overall negatively charged surface. An image is written on the drum this way, line by line, in a series of positive dots against a negative surface, until the entire image is stored. In its default state, the drum surface has no electrical charge. The stored image is the latent image mentioned earlier.

To remove the previously charged dots from the drum, a series of *erase lights* are set up near the drum's surface. The erase lights are filtered to provide a specific wavelength that bleeds away any electrical charge from the drum. After the drum has been erased, it has a *neutral charge*—that is, no electrical charge at all.

An area that can be confusing during the exam is the difference between "cleaning" old toner particles from the EP drum, and "erasing" an image from the drum. Think of it this way: You erase a picture; you don't clean a picture.

Conditioning

The neutral surface of the drum has no sensitivity to light at this point and can't store any kind of image. The drum must be given a negative charge that's completely and evenly distributed across the entire surface of the drum. That electrical charging is called *conditioning*.

To condition the surface of the drum, an extremely powerful negative charge of electricity is swept across the surface of the drum. This voltage is about -6,000 volts (negative charge) and is distributed by a very thin wire called the *corona wire*, which is located close to the drum. The drum and the corona wire share a "ground" with the high-voltage power supply, and their proximity generates the electrical field. After the conditioning and a negative charge has been applied to the drum, it again becomes photoconductive.

Corona Ionization

Essentially, the high voltage being sent through the corona wire causes a short circuit between the wire and the image drum. The air around the wire breaks down, causing a corona to form. The corona ionizes the molecules in the air surrounding the drum, and negative charges migrate to the drum surface.

Because a short circuit isn't healthy for high-voltage power supplies, a primary grid is put between the wire and the drum, allowing for a regulating process of controlled voltages—the regulating grid voltage, or typically -600 to -1,000 volts. The charge on the drum is set to this regulating voltage.

Writing

When a beam of light touches the surface of the drum, it discharges a small amount of electricity, usually about -100 volts. Because the surrounding area of the drum is between -600 and -1,000 volts, this spot (or dot) is "more positively charged" than the surrounding area. In other words, the dot is less negatively charged, and we say that it has a *relative positive charge*. In other words, the spot charge is somewhat positive, relative to its surroundings.

Because we've started with negative charges (i.e., -600 to -1,000 volts) and the light from the laser beam siphons off about 100 volts, there is a more negative charge where the light missed, and a higher (less negative) charge where the light touched. The background charge is the -600 volts, and the lower charge (-600 volts with 100 volts siphoned off) is -500 volts.

The image held in memory, which was sent there by the software program, is transferred to the *writing mechanism*. This is a sophisticated device that controls the way in which the laser beam moves over the surface of the drum. It also controls when the beam is lit or turned off. The beam produces a dot on the drum each time that the beam is on.

Developing

At this point, an invisible pattern of electrostatic charge differentials is sitting on the surface of the drum. Overall, the charge is negative, but at each data point, there's a relatively positive dot standing out from the surrounding area.

Somehow, we're going to have to move toner from the cartridge onto the drum, in such a way that an image is made visible. ("Visible" is a debatable term because it's pitch black inside a laser printer after the laser beam has finished writing the latent image.) To do this, we use a long metal sleeve with a permanent magnet inside. This sleeve is called a *toner cylinder*, or sometimes a *developer roller*.

The toner cylinder is constantly turning in the middle of all the toner powder. Toner powder is held in the toner trough. As the cylinder turns, it attracts particles of toner to its metal sleeve. Now the high-voltage power supply sends current, but this time through the toner cylinder, which charges the toner *particles* with a negative charge. The charge is somewhere between the charges on the drum, averaged for the places where the light touched and where no light touched.

The toner on the toner cylinder is kept at one microscopic layer by a *restricting blade*. The rotation of the cylinder is moving charged toner on the cylinder ever closer to the drum. Where there was no light, the higher negative charge repels the less negatively charged toner particles. Where light touched the cylinder, there's less of a charge than the charge of the toner particles, so the toner particles are attracted to the surface of the drum. (A fluctuation mechanism helps ensure that toner particles are more attracted to the drum than the cylinder.)

Stop for a second. Think of the drum surface as a flat surface. It's clear in color. Wherever the laser beam touches, the surface sinks downward. This leaves a sort of hole, or "dip" in the surface. The dips are also clear, without any toner in them.

Toner particles are attracted only to the dips, and they're pushed away from the main surface area. Therefore, the developing process is sort of like shoveling toner particles into the holes until the surface of the holes reaches the same level as the original flat surface. An image develops wherever the black toner particles fill in the electrostatic holes on the drum.

 Remember that you can't develop an image unless you first write it to the EP drum. The process is very much like taking a photograph, and you can't develop an image unless you first "snap the picture" (write the image).

Transferring

The surface of the drum now has a layer of toner powder in an image pattern. The powder has to be laid down on a piece of paper in that precise pattern—that is, it has to be *transferred* to the paper. The problem is that although the toner was originally attracted to the drum by feelings of electromagnetic love, it now has to be pried away from the drum, kicking and screaming.

A different corona wire, this time called the *transfer corona wire*, charges the paper at this point, similar to the way the drum was charged. This time, the paper takes on a very high *positive* charge. If you've ever rubbed a comb against cloth and then held the comb over a piece of tissue paper, you saw how the comb attracted the tissue. This is a problem with laser printers: The paper must be charged enough to pull the toner particles off the drum, but not so much that the paper wraps itself around the drum.

The size and stiffness of the paper, along with the relatively small size of the drum, work to prevent the wrapping problem. Additionally, a static charge eliminator called an *eliminator comb* works to counteract the attraction between the paper and the drum. Just like in rock music, everything is attracted to the drum(mer).

Fusing

Once the toner particles get onto the paper, they're held there only by a combination of gravity and a residual electrostatic charge in both the paper and the toner. If you've ever had a printer jam and pulled a piece of paper out of a laser printer before it was fused, you've seen how easily the toner rubs off onto anything it comes in contact with. Toner must be bonded to the paper before the print process is complete. This bonding process is called *fusing*.

The *fusing assembly* is a quartz heating lamp inside a roller tube, positioned above a rubber *pressure roller*. This *heating roller* is made of a high-quality, nonstick material. As the paper with the toner on it is drawn between the heated upper roller and the rubber lower roller, the toner is subjected to enough heat to melt it (180 degrees Celsius) and is then pressed into the paper by the bottom roller. The combination of the fusing roller and pressure roller is called the *fusing rollers*, but only the upper roller produces the heat.

 The temperature of the heating lamp must be highly controlled to prevent fires and internal damage to the printer. Remember that the temperature sensor on the heated fuser roller is designed to shut down the system in the event that the temperatures get high enough inside the printer to cause a fire.

End of Cycle

Finally, a fabric cleaning pad, located on the opposite side of the heated upper roller, rubs off any residual melted toner. The paper with its fused image is rolled out of the printer and deposited in the output tray. During the final stages, the drum is in the process of being cleaned and erased, as we saw at the beginning of the cycle.

An even distribution of light is passed over the entire surface of the drum, causing the entire drum to bleed away all electrostatic charges. The drum is then ready to be conditioned and the next page printed. This happens for every sheet passing through the laser printer.

 Be sure to remember the difference between the primary corona and the secondary corona wires. The primary wire charges the EP drum so it can attract toner. The secondary wire charges the paper so it can pull toner away from the EP drum. First comes the drum, then comes the paper. There's no logical sense in running the paper under a blank drum.

Paper Feed Process

When you send a **PRINT** command to the laser printer, the main motor begins to turn. This starts the EP drum, the fusing rollers, and the feed rollers that move the paper along. However, three mechanical rollers aren't part of this process: the paper pick-up roller and the pair of registration rollers. They are controlled by a separate clutch mechanism and stay stationary.

Figure 7.4 shows the outside of a typical laser printer. We've made the larger pick-up roller and the two registration rollers a darker shade. Once the printing cycle is under way, a clutch engages the pick-up roller, dropping the roller down

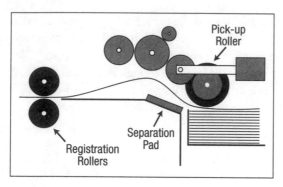

Figure 7.4 The laser printer's paper feed process.

onto the surface of the top piece of paper in the paper tray. The pick-up roller is "notched" and only makes one turn—just enough to pull the edge of the paper in between the registration rollers.

Just as the paper leaves the paper tray, a small rubber *separation pad*, right below the pick-up roller, tries to ensure that only one piece of paper is pulled into the printer. One of the most common causes of paper jams in laser printers is when more than one piece of paper moves between the registration rollers, and tries to go through the printer. The registration rollers continue to turn until the entire sheet of paper has passed between them.

 When a paper jam occurs and no paper is in the paper tray, the most common cause of the jam is either more than one page entering the system, or the paper separation pad. Typically, if the wrong type of paper is being used, the pick-up roller can't move the first page. If the pick-up roller can move the paper, then the most likely problem is that the separator pad can't separate two sheets.

Practice Questions

Question 1

> A black band around the screen image of an LCD panel can indicate what type of problem?
>
> ○ a. The resolution has been set lower than the panel maximum.
>
> ○ b. There is a device driver mismatch.
>
> ○ c. More colors have been selected than the panel can display.
>
> ○ d. The scan rate is too slow for the resolution.

Answer a is correct. On an LCD panel, changing the image resolution can potentially cause a black band to appear around the edge of the panel. Because the display is designed to match the number of pixels in an image, the LCD process turns on crystals based on usage, and if the resolution is set too low for the panel, the images would be too small to go all the way to the edges of the panel.

Question 2

> What is the standard resolution for a VGA monitor?
>
> ○ a. 480 horizontal × 640 vertical
>
> ○ b. 800 horizontal × 600 vertical
>
> ○ c. 640 horizontal × 480 vertical
>
> ○ d. 600 horizontal × 400 vertical

Answer c is correct. A standard VGA monitor has a resolution of 640 pixels horizontally and 480 pixels vertically. We use the × to mean the word "by," so the measurement is commonly written as 640×480. The other answers are invalid screen resolutions.

Question 3

What is a pixel?

○ a. A dot of ink on a page

○ b. A 1-micron unit of image

○ c. A fairy-like creature

○ d. A single picture unit

Answer d is correct. Microsoft invented the term "pixel" to mean a single picture unit. Pixels are used mostly in image resolutions where some kind of light is involved. Dots per inch (dpi) are used where some kind of ink is involved.

Question 4

How many times does the electron beam sweep from top to bottom to fully refresh an interlaced monitor's screen?

○ a. Two

○ b. One

○ c. Four

○ d. None of the above

Answer a is correct. Interlaced mode means the electron beam sweeps from top to bottom, taking two passes to do so. First it refreshes the odd lines, then the even lines. Noninterlaced mode is where the beam moves across the tube only one time.

Question 5

What is the purpose of the erase lamp in a laser printer?

○ a. The erase lamp places spaces between dots.

○ b. The erase lamp removes toner from the drum.

○ c. The erase lamp allows printing of special fonts.

○ d. The erase lamp resets the photosensitive drum to clear.

Answer d is correct. The laser beam writes a preliminary, or latent, image to the drum before transferring the image to paper. To clear the latent image, an erase lamp resets the drum to clear. Remember that toner is removed by the cleaning blade.

Question 6

> The main motor in a laser printer turns which of the following subsystems? [Choose the three best answers]
>
> ❑ a. EP drum
>
> ❑ b. Fusing rollers
>
> ❑ c. Paper pick-up roller
>
> ❑ d. Feed rollers
>
> ❑ e. Registration rollers

Answers a, b, and d are correct. The paper pick-up roller is used to move the top sheet of paper in a paper tray far enough that the registration rollers can grab it and pull it into the printer. The EP drum, fusing rollers, and feed rollers are all part of the main assembly being moved by the main motor.

Question 7

> Print rollers should be cleaned with what type of solvent?
>
> ○ a. Alcohol
>
> ○ b. Mild soap and water
>
> ○ c. Thinner
>
> ○ d. Print rollers are brushed clean; solvents are not recommended

Answer a is correct. Print rollers need friction to work properly. Therefore, they must be cleaned with a solvent that will dissolve grease and leave no residue. Alcohol has these properties and is an excellent solvent for cleaning print rollers. Answer b is incorrect because soap will leave a sticky residue. Answer c is incorrect because thinner is a corrosive solvent. Answer d is incorrect because a brush will not remove the grease that causes a loss of friction.

Need to Know More?

Bigelow, Stephen. *Easy Laser Printer Maintenance and Repair.* New York, NY: McGraw-Hill, 1995. ISBN 0-07-035976-8. This book has more information than you need for the exam, but it is a great reference for technicians.

Bigelow, Stephen. *Troubleshooting, Maintaining, and Repairing Personal Computers: A Technical Guide.* New York, NY: TAB Books, 1995. ISBN 0-07-912099-7. This book contains detailed information from a break-fix standpoint for displays; LCD panels; and dot matrix, ink jet, and laser printers.

Messmer, Hans-Peter. *The Indispensable PC Hardware Book.* Reading, MA: Addison-Wesley, 1995. ISBN 0-201-87697-3. This book contains much greatly detailed information about monitors and displays.

Minasi, Mark. *The Complete PC Upgrade and Maintenance Guide.* San Francisco, CA: Sybex Network Press, 1996. ISBN 0-7821-1956-5. This book is a great source of information on peripherals from a repair standpoint.

Rosch, Winn. *Hardware Bible.* Indianapolis, IN: Sams Publishing, 1994. ISBN 0-672-30954-8. This book covers everything you'd want to know about computer hardware.

8

Networking

. . . .

Terms you'll need to understand:

✓ Small Computer System Interface (SCSI), Universal Serial Bus (USB), FireWire

✓ Megabits per second (Mbps) and megabytes per second (MB/s)

✓ Network interface card (NIC)

✓ Ethernet and token ring architectures

✓ Collisions and collision domains

✓ Backplane

✓ Hub, bridge, router

Concepts you'll need to master:

✓ Serial connectivity

✓ Client/server and peer-to-peer network

✓ Baseband versus broadband

✓ Star, ring, and bus topologies

Before you start stressing about the complexities of networking, remember that a computer is only a bunch of parts put together by human beings just like you. Someone wanted to do something with information, and was inspired to invent a particular way to do it. When it worked, lots of people started using it, and they soon started complaining that it was too slow and too expensive, or that it had some problems. Then, someone came along and figured out a better way. Part by part, each area of computer technology grew out of previous problems.

Let's start our network section by reviewing three technologies that are not networks. Strange, right? Well, the reason is that these three are so similar to networks that, by the time we finish, you'll have a much better understanding of how networking began. The technologies are the Small Computer System Interface (SCSI), the Universal Serial Bus (USB), and the Institute of Electrical and Electronic Engineers (IEEE) 1394 specification, which is also called Apple Computer's *FireWire* or Sony's *i.Link*.

Chaining Devices

When peripheral controllers began taking on more intelligence, devices began to change to allow several devices to access a given controller. Rather than add more and more sockets to the controllers, a "pass-through" connection was added to the device. This means that a second connector on the device allows a downstream device (added afterward) to send and receive data to or from a *host*, usually the PC.

If a removable drive uses the parallel port controller as an interface, a pass-through connector allows a printer to be connected to the removable drive in a *chain*. The controller handles the prioritization of the data stream and sends appropriate information to either the drive or the printer. The port controller is the host, and both the drive and printer are *chained devices*.

Note: An IDE or EIDE disk must be mounted inside the computer. There is no standard provision for an IDE ribbon cable to run to external devices. For a while, kits were available on the market that allowed a connection to an external IDE drive using the parallel port, but the wide acceptance of Iomega's Jaz and Zip drives have relegated these kits to novelty status.

When two or more devices are chained together in this manner, we call it a *daisy chain*. The problem with pass-through connectors is that only two devices can be connected to the host, much like an IDE controller.

Typical floppy drive controllers for IBM PCs and clones allow a maximum of two floppy drives to be connected with a single cable. On the exam, you'll likely be tested on how many devices can be attached to certain types of cable interfaces. For example, SCSI allows up to eight devices—one host adapter and seven peripherals. A floppy disk, IDE, or EIDE controller allows two devices.

SCSI Interface

The SCSI interface (pronounced "scuzzy") is one of the occult mysteries of computerdom. Like any of the PC technologies, the interface could take up an entire chapter, but our purpose here is to help you understand SCSI enough to pass the exam. (See Chapter 9 for more on SCSI connectors and other cables.)

SCSI is used by many manufacturers and supports a mixture of drives and devices within the same system (e.g., disk drives, tape backups, and scanners). Aside from a mandatory *host adapter*, there can be up to seven additional devices on a SCSI chain. SCSI is available in three versions: SCSI-1, 2, and 3.

 The SCSI bus also allows computers that aren't IBM compatible to use hard drives that were developed specifically for IBM-type PCs. An important thing to remember about the SCSI interface is that the bus allows both hard drives and other devices to be connected to an external cable.

The IDE and EIDE controller also uses drives and other devices, but allows only two devices in a chain and does not support external devices.

The SCSI Chain—Eight ID Numbers

SCSI is completely different from IDE in the sense that it isn't restricted to disk drives. SCSI is not a controller/adapter like the IDE; it is a complete and separate bus. The bus connects to the system bus on the motherboard through a host adapter. This is how you can see references to a PCI SCSI adapter. In that case, the host adapter fits a PCI slot on the motherboard bus.

A single SCSI bus can hold up to eight devices, each with a unique SCSI identification (ID) number from 0 through 7. Be sure to remember that hexadecimal counting begins at zero. The host adapter takes up one of the ID numbers, leaving seven IDs for the other hardware devices.

The main thing to remember about configuring a SCSI device is that the host adapter and every device must have a SCSI ID number. The ID number is almost always between 0 and 6 (seven choices), with the host adapter usually set to

7 at the factory. ID 7 is the highest priority, and the adapter is critical. If the adapter ID is 7, that means it's the eighth device—leaving room for seven more devices.

 Don't be confused by the eight ID numbers and seven devices on the overall SCSI bus. Remember that the host adapter automatically takes up one ID number. The remaining seven hardware devices take up the remaining seven identification numbers.

The ID is set in much the same way that master/slave jumpers are set on an IDE hard drive. For no reason at all, and instead of making it simple, SCSI manufacturers use binary numbers represented by three jumpers. One SCSI manufacturer might have binary 000 as SCSI ID 0 and binary 100 as SCSI ID 4. Just to be diabolical, another SCSI manufacturer might reverse the jumper settings, so that ID 4 could just as easily be 001.

Note: A SCSI cable must be terminated at both ends, just like a network bus. Because the host adapter is usually at one end, it typically has a built-in terminator. If the host adapter is in the middle of the chain, you need to remember to remove the terminator mounted on the controller and install terminators at both ends of the cable.

SCSI-1

The first set of standards, SCSI-1, included 18 commands, but the interface could send only one command at a time. The bus required a host adapter and used a unique SCSI ID number for each drive. It introduced the seven-device limit to a daisy chain, other than the host adapter device, where the remaining devices could only be different types of hard drives. SCSI-1 was very strict about termination and used a 132-ohm passive terminator. The terminator didn't work well with high-speed transfer rates, sometimes causing data errors when more than one device was on a chain. Another problem with SCSI-1 was that the cable length was limited to 6 meters, which is approximately 19 feet.

SCSI-2

Release 2 of the specification lowered the terminator resistance and used an active (voltage-regulated) terminator. The lower impedance (ohms) helped improve reliability. SCSI-2 included the original 18 commands (rewriting some of them) and added new commands, including specific support for drives other than hard drives (e.g., CD-ROM, DAT, floptical, removable disk, standard QIC tape, magneto-optical, WORM drives, and scanners). Some drives still required third-party software drivers, but the seven-device limit stayed.

SCSI-2 also introduced support for a bus-mastering controller (onboard CPU/DMA controller) and support for multitasking environments. Up to 256 commands could be sent at one time to a device, which stored them in a buffer and reordered them for better efficiency.

SCSI-3

SCSI-3 is actually a collection of evolving specifications for device operation. Currently, three subsets of SCSI-3 are referred to as the SCSI Parallel Interface (SPI). In fact, we often do not refer to SCSI-1, 2, or 3 anymore, but rather reference the specific subsets as follows:

➤ *SPI–1 (Ultra SCSI or Fast 20)*—Uses a 68-pin "wide" connector and runs at 20Mbps or 40Mbps.

➤ *SPI–2 (Ultra 2 SCSI or Fast 40)*—Uses a Very High Density (VHD) connector and runs at 40Mbps or 80Mbps.

➤ *SPI–3 (Ultra 3 SCSI or Ultra 160)*—Uses double clocking and "packetization" to achieve a transmission speed of 160Mbps

Universal Serial Bus (USB)

The old COM and LPT ports are far too slow for modern processors, and although parallel transfer is faster than serial transfer, parallel bits get out of synch when they have to travel too far. This is known as *signal skew* or *jitter*, and is why both parallel and SCSI interfaces require fairly short cables. Serial cables can be much longer, but the COM port is very slow (approximately 100KB/s). If we could boost the speed of serial transfers, we'd get the best of both—faster transfer and longer cables.

Another problem is that, for a long time, too many devices were available for the limited number of basic I/O ports on the motherboard. A modem took one of the COM ports, regardless of whether it was internal or external. The mouse is now as critical as a keyboard, but although the back panel added two new PS/2 connectors, the mouse was still using one of the serial controllers on the board. If anyone used two printers, they used an A/B box, so the back panel eliminated all but one LPT port.

On top of all this, when you added an expansion card to an internal bus slot, you'd have to reconfigure the system to deal with IRQs and DMA lines. Plug and Play (PnP) (discussed in its own section later in this chapter) went a long way toward making cards and devices more intelligent, but even today, online connections can mysteriously freeze or disconnect due to the vagaries of an internal modem. To get around the limited I/O ports and the need to configure add-on device cards, the industry developed two new serial transfer architectures: the Universal Serial Bus (USB), and IEEE 1394. We'll discuss USB first and then take a look at IEEE 1394 (FireWire and i.Link).

The advantage of USB is that it removes the need for dedicated cards and slots. PnP devices using a USB design allow the operating system to understand the peripheral as if it were installed in an expansion slot. This means (presumably) that no more configuration problems will be associated with a limited pool of memory addresses and IRQ lines. The USB mark is shown in Figure 8.1.

Version 1.0 and 1.1

The first USB specification was released in January 1996, and Intel decided to support it in chip sets starting with the Pentium II. Windows 98, Windows 2000, Windows ME, and Windows NT (4.x and later) include full support for USB. Version 1.0 pioneered a way to daisy-chain more than two peripheral devices to a single USB controller, called a *hub*.

There is a small bus inside a hub, with terminators at both ends and wires leading to connectors on the outer casing of the hub. The hub connects to a cable, and other cables then connect computers or resources to the hub. When a hub can be connected to another hub, which in turn connects to a main USB cable, this is a *tiered-star topology*. We'll discuss topologies for networking in the "Token Ring (IEEE 802.5)" section later in this chapter.

In September 1998, version 1.1 of the specification further clarified how USB ports would work. USB 1.1 runs at 12Mbps or 1.5MB/s).

You'll most likely be tested on values in terms of bits per second. If you remember those, all you have to do is to divide by 8 in order to calculate the bytes per second. Divide 12 megabits by 8 bits, and the result is 1.5 megabytes per second.

A maximum of 127 devices can be chained to a Universal Serial Bus in a tiered star topology. *Star* means that all devices are linked to a central point. *Tiered* means that within the star, devices can be plugged into additional hubs—one after another, in several levels. Figure 8.2 shows the way this is done; in the figure, the tiers are numbered 1 through 5. The rules for USB hubs are as follows:

➤ Hubs can be plugged into the cable, and multiple devices can then be plugged into each hub.

➤ You can have as many as five tiers of hubs.

Figure 8.1   The USB mark on cables, connectors, hubs, and peripheral devices.

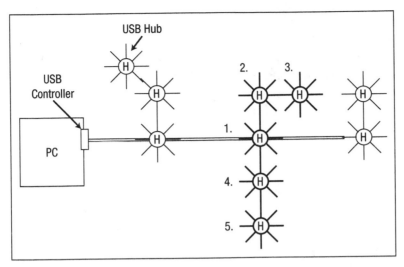

Figure 8.2   USB tiered-star topology.

Powered USB Hubs

USB hubs provide both connectivity and power. Most peripheral devices are powered through the devices' cables. This can overload power circuits, particularly in portable laptops where battery life is limited. To overcome this, USB hubs include a power supply, allowing the hubs themselves to provide power to their devices.

Hubs also provide a *bidirectional repeater*. A repeater receives a signal, rebuilds it, and sends it out again. This is important because a USB cable has a limit of 5 meters (approximately 15 ft.). If you want to go any farther than 5 meters, you need a repeater to rebuild (and retime) the signal.

The important things to remember about USB versions 1.0 and 1.1 are that:

➤ The topology is tiered star.

➤ 1 USB controller can sustain up to 127 devices.

➤ There are two channels: High and Low.

➤ The high channel transfers at 12Mbps.

➤ The low subchannel (e.g., pointing devices and keyboards) transfers at 1.5Mbps.

Version 2.0

The current modification to the USB specification includes backward compatibility with both versions 1.0 and 1.1. If you look at Table 8.1, you can quickly see the different data rates of all three versions. USB 2.0 allows for a data stream of 480Mbps (60MB/s). This speed was developed using a process called *Non-Return-to-Zero-Inverted* (NRZI) signaling, which we discuss in the next section.

Version 2.0 hubs have also been made faster, but they continue to work with older devices. They will adjust the signal speed on a per-device basis. This is done by buffering, where a high-speed bit stream can be stored in a buffer and is then parceled out to a version 1.x device.

Like an IDE drive controller, if you mix 2.0 and 1.x hubs, any device downstream from the 1.x hub will be limited to the lower speed of the 1.x hub. USB version 2.0 brings about improvements in three areas:

➤ Speed

➤ Power

➤ Buffering

Non-Return-to-Zero-Inverted (NRZI)

In Chapter 3, we mentioned that AMD created faster throughput by using a change in *state* of the clock. You may recall that it wasn't the clock tick itself that was used for timing, but rather the change in voltage as the clock went from a *pause* to a tick. The increasing voltage was one state, and the tick itself was a different event. As the clock returned to its pre-tick condition, the reducing voltage was a second state. This allowed for two instructions per clock tick, rather than only one instruction being linked to the tick.

The "pause" condition, where zero voltage is being applied to the clock, constitutes a *reference point*. When the voltage goes up in order to generate a tick, that event is distinct from when the voltage returns to zero. Up until USB, this was how many digital processes worked with voltage changes.

NRZI encoding means that only the *variation* of the voltage produces a change in state. A steady voltage represents a 1, and any change at all in voltage repre-

Table 8.1	USB signal transfer rates.	
Version	Mbps	MB/s
1.0 (low)	1.5	0.1875
1.1 (high)	12	1.5
2.0	480	60

sents a 0. The change could be a drop in voltage or a return to zero voltage, but with NRZI, the return to zero is no longer required—no reference point is necessary. This works both ways. If the voltage changes a lot, it causes a string of 0s. If the voltage stays steady, it causes a string of 1s. On the other hand, a string of 1s or 0s can set the voltage to a steady state or a varying state, respectively.

NRZI is one of the ways that USB can generate much higher throughput than earlier serial transfer protocols. NRZI encoding is unique to USB.

Plug and Play (PnP)

PnP comes from the expression Plug and Play (spoken as "plug 'n' play"). It was first introduced in Windows 95, but the concept originates with the old EISA bus. PnP is shorthand for a process in which the operating system works with the underlying hardware in an attempt to automatically configure peripheral devices.

The PnP standard is an agreement among hardware, software, and operating systems developers regarding how to "plug" (install) something into the system and have it "play" (work) automatically. Keep in mind that a truly workable autoconfiguration process involves more than just the operating system.

PnP is both a hardware and a software solution. Not only do PnP devices have to be built according to the specification, but they also require a compatible operating system and a compatible BIOS. The three aspects described in the PnP industry specification are:

➤ PnP-compatible hardware

➤ PnP BIOS

➤ PnP operating system

After a device has been configured, the PnP operating system assigns various system resources (such as memory and time slices) as long as the computer is running. The interactivity of the PnP technology allows the device to tell the operating system what it needs, and the OS gives the device those resources.

Older (non-PnP) devices installed in a PnP system have their expansion cards configured manually. In that case, the operating system can't work with the device to manage system resources. As far as the operating system is concerned, it doesn't "see" the device, and it may end up assigning those resources to some other card—a PnP-compliant one. This could shut the older card out of the resource pool, leaving the device that it controls dead.

A PnP operating system does not require PnP hardware. Older hardware won't be autoconfigured by a PnP operating system, but this means only that it must be configured manually. Non-PnP hardware can still run on a PnP system.

Although the technical standard describes only the three major components, Microsoft also includes a fourth component. A question may be on the exam concerning PnP-aware application software, which refers to this fourth specification.

IEEE 1394

We said earlier that FireWire and i.Link are both part of the IEEE 1394 standard. IEEE (the Institute for Electrical and Electronics Engineers) and ANSI (American National Standards Institute) set the technical standards for these kinds of things, and they never can agree on anything for sure. That's why the nice thing about standards is that there are so many of them.

IEEE 1394 was designed around video applications, particularly video cameras and video software. Motion video requires extremely high processing speed and bandwidth, and although the architecture is also designed for linking many devices together, we typically see an IEEE 1394 cable used to connect a camera or video-editing equipment to a PC.

IEEE 1394 is faster than USB technology. The current standard calls for three signal rates of 100Mbps (12.5MB/s), 200Mbps (25MB/s), or 400Mbps (50MB/s). Although most cards support the 200Mbps rate, most of the devices on the market run at up to only 100Mbps. FireWire and i.Link, like SCSI and USB, allocate bandwidth to the speed of the designated device. To that end, not all the connected devices are required to run at 400MB/s.

Note: A proposed modification to the current specification indicates an upgrade to gigabits per second (Gbps) bandwidth.

IEEE 1394 uses what's called a *daisy-chained and branched topology*, where each adapter card allows for up to 63 nodes, with 16 devices chained from each node. IEEE 1394 provides a performance improvement over ultra-wide SCSI and costs significantly less. However, the devices all use power from the computer, unlike the powered hubs of USB. IEEE 1394 is fully PnP-compatible, including a capability for what's called "hot swapping," which allows for connecting or disconnecting a device without shutting down the PC.

Networking Overview

Networks typically connect both computers and peripherals together. USB and IEEE 1394 are designed to connect peripherals to a single computer. Networking is done to share resources, either for convenience or to save money. Connecting computers together in a network requires three things: a network interface card (NIC); a network operating system (NOS)—technically called a *redirector*— and a medium for transmitting data from one computer to another (usually some type of wire). We will focus most of our attention on wire (cable) transmission mediums.

Categories and Types

Networks fall into two broad categories: *peer-to-peer* and *client/server*. We can also divide each category into two types: *Ethernet* and *token ring*. All computers are equal in a peer-to-peer network (think of a "jury of your peers"), and you can choose what data and resources you want to share. Client/server networks are configured in such a way that one or more computers act as *file servers* (or just *servers*), with the rest acting as *clients*. Servers, which control the overall network, are usually dedicated to storing data. A file server is like a lawyer, serving clients with filing, applications, and processing.

Peer-to-peer networks don't have dedicated servers and therefore are less expensive to set up. Instead, each PC shares its own resources with the other PCs connected to the network. For example, you might access Sue's hard drive to retrieve a spreadsheet, and she might choose to print a document using a printer connected to your PC. Although security is provided to determine who can use what resources, peer-to-peer networks don't have the same level of security as client/server networks.

 Peer-to-peer is where each computer is a peer (equal) to the other. Client/server is where a central file server provides services to many clients. Windows 95, 98, and ME provide built-in peer-to-peer networking. Windows NT and 2000 (in their server versions) can also provide client/server networking.

Both peer-to-peer and client/server networks use software that performs the redirector function, but that software is called different things depending on the category. Beginning with Windows for Workgroups (version 3.11), Microsoft provided a peer-to-peer redirector as part of the operating system. Because of this, we rarely talk about redirectors in peer-to-peer networking, but refer to whether the feature is activated or not. Reference to a redirector usually means client/server networking.

Network Interface Card (NIC)

A network interface card plugs into the expansion bus of a motherboard and provides several necessary networking features. Initially, a NIC provides a unique network address for the PC. This address is stored in ROM on the card and is a unique code assigned by the manufacturer. Secondly, the NIC provides a connection to the media or cable used for the network. Finally, it provides the processor and buffers required to send and receive packets of data over the network cable.

 The NIC provides the network address for the PC. If you change the NIC, you change the address of the PC on the network. This can have interesting repercussions, depending on the network's configuration and security.

The Redirector

File servers run on a network operating system, which includes a redirector. The redirector monitors the CPU and determines whether data requests are *local* (in the server setup) or *remote* (outside). If the data is on a local hard drive, the request is routed to the drive. If the data isn't on the server's drives, the request is redirected to the NIC for transmission over the network.

All the machines running the operating system's *client software* also have a redirector as part of that software. When the file server broadcasts a signal, the redirector on the individual PCs checks to see whether the request is meant for that local setup.

Media

All networks communicate over some kind of media. This can be as simple as a pair of twisted wires, or as exotic as fiber optics and radio transmission. For the purposes of this discussion, we refer to the central media cable as the *backplane*. This isn't technically correct, but we're using it to refer to the main network "highway" where signals move around to various terminals. Ethernet is one of the first network types and one of the most popular, so let's start there.

Ethernet (IEEE 802.3)

Ethernet is a *baseband* network, meaning that only one signal can be on the network at a time and that the signal takes up the entire *bandwidth*. Originally, Ethernet ran at 10Mbps over a thick coaxial cable. At network transmission speeds, the wire was using frequencies well into the radio range, and the shielded wire prevented the cable from becoming an antenna and interfering with data transmissions. The cable was terminated by a resister at each end (called a terminator), which prevented signals traveling along the wire from reflecting back onto each other from the cable ends. All devices on the network attached to this cable using a *tap* and shared the cable as a transmission media.

In an Ethernet network, the NIC "listens" to the cable, checking to see if anyone else's PC is talking. If no other PCs are transmitting at that moment, your card sends out a data transmission. As more terminals come online (join the network), each new card waits for a quiet moment (when no signal voltage is on the line) before transmitting data. If data signals moved instantaneously, each card would know when any other card was sending, but signals take time. However, data signals don't move instantaneously, and there's a time delay over the length of wire from one end of the network to the other.

When the two NIC cards transmit at the same time and the signals meet in the middle somewhere, we have what's known as a *collision*. A collision creates a spike, or bump, in the voltage that the transmitting NIC detects. That NIC then sends out a *jam signal*, which is nothing more than a stream of 0s and 1s designed to fill up the network. All the cards on the network stop transmitting, and a random number generator on each of the transmitting cards picks a random time to begin transmission after an initial silence. This is why Ethernet is often called a Carrier Sense Multiple Access/Collision Detection (CSMA/CD) network.

The IEEE soon developed the 802.3 standards around this network, and the cable was named 10Base5 cable. The exact meaning of 10Base5 is discussed in Chapter 9.

Note: Fast Ethernet, using Category 5 wiring, runs at 100Mbps.

Throughput and Bandwidth

We introduced throughput in Chapter 2, saying that it's essentially how much data we can move through a bus. If you think of a byte as eight horses at the racetrack, then an 8-bit bus would be like the starting gates, where each horse (a bit) has its own gate. Suppose you have 100 rows of horses, and the gates only open and close for each row. Each time a row of horses goes through the gates, that's 1 *cycle*. The *bus clock* tells the gates when to open and shut. The number of times that the gates open and shut in a given time period is the *frequency* for that cycle.

If you think of bus throughput as *bits per cycle*, then you can begin to think of frequency as something like *cycles per bit*. Let's suppose that it takes 5 cycles to describe 1 bit. If each cycle takes 12 seconds, then it would take 60 seconds (1 minute) to produce 1 bit (5 cycles × 12 seconds per cycle = 60 seconds). The number of cycles in a given second is the frequency of those cycles, and this frequency is expressed in hertz (Hz).

If you could make the cycles go faster, you could describe more bits. By "compressing" the frequency to 5 cycles per second, it would take 1 second to describe 1 bit. If 1MHz is 1 million cycles per second, that would allow for 200,000 bits, or 25,000 bytes (25KB or 2.5MB).

Bandwidth is a measure of the "capacity" something has to move data. For instance, our racetrack can only handle a burst of 8 horses going through the gates, but part of that is due to the dirt on the track, the weather, and the nature of the track. The something through which the data is moving could be a bus, an Ethernet cable, or even air.

Although the throughput is the actual data being moved, the bandwidth is the property of the medium to accept frequency compression. We almost never refer to bandwidth in conjunction with moving data through a bus. Usually we're referring to radio, or a cable of some kind.

Note: Baseband Ethernet bandwidth has the capacity to move only one signal at a time, with that signal taking up the entire bandwidth. Technically, bandwidth is the difference between the highest and the lowest frequency being transmitted. High bandwidth allows for the transmission of a lot of information in a high frequency. Low bandwidth is a lesser capacity, allowing for less information to move at a lower frequency.

Broadband allows many different frequencies to travel over the transmission medium. Until recently, the most common example of broadband technology was radio, where many different signal frequencies (radio stations) could transmit at the same time. Amplitude Modulation (AM) radio is broadband technology, so when you hear about WAEC at 890 on your dial, the station is transmitting at a frequency of 890MHz. Fiber-optic cable allows for broadband data movement.

Note: Baseband (time-division multiplexing) allows many signal frequencies, but each signal gets only a tiny slice of time for itself, and that signal uses the entire bandwidth. Broadband (frequency-division multiplexing) has a broad range of frequencies moving continuously, but any given signal gets only one frequency.

Terminators

Any electronic media or cable that carries a signal of any type must be terminated properly at each end. To maintain error-free data travel along the bus, *terminating resistors* absorb any signal that reaches the end of the cable. This prevents the signal from "bouncing back" along the cable and crashing into other signals traveling along the bus (collisions). In a long backplane, it isn't unusual for a PC to transmit from one end while a PC at the other end still hears silence and transmits at the same time.

Remember that electronic cables or media that carry data or signals are essentially a *bus.* To prevent errors caused by signals bouncing back along the bus from the ends of the cable, a terminating resistor must be at both ends. These are called *terminators.* Terminators absorb signals to keep them from reflecting back along the cable.

Token Ring (IEEE 802.5)

Ethernet networks using transmissions and quiet times are called *probabilistic*, in that moving data is a matter of probably avoiding a collision. IBM wanted to develop a *deterministic* way of making sure that data would avoid a collision, so it invented the token ring network.

A *token* is a sort of placeholder for something that it represents, like a token of appreciation. A token ring network connects PCs in a ring and then passes an empty data packet from one PC to another. This symbol (the empty data packet) of what could become data is the token. When a terminal requires data from another terminal, it waits for the token to come around, then places its request (along with the NIC address of the PC from which it wants information) in the token. The token then becomes an actual data *packet*, and it passes around the ring to the appropriate PC.

Token ring networking is like a group of people sitting around a dinner table. If someone wants mashed potatoes, they wait for a pause in the conversation, then pass a note with their request to the person nearest the potatoes. That person reads the note and hands the potatoes to whoever is near them in the ring, and everyone passes the mashed potatoes along. When the person who sent the request gets the bowl, they dish out some potatoes onto their plate—the local hard drive. With every resource waiting for the token before it transmits, there are no longer any collisions.

Bus and Star Topology

Ethernet is a little like an old telephone party line. Regardless of how many people are talking on the phone, each person can hear every other person. The trick is to listen for the specific voice of the caller who's addressing you, and ignore all the rest. Networks are a little more sophisticated than that, as we'll see in this section.

An Ethernet backplane is one long, heavy piece of coaxial cable that snakes its way through an office suite. This type of topology, which has only one wire, is called a *bus topology.* The cable can transport only one signal at a time, which means that only two devices can "talk" back and forth at any given time. All the PCs share that one cable, and any given PC can transmit when the bus isn't moving someone else's signal. All PCs on the bus can hear the transmission, but only the addressed PC copies the transmission into its buffer for processing.

In many cases, we use shorter *twisted-pair* cables to connect several terminals to a hub. Even though the hubs may be connected to a single bus, the wires branching out from it look much like the legs of a starfish. Because of these hubs and branches, we call this type of installation a *star topology*. Figure 8.3 shows a linear bus topology and a hub and star topology. Note the terminator resistors at each end of the bus.

Bridges and Routers

As networks became larger and larger, various limits began showing up. Signal strength and quality would decay with distance, and people wanted to add more computers to the network. Keep in mind that more transmissions lead to more signals, which in turn increases the probability of jam signals and slowdowns.

The Bridge

A *bridge* is a way for a large network running at full capacity to be broken into smaller groups of segments. Bridges work with only the addresses of the network cards on a specific network. When a bridge is installed in the middle of a network, it logs all of the NIC addresses on either side of it, only passing traffic if that traffic has a destination address on the other side of the bridge. This is how a bridge segments a network and allows for more PCs to be connected without creating traffic bottlenecks.

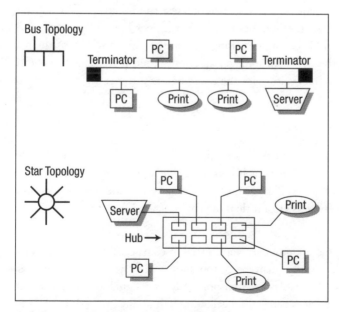

Figure 8.3   Outline of bus and star topologies.

However, even with bridges, there is a limit to how many network addresses can be maintained and processed by a given device. Because of this, another level of addressing was established at the network level, and *routers* (rhymes with "shouters") were developed to operate at the network level (not at the individual resource level).

A *bridge* segments a network. It does not create two networks. This is a key point to remember.

The Router

With the introduction of the bridge, networks became so huge that individual NICs began running into trouble trying to figure out how to address a specific machine. If you think about it, the phone system (network) had a similar problem. At first, only four digits were used because only a couple of thousand phones existed. Then, each town (network) began having enough phones that the towns had to be broken into segments, and three exchange (bridge) numbers were added.

Routers are a way to list entire network addresses and the subsequent network segments. When the number of phones went beyond a seven-digit number capacity, we added an area code. A router is like a phone book that holds only area codes. Networking was becoming so complicated that the Open System Interconnection (OSI) committee was formed to create the OSI model for networking, which is yet another set of standards.

When a router is installed between two networks, it passes traffic with a network address to that network. Routers don't care about each NIC address because they're only concerned with networks as a whole. This is how many networks can be connected together to form one big internetwork like the Internet.

The Internet uses a protocol called Transmission Control Protocol/Internet Protocol (TCP/IP), which establishes the format for addressing networks and stations on the network. In this environment, every PC has two addresses: The NIC has its built-in address, and the card is assigned a second, TCP/IP address.

TCP/IP is actually made up of two layers. At the higher layer (the Transmission Control Protocol), messages or files are broken into smaller packets that can be sent over the Internet. At the receiving end, the packets are reassembled into the original message. The lower layer (the Internet Protocol or IP layer) assigns an address to each of the smaller packets created by the TCP layer, to make sure that each packet gets to the right destination. Note that IP addresses don't apply to the Internet exclusively, but are also used in other networks.

The OSI Model

Seven layers are defined in the OSI model. We don't need to go into detail on each layer, but their names and basic functions are as follows:

➤ *Physical layer*—Electrical, mechanical, and transmission functions, along with specifications for wire (e.g., voltage, connectors, and data rates)

➤ *Data Link layer*—Physical (not logical) addresses for NICs, and related addressing within segments (bridges)

➤ *Network layer*—Network services and logical address specifications for "best path" connection (routers)

➤ *Transport layer*—End-to-end connection; sends segments from one host to another

➤ *Session layer*—Communication sessions; establishes, manages, and terminates these

➤ *Presentation layer*—Sound, video, graphics, text, and data

➤ *Application layer*—Program (e.g., spreadsheet or word processing)

If an engineer asks whether a device is a Layer 2 or Layer 3 device, it's another way of asking whether the device is for either a local area network and the addresses on that LAN, or multiple networks. Once again, a bridge creates segments in a network. A router handles addressing for whole networks.

 Bridges manage traffic on the network by filtering data. Routers then route data between networks based on network addresses.

Under this format, every station is assigned a 12-digit network address that is broken into four 3-digit blocks. This is the IP address. For example, a specific PC may have the address 192.168.001.115. Some of these digits represent the network address, and the others represent the PC itself. A *subnet mask* determines what the digits represent. A Domain Name System (DNS) server, which cross-references names with numeric addresses, is usually somewhere on the network.

Note: A firewall is a router that can be programmed to accept or reject traffic based on IP addresses and content, such as packet contents. A firewall can also be set up to accept or reject certain protocols.

The Internet

Although you don't need to know the details of TCP for the exam, you should know that an IP address is 12 digits long and difficult to remember. *Domain names* are a way to cross-reference the address number to an actual name. A DNS server keeps track of these references, allowing people to use address names that are much easier to remember.

When you type a Universal Resource Locator (URL) into your Web browser, the DNS server translates it to an IP address and then passes the request along to the Internet. One of the subdivisions of the overall Internet is the World Wide Web (WWW). The HyperText Markup Language (HTML) was created to preserve nicely formatted documents, instead of typing plain old text files. The HyperText Transfer Protocol (HTTP) was invented to transmit those HTML documents over the World Wide Web.

A typical URL is written as **http://www.*symbolics*.com**. The *symbolics* is the domain name, and the "com" is the type of domain. The periods ("dots") are separators, as are the colon and two forward slashes. In 1985, symbolics.com was assigned as the first registered domain name. Until recently, a limited number of domain types—for example, com (commercial), net (network), org (organization), edu (education), gov (government)—were available.

In the URL **http://www.jamesgjones.com**, the James G. Jones domain is a *com*mercial domain and therefore has a com suffix. The URL **http://www.comptia.org** indicates that CompTIA is an *org*anization because it has the org suffix. *Gov*ernment agencies typically use gov as their suffix, and *edu*cational institutions use edu.

With the explosive popularity of the Web, we started running out of addresses. The Internet Network Information Center (InterNIC), funded by the National Science Foundation, came together to coordinate a whole series of new extensions—for example, bus (business), co (country), tv (television), ws (Web site). We now have enough addresses to last until at least next week.

Email Addresses

An email address requires an additional user name to go along with the domain name. The separator between the two is the @ sign. The user name is to the left of the separator, and the domain name is to the right. A typical email address would be **a-plus@jamesgjones.com**. In this case, the user name "a-plus" comes first, then the @ separator, then the "jamesgjones" domain name, then the dot separator, and finally the "com" to signify the type of domain.

An email address has a user name and a domain name, with the user name to the left of an @ sign, and the domain name to the right of the @ separator.

Cable Networking, ISDN, and DSL

Very few people accessing the Internet have routers, networks, or assigned IP addresses, so how do they get on? In most cases, when you access the Internet through a dial-up telephone line and modem, you're actually calling an Internet service provider (ISP) over an analog line. The ISP connects your call, assigns a TCP/IP address to your PC for that session, and routes your data (using its router) to the Internet. Even with a 56.6Kbps modem, this is a slow task, so many people and small businesses are moving to faster broadband service, such as cable modems, Integrated Services Digital Network (ISDN), digital subscriber lines (DSLs), satellite wireless connections, or Multichannel Multipoint Distribution System (MMDS).

Where any kind of transmission system could be used to connect a PC to the Internet, broadband connections are changing constantly. We already know about fiber-optic connections, but there are cellular towers, laser beams, microwaves, and even electrical power lines. Even broadband itself is pointing a way to the next *ultraband* step for even faster connections.

Cable

Remember the first Ethernet networks and the coaxial cable? Your cable television service uses a big, thick cable to connect from the wall to your TV or video cassette recorder (VCR). There's no reason a digital signal can't be transmitted across the cable. Everyone's got cable. (You are on cable, aren't you?). One of the reasons AT&T has been buying up cable television companies is to provide this Internet connection service to cable clients. The cable provides a bus network, much like Ethernet, and your PC connects to a special cable modem that becomes the tap.

The coaxial cable connects to a *node* (intersection point) in your neighborhood, and from there the cable changes to fiber optics. Information travels at very high speeds from the node to the cable company, and then out to the Internet. Cable modem connections are "always on," with typical speeds in the 1.5Mbps range.

Integrated Services Digital Network (ISDN)

ISDN is a set of standards that can provide up to 128Kbps of digital transmission over an ordinary phone line going into homes and small businesses. The service is provided over one of the pairs of wires already installed at your location. Unlike modems, which are affected by the vagaries of analog phone lines, ISDN uses a special adapter in place of the modem. The adapter (NT-1 or "network terminator 1") is usually built into the ISDN router or bridge.

The throughput in an ISDN line is exactly as rated; however, in the case of ISDN, you need an inexpensive router or bridge at your location. This is often provided by the telephone company and connects using a NIC with a straightforward and easy installation. After the service is operational, you don't have to wait for dialing, and you are permanently connected to the Internet.

Digital Subscriber Line (DSL)

DSL is provided in many variations and speeds. Although the local telephone company provides the service, many individuals contract through an ISP for a total service. As with ISDN, you need a local router or bridge (often provided by the ISP) and a modem. This service also uses an existing pair of wires, if they're available at the location, but unlike ISDN, if a pair of wires is not available, the signal can be transposed over your active telephone line.

A DSL connection is always on, meaning that you're always connected to the Internet. It typically provides download speeds (reading a Web page) of 1.5Mbps and upload speeds (sending a file) of 128Kbps. To be eligible for a DSL connection, a PC must be within three miles of a central telephone office; otherwise, the signal begins to degrade beyond the value of the specialized connection. Unlike a cable connection and its neighborhood node, the phone line is a direct connection to the home or business, so speeds aren't subject to how many people are using the line at any given time.

Satellite Wireless

A broadband wireless connection to the Internet works like a satellite television account, using a small satellite dish to send and receive signals. The satellite relays signals to a service provider with a connection to the Internet. Once again, a specialized modem handles the encoding and decoding of signals between your PC and the satellite, and the connection is always on. Also, like some DSL and cable connections, your service can be one way only, where surfing the net (downloading) takes place through the satellite connection and uploading is done with the regular phone line.

Current satellite wireless isn't as fast as other types of connections, with a typical transmission rate of around 395Kbps. Even so, this is about seven times faster than a dial-up modem, and the system doesn't rely on any ground wires between the computer and the ISP. On the other hand, you have to have a clear view of the sky in the direction of the satellite, and there's a small amount of delay time as signals pass through the satellite relay.

Multichannel Multipoint Distribution System (MMDS)

One of the newer technologies appearing on the scene is based on a line-of-sight transmission from a digital transceiver at the PC location to a tall transmission tower. Signals from the tower are decoded through a wireless modem with speeds of up to 5.6Mbps. Although this is an exciting possibility, signals can't pass through or around solid objects. The transceiver must be within 35 miles of a tower, and because the system uses wireless transmission frequencies, speeds can be affected by how many people are using the connection at any one time.

Practice Questions

Question 1

What are two major benefits of using USB?

☐ a. Ability to use Plug-and-Play components external to the PC

☐ b. Speed of transmission

☐ c. Ability to connect many computers together with a single cable

☐ d. Ability to fully use parallel transmission

Answers a and b are correct. USB uses high-speed serial transmission to connect peripheral devices to a PC. USB does not use parallel transmission and is not designed for connecting multiple PCs.

Question 2

The IEEE 1394 standard made home networking practical.

○ a. True

○ b. False

Answer b, false, is correct. IEEE 1394 technology, also called FireWire or i.Link, is used primarily to interface video equipment with PCs and to connect many devices to a single PC. Networking connects many PCs together.

Question 3

What are the two major types of network architecture?

☐ a. Broadband

☐ b. Peer-to-server

☐ c. Bus

☐ d. Token ring

Answers c and d are correct. Bus and token ring networking are two very general categories of networking, not to be confused with bus and star topologies. Broadband is a description of transmission capacity. "Peer-to-server" doesn't exist, although client/server networking uses a file server. Although peer-to-peer and client/server could also be two major categories, the inclusion of the false peer-to-server as an option points to the c and d combination.

Question 4

How many simultaneous signals can travel on an Ethernet network without error?

○ a. One

○ b. Two, when early token release is implemented

○ c. 1,024

○ d. Up to 10, on a 10MHz network

Answer a is correct. An Ethernet bus (wire) allows only one signal at a time to use the network. More than one signal can easily create an error condition known as a collision.

Question 5

Which device is most typically used to control traffic between different networks?

○ a. A router

○ b. A bridge

○ c. A NIC

○ d. A TCP/IP

Answer a is correct. A router is used to control the flow of data between two or more separate networks. A bridge is used to segment an existing network; it does not create two networks. NIC is the abbreviation for network interface card; NICs function within a network. TCP/IP is a protocol used in moving data between and within networks, but it does not actually control the flow of data.

Question 6

A SCSI card can have up to how many storage devices attached to it?

○ a. 2

○ b. 8

○ c. 7

○ d. 5

Answer c is correct. The SCSI bus requires that every device has a unique ID number. The card itself will take one identifier for the host adapter ID, leaving seven numbers to be assigned to other devices. In this case, the devices are separated from the host adapter because the question asks about storage devices. SCSI cards can have eight ID numbers, but a host adapter is never a storage device.

Need to Know More?

 Craft, Melissa, Mark A. Poplar, David V. Watts, and Will Willis. *Network+ Exam Prep*. Scottsdale, AZ: The Coriolis Group, 1999. ISBN 1-57610-412-5. This resource covers all the networking basics.

 Derfler, Frank J. *Guide to Connectivity, 3rd Edition*. New York, NY: Ziff Davis Press, 1995. ISBN 1-56276-274-5. This is a very good basic text on how networks are wired and how they operate from a hands-on standpoint.

 Derfler, Frank J. Jr., Les Freed, and Frank Derfler. *How Networks Work, Millennium Edition*. New York, NY: Ziff Davis Press, 2000. ISBN 0-78972-445-6. This is an introductory text for people who have had no previous exposure to networking.

 Freedman, Alan. *Computer Desktop Encyclopedia, 2nd Edition*. AMACOM, 1999. ISBN 0-814-479-855. This is great for a fast look-up or a refresher.

 Minasi, Mark. *The Complete PC Upgrade and Maintenance Guide, 11th Edition*. San Francisco, CA: Sybex Network Press, 2000. ISBN 0-782-128-009. This is considered one of the best reference books available. In fact, Minasi's book was instrumental in the formulation of the first A+ exam.

 Muller, Scott. *Upgrading and Repairing PCs, 12th Edition*. Indianapolis, IN: Que, 2000. ISBN 0-7897-2303-4. This is one of our favorites. If you are only going to have one reference book, give this one serious consideration.

 Reeves, Scott, Kalinda Reeves, Stephen Weese, and Christopher S. Geyer. *A+ Exam Prep, 3rd Edition*. Scottsdale, AZ: The Coriolis Group, 2001. ISBN 1-57610-699-3. This is a good reference that concentrates on providing exam-required information.

 www.webopedia.com—This online encyclopedia devoted to technical terms features additional links to other Web-based articles, research, and white papers.

 www.whatis.com—This technical Web site resource with short articles describes many aspects of information technology.

Cables and Connectors

Terms you'll need to understand:

✓ Interface and port

✓ Input/output (I/O) bus

✓ COMmunications (COM) port and Line Printer Terminal (LPT)

✓ Serial and parallel

✓ Operating system device names

✓ DIN, mini-DIN, PS/2, and USB connector

✓ RJ-11 and RJ-45 modular connector

Concepts you'll need to master:

✓ Plug (male) and socket (female)

✓ Connector, cable, back panel (of the PC)

✓ Serial and parallel data transfer

✓ Coaxial cable naming conventions

✓ Categories of twisted-pair wire

✓ Shielding and insulation

When we turn on a computer by pressing the AC switch, the monitor lights up, drives begin to whirl, lights blink, and speakers beep until, eventually, a bit of music plays and the computer system is ready to go (you hope!). Beginning with the AC power connector that plugs into the wall outlet, everything connecting to the CPU uses a particular type of wiring scheme and connecting device. The point where something meets something else is the *interface*, and in a computer system, there is an interface between every different hardware component. An interface is often called a *port*.

The spaghetti mess of cables around a computer can be sorted into various wires and connectors, grouped by the plugs and sockets at either end. A plug has pins that stick out, and we refer to it as a *male* connector. A socket has holes for seating pins, and we refer to it as a *female* connector. This has nothing whatsoever to do with gender; they are merely technical terms.

Certain I/O interfaces that have been on computers from the very start constitute our first group of interfaces. The second group is made up of those connections and interfaces that have changed through the years, and that mostly move data to or from a *device*, which is any piece of hardware that does something specific. For the third group, we touch briefly on various connections used for interfacing two or more computers together, but a more thorough discussion on networking is found in Chapter 8.

Basic I/O Interfaces

The XT motherboards, on through the AT and Baby AT form factors, used a basic set of data connections to move data in and out of the processors. This basic input/output system, known as the BIOS, includes the rudimentary instruction programming that tells the CPU how to work with the hardware. The keyboard and mouse (input) connected through the serial ports or through dedicated interface cards. The video console and printers (output) used the video and parallel ports. Some printers used interface cards, as did tape backups and scanners. Some printers even used a serial port.

The device names that the operating system continues to use for basic hardware interfaces are:

➤ *Serial ports*—COMmunications (COM)1, COM2, COM3, COM4, and AUXiliary (AUX)

➤ *Parallel ports*—Line Printer Terminal (LPT)1, LPT2, LPT3, and PRiNter (PRN)

➤ *Video monitor*—CONsole (CON)

Note: Another type of device is the NUL device, used as a sort of black hole in space. Any data sent to the NUL device simply vanishes, making this a place to send text messages you don't want the person using the computer to see. For example, typing "Pause > NUL" in a batch file will send all output from the Pause command into oblivion, leaving a paused blank screen with a blinking cursor.

Each I/O connection uses a specific plug or socket on the back panel of the computer, along with a *controller interface* to the motherboard. The connector joins the device to the computer's box, and the controller interface connects the data coming from the device to the motherboard. Early machines used a separate controller board, some of which took over bus slots.

Today, many of these basic I/O device controllers are built right onto the motherboard, eliminating the need for a specific adapter slot. Usually, these include a primary and a secondary IDE controller, a floppy controller, the two serial ports, and the parallel port. This joining together and mounting on the motherboard created a single new chip called the *Super I/O chip*. Some systems add other peripherals, such as a SCSI host adapter, a video adapter, an integrated mouse port, and/or a network interface card (NIC).

Note: The floppy drive controller, having been one of the very first devices installed on early PCs, is still assigned to IRQ 6 by default.

Although these controllers and ports are built in, they act just like cards that plug into an expansion slot. A potential problem of this type of convenience is that it can limit the "upgradability" of a system because the original devices can't be removed. Some motherboards allow for disabling the built-in devices, but many motherboards, such as Compaq's, do not.

Floppy and Hard Disk Controllers

Originally, these controllers, due to their many variations, almost always used an expansion slot. However, when IDE and EIDE drives finally became standardized, the controllers were integrated onto the motherboard. Today, most IDE and EIDE (as well as some SCSI) controllers are on a Super I/O chip. Almost every disk drive has two connectors: one for electrical power and one for control/data signals. These connectors are fairly well standardized across the industry and across drives.

Typically, the control cable connector is a 34-pin design and uses either an edge connector or a pinhead connector. Because these cables have so many wires running through them, they're designed to be flat and flexible to save space. They're usually called *ribbon cables* because of their similarity to ribbons. Obsolete 5 1/4-inch drives used a larger-edge connector, and 3 1/2 inch drives use a smaller, pinhead connector.

Note: Don't confuse a smaller floppy drive ribbon cables with the typical 50-pin SCSI ribbon cable.

Accelerated Graphics Port (AGP)

A video monitor originally used a display adapter that was either inserted into one of the PC's expansion slots or built into the motherboard. Although built-in display adapters are efficient and economical, the actual monitors have evolved very quickly, along with the increasing requirements of 3D animated graphics. Built-in adapters are almost impossible to upgrade without swapping out the motherboard. Plug-in adapters are easy to upgrade, but because they're plugged into expansion slots, they're slower. The Accelerated Graphics Port (AGP) is a unique type of port that provides a dedicated bus to the processor for speed, and the flexibility of quickly upgrading a video card.

Parallel (LPT) Ports: 8 Bits Across

Nowadays, the majority of printers sold on the market use a *parallel* interface. The parallel port transfers information in a sort of wave, 8 bits across, in which each bit goes in the same direction at the same time. You can think of parallel transfer as an army of soldiers moving through a street, eight across, in columns. Serial ports (discussed in the next section) transfer information 1 bit at a time, in a line—a series.

Note: In Chapter 4 on memory, we spoke of the RDRAM modules working in series, using a continuity module. We mentioned Christmas tree lights, where sometimes the whole string goes dark if one bulb burns out. This is series wiring, where current must pass through one bulb before it can get to the next. Parallel wiring is where each bulb and socket connector acts as a sort of rung on a ladder. If one bulb burns out, current still continues up the sides of the ladder through the terminals in the sockets, and the rest of the lights glow.

Standard parallel cables have a DB25 male connector on one end, and a 36-pin Centronics male connector on the other. Figure 9.1 shows an outline of each type of connector. The parallel connector on the back panel of the computer is female, and you should remember that the printer cable uses a 25-pin *male* plug. The usual printer cable connects to the back panel of the computer with a connector 25 pins wide.

 Be very careful that you read a question correctly. A printer port is a female connector often found on the back panel of a computer. A printer connector is a male, 25-pin plug. If you find a 25-pin male connector on the back panel of a PC, it's almost always a serial connection. The 25-pin serial connectors are rare, but they do exist.

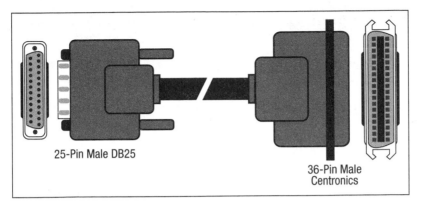

Figure 9.1 A typical parallel cable connecting a PC to a printer.

SCSI Connectors

SCSI devices can be internally connected, but can also be external to the computer, where they can be mounted in individual boxes or mounted together in larger, tower enclosures. Newer devices use what is considered the preferred connector according to the SCSI-2 standard: a smaller 50-pin SCSI connector with two rows of 25 pins, frequently referred to as a 50-pin mini D shell (MDS50) connector.

 There isn't any easy way to remember the number of pins in the various connectors. You'll be tested on the 9-pin serial, 15-pin video, 25-pin parallel, 36-pin Centronics cable, and the 50-pin SCSI cable for sure, so be sure to remember them.

Centronics Connector

Centronics Corporation was one of the original printer developers. At the time, it created a parallel interface for its dot matrix printers that became the standard connection. A typical printer cable connects to the *printer* with a Centronics male connector that is 36 pins wide.

 On the exam, Centronics is used only for printer connectors. Don't confuse a 36-pin Centronics connector and a 50-pin SCSI connector.

Types of Parallel Ports

Because we know 8 bits equals 1 byte, we can see how parallel wiring puts 1 byte through the interface at a time (8 bits across). Depending upon how fast those bytes move through the interface, the throughput goes up in terms of kilobytes, megabytes, or gigabytes. Parallel ports are available in the following types:

➤ *Unidirectional (original parallel port)*—Data flows out, but can't come back in. (Printers could not communicate with the CPU.)

➤ *Standard bidirectional*—Peripherals can send status messages back to the CPU for action.

➤ *Standard Parallel Port (SPP)*—This is a setting often found in laptops and notebooks.

➤ *Extended Capabilities Port (ECP)*— ECP ports are about 10 times faster than the standard bidirectional port.

➤ *Enhanced Parallel Port (EPP) (also called fast mode parallel port)*—ECP ports are also about 10 times faster than the standard bidirectional port.

Serial (COM) Ports: 1 Bit after Another

As we've said, serial ports transfer information one bit at a time, much like ants following one another. Because only one bit moves through the interface, serial ports are much slower than parallel ports. If a parallel port is like an army of ants marching eight abreast in columns, the serial port can be thought of as "the ants go marching one by one."

Note: Microprocessors work with bytes (8-bit units). Serial devices work with bits (1-bit units). Bus connections are often involved in converting bytes to bits, or bits to bytes.

Newer computers almost always have a dedicated PS/2 connector (mini-DIN) for the mouse and keyboard, but many older computers used either a 9-pin or a 25-pin *serial male* port. The top panel in Figure 9.2 shows how closely the serial and parallel ports on many older computers resemble each other. The DB25 connectors were next to or above each other, and the only way to remember which was the printer port was that it had a female connector.

Bits, Bytes, and Baud

Bits are binary digits (0s and 1s). Eight bits make up one byte, which typically corresponds to one character (i.e., a letter or number).

Today, data rates are measured in kilobytes per second (KB/s) and megabytes per second (MB/s). The term *baud rate* refers to the number of discrete signal events per second in a data transfer, not bits per second. The term *baud* has fallen out of use. In the early days of 300 and 1,200 baud modems, the baud rate equaled the kilobytes per second. The term remained until 14.4KB/s modems entered the market, even though it was no longer technically correct to refer to the modem speed by its baud rate.

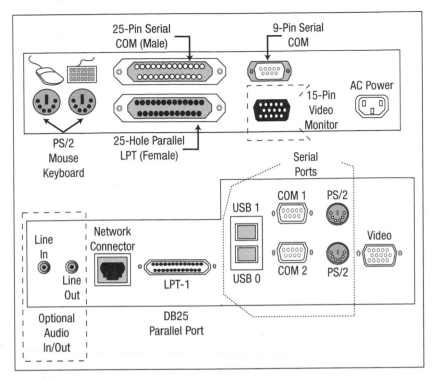

Figure 9.2 Typical back panels.

 Remember the relative sizes and shapes of the connectors. You may have to recognize them by their outlines.

Consistency has never been a strong point in the computer industry, so you can't just assume that a serial connector has nine pins. Neither can you assume that serial connectors are always used for modems. Serial connectors can be:

➤ DB9 (nine-pin)

➤ DB25 (25-pin, male)

➤ Keyboard or mouse

Keyboard or Mouse Connector: PS/2

The original AT motherboards used two types of connectors for keyboard cables: either a five-pin DIN, or a six-pin mini-DIN. The bigger five-pin connector, known as an AT connector, gave way to the smaller PS/2 connector developed by IBM. Eventually, AT keyboards switched to the PS/2 style connector, and until

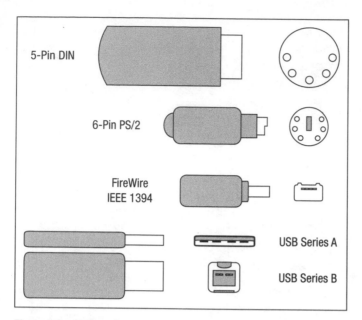

Figure 9.3 Keyboard, mouse, and USB connectors.

recently, both keyboards and mice routinely used the smaller connector. Today's motherboards often come with two PS/2 connectors and two USB connectors. In Figure 9.3, you can see the relative size differences between the AT DIN connectors and PS/2 connectors, along with the different shape of USB and FireWire cable ends.

 The difference in all these connectors is in both the number of pins and their shape. Keep in mind that the keyboard/mouse connection is often still configured as a COM port, even though it's installed as a PS/2 connector.

If a motherboard does not have serial ports available or a direct motherboard mouse port, you can install a mouse that uses an expansion slot. This might be necessary when older software is using both COM1 and COM2; the mouse then has to be configured to COM3 or COM4. A mouse using an expansion slot of its own is generally referred to as a *bus mouse*.

Network Cables and Connectors

We said that the wires around a computer can be sorted by groups, depending on their connectors. Networking wire can also be sorted by groups, but in this case, the grouping is more often the physical structure of the wire and/or the transmission rate for data. The three groups we discuss here are coaxial cable, twisted pair, and fiber optics. We also touch on wireless networking, which doesn't use wire (obviously).

Coaxial Cable

The first coaxial (coax) cable was quite thick and heavy, and was standardized at *10Base5* Ethernet (Thicknet). Breaking this down, it means that 10 megabits can travel across a baseband piece of cable to a maximum distance of 500 meters (i.e., the "5" x 100), or approximately 1,500 feet. This naming convention continued forward, so remember megabits per second (Mbps) + "Base" + distance (in hundreds of meters the signal can travel).

Originally, each terminal connected to a 10Base5 cable with a *tap* (sometimes called a *vampire tap*). These connectors ($65 to $95 apiece) look like tiny jaws with a pair of long, sharp teeth. The teeth drive right through the insulation and into the core wire.

Thicknet gave way to a thinner wire called 10Base2 (Thinnet). The reduced thickness was easier to handle, but meant a subsequent reduction in the maximum transmission distance. Although the wire could still move a single 10Mbps baseband signal, the maximum distance dropped to 200 meters (approximately 600 feet). Taps gave way to the bayonet nut connectors (BNCs), and terminal connectors or *T-connectors* ($1 to $3 apiece).

Note: Both 10Base5 and 10Base2 require terminators at the end of the cable. If the cable breaks or a terminator isn't installed, the entire network can perform erratically and fail.

Twisted Pair

Because of cable-length limits and the difficulty of installing stiff coax cable, most Ethernet networks today use a type of wire called 10BaseT. The "T" in 10BaseT stands for twisted-pair wiring, which is exactly what it sounds like—pairs of wires twisted together. Twisted-pair cables are short and connect several terminals to a hub.

Wire carries some amount of electricity, and in this case, carries fragile data signals made up of fractional changes of voltage and frequencies. We've spoken of electromagnetic interference (EMI) and electrostatic discharge (ESD), and the first level of defense against them is the insulation around the metal core of a wire. That core can be many thin strands braided together, or it can be solid metal. The insulation wraps around the outer layer of the wire, but between the insulation and the core, we can put a second line of defense called *shielding*. Shielding is a braided metal or foil that, together with an underlying insulator, wraps around a conductive material and intercepts radio and electromagnetic energy.

10BaseT cable comes in two basic groups: Shielded Twisted Pair (STP) and Unshielded Twisted Pair (UTP). Both are still 10Mbps baseband cable, but UTP uses four pairs of wire (eight wires), where each wire spirals around its partner and then all four pairs are twisted together. Unshielded Twisted Pair is frequently used in both the telecommunications (telco) industry and the computer industry. If we're speaking of telephone wire, we'll usually say twisted pair. To distinguish the same wire in networks and data transmission, we'll use 10BaseT.

Note: A so-called drop ceiling (acoustical tile suspended on a frame), also called a plenum-type ceiling, allows air to circulate. Twisted-pair wire can have regular insulation or Teflon insulation. Regular insulation gives off toxic fumes when it burns, so the U.S. Fire and Safety Code requires Teflon insulation for all plenum ceiling installations. Therefore twisted-pair wire comes in either plenum-type or nonplenum.

Twisted-Pair Categories

We use five *categories* to distinguish the gradation in quality (grade) of what looks like the same wire. Category 1, 2, and 3 (C1, C2, and C3) are used almost exclusively for analog telephone signals. Category 4 (C4) is good enough for digital data signals and can be used in either industry. C4 introduces some errors, but Category 5 (C5) is data grade wiring. C5 wiring is used almost always in networking situations where reliable data transmission is required.

Wiring Problems

UTP 10BaseT wiring pairs are not connected in a pins 1 to 8 series. Rather, the first pair connects to pins 1 and 2, while the second pair connects to pin 3 and 6. This "skipping" is used to maintain better data integrity. Cross-wiring the pairs to the wrong pins produces an unusable cable, or *patch cord.*

Two standards for wiring are used within a building where patch cords connect to the wiring inside the walls. Northern Telecommunication, Inc. created the 568-A standard, and American Telephone and Telegraph (AT&T) created the 568-B standard. The difference between the two standards is in the pairs that are used to transmit data after the signal reaches the wall. Because the standards are incompatible, only one may be used throughout the installation site.

RJ-45 Modular Connectors

At the end of a C5 patch cable, you'll find two *modular connectors* that look very much like the RJ-45 connectors used for phone cords. However, data modular connector plugs are wider than RJ-11 four-wire phone connectors and designed to a much higher specification, using gold contacts to eliminate tarnish. RJ-45 data connectors are more expensive (55 to 80 cents) than phone connectors (8 to 10 cents), and low-bidding network installers sometimes use the RJ-45 phone connectors to cut costs. The only way to tell the two connectors apart is either with a testing machine or by observing whether, in six months, the connectors have tarnished. Tarnished connectors cause increasing network crashes.

Twisted-pair wiring generally uses stranded core for patch cables connecting a device to the wall, or a device to another device. Stranded-core wire is flexible and more "forgiving" than solid-core wire. "Forgiving" means a more relaxed tolerance, where signals don't have to be as exact. Solid wire is more efficient at transferring data, but is stiffer and harder to work with. Solid-core twisted pair is usually used for the wiring inside the walls.

Shielded Twisted Pair (STP)

STP 10BaseT, used mostly in token ring networks, uses an expensive IBM data connector. Each pair of wires is twisted and then shielded with foil. After the individually shielded pairs are twisted together, more foil wraps all four pairs. Finally, insulation is wrapped around the outer shielding.

Fiber Optic

Fiber optic cable (or simply *fiber*) is a bundle of glass fiber optic tubes, each wrapped in a plastic shield, with the bundle wrapped in an outer jacket. It looks like wire, but conducts light, not electricity. "Long-haul" fiber optic uses a laser beam as the light source, which has a very low *skew* factor and stays coherent (straight line) over longer distances than light-emitting diodes (LEDs). The two main types of fiber optic cable are:

➤ *Single mode*—Uses a laser source and can travel 22 kilometers (km) before requiring a repeater. Its transmission path is 5 microns wide.

➤ *Multimode*—Uses an LED source and can travel only 6 km. Its transmission path is 62 microns wide.

A fiber optics communication path requires two fibers. Light is unidirectional, meaning that one beam can send (transmit) information, but another beam must return (receive) information. Synchronous Optical NETwork (SONET) is a protocol based on multiples of a *base rate* of 51.84Mbps—called Optical Carrier (OC)-1—going up to 9.6 gigabits per second (Gbps) (OC-192). Typically, fiber optic cable runs in excess of 10 times the speed of its copper counterpart.

As is true of optical disks, dirt smudges and other interference can stop the transmissions. Although some people think a fiber cable cannot be repaired, this isn't true. A break can be fixed using a *fusion splicer*, and certain instruments can tell a technician how far away a break has occurred.

Wireless Networking

A wireless network uses radio frequencies and has been finalized as IEEE 802.11. A device uses an *access point* (bridge) and a network interface card with a transmitter and receiver. Often, these NICs are very small and can fit on a PC card.

Signals move at 11Mbps and can typically travel 100 to 200 yards. Special antennas can extend the transmission distances to more than a mile (used in corporate networking).

Infrared wireless uses light frequencies and also works with a transmitter and receiver. A wireless mouse uses this technology, as do common television remote controls. The transmitter and receiver are often built into modern motherboards and devices, using a small plastic window to radiate the infrared light. Infrared Data Association (IrDA) specifications indicate that data can be transmitted from 0 to 3.3 yards. Speeds range from .9 to 1.1Mpbs.

Practice Questions

Question 1

A DB25 _____ connector is used to connect the _____ port to a printer.

○ a. male, COM

○ b. female, COM

○ c. female, LPT

○ d. male, LPT

Answer d is correct. The "25" in DB25 references the number of pins on the cable connector or back panel connector. When the cable has 25 pins, it fits into an LPT socket with 25 holes and is called a DB25 parallel cable. This question is ambiguous because the connector can refer to the cable connector or the back panel connector. In such instances, we believe that CompTIA will always mean the cable connector.

Question 2

A modem connects to the serial COM2 port using a _____ connector.

○ a. DB15

○ b. DB9

○ c. Centronics

○ d. DB25

Answer b is correct. The COM port serial cables use a nine-pin connector. Video connectors are usually 15-pin connectors, and the Centronics connector is used to connect a 25-pin DB25 to a printer at the printer end.

Question 3

Which of the following designations do not apply to parallel interfaces?
[Choose the two best answers]

❑ a. ECP

❑ b. EPP

❑ c. ECC

❑ d. UTP

Answers c and d are correct. Answer c is correct because ECC is a type of parity and does not apply to parallel interfaces. Answer d is correct because UTP is a type of twisted-pair wiring (unshielded) and does not apply to the parallel interface. Answer a is incorrect because ECP is the Extend Capabilities Port. Answer b is incorrect because EPP is the Enhanced Parallel Port.

Question 4

A Centronics printer cable uses a _____ pin connector, and a typical SCSI-2 cable uses a _____ pin connector.

○ a. 25, 36

○ b. 36, 50

○ c. 50, 25

○ d. 25, 9

Answer b is correct. A Centronics cable is a 36-pin connector, and a SCSI cable is usually a 50-pin mini D-shell connector. Parallel cables are 25 pins, and serial cables are 9 pins. You'll have to remember these in whatever fashion suits you.

Question 5

10Base2 Ethernet coaxial cable is sometimes referred to as _____ and has a distance limit of _____ meters.

○ a. Thinnet, 200

○ b. Thinnet, 500

○ c. Thicknet, 500

○ d. Thicknet, 200

Answer a is correct. 10Base2 Ethernet coaxial cable, sometimes referred to as Thinnet, has a distance limit of 200 meters. 10Base5, the original coaxial cable, was thicker than 10Base2. Thicknet and Thinnet refer to the relative thickness of the cable wire. The 10 refers to the megabits per second transmission rate, and the last number is how many hundreds of meters the signal can travel. 10Base5 is 500 meters, and 10Base2 is 200 meters.

Question 6

In a wireless networking environment, data is transmitted using which medium?

○ a. Infrared light

○ b. Radio frequencies

○ c. SONET protocols

○ d. UTP

Answer b is correct. The clue in the question is both "networking" and "data." Wireless networking is done with radio frequencies. Mice and remote control units use infrared light to transmit simple commands. SONET refers to the Synchronous Optical NETwork protocols used in fiber optics, and UTP is Unshielded Twisted Pair wire.

Need to Know More?

 Bigelow, Stephen. *Easy Laser Printer Maintenance and Repair.* New York, NY: McGraw-Hill, 1995. ISBN 0-07-035976-8. This book, which contains more information than you need for the exam, is a great reference for technicians.

 Bigelow, Stephen. *Troubleshooting, Maintaining, and Repairing Personal Computers: A Technical Guide.* New York, NY: TAB Books, 1995. ISBN 0-07-912099-7. Detailed information from a break-fix standpoint for displays; LCD panels; and dot matrix, ink jet, and laser printers.

 Messmer, Hans-Peter. *The Indispensable PC Hardware Book.* Reading, MA: Addison-Wesley, 1995. ISBN 0-201-87697-3. This book contains much information, in great detail, about monitors and displays.

 Minasi, Mark. *The Complete PC Upgrade and Maintenance Guide.* San Francisco, CA: Sybex Network Press, 1996. ISBN 0-7821-1956-5. This resource is a great source of information on peripherals from a repair standpoint.

 Reeves, Scott, Kalinda Reeves, Stephen Weese, and Christopher S. Geyer. *A+ Exam Prep, 3rd Edition.* Scottsdale, AZ: The Coriolis Group, 2001. ISBN 1-57610-699-3. This is a good reference that concentrates on providing exam-required information.

 Rosch, Winn. *Hardware Bible.* Indianapolis, IN: Sams Publishing, 1994. ISBN 0-672-30954-8. This book contains everything you'd want to know about computer hardware.

DOS

Terms you'll need to understand:

✓ Command interpreter, command line, switch

✓ Environment memory

✓ Search path, parent and child directories

✓ File allocation table (FAT)

✓ File fragmentation (DEFRAG.EXE)

✓ Hidden and system file attributes (ATTRIB.EXE)

✓ Wild cards, variables

✓ Shells

Concepts you'll need to master:

✓ Command interpreters and operating system kernels

✓ Partitions and logical drives versus physical disks (FDISK.EXE)

✓ Directories (folders) and subdirectories (subfolders)

✓ File systems, file management, file names

✓ Tracks, sectors, and clusters (SCANDISK.EXE)

✓ File searches (**DIR**)

✓ Operating systems versus shells

DOS is so old it has whiskers, so why are we reading this stuff? Three answers come to mind:

➤ Windows 3.x, 9x, and ME all start by loading the files IO.SYS and MSDOS.SYS, which are DOS files.

➤ Many of the key troubleshooting utilities you will be using for network and PC diagnostics are based on DOS.

➤ The scope of the operating systems covered in A+ is so broad that you cannot memorize all of the variations. The best way to gain a sense of how these systems operate is to understand how they developed.

So do not skip this chapter! This one and the next are two of the most important chapters in the book. On the current market, we now have machines running Windows 3.11, Windows 95, Windows 98, Windows ME, Windows 2000, and Windows NT. DOS is still around, and some machines use IBM's Operating System 2 (OS/2). Unix (commercial) is an operating system, although Linux (free) is gradually developing a powerful market presence.

There's no doubt that if you want to understand how Windows evolved, you must know something about DOS. If you understand how Windows developed as a graphical user interface (GUI), then you'll be able to focus on the differences in 32-bit Windows.

For that reason, we refer to DOS and Windows 3.x as a 16-bit concept. We refer to Windows 9x—which includes Windows 95, 98, and ME—along with Windows 2000 and Windows NT, as a 32-bit concept. Windows 9x actually fits into both categories. The overall division is between 16-bit (Chapter 11) and 32-bit Windows (Chapters 12 and 13). Yes, this seems complicated at first, but when you've seen the essential differences, you'll understand the basis for the groupings.

Operating Systems

A software *program* is a set of instructions put together in an organized way that tells a microprocessor what to do. When a program is written in English, a human being can understand it. A *programming language* is a special way of using human language so that the instructions written by the *developer* (programmer) can later be turned into *machine language*—that is, compiled. COBOL, Basic, FORTRAN, Pascal, C++, and Assembler are examples of some of the programming languages.

We usually divide software programs into two categories: operating systems and applications. *Applications* are groups of program files that make up a tool of some kind and that create user data (files). Human beings use application tools to produce documents, spreadsheets, databases, mailing lists, new airplane designs, virtual realities,

---

Compilers and Machine Language

What are compilers? Programs must spell out, in excruciating detail, every single instruction to the microprocessor. No matter how short a speech-based language might be, it still takes far too much space to write even a simple program. Therefore, computer languages use shorthand words to cram as much information as possible into the smallest amount of space. "Move" becomes **MOV**, "jump to" becomes **JMP**, "delete" or "erase" becomes **DEL**, "remove directory" becomes **RD**, "list a directory of files" becomes **DIR**, and so on.

After a program has been written so that a human being can understand it, the result can be reduced even further into something that a machine can understand— machine language. Machine language is composed entirely of 1s and 0s. The process of final reduction is called compiling the program. After the program has been compiled (using a separate application called a compiler), the instructions are run as fast as possible. Compiled (binary) programs in DOS have one of two extensions: .COM (command program) or .EXE (executable program).

Batch programs, with .BAT extensions, are not compiled and are entered as plain English lists of commands. AUTOEXEC.BAT is a batch file, and the name is a reserved name used from within COMMAND.COM.

---

and test scenarios (simulations), to name a few. America Online is an application, as are the component applications (pieces) that make up Microsoft Office. In many cases, smaller programs have been created for the purposes of augmenting the primary programs that make up an operating system. These kinds of tools are called *utilities*. ScanDisk, Defrag, SYSEDIT, and HwDiag are examples of utilities.

DOS

We believe that you'll find it easier to remember some of the details of DOS if you have a mental picture of how it came into existence. The history of DOS is somewhat hazy because of the amounts of money and the various egos that have been involved, but this section should give you a good idea of how it all came about.

A long time ago, in a place far away, a young girl suggested to her father that a new toy for electronics hobbyists should be called the Altair, after a star system named in a *Star Trek* episode. The Altair, released in 1970, was based on the Intel 8080 chip and was the first computer a person could take home. It had 256 bytes of memory, could hold about four lines of text instructions, and was operated by flipping switches on and off. Even though it had no keyboard, Bill Gates and Paul Allen were fascinated with it and spent long nights writing a version of

Beginner's All-purpose Symbolic Instruction Code (Basic), a computer language that would work with the Altair. They called it Altair Basic.

Note: When a switch was flipped to either on or off, the computer circuitry could use that information in some way. A series of switches taken together could form a binary number. When the computer looked at a number of switches to find a number, they were called the first registers. Registers have now become very small transistors on a microprocessor, and they continue to store binary numbers.

Gates decided that Altair Basic should have some sort of *file management* and disk storage capability, so he upgraded the original system. This was the first conceptual hint of the File Manager, which went on to become Windows Explorer. Gates's and Allen's interest in operating languages and their belief that microprocessors would change the world led them to incorporate Microsoft in 1975 (to market a traffic-counting machine) and—as early as 1976—to start complaining about software piracy. At the time, software was stored on cards by punching holes in them.

CP/M

The Intel 8080 processor found its way into another computer called the Imsai 8080, which came with a floppy drive and was targeted at small businesses. The floppy drive circuitry was controlled by an operating system called CP/M, designed by Gary Kildall.

Kildall was working for a company called Intergalactic Digital Research and wanted a scaled-down language that would work with microprocessors rather than mainframe computers. Perhaps because of a government coverup or something else, the company eventually dropped "Intergalactic," leaving only the name Digital Research. Intel didn't think there was much use for CP/M, so it granted Kildall full rights to it. Features of CP/M included the following:

➤ Used only 4KB of memory space.

➤ Introduced a 64KB command file and used a dot (period) plus three-letter (.COM) *extension* to signify the type of file. (COM files, short for COMmand files, still have a maximum size of 64KB.)

➤ Used a command interpreter, or command processor program, called CCP (short for console command processor).

➤ Used two fundamental files called Basic DOS (BDOS) and BIOS to handle files and I/O processing.

Apple

Back in 1974, the most popular microprocessors were the Intel 8080 and the Motorola 6800. One of the 6800's inventors, Chuck Peddle, quit Motorola in 1975 and started a new company called MOS Technologies. MOS began manufacturing the 6501 microprocessor, which resembled Motorola's 6800. In 1976, Steve Wozniak and Steve Jobs took some MOS 6502 chips and built the first Apple computers—the Apple I.

At the time, Charles Tandy, who had been unsuccessful buying Imsai computers, created his own Tandy TRS-80 product line based on another chip—the Zilog Z-80. Both the TRS-80 and the Apple I computers came fully assembled and, to help keep costs down, used only uppercase letters. Neither Radio Shack nor Apple Corporation could keep the computers in stock. An immediate problem that began to crop up between the Apple and the CP/M systems was that:

➤ Operating systems don't necessarily work on all microchips.

➤ The Apple MOS-6502 was an 8-bit processor and couldn't run CP/M.

The Apple II model upgrade added an optional floppy drive and ran a program called VisiCalc—the first real spreadsheet application—created by Dan Bricklin, Dan Fylstra, and Bob Frankston. Businesses could use small PCs to create spreadsheets, and suddenly the PC market came alive. Meanwhile, Gates and Allen were writing Basic and other programming languages that worked on Intel and Zilog chips. Eventually, Apple turned away from the MOS chips and went to Motorola chips.

CP/M was a hot programming language, and some very exciting software applications based on the language were arriving on the market. However, these programs would run only on Intel and Zilog chips. Therefore, rather than spend the long hours necessary to translate Basic into a form that would work with the Apple computers, Gates and Allen chose to license CP/M from Kildall. They began selling CP/M, along with an add-on board that had a Zilog chip, so that Apple customers could put the Microsoft card into their computers and run CP/M-based programs.

86-DOS

Meanwhile, in Seattle, Tim Patterson was making motherboards for a company called Seattle Computer Products. Intel had just produced its first 16-bit 8086 chip, and Patterson needed a 16-bit operating system to go with the 8086. Kildall was saying that he would soon be finished with the CP/M-86 (the first vaporware). Patterson decided that he couldn't wait, so he wrote his own operating system.

In 1980, Patterson created a quick and dirty operating system (QDOS). QDOS soon became 86-DOS (for the 8086 processor), then SCP-DOS (after the company), and then simply the disk operating system (DOS).

To simplify matters for the growing number of programmers who were writing for the CP/M operating system, Patterson kept the basic CP/M file management structure, the way CP/M looked, and the way it loaded itself and programs into memory. This compatibility is often referred to as the "look and feel" of an operating system. Along the way, he added something called a file allocation table (FAT), which he found in Gates's Altair Basic.

Keep another eye on the FAT, because it too carried all the way into Windows 9x. FAT32 and all the other file management systems started here.

PC-DOS

At about the same time, in 1980, IBM approached Microsoft about a possible 8-bit PC (microcomputer) that IBM was considering manufacturing. IBM was making mainframes for the most part and looked to young Microsoft as one of the leading (if not only) businesses creating computer languages for microcomputers. IBM thought that PCs were mainly a passing hobby, but Gates and Allen were convinced that the microprocessor and the so-called *personal* computer would change the world. They convinced IBM to change its design to a 16-bit processor, and when IBM asked who had a 16-bit operating system, Gates is said to have replied "Gary Kildall." At that point, history gets a bit fuzzy, but somehow Kildall either wasn't available or chose not to sell IBM the rights to CP/M.

Gates and Allen purchased Patterson's 86-DOS for around $50,000 and suggested to IBM that Microsoft become the vendor for Basic, FORTRAN, Pascal, COBOL, and the 8086 Assembly language. They also proposed to license 86-DOS to IBM as the operating system for IBM's new PC. IBM agreed (another historical blunder), and in 1981, released the first personal computer with Microsoft's DOS 1.0, which IBM called PC-DOS. (Patterson became successful in his own right and eventually went to work for Microsoft.) It wasn't until the release of DOS 5.0 that Microsoft finally started selling its own generic version of MS-DOS on the open market.

PCs using IBM's PC-DOS still continued to use COMMAND.COM (the command interpreter), along with IBMDOS.COM and IBMBIO.COM. PCs using Microsoft's MS-DOS went on to use the COMMAND.COM interpreter, and changed the two other system files to IO.SYS and MSDOS.SYS.

Keep an eye on MSDOS.SYS, because it carried through all the way into Windows 98 and Windows ME.

CP/M into DOS

Without applications, few people would be interested in computers. At the time of the first IBM PC, the most popular applications were dBase II and WordStar, both of which ran on CP/M. Because IBM didn't have much in the way of interesting software, it pushed very strongly to make DOS similar enough to CP/M that it could run those other applications. Among the changes that DOS brought to CP/M were the following:

➤ Variable record lengths

➤ Large EXEcutable (EXE) format files, along with smaller 64KB CP/M-style COM files

➤ Terminate and stay resident (TSR) programs that could end (terminate), but stay (reside) in memory and snap back onto the screen without reloading

➤ A FAT, which could keep track of all the pieces of files on a disk

➤ The ability to use device names to perform I/O operations on peripheral devices (e.g., screens and printers) the same way that it worked with files

*Note: Even today, we can use the DOS **COPY** command to copy a file to the screen (CONsole) and show the results on the monitor (**COPY CON FILENAME.TXT**). Likewise, we can copy a file to a printer and have the hardware device produce a printed output (**COPY FILENAME.TXT PRN**).*

DOS kept the CP/M-style file names of eight characters, followed by a period, then a three-character extension. DOS also kept the C> prompt format at the command line. Compatibility also meant keeping the CP/M-style file control blocks (FCBs), program segment prefixes (PSPs), and the way in which CP/M used memory addresses for loading.

Note: Although it may appear that Windows bears little resemblance to DOS, the continued use of the C:\ annotation for the root directory (folder) of drive C: traces all the way back to CP/M.

DOS also kept the CP/M representation of a directory as a *dot* and the parent directory (the directory one step above) as two dots, or *dot-dot*. We discuss the two dots in more detail later in this chapter when we look at *directories* and *subdirectories*, which are exactly the same as *folders* and *subfolders*. DOS also introduced the ability to use a specially reserved extension for files that contained plain English scripts that a user could write. These special *batch files*, with the .BAT extension, use rudimentary reserved words and need not be compiled into machine language.

MS-DOS and PC-DOS

Beginning with the release of DOS 5.0, two versions of DOS were sold in the consumer market: the IBM version and the Microsoft version—PC-DOS and MS-DOS, respectively. Any DOS questions on the exam will use the MS-DOS version.

> The **VER** command (internal) is used to discover which version of DOS is running on a PC. At the command prompt, type "VER" and press Enter. The screen returns the version number and tells you whether the computer is using PC-DOS or MS-DOS (or some other variation). This command continues into all versions of Windows, although you must go to a command prompt to run it.

A fundamental difference between the IBM and the Microsoft versions of DOS is that they use two system files with different names. MS-DOS uses IO.SYS and MSDOS.SYS, and PC-DOS uses IBMBIO.COM and IBMDOS.COM.

> IO.SYS and MSDOS.SYS are the two hidden system files that combine with COMMAND.COM (not hidden) to form the fundamental DOS operating system.

From DOS to Windows 9x

Windows 3.0, 3.1, 3.11, and Windows for Workgroups (3.11) are *not* operating systems. Windows is a GUI using a *shell*, which, theoretically, makes the daily operation of an IBM-compatible computer somewhat easier than using the DOS command line. However, Windows 3.x and Windows 9x still require DOS to run.

The release of Windows 95 included DOS 7.0, which made a real break from all prior DOS versions. Windows 95 isn't a true operating system either, but more of a hybrid of DOS and Microsoft's New Technology (NT). Nevertheless, many people have accepted Microsoft's claim that Windows 9x is an operating system. Windows 2000 narrowed the gap between DOS and Windows NT.

The Command Interpreter

An operating system includes many individual component programs that tell a computer how to work with all of its parts. Therefore, either an operating system (OS) or an OS kernel makes all the computer hardware work. Applications are designed for human beings to use the computer. The point where human beings meet the operating system is the *user interface*. DOS is a *text-based* interface in that you type words and letters. Windows is a *graphical* user interface, in that you use representational graphics.

CompTIA proposes that an operating system (software) is made up of two things: a *command interpreter* that works with program and system files, and a *user interface* that allows a human being to instruct the command interpreter what to do. In our opinion, an operating system requires a file system and several other critical components, but we'll focus your attention on what CompTIA calls an operating system.

For the exam, remember that an operating system may be referred to as three components: system files, a command interpreter, and a user interface.

When you issue a *command*, you're using one of the operating system program files to gather computer-related instructions and apply them to the components making up the system. A command is somewhat different than a program in that the command is what a user types (often a program file's name) onto a command line. A program is the set of instructions the computer actually uses to execute a sequence of events. A command is usually word(s) of some kind (**FORMAT A:**) as opposed to a program, which is a file (FORMAT.COM).

Note: A computer can only do exactly what it's told to do. A human being creates every single detail of what a computer knows how to do. The human being using a computer is either a programmer or an operator. An operator relies on what the programmer told the computer to do by using special instructions built into a program. Those special instructions are the commands.

FORMAT.COM and FDISK.EXE are command programs, whereas REGEDIT.EXE is more of a *utility* program designed for the specific purpose of editing a Windows Registry (sometimes called the system registration). WP.EXE is an *application* program that runs a word processor and borrows part of the operating system whenever it copies a paragraph or file from one place to another.

After you've issued a command through the interface, the next part of an operating system is the *command interpreter* (also a program). With so many separate files making up an operating system, there must be an oversight manager of some kind to distinguish a letter you're typing to your mother from a *string* (line or group) of characters you're typing to instruct the computer to do something. COMMAND.COM is the DOS command interpreter, which is also used by both Windows 3.x and 9x to control the computer.

COMMAND.COM continues to open a so-called Windows 2000 DOS window in Windows 2000. This can be done by selecting the Start|Run option and typing "COMMAND". However, a command line is now run from a program file called CMD.EXE and generates a command line window. Note that depending on which of these options you choose, you get different results. (When you are in DOS, remember to type "EXIT" and press Enter to return to Windows.)

COMMAND.COM includes a number of *internal commands* and instructions on how to use *batch files*. Some examples of internal commands are **COPY**, **DEL**, **DIR**, and **ECHO**. *External commands* are the many other program files included in the overall operating system. Examples of external commands in DOS include **ATTRIB**, **FDISK**, **SCANDISK**, or **DEFRAG**.

The command interpreter literally interprets keyboard or mouse input and makes decisions as to whether to change the computer or pass the input on to an application program.

Keep in mind that in an open operating system, the command interpreter is directly associated with a number of low-level system files. DOS uses two critical system files and keeps them hidden from the casual user. There is a specific attribute assigned to system (S) files, and SYS.COM is a utility command written to specifically operate on those system files. (We'll discuss SYS.COM in a moment, and ATTRIB.EXE at the end of this chapter.)

Running a Program

One of the fundamental (and often confusing) principles of using a computer is the idea that a program "loads" into memory in order to "run." Running a file is when the system executes the instructions contained in a program. Program files are a way to store instructions on a computer without needing a constant supply of power. We've seen how RAM loses data when the power is turned off, and we've also seen how disks store data without requiring a constant power supply.

Note: Windows NT uses the word initialize to distinguish between loading a device driver and running it at a later time.

A program is *executed* (run) either when we type something on a command line (and press Enter) or when another program *calls* (programming word) the first program. Upon execution, the instructions that the computer needs at any given moment are *copied* (not moved) into memory from the program file. This is what we mean by loading a file. The original file remains stored on the disk, untouched and unchanged unless certain instructions make a change to the stored file.

Note: Viruses often copy themselves into RAM and use programming instructions to change the original file on the disk. Understand that the file itself doesn't go into memory, but that a copy of the programmed instructions goes into memory.

The entire process of saving data on a computer revolves around the basic fact that data is always changed in memory, but the changes are only retained if the data is stored back to a storage media of some kind (for example, a disk). Memory is not the same thing as storage, even though many novices use the terms interchangeably.

Error Messages

People sometimes forget that a computer doesn't have a conceptual mind, and it can't actually harbor a grudge or get angry—at least not yet. Everything that happens on a computer is created by a human being. When something goes wrong, a message of some kind might show on the screen. That message isn't simply a casual expletive that the computer thought up on the spur of the moment.

The actual text of the error messages must not only be written into a program, but it also ought to have a connection to an event. Connecting an error message to an event is sometimes called *trapping* an error in a program. The programmer uses what's called an **IF...THEN** logic statement to display an error message on the screen.

For instance, the following statement might be used to trap for a missing file error: **IF** *filename* X on the command line doesn't match *filename* X in the directory allocation table (DAT), **THEN** type the message "File not found" to the screen.

Error message text on the screen can often be either misleading or completely wrong in terms of the error being reported. The text itself is not the computer scratching its head and dreaming up a statement, but rather a specific line of text that a programmer told the operating system to write to the screen when an explicit set of circumstances occurs. (A proposed error message we've seen recently as a candidate to be written into the Windows interface is "Closing current Windows session. Would you like to begin another game?")

The "Any Key" (PAUSE)

The most common way to allow time for a user to read an error message entered on the screen is to temporarily *pause* the screen until the user provides further input. Remember that the keyboard processor is constantly scanning the keyboard for status changes and key-press activity. When the error message reads, "Press any key to continue," it literally means that you can press any key on the keyboard. The most common keys to press are the spacebar, the Enter key, or the ESCape (ESC) key. In DOS, one of the internal batch file commands is **PAUSE**.

COMMAND.COM

DOS is really a package of many programs and utilities that take up a lot of space in a default directory called C:\DOS (C:\WINDOWS\COMMAND in Windows 9x). When we talk about DOS, we're referring to the whole package and all the various subprograms. However, the essence of the operating system is the command interpreter and the two hidden *system files* that handle basic I/O.

One of the ways we'll be tracking the gradual elimination of DOS and the evolution of Windows into a true operating system is by keeping tabs on what happened to the system files and the use of an OS kernel. Even in Windows 2000, a file called COMMAND.COM is still installed on the hard drive. Opening a DOS window with this file produces a notice that you are now running Windows 2000 DOS.

COMMAND.COM is usually loaded into RAM when a computer boots up, and parts of it stay in RAM during the session (the time during which the computer is turned on). COMMAND.COM uses a number of routines almost constantly, and they can be accessed faster if those parts of the program stay in fast RAM. The parts of the interpreter that stay in memory are called the *resident* parts. The parts of COMMAND.COM that move back and forth between the disk and memory are called the *transient* parts.

When a computer is running, we call that a session. Windows opens up a DOS session as a virtual machine. Keep an eye on how a real machine works, because you'll have a lot easier time understanding what Windows is doing when you run a 16-bit application under Windows 2000.

The DOS Command Line

Being text-based, DOS uses a series of letters entered in a row as commands. These character strings contain *reserved words*, which are the starting points for a set of instructions that command the computer to do something. An example of a reserved word is "copy." An example of a reserved character is the colon (:).

The text that you enter to spell out commands is called a *command line*. The A> or the C> next to a blinking cursor is called the *prompt*, or *DOS prompt*. A blinking cursor that shows you where the next character you enter will appear is the *command prompt*. You type out a character string at the command prompt and press the Enter key. The command interpreter looks at the string you typed and decides what to do about it.

When you enter a command, DOS breaks up the letters, symbols, and numbers into units that match internal patterns of characters. Breaking apart a line of characters into a particular pattern of meaningful pieces is called *parsing* the line. The patterns of characters are commands, and the commands are part of either the DOS system files or a program file.

The DOS prompt is the combination of symbols at the left-most column of a plain screen and the blinking cursor, or *insertion point* of the command prompt. The default prompt is the A> or the C> symbol from CP/M, but you can change the way the prompt looks (with the **PROMPT** command).

As we've seen, a fundamental part of COMMAND.COM is its ability to read a command line and pass the information contained in the characters back to MSDOS.SYS and IO.SYS for processing. If the command line fails to match exact patterns, COMMAND.COM contains a number of error messages that it sends to the screen. Command lines are still an important part of troubleshooting a computer, and although we're speaking here of COMMAND.COM, the concepts also apply to CMD.EXE and the Recovery Console.

Note: The Recovery Console is an administrative tool found in Windows 2000 that essentially provides a way to bring up a nontransient DOS environment. CMD.EXE is transient, meaning that once the program or command you run from this command line terminates, the command window disappears and you're returned to the Desktop.

Switches

A command line uses words, numbers, and symbols to produce specific results. The words represent program files that DOS can find along the search path. Usually, the numbers are variables designed to produce different results, depending on the number. *Switches* are certain symbols that call on variations of the specific command. The important things to remember about switches include the following:

➤ Switches almost always start with a single forward slash (/) and are immediately followed by a letter or a character.

➤ Some programmers use the dash (-) as a switch indicator.

➤ A space separates the command word from the switch.

When you use the DIRectory **(DIR)** command to list the directory, you see the entire directory. However, a 512-file directory will zoom right up off the top of the screen. To make it stop, use one of the following switches:

➤ **DIR /p**—Tells DOS to stop the list every 23 lines, which make up a screen page. ("P" is short for "by the page.")

➤ **DIR** /w—Tells DOS to show the files in a "wide" format (that is, across the screen).

➤ **DIR** /s—Tells DOS to show not only the current directory's files, but also all the files in every subdirectory below the current one.

Switches can often be combined to provide combined variations of any command that supports multiple switches. In the case of **DIR** /s /p, you're asking DOS to show you all the files in this directory and any subdirectories, and also to stop the display every 23 lines until you press any key.

The /? Switch

DOS versions 5 and later include a rudimentary built-in Help feature that acts as a quick reminder of how a command can be used. As far back as version 3, MS-DOS provided a complete help file with an expanded Help feature on how to use commands. PC-DOS didn't include the expanded Help feature until later versions.

At a DOS prompt, you can almost always type "[*command*] /?" to obtain a cheat sheet on how to use that command. For example, **DIR /?** gives you all the switches and a brief explanation of what each does.

Syntax

The dictionary defines *syntax* as "the way words are put together in order to form sentences, clauses, or phrases." A DOS command line is an instruction to DOS to do something, and DOS reads it much like you or I read a sentence.

The conventional standard for listing the syntax of a command is to begin with the command followed by square brackets ([ ]), which enclose each and every possible switch. Italicized words that come after the command usually refer to some additional characters that you're supposed to enter to replace the word. For example, **DIR [d:]** [*path*] [*file name* [*.ext*]] [/P] [/W] [/S] means that the **DIR** command can (but need not) be followed by any of the items listed in square brackets.

The Environment

The environment is an area of memory that DOS keeps aside to store system settings. Because the information being stored changes, we call them environment *variables*. **PROMPT, PATH,** and **COMSPEC** are both environment commands and environment variables. The common way to set the environment variables is with the AUTOEXEC.BAT file. This batch file is discussed in its own section later in this chapter, as well as in Chapter 11.

Variables

A mathematical or computer variable is an interesting device, and one that you already know how to use—you just don't know that you know it. As is often the case, confusion can arise when someone uses a formal word to describe a common event.

Variables are *placeholders* that act as stand-ins for something real that will happen later. You probably took algebra in high school and used the symbol "X" in equations as a variable.

A classroom containing a number of desks is a variable situation. Suppose that 15 desks are in the room. Each semester, those 15 desks sit in the same place. If you were asked what those were, you would say, "Those are desks." However, each semester, 15 students enroll in the class and sit at the desks. The desks are the *variables,* and the students are the *data being held by the variable.*

Depending on which semester it was, if you were asked what those desks were, you would say, "That's Bill's desk" or "That's Sharon's desk." Bill and Sharon are the data being assigned to the variables (desks) at a particular moment in time. The next semester you would point to the same desks and say, "That's Donna's desk" or "That's Phillip's desk."

If you number each desk 1 through 15, you're *naming* the variables. Therefore, a computer programmer could say "Go get the data in '12.' **IF** '12' is empty, **THEN** '**ANSWER**' = 0. **IF** '12' is not empty, **THEN** '**STUDENT**' = '12.'" The number 12 is a variable representing desk number 12, which is either empty or contains a student. **ANSWER** and **STUDENT** are additional variables that also hold information that can change.

By providing the computer with a list of student names and their desk numbers each semester, the computer can tell you whether the desk is empty, whether the student is present, and what the student's name is.

The DOS environment is a small, 256-byte area of memory set aside to store configuration settings for the operating system to use. One way to use up the 256 bytes is by a *path* containing that many characters. Another way is by running several instances of COMMAND.COM at the same time.

16-bit Windows created its own little area of environment memory called *resources*. Windows resources can run out of room just like the DOS environment could run out of room.

SET [*variable*]

The important variables to note are **COMSPEC=**, **PATH=**, **PROMPT=**, and **TMP=**. All of these are set manually, except for **COMSPEC=**, which tells DOS where COMMAND.COM is located. When we say *manually*, we mean either that the user enters a **SET** [*variable*]=[*value*] command at the command line or that the **SET** commands can be listed in the AUTOEXEC.BAT batch file. For instance, **SET Temp=c:\dumb** assigns temporary files to the "dumb" subdirectory in the root of drive C:. Applications will look for a **TEMP** variable in the environment to find the location for their temporary files.

An environment variable can be manually set by typing "SET [*variable name*]=[*value setting*]" at the command line. To change the **PROMPT** variable at any time, type "SET PROMPT=Hello World" at the command line and press Enter. This means that instead of the DOS command line starting with C:\WINDOWS>_, it would start with Hello World_. Typing "PROMPT=$p Hello World$g" and pressing Enter would cause the command line to start with C:\WINDOWS Hello World>_.

To change the search path to only the \Windows and the \Exam directories, type "PATH=C:\WINdows;c:\eXAm" and press Enter. Note that it doesn't matter how you mix uppercase and lowercase letters; DOS will change all the letters to uppercase.

 The **COMSPEC=** environment variable is automatically set by COMMAND.COM during the boot process. The default value for this variable setting will always be the drive containing the boot disk and the name of the command interpreter file (almost always COMMAND.COM).

Both DOS and Windows can work with the environment. COMMAND.COM looks in the environment for a number of variable settings, whereas DOS batch files move information in and out of the environment in a rudimentary programming capability.

 Batch files are plain ASCII text files containing DOS commands on separate lines. Batch files must have a .BAT extension and are considered executable program files. COMMAND.COM contains a number of internal commands that can be used by batch files. Some of the internal commands include **ECHO**, **@**, **ERRORLEVEL**, **PAUSE**, **FOR**, and **IF**.

The exam sometimes refers to COMMAND.COM as a "batch command processor," although the proper name is "command interpreter."

The only time that the **SET** command itself is required is from within a batch file. Otherwise, entering only the variable's name and a DOS character separator is sufficient at the command line. However, it's good practice to always use the **SET** command when changing environment variables. Another example at the command line would be to type "SET PATH=C:\;d:\Utils;E:\windows\ ComMaND". Note again that in the **PATH** variable, the case of the letters is ignored.

 The semicolon is the formal separator used to separate out multiple "requests" (as in requesting different directories in a search path). The equal sign or a space is the formal character separator following a command (in this case, the variable name).

Typing the **SET** command and pressing Enter at a DOS command prompt produces a report of the current settings. For example, a typical environment **SET** report shows the following:

```
TMP=C:\WINDOWS\TEMP
winbootdir=C:\WINDOWS
COMSPEC=C:\COMMAND.COM
WINPMT=$P$G
PROMPT=Type EXIT to$_Return to Windows$_$p$g
PATH=C:\WINDOWS;C:\WINDOWS\COMMAND;C:\;C:\DOS;D:\UTILS;D:\BATCH;
    D:\WINUTILS
```

An interesting property of the DOS environment is that the names of the environment variables are automatically converted to uppercase in all instances. After you've passed the certification exam, you might be interested in researching how the **winbootdir=** and **windir=** variables can show up as lowercase.

PROMPT is a reserved word for an internal DOS command, and it is known as an *environment command* in that it affects the way that DOS looks on the screen when you're not doing anything. The prompt to the left of the blinking cursor simply exists, waiting for you to do something.

PROMPT uses special symbols called *metastrings* in conjunction with the word "prompt". When you type "PROMPT" with a dollar sign ($) and a metastring, DOS sends the information you entered to ANSI.SYS (an auxiliary system file that comes with DOS) and changes the environment. The **PROMPT** command and switches are case insensitive, meaning that you can enter them in uppercase, lowercase, or any combination of the two.

The case-insensitive command **PROMPT=PG** makes the prompt show the default drive, directory, and the > character, C:\DOS>_. The command

PROMPT=Type "EXIT" to$_return to Windows$_pg (without spaces in Windows$_$p$g) produces a three-line prompt at a DOS screen as follows:

```
Type "EXIT" to
return to Windows
C:\DOS>_
```

The = character is used by DOS to signify a space. Therefore, you need not enter it, but it's good practice to use it so that you don't accidentally omit a space. The command **PROMPT=pg** works the same as the command **prompt Pg** because these commands are not case sensitive.

SET TEMP=

Both Windows and DOS applications use a temporary directory to store overflow files, swap files, and other temporary files. DOS and Windows know where to put those files by looking at the **TMP=** or the **TEMP=** setting, respectively.

The temporary directories are not required to be called \TMP or \TEMP. They can be called anything you like and can be located anywhere on any accessible drive. The important thing is that the **SET TEMP=** line of the AUTOEXEC.BAT file places the **TEMP** *variable* in the environment and names the variable's setting. Windows and DOS look for a variable called **TMP** and **TEMP**, respectively, but the directories being used can be any valid directory on any drive accessible to the local machine.

Note: If you have enough RAM, you can locate a temporary directory on a RAM drive (a virtual drive created with the RAMDRIVE.SYS program).

Logical Formatting and Partitions: FDISK

Before we get into this topic, let's make sure we all understand that a physical disk is a bunch of machinery with platters that store magnetic information. Up until now, we've used the word "drive" interchangeably with "disk," but in this segment, it's critical that you understand the difference. A disk is not a logical drive.

In Chapter 6, we said that many people refer to the disk in a mechanical drive as a drive. In this discussion, you must understand that a drive is a logical designation created by an operating system. For instance, a floppy disk is a physical item that you insert into a floppy disk mechanism. For the operating system to recognize the disk, that mechanism is given a symbolic name. DOS and Windows designate a mechanical disk subsystem by the letters A through Z.

A *partition* is an area on a drive. If that area has been formatted by an operating system, it becomes a *logical drive*. Logical drives are assigned both a drive letter and a *volume* name. *Low-level formatting* is where a manufacturer actually magnetizes the tracks on a disk. *Logical formatting* is where an operating system installs its file management system.

 The Installable File System (IFS) in Windows 3.x uses a helper program to load into memory. That helper program is a device loaded through CONFIG.SYS and is called IFSHLP.SYS.

Logical formatting means that some amount of space is set aside on a physical disk (what we've previously called a "hard drive") as a discrete area in which to store data and program files. These areas are the partitions, but they are routinely referred to as *volumes*. Each partition must have a volume name, and after a volume is formatted, it becomes a [logical] *drive*. Effectively, and for the sake of clarity, partition and volume mean the same thing in this section.

Note: The volume name is used to explicitly designate a partition, and is assigned during the FDISK "Create a Partition" procedure. As a safety measure, to avoid accidentally deleting a partition and wiping out any information on that area of the disk, you must enter the volume name of the partition before you delete it. The FORMAT command allows you to create a volume name on a floppy disk. Windows Explorer uses the FORMAT command when you right-click on the floppy drive icon and select Format.

The Windows 9x Explorer will not let you format a hard drive containing files. To partition and format a hard drive, you must use a DOS command line. FORMAT is also one of the commands available in the Windows 2000 Recovery Console.

A physical disk can contain a number of partitions that DOS recognizes as logical drives. Almost all PCs have a physical hard drive (disk) and at least one logical drive (partition). An exception would be a diskless network terminal, from which the hard disk is removed and from which the terminal is booted up with a floppy disk. Microsoft created certain names for the various conceptual areas of a fixed disk as follows:

➤ *Fixed disk drive*—The actual set of platters attached to a drive controller. Disk drives are listed with numbers.

➤ *Partition or logical drive*—An area set aside on a disk for storage. Logical drives are assigned the letters A through Z by the operating system.

➤ *Volume label*—The actual 11-character name of a logical drive.

➤ *Primary partition*—A bootable area of a fixed disk, assigned a drive letter (C:, D:, etc.). Primary partitions may not be subdivided. The maximum number of primary partitions in Windows 9x is three.

➤ *Extended partition*—A nonbootable area of a disk. Extended partitions are not assigned a drive letter. Extended partitions may be subdivided into logical drives, which are then assigned a drive letter.

➤ *Status*—The letter used to show which partition is active (A). The Active partition defines which Primary partition is being used to boot the system.

➤ *Type*—The term used to list either a primary (PRI), extended (EXT), or non-DOS partition.

➤ *System*—The term used to list the type of file system being used. DOS partitions are FAT16. Other types include FAT32, HPFS, and NTFS.

The absolute and technical maximum number of logical drives is 26 (A through Z). However, the A: and B: drive designators are built into DOS, and are always considered floppy disk drives. The letter C is always the first letter assigned to a hard disk, so drive C: is considered the first bootable logical drive (active, primary partition) on a hard disk. That makes three letters being used in almost every situation. A printout of an FDISK information report shows how each word is used:

```
                  Display Partition Information

Current fixed disk drive: 1

Partition  Status   Type   Volume Label  Mbytes  System  Usage
    1        A     Non-DOS                  2               %
    2              Non-DOS                250              24%
C:  3              PRI DOS  W95_5-8-97    300    FAT16    29%
    4              EXT DOS                478              46%

Total disk space is  1030 Mbytes (1 Mbyte = 1048576 bytes)

The Extended DOS Partition contains Logical DOS Drives.
Do you want to display the logical drive information (Y/N)..?[Y]
- - - - - - - - - - - - - - - - - - - - - - - - - - - - - - - - - - -
                  Display Logical DOS Drive Information

Drv Volume Label  Mbytes  System  Usage
D:  ALL-DATA       300    FAT16    63%
E:  DATA           178    FAT16    37%

    Total Extended DOS Partition size is 478 Mbytes
       (1 MByte = 1048576 bytes)
```

In Windows 2000 and Windows NT, the FDISK.EXE program became part of the Computer Management utility. This provides a graphic, interactive way of partitioning a disk, much like the Powerquest Partition Magic utility program.

Primary and Extended Partitions

Partitions are categorized as either *primary* or *extended*. Now here's where it gets tricky. If you have a PC with a fixed disk (hard drive), that means it *must* have a set of platters for storing information. One way or another, a useable computer will boot up from either drive A: or drive C: (or a bootable CD-ROM). That means three letters are taken, because A and B are built into COMMAND.COM, and C is automatically assigned to the fixed disk.

When you lay this all out, it means that a hard "drive" can technically have a maximum of 24 logical drives. To make things even more confusing, a logical drive (in the real world) often refers to either the primary or extended partitions. If you have a primary partition (required to boot a machine) *and* an extended partition, the extended partition can have a maximum of 23 logical drives. The floppy disk drive takes up 2 drive letters, and the primary partition takes up 1 drive letter (A:/B: floppy; C: primary), leaving 23 letters in the alphabet.

Formatting a disk (technically called logical formatting) means that the DOS file system is used to create the FAT, the DAT, and the root directory. Formatting also defines the number and size of clusters on the volume.

Be sure to remember that COMMAND.COM can recognize 24 drives beyond drives A: and B:, but that an extended DOS partition can contain a maximum of only 23 logical drives. Drive C: is almost always a primary partition.

Because the volume (logical drive) might be smaller than the physical disk, the names "volume" and "drive" are not interchangeable with "disk."

You can partition a disk into logical drives or volumes, but you can't partition a drive into logical disks.

The external DOS program used to partition a physical disk is FDISK.EXE. The external DOS program used to format a logical drive is FORMAT.COM. Partitioning a disk completely destroys not only all the data on a disk, but any logical formatting on that disk as well.

LASTDRIVE=

Certain DOS settings are automatically set to a default value. As mentioned previously, this is done in the environment with an environment variable. The DOS environment shell is 256 bytes by default, and the prompt is C> or A> by default. **LASTDRIVE** is the environment variable that contains the last letter of the alphabet you will allow DOS to use to assign recognition to a logical drive. The default number of logical drives is set to five. Drives A: and B: are automatically set as floppy drives, and the first nonremovable disk (drive 0) is set to C:. For example, LASTDRIVE=K increases the number of logical drives that DOS can "see" to 11, with drive K: being the last.

The default setting of five drives for **LASTDRIVE** leaves D: and E: open as additional, available logical drives following drives A:, B:, and C:, which are found on a system with a hard disk.

LASTDRIVE is set in the CONFIG.SYS file in a DOS and Windows 3.x machine. The directive still exists in MSDOS.SYS on a Windows 9x machine (the default is still five drives), but **LASTDRIVE** can be increased in only an optional CONFIG.SYS file.

We said there was a limit to how many logical drives a fixed disk could contain. There's also a limit to the number of logical drives LASTDRIVE will recognize. The reason for the limit of 24 logical drives in this instance is that drives A: and B: always exist in the system, even if they don't physically exist on the PC. There are 26 letters in the alphabet, so 26 minus 2 (A: and B:) leaves 24.

An interesting fact to keep in mind is that Novell uses the default drive F: to search for the LOGIN.EXE command. However, during the installation of the client software, Novell requires that the LASTDRIVE be set to Z: (usually done in a CONFIG.SYS file). Note that whereas drives are always accessed by using the drive letter and a colon, the LASTDRIVE= statement doesn't require a colon, as in LASTDRIVE=K.

LASTDRIVE is an important (though not required) CONFIG.SYS file directive for networks and is important when many partitions exist on a big hard drive. If no line for **LASTDRIVE** exists, DOS assumes that only five logical drives exist on the system.

If a disk is partitioned into 12 logical drives—two primary partitions, and an extended partition with 10 logical partitions—you must create a CONFIG.SYS file (with a text editor) and include the LASTDRIVE=N line. Whether you use DOS, 16-bit Windows, or Windows 9x, the extra drives can be made visible only in a CONFIG.SYS file.

In the 12-drive example, the actual value for LASTDRIVE= can be any letter from N to Z. However, if it appears earlier in the alphabet than N (e.g., L), DOS won't see whatever drives exist that would have had the letters you forgot. In this case, the last drive is N (the fourteenth letter) because A: and B: are the floppy drives; therefore, 12 logical drives exist in addition to the floppies.

SET in AUTOEXEC.BAT

Some of the environment variables are set after the system has booted up. Others are set during the boot-up process (covered in Chapter 11). If the variable controls how COMMAND.COM understands the system, it has to be set in a CONFIG.SYS file, which loads before the command interpreter. **LASTDRIVE** and **SHELL** are examples of these variables, and when they are set in a CONFIG.SYS file, they are called *directives*. Directives do not use the **SET=** prefix.

If a variable applies to a session, it must be set in either the AUTOEXEC.BAT file or from a command line. **PROMPT, PATH,** and **TEMP** can all be changed during an active session. When the variable is set in this fashion, it is called a **SET** command. The **SET=** prefix is required only from within a batch file.

FORMAT.COM

Partitioning a disk tells the operating system only how the disk is divided into potential drive space. No matter which operating system (e.g., DOS, OS/2, or NT) you choose to install on any given partition, you need to set up the partition as a logical drive with some kind of file system. The DOS **FORMAT** command prepares the drive's file system in the following manner:

➤ Creates a boot sector, two copies of the FAT, and the root directory

➤ Performs a low-level check for bad sectors, marking any that it finds as unusable

➤ Provides an optional single-step system files transfer to make a disk bootable

➤ Allows the user to label a disk with a volume name at the end of the **FOR-MAT** process

During a *quick format* (**FORMAT [d:] /Q**), the program changes only the FAT on the disk and tells DOS that every sector on the drive is now available for data. The data still resides on the disk, but DOS has been told that it can write over anything and put a new entry into the FAT. Unconditional formatting (/U) erases data from the entire disk. Safe formatting places a hidden file on a floppy disk, reducing the entire storage area of the disk.

Note: To completely format a disk and have FORMAT.COM examine the entire disk, use the FORMAT [d:] /U switch (for Unconditional).

LABEL.EXE

Oddly enough, a DIR listing (since the time of DOS 1.0) includes a line that states "Volume in Drive X:" and possibly a label of up to 11 characters. However, there was no way to label a disk other than running a format on it and putting the label on at the end. DOS 3.0 introduced the **LABEL** command, which allowed a volume label to be put on a disk without formatting it.

SYS.COM

When a working hard drive suddenly produces an error at boot-up that reads "Non-system disk or disk error. Replace and press any key when ready," it may mean that the system files have become corrupted. It could also mean that someone forgot to take a data floppy out of drive A: when he or she shut down the system the last time. SYS.COM is the first step to try to fix the problem (after you check to see if there's a floppy in the drive).

The boot sector includes the Master Boot Record (MBR). You can't just copy the DOS system files using the **COPY** command because of the specific location of both the files and a special bootstrap loader (discussed in Chapter 11). Additionally, both IO.SYS and MSDOS.SYS are hidden files, and **COPY** won't see them.

SYS.COM is a special DOS program that has one purpose only: to copy the system files to another bootable disk. The destination disk must first have been formatted as a bootable disk. SYS.COM replaces corrupted system files on a hard drive by copying clean versions of the system files from a working, virus-free bootable floppy.

SYS.COM is indicated when a hard drive stops (following the POST) and the message "Bad or missing command interpreter" appears. The command to copy the system files from drive A: (bootable disk) to drive C: (with corrupted files) is **SYS C:** or **SYS A: C:**.

An even more frightening message following the POST is "Non-system disk or disk error" when you're booting from a hard drive. Boot from your emergency boot disk and see whether you can log on to drive C:. If you can, try SYS.COM.

A bootable floppy starts the operating system and provides a way to test for access to the hard drive. If the system boots and you type "C:" and press Enter, you should log on to drive C: regardless of whether that drive is bootable. If you can't log on to drive C:, a more serious problem exists.

Logical Block Addressing (LBA)

When DOS 1.0 was released, the hard drive wasn't available for PCs. Version 2.0 was released partly to support the introduction of the newly developed 10MB and 20MB hard drives. Through version 3.3, the maximum amount of space that DOS could handle was 32MB. Although larger hard disks were available, the only way to use them with DOS was to partition them into logical drives of 32MB or less.

DOS 4.0.1 broke the 32MB barrier, allowing for 256MB partitions. Hard disks were beginning to enter the range of gigabyte capacity and could now be broken up into larger logical drives. When DOS 5.0 finally arrived, it included support for 2GB logical drive partitions. However, the BIOS for the drive controllers in many computers (e.g., the 80486 chip) couldn't always support the large drives.

The original IDE specification handled logical drive space up to 512MB. The IDE controller-addressing model didn't allow addresses large enough to work with larger drives. Logical block addressing (LBA) allowed an older IDE controller to access logical drives up to 8.4GB as long as the computer's ROM BIOS included LBA support.

File Systems

Many people think of day-to-day file management as saving, copying, deleting, moving, and modifying files. For clarity, we'll use the term *maintenance* to mean what a user does with files. We'll use the term *management* to mean fundamental operating system processes.

An operating system must include a file system to make sense of the bits of magnetized coating on a disk. The file system keeps track of where all the parts of files are located; the directories and file names; and the used and unused space on a disk—allocated space and free space, respectively. The file system continually updates the cluster locations of all the parts of a file. When we speak of DOS, we'll use the term "directory." When we speak of Windows, we'll use the term "folder." Both terms mean the same thing, but understanding a directory will show you why a command line uses the Change Directory (**CD**) command.

Note: The Windows 9x Long File Names feature uses the DOS file system to actually store the data on the physical disk. However, Windows controls how the FAT is used.

The original disks were able to store only 160KB of information, and programs and PCs were using only 64KB of RAM at that time. Engineers had to make a decision regarding how much space to set aside on a disk to hold all the information in a file structure (the FAT) as well as the directory allocation table used for the directory structure. They needed to strike a compromise between the expected size of future disks and the amount of space to take away from programs and data files.

DOS was set up to work with 16 bits worth of addresses, allowing for 65,525 clusters. Back then, no one ever imagined that PCs would be important or useful enough to need more than this 32MB of space. The original 16-bit FAT continues to this day, and Windows 9x still relies on it. The FAT32 system is an actual change to the the basic 16-bit file allocation table, and it uses 32-bit addressing along with adjustable cluster sizes. We discuss FAT32 in Chapter 12.

Directories (Folders)

A DOS *directory* is a special type of file. Directories and their subdirectories are used to keep together files having a common purpose—to organize a disk. For example, C:\DOS usually contains all the DOS operating system files, and C:\MSOFFICE contains the files that pertain to Microsoft Office. Today, we speak of folders and subfolders, but many of the routine operations involving running a computer are still linked to the concept of directories.

All files have names. All files also contain data. Commonly, a file contains data, so we use a *directory name* to contain file names. These are fundamental principles of files, and DOS uses one way (the file allocation table) to keep track of the data, and another way (the directory allocation table) to keep track of the file names.

Directory Tree

A directory and all its subdirectories are an example of a hierarchy. The original designers thought it looked like a tree, and the first part of a tree is the root. If you suppose that a *directory tree* looks somewhat like a root system, then smaller and smaller roots *branch* off of a larger root. The left pane of Windows Explorer shows the directory tree, while the right pane shows both the files and the subdirectories contained within a highlighted directory.

The FAT uses one directory—the root directory—as the starting point for all the files on a given drive (volume). The root directory can contain only a limited number of files, including both data and program files and subdirectory names.

The root directory, with its representative backslash (\), is at the top of the tree (level 1). The root directory is still a file, containing both data files and other directory files—subdirectories. When a subdirectory contains files, it becomes a lower level in the hierarchy. Level 2 is represented by an indented line coming down from the root, and there are smaller horizontal lines branching to the right. This stepladder design of lines and branches unfolds when you click on the little + or − sign to the left of a directory name in Explorer.

Every FAT16 volume must have its own root directory on the first track and sector of the active, primary partition. The maximum number of directory entries in the root directory is 512. To have more than 512 file and directory names, you must use at least one subdirectory. Subdirectories can have as many directory entries as there is room on the disk.

An interesting problem on some hard drives occurs when DOS prevents the user from creating a new file. An error message referring to insufficient disk space appears, but the user knows that he or she has a 500MB partition available. This might happen when users have put all their files into the root directory. With no subdirectories, the directory table has run out of room for a new file name and issues the out-of-space error.

Directory Management

To create a directory, DOS uses the command **MD** (Make Directory). To create a directory called "example" branching from the root directory, the command is **MD\EXAMPLE** (note the backslash). To create a directory one level below whichever is the current (default) directory, the command is **MD EXAMPLE** (note the space). In the first example, the backslash explicitly names the root directory as the directory that will contain the new "example" subdirectory.

To delete a directory, the original command was **RD** (Remove Directory). If there were files in the directory, the files had to be removed first (**DEL *.***). Only then could the directory be removed (**RD C:\EXAMPLE**). DOS 6.0 introduced the **DELTREE** command, which could take out a whole directory and all its subdirectories in one step.

To change from one directory to another, DOS used the **CD** (Change Directory) command. Used with an absolute name, **CD** would take you to that exact directory. Used with a space before another directory name, the command would take you down to the next subdirectory from the current location.

Relative Locations

If we all are facing the same direction to begin with and someone yells, "Turn left!", we'll all end up facing the same way. On the other hand, if we're all facing different directions and someone yells the same thing, we'll still be facing different directions. However, no matter how many of us are facing in different directions, if someone yells, "Turn north!", then we'll all end up facing one way (assuming everyone has a compass and understands basic geography).

North, south, east, and west are absolute directions on the planet Earth. No matter which direction you're facing, north is always in a specific direction. Left and right, on the other hand, are relative directions. When someone is talking about "left" or "right", you need to know which way they're facing to determine what absolute direction they're talking about.

If you issue the command **CD\WINDOWS\SYSTEM**, you'll be taken to the root directory (the first backslash) and then moved down through WINDOWS to SYSTEM. However, if you issue the command **CD SYSTEM** (using a space after the **CD**), DOS starts from wherever you are and tries to go down one level to a subdirectory called "System." If you happen to be in the Windows directory, this command will work. If you happen to be in some other directory and there isn't a SYSTEM subfolder in that folder, you'll get a "File(s) not found" error.

*Note: A space after the **CD** command is a relative "down" designation. Before issuing such a command, be sure there is a location to go down to; if there isn't, DOS returns an error message. The **CD..** command always moves up toward the root. Even at the root, DOS will not return an error message.*

Dot and Dot-Dot

The **CD** command (once known as **CHDIR**) is used to change the *default directory* to another directory. The default directory is the directory where COMMAND.COM first looks for any referenced program entered on a command line. If you type "CD" and press Enter, DOS returns the name of the default directory.

If you are logged in to the C:\WINDOWS\SYSTEM directory, you have made that directory the default directory. If you then type "CD.." (two dots in a row), DOS changes the default to the directory immediately above the existing one—the parent directory.

When you type the full pathname to a file, you're giving DOS an absolute name. If you say "Change directories (**CD**) to the C:\WINDOWS\COMMAND directory," DOS knows exactly where that is. On the other hand, you can use what's called the "dot-dot" (..) to tell DOS "**CD** to the next directory up from here." The dot and the dot-dot are still there from CP/M.

From the C:\WINDOWS\SYSTEM directory, you could type the absolute location by issuing the command **CD** <space> **C:\WINDOWS**. This would change the default location to one step above where you are, but it means typing a lot more characters.

 Typing two dots after the **CD** command moves you up one level from where you are, to the parent directory.

The single dot represents "here" to DOS. You can use it as a shortcut with a program command such as **XCOPY** when you want to copy all the files in a single directory of drive A: (floppy disk) to the current directory. Instead of typing out the whole location, you can enter "XCOPY A: ." with the single dot after the A: to tell DOS that you want the files to arrive "here." This is handy if you're copying a lot of files from drive A: to a network location like J:\pdj16\US\station5\1998\edu-work\process\managers\march. In this instance, you can log in to the network location and use the single dot rather than retyping the entire path.

Subdirectories (Subfolders)

Subdirectories are symbolized by the name of the *parent* (containing) directory, followed by a backslash. For instance, in the case of C:\WINDOWS, the parent directory is the root directory of drive C:. The first backslash follows to the right of the drive name. Therefore, WINDOWS is a subdirectory of the root directory.

Note: The DOS indication for "drive" is the colon (:). Therefore, the C drive is written as C:.

C:\WINDOWS\SYSTEM is the name of a subdirectory called SYSTEM. (It could also be the name of a file called System.) The SYSTEM subdirectory is under its parent, the WINDOWS directory. WINDOWS is under the root directory.

Directory or File Name?

In the name C:\WINDOWS\SYSTEM, "SYSTEM" can be either a file name or a subdirectory name. The last name in a path, or complete file and directory listing, is somewhat ambiguous. You can see this uncertainty when using the **XCOPY** command to copy a series of files to a different subdirectory. **XCOPY** asks you whether you want the destination to be a file or a directory.

Even though subdirectories can have an extension, convention has it that file names use from one- to three-character extensions, whereas subdirectories stay with just the eight main characters of typical file names. This helps keep subdirectories and files separate. Additionally, because subdirectories are files (albeit of a special type), DOS provides angle brackets (< and >) and the DIR abbreviation (<DIR>) to indicate that something is a subdirectory.

Because subdirectories are files, they can also have one- to three-character extensions. However, many applications programmers forget to consider this, and those applications can't show the 8.3 type of subdirectory names in their File|Open dialog boxes.

File Management

We've said that, technically, an operating system includes a file management system and a command processor. File management involves controlling file names and keeping track of the files on a hard disk. The file management system must have a way to write to, read from, and locate tracks, sectors, and clusters. DOS and Windows use some version of a FAT, along with a root directory, as part of its file management system.

We saw in Chapter 6 that disk manufacturers perform a low-level format on brand-new hard drives, whereby they divide the disks into *tracks* and *sectors*. A sector is almost always a 512-byte piece of a track—a half of a kilobyte. The manufacturer's *physical formatting* creates many circular bands of magnetic strips on the platters of the disk called tracks. Each platter has a set of concentric tracks stepping outward from the center, and each platter is vertically aligned. All of the vertically aligned tracks (one above the others on every lower platter) taken together are called a *cylinder*.

Tracks are divided into sectors. Sectors can contain 512 bytes of data. Some number of sectors are used to make up a cluster.

In Figure 10.1, we've taken the top platter of a typical hard drive (disk) and outlined the tracks, sectors, and clusters. Note that the black ring in the drawing is a cylinder. Below this platter is another platter, and if you could see the black ring on that platter, it would be exactly the same distance from the spindle motor. Note also that in this example, 1 cluster is made up of 4 sectors (2,048 bytes).

Observe that in the center of this platter is the spindle motor. The very first track next to the motor is track 0. The adjacent track outward from 0 is track 1, and so on. In Figure 10.1, the example track is the fourth out from the spindle. This is the top track of cylinder 3, track 3.

Each platter has its own set of tracks, each beginning with track 0. During the **FORMAT** process, all the tracks of a given number (for example, cylinder 1) are formatted at once, and the screen shows you which cylinder is being worked on. Moving down from (read/write) head 0, the next platter would have head 1, then head 2, and so on. Head 2 would be the third set of read/write heads down, working on the third platter of the hard disk.

Note: If a hard drive is manufactured to have read/write heads on both the top and bottom sides, then head 0 would be the top read/write heads on platter 0, head 1 would be the bottom read/write heads on platter 0, head 2 would be the top read/write heads on platter 1, and so on.

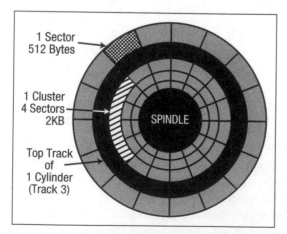

Figure 10.1 The basic division of a hard drive into tracks, sectors, and clusters.

Logical Formatting: Clusters

The next step in the process is to prepare the disk for an operating system of some kind. In this case, we'll discuss and work with DOS. Windows uses the same set of basic principles.

A logical (as opposed to a physical [low-level]) formatting process creates a FAT (discussed shortly) and defines the *minimum* number of sectors a cluster can use to store data on that drive volume. If any group of sectors has been allocated (reserved and set aside) for use by file data, that group is called a *file allocation unit*. If there is actual data stored in file allocation units, we call that group of sectors a *cluster*. Depending on how a disk is formatted, clusters can contain a varying number of sectors.

Note: Today, when you buy a computer from a store, the low-level formatting has been done by the drive original equipment manufacturer (OEM). Typically, the logical formatting has also been done by the dealer. Most dealers format a hard disk as one logical drive—a single partition. The larger the partition, the larger the clusters needed to fill up that space. Large clusters mean wasted space when a small 2,000-byte file takes up 1 cluster composed of 16 sectors (8,192 bytes).

The file allocation *table* keeps track of the clusters. Always remember that clusters consist of a specific number of sectors, and that clusters can contain more sectors as the *volume* grows larger. A volume is the formal name for a logical drive. In the "FDISK" section, we discuss the absolute difference between a volume and a disk.

 The formatting process determines how many sectors will be inside each cluster, depending on the size of the logical drive (volume), not the physical disk.

Let's review the differences among tracks, sectors, and clusters. Clusters are made out of sectors, and sectors are half-kilobyte pieces of tracks as follows:

➤ Tracks are divided into sectors of 512 bytes.

➤ Sectors are combined into clusters, starting at 2KB (2,048 bytes), or 4 sectors.

➤ Clusters must fill the entire volume from beginning to end.

➤ The size of the volume (logical drive) dictates the size of the clusters. Clusters will grow larger in order to fill the entire logical drive.

➤ The largest cluster DOS can make is 32KB, making 2GB the largest logical drive that DOS can address with FAT16. (Larger disks must be partitioned.)

➤ The maximum number of FAT16 (DOS) clusters is 65,525.

Sectors are the basic storage unit on tracks; they are not clusters. Sectors can hold 512 bytes (not kilobytes) of information. Tracks are divided into sectors, and drives are divided into clusters.

File Allocation Table (FAT)

The formatting process creates a *root* directory (folder) that must be at a specific physical location on a logical drive. The FAT is designed for a maximum number of *entries* (file names) in that root directory, which limits the maximum number of clusters (not sectors) in the root directory. The directory allocation table (DAT), along with the FAT, keeps track of the *directory structure*. DOS uses a particular format for making directories on a disk.

The file allocation table is literally a table with bits of information about files. The first piece of data is the name (address) of the cluster that holds the beginning 2KB of a file—about one page of typing.

The FAT is absolutely critical to the maintenance of all the data on a given disk. Without an allocation table, there's no way to know where anything is on that disk. For this reason, DOS maintains two copies of the FAT in case one of the copies becomes corrupted. Some third-party software tools can recover a disk through the use of the second copy of the FAT. However, this assumes that the second copy isn't corrupted, which usually is not the case.

Time and wear and tear eventually affect the magnetic layers used to store data on disks. Even if no outside interference (e.g., speaker magnets or frigid cold) wipes out data, physical properties of magnetism can cause a loss of data. When this happens and the drive heads can't read or write data to the sector, the DOS **FORMAT** command marks the sector as bad and, from that point, as unavailable. If the boot sector goes bad, the disk is no longer usable. If the FAT becomes corrupted, most often it's because the entire area where both copies of the FAT are stored has failed.

The 16-bit FAT (FAT16) addressing structure has a maximum of 65,525 clusters, each limited to a maximum size of 32KB. Therefore, the largest drive using a FAT16 partitioning and formatting scheme is 2GB. LBA (discussed in its own section later in this chapter) provided a way to work with newer BIOS to support up to 8GB of physical disk space. With a combination of FAT16 partitioning, formatting, and Windows 9x, the largest physical disk can be greater than 8GB, but the largest logical drive is still limited to 2GB.

FAT32 Clusters

Clusters are fixed at a minimum of 2KB (four 512-byte sectors), meaning that even a 3-byte file would take up a 2,048 bytes worth of space on a small logical drive. As the size of the volume grows larger, the formatting process increases the size of the clusters. FAT16 tries to fill up a volume with clusters, meaning that on a 2GB disk, each cluster will have expanded to 32KB in size. That same 3-byte file would now take up 32,768 bytes of storage space. When a small file on a large disk uses up a whole cluster, the unused portion is called *slack space*. It isn't at all unusual for a large volume with many small files to have many megabytes of slack space.

FAT32 uses a different cluster size adjustment and can work with a volume 2TB (terabytes) in size. The same 32KB cluster created by FAT16 uses only 4KB of space on a 2GB volume formatted with FAT32. FAT32 makes more efficient use of a disk by cutting down on slack space. Additionally, the smaller cluster size on large hard drives shortens the amount of time needed by the read/write heads (seek time) to find a file.

SCANDISK and CHKDSK (Check Disk)

From the beginning (DOS 1.0), there had to be a way to reconcile the FAT with what was actually on the disk. One of the external programs that came with DOS was the program CHKDSK.EXE (Check Disk) that checked the disk for discrepancies between the allocation table and file clusters.

CHKDSK looked at the FAT for a beginning and ending cluster address for a file. Then DOS went to that address on the disk (the cylinder, track, and sector) and checked to see whether any readable information was in the cluster. DOS didn't read the file for news about how Granny was doing in Oshkosh; rather, it used the drive's read/write heads to copy the information into RAM and write it back again. It then checked the directory listing and name against the records in the FAT. If all went well, CHKDSK went on to the next entry in the FAT and did it all over again. CHKDSK has been completely replaced by SCANDISK (SCANDISK.EXE).

Note: CHKDSK is an obsolete program and can wreak total havoc on a Windows computer. Never run this program! Always use SCANDISK or a proven third-party utility.

Having said the above, Check Disk (a revised version) makes its reappearance as one of the available commands under the Windows 2000 Recovery Console.

If a cluster address in the FAT does not match the data on the disk, SCANDISK returns a message to the user that there are lost clusters or cross-linked files. *Lost clusters* are areas of the disk that have been allocated to a specific file when the file itself wasn't closed correctly (maybe because of a crash or a lockup). Cross-linked files are more scary. Cross-linking means that, according to the FAT, two files occupy the same space somewhere in a group of clusters. Possibly, either the FAT or the DAT has been corrupted. This can sometimes happen when the power goes out or is turned off while the computer is running an application.

CHKDSK was the only way (without third-party utilities) to validate the FAT and the DAT prior to DOS 6.0, when ScanDisk was introduced. One of the first utilities provided by Symantec's Norton Utilities was Disk Doctor, which allowed a user to check a disk for sectors that were either bad or becoming bad. If bad sectors were found, Disk Doctor would attempt to move any data within them and mark the sectors as bad. CHKDSK does not check for bad sectors in which the physical disk is damaged or unusable.

ScanDisk finally allowed a way for DOS owners to attempt to fix cross-linking, lost clusters, and bad sectors. You don't have to reformat a hard drive just to set aside bad sectors anymore. ScanDisk can't be used on a network drive, but it can be used under Windows. We will discuss DEFRAG (defragmenting) in the following section.

 ScanDisk is a way to scan a disk for problems and then work toward repairing some of those problems. DEFRAG is a way to speed up disk access by combining parts of files from all over a disk into organized, continuous *blocks* of clusters.

DEFRAG.EXE

If you write a two-page letter and save it as NAME1.DOC, the file system notes the name of the file and puts the two pages onto the hard drive in a set of clusters. Suppose that you then write another two-page letter and save it as NAME2.DOC. Again, the file system keeps track of the name and the clusters containing the second file. How does the file system know which clusters have which data in them?

Keep the picture of your two letters in mind. Suppose that you decide to make some additions to the first letter. You open your application (say, a word processor) and load NAME1.DOC into memory. You add another two pages of text and then resave the letter. It still has the same name, but now you have two additional pages of data.

If the file system tries to store the added two new pages next to the original two pages, there isn't any room. Your second file, NAME2.DOC, has taken the neighboring set of clusters. Therefore, the file system skips the two pages of NAME2.DOC and puts the additional pages of NAME1.DOC after the end of NAME2.DOC. If you look at Figure 10.2, you can see how your files can eventually end up in pieces and scattered all over the hard drive. When many files are scattered over a drive, we say the drive is fragmented and is in need of defragmenting, or "defragging."

DEFRAG.EXE was added to DOS 6.0 as a way to put all the parts of files into one continuous group of clusters. This is a typical maintenance chore and should

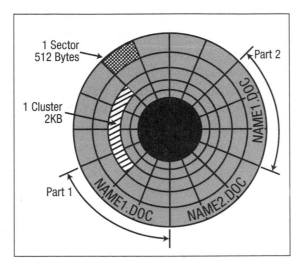

Figure 10.2 Stylized disk showing a file splitting up another file.

be done on a regular basis. Prior to DOS 6.x, the only way to defragment a file was to use a third-party software utility tool. Because DOS originally included almost no utilities, an entire industry of utility companies sprang up around this void. The Norton utility was called Speed Disk.

The revenues from the utilities eventually reached high enough numbers that, for DOS 5.0, Microsoft contracted with some of the largest companies to add scaled-down versions of a few of its utilities into DOS itself. For example, MEMMAKER.EXE was a subset of Helix Corporation's memory manager. SCANDISK and DEFRAG are other examples of utilities. Before DOS 6.0, most people either didn't know that you should defragment your disk periodically, or they used the Norton SPEEDISK.EXE utility.

Note: The nice thing about third-party utilities is that they're not tied to the operating system's command interpreter. DEFRAG.EXE could run only if it was the correct version, based on a matching version of COMMAND.COM. Even copying DEFRAG.EXE from Windows 95 OS/R-A to OS/R-B won't work. Norton Utilities' SPEEDISK could be run on any system, regardless of what version of COMMAND.COM was installed.

The DOS version of DEFRAG.EXE is run from the command line. DOS 7.0 (Windows 95) includes DEFRAG.EXE in the C:\WINDOWS subdirectory, but could also run it from within a window. Following Windows 95, DEFRAG became a graphics-only application, meaning it could be run only in a window, not from the command line. In each ensuing discussion of specific operating systems, we'll focus on the different maintenance utilities that were added to help troubleshoot a problem.

Defragmenting a disk means that parts of files are brought together into contiguous sectors. ScanDisk (SCANDISK.EXE) is used to check the validity of the FAT and the integrity of the sectors. DEFRAG uses the valid FAT to find all the parts of a file and bring them together.

The DEFRAG process is automatic and requires a perfect FAT and a perfect disk. If, at the beginning of the process, DEFRAG finds an error in the FAT, the program halts, and the user is given a message to run ScanDisk.

File Names

Information can't be saved without a name. Certain file-naming conventions were developed in the DOS world, and computer people are often judged on the elegance of their procedures. You *can* create an archive file with something like WinZip or PKZip and call it ARCHIVE.698 (instead of ARCHIVE.ZIP). However, if another technician needs to conduct research into which type of file it is, you'll probably be considered ignorant (at best).

This system has carried forward to the extent that many applications routinely assign a specific extension to their data files. You can override the process if you know how, but most people haven't learned how. Even in Explorer, the default installation is to hide the "type" extensions, and you must choose a specific option to unhide file types.

Some file names are absolute in their names—for instance, AUTOEXEC.BAT, CONFIG.SYS, SYSTEM.DAT, and USER.DAT. If you spell these in any way other than the required way, they won't work in the expected manner. The best policy is to learn the common extensions and stick with the program. Computers are hard enough to deal with, and you don't need to spend extra time decoding someone else's surrealistic file-naming ideas.

Nondisplayed Periods

One confusing aspect of DOS is that when a DIR listing of files in a directory is sent to the screen or printed, no periods appear. It looks like the file names are split into one to eight characters, a big empty space, and then one to three characters, or the <DIR> notation.

Although the screen or printer doesn't print the periods in the file names, DOS needs those periods. If you try to find a file name without using the period, you will receive a "File not found" response.

Characters Allowed in DOS File Names

We've spoken about the 8.3 file name format. Which characters, then, can you use for file names? These characters are found in the ASCII character set. The original set was 126 characters; for the extended ASCII character set, IBM added another 126 characters (high-bit). DOS allows any character between ASCII decimal number 33 and 255.

Windows 95 (borrowing a Macintosh and networking idea) wanted to overcome the limits of DOS characters, particularly the space character. Long File Names can be seen in any 32-bit version of Windows, but DOS (7.x) keeps track of the files through the use of a tilde (~) and consecutive numbers to truncate the long file name into its first eight characters (i.e., prior to the extension). We'll discuss how this happens when we describe the VFAT in Chapter 12. The allowed characters in DOS are:

➤ The letters A through Z

➤ The numbers 0 through 9

➤ ', ~, ", !, @, #, $, %, ^, &, (,), -, _, {, }

➤ High-bit characters from 127 through 255

The lower the scan code number of a character, the higher the file name will be on a directory listing sorted by name. This is confusing to some people who expect a list sorted by name to have all names beginning with "A" at the top and all names beginning with "Z" at the bottom. Because 1 is a lower number than 2, all files beginning with 1 will move to the top of a directory listing. For example, 11NOV98.DOC will appear directly below 1JAN98.DOC, and 2FEB98.DOC will be third.

To force a file name to the top of a directory listing, begin the name with something like !, @, or # because these have very low scan codes.

By convention, temporary deletable files often start with a tilde (~), an underscore (_), a percent sign (%), a dollar sign ($), or an ampersand (&). Table 10.1 shows common file name extensions in DOS.

Note: The use of the tilde (~) is a configuration option in the Windows 9x setup.

Table 10.1	Common DOS file name extensions.
Extension	**Type of File**
.BAK, .OLD	Backup file
.BAS	Basic program file
.BAT	ASCII plain-text batch file
.BMP	Windows bitmap graphics file
.CAB	Windows 9x cabinet file
.COM	64KB compiled command file
.DAT	Data file
.DIZ	Internet shareware description text
.DLL	Windows dynamic link library
.DOC	Document file (full character sets, formatting)
.DRV	Driver software file
.EX_, .CO_	Microsoft expand/extract archive
.EXE	Large, compiled executable file
.GRP	Windows program group file
.HLP	Windows HELP hypertext file
.HTM	Internet HTML (Hypertext Markup Language)
.ICO	Windows icon file
.INF	Windows 9x autoscript setup program
.INI	Initialization file (DOS and Windows)
.LNK	Windows shortcut file
.MID	MIDI sound file
.OVL	Program overlay file
.PCX	MS Paint raster image
.SCR	Script file or screen-saver file
.SYS	System driver software/instruction file
.TMP	Temporary file (usually deletable)
.TTF	TrueType font file
.TXT	Plain ASCII file created by text editor
.VXD	Windows and DOS 7.x virtual device driver file
.WAV	Waveform sound file
.WMF	Windows metafile graphics file
.WRI	Windows 3.x MS Write file
.ZIP	Archive file

DOS Commands

The main thing to remember about DOS is that COMMAND.COM is the command processor (command interpreter) and that it uses MSDOS.SYS and IO.SYS to make up the trio of the DOS operating system. DOS comes with many other programs besides the main trio. Anything that comes with DOS but that isn't inside COMMAND.COM is an external command. If it can be entered on the DOS command line (MS-DOS prompt) or used in a batch or an AUTOEXEC.BAT file, it's a command.

Note: Device drivers (SYS files) could be called commands, but they're more accurately called drivers. The 16-bit device drivers are almost always loaded in a CONFIG.SYS file.

DOS also comes with some generic device names that can be used to instruct the basic devices that come with any PC. Some of these devices are PRN (printer), CON (video console), COM (communications), and LPT (line printer). When you type "COPY FILENAME.TXT PRN" and press Enter, you tell DOS to copy a file called filename.txt to the printer. The file will then be printed.

Note: The right angle bracket (>) is also called a redirector. Issuing the ECHO ^L >PRN command redirects a carriage return and line feed to the printer, causing a laser printer to eject a sheet of paper. Another example is where you issue a TYPE AUTOEXEC.BAT > [somefile].TXT command, and DOS types out the contents of the batch file but redirects the output into a new file ([somefile]). If that new file exists, the contents will overwrite whatever was in it. If it doesn't exist, DOS will create it. Using the TYPE AUTOEXEC.BAT >> [somefile].TXT command tells DOS to append (add) the contents to the redirected file.

ATTRIB.EXE

When data is created either in programs or in the files created by programs, the result is a file. Files, which are stored on disks, contain the data and instructions that a user has created, as well as additional data that can be used by the operating and file management systems.

A file's header information generally contains identification data that other programs can read. This is how file viewing applications (e.g., Quick View and Outside In) can identify the correct viewer to show the file. Every file has an important piece of data, its *attribute bit*, attached to it.

The DOS and Windows basic file attributes come in four flavors: R (read-only), A (archive), S (system), and H (hidden). Network operating systems include several additional attributes for the purposes of rights and permissions. Each attribute can be turned on or off using the plus (+) or minus (–) sign associated with the external **ATTRIB** command. If an attribute is turned on, it shows in the results of issuing the command. The syntax for ATTRIB.EXE is:

```
ATTRIB [+R | -R] [+A | -A] [+S | -S] [+H | -H] [[drive:]
   [path]filename] [/S]
```

```
+    Sets an attribute.
-    Clears an attribute.
R    Read-only file attribute.
A    Archive file attribute.
S    System file attribute.
H    Hidden file attribute.
/S   Processes files in all directories in the specified path.
```

The results of using the **ATTRIB** command show the current attribute of a given file or set of files. DOS 6.x added several switches to the **DIR** command, where specific files could be shown on the basis of their attribute. For example, **DIR /A:H** shows a listing of all hidden files in a directory. Another switch added to **DIR** is the /S for subdirectories. Prior to these changes in **DIR**, the only way to see every file in every subdirectory was to use **ATTRIB, CHKDSK,** or **TREE**.

Look at the following example of the **ATTRIB** command:

```
      SHR    IO.DOS        C:\IO.DOS
      SHR    MSDOS.DOS     C:\MSDOS.DOS
A     H      BOOTLOG.PRV   C:\BOOTLOG.PRV
      R      COMMAND.DOS   C:\COMMAND.DOS
      R      WINA20.386    C:\WINA20.386
A            CONFIG.DOS    C:\CONFIG.DOS
A            AUTOEXEC.DOS  C:\AUTOEXEC.DOS
      HR     SUHDLOG.DAT   C:\SUHDLOG.DAT
      H      MSDOS.-       C:\MSDOS.-
      H      SETUPLOG.TXT  C:\SETUPLOG.TXT
A            COMMAND.COM   C:\COMMAND.COM
```

Note that examples of all the types of attributes are listed by typing "ATTRIB" and pressing Enter. In this case, IO.DOS is a system, hidden, read-only file. The **DIR /A:[option]** command lists only those files with the specific attributes you state. The **ATTRIB** command also shows the subdirectory where the file is located and can use the /S switch to list subdirectories. In older as well as modern PCs, issuing the **ATTRIB *.* /S >PRN** command is one of the only ways to get a full printout of every file on the disk. The > redirector sends the results of the command to the printer.

*Note: The **TREE** command in versions prior to DOS 7.0 could be used to produce a full listing of files or a graphical report of all directories on a logical drive. Microsoft removed the **TREE** command in DOS 7.0, leaving shareware utilities as the only way to meet this need. Strangely enough, the **TREE** command makes a reappearance in Windows 2000.*

Hidden Files

Certain files on a drive are so important that if they don't exist, the system will fail to boot. On the other hand, the **DEL** command makes it very easy to delete the files. One of the more dangerous aspects of Windows File Manager and Windows Explorer is that files can be easily deleted, regardless of whether they are hidden or otherwise protected.

The R (read-only) attribute means that a file can be opened and read, but not changed. Read-only does *not* protect the file from being deleted. The hidden and system attributes make the file undeletable by a normal **DEL** command. If you type "DEL IO.SYS" and press Enter, the result will be "File(s) not found." IO.SYS is hidden, and you can't delete a file unless DOS can see it.

 Remember that a hidden file is only more difficult, but not impossible, to delete. Using Windows Explorer or File Manager, or changing the attribute to -H, will make the file visible to DOS, after which it can be easily deleted.

The Path

The path—a file's formal, full name (*pathname*)—is perhaps one of the most common causes of trouble at the software level. **PATH=** is an internal environment command. The path is also the true name of a file. When we tell someone about a file name, we imply the rest: the drive and the subdirectory chain. When you talk to DOS about a file, you must write out the entire file name, or you can make a specific subdirectory the default location. This is still true when you work with a command line in any version of Windows.

Directories can contain subdirectories, each of which can contain more subdirectories, each of which can contain more subdirectories, and so on down until the entire name of a subdirectory and file reaches a limit. DOS created this limit, setting it to 256 characters. The entire name of a file (including every directory needed to get to that file, and the drive where the file is located) is called its full pathname.

Note: Windows' Long File Name limits are set by keyboard buffer and command-line character limitations. The default command line is 127 characters. Batch files and environment variables support up to 244 characters. To increase the default command-line buffer, place the following line in a CONFIG.SYS file: SHELL=c:\windows\command.com /u:255 (where /u: increases the environment space). If no other characters are necessary in a variable name or command-line statement, a Long File Name can be up to 255 characters.

DOS FAT16 directory names must follow the 8.3 (read "eight dot three") naming convention. DOS has no way of storing Long File Names, but Windows can go beyond the 8.3 convention. Special provisions were made to link a DOS name to a Windows file name. We'll discuss this in the "VFAT" section of Chapter 12.

Keep in mind that the maximum number of characters in the full name of all the directory levels and the file name is 256. (This is a different 256 than the default environment size.) If you have a file named C:\level2\level3\4thlevel\level5\onemore\yikes\toolong\MYFILE.DOC, there are 66 characters in the entire file name (the path). This example contains eight directories—one root directory and seven subdirectories. MYFILE.DOC is a data file in the directory at the eighth level.

Each directory is symbolized by the backslash at the right end of its name. The root directory is a plain \ to the right of a drive letter. In C:\, the backslash represents the root of drive C:. In the previous example, "level2\" has a backslash at the end of its name, showing that level2 is a directory name. This continues all the way to MYFILE.DOC, which has no backslash, signifying that this is a data file.

Note: Unix uses the forward slash (/) to represent the division in directories. Because the people who actually invented the Internet (not Al Gore) were familiar with Unix, Web addresses show the directory level on the computers hosting the Web site with these symbols. For instance, in http://www.coriolis.com/store/default.asp, you can see that "store" is a subdirectory of the main data directory for the overall site. The data file containing the Web page for the bookstore areas of the site is "default.asp."

Search Path

When you enter a word in a command line, COMMAND.COM parses (splits apart) the line and looks for a *command file* (program file) matching that word. If the command word is not found internally, COMMAND.COM looks elsewhere for a file with a .COM, an .EXE, or a .BAT extension. But where does DOS look? It looks in any directory listed in the *search path*.

Suppose that we've made the D:\JUNK directory the default directory by typing "D:" and then pressing Enter, then typing "CD\JUNK" and pressing Enter once again. Our current location, then, is D:\JUNK. Now suppose we type "FOURMAT A:" and then press Enter. What will happen? (Pay attention, and check the spelling.)

COMMAND.COM parses the line, finds A: to be a valid drive location, and expects FOURMAT to be a program file or internal command. DOS will attempt to execute the command through COMMAND.COM in the following order:

1. It first looks inside itself for the character string FOURMAT (which it won't find) and then in the current directory for a program file that begins with FOURMAT. Here, it will look first for FOURMAT.COM, then for FOURMAT.EXE, and finally for FOURMAT.BAT.

Note: If FOURMAT.COM and FOURMAT.EXE both exist in the same directory, COMMAND.COM will execute the COM file first and never know that the EXE file exists alongside it. COM files come first, then EXE files, and finally BAT files.

2. If FOURMAT.COM/EXE/BAT does not exist in the current directory, COMMAND.COM turns to the DOS environment and looks for an environment variable named **PATH**.

3. If **PATH**= exists, COMMAND.COM starts with the first directory listed and repeats Step 1.

4. If FOURMAT is still not found, COMMAND.COM starts with *each directory after each semicolon* and repeats Step 1.

5. If FOURMAT is not found in any of these places, DOS writes an error message to the screen that reads "File(s) not found". In this instance, the odds are that DOS wouldn't find FOURMAT.COM because the actual file name is FORMAT.COM and that command is located in the DOS subdirectory.

A search path is a list of directories that DOS can search to find a program name entered on the command line. The advantage of **PATH** is that the command can be entered without being logged in to the specific directory containing the program file.

The **DIR** Command: File Searches

One of the commands used almost routinely in DOS and Windows is the **DIR** command, which shows a directory listing. You may think that Windows doesn't use this command, but every time you call up the File Manager or Explorer, Windows is using the **DIR** command properties to get a listing of the files you're seeing.

If you try to find a file using the Search or Find options in Windows, you're presented with a field in the dialog boxes where you enter some parts of a file name, and something having to do with asterisks (also called the "star"). If you've ever used the Save As or Open command in almost any application, your options for the *type* of file include the DOS names. For example, the default in Microsoft Word is to open all Word documents (*.doc).

In the following section, we'll look at the DOS wild cards, but for now, just remember that the **DIR** command does two things. It shows a listing of files on a drive or in a directory, and it is used to search for files on a drive or in a directory.

Wild Cards

If you've ever played poker, you know that in certain games, the dealer can make a card "wild." The wild card can represent any other card. The wild card becomes a variable just like the blank tile in a Scrabble game, or one of our previously mentioned student's desks. You can use the card, and it can represent whatever you'd like it to.

DOS has two reserved symbols that represent this sort of variable: the asterisk (*) and the question mark (?). You can use the wild cards in Explorer's Find: All Files|Named: dialog box, exactly the way they've always worked in DOS. The asterisk and question mark each have a slightly different way of working, though, which works out in the following manner:

➤ The asterisk symbol represents one or more characters to the right of the point where the asterisk is used. Its results can be limited to the first eight characters in a file name by placing a single dot (period) after the asterisk (i.e., *.).

➤ The question mark symbol can represent only a single character. If more than one character is needed, more than one question mark must be used. When the question mark is used, it means one character must be available for every question mark typed.

Perhaps the easiest way to demonstrate wild cards is to show various ways they would be used with the **DIR** command. Let's suppose we have a number of files with a .WKS extension in a directory and another set of files that have an .XLS extension. The main part of the file name can be anywhere from one to eight characters; however, a number of the files start with REP for report, followed by a date (e.g., REP1998, REP1999, REP00).

Let's further suppose that this directory has a number of files with many different extensions. There might be a THISONE.TXT, THATONE.MIS, NEWFILE.DLL, OLD.BAK, REAL.DOC, RUSS.DOC, and MY.WRK.

If we were to try and find every file that was an Excel spreadsheet (.XLS extension), we would have to use one of the wild cards. The way that we look specifically for every file with the .XLS extension is to use **DIR *.XLS** as the command. Note that the default in Windows Explorer 4.x is to search for all subdirectories. This can be limited to a single directory by deselecting the Include subfolders checkbox. The DOS command to search subdirectories would be **DIR *.XLS /S**.

If you were to use **DIR ????????.XLS** under the assumption that you would find anything in the main name, it wouldn't work. The reason is that the question mark doesn't just represent any single character, but it means that some character *must* exist as well. In this instance, you would be telling DOS to look for a file that must have eight characters, a period, and the .XLS extension. Although there may be a few files with both an eight-letter name and an .XLS extension, there may also be many files with seven, five, or four characters to the left of the dot.

If you were to use **DIR ?.***, you would have to have a file with one character in the name, along with an extension. There might be 200 files in a directory, but if none of them had only one character and an extension, DOS would return the "File(s) not found" message.

If you wanted to find every file that was a report file, you would use **DIR REP*.*** because all these files begin with the letters REP and the company's naming standards require that all reports begin with the letters REP.

Developing a consistent way to name your files allows you to use the DOS wild cards to search for those files in a logical manner.

To find all the temp files on drive C:, you would have to know that almost all Windows temp files end with .TMP. Another form of temporary file has the ~ (tilde) as the first character. You can't use the command-line **DIR** to find two different types of files. For instance, you can't use **DIR ~.*;*.TMP**. The semicolon isn't allowed on the command line. However, you *can* type *.TMP; ~.* in Explorer, using the semicolon as a separator.

Using DOS in the situation just described, you would have to issue two **DIR** sequences. The first would be **DIR C:\~*.* /S** to find any file that began with a tilde, starting from the root directory of drive C: and looking in every subdirectory on the drive. The second would be to use **DIR C:*.TMP /S** to find any file in any subdirectory on drive C: with a .TMP extension.

Saving Search Results

There is another use for the > symbol. Whenever you issue a command, that command performs an action. Many times the command also *outputs* some type of result. The result can be in the form of messages or, in the case of the **DIR** command, the listing of your directory.

If you use the > redirector, you can send the output results from **DIR** to either a printer or another file. Using **DIR C:*.TMP /S > PRN** would redirect the results of searching for every .TMP file on the entire drive C: to the printer, where you could go over the list at your leisure. Using **DIR C:*.TMP /S > C:\\SOMEFILE.TXT** would create a file called SOMEFILE.TXT in the root directory of drive C: that would contain all the files listed in the search result. Later, you can open C:\\SOMEFILE.TXT with Microsoft Word, Notepad, EDIT, or any other application that can read a plain, ASCII text file.

Note: What's sad about Windows is that it's extremely difficult to save the search parameters (file names and types) as an icon on your Desktop. Windows says it will save the search, but it won't save the *.TMP or A*.EXE parameters in the shortcut.

Web browsers routinely cache Internet site information such as graphics, cookies, and pages. This sort of caching (as opposed to L-1 or L-2 memory caches) downloads a page from a Web site under the assumption that you'll want to go back to it. However, "cleaning out the cache" is a manual process in most cases. If the cache isn't emptied, it can grow to thousands and thousands of files. Additionally, temporary files aren't always deleted as an application cleans up after itself. This, too, can lead to thousands of files slowing down the system.

To clean out a cache is a fairly simple thing. Find the cache directory (folder) assigned in the Preferences of your Web browser. Do a search of that folder for *.* files (every file with any name). Select them all with either Ctrl+A (Select All) or "Shift Select." To use the Shift key to select every file between one file and another, highlight the first file, hold down the Shift key, scroll to the last (or other) file, and click to highlight it while still holding down the Shift key. Then press the Delete key.

Note: Windows 2000 provides the Disk Cleanup utility tool to help clean out cache files.

Finding temporary files is where knowing wild cards comes in handy. From the Search dialog box, you can enter

```
~*.*  ;  *.TMP
```

to find all files that begin with the tilde, and all files that end with .TMP. When they've been found, you can delete them all.

Vanilla ASCII (Plain Text)

Batch files, AUTOEXEC.BAT, CONFIG.SYS, and many generic reference files require that only characters from ASCII 0032 through 0126 be in the file. These basic characters are called *plain*, or *vanilla*, ASCII characters (from plain, good ol' vanilla ice cream). Books often mention using a text editor or your favorite word processor to create these files.

A *text editor* is a word processing program that allows only plain ASCII characters and no formatting whatsoever. A text editor might allow you to use the Tab key, but when you save the file, the tabs are converted to a number of spaces. The original text editor that came with DOS was called EDLIN.COM (for "edit lines") and drove most early DOS users insane.

Most upscale word processors allow you to choose the File|Save As feature and pick a *.TXT file type. This combination gives you all the search-and-replace, copying, moving, macros, formatting, and other features of a powerful word processor to create a document; a plain ASCII TXT file is the result. Common text editors include EDIT.COM (introduced with DOS 5.0 and higher), NOTEPAD.EXE (the Windows 3.x text-editing utility), and WORDPAD.EXE (the Windows 9x replacement for Notepad).

 If you have a copy of it, you can copy NOTEPAD.EXE to the Windows 9x Send To folder, after which it will show up as an option on the Properties *Send To* menu. If you highlight a file in Windows Explorer and right-click for the properties, you can send that file to Notepad, often getting an idea of contents of that file. This is particularly useful if a file extension isn't registered in the Explorer's File Types option.

Operating Systems vs. Shells

For many years, people were marketing *menu* programs and *shells* for the text-based DOS, hoping to make *using* computers one thing (user interface) and *configuring* them another. A computer menu is a list of options (choices) written to the screen. The user selects one of the options and presses keys or clicks a mouse button to pick one of the options. Menu choices are essentially the same as *program items* in 16-bit Windows and *shortcuts* in 32-bit Windows.

Note: Even today, when you run CMD.EXE or choose Start\Run and enter "COMMAND.COM", you are creating a DOS shell. It appears to you as a DOS or text-based window, but it is, in fact, a small shell.

In time, menu programs became more sophisticated. Some companies included security features in their menu programs where a user could access the command processor only through the menu. By controlling how the menu program passed commands to the command processor (the file's properties), menu programs began to become more and more like shells.

File Properties

These days, the defining characteristics of a menu choice are often included in what we call *properties*. Borland's Quattro Pro spreadsheet introduced the idea of using the mouse's right button to call up a menu for changing the properties of whatever the mouse was pointing to. The idea quickly caught on, and now most Windows-based applications access a properties menu from the right mouse button.

On the main Program Manager menu in 16-bit Windows, File|Properties lists the essential properties of a program. 32-bit Windows incorporates the right-click of the mouse (alternative mouse click) to create a context-sensitive properties menu, meaning that the properties change depending upon the context of what the mouse is pointing to.

Shells

A *shell* is where the command processor (COMMAND.COM) loads another instance of itself, resulting in two or more separate command processors being "resident" in RAM. Both Windows File Manager and the Windows 9x Explorer are programs that pass a user's intentions to the underlying DOS command processor. They place a *layer* between the user's actions and the underlying operating system. This layer is what we mean by the term *shell*.

In a DOS session, the resident part of COMMAND.COM sitting in conventional memory intercepts keystrokes from the keyboard and then passes them on to the CPU. Strictly speaking, COMMAND.COM is creating a shell around the operating environment where any instruction that enters the environment is tracked by COMMAND.COM before the instruction can move out of the environment.

Another way to think of a shell is that it acts like an executive secretary screening calls to the boss. Anyone (i.e., the program instruction) who wants to contact the executive must first go through the secretary. The secretary has a list of high-priority people who get passed through immediately. Other people are directed to someone else, depending on their business. Network operating systems often use a shell that works alongside the COMMAND.COM interpreter. Both shells look at incoming program instructions to see which operating system should take the call.

A CONFIG.SYS file uses an optional *directive* (statement) called **SHELL=** to tell COMMAND.COM to increase the size of the environment space in memory. **SHELL=C:\COMMAND.COM /E:1024 /P** increases the environment to 1,024 bytes and keeps it permanent (the P). The **SHELL=** directive also sets an environment variable that tells the operating system where to find its command processor. In this case, DOS always knows that COMMAND.COM is in the root directory of drive C:.

Note: The memory environment is still a configuration option for 16-bit DOS sessions under Windows 9x. To see this, locate the DOSPRMPT.PIF shortcut to COMMAND.COM and examine the properties (right-click). On the Memory tab, each type of memory can be configured, along with the environment size. Types of memory are discussed in Chapter 11.

The word *shell*, like many words in the language of computers and operating systems, has been modified to include menus. Remember that when someone talks about making a computer more "user friendly," this can be done by either changing the way an operating system works or by changing the words used to describe the computer. It's a lot cheaper to change a word than it is to change a basic operating system installed on hundreds of millions of computers.

To create a *transparent* (unnoticed) interface with the computer, Microsoft introduced a Windows applet called File Manager (WINFILE.EXE) as a replacement for the **DIR, COPY, MOVE, RENAME (REN), DELETE (DEL), MD, CD,** and **RD** commands. An *applet* is a self-contained program application that works from within an overseeing parent application. For instance, in the overall "application" of your kitchen, a can opener would be analogous to an applet. In time, the distinction between an application and an applet has become blurred.

The Windows 3.x File Manager is an applet under the Program Manager (PROGMAN.EXE) domain, its companion interface program. PROGMAN.EXE runs first and then offers the opportunity to run the File Manager interface from within it.

Windows Explorer (EXPLORER.EXE) creates the Windows 9x Desktop interface (folder) and runs constantly during a Windows session. On the other hand, File Manager must be explicitly run and closed from within PROGMAN.EXE. To see this, press Ctrl+Alt+Delete in a Windows session from a plain Desktop. Task Manager (TASKMAN.EXE) runs, and Windows Explorer is one of the tasks. Both 16-bit and 32-bit Windows have the Task Manager utility program.

SYSTEM.INI and SHELL=

The **SHELL=** line in the SYSTEM.INI file defines the interface program that Windows presents to the user at startup. In Windows 3.x, the two shells are Program Manager and File Manager. By default, the line reads **SHELL=PROGMAN.EXE**, which loads Program Manager as the user interface for Windows 3.x.

By editing the SYSTEM.INI file and changing the line to **SHELL=WINFILE.EXE**, Windows 3.x starts with File Manager as the primary interface. However, File Manager doesn't include a Desktop area for creating program groups and icons. The Microsoft Web site still offers MSDOS.EXE (the old MS-DOS Executive from Windows 2.x) for use as a shell interface.

Windows 95 first extended the File Manager's capabilities to include the Desktop, icons, and program groups (folders). File Manger became EXPLORER.EXE.

SHELL=

Ordinarily, 256 bytes is enough to handle the few configuration settings DOS uses during a session. In some cases, a larger environment is used for tweaking the speed of the machine (enhancing performance by experimental settings changes). The DOS environment is technically called the DOS *shell*. The line that changes the environment size is:

```
SHELL=C:\COMMAND.COM /P /E:1024
```

The **SHELL=** environment variable can be set only from within an optional CONFIG.SYS file or from the Properties menu of a PIF file (Program Information File) used to run a Real Mode DOS session under Windows. In this case, the shell is set to the COMMAND.COM interpreter. The **/P** switch loads COMMAND.COM and keeps it permanent. The **/E:** switch tells COMMAND.COM to change the environment, and 1,024 is the value for the number of bytes. The environment has been increased from the default of 256 bytes to 1,024 bytes.

Batch Files

The underlying programming and operations of a menu control how an option is executed. Some menus include the ability to combine the selection and key-press process into a single event. Simple menus can be created by using *batch files*. Menus reduce the number of keystrokes necessary to run a program and store complicated configurations used in running certain programs.

A batch file is a file containing a list of commands, one on each line of the file. Naming the file with the .BAT extension tells DOS that this file is an executable program file. DOS then reads each line of the file as though a user were entering that line. DOS menus use file names such as 1.BAT, 2.BAT, A.BAT, B.BAT, WP.BAT, and LOTUS.BAT, and the files are usually saved to a subdirectory in the search path. When the user turns on the computer, the last command in the AUTOEXEC.BAT file might call, for example, MENU.BAT, which draws a menu on the screen.

For the exam, remember that when statements are put into a text file that can be interpreted by COMMAND.COM (a command processor), we refer to that file as a batch file. AUTOEXEC.BAT is a batch file. CONFIG.SYS is a configuration file. Both files can also be called startup command files.

By storing complex configuration switches, batch files are used to automate the process of running a program. Some programs require configuration switches to be entered at a command line. Batch files allow the computer to literally type commands to itself in exactly the same way a human being uses the command interface. Other programs can be configured only from within a CONFIG.SYS file.

AUTOEXEC.BAT

If you ever look inside COMMAND.COM, you'll find a reference to a file with a specific name: AUTOEXEC.BAT. This is a batch file just like any other batch file that can be created using a text editor. If the file has this name, spelled this way, and it resides in the root directory, DOS processes any instructions in this file as the final step in the boot process. Like CONFIG.SYS, AUTOEXEC.BAT is not required to boot the computer. If AUTOEXEC.BAT does exist, COMMAND.COM processes it as the last step in the boot process.

Note: Observe the way a programming sequence in the command processor looks for a specific file in a specific location. This example of "hard coding" a set of events will show up again during the boot process, and later with Windows NT and Windows 2000.

The AUTOEXEC.BAT file is used to run commands that you want to have processed every time you start the computer. Typically, you want to set a **PATH** each time you use the computer to tell DOS and Windows to use the TEMP and TMP directories for various overflow files.

AUTOEXEC.BAT files may still be necessary on a Windows 9x or even NT machine. They're particularly useful in configuring 16-bit device drivers that require a CONFIG.SYS file. These configuration switches might be for non–PnP-compliant 16-bit devices, such as CD-ROM drives and sound cards. The character strings following a command name can be exceptionally complicated and arcane. A batch file is a good way to store this kind of complexity within a file with a simple one-word name to enter.

Note: AUTOEXEC.BAT files were routinely used to configure networking connections, search paths, and sound cards in DOS and Windows 3.x machines.

After the last command line in the AUTOEXEC.BAT file has been processed, control returns to COMMAND.COM, and the computer is ready to begin a working session. If an application's startup program file is the last command, the last thing AUTOEXEC.BAT does is start the application, placing the user at whatever startup location that application normally provides.

A Sample Batch File

A batch file is a plain-text file composed of command lines and saved with the .BAT extension. Using DOS's Edit or the Windows Notepad, you can create a new file with the following lines:

```
DIR C:\ /P
ECHO This is a test line
PAUSE
REM I don't want this line to show
DIR C:\ /W
```

When you are finished entering these lines, press Enter at the end of each line and save it as some file name with the .BAT extension—for example, C:\BATCH\TRYTHIS.BAT. Remember that it *must* be plain ASCII text. Open a DOS window by choosing Start|Run and typing "COMMAND" as the program you want to run.

When you type "TRYTHIS" and press Enter, this batch file gives a directory listing of the root directory on drive C:, pausing every 23 lines for a keypress (**DIR C:\/p**). When the DIR is finished, it displays the on-screen message "This is a test line".

*Note: The **ECHO** command is a batch file command that tells DOS to type to the screen whatever follows **ECHO** and a space.*

The **PAUSE** command (internal to COMMAND.COM) pauses the process and places the generic message "Press any key to continue..." at the next line below the test-line row. When you press a key, the batch file skips the following line:

```
REM I don't want this line to show.
```

REM (short for *remark*) is an internal DOS batch file command that must begin in the first column of a new line. **REM**, followed by a space, causes COMMAND.COM to bypass the line and move processing to the next line.

REM is often used to *remark out* a line in the AUTOEXEC.BAT or CONFIG.SYS file in a test situation where you might want to keep the commands in the line, but bypass them for a number of sessions until you've figured out some particular problem. Then you can delete the **REM** from the file.

Windows allows this type of "commenting out" in the WIN.INI and SYSTEM.INI files by using a semicolon (;) followed by a space in the first column of the line. **REM** won't work in a Windows INI file, and a semicolon won't work in a DOS batch file.

Because the line following the **PAUSE** command has been "commented out" and won't be processed, you won't see "I don't want this line to show" on the screen. The next thing you *will* see is another DIR listing of the root directory, but this time in wide format and without the pause (**DIR C:\ /w**). When the DIR is finished listing, the batch file turns control back over to COMMAND.COM and returns the DOS prompt.

This is exactly how the AUTOEXEC.BAT file works, and you can edit the file with DOS's Edit, the Windows Notepad, WordPad, or any other word processor that creates TXT files. Be sure that you save the file in plain ASCII, because it's not unusual for someone to edit the CONFIG.SYS file or AUTOEXEC.BAT file with Microsoft Word and then save it as a DOC file, which contains all kinds of extended, non-ASCII characters. When this happens, the computer either throws up and dies when it hits the non-ASCII file, or it bypasses the file completely. If the AUTOEXEC.BAT file contains network login commands, the user can end up mystified as to why he or she can't log on to the network.

Note: Always make a backup copy of the latest working CONFIG.SYS and AUTOEXEC.BAT files before editing them so that you have a current, uncorrupted version in case of emergencies.

Practice Questions

Question 1

When a PC is first powered up, COMMAND.COM, AUTOEXEC.BAT, and CONFIG.SYS files load in which order?

- ○ a. AUTOEXEC.BAT, CONFIG,SYS, COMMAND.COM
- ○ b. COMMAND.COM, CONFIG.SYS, AUTOEXEC.BAT
- ○ c. CONFIG.SYS, COMMAND.COM, AUTOEXEC.BAT
- ○ d. COMMAND.COM, AUTOEXEC.BAT, CONFIG.SYS

Answer c is correct. CONFIG.SYS initializes 16-bit Real Mode devices and sets the environment, and then the command interpreter, COMMAND.COM, loads. After the interpreter is loaded, commands contained in the AUTOEXEC.BAT batch file are processed.

Question 2

Which files does MS-DOS require to be present on a disk in order for it to boot? [Choose the two best answers]

- ❑ a. **IBMBIO.COM**
- ❑ b. **IO.SYS**
- ❑ c. **COMMAND.COM**
- ❑ d. **DOS.SYS**

Answers b and c are correct. MS-DOS requires IO.SYS and MSDOS.SYS as the two basic system files, with COMMAND.COM being the fundamental command interpreter. Answer a is incorrect because IBMBIO.COM was a system file from IBM's version of DOS. Answer d is incorrect because DOS does not use a file called DOS.SYS.

Question 3

Files with which of the following extensions can be executed from the DOS command prompt? [Choose the three best answers]

❑ a. .TXT

❑ b. .EXE

❑ c. .COM

❑ d. .BAT

Answers b, c, and d are correct. Executable (EXE), command (COM), and batch (BAT) files can be executed from the command prompt. Answer a is incorrect because text (TXT) files contain text data and must be accessed by another program application.

Question 4

Which **DIR** command would find all files that begin with "A" and are device drivers?

○ a. DIR *A.SYS

○ b. DIR A?????.SYS

○ c. DIR A.*

○ d. DIR A*.SYS

Answer d is correct. The asterisk (*) wild card overrides anything to the right of the symbol in either the main file name or the extension. Answer a is incorrect because it would find all files with a .SYS extension, regardless of what letter they started with. Answer b is incorrect because it would find only files that begin with A and contain six characters in their main file names. There may be some files with fewer or more characters than six. Answer c is incorrect because it would find any file beginning with "A" regardless of what extension it had (such as .EXE or .DOC).

Question 5

DEFRAG.EXE is used to scan a disk for bad sectors, mark them as unusable, and bring all files into contiguous sequence.

O a. True

O b. False

Answer b, false, is correct. Defragmenting a disk brings files into contiguous blocks, thereby improving the efficiency of the system. SCANDISK.EXE is used to check for disk-level problems, such as bad sectors, cross-linked files, or corrupted FAT listings.

Question 6

A hard drive can have up to _____ logical drives, and an extended partition can have up to _____ logical drives.

O a. 24, 23

O b. 26, 24

O c. 1, 26

O d. 23, 1

Answer a is correct. Note the reference to a hard drive, meaning a fixed disk not including a floppy drive. A: and B: are reserved drive names for floppy disk mechanisms. A single fixed disk can take all the remaining letters of the alphabet (24). An extended partition can be created only after a primary partition has been created, and the primary partition takes up one letter. If the primary partition uses the C: designation, that leaves 23 letters in the alphabet remaining. Answer b is incorrect because the floppy disks take two letters. Answer c is incorrect because it's possible for a fixed disk to have many more than just one logical drive. Answer d is incorrect because in addition to any logical drives contained within an extended partition, a primary partition is considered a logical drive.

Question 7

> DOS system files must be located in the _____ partition, and that parti-
> tion must be set to _____ for the computer to start DOS.
>
> ○ a. first, primary
>
> ○ b. primary, active
>
> ○ c. current, initialize
>
> ○ d. extended, DOS

Answer b is correct. The DOS system files must reside in a primary partition, and that partition must be made active. Answer a is incorrect because the primary partition does not have to be the first partition on the disk. Answer c is incorrect because, until the system boots up, there is no "current" or default partition or drive. Answer d is incorrect because DOS cannot be booted from an extended partition.

Question 8

> A sector is located on a _____ and contains _____ bytes of information.
>
> ○ a. cluster, 512
>
> ○ b. track, 512
>
> ○ c. platter, 16
>
> ○ d. track, 16

Answer b is correct. A cylinder is low-level formatted by a manufacturer to contain tracks and sectors. Each cylinder is the vertical stack of tracks at the same distance from the spindle motor. Tracks are divided into sectors of 512 bytes. Answer a is incorrect because a cluster is composed of some number of sectors, defined during the formatting process. Answer c is incorrect because, although a track is on a platter, it does not contain 16 bytes of information. Answer d is incorrect because a sector contains 512 bytes of information, not 16 bytes.

Need to Know More?

DOS books are getting harder to find, and they all cover this operating system in far more depth than required by the A+ exam. However, if you really want to get into it, here are three in particular that we like:

 Gookin, Dan. *Batch Files and Beyond: Your Path to PC Power.* Blue Ridge Summit, PA: Windcrest, 1993. ISBN 0830643850. If you want to be able to really tune a system, this book is for you. However, it provides much more information than you will ever need for the A+ test.

 Minasi, Mark. *Inside MS-DOS 6.2.* Upper Saddle River, NJ: Prentice Hall, 1993. ISBN 1-56205-289-6. This detailed reference of DOS commands covers many that are still used in Windows systems today.

 Norton, Peter. *Peter Norton's Complete Guide to DOS 6.22.* Indianapolis, IN: Sams Publishing, 1994. ISBN 0-67230-614-X. Norton has always been able to explain the logic of DOS. This is a good reference to have on your shelf.

Booting,
Windows 3.11,
and Memory

Terms you'll need to understand:

✓ Bootable disk

✓ Virtual, emulate, and simulate

✓ Program information files (PIF files)

✓ WIN.COM

✓ SYSTEM.INI and WIN.INI

✓ Conventional memory and extended memory

✓ Swap files

✓ HIMEM.SYS and EMM386.EXE

✓ System resources

Concepts you'll need to master:

✓ Booting and system files

✓ CONFIG.SYS

✓ Starting 16-bit Windows

✓ Virtual Real Mode and the virtual machine (VM)

✓ Initialization (INI) files

✓ Virtual memory

✓ Virtual device drivers (VxD)

✓ Windows 3.x global heap

We'd like to take a moment to emphasize how important it is for you to understand the underlying concepts of DOS and the Windows 3.11 shell system. Everything Microsoft has done to bring about Windows NT and Windows 2000 is directly linked to the problems of backward compatibility with DOS. We understand that some readers may be encountering both DOS and 16-bit Windows for the first time.

In this chapter, we're going to take a look at the original boot process as it runs following the power-on self test (POST). We'll also follow the startup process for Windows 3.11 as it loads itself and takes over some of the underlying DOS chores. Windows 95 and Windows 98 were modifications of Windows 3.11, where code was added on an as-needed basis to move the customer base over to a true, 32-bit operating system (Windows NT).

Booting and System Files

Everything about starting a PC revolves around something called the *Master Boot Record* and the way the startup process joins the motherboard BIOS to the operating system. DOS works with the IO.SYS file and a CONFIG.SYS file before passing control to MSDOS.SYS, the third of the three critical system files. We've tried to focus your attention on important points by using Exam Alerts, but you should also work with a computer and pay attention to everything that goes on when you turn on the power.

When the PC's power switch is turned on, the POST routine in a ROM BIOS chip *initializes* the system and runs a test of all the components built in to the computer. Therefore, you should physically turn off the computer if you plug in a new peripheral. In most cases, you'll want the POST to access the device at power-up.

 The POST is run only when power to the CPU is turned off and then turned on again. A *system reset* (accomplished with the Reset button) or a *warm boot* (accomplished with Ctrl+Alt+Del) does not always include the POST.

The Three-Fingered Salute

When an irreversible error occurs in memory, the CPU becomes frozen, and the computer won't accept input to one degree or another. Sometimes, the mouse pointer moves around, but clicking won't do anything. Other times, even keystrokes fail to get recognized. In either case, if this happens to you, you're experiencing a computer crash.

If the computer's display is frozen or locked, but the system accepts keyboard input, the universal key combination of pressing and holding the Ctrl key, then pressing and holding the Alt key, and then pressing and holding the Del key—keeping all three keys pressed simultaneously—generates a restart, or system reset command from ROM BIOS. This three-key combination—a warm boot—is abbreviated Ctrl+Alt+Del.

If the computer is so locked up that even the keyboard can't access the system, the only way to restart the computer is either to turn the power off and then back on, or to use the Reset button on the face of the casing. This type of lockup is called a *hard crash*, and it requires a *cold boot* to restart the computer. Until recently, pressing a Reset button would not call a POST routine, and a cold boot includes this routine. Modern systems often do call the POST from the Reset buttons, making no distinction between a system reset and a cold boot.

Note: The cold boot, not a warm boot or reset, calls the POST, although some third-party software utilities can call the cold boot instruction set from ROM BIOS. Windows often generates a cold reboot during certain installation procedures.

Booting Overview

There's an old saying that relates to pulling yourself up by your own bootstraps. The saying refers to bettering your position in life by relying completely on your own talents and capabilities, not waiting for someone else to lend a hand. Because DOS loads itself (sort of by its own bootstraps), the startup process has come to be known as the *boot* process, or *booting up* the computer.

Following the test for what's connected, the POST looks to the ROM BIOS on the motherboard and begins a parity-checking program to test the main memory chips. The parity program writes information to each chip and then reads the information and compares it. Sometimes you can see this parity-checking process take place by the rapidly incrementing numbers at the top of a black startup screen.

Each version of DOS and the BIOS contains *fixes*, or *patches*, for problems. The system moves some of these patches to lower memory, so they won't have to be constantly read from the ROM chip. This is the reserved motherboard BIOS area of memory (how DOS uses memory is discussed in the "Memory" section later in this chapter). Patches routinely overwrite instructions in the ROM chip.

Finally, the BIOS looks for the first sector (track 0, sector 0) of a floppy disk in drive A: for a bootstrap loader built into the operating system. If it finds the bootstrap loader there, it transfers control to the bootstrap loader to load the operating system. Otherwise, depending on the CMOS settings (in newer computers), BIOS looks at the first sector on drive C: for the bootstrap loader.

ROM BIOS Looks at the Boot Sector

Formatting divides the disk into two specific areas: a *system* area for DOS system files and a *files* area for data and programs. The system area is called the boot sector. Formatting also sets up the two copies of the FAT and creates the root directory. If the disk is to be made bootable (able to start the operating system), COMMAND.COM and the two system files must be in the root directory of that disk. The boot sector is:

➤ Always the first sector (sector 0) of the first track (track 0) of the first cylinder (cylinder 0) of the disk

➤ 512 bytes long, just like any other sector

➤ Contained on all disks, regardless of whether they are bootable

Note: In a moment, we'll discuss the partition loader. The Master Boot Record is the first available track and sector of a partition. The boot sector is the first sector on the disk.

The FAT (and directory table) comes directly after the boot sector and takes up different amounts of room, depending on how large the drive is. There are two copies of the FAT, to protect against one being corrupted. A *boot-sector virus* is where the boot sector of the disk has become infected (corrupted). We discuss viruses in the "Viruses" section of Chapter 14.

The root directory comes after the FAT and, in FAT16 systems, is 16KB. The 16KB limit on a FAT16 file system format is what makes the 512-name limit in the root directory. The general file storage area comes after the space set aside for the root directory. Make a note that Virtual FAT (VFAT) uses the FAT as a *vector* table. Vectors are discussed in the "Memory" section of this chapter.

Basic Bootstrap Loader

If the disk has been formatted to be a bootable disk running DOS, Windows 3.x, Windows 95, Windows 98, or Windows ME, the system area must contain the DOS system files. These files can be installed during formatting by using the command **FORMAT A:/S** or can be copied over using the external SYS.COM command, which is either **SYS A:** or **SYS C:**. (The **SYS** and **FORMAT** commands are discussed in Chapter 10.)

The boot sector also contains a very small program written in Basic. This program calls a small part of IO.SYS called the *bootstrap loader,* which either copies (loads) the so-called DOS *kernel* (system files) into memory at startup or writes the message "Non-system disk or disk error. Replace and press any key when ready" to the screen. The MS-DOS system files IO.SYS and MSDOS.SYS must be in a root directory for the DOS kernel to be loaded.

Note: The bootstrap loader works in conjunction with the system files and must be in the boot sector. Simply copying COMMAND.COM and the two hidden system files to a floppy disk won't extract the bootstrap loader. The only way to install the bootstrap loader into the boot sector is with FORMAT.COM or SYS.COM.

The bootstrap loader contains a *BIOS parameter block (BPB)*, which contains information about the physical structure of the disk. If it's a hard disk, the BPB is read only once because the disk won't be removed. If it's a floppy disk, every time the disk is accessed, DOS works with the change-line process (see the "Change Line Jumper" section of Chapter 6) to read the BPB if a new disk is in the drive.

*Note: An interesting problem occurred when DOS was loaded from a floppy disk in dual-floppy computers. COMMAND.COM would partially load into RAM and would keep track of where the rest of itself was stored (using the **COMSPEC** environment variable). A user would replace the COMMAND.COM disk with a word processor or other application disk and use the computer. At the end of the application session, the user would exit the application and discover an error message: "Missing or bad system files." COMMAND.COM was trying to find itself on the now-removed boot disk.*

Partition Loader

If the boot disk is a fixed disk, the boot sector also has a small *partition loader* program with 16 bytes of information per partition, identifying the operating system, the starting and ending sector of the partition, and which partition is bootable. The partition loader points the process toward the active, primary partition for that fixed disk. The active partition is what makes the hard disk bootable.

The BPB and partition loader, taken together, are what is properly called the *Master Boot Record (MBR)*. An undocumented switch for FDISK can sometimes re-create the MBR. In some cases, this may be a way to eliminate a boot-sector virus if a virus protection program isn't available. To use the switch, type "FDISK /MBR" from a DOS screen (not from a DOS window running within the Windows shell). You should be extremely careful using the /**MBR** switch with a suspected virus because certain viral infections can cause the total loss of an entire partition and all its data.

The boot sector, sometimes improperly called the Master Boot Record (MBR), is found on cylinder 0, head 0, track 0, sector 0. The boot sector is the absolute first sector on a disk. Whether a disk is bootable or not, all disks have a boot sector. The boot sector contains the partition loader.

Technically, the Master Boot Record is the BPB and partition loader. On the exam, though, the Master Boot Record probably refers to the entire boot sector.

Bootstrap Loads IO.SYS

ROM BIOS runs the bootstrap loader, which loads the I/O device management system, IO.SYS and MSDOS.SYS. The DOS kernel manages system-level functions, such as file management and memory management. For the computer to understand itself and for the kernel to be loaded, the two DOS system files must be present in the root directory of the boot disk, either A: or C:, of a FAT16 formatted drive.

The two DOS system files have their attributes set to Hidden, Read-Only, System. ATTRIB.EXE is the DOS program used to change file attributes: Archive (A), Hidden (H), Read-Only (R), and System (S). In DOS 7.0, Windows 9x uses MSDOS.SYS and IO.SYS differently.

IO.SYS Checks for CONFIG.SYS

Following the bootstrap loader, IO.SYS loads first. IO.SYS contains generic device drivers for the basic peripherals expected to be used on the computer, such as the monitor, disk drives, keyboard, communications and printer I/O ports. It also contains a module called **SYSINIT**, which runs through a startup procedure and device driver initialization. **SYSINIT** (inside IO.SYS) calls the CONFIG.SYS file (if it exists) to initialize 16-bit devices.

 IO.SYS always loads first, *no matter what.* Whether it's DOS, Windows 3.x, Windows 9x, or Windows ME, IO.SYS is always the first program file that loads following the POST and bootstrap routines. In Windows 9x and ME, IO.SYS contains a hard-coded device driver loading instruction for HIMEM.SYS.

SYSINIT

We just said that IO.SYS takes care of the generic instructions involving hardware devices. After IO.SYS is loaded into memory, the computer begins to wake up a bit and discover what it is. Up until this point, the motherboard and ROM BIOS have, for the most part, controlled the startup process. This is like when you first realize you're starting to wake up in the morning, but haven't opened your eyes yet. All you know is that you're alive—you're not sure yet who you are (depending on what kind of night you had).

Part of the **SYSINIT** module contained within IO.SYS is a set of instructions that looks for a file named \CONFIG.SYS (with the backslash). This name, which is explicitly written into the program, is spelled exactly that way and contains a specific reference to the root directory (\) of the boot disk. The following are true of CONFIG.SYS:

➤ It is *not* a required file for booting up.

➤ It contains references to the location and configuration of software programs that contain additional instructions on how to run hardware devices (such programs are called software *device driver files,* or *drivers*).

➤ It must be a plain ASCII text file created by the user or sometimes by an installation routine.

The CONFIG.SYS File

If CONFIG.SYS exists, IO.SYS reads the file line by line. DOS specifies the way in which each line of the CONFIG.SYS file is written. The file is much like a batch file in that DOS has the capability to examine each line of text as a line of instructions. Because this is a .SYS file and not a program, we use the term *directives* rather than *commands* to refer to the reserved words used in the CONFIG.SYS file. The CONFIG.SYS file is discussed throughout this chapter.

Windows 95 joined a generic CONFIG.SYS file to the IO.SYS. Most of the directives were moved into the updated file, and CONFIG.SYS (theoretically) went away. However, compatibility issues with legacy systems (older systems) forced knowledgeable users to create a configuration file on their own, and to often create a subsequent AUTOEXEC.BAT file.

Note: IO.SYS only began loading device drivers with Windows 95. The initial programming for HIMEM.SYS and other directives can be seen in IO.SYS all the way back in DOS 6.x, but it wasn't activated until Windows 95.

Many people have discovered that CONFIG.SYS may still be necessary, even with Windows Plug and Play. CONFIG.SYS is not required by 32-bit Windows; however, the implication for people learning about operating systems is that CONFIG.SYS was required by earlier versions of DOS and 16-bit Windows. This is not true.

A computer can be started without a CONFIG.SYS and an AUTOEXEC.BAT file. If there are CD-ROM drivers or sound card drivers in the file, those devices won't operate unless the ROM BIOS recognizes a bootable CD-ROM, but the basic computer will start and run. Read any exam questions about CONFIG.SYS very carefully.

The only files absolutely required to boot a computer into DOS are IO.SYS, MSDOS.SYS, and COMMAND.COM.

The DOS F5 Key

Beginning with DOS 5.0, the boot process could be interrupted by pressing the F5 function key at the point where the message "Starting MS DOS..." appears on the screen. This interruption allows the user to choose from a menu on the monitor's screen. The menu provides choices such as:

➤ Bypass the CONFIG.SYS and AUTOEXEC.BAT files completely.

➤ Pause at each line of the CONFIG.SYS and AUTOEXEC.BAT files and choose whether to execute the program line.

➤ Choose different types of configurations based on specific formatting within the CONFIG.SYS text file.

For those of you who are familiar with the DOS F5 key, the exam room can be a confusing place to try to remember which key does what across all the environments of DOS, Windows 3.x, Windows 9x, and 32-bit Windows.

You should know how to arrive at the Safe Mode text menu in Windows 9x. Pressing F8 between the "Starting Windows 9x..." message and the Windows 9x logo splash screen interrupts the boot process and allows you to choose various options from a Startup menu. (A *splash screen* is jargon for anything that appears on the screen prior to the actual program environment. This can often be a corporate logo, a shareware registration screen, or simply a notification screen that the program is still being prepared to run.)

CONFIG.SYS and MSDOS.SYS

The DOS system files attempt to find each device driver listed in CONFIG.SYS and to execute the instructions in that driver (in the order in which they're found). Remember that a software driver is a special file that contains instructions from a manufacturer regarding how to operate its piece of hardware. PnP specifications generally allow for new devices to be folded into the operating system through Internet downloads. However, prior to PnP (and in some cases, even with PnP), device drivers are often required for 16-bit devices.

*Note: CONFIG.SYS is examined before the full operating system has loaded. There has been no opportunity to issue a **PATH** statement, so each device must be listed by its full pathname.*

In a DOS machine, after all the device drivers have worked out their differences, found one another, and settled down into RAM, control passes to MSDOS.SYS, which loads into a lower area of DOS memory. (We discuss the divisions of memory in the "Memory" section at the end of this chapter.) The MSDOS.SYS file contains all the support functions necessary to run programs and to allow program development. This is where the interrupts listing is held, along with various patches, fixes, and updates to DOS.

When DOS runs through the lines in the CONFIG.SYS file, the files referred to are either found or not found. Assuming that all the device drivers are found and loaded into memory, the CONFIG.SYS file eventually ends, and control returns to IO.SYS.

CONFIG.SYS Confusion

Let's take a moment to mention HIMEM.SYS here; we'll discuss it in greater detail later in this chapter. HIMEM.SYS is technically a software driver designed to allow access to any memory beyond the first 1MB. It originally loaded from a CONFIG.SYS file, back when all device drivers were being installed from this file. When the market reached a point where nearly every machine had more than 1MB of memory, HIMEM.SYS became a critical file. DOS 7.0 (Windows 95) folded the loading directive into IO.SYS, thereby ensuring it would be always installed and eliminating the possibility of accidentally failing to load it from an optional CONFIG.SYS file.

IO.SYS runs *once* to determine whether a CONFIG.SYS file should be read. If a configuration file exists, then IO.SYS drops out to allow the CONFIG.SYS file to load any existing Real Mode device drivers. After the CONFIG.SYS file has completed, IO.SYS returns to read MSDOS.SYS *again* for the rest of the startup process.

As we've said, this quick pass into CONFIG.SYS can lead to some confusion on the exam. Our information comes from the Microsoft technical description of the Windows 95 startup process, although we found it to be difficult to find. In our opinion, the exam makes an assumption that this first look at CONFIG.SYS doesn't happen.

 Before loading hardware device drivers from a CONFIG.SYS and an AUTOEXEC.BAT file, try commenting them out to see whether the Windows 9x autodetection capabilities can run those devices with VxDs. (VxDs are discussed in the "Virtual Device Drivers (VxDs)" section of this chapter.)

DOS 7.0 changed the basic system files, using the hidden IO.SYS to read configuration and device information from either the MSDOS.SYS hidden file, a CONFIG.SYS file (if one is present), or *both*. IO.SYS must still be in the boot sector of the bootable partition, and MSDOS.SYS (also hidden) is still placed in the root directory. COMMAND.COM is also carried forward in DOS 7.0 and installed in the WINDOWS directory.

Technically speaking, IO.SYS reads CONFIG.SYS, then MSDOS.SYS, and then passes control to MSDOS.SYS. After MSDOS.SYS, control passes to COMMAND.COM, which reads CONFIG.SYS *again* before passing control to AUTOEXEC.BAT.

Although, technically, CONFIG.SYS is read twice, we believe the exam expects CONFIG.SYS (if it exists) to process following COMMAND.COM. This is one of those ambiguous, imprecise questions where Microsoft says what happens, but the proper response isn't listed on the exam.

Note: Windows 9x looks in the boot sector, where it finds IO.SYS. Windows NT and OS/2 can be booted from a boot track, making it possible to boot them from a different partition than the primary, active one. In Windows 9x, the "Starting Windows 9x..." message is displayed on the screen following the initial POST and parity check, and is written into IO.SYS.

IO.SYS and 16-Bit Device Drivers

IO.SYS in Windows 9x and ME, does the same thing as in DOS. It sets up *segment addressing* in conventional memory and loads low-level Real Mode device drivers into the first segment of memory (low memory). IO.SYS then reads MSDOS.SYS or an existing CONFIG.SYS file.

Windows 9x uses a preliminary hardware profile from the hardware detection phase to attempt to start the computer (e.g., interrupts, BIOS serial and parallel ports, and CMOS or BIOS system board identification). After the computer is started for the first time, the Registry tells Windows 9x which settings to use at startup. IO.SYS reads both the MSDOS.SYS file (to process specific devices) and the Registry (SYSTEM.DAT) for the device settings.

If a CONFIG.SYS file, an AUTOEXEC.BAT file, or both are supposed to run, IO.SYS loads the COMMAND.COM command interpreter to run the two files. Depending on which lines are found in these files, COMMAND.COM runs various Real Mode commands and programs.

Remember that whatever is loaded into the DOS environment at this point descends to any DOS sessions run from within Windows.

MSDOS.SYS

Whether or not CONFIG.SYS, AUTOEXEC.BAT, or both exist, IO.SYS reads the MSDOS.SYS file first, then reads it again for VxDs and other configuration settings. MSDOS.SYS is a plain ASCII text file that can be edited by DOS's EDIT.COM or Microsoft's WordPad. The important point is that all attributes are set on the file, making it hidden, system, and read-only. Before you can edit MSDOS.SYS, you're expected to know what you're doing and how to change the file attributes.

The MSDOS.SYS file tells Windows 9x about multiple booting options, Startup menus, which mode to start in, and whether the Windows GUI is supposed to start at all following boot-up.

Note: If you press and hold the Shift key, instead of the F8 key, before the Windows splash screen, MSDOS.SYS is bypassed and not read at all.

Keep in mind that neither the CONFIG.SYS nor AUTOEXEC.BAT are required, but if they exist, they run at the points just listed. Windows 9x still uses the same steps, and although most of what used to be in the CONFIG.SYS file has now been coded into IO.SYS, the process still follows this same set of steps.

MSDOS.SYS Passes to COMMAND.COM

If no CONFIG.SYS file can be found, IO.SYS hands off to MSDOS.SYS, which looks for COMMAND.COM in the root directory of the boot disk. COMMAND.COM must be from the same version of DOS as the system files are, or the process comes to a screeching halt with the message "Incorrect DOS version". The DOS kernel (system files) loads COMMAND.COM into memory following any device drivers from IO.SYS and CONFIG.SYS.

Beginning with DOS 5.0, COMMAND.COM could be loaded into conventional memory or upper memory, depending on whether a memory device manager (HIMEM.SYS) was run from CONFIG.SYS. However, regardless of the area of memory, COMMAND.COM is run and installs into some part of the first 1MB of RAM (conventional memory).

After all the device drivers have been accounted for, the last step in booting up a DOS machine is to load the command interpreter itself. COMMAND.COM moves its resident portion into RAM and checks to see if an AUTOEXEC.BAT file exists (spelled exactly that way) in the root directory. If AUTOEXEC.BAT is there, COMMAND.COM runs the batch commands in that file.

When the last command in the AUTOEXEC.BAT file has been run, COMMAND.COM returns a prompt on the screen, and the machine is ready to work. If the last command of the AUTOEXEC.BAT file is WIN.COM, the process continues and loads Windows 3.x.

Beep Codes

We've seen that the POST routine resides in ROM BIOS and executes when power is supplied to the motherboard at startup. During the time the POST runs and completes, no operating system is loaded, and no device drivers have been put into memory. Therefore, the PC has no way of working with a disk, a monitor, floppy drives, or any other device that requires a driver, including a keyboard. There's only one way for the POST to communicate with you.

The POST produces a pattern of sounds, depending on the exit condition it finds on completion of the program. These sounds access the motherboard's speaker and produce a *beep*. Most programs use *error codes* to provide a way to tell the world what happened when the program finished. In DOS, the **ERRORLEVEL** batch command uses these error codes. An error code can include a code for successful completion with no errors.

Table 11.1 lists some of the main beep codes (sound patterns) associated with a POST exit. The PC's speaker beep is a DOS bell control signal (decimal .007, or ^G). *Bell* refers to the old teletype machine bells.

Table 11.1	**The main AMI BIOS beep codes.**
Number of Beeps	**Meaning**
None	There must always be at least one beep. If you don't hear a beep when the POST has completed, then the PC speaker may be bad. Otherwise, the motherboard has failed, or the power supply is bad.
1	Successful. The POST has completed successfully. If you can see everything on the monitor, then the system started okay. The most common problem for a successful POST, but no monitor, is lack of power to the monitor. Check the monitor's fuse and power supply. If the monitor still has no picture following a 1-beep successful POST, then the video card may have a bad memory chip. To check the video memory, try reseating the SIMMs and rebooting the machine. If the SIMMs are in tightly and there's still no image, then you'll probably need to buy a new video card, because the SIMMs are usually soldered onto the IC board.
2, 3, or 4	Memory. The POST checks the first 64KB of main memory. If you hear 2, 3, or 4 beeps, then either video or main memory has a problem. If the video is working, then there was a parity error in the first 64KB of system memory (low memory). Try switching SIMMs between memory banks. If a reboot generates 1 beep, then you have a bad memory module in the switched bank.

(continued)

Table 11.1	The main AMI BIOS beep codes *(continued)*.
Number of Beeps	**Meaning**
4	Clock. 4 beeps can also mean a bad timer oscillator.
	If you hear more than four beeps at startup, you have a precarious situation. The motherboard could be smoking, or the CMOS could have lost its mind. Generally, a repeating series of beeps indicates that a network configuration file or user's logon script is failing to find various devices and drivers. Another possible cause, not related to the POST, is that following a successful startup, something is resting on the keyboard, and the keyboard buffer is sounding an alert.

The Bootable Disk

Back when every PC used DOS, making a bootable disk was a simple process. You would insert a disk into drive A: and format it with system files (**FORMAT A:/S**). You would copy over a few useful DOS utilities, and from that point on, you could access just about any machine that could spin the floppy drive. Today, bootable disks have different purposes, and they're created in different ways, depending on the operating system and the user interface.

DOS Bootable Disk

Making a disk bootable means that the three system files (IO.SYS, MSDOS.SYS, and COMMAND.COM) are copied to the disk. Along with the system files, the bootstrap loader (see Chapter 11) is placed in the boot sector. If the disk can start the operating system, the disk is bootable. The steps to make a bootable DOS disk are:

1. On a working PC, insert a 1.44MB standard floppy disk into drive A:. Exit all applications, or otherwise set the system to a DOS prompt (command line).

2. Type "FORMAT A: /S /U" and press Enter to format drive A: and transfer the system files, formatting the disk unconditionally. Allow the process to complete.

3. Leave the new disk in drive A: and restart the machine. If the machine successfully boots up, you are asked for the date (press Enter) and the time (press Enter), and you then arrive at an A: prompt.

Making a DOS-Bootable Disk from Windows Explorer

Creating a bootable disk in Windows is a fun way to work in the graphical environment, but you don't have the opportunity to choose the /U (unconditional) switch, nor do you have as much control over the process as you do in DOS. To make a bootable DOS disk from Windows Explorer:

1. Insert a disk into drive A:. Execute the EXPLORER.EXE program or select Start|Programs|Explorer. Windows 9x won't allow you to format a hard drive, and the Format Disk option does not appear unless you have a disk in drive A:.

2. With a disk in drive A:, right-click on the drive A: icon. In the Properties dialog box, select Format. Make sure that you click on the Copy System Files radio button.

Remember that you can create an emergency startup disk in Windows 9x by selecting Start|Settings|Control Panel|Add/Remove Programs and by clicking on the Startup Disk tab.

Neither Windows 3.x nor Windows 9x allows you to format a disk unconditionally (completely wiping out any preexisting information). Windows Explorer won't allow the format option when you right-click on a nonremovable disk drive. Fortunately, we still have the option of either going to an MS-DOS prompt in a window, running a command line, or restarting the machine in DOS Mode. As long as you can get to a command line, you can still format any disk unconditionally.

Note: The technical term for right-clicking (on the exam) is alternative-clicking. Don't confuse this with Alt-click or the Alt key.

Bootable Disk Utility Files

You can assume that the only time you'll need a bootable disk is in an emergency, in which case you'll need to do some detective work and probably some repair work as well. The repair work could simply be editing a CONFIG.SYS file, or it could be as drastic as performing an FDISK repartitioning of the hard drive.

Note: In Windows 2000, FDISK operations take place under Disk Management.

A Windows 9x emergency startup disk isn't quite the same as a DOS bootable disk. The emergency disk boots the system using IO.SYS, MSDOS.SYS, and COMMAND.COM. However, it includes a number of utility programs that the process automatically copies to the emergency disk. If Windows 9x is work-able and the problem involves accessing the hard drive, the emergency startup disk boots the system and tries to load Windows.

 When you run FDISK and partition a hard disk, you totally and irrevoca-bly wipe out all information on the disk. You remove not only applica-tions and data, but also the logical drives themselves.

FDISK is used *only* to view the existing partition setup of a hard disk or to completely destroy all information on the hard disk; there is no in-between. If you can think of *any* other option for solving a problem, you should attempt that before using FDISK to completely reinstall the disk.

If Windows 9x can be loaded at all, the emergency startup disk attempts to load in Safe Mode if it can't load normally. The emergency disk contains a number of programs that can be run only from within Windows (e.g., ScanDisk).

Note: If Windows 9x can't load, IO.SYS still produces a "Starting Windows..." message, but the start sequence ends at a plain DOS prompt. In this case, no text-based F8-type Startup menu appears, and you'll need to know DOS commands to continue solving the problem.

Some of the utility files that should be copied to the DOS bootable disk include: FORMAT.COM, FDISK.EXE, EDIT.COM (for editing ASCII startup files), SYS.COM, SCANDISK.EXE, ATTRIB.EXE, and DEBUG.EXE (for destroy-ing a boot sector).

Note: DEBUG.EXE is a program for creating Assembler (COM) files. In very special cases, the only way to ensure that a boot sector virus has been totally destroyed is to use Assembler language. Also note that if you use EDIT.COM on any system prior to Windows 95, you must include QBASIC.EXE as the support file for the editor (or it won't run).

Bootable Disk Configuration Files

A specific PC should have its own dedicated bootable disk. That disk should include up-to-date copies of critical startup files used to start the PC in a normal condition. If the PC has a CD-ROM drive, but no BIOS to support it, a device driver must load in the CONFIG.SYS file. References to the device driver might exist in the AUTOEXEC.BAT file as well.

Place the PC's emergency boot disk in that PC's *system binder* along with a cur-rent printout of MSD.EXE and HWDIAG.EXE. If you had to back up driver files in subdirectories, put those disks in the system binder as well.

Note: A system binder is a three-ring binder containing configuration printouts, unusual instructions relating to a PC, and a number of vinyl disk-sized pocket pages. These vinyl pages hold critical installation disks for drivers, the operating system, and other important devices. The system binder is a good place to keep current backup copies of the SYSTEM.DAT and USER.DAT Registry files, along with CD-ROMs.

If the PC has a sound card, scanner, mouse, printer, or any peripheral that isn't absolutely critical, the device drivers can probably be replaced in the event of an FDISK-type catastrophe. You should examine the system for SCSI device drivers and other driver files that will be necessary when the problem is fixed.

Note: Make sure that you have copies of any device drivers on the hard drive (if you can access the drive). If you can't find original installation disks for SCSI, sound card, mouse, or other devices, back up copies of any subdirectories with driver files to disk.

Important configuration files to include on a PC's bootable emergency disk include CONFIG.SYS, AUTOEXEC.BAT, CD-ROM device drivers (manufacturer specific) or MSCDEX.EXE (generic CD driver), and WIN.INI and SYSTEM.INI (if necessary).

Note: There's no point in making a backup copy of the Registry because the entire disk will have to be reinstalled. A "disk image" program is very useful in situations like this. We mention disk images in Chapter 13.

Windows

With the success of PCs, everyone was looking for a better way to network them. The Unix and Macintosh systems use a different file structure and were designed from the ground up to be a network operating system (NOS). On the other hand, DOS was never designed for real networking. IBM and Microsoft were urgently trying to create a new version of an operating system that would handle more files, larger disks, and better networking. OS/2 (the new, "second" OS) was going to be that messiah of the IBM PC world.

We've seen that a 16-bit FAT limits the number of clusters on a single logical drive and that those clusters increase in size, depending on the size of the drive. OS/2 was going to feature a completely redesigned 32-bit file management system and better control over cluster size. Additionally, the new operating system was going to be designed for networking.

At the time, Microsoft and IBM were partners, and they noticed that they were losing customers who wanted something called *task switching*. Microsoft was looking at how many customers were buying into the easy-to-use graphical environment of the Macintosh, and they wanted something to lure those customers away from Apple Corporation. IBM promised to provide an operating system for the so-called multitasking 80286 chip and, in 1984, released Top View, a text-based task switcher.

IBM was also working on a *multitasking* environment for the new 80386 chip that Intel was researching. The 386 would correct the protected memory problems of the 286, and both IBM and Microsoft wanted an operating system that could take advantage of this, both for multitasking and for the user-friendly interface of the Mac's graphics. Both companies wanted safe multitasking, network capabilities, large disk- and memory-handling abilities, and a user-friendly graphical interface.

The two companies decided that an idea Microsoft was developing for something called "Windows" would be the front-end interface of this new, second-generation operating system (OS/2). The Windows interface had some memory management functions built into the overall menu. IBM would take care of changing the underlying operating system and would provide a way for software to use *threads* for multithreaded pre-emptive multitasking. The two companies agreed to release individual products, but for compatibility and to save costs, they also agreed to share their underlying work, research, and code.

IBM and Microsoft began rewriting DOS to run in both Real and Protected Mode when software developers were slow to write programs for the 286. The results of these projects were OS/2 v1.0 and Windows 286, which could run most DOS programs in Real Mode just as they had run before, but in multiple instances.

In Protected Mode, OS/2 provided true multitasking (as opposed to task switching) as well as access to 1GB of *virtual memory* and 16MB of physical memory address space. This word "virtual" means temporarily simulated, and is similar to "emulate," which means to imitate.

Microsoft Windows took advantage of something called *page frame switching* in both the 80286 and the 80386 chips to provide high-speed task switching. The better protection built in to the 386 helped make Windows more stable. (We discuss page frames in the "HIMEM.SYS and EMM386.EXE" section later in this chapter.)

Windows 3.0, in Standard Mode, used the page frame memory-swapping capability of the 286 to switch among several running programs (tasks) without being able to run the programs concurrently. By the time software arrived on the market for Windows 3.0 Standard Mode, the new 386 chip was rapidly replacing the 286 chip.

Virtually Real

Existence can be broadly divided into physical and metaphysical reality. Metaphysical (from *meta*) is literally greater than physical. In physical reality, all things have attributes, or characteristics. When we point to an object and define it, we're taking out and using the single, unique attribute that distinguishes it from any other object in existence. Physical objects are accessible through our senses (perceptions) and can be touched, smelled, heard, seen, or tasted.

A virtual object is a thing that exhibits all the attributes of the same objects in its class (or set) except for one: physical existence. Virtual objects are not "sensible" to physical perceptions (yet). A virtual machine is a machine that works and acts exactly the same way as a physical machine, except that you can't reach over and pick it up with your physical arms.

Virtual reality (VR) can provide you with virtual arms. In this situation, your nonphysical arms work the same way as your physical arms. The difference is that you can use virtual arms to pick up a virtual machine. The end result is then reflected in the virtual reality as having consequences just like in the physical world. For instance, you could end up with a virtual hernia.

Both 16-bit Windows and Windows 9x continue to use page frame task switching. Windows NT is Microsoft's true multitasking operating system, and Windows 2000 is the place where 16-bit and 32-bit Windows finally come together. We discuss Windows NT and 2000 in Chapter 13.

Multitasking

Computer multitasking is the ability to run multiple programs at the same time. In other words, if you upload a file from America Online (AOL) and then switch to Microsoft Excel and print a spreadsheet, both tasks should happen simultaneously—at exactly the same time—and have no effect at all on each other.

If the upload crashes in the middle of the process and AOL halts, the spreadsheet shouldn't even notice that anything has happened. AOL should be dropped out of memory with no fuss, and any gaps in RAM should fill in as smoothly as the ocean covers a sinking ship. If you're playing a musical CD at the same time, you should hear the music as smoothly as if you were playing it on a home stereo system. There should be no jerky pauses—indications of *time slices*—in the music.

Time Slices

Something like recalculating a spreadsheet can force the CPU into full-time work. In that case, the CPU can give only a few *time slices* to a CD every other couple of microseconds if you're playing music while you're working on your spreadsheet.

If controlling the data passing from a modem through a UART chip is also taking up the CPU's time, you begin to see something like a picture of a harried mother trying to control four young children in the middle of a mall during the Christmas rush. The CPU's attention can only rotate among all the tasks in some fraction of time—a time slice.

Microsoft Windows is a management software program that takes advantage of Virtual Mode, and programs designed for Windows can run alongside multiple DOS programs in multiple virtual machines. Because the processor can service only one application per clock tick, Windows manages the amount of time the CPU gives to each program in time slices, usually measured in milliseconds. Because the chip is so fast and time slices are so small, the multiple applications running under Windows appear to be running concurrently.

Processes

As instructions move back and forth between software, hardware, and the CPU, we say that they all have a *process* of some length of time (time slices). A program file is a complete set of instructions. When that program runs, we can think of the process as complete. It begins and ends, and it expects not to have any interruptions in memory addresses.

If a user wants to run two or more programs at the same time, a way must be set up to overcome a program's expectation of having the whole world of RAM to work with, and no unexpected memory gaps. Putting part of a program in base memory (the 640KB of the first 1MB of conventional memory) and another part in expanded memory leads to confusion, lockups, and crashes. Memory can become fragmented, just like a disk full of files can be fragmented. Although DOS includes DEFRAG.EXE for disks, it doesn't include a way to defragment memory itself.

Note: Some third-party software utilities can defragment the area of memory used for Windows resources. This can sometimes be helpful when many applications have been opened and closed in a session. Sometimes, Windows reports there is enough memory to run an application, but the application returns an "insufficient memory" error. Defragmenting, or compressing, the Resources area may fix the problem. This problem continued through Windows 9x and Windows ME.

We see a similar problem when hardware or software runs a process and calls for work from the CPU. In this case, interrupts are sent to the CPU to interrupt whatever it's doing and reorder the priorities of action. If a process in the CPU hasn't finished, a snapshot of the whole process is switched into a *stack* and is retrieved when the new process has run its course.

Threads

Threads are a way for an application process to be divided into precise subprocesses that happen at the same time. You can think of a thread as the smallest amount of time required by the CPU to complete a single set of instructions. Threads operate very fast because they're very small pieces of code. Because threads are written into an application, they have full access to the entire program. They also share address space, file access paths, and other system resources associated with the application.

You can also think of a thread as a kind of interrupt written into an application by the programmer. The programmer decides, thread by thread, what the smallest piece of code is. The program can then send only the necessary instructions at a given moment. Threads also allow different areas of the same overall application to use only the instructions specific to those areas (e.g., to recalculate while redrawing the screen).

Threads can be moved into RAM at the same time, carrying with them (within the thread) a piece of code that tells the CPU how important that piece of code is in the overall scheme of things. This provides some help to the CPU as it moves processing in and out of the stack and allows one thread to interrupt (pre-empt) another thread.

The importance of a given thread is therefore prioritized,allowing one thread to *pre-empt* the time that is being called for by another thread from the CPU. This capability is called *pre-emptive multithreaded multitasking*. True pre-emptive multitasking requires that software be written with threads and that the operating system be written to understand threads.

Tricky Semantics

Because Windows decides (on the basis of time slices) whether and when a DOS application will have access to the CPU, the term *pre-emptive multitasking* for DOS applications crept its way into the language with the arrival of Windows 3.x. Because DOS applications aren't written in a threaded format, this use of the term isn't really accurate. It's true that Windows is literally pre-empting the DOS application's access to the CPU, but that doesn't mean that Windows is using pre-emptive multitasking in the way that it's formally defined.

Microsoft tends to advertise Windows 3.x as having pre-emptive multitasking capabilities. This is true semantically, but not in the generally accepted meaning of the term. In terms of the exam, you should think of Windows 3.x, Windows 9x, and Windows ME as offering real multitasking (without reference to its being pre-emptive).

Windows 2.x

In 1987, IBM released OS/2 version 1.0, which included the text-based Presentation Manager front-end interface. IBM designed this version to run hardware-based (chip) multitasking to take advantage of the 80286, but had the much better 80386 in mind. IBM deferred the development of the graphics to Microsoft, and Windows 2.0 arrived on the market with the ability to create so-called virtual 8086 computers (virtual machines) out of 640KB snapshots of memory.

Meanwhile, IBM was having serious trouble developing its operating system, and Microsoft was becoming impatient because of Apple Corporation's constant increase in computer sales. Windows used MS-DOS Executive as its user interface, and version 2.x offered the ability to create a virtual 8088 memory environment called *Real Mode*.

Memory addressing in Real Mode is done directly, in the same way that original memory addressing was handled by the 8088/86 processors using conventional memory. Windows 2.x also introduced the concept of Dynamic Data Exchange (DDE), whereby applications running together under Windows could communicate with one another.

Note: DDE led to Object Linking and Embedding (OLE), which eventually led to an incredibly confusing world of ActiveX and DirectX, none of which is part of the exam.

Virtual Real Mode and the Virtual Machine (VM)

Using Virtual Real Mode, the CPU can simulate the way an actual 8088/86 does real operations with real memory addresses. At the same time, Windows can run hardware-based (80386) memory protection. This allows a true multitasking operating system to load multiple copies of DOS, while making the CPU think it's working with only one machine. There is only one physical machine present, but each copy of the DOS command processor is running in its own simulated world—a virtual machine.

If the system is using appropriate memory management software, the 386 chip could create several *memory partitions*. Each of these memory partitions can have its own copy of DOS and use the full range of DOS services, thereby functioning as if it were a standalone PC. When this type of organization is in place, the computer is often said to be running virtual machines. As we examine Windows, we see how the *Virtual Machine (VM) Manager* is a basic component of all versions of Windows. We'll also see how virtual machines can use *virtual device drivers*, called VxDs (files).

Note: A virtual machine is a simulated PC. It "comes with" an 8088/86 CPU that can address only 1MB of RAM. Session configuration settings can "install" more memory in that virtual (fake) machine, making the configuration of a DOS session under Windows an exercise in the history of PCs.

Virtual Machine (VM)

A VM is an executable task. It's an actual program that combines application, support software such as ROM BIOS and DOS, memory, and CPU registers. Running COMMAND.COM or CMD.EXE at the Run line under a Windows Start menu creates a generic virtual machine. The properties in the DOSPRMPT.PIF (Program Information File) file in the Windows subfolder (the MS-DOS shortcut) allow you to configure a VM.

Windows uses a single virtual machine called the System VM to run the Windows kernel, its other core components and extensions, as well as all Windows-based applications. Each time a DOS application is run, it creates a separate VM that exists for only the length of time that the DOS application is running—a *session*. Windows 3.x uses an applet called the PIF Editor to control how each session's VM ran.

Microsoft released a 2.01 incremental upgrade shortly after releasing version 2.0. The main reason for the upgrade seems to have been that Windows took on IBM's System Application Architecture (SAA) standard for how a program looks to the user. This standard for a "look" describes how windows, menus, and dialog boxes should look for any and all programs running in a graphical environment. The idea was that, as with Macs, users shouldn't be required to relearn the skills they acquire from one program when learning a new one. The SAA standard became the standard for all IBM-type computers running a graphical, Windows-style interface.

Note: The SAA for the "look and feel" of an application is not the same as the application program interface (API). The API is how a program developer works with an operating system to develop new applications.

Another important aspect of Windows 2.x was that, after it was loaded, it took on some of the underlying DOS operations. In other words, while Windows was looking like a menu system and acting like a shell, it was also reaching down into the basic operating system to control how memory addressing and management was being done.

Windows uses something called *resources* that are called for by a program. These resources are the amount of memory a program or screen item needs at any given time it's active. The resource instructions to Windows were originally contained within EXE files and dynamic link library (DLL) files. Rather than leaving the moment-by-moment control of memory to DOS, Windows took over the management tasks. (Resources are discussed in more detail later in the "The Windows 3.x Environment: Global Heap" section of this chapter.)

Dynamic Link Libraries (DLL Files)

Along with the Windows kernel and core files, Microsoft provides the Windows *extensions* that are meant to standardize many Windows functions, including the look and the feel of the interface. COMMDLG.DLL is a generic way for a programmer to work with Windows to create standardized dialog boxes. DDEML.DLL is a library of management tools for DDE (Dynamic Data Exchange), and MMSYSTEM.DLL is a library of management tools for sound and multimedia.

The Windows extensions are designed to make the Windows environment as flexible as possible. DLL files are Windows-executable files that allow applications to share program code and necessary resources. A programmer can extend the basic Windows environment by writing a DLL file to make it available to other Windows applications. Dynamic link libraries commonly have the .DLL extension, but they can also have an .EXE or other extension. KERNEL.EXE, USER.EXE, and GDI.EXE are dynamic link libraries that have an .EXE extension.

The SHELL.DLL library provides the drag-and-drop capabilities used with File Manager. Such routines can be used by other applications without needing to rewrite the code. The programmer calls up the routines from the SHELL.DLL file (which installs with Windows by default).

Program Information Files

Windows provides memory to a DOS application in the same way that any PC comes with base memory to run programs. The amount of DRAM memory on a real PC is determined by chips and buyer choices. The amount of virtual memory on a virtual PC is determined by the requirements of the application asking for a virtual machine. If no one does anything, the default settings are created by the DEFAULT.PIF file that comes with Windows 3.x and the DOSPRMPT.PIF file that comes with Windows 9x. COMMAND.COM has its own properties in Windows 9x, and this property menu works much like the original PIF files did.

Originally, a program information file was stored in a proprietary format and couldn't be edited using a typical ASCII text editor. The PIFEDIT.EXE applet was used to edit PIF files, much like REGEDIT.EXE is a specialized editor for the Windows 3.x Registration database and the Windows 9x Registry.

The PIF Editor dialog box asks for information about the program, including its full pathname and command file name, along with any startup switches that you want to use for that program. The **PROGRAMS**= line in the WIN.INI file (in the "WIN.INI" section later in this chapter) specifies that .EXE, .COM, .BAT, and .PIF file extensions are to be considered executable by Windows. Note that a PIF file is an executable file in the Windows environment.

Rather than pointing a shortcut to an EXE or COM file, the properties can be used to point to the PIF file associated with the actual executable file (as in the case of **DOSPRMT**). A PIF file can also tell Windows how much time (in time slices) to give to the processes generated by the DOS application. Windows 9x properties can't do this.

Windows 3.0 and New Technology (NT)

For a while, Microsoft and IBM were working together to improve both the OS/2 operating system and the Windows interface. IBM was primarily focusing on an operating system that communicated directly with the CPU. Microsoft was focusing more on the way in which the user was working with the computer. IBM has always tended to pay more attention to hardware (how things work), while over the years, it seems as if Microsoft has been more interested in appearances (how things look to the user).

OS/2 version 1.x was a whole new way of programming, and the API was difficult to learn. However, even in that version, OS/2 changed the FAT to support much larger drives. In 1989, IBM released OS/2 1.20, which had an improved Presentation Manager. Shortly thereafter, version 1.2 EE introduced something called the High Performance File System (HPFS).

HPFS is much more efficient and faster than FAT, and it keeps track of data on disks with fewer errors and better security. HPFS would eventually grow to be a true 32-bit file management system that could be located anywhere on a logical drive, not exclusively in the root directory. HPFS is not the same thing as the Windows NT File System (NTFS) or Windows 9x FAT32, however.

Although IBM's HPFS is a true 32-bit file management system, the Windows 9x Installable File System (IFS) is a virtualized 32-bit FAT (virtual FAT, or VFAT) that relies on the DOS 7.0 16-bit FAT for actual file management. Chapter 12 discusses the VFAT in greater detail.

IBM had begun work on two new OS/2 products: OS/2 2.0 and 3.0. Version 2.0 was going to be the first 32-bit operating system for PCs. It was designed specifically for the Intel 80386 and later chips, and would no longer be compatible with the 80286 processor. Version 3.0 was going to be a network server version of the operating system. It was also intended to be *platform independent*, meaning that the same operating system could run on PCs using different types of chips. Version 2.0 would focus on the individual user—the consumer market—whereas version 3.0 would focus on the business world and networks.

Because OS/2 was going to be built on top of something called a *microkernel,* it wouldn't matter what type of hardware it was running on. Therefore, it could run on Intel processors and on other types of chips made by Sun, Digital Equipment Corporation (DEC), and Motorola. Everything was fine, except that IBM was way behind in its work, and Microsoft was ready to go with an interface that looked almost exactly like a Mac screen.

In 1990, Bill Gates decided to release Windows 3.0, without IBM's agreement, in a move to lure customers away from the Macintosh to the Intel-based operating systems. DOS was *the* operating system in this market, and Microsoft wanted the Mac customers. IBM decided to step in to try to keep Microsoft from dominating the entire operating system market, and a great divorce battle ensued.

When the dust settled, an agreement had been made that IBM would continue to develop OS/2 2.0 for personal computers and Microsoft would take over development and funding for OS/2 3.0 (the network server version). Microsoft renamed the experimental network operating system Windows New Technology (NT).

Program Manager and File Manager

One of the fundamental differences between Windows 2.x and 3.0 was the way they showed themselves to the user. The MS-DOS Executive was like a two-dimensional version of File Manager. It had no colors, and it looked very similar to the results of a **DIR** command printed on paper. The difference between the directory command and MS-DOS Executive was that you could double-click on an application file's name, and the program would actually run. Windows 3.0 allowed running a mixture of Windows and DOS programs at the same time. It had its bugs, but it was progressing.

Another basic change in the look of Windows 3.0a and 3.0b was the introduction of *icons* and *program groups.* A program group is much like a subdirectory, but it looks almost exactly like the folders and subfolders of the Macintosh operating system (Mac OS). Icons incorporate a program item properties dialog box, where information is entered about the location of a program and how it starts—a graphic menu option. In Windows Explorer, the "look and feel" came so close to that of the Macintosh that Apple Corporation sued Microsoft in a legendary court battle. Microsoft won, so today's folders and subfolders continue to look and work the way they do.

Windows 3.1

Windows 3.0 and OS/2 2.0 included TrueType fonts (another war was being waged about who had the best way to draw letters on a screen and print them to printers). The idea of What You See Is What You Get (WYSIWYG) became a reality as Windows took on the ability to display characters the way they would actually look on the printed page. Microsoft wanted everything to connect to everything, and its new rallying cry became "Windows everywhere!"

In 1992, Windows 3.1 was released with all the improvements that were needed as a result of the somewhat rushed release of 3.0. Windows 3.1 improved the File Manager shell/applet interface and added internal fonts. Another improvement was the Object Linking and Embedding technology for interconnecting data produced by different applications.

The instructions and connections used in OLE were moved to a special database called the *Registration database* (REG.DAT). To prevent unsophisticated users from accidentally breaking links between programs, this database took on a proprietary form and could be edited only with a program call REGEDIT.EXE.

Note: The Windows 3.x Registration database was the precursor to the 32-bit Windows Registry. REG.DAT eventually became SYSTEM.DAT and USER.DAT. The editing program is still called REGEDIT.EXE.

Windows 3.1 featured many improvements, making it more of a full version upgrade than the minor point revision implied by the number. The stability was significantly improved, and the way in which programs were isolated in memory became much more secure. Windows 3.1 finally took on the ability to shut down a frozen window without rebooting the entire computer (some of the time).

Another preview of the standardization to come was the *common dialog box* (COMMDLG.DLL) programming library, so that the programmer didn't need to "re-create the wheel" every time they needed a dialog box. It's important to note that these common dialog features are held in certain files that change with various versions of Windows.

Note: The 16-bit files were COMMDLG.DLL, VER.DLL, SHELL.DLL, DDEML.DLL, and LZEXPAND.DLL. Although you won't be tested on these names, keep in mind that 32-bit and 16-bit Windows applications might use different versions of these files and that, therefore, they aren't interchangeable.

Starting 16-Bit Windows

We've discussed the basic loading of the operating system, ending with the DOS command prompt that generally appears after the final line of an AUTOEXEC.BAT file. Typically, on a computer set up to run Windows 3.x, the last line of that AUTOEXEC file is WIN. This means that a program must be somewhere on the disk called WIN.* (using a DOS wild card). It just so happens that Windows has such a program, called WIN.COM, and it's located in the C:\Windows directory.

MS-DOS 4.0 introduced something Microsoft called the DOS shell, which was really a rudimentary graphic file maintenance and menu program. This complicated menu system was run from DOSSHELL.BAT, which used a very small stub program loader (SHELLB) to push the main program (SHELLC) into memory. SHELLB was about 3.5KB, whereas SHELLC was 150KB. This began the process of using a loader program.

WIN.COM is the next iteration of that loader stub. It calls into memory USER.EXE, GDI.EXE, and KERNEL.EXE—the core Windows files.

 The three core Windows 3.x files are USER.EXE, GDI.EXE, and KERNEL.EXE.

During the setup process, SETUP.EXE combines VGALOGO.LGO and VGALOGO.RLE (the Microsoft logo screen) with WIN.CNF and creates WIN.COM, which loads the Windows program into memory and continues forward in graphical mode. Depending on whether an automatic or custom installation was chosen, the routine pauses at various points to allow further choices in terms of which applets will be installed.

Note: VGALOGO.* are the two files Windows uses on systems with VGA graphics capabilities. Where the system used a CGA or EGA monitor, Windows had two files each for CGALOGO.* and EGALOGO.*, which it could compile into WIN.COM.

SETUP.EXE

DOS programs often included a separate installation *routine* (program) to make sure that every step of the installation was followed correctly. You can usually tell whether you're looking at a DOS- or Windows-based application by the name of its installation program. DOS programs continue to use INSTALL.EXE as the first file to run in setting up the program. Windows programs use SETUP.EXE.

Windows itself uses a SETUP.EXE program, which goes farther than the DOS installation routines. SETUP.EXE not only copies (and expands) files to various locations on the disk, but it also examines the hardware and software in the system. The theory behind this examination is that users shouldn't need to know how their computers run. Following the Microsoft lead, most modern installation programs attempt to identify the existing system before installing their application.

Most installation and setup programs make a number of assumptions about the destination computer—the default setup—and offer the computer owner a way to take only some control over the installation. Typically, the installation routine offers a somewhat misleading Express and Custom pair of setup options.

 You should always choose the Custom or Advanced option if the setup routine offers one. In every case we've ever seen, there is a default setting for any steps in the program where you're given a choice. In situations where you don't know what you're looking at, you can choose the default. However, in places where you do know what you're looking at, you may often disagree with what some faraway programmer has decided to do to your system.

The Windows 3.x SETUP.EXE does a rudimentary examination of the type of hardware and memory available on the computer. It offers some basic configuration options, such as the directory to install Windows in and which kind of display, keyboard, mouse, and network configuration to use.

The key file used by SETUP.EXE is SETUP.INF (information file). SETUP.INF contains entries that determine which files will be copied during the installation. SETUP.EXE also uses EXPAND.EXE to decompress the files on the Windows installation disks. Because the files are stored in a shrunken (compressed) format, the **DOS COPY** command isn't enough to fully install Windows from original disks.

Note: You can usually tell that a file has been compressed by Microsoft by looking at the last character in the file's extension. Microsoft's proprietary archive process usually makes this last character an underscore (PROGRAM.EX_).

The initial options offered at the beginning of the custom installation can be changed later from within Windows by the Win Setup applet in the Main program group. If the automatic (default) setup is chosen, Microsoft decides which files to install and where to install them. Windows 3.0 didn't offer a choice, providing automatic installation only. Windows 3.x returned some control of the setup process to the user. Windows 9x pretty much removed that control, and it was never seen again.

All the way back in DOS 5.0, Microsoft began installing a program in the root directory of the primary, active drive that tells Windows that the computer (processor) can support 386 Enhanced Mode. That file is WINA20.386 and is located in the C:\ root directory (read-only). After SETUP.EXE determines that Windows can be installed on the computer and determines if there's enough room on the disk, it copies the core files and many of the required files to the hard drive.

SETUP.EXE creates a \WINDOWS subdirectory (typically on drive C: at the root directory). It also creates a \WINDOWS\SYSTEM directory that Windows searches regardless of which other subdirectories are listed in the **DOS PATH=** environment variable.

Windows 3.x SETUP.EXE allowed various switches at startup. You could always get a quick reminder of the switches by using the **SETUP /?** switch for DOS online help.

Three of the switches that you might need to know for the exam are:

➤ **/N**—Sets up a shared copy of Windows for Workgroups from a network server.

➤ **/O:file**—Specifies the SETUP.INF file.

➤ **/A**—Places Windows for Workgroups on a network server (administrative setup).

WIN.COM

Typing "WIN" at the command prompt or having the AUTOEXEC.BAT file enter it for you runs a small COM file (WIN.COM) that does some preliminary checking before it begins to search for the necessary core files for the Windows program. WIN.COM checks to see what type of computer, CPU, and memory are installed. The memory might be real, extended, or expanded.

Next, WIN.COM checks to see which device drivers have been loaded—especially virtual memory devices (HIMEM.SYS)—and then makes a decision regarding the mode in which Windows should start. WIN.COM also allows switches on its command line to force certain ways of loading. These different ways of running are called *modes* of operation. Depending on the amount of memory, the type of processor, and whether an extended memory device driver is present, 16-bit Windows' WIN.COM could use:

➤ /R—Real Mode

➤ /S or /2—Standard Mode

➤ /3—Enhanced Mode

➤ /B—To keep a boot log text file of any problems encountered during startup

Note: Additional switches can be used, but the details of these are beyond the scope of this book. Typing "WIN :" (note the space before the colon) starts Windows 3.x without the Microsoft logo screen (or splash screen) during the startup process.

Real Mode (WIN /R)

Real Mode Windows 3.0 was designed to run on 8086-based computers. Microsoft offered this mode, but those computers were so limited that Windows ran too slowly for all practical purposes. Real Mode was a 100-percent–compatible mode for running pure DOS. Some games that run under DOS environments had a problem running under Windows 3.0. DOS programs, especially these kinds of games, often write directly to the screen, and with Windows trying to handle device operations, the confusion caused lockups and crashes. Real Mode required at least an 8088/86 processor and 640KB of conventional memory, was used mainly for running Windows 2.x applications that hadn't been converted to Windows 3.0, and was eliminated in Windows 3.1.

Standard Mode (WIN /S)

We saw that Windows grew out of changes in the way in which the processor manages memory. In a way, Windows does send instructions directly to the CPU. Remember that 286 Protected Mode is really what started everything. WIN.COM transfers control to other programs that take over management of expanded memory, extended memory, or both.

If WIN.COM finds the extended memory manager HIMEM.SYS in memory, and at least 256KB of conventional memory and 192KB of extended memory, Windows can start in Standard Mode. Windows uses Standard Mode when the computer has an 80286 chip with 1MB or more of memory or a 80386 processor with more than 1MB, but less than 2MB of memory.

 If the computer has more than 2MB of memory and a 386 CPU or later, Windows uses Enhanced Mode by default. Because this is almost universally true on modern machines, HIMEM.SYS became a fundamental and critical file and is now called from IO.SYS.

One of the main differences between the 286 and the 386 chips was that although the 286 could switch into Protected Mode during a session, it required a system reset to switch back to Real Mode. This may be the reason that Bill Gates called the 80286 chip "brain-dead" and tried to push IBM into skipping development efforts to the 80386 rather than waste time with the 286. IBM's corporate policy of always keeping its promises is what set back the development of OS/2 and eventually led to the split between the two corporations—yet another legendary management decision.

386 Enhanced Mode (WIN /3)

The 386 Enhanced Mode is usually referred to simply as Enhanced Mode. Its startup sequence is the same as the one for Standard Mode, except that Windows switches the 386 chip into 32-bit Protected Mode. Instead of calling the 286 kernel, WIN.COM loads KRNL386.EXE, which then loads the rest of Windows. Windows Enhanced Mode requires a 386 or faster processor and can, therefore, switch between Protected Mode and Real Mode without the problem of resetting the computer.

The 80386 processor chip introduced virtual memory by creating an illusion for DOS that 1MB of memory stayed constant. The chip would change the addresses to point to extended memory (vectoring) and report back to DOS that nothing was different—the memory was the same as it was a minute ago. Each new 1MB of memory is placed in front of DOS, page by page, using the page-frame segment of conventional memory.

In the same way that the 386 chip was fooling the old DOS into thinking that only 1MB of RAM was present, it fools Windows into thinking that many virtual 8086 PCs are running in the same place. The 386 Enhanced Mode also takes better control of DOS programs that bypass BIOS with video functions and intercepts those function calls (e.g., games). This allows most DOS programs that use a Graphics Mode to be run under Windows in Enhanced Mode.

The 80386 and all later chips protect both memory areas and hardware process operations by intercepting all memory addressing and hardware calls. Windows and the CPU get together and intercept *everything* an application tries to do. When two applications try to access the same device at the same time, Windows arbitrates and decides which one gets access first.

Windows 3.x Core Files

After WIN.COM has defined a running mode, it transfers control to DOSX.EXE and WIN386.EXE, which then load the Windows core programs into memory. Windows also loads its own device drivers from the SYSTEM.INI file, just as DOS uses the CONFIG.SYS file to load device drivers. The core Windows files are as follows:

➤ *USER.EXE*—Creates and maintains windows on the screen and handles requests to create, move, size, or close windows. Also controls the user interaction with icons and other interface components, including input devices such as the keyboard and mouse.

➤ *GDI.EXE*—Controls the graphics device interface, which is responsible for graphics operations that create images on the monitor or other display devices.

➤ *KRNL286.EXE or KRNL386.EXE*—Controls memory management, program loading, program code execution, and task scheduling. KRNL286.EXE is specific to the 80286 processor, and KRNL386.EXE applies to all later chips.

Initialization (INI) Files

The so-called Windows operating system environment includes a number of support files, just like DOS does. Windows was designed to succeed DOS and become the main (and only) interface between the computer and the user. As a result, Microsoft tried to gather as many device drivers as possible and pull them together under a single umbrella. Additionally, as program files became larger, some of their supporting code was moved outside the EXE or the COM file to additional files. These files are required to run the application because the main executable file contains internal references to those files. Generally, these support files are located in a specific directory called a *working directory*.

For various reasons, PC users found that it was useful to locate the main program files in one place and some of the auxiliary files somewhere else. Not only that, but the data files created by an application are often placed on completely different drives (as in networks). To make some sense out of all this, certain types of configuration files were created to hold information regarding how the main executable file was supposed to run. These particular configuration files are called *initialization files* and almost always have a .INI extension (read "dot eye-en-eye").

We've seen that in a menu or shell, properties describe important information about the location of the main executable file and how to run it. Initialization files, on the other hand, describe to an *executable file* important information about how that program should run and where to find external support files.

The two fundamental INI files used by Windows 3.x are the WIN.INI file and the SYSTEM.INI file. Both files are plain ASCII text files located by default in the \WINDOWS directory. New sections can be added to INI files either by other program installations or by the user. Sections are enclosed in square brackets (e.g., [restrictions]) with a unique name.

SYSEDIT.EXE

SYSEDIT.EXE, located in the \WINDOWS\SYSTEM directory, is a small editing utility applet that opens and cascades the primary configuration files for Windows 3.1x and Windows 9x. In 16-bit Windows, the main files are CONFIG.SYS and AUTOEXEC.BAT for DOS, and SYSTEM.INI and WIN.INI for Windows. All four files are opened and arranged (cascade style) and can be viewed and edited. If Windows for Workgroups is installed, SCHDPLUS.INI is included in the editor for Schedule Plus (a workgroup schedule management program). Windows 3.x and Windows 9x also include PROTOCOL.INI for Real Mode networking protocols and configuration settings.

Note: SYSEDIT can be set up in any program group window by using the File\New\ Program Item dialog box in Program Manager. Likewise, you can drag the SYSEDIT.EXE program onto the Start button to put it into your Programs menu.

SYSTEM.INI

Anyone who installs a new piece of hardware or a new software application under Windows 3.x is touching the SYSTEM.INI file. This is the initialization file that Windows looks at after all the necessary and core system files have been installed. The SYSTEM.INI file contains the controls for the interface between Windows and DOS and, as we just saw, is where Windows VxDs are loaded into memory.

The SYSTEM.INI file is a plain ASCII text file that can be edited by WORDPAD.EXE, NOTEPAD.EXE (Windows applets), the DOS Editor (EDIT.COM), SYSEDIT.EXE, or any word processor that saves files in plain ASCII low-bit format.

Note: WordPad is capable of saving to file types other than TXT (plain text). Be sure you choose the text format, or SYSTEM.INI becomes unreadable to Windows.

SYSTEM.INI is divided into *sections*, each of which has a heading enclosed in square brackets ([ ]). The most common areas of user interest are the [386Enh] section for 16-bit device drivers and the [boot] section, where the **SHELL=PROGMAN.EXE** line points to the shell file that runs the Program Manager at startup. This shell statement was moved into MSDOS.SYS for Windows 9x and calls the Desktop. The Program Manager still runs just fine under Windows 9x, and you can see a miniature version of how it used to look by right-clicking on the Start button and choosing Open.

Note: Changing SHELL=PROGMAN.EXE to SHELL=WINFILE.EXE causes Windows 3.x to start up with the File Manager as the first window.

The only unusual thing to remember about the SYSTEM.INI and WIN.INI files (or any other Windows INI file) is that **REM** (Remark) isn't the way to comment out a line in the file. To skip over the line in an INI file, you must use a semicolon (;) in the first column of the specific line, followed by at least one space. **REM** is used for DOS batch files.

SYSTEM.INI can run alongside the Windows 9x Registry (SYSTEM.DAT and USER.DAT), and in Chapter 12, we discuss the differences among the three files. Until there are no more 16-bit legacy devices, there may still be a need for this particular file.

Remember that SYSTEM.INI installs device drivers and VxDs. Windows 9x continues to use the SYSTEM.INI file to load certain types of 16-bit device drivers, so even Window 9x machines may often have a SYSTEM.INI file.

WIN.INI

The second basic initialization file that Windows looks through at startup is WIN.INI. WIN.INI isn't required, but if it doesn't exist, Windows creates a default version. The WIN.INI file is where all the information about the overall user environment for Windows is stored. Whereas SYSTEM.INI is similar to the CONFIG.SYS file in the DOS startup process, WIN.INI is similar to the AUTOEXEC.BAT file at the end of the booting process.

WIN.INI contains the [windows] section, where programs can be set to run automatically without putting them in the Startup group window. **LOAD=** tells a program to run minimized on Windows startup, and **RUN=** tells a program to run normally at Windows startup.

Note: When you can't find a reference to some program that seems to run from the Startup program group, you'll almost always find it referenced in either the LOAD= or RUN= line at the top of the WIN.INI file. Screen savers and antivirus programs typically use this line, as do mouse configurations.

The WIN.INI file also contains a listing of all the fonts installed into Windows, along with associated extensions for programs—file associations. For example, the [extensions] section of the WIN.INI file might have the line

```
bmp=C:\windows\ mspaint.exe ^.bmp
```

which tells Windows that, any time it sees a DOS file with a .BMP extension, it can make an assumption that the program MSPAINT.EXE will be used to open that file.

What Happens If Certain Files Are Missing?

There may be some peculiar scenarios on the A+ exam, and one of the more unusual ones that you may encounter is a situation in which either the SYSTEM.INI or WIN.INI file is missing. If the SYSTEM.INI file is missing, Windows simply won't start at all, and it produces an error message to that effect. If the WIN.INI file is missing, Windows starts in a default VGA Mode (assuming Enhanced Mode is possible). This is the precursor to the Windows 9x Safe Mode (discussed in Chapter 12), where Windows starts with a basic configuration. When Windows can't find a WIN.INI file, it creates one when it starts. Any environmental customization (e.g., colors, icon spacing, or mouse configurations) will be missing, but you will at least be in Windows.

File Associations

Have you ever used the F2 key or the Properties menu to rename an executable file in Windows Explorer? If you change the extension (assuming it's even visible) you'll get an "Alert!" message telling you that you may be unable to run the program and that the file naming police have been dispatched to arrest you immediately. Why is there an alert message at all?

Files are *associated* in the [extensions] section of the WIN.INI file by selecting File|Associate in File Manager. This used to be a simple process in Windows 3.x and is typically far more complex under Windows 9x. Associating a program means that you can double-click on a file name in either File Manager or Windows Explorer, and Windows runs a program that can work with the file. But how does Windows know which program to run?

Here's where you really need to know all about *file extensions*, those three letters to the right of the period in a file name (see Chapter 10). A common association is that any file ending with a .DOC extension automatically opens Microsoft Word. Both Windows 3.x and Windows 9x install certain predefined associations. Typically, INI files, BAT files, and TXT files are associated with the Notepad or WordPad text editors. Many shareware programs (try before you buy) include a DIZ description file. If you download a lot of shareware, you can easily associate the .DIZ extension with Notepad, thereby making it easy to double-click on the description and read it.

A default installation will typically hide the extensions in Windows Explorer. Whether or not you unhide the extensions, the associations are what produce the icon and description in the Explorer window. The Windows 3.x File Manager shows all file extensions by default, and choosing File|Associate immediately calls up a dialog box. Windows 9x, on the other hand, requires that you either do some detective work to find out what program is already associated with an extension, or fill out a nearly incomprehensible description form.

PROGMAN.INI

The poorly documented PROGMAN.INI file is a configuration file that controls the way the 16-bit Windows Program Manager appears to the user. The default INI file contains a list of the *program groups* and very little other data. However, this file can be used to provide basic security on a system by removing certain options from the shell.

Usually the last line under the [Groups] section begins with **Order=**, specifying the order in which Program Manager loads various groups. An optional section can be *added* by editing the PROGMAN.INI file and typing "[Restrictions]". The *xxxx=* lines added to this section can tell Program Manager whether to allow a user to run a program (**NoRun=**), change settings (**NoSaveSettings=**), or use the File menu (**NoFileMenu=**), among other things. Using the [Restrictions] section is a way to prevent someone from accidentally deleting (and/or creating) program groups.

The rapid onset of corporate networking and computer crime produced an industry-wide boom in security programming. Microsoft began including various security functions in Windows with the PROGMAN.INI file, but quickly moved into a full-featured set of security options. Typically, the person controlling computer security is a systems administrator or network administrator.

Group (GRP) Files

Within the Program Manager, a number of additional windows are installed by default and can be added by the user. Each of these smaller windows is a program group. Each program group contains graphic symbols (icons) representing individual *program items*. Both program groups and program items can be created with the File|New option of the Program Manager menu. Windows Explorer works the same way, but choosing File|New offers an option for either a new file or a new folder (program group).

In almost the same way that a directory contains subdirectories and files, program groups contain icons pertaining to related programs (shortcuts), or they act as a sort of bucket to hold programs the user wants easy access to. Either way, Windows stores the information about what icons are in any given program group, along with each icon's properties. The files where this information is stored generally use the first eight letters of a window's title (found on the title bar) and a GRP extension.

Group files were the precursor to the shortcut link (LNK) files and are normally stored somewhere in the \WINDOWS directory. During the creation process, program groups offer the user an opportunity to name a specific location and file name, but most people don't use this option. The properties menu on a LNK file continue to provide information about the actual executable program being pointed to.

A common problem found on Windows 3.x systems occurs when a user has accidentally highlighted a program group icon and deleted it. Although the group file has been deleted, the underlying programs are not affected at all. Create an \INIBACK directory (or some other name) and copy the group files and INI files to it. In the event a GRP file is accidentally deleted, you can restore the program group by simply copying it back to the \WINDOWS directory.

For the exam, remember that before you upgrade a Windows 3.x system to a Windows 9x environment, you should back up all GRP files, along with all INI files (*.GRP and *.INI). Windows 9x can interpret both types of files and carry the previous configuration through the upgrade.

The DOS commands **DIR [*d*:]*.GRP /S** and **DIR [*d*:]*.INI /S** will find all GRP and INI files on a drive (where [*d*:] is the drive letter). *.GRP and *.INI can also be used within File Manager (File|Search) and within Windows Explorer (Tools|Find).

Memory

An operating system is software and, as such, loads into memory. It's important to understand the memory environment and how DOS, Windows, and any other software lives in that environment. In this context, the three main types of memory are:

➤ Conventional memory

➤ Expanded memory (EMS)

➤ Extended memory (XMS)

Basic Memory Divisions

You can think of memory as divided into two basic worlds: the world of what used to come with 8088/8086 PCs and the world of everything that was invented later. Remember that computers still often face day-to-day limitations that are based on the way in which the first XT worked. These limitations have been forced on the manufacturers by the entire concept of *backward compatibility*.

Microprocessors have many switches on their silicon layer and something called *microcode*, which is an extremely small machine language that is designed to process basic logic, arithmetic, and control signals. In addition to the switches, there are *data banks* that keep track of calculations in progress and *registers* that keep track of control data. The registers have a tiny amount of memory capability, allowing them to store only 2 bytes of information at a time.

If you recall that a byte is 8 bits, then 2 bytes would be 16 bits. A byte is something like the letter "G" or the number "5," and a register can contain 2 bytes. When the 2 bytes are put together, the combination is called a *word*.

A CPU has 14 registers, each of which is 2 bytes long, or 16 bits. The largest number that all these registers can hold (if every one of them had a hexadecimal F) would be 65,536. If you divide 1,048,576 (1MB) by 65,536, you get 16. Coincidentally, the first megabyte of RAM, as we'll see shortly, is divided into 16 segments.

The Costs of Doing Business

Technical people sometimes forget that a computer is a tool that often is used in business to earn profits. A fundamental principle of business is that everything must pay for itself and that whatever remains is profit. Imagine a company using 30,000 computers with Windows 95 as the operating system.

Say that the price of a single copy of Windows 2000 is $50 (taking into consideration volume discounts, upgrade discounts, and so on), and then multiply $50 by the 30,000 computers. Simply purchasing the software would cost $1.5 million, which doesn't include shipping, taxes, and other incidental charges.

This company has an entire information systems (IS) staff and can assign five full-time employees the task of installing the upgrade on every computer. The rest of the staff must handle day-to-day problems and questions. Suppose that these five employees each make a salary of $16 per hour.

If it took only 30 minutes per computer to back up the original machine and install the upgrade, each computer would cost $8 in labor for one IS employee and possibly an additional half-hour of the person whose desk had the computer. Considering only the IS staff, 30,000 machines at $8 each would cost $240,000 in time and labor. With no problems, no errors, and a perfect first-time installation, it's already costing the company $1.74 million. We haven't even looked at the downtime of every salaried employee whose computer is unusable during the upgrade, from the $8-per-hour clerk to the $175,000-per-year executive (assuming $84 per hour with a loss of $42 of computer time). Nor have we looked at the time costs that the mailroom uses to process all those incoming copies of Windows 2000.

Those 30-minute-per-machine upgrades mean 15,000 work hours divided by the 5 IS employees, or 3,000 hours per IS employee. Assuming an 8-hour workday, it would take each IS employee 375 days to accomplish the upgrade. Naturally, with time off for weekends and sleep, you can see that it would take more than a year simply to change the company from Windows 95 to 2000. Then, think of what this would mean if the main spreadsheet program didn't work on the upgrade—if Windows 2000 wasn't backward compatible.

The BIOS contains tables of interrupts, copyright information, testing routines, error messages, and some instructions to put characters on the screen in color. The ROM chips also hold a scaled-down version of Basic that the chip can use to execute instructions on how to move all the stored information into lower memory. Because DOS doesn't start running until after startup, this Basic code in the ROM chips controls the lights and beeps and initializes the printer and the keyboard.

Conventional Memory

ROM BIOS assigns and keeps track of specific locations in memory. These memory addresses are constantly being attached to bits of data and shuttled across buses and through the system. If the CPU can move 16 bits of information around in its own registers (internal bus), it stands to reason that it should be able to pass 16 bits of information to everything around it (external). Reason, however, has never been a strong point in the computer world.

The 8088 could keep track of a bit more (no pun intended) than a million separate addresses in memory, or 1MB (1,048,576 bits). Almost everything involved with moving data around a computer is done by its address. This is like mailing a picture of your new car to a friend. The post office has no interest in the picture, only in the address on the envelope. Imagine that you were a single mail carrier and had a million addresses to work with *every day*.

To make it easier to keep track of the first megabyte of memory, the 8088/86 CPU used 16 "regional ZIP codes," called *segments*. Each segment of memory is 64KB long. Because the 8088/86 could address only 1MB of memory, this was fine. Newer chips have the capability to address far more than 1MB of memory and to do so more directly.

Memory segments are numbered, and the smaller numbers are said to be lower than the larger, higher numbers. For this reason, data stored in the first segments of RAM is said to be in *low memory*.

 The original addressing scheme of the 8088/86 chips, using 16 segments of 64KB of memory, is the foundation of all later memory organization. This 1MB of RAM, divided into segments, is referred to as *conventional memory*. Memory addresses are expressed in hexadecimal numbers.

If you use binary math to calculate the number of addresses available to a 16-bit processor, you'll see that the number is less than the actual number available. Binary math alone won't go the whole distance (it would take 20 bits) because of the two-part address involving the segment and the *offset*. Without going into the details, you should know that memory error messages are reported using both parts of the address.

The *segment address* is one of the 16 regional segments of the 1MB. The *offset address* is the specific address within the 64KB length of the segment. The combination of segment and offset addresses is how a 16-bit processor can address 20 bits of addresses, or 1MB.

Although you might not be tested on this low level of detail, if you plan to work on computers, you should at least know what a segment address and an offset address look like. A typical example presented on the screen would be SEGMENT:OFFSET and appear as 30F9:0102.

80286 and Real Mode

The 8088/86 chips used single addresses for each segment:offset location in memory. The registers in the chip hold the actual hex number of the address as it directly relates to a *real address* in 1MB of memory. This direct, real, one-to-one relationship is known today as the Real Mode use of memory. The need for compatibility has kept Real Mode, along with the original 1MB of directly addressable memory, alive to this day (in 16-bit virtual machine windows).

The 286 chip changed from segment:offset addressing to something called *selector:offset addressing*. Instead of using a real segment, the registers held a pointer, or *vector*, to some other segment. Because the selector pointer is a smaller number than the full segment address, more selectors can fit into the same number of registers. This concept of using one address to refer to another address is used throughout the computer world. The words that describe this process are *mapping* and *aliasing*.

Aliasing and Mapping

When you rent a box at the post office, you're telling the post office that instead of putting an address on your big house, you want to put your address on a small box that will *refer* mail to your house. Instead of having to walk all the way to your house, the postal service can immediately move an envelope into your box, and *you* can then come pick it up. The box is vastly smaller than your house, and the distance from the incoming mail dock far shorter.

A cooperative venture between the post office (the CPU), which *could* deliver all the way to your house, and you (the hardware), who walks to the post office, results in faster processing and access to a larger storage area—the whole post office. In a nutshell, this is how expanded memory works.

The external **DOS SUBST** command (for *substitute*) is a way to shrink a long path of many subdirectories (with many characters) into the two characters of a drive letter. If you substitute C:\WINDOWS\SYSTEM\VBRUNS\100 with G:, instead of entering the full path, you can refer to it by using the aliased drive letter, G:. This is called *drive mapping*.

The 286 chip used part of its register group to provide an indicator to a real segment in additional sets of 1MB of memory. In other words, instead of a real address in a single megabyte of real memory, the register holds a sort of P.O. box number that refers to a whole new megabyte of memory. When the address is called, the CPU is pointed to this new megabyte and gets the segment:offset address of that new megabyte. Using this scheme, the 286 could address up to 16MB of memory.

Aliasing and mapping are used in expanded memory, interrupt vector tables, and most importantly, in the pseudo-32-bit FAT of the Windows 9x Installable File System (IFS) and VFAT. It is also used in networking, where very long path names (which include volumes and drives) are mapped to single drive letters.

If you think of air-traffic control as assigning a vector to an airplane, the controller is essentially pointing the pilot in a certain direction. The interrupt vector tables tell DOS where to look to find a particular set of interrupts. An undocumented command in DOS is the **TRUENAME** command, which returns the formal name of a subdirectory, regardless of how it may masquerade as a mapped or substituted drive letter.

Mapping is commonly used to create network drive letters out of specific subdirectories. Aliases are commonly used in Windows shortcuts (LNK files), which are iconic representations of pointers to executable files somewhere on the drive.

Low Memory (Segment 1)

When DOS begins to load, even before the system files are hauled up by their bootstraps, BIOS installs its main I/O tools, tables, and instructions in the area of conventional memory that IBM originally reserved for it. The DOS system files "kernel" is also put into low memory—the first segment of the conventional 1MB of RAM (0000h to 9000h). Remember, this first megabyte is *conventional memory* and is addressed in the old, 8088/86 *real* way—Real Mode.

DOS uses a low-memory control process to map out the first megabyte of memory and stores this map in a location within the first segment of RAM. The first segment can easily be very crowded, containing device drivers, parts of COMMAND.COM, pieces of TSRs, disk buffers, and environment and file controls. The first segment of memory goes to:

➤ The interrupt vector table and DOS BIOS low-memory control

➤ IO.SYS and MSDOS.SYS

➤ Device drivers, such as MOUSE.SYS and ANSI.SYS

➤ Disk buffers

➤ Stacks (the way the CPU prioritizes and keeps track of tasks that were interrupted by more important tasks)

➤ The environment and file control blocks (FCBs)

➤ The resident part of COMMAND.COM, which is always in memory and produces the message "Abort, Retry, Ignore, Fail?"

➤ Pieces of the transient part of COMMAND.COM, which periodically drops out of memory to disk and then returns when it's needed

➤ The stack and data parts of programs, which are running but lurking in the background waiting to be called on (e.g., the **MODE** or **PRINT** commands from DOS or Borland's Sidekick)—TSR programs

When an event needs to interrupt the CPU, whatever generated the interrupt first checks the *interrupt vector table* for directions on where to look for the actual interrupt instructions. This table is in the first segment (low memory) from 0000h to 1000h. The interrupt vector table is used by BIOS, DOS, the interrupt controller chip, the main CPU, and any software programs that are running.

COMMAND.COM is a fairly large file, and for efficiency's sake, it doesn't load completely into RAM and remain there using up space. You need some parts of COMMAND.COM only rarely, whereas other parts must be available constantly. For example, the part that watches for a missing disk must be in memory all the time because the event causing the missing disk can happen at any time. This part of COMMAND.COM is *resident* because it's always resident (living) in memory.

The resident part of COMMAND.COM is like a sentry. It keeps an eye out for a commanding officer while the rest of the command is taking a break. When you exit an application and go to a DOS command line, the resident part calls the *transient* part of COMMAND.COM, which hurries back from the disk and jumps into memory just in time to produce the C:\> prompt and begin parsing the command line.

Upper Memory (Segments 10 through 16)

Passing over the 640KB of applications memory, the very top segment of memory, from F000h to FFFFh, is also grabbed at the beginning of the startup process. The motherboard's system BIOS installs to this segment to run the self tests generated at the time the power is turned on (the POST). This is also where the ROM-level BIOS instructions are stored for drive controllers, keyboard polling, the system clock, I/O ports (serial and LPT), and a map of the addresses of the memory itself. System ROM (motherboard) and Basic go to segment 16.

IBM originally left a small 64KB gap directly above the area set aside for running programs. This area occurs at segment A000h and was quickly grabbed by enterprising memory management software utilities or was sometimes configurable by DIP switches. Instead of 640KB of user memory, this allowed for an additional

64KB, making 704KB available. Because this extra segment has always been there and has always been unclaimed, 32-bit operating systems routinely provide 704KB of usable memory for a virtual PC running in a DOS window.

Video RAM (B000)

The 64KB block after A000h was intended for EGA and VGA video extensions. IBM's common monochrome adapter (CMA)—also known as monochrome display adapter (MDA)—also laid claim to this area. However, as soon as CGA and color monitors arrived on the market, B000h to B800h became available to be stolen. Early memory managers could grab the 32KB between B000h and B800h for extra RAM on top of the previous 64KB.

Working with a CGA monitor was like looking through a screen door through silk underwear at a pine tree blowing in the wind without your glasses on. Aside from a resolution problem, the adapter card didn't have enough memory, and any scrolling would cause the screen to go black before it redrew itself. CGA vanished as soon as it could, leaving its IBM-reserved memory area free for memory management software.

Note: The most commonly used DOS command with a CGA monitor was the CLS (clear screen) command. This command not only clears all text from the screen but also converts any residual color back to black and white. CLS is an internal DOS command that is built into COMMAND.COM.

Shortly after the failed CGA attempt, IBM introduced EGA, VGA, and the 8514/A color monitors. EGA and VGA demanded memory and went back to the A000h block to start high-resolution memory processing.

The 640K Barrier

DOS functions take up the first 64KB segment of the basic 1MB of conventional memory. ROM BIOS, the motherboard, COMMAND.COM, and other parts of DOS take an additional set of segments at the top of the conventional memory. Below these upper functions, video adapters, network cards, and certain drive controllers take up even more space. Because the top and the bottom of the 640KB user area is locked in by these other memory tenants, with most of the space taken at the top, people refer to the 640KB limit as the "640K barrier" or as hitting the "640K wall."

The *base memory* is whatever memory from the 640KB of user memory is left to the user after everything has loaded and all drivers and TSRs are in place. DOS 6.2 included a memory optimization software utility (MEMMAKER.EXE) that could provide close to 600KB of base memory. This optimization process took advantage of every unused piece of memory in the 1MB of conventional memory.

Virtual Memory

When Windows runs an application, that application looks at what it *thinks* is DOS and works with various memory addresses. In fact, Windows intercepts every addressing call from the program and hands the program an address based on Windows' own memory decisions. If a lot of memory has been used, Windows starts using disk space as additional, virtual memory.

When Windows puts an application's memory addresses on the disk, it uses 4KB chunks, and it doesn't tell the program that the apparent memory is somewhere on a disk. The application thinks it's addressing a continuous set of addresses in a RAM segment. When the application calls for memory addresses that aren't in actual RAM, it generates a *page fault request*, telling Windows to go to the disk and find those addresses. Windows then *pages* (loads) those addresses back into RAM and hands them to the application as though everything were completely normal.

Swap Files

Windows has two ways to set aside space on a hard drive to handle page overflow: *temporary* and *permanent* swap files. Windows 3.x could manage a maximum of only 16MB of installed RAM, but it could use far more virtual memory by saving 4KB pages (chunks) of memory to the disk as a swap file.

Note: The default location of the swap file is the root directory of the drive where Windows was installed, usually drive C:. This is true of Windows 9x as well as Windows 3.x.

The difference between a permanent and temporary swap file is mostly speed of access, leading to system performance issues. If Windows is going to swap out memory to the disk, it has two options: It can create a file somewhere on the disk and put memory there, or it can go to an already existing file. If it has to create the file at the moment, then it's a temporary swap file and is deleted when the session ends. You can create a permanent swap file out of contiguous sectors and save some time by not making Windows have to create the file when it needs it.

Windows 3.x created two files when it set up the drive's swap file. The first file, SPART.PAR, was a small read-only file in the Windows subdirectory. The sole purpose of this file was to tell Windows the location and size of the other file (the actual swap file). The swap file is usually in the root directory of the installation drive, but it can be on another, larger drive.

In Windows 3.1x, the permanent swap file is called 386PART.PAR and can be seen with File Manager if the View (by file type) options are set to show hidden files. The temporary swap file is usually called WIN386.SWP. A disadvantage of the temporary file is that it grows or shrinks depending on Windows' needs. The permanent swap file is fixed and doesn't grow to take over your disk.

Note: If Windows is running in Standard Mode, a third type of temporary swap file—an application swap file—is created whenever a DOS application is started from within Windows.

Controlling Swap Files

Windows recommends a file size for the virtual memory swap file, and this recommendation can be changed. Windows 9x decided to drop the "swap file" name in favor of the more sophisticated-sounding "virtual memory." Either way, the file calculates all *available space* on the Windows installation drive, together with the largest block of contiguous, unfragmented space, to recommend a file 2.4 times the size of the *physical memory* installed on the computer.

User control over the type and size of the swap file is handled by the Control Panel applet (in the Main program group of Program Manager for Windows 3.x, or in Start|Settings under Windows 9x). Control Panel is run by the CONTROL.EXE program in the \WINDOWS directory. Any changes are stored in the CONTROL.INI file and in the \WINDOWS directory.

You can always get to the Control Panel quickly by clicking on the Start button (or pressing Ctrl+Esc), choosing Run and typing "control", and then pressing Enter. By the way, if you right-click on the Start button, you can quickly go to the Explorer or the Find (Explorer|Tools|Find|Files or Folders) option. To get a fast Desktop (Program Manager Window), click on Start, choose Run, type a period (dot), and then press Enter.

The Control Panel icon opens to the Control Panel window, which contains icons for the internal subroutines held within CONTROL.EXE. In 16-bit Windows, one of the available icons is the Enhanced icon (a graphic picture of a CPU) through which virtual memory settings can be changed. The Enhanced option in the Control Panel is used to change virtual memory settings, swap file size and type, and device contention between I/O ports. The Enhanced option also provides for configuring task scheduling and Windows foreground, background, and exclusive processing.

In Windows 9x, virtual memory is accessed through the Control Panel's System icon, by double-clicking on the My Computer icon and opening Control Panel, or by right-clicking to the Properties menu on the My Computer icon. At the System Properties dialog box, the Performance tab has a button for virtual memory. This is only slightly more sophisticated than the original Windows 3.x swap file.

Allowing Windows to manage memory (recommended) is merely giving Windows a temporary swap file (which can take over the entire logical drive). Permanent swap file configuration is under the Let Me Manage... checkbox.

Note: Because Windows would like to take total control of the user's system, the alert message following a reconfiguration to permanent swap file status is terrifying. It speaks of the end of the world and total collapse of civilization as we know it. Disabling virtual memory on this tab window merely disallows Windows from creating swap files.

A permanent swap file is a bit faster than a temporary swap file because it contains contiguous clusters and need not be created before Windows can use it. A temporary swap file must be created and saved before Windows can transfer the first 4KB memory block to the disk. It's better to defragment (DEFRAG.EXE) the disk before loading Windows and changing virtual memory to make the swap file permanent.

HIMEM.SYS and EMM386.EXE

Properly speaking, any memory beyond the first 1MB of conventional memory is extended memory. However, because there was no way to use this memory until the Lotus/Intel/Microsoft (LIM) specifications and hardware cards arrived on the market, the residue of expanded memory still exists. Even under Windows 9x, extended memory can be configured so that a part of it is used as expanded memory.

For any kind of memory beyond the conventional 1MB to be accessible by DOS, a memory manager device driver must be loaded from the CONFIG.SYS file. Originally, the device was only an expanded memory manager. With DOS 5.0, Microsoft began selling DOS directly to the customer. This generic DOS used HIMEM.SYS as a doorway manager to extended memory. Part of HIMEM.SYS is its ability to access unused parts of the conventional 1MB, which it calls *upper memory blocks (UMBs)*.

HIMEM.SYS does not provide expanded memory configuration. EMM386.EXE is the expanded memory device drive and will not run unless HIMEM.SYS has been loaded first. In DOS and 16-bit Windows, all this was done in the CONFIG.SYS (Configure the System) file. Windows 95 incorporated the loading of HIMEM.SYS into the IO.SYS system file. If an old legacy program requires expanded memory, then EMM386.EXE still loads from a CONFIG.SYS file, and one will have to be created. Windows 9x did away with creating this file automatically, along with the AUTOEXEC.BAT file. That doesn't mean the CONFIG.SYS and AUTOEXEC.BAT aren't still necessary in some instances, however.

Do whatever you need to do to separate the correct names and characteristics for *expanded* (EMS) and *extended* (XMS) memory from conventional memory. The exam will contain questions about how each type of memory works and their correct names. You might use the *386* in EMM386.EXE to think of the old days, back when the 80386 processor was a hot item. Today, practically nothing uses expanded memory, so perhaps you can associate *expanded* with *old* and *386*. Another way might be that the "X" in XMS is the Roman numeral "TEN" and X-TEN sounds a lot like extended.

Upper Memory Blocks (UMBs)

DOS and Windows 3.x machines want to have as much base memory (640KB application memory) as possible for running DOS applications. DOS 5.0 introduced a change to COMMAND.COM that allowed it to use high memory and upper memory blocks to store parts of itself.

Upper memory blocks are managed by EMM386.EXE, which can run only after HIMEM.SYS has opened the door to extended memory. Therefore, the only way the **DOS=UMB** directive can be used is if the HIMEM.SYS driver is used first.

After HIMEM.SYS opens access to all memory above the 1MB of conventional memory, COMMAND.COM can be loaded into the *High Memory Area (HMA)*. **DOS=HIGH** places most of the command processor into the HMA (above A000h). To use even more extra memory, the UMBs can be made accessible only through the expanded memory driver (EMM386.EXE).

EMM386.EXE allows high memory and UMBs to be used for applications and drivers. High memory can hold programs by using **DEVICEHIGH=** (in CONFIG.SYS) and **LOADHIGH=** (in AUTOEXEC.BAT).

Translation Buffers

Windows still requires DOS to handle certain functions, such as reading or writing a file to disk. To do this, Windows switches the CPU back to Real Mode so that DOS can run in Real Mode and read the conventional memory for instructions. To communicate with DOS, Windows places *translation buffers* in the upper memory 384KB area.

Translation buffers act as a kind of vector table for Windows to hand addresses to DOS. Windows also uses translation buffers to make Real Mode networking calls to a network operating system. Windows allocates two 4KB translation buffers (8KB) for each virtual PC. Running an application creates a virtual PC, so each running application uses 8KB of real memory in the form of translation buffers.

Note: Networked physical computers use six 4KB translation buffers per virtual PC, which is 24KB per application.

Because all adapter cards, including network interface cards, use some address space in upper memory, a physical computer with a number of adapter cards can eventually take up all the upper memory. In this event, Windows can be told to use *base* memory for translation buffers. Translation buffers can't be split between upper and base memory. If the translation buffers end up in base memory, every virtual PC that Windows creates will inherit the buffers, leaving less memory for the application to run.

Remember that Windows creates virtual PCs out of the existing environment when it loads. Therefore, when an application runs and Windows 3.x creates a virtual PC for it, the VM inherits the DOS environment that was in existence when 16-bit Windows was started.

System Resources

All *free memory* (not conventional memory) available from the first DOS prompt is referred to as *base* memory (640KB), the High Memory Area (HMA) above A000h, and *extended* memory (beyond 1MB). After Windows (all versions) is up and running, it takes control of memory on the system and loads device drivers, program code, and data files into free memory. DOS is out of the loop except for file management at the disk level and hardware management at the interrupt level.

For the exam, remember that, although there is a formal distinction between base memory and conventional memory, questions will usually apply the term "conventional" memory to the 640KB used for applications, and will refer to high memory by name.

The names used for memory in a DOS session change after Windows is running. All of memory becomes the global heap, or simply "the heap."

The Windows 3.x Environment: Global Heap

The *global heap* in Windows 3.x is the entire amount of memory available at startup. Windows reads the existing environment created by CONFIG.SYS (if it exists) and HIMEM.SYS (if it was loaded). Whatever programs have been installed by DOS prior to running Windows are recognized by Windows, and whatever memory is actually available for programs is taken by Windows.

The global heap is all available memory that Windows 3.x can see at startup. The maximum amount of actual memory Windows 3.x can use is 16MB. The global heap is divided into three main areas:

➤ *Conventional memory*—This is the same as base memory in DOS real sessions, (i.e., segments above low memory and below A000h).

➤ *High memory*—If DOS has set aside areas above the A000h segment for use by applications, Windows takes control of that area and adds it to the global heap of memory.

➤ *Extended memory*—After Windows starts, it already knows how much memory you have in your system by reading the virtual memory driver (HIMEM.SYS), and it takes over control of that memory from DOS and accesses it directly.

After Windows has taken over the management of RAM, it makes no difference whether the memory is extended or conventional. Windows sees all memory up to 16MB as part of the global heap. The theoretical limit to extended memory available to Windows 3.x is 15MB: 16MB minus the 1MB of conventional memory.

Windows loads program code into the heap by putting it first into lower segments and then into increasingly higher segments. The global heap is divided into two areas: USER.EXE and GDI.EXE. Each smaller area also has a *local* heap of memory.

The local heap is reported as the *system resources*, some of which is used and some of which is freed up as code moves in and out of memory. In Windows 3.x, each area is limited to one 64KB segment for a total of 128KB for the heap. The following system resources (memory) are a special area set aside by Windows:

➤ The USER and GDI local heaps together make up the Free System Resources percentage seen under the Help|About|(System) menu option from any main menu in a Windows-compliant application.

➤ Everything in the Windows environment (both 16-bit and 32-bit) uses a percentage of the system resources, including icons, windows, programs, applications, data, menus, program tools, and screen savers.

➤ System resources are reported as a percentage available. Typically, between 50 percent and 85 percent of the resources should be available at any given time (taking into account all programs running in that session).

Note: So-called memory doubler software does not double the amount of installed RAM; rather, it doubles the amount of system resources available from the two local heaps.

Programs are supposed to be written in such a way that resources are taken from the free system resources and given up again when the code for that program terminates. Unfortunately, not all programmers follow the rules, and not all programs work the way they were intended to work.

If something takes up resources, but fails to release them back to the heaps at conclusion, those resources never return to the Windows resources memory. This problem is sometimes referred to as a *resource leak*. Windows must be exited and restarted to re-create a new heap and start again with maximum free resources. This problem can occur as easily in Windows 9x as in Windows 3.x, although fewer programs written for 32-bit Windows steal resources.

An "Out of memory" error in Windows often refers to the lack of enough free system resources, not to the amount of total free memory on the computer.

LIM 4 Expanded Memory

By the time the AT-class computers were arriving on the market and the 80286 chip was getting organized, the hottest application driving the sale of PCs was the Lotus 1-2-3 spreadsheet. Lotus was getting tired of hearing complaints from its customers with big spreadsheets running out of memory, so it decided to do something about it. Lotus got together with Intel and worked out a process (bank switching) that they decided to call the Expanded Memory Specification (EMS) 3. No one knows what happened to specification 1 or 2, but eventually Lotus and Intel brought pressure to bear on Microsoft to join with them and release LIM (Lotus-Intel-Microsoft) EMS 3.2 memory.

LIM 3.2 *expanded memory* introduced access to 8MB of additional memory, allowing the 80286 to address up to 16MB of additional memory. LIM expanded memory required a special hardware expansion card, and software had to be written specifically to work with both the EMS memory and the cards.

Not long after the release of the EMS LIM specification, AST (a large motherboard manufacturer) got together with Ashton-Tate, one of the largest software companies and the maker of dBase. Together, these two companies released a far more flexible version of expanded memory specifications called Enhanced EMS (EEMS). Lotus, Intel, and Microsoft then one-upped the AST-Ashton-Tate group and enhanced their specification to version 4. LIM 4 EMS provided 32MB of addressable memory.

Think about it: Starting with the 80286, processors could address 2MB or more of memory, but DOS could address only the 1MB of real memory. There had to be a special way to work around that limitation. The workaround, once again, had to do with the selector:offset mapping process. One last segment of real memory was set aside and configured as the EMS page frame segment—a 64KB *block* that was set aside somewhere between C000h and E000h—above 640KB base memory, but below video RAM.

The 64KB page frame was divided into four 16KB blocks called *pages*. When a program wanted to put data into expanded memory, it assigned an address to the data and then assigned a pointer vector to that address, kind of like renting warehouse space. The program put the data in the warehouse, making a note of the warehouse's location in the EMS page frame segment.

When the application called the data, it looked up the storage bin's address (the page of memory) in conventional memory and then switched DOS into thinking that the 1MB of memory it was looking at was one of the extended megabytes. DOS used the data while still thinking that it was in the original 1MB. When the data was sent back to memory, EMM386.EXE picked it up and drove it back to its remote storage bin in *extended* memory.

EMM386.EXE

In Chapter 8, we discussed how commands are used. The syntax of any command includes the command and the variables (switches) that can be used to set various configuration values. EMM386.EXE offers a good example of the convention used to describe a command's syntax. The complete syntax for EMM386.EXE is as follows, where each of the settings enclosed in square brackets ([ ]) can either have a value or represent a value:

```
EMM386.EXE [memory] [L=minXMS] [NOEMS] [RAM] [ON|OFF|AUTO]
  [I=address-address] [X=address-address] [W=ON|OFF] [Mx]
  [FRAME=address] [/Paddress] [Pn=address] [B=address]
  [A=altregs] [H=handles] [D=nnn] [N=path]
```

Note: EMM386.EXE RAM (using the RAM switch) provides whatever expanded memory is needed for any DOS applications that require it.

Conventional memory technically refers to the full 1MB of RAM installed on almost every computer sold in the last 10 years. The lower 640KB of application memory is technically called *base* memory. The upper 360KB is technically called *high* memory.

DEVICEHIGH and **LOADHIGH** can take advantage of high memory and UMBs to store device drivers. **DOS=HIGH,UMB** can load parts of COMMAND.COM into high memory and upper memory blocks.

 The certification exam generally uses the conventional memory designation to mean the first 640KB and the high memory designation to mean the upper 360KB, including UMBs.

Task Switching

The 80286 not only increased addressable memory to 16MB, but also introduced the concept of Protected Mode. In theory, Protected Mode keeps a given area of memory isolated from another area of memory. People using plain DOS were already coming up with ways to do more than one thing at a time on computers, and the most popular way for doing so was by *task switching*. Some commercial menu programs even provided a way for the user to do this. This integration of the menu program and the ability to do task switching made PCs easier to use and more versatile.

Task switching means that the loaded parts of a program and its data files are taken out of RAM and stored to the disk as a kind of photographic snapshot. All the program code for a word processor is saved out of RAM onto a special area of the hard drive called a *swap file*. The data or documents being worked on at the moment of the switch are also stored to the swap file.

Sometimes the CPU is in the middle of doing something when an IRQ comes along with an interruption. Depending upon how important that interruption is, the CPU has to put down whatever it was doing and pick up whatever the IRQ needs. The "place" in memory where the CPU keeps track of what processing it puts down is called a *stack*. If there are too many interruptions, the CPU can generate a *stack overflow error*. Task switching uses a process similar to that of the stacks used by the CPU.

Because it takes a certain amount of time to spin the disk, move the read/write heads, and store the information on disk, task switching is relatively slow. Not only must the contents of memory be stored, but a new program must be loaded into RAM and prepared for the user. Each new task being loaded into RAM requires a new snapshot of RAM: a *window*.

A way was needed to keep every program in memory and go beyond the 640K barrier of conventional memory so that the slowness of disk swapping RAM could be overcome. Then, the *page frame* and expanded memory arrived. Now, a program could be saved into expanded or extended memory just as easily as it could be saved to disk, and the 286 Protected Mode would (theoretically) keep everything nice and separate.

Page Frame Memory and Page Swapping

The 286 chip's Protected Mode and a LIM expanded memory card gave users access to 16MB of memory for use by programs and data. The idea was that if something could keep track of those snapshots of conventional RAM and shift them up into expanded memory, several programs could be run at once in the same base memory area. The 80286's protection features would make sure (in theory) that each program in memory had its own specially protected area and that, if something went wrong, the program could be shut down only in that area while everything else continued to run.

If you think of expanded memory as a sort of warehouse on the second floor of a building, then you can imagine a loading dock on the first floor. When a program is running, it's like a truck being loaded from the dock. If another truck (program) has to be loaded (run), then in our imaginary warehouse, all the boxes (program code) from the first truck have to be sent back up to the warehouse (expanded memory) on an elevator. New boxes have to be sent down the elevator, and the second truck has to change places with the first. The elevator is like the page frame. (We discussed memory pages in Chapter 4.)

Task switching is like a Lazy Susan on a dining room table. Someone who wants an item spins the rotating platter until the choice comes around. However, instead of the other choices becoming available to the other side of the table, the other programs are spun through the page frame doorway into expanded memory or are saved to the disk.

Task switching to expanded memory was a nice idea, but it didn't work out quite as planned. DOS had a hard time keeping the various balls it was juggling in the air and tracking which parts of memory were supposed to be used for what. Aside from that, the 64KB page frame area was becoming a bottleneck because users had to move a 550KB process through it during a switch and another 612KB process back up into EMS memory.

The 286 had some internal problems as well. For example, when a program crashed in a so-called protected area, it usually brought the entire system tumbling down with it, regardless of how well the program area was protected. This led to a reboot, which would cancel whatever had been going on with any other programs. The swap file would be erased during the reboot, and any data that hadn't been saved would be lost.

Virtual Device Drivers (VxDs)

The lowest area of the global heap (memory) is set aside for Windows to load Windows-based device drivers that handle the interface between Windows, DOS, and hardware devices. We saw that the CONFIG.SYS file in DOS installs device drivers in the first segment of conventional memory prior to loading Windows. The Windows device drivers are loaded into the lowest segment of the global heap, which is usually just above the low-memory area set aside by DOS.

Windows has its own device drivers that handle the keyboard, mouse, printers, video monitors, sound cards, scanners, and anything else that connects to the motherboard. All these device drivers are listed in the SYSTEM.INI file with any additional information they might need during startup.

For the exam, remember that a virtual device driver (VxD) is a 32-bit Protected Mode .DLL that manages a system resource (i.e., a hardware device or installed software) such that more than one application can use the resource at the same time. The 32-bit Protected Mode comes from the 32-bit 80386 chip architecture and therefore is available only for a 386 or faster CPU.

The V*x*D abbreviation is used to refer to any (V)irtual *device* (D)river, where *x* is used as a stand-in variable. The specific device driver replaces *x* with a character or characters referring to the specific type of driver. For example, a V*DD* is a virtual *display* driver, where *D* represents *display*.

VxDs work together with DOS to support multitasking in that more than one application can access the device at the same time in an arbitrated (managed) way. The VxDs work together with Windows to process interrupts and to carry out I/O processes for a specific application without interfering in another application's use of the same device. All the hardware devices on a typical computer have a VxD, including the motherboard program interrupt controller (PIC), the timer oscillator, DMA channels, disk controller(s), serial and parallel ports, keyboard and input devices, math coprocessor, and monitor display.

A virtual device driver is generally written to hold code for specific operations of a device that might not be included in the basic Windows installation. However, a VxD is required for any device that can retain settings information from an application that might mess up a request from another application. VxDs can also be written for any driver software that was installed by DOS during the CONFIG.SYS process.

When a VxD is a software driver, it usually surrounds the existing device (or TSR) and provides a specialized environment coming from Windows. This fools the existing device into thinking that only one computer running one application is present and that only that application will be using the hardware device controlled by the real driver. Again, the VxD is acting as a liaison between the Windows control management system and the individual device that is looking for a secure set of memory addresses.

 For the exam, remember that VxDs are installed from the SYSTEM.INI file, usually in the [386Enh] section of the file, and begin with **DEVICE=**, the same as they do in the CONFIG.SYS file. Windows 95 extended this process and tries to substitute a VxD for any device listed in a CONFIG.SYS file.

An Example CONFIG.SYS File

The following CONFIG.SYS file was processed by MEMMAKER, a DOS memory-optimization utility. Let's again discuss the fundamental directives and what they do using a real-world example.

 Be sure that you don't get caught saying that MEMMAKER speeds up the overall system performance. MEMMAKER only increases the amount of conventional memory available to DOS applications by moving whatever it can into high memory and UMBs (if they're available). Technically, this can speed up some applications, but for the exam, MEMMAKER affects space, not performance.

```
DEVICE=C:\DOS\SETVER.EXE
DEVICE=C:\WINDOWS\HIMEM.SYS /TESTMEM:OFF
DEVICE=C:\WINDOWS\EMM386.EXE RAM I=B000-B7FF WIN=CD00-CFFF
BUFFERS=40,0
FILES=70
DOS=UMB
LASTDRIVE=K
FCBS=16,0
DOS=HIGH
STACKS=9,256
SHELL=C:\COMMAND.COM /P /E:1024
DEVICE=C:\BUSLOGIC\BTDOSM.SYS /D
DEVICEHIGH /L:3,19344 =C:\BUSLOGIC\BTCDROM.SYS /D:MSCD0001
DEVICEHIGH /L:1,22576 =D:\IOMEGA\ASPIPPM1.SYS FILE=SMC.
     ILM SPEED=10
DEVICE=D:\IOMEGA\SCSICFG.EXE /V
DEVICE=D:\IOMEGA\SCSIDRVR.SYS
DEVICEHIGH /L:1,5888 =C:\DOS\RAMDRIVE.SYS 2048 /E
DEVICE=C:\WINDOWS\IFSHLP.SYS
```

A quick (but subtle) indication that this PC is not running Windows 9x is the fact that EMM386 has no **REM** (remark) in front of it, and the existence of the line **DOS=UMB**. In Windows 9x, SETUP.EXE automatically removes any expanded memory drivers from an existing CONFIG.SYS file during the installation process.

 Remember that Windows 9x requires HIMEM.SYS to access extended memory for virtual memory management. HIMEM.SYS has been hard-coded into the IO.SYS file, which took over configuration from CONFIG.SYS. Windows 9x also uses **REM** to cancel any reference to SMARTDRV or EMM386.EXE.

Points of Interest

Notice that the **DEVICEHIGH=** directive has been put in by MEMMAKER. The /L:# value is automatically configured when MEMMAKER optimizes the specific addresses. The BusLogic SCSI adapter driver controlling the CD-ROM has been moved to high memory, as has an Iomega driver.

EMM386.EXE (expanded memory) has been told that Windows 3.x is present and to include (/I=) a range of memory addresses for use by devices. This is the **I=B000-B7FF** switch on the EMM386 line.

A RAM drive has been installed using the following line:

```
DEVICEHIGH /L:1,5888 =C:\ DOS\RAMDRIVE.SYS 2048 /E
```

The **/L:1,5888** was added by MEMMAKER to put the device driver in high memory. RAMDRIVE.SYS loads the RAM drive device driver and creates a 2MB RAM drive in extended (/E) memory. A companion line in the AUTOEXEC.BAT file could then be used (**SET TEMP=G:**) to tell DOS to use the RAM drive for temporary files.

Note: RAMDRIVE.SYS comes with both DOS 6.x and Windows 9x and can create a virtual disk drive out of RAM. Because a RAM drive moves at the speed of memory, it can sometimes be useful for temporary files. However, the drive vanishes when the system is powered off.

Finally, HIMEM.SYS is used with an unusual **/TESTMEM:OFF** switch. During boot-up, when HIMEM loads, it tests the memory in almost the same way that the parity check is done during the POST. This second memory integrity check can take enough time that it can be turned off. **/TESTMEM:ON|OFF** is the settings switch to either turn off the memory checking or force it (useful with nonparity memory).

Windows 3.x could address a maximum of only 16MB of memory. Even though DOS could recognize more than that, 16-bit Windows would show "3% Remaining Resources" and fail almost as soon as it loaded. An undocumented way around this was to borrow the HIMEM.SYS file from Windows 95 OS/R-B and install it in place of the version that came with DOS 6.x. This would fool Windows 3.11 into believing it could use more than 64MB of RAM.

DEVICE= and DEVICEHIGH=

The **DEVICE=** directive means that a device is attached to the system. In this case, the device driver (usually a SYS file) can be found on drive D: in the \IOMEGA subdirectory. The specific name of the device driver file is ASPIPPM1.SYS. With a little experience, we might guess that this refers to an Iomega Zip, Jaz, or Ditto (tape) drive. A typical statement in the above CONFIG.SYS file appears as follows:

```
DEVICE=D:\IOMEGA\ASPIPPM1.SYS FILE=SMC.ILM SPEED=10
```

Remember that the CONFIG.SYS file is executed prior to the AUTOEXEC.BAT file during the boot process. The **PATH** environment variable can be set only after the system is under the control of the operating system. The **PATH** command can be run only in a batch file or at the DOS command line. **PATH=** is always found in the first few lines of the AUTOEXEC.BAT file.

Because no search path has been set when the CONFIG.SYS runs, every device must have its full path and file name in the directive. Because no path has been set, DOS can look for the driver file only in the root directory of the bootable disk in the boot drive. This is the directory that DOS is logged in to as the current directory at boot-up.

If enough memory was available in high memory (above conventional memory, according to the exam), the **DEVICEHIGH=** directive (DOS 5.0 and later) would attempt to load the Iomega (device) driver above the 640KB of base memory. In this case, the **DEVICE=** directive means that the driver is intended to load into conventional (base) memory.

MEMMAKER automatically runs hundreds of configuration settings to see which programs can make the most efficient use of high memory, UMBs, or both. In this case, it determined that the Iomega driver should stay in conventional base memory.

DOS marks an intentional space between characters with an equal sign (=), a semicolon (;), or a space (spacebar or ASCII decimal .0032 scan code). An equal sign or a semicolon is used most often to ensure that a space is marked and to leave no room for misinterpretation. ".0032" can be entered using the Alt key at the same time as the digits are entered on the numeric keypad of the keyboard.

Again, the line we're examining is:

```
DEVICE=D:\IOMEGA\ASPIPPM1.SYS FILE=SMC.ILM SPEED=10
```

A space and more information follow the device driver. **FILE=SMC.ILM** probably refers to a data file in which either further configuration settings are stored through customer configuration or the device reads factory-configured values.

During SETUP.EXE (all Windows versions) or INSTALL.EXE (DOS) for a new device, a typical detection program uses simple tests to check for the existence of certain hardware and software. This is not the same as the POST looking at CMOS settings.

Depending on whether Yes or No returns from a setup test, the new device's installation routine often chooses one of several files containing factory-configured values. These files are usually taken from the installation disk that comes with the device. Some knowledgeable guesswork would indicate that SMC.ILM is one of these factory configuration files relating to some device made by Iomega.

 The exam might ask you to explain why Windows 9x notices a particular device attached to the system but can't provide the manufacturer's information and settings. Windows 9x has a large internal database of many devices made by today's hardware manufacturers.

If Windows 9x can read settings information from a BIOS chip on a PnP-compatible device, it configures the device with its correct settings. If Windows 9x can recognize that a generic type of device is attached to an I/O port, it tries to use generic settings, which might work.

If Windows 9x notices only that a device exists at an I/O port, but can't even tell which general class (Registry) the device falls into, it tries to prompt the user for specific configuration settings by using the Have Disk option dialog box during installation.

If neither PnP processing nor generic device awareness takes place, the device is ignored in a full PnP-enabled configuration. If PnP is not enabled, Windows 9x resource management stops short of managing device resources.

At the end of the SMC.ILM file name is yet another space and the **SPEED=10** setting value. Note that no internal way exists of knowing what this refers to beyond some sort of speed setting with 10 being the value. The **SPEED** setting is explained only in the device's technical reference documentation.

MSDET.INF

Windows 9x uses detection modules called by MSDET.INF during setup. These DLL modules contain general settings information about classes (general categories) of devices. The specific .DLL files that MSDET.INF calls, try to read information from a device through PnP BIOS chips on the device. If PnP won't work, the .DLL generates common settings for that class of device. The settings are stored in the Registry following completion of the setup routine. This so-called autodetection became available starting with Windows 95.

The data resulting from the checking process is stored in the DETLOG.TXT file (detection log text file), and the device has either a manufacturer's name and settings stored in the Registry or a generic class name. To distinguish between true PnP compatibility and the best-guess capabilities built into Windows 9x, we use the term *autodetect* here, although it is not the formal name of a feature in Windows 9x.

A classic way to troubleshoot a PC is to bypass every reference to any device from all configuration files. Inexperienced technicians tend to use the Delete key to delete the entire file or to delete a line in a configuration file. In this situation, if it should turn out that the device was a critical system driver (such as a SCSI controller), the technician is left with only his or her memory to replace the line.

Regardless of whether CONFIG.SYS supports the **REM** statement, typing "REM" followed by a space at the beginning of any line in CONFIG.SYS or AUTOEXEC.BAT causes DOS to bypass the line without executing any instructions. In Windows INI files, use the semicolon (;) followed by a space to accomplish the same bypass.

If it should turn out that a configuration line is necessary, it can be reactivated by deleting the **REM** or the semicolon, removing the necessity of trying to remember what you've deleted at a later date.

Practice Questions

Question 1

A Windows ME machine no longer uses either a POST or a command interpreter because the Registry controls the entire process for the machine.

○ a. True

○ b. False

Answer b, false, is correct. All computers use a boot process involving a power-on self test (POST), regardless of what operating system is installed. The Windows Registry manages system configuration for Windows 9x machines running a Microsoft operating system and can only begin to operate after the system files have taken charge of the system.

Question 2

Windows 9x uses SYSTEM.DAT and USER.DAT to run driver software. Which initialization file is used in the case of a 16-bit legacy device?

○ a. WIN.INI

○ b. SYSTEM.INI

○ c. WIN.COM

○ d. PROGMAN.INI

Answer b is correct. SYSTEM.INI must be present for certain 16-bit hardware devices to be recognized by any version of Windows 95, 98, or ME. Answer a is incorrect because WIN.INI stores user configurations in a 16-bit Windows (3.x) environment. Answer c is incorrect because WIN.COM is the loader program for Windows and doesn't store any settings. Answer d, PROGMAN.INI, refers to the Windows 3.x Program Manager Desktop shell and was sometimes used for rudimentary security.

Question 3

Windows 95, 98, and ME all load the _____ memory manager from the _____ system file.

- ○ a. EMM386.EXE, MSDOS.SYS
- ○ b. EMM386.EXE, CONFIG.SYS
- ○ c. HIMEM.SYS, IO.SYS
- ○ d. HIMEM.SYS, MSDOS.SYS

Answer c is correct. Beginning with Windows 95, HIMEM.SYS was loaded from within the IO.SYS system file. In DOS and Windows 3.x, extended memory was accessed through the **DEVICE=** line in the CONFIG.SYS file. Answers a and b are incorrect because EMM386.EXE is an expanded memory manager, not extended memory. HIMEM.SYS accesses XMS memory. Answer d is incorrect because MSDOS.SYS is concerned with how Windows starts up, not basic system access.

Question 4

Virtual Real Mode creates a _____ based on an _____ chip.

- ○ a. Virtual XT, 80286
- ○ b. Command session, 80386
- ○ c. Real machine, 80286
- ○ d. Virtual machine, 8088/86

Answer d is correct. The virtual machine (VM) is a software-generated copy of the first XT machine that was based on the 8088/86 CPU. It addresses memory in a "real" way. Answer a is incorrect because a VM is not a virtual XT, and the chip emulation is not a 286. Answer b is incorrect because of the 386 chip and the improper term "command session." Answer c is incorrect because of the 286 chip and the improper term "real machine."

Question 5

The utility program most used in a preliminary diagnostics session in order to examine settings and startup problems is _____.

- ○ a. PIFEDIT.EXE
- ○ b. SYSEDIT.EXE
- ○ c. REGEDIT.EXE
- ○ d. WINEDIT.EXE

Answer b is correct. Running SYSEDIT.EXE produces a cascade of windows showing the various basic text files the system uses during startup. Answer a is incorrect because PIFEDIT.EXE is used to configure a PIF file for a DOS application. Answer c is incorrect because REGEDIT.EXE is used to open the Windows Registry and reconfigure basic elements of the Windows 9x system, not to do a preliminary diagnostics on a faulty system. Answer d is incorrect because there is no system editor called WINEDIT.EXE.

Question 6

IO.SYS is loaded into the _____ memory area of _____ memory.

- ○ a. low, conventional
- ○ b. high, low
- ○ c. base, conventional
- ○ d. conventional, low

Answer a is correct. IO.SYS contains basic functions and tables required by the BIOS and motherboard. It loads into the low area of the first 1MB of conventional memory. Answer b is incorrect because the high and low areas of memory are contained within what's called conventional or (incorrectly) base memory. Technically, base memory is whatever memory is left to the user for applications. Answer c is incorrect because base and conventional memory refer to the overall first megabyte of memory. Answer d is incorrect because the terms are in reverse order of proper usage.

Question 7

Windows 98 creates a permanent swap file when you choose to specify virtual memory settings in the system's Performance dialog box.

○ a. True

○ b. False

Answer a, true, is correct. The Performance tab of the System properties dialog box under the Control Panel allows user configuration of temporary or permanent swap files. When Windows manages virtual memory, it usually uses a temporary swap file that can grow to take over all empty (contiguous) space on a hard drive. Specifying the virtual memory settings creates a permanent swap file, both limiting the amount of drive space Windows will take over and saving the time it takes to create the temporary swap file during each session.

Need to Know More?

 Freedman, Alan. *Computer Desktop Encyclopedia, 2nd Edition.* AMACOM, 1999. ISBN 0-814-479-855. This is great for a fast look-up or refresher.

 Messmer, Hans-Peter. *The Indispensable PC Hardware Book, 3rd Edition.* Reading, MA: Addison-Wesley Publishing Company, 2000. ISBN 0-201-403-994. This is a comprehensive, up-to-date reference book that covers far more than you will need to know for the exam.

 Microsoft Windows 95 Resource Kit. Redmond, WA: Microsoft Press, 1995. ISBN 1-55615-678-2. This is the definitive resource for all Windows 95 questions. It assumes that you have a good working knowledge of Windows 95.

 Minasi, Mark. *The Complete PC Upgrade and Maintenance Guide, 11th Edition.* San Francisco, CA: Sybex Network Press, 2000. ISBN 0-782-128-009. This is considered one of the best reference books available. In fact, Minasi's book was instrumental in the formulation of the first A+ exam.

 Muller, Scott. *Upgrading and Repairing PCs, 12th Edition.* Indianapolis, IN: Que, 2000. ISBN 0-7897-2303-4. This is one of our favorites. If you are going to have only one reference book, give this one serious consideration.

 Reeves, Scott, Kalinda Reeves, Stephen Weese, and Christopher S. Geyer. *A+ Exam Prep, 3rd Edition.* Scottsdale, AZ: The Coriolis Group, 2001. ISBN 1-57610-699-3. This is a good reference that concentrates on providing exam-required information.

 Rosch, Winn. *Hardware Bible, 5th Edition.* Indianapolis, IN: Sams Publishing, 1999. ISBN 0-789-717-433. This is a well-organized reference book that covers software issues as well as hardware.

Windows 95, 98, and ME

Terms you'll need to understand:

- ✓ Version release number
- ✓ FAT32, FAT16, 32-bit, 16-bit, and Virtual FAT (VFAT)
- ✓ Properties and Settings tabs
- ✓ File attributes (Hidden, System, Read-only, and Archive)
- ✓ INI files and log files (LOGVIEW.EXE and BOOTLOG.TXT)

- ✓ Safe Mode, Real Mode, the virtual machine (VM) and Virtual Memory Manager 32 (VMM32), and MS-DOS Mode
- ✓ Vectors (pointers), aliasing (mapping), and truncated file names
- ✓ History log and version control

Concepts you'll need to master:

- ✓ The Registry (SYSTEM.DAT and USER.DAT)
- ✓ HKey handles and keys
- ✓ The installation and startup process for Windows
- ✓ Static and dynamic virtual device drivers (VxDs)
- ✓ Configuration settings (CONFIG.SYS and AUTOTEXEC.BAT)

- ✓ Long File Names (LFNs) and Installable File System (IFS)
- ✓ Network redirectors and interrupt requests (IRQs)
- ✓ Windows Explorer (EXPLORER.EXE) and the Windows Desktop
- ✓ System administration tools, utilities, and application suites

When Windows 95 was released (to much fanfare and rock-and-roll music), the world stood back to wonder at the final integration of DOS and Windows NT in a fully backward-compatible 32-bit operating system. Software boxes carried a Windows 95 logo indicating that the software developers had complied with all the proper Microsoft coding instructions. So why do we still have Windows NT? And how come there's a Windows 98, a Windows ME, and a Windows 2000?

It turned out that, although Windows 95 is usually described as an operating system, the technical fact remained that Windows 95 required DOS 7.0 and a 16-bit FAT for file management precisely for that backward compatibility with older DOS and Windows 3.11 systems. In this chapter, we'll continue to refer to Windows 95, Windows 98, and Windows ME as *Windows 9x* or simply *Windows*. Otherwise, we'll refer specifically to the version names that we're differentiating.

Windows 95 introduced a simplified user interface, new system management tools, and the Windows Desktop. Several other new features included:

➤ Pre-emptive multitasking

➤ Protected Mode device drivers

➤ Multithreaded 32-bit application support

➤ Integrated email (Exchange) and dial-up networking

➤ Plug-and-Play (PnP) support

➤ Enhanced multimedia and video support

➤ Long File Names (LFNs) or Virtual FAT (VFAT)

➤ System policies held in user profiles for better individual security management of the computer

➤ IO.SYS and MSDOS.SYS as the primary device driver loader, with CONFIG.SYS and AUTOEXEC.BAT as secondary configuration files

➤ Dynamic 32-bit virtual device drivers (32-bit VxDs)

➤ System settings and internal configuration going to the Registry as opposed to INI files

Windows 95 also brought the concept of installation and administration *wizards* to the home PC to make it easier to do system tasks. A wizard is a set of software decision branches that produce related dialog boxes asking a user for input. Depending upon what the user inputs, the underlying wizard program makes a decision and presents the next dialog box in that decision branch. When all responses have been entered, the wizard takes care of applying all the configuration information to the underlying system.

One of the benefits of the Windows 95 Installation Shield (which also uses a wizard) was that it brought a rudimentary *uninstaller* into the operating system. If a program's installation routine was written to take advantage of the Installation Shield, the user could uninstall the program at a later date and be assured that most of the ancillary files for that program would be removed, regardless of their location on the hard drive. To use the Installation Shield's uninstaller, choose Start|Settings|Control Panel and double-click on the Add/Remove Programs icon. Highlight the application you want to uninstall, and click on the Add/Remove button.

Supplemental Releases

The old **VER** (version) command is still available in any Windows environment, from Windows 95 to Windows NT. To open the command line, you can:

➤ Double-click on an MS-DOS prompt.

➤ Restart the machine in MS-DOS Mode.

➤ Choose Start|Run, type "COMMAND", and press Enter.

After you have opened the command line, you can type "VER". Another way to see the version number is to access the General tab of the System Properties window by either right-clicking on the My Computer icon and choosing the Properties menu option or, in the Control Panel, clicking on the System icon.

Windows 95 is version 4.00.950 in its first release. This makes sense, given that the previous version of Windows was version 3.11 (Windows for Workgroups). Operating System Release-1 (OSR/A) was the first release of the operating system, with a Plus Pak soon to follow. The Plus Pak was a series of patches and bug fixes, and included several add-on utilities and features. OSR/2 (OSR/B) was released after the initial Windows 95 4.0 release. The way to see these minor version releases is through the **VER** command, through the System Properties dialog boxes, or on the Version tab of the EXPLORER.EXE Properties menu. There was an obscure OSR/D release, and nobody knows what happened to OSR/C.

Each of the minor version-number releases introduced various new features, and they also fixed a number of problems (bugs) with the previous version. Microsoft seems to have begun this policy of using minor release numbers for substantially different platforms all the way back with Windows 3.1. Somewhere between Windows 3.1 and Windows 95 OSR/B, Microsoft also seems to have begun to segment the buying market into technically knowledgeable users and general computer users.

Windows 95 OSR/A had enough problems and missing features that a Plus Pak was released as an *add-on*. Installing the add-on package changed Windows 95 at a system level, producing an oddly confusing semi-subrelease that wasn't version A anymore, but wasn't OSR/B either. OSR/B introduced a FAT32 partitioning capability that changed the way the system stored files.

Note: Although FAT16 could be upgraded to a FAT32 system without losing files, the only way to change a FAT32 system back to FAT16 was to repartition and reformat the hard drive.

As Windows 95 was incrementally updated with add-on packages, minor version releases, and downloads of *patches* and bug fixes (adjusted program code), the increasing variation became a problem. Corporate information technology (IT) managers were having difficulties tracking which computers were running what version of Windows. These changes had taken place over a couple of years, and the "95" in Windows 95 (1995) was making the operating system appear dated.

Windows 98 was a major release update, again using the year (1998) in the name rather than a version number, but keeping the version numbering as a minor release (Windows 4.1.x). Windows 98 incorporated all the changes that had been previously put into the various versions of Windows 95, such as FAT32, USB support, disk partitioning support, expanded Internet capabilities, and expanded hardware support.

FAT32

Windows 95 version 2 (OSR/B), as well as Windows 98 and Windows ME, include an option to format a logical partition for a 32-bit FAT called FAT32. This allows for multithreaded Protected Mode access to the disk through VFAT and a faster, more efficient method of disk caching. Windows 2000 supports both FAT32 and NTFS.

The Virtual File Allocation Table (VFAT) is not the same thing as a 32-bit FAT system. VFAT is part of the Windows 9x Virtual Memory Manager (VMM) and uses the existing FAT16 file structure. FAT32 is an actual enhancement to the underlying disk-based file management system being created through FDISK and taking place long before Windows ever loads.

Because FAT16 uses 16-bit numbers for cluster addressing, the maximum allowable size for a FAT16 partition is 65,536 clusters, or 2GB. Current systems routinely come installed with huge hard disks far larger than that, so the FAT32 feature in Windows 9x allows for these single, large partitions. However, after a disk is set up with the FAT32 feature, it can't be changed back to a 16-bit FAT. Unfortunately, most new computer buyers haven't the slightest idea (or interest) in the underlying decisions being made for them by their system dealers.

FAT32 works the same way as FAT16, but uses the larger 32-bit numbers in the data addressing scheme. The larger numbers mean that FAT32 can manage more clusters on a disk. The maximum number of clusters a FAT32 partition allows is 268,435,456, or 2 terabytes (TB). FAT32 requires that a disk have a partition table, so for that reason, FAT32 cannot be installed on a floppy disk or any other removable disk that doesn't have a partition table.

Drive Converter (FAT32)

Windows 98 provides Drive Converter as a conversion utility to convert an existing FAT16 to FAT32 without data loss. In Windows 95, a drive can be set up with either FAT16 or FAT32 during the FDISK process. Windows 98 allows for a conversion after the disk has been previously partitioned. Although the conversion utility allows a drive to be converted from FAT16 to FAT32 (or NTFS, in the case of Windows NT), the user is unable to revert to FAT16 without reformatting the partition.

Windows 9x vs. Windows 3.x

Backward compatibility isn't an easy thing to accomplish, and because Microsoft told Wall Street that it would release its new operating system on a certain date, Windows 95 simply had to go to market—regardless of whether it had compatibility issues with older systems.

Many of the more powerful commands and utilities remained in DOS 7.0, redesigned to work directly with a companion graphic component of the operating system. All this was necessary because no one could afford to write off the massive installed base of 16-bit PCs and existing Real Mode applications.

As a result, many of the DOS 6.x executable programs have their same-name counterparts in Windows 9x, but can be run only from within Windows as a graphical application. Defrag (DEFRAG.EXE) is an important program that can be run only under the GUI, but ScanDisk, XCOPY, EDIT, and MSD.EXE still run in either plain MS-DOS or an MS-DOS window. In fact, Windows 95, 98, and ME still allow the user to start the system in a plain MS-DOS Mode. It wasn't until Windows 2000 (see Chapter 13) that this feature disappeared.

Note: The feature didn't actually disappear, but was renamed Recovery Console and stored on the installation disks as an optional feature.

SCANDISK.EXE is an example of the transitional aspect of Windows 9x. Originally, ScanDisk was a plain DOS program. The version offered with DOS 7.0 can now be run as either a text-based program or a Windows-based program, depending on which interface the program starts from.

Note: The fact that SCANDISK.EXE runs before Windows 9x is even set up, and that in OSR/B, a crash and improper close will automatically run ScanDisk, shows you how important DOS continues to be.

The startup process still opens into DOS before loading Windows, and starting Windows from the DOS Command Mode still requires running WIN.COM. The old QBASIC (DOS 6.x) that supported EDIT was folded into the base operating system, with the new Windows 9x version allowing full Windows functionality (e.g., scrollbars, mouse pointer, and cut-and-paste) to seamlessly carry into DOS windows (unlike Windows 3.x). The MS-DOS windowed sessions, in Windows 9x, took on the GUI functions of a Windows application and had copy and paste functions, along with resizable text fonts.

It might help to think of the Windows 9x versions as a transitional movement from DOS to NT. Windows 9x moves further toward the GUI environment, but it is still composed of two intertwined components: the DOS component and the graphical interface component. The GUI component can't work without the DOS component, but the DOS component has such limited functionality that it's almost not worth running alone. The important thing to know about the DOS component is that it controls the physical file locations on the disk and is required for disk partitioning.

Note: In the event that you think all this information about DOS is irrelevant, remember that the Windows 2000 command line (CMD.EXE), startup files, and the Recovery Console are all based on DOS.

Windows 9x came with many of the features found in Windows NT, making it superior to Windows 3.x in memory management and device control. In fact, the improved device handling of the new VxDs made it more efficient to run almost any DOS program (including difficult game software) in a Windows MS-DOS window, or *session*—the virtual DOS machine (VM). We've mentioned that the primary shell, EXPLORER.EXE, is an upgraded File Manager, incorporating elements of a Desktop that was once unusable space sitting behind Program Manager.

The Windows 3.x Desktop wasn't completely unusable. When an icon was minimized, Windows put it on the Desktop area outside the Program Manager. However, the Windows 3.x Desktop was really only a place to store minimized icons rather than a place to organize work and applications. Windows 9x uses the Desktop as the main *metaphor* (symbol) and the Start button, Taskbar, and System Tray in place of the old Program Manager and Task Manager.

When several programs are open and running in Windows 9x and Windows 2000, the old Alt+Tab keystroke combination still toggles from the current program to the next program listed on the Taskbar. However, the Windows 9x Task Manager (Ctrl+Alt+Del) no longer holds a Switch To option.

When you start Windows 95, the new Desktop is nearly empty. The only icons that Setup installs are My Computer, Network Neighborhood, and the Recycle Bin. To provide interactive help to a novice user, the Taskbar is at the bottom of the screen, and the Start button is prominently displayed. Rather than having Program Groups with icons sitting inside them, Windows 95 groups the programs in a cascading series of menus, growing from each menu item on a previous list, originating from the main Start menu.

Windows 95 can read GRP files and INI files from a Windows 3.x installation and can convert all Program Groups to cascading menus. For this reason, you should back up these existing sets of files before running an upgrade installation.

Primary Differences

Windows 9x differs from Windows 3.x primarily by:

➤ Using IO.SYS and MSDOS.SYS, rather than CONFIG.SYS and AUTOEXEC.BAT, as the primary device-loading programs

➤ Using loadable, dynamic, 32-bit virtual device drivers alongside static, fixed, 16-bit VxDs

➤ Using OLE *shortcut objects*, with links to data and/or the programs that created the data

➤ Using a floating Properties menu accessed by right-clicking the mouse or using a special Windows key on a Windows keyboard (not unlike the special command key used on Apple keyboards)

➤ Allowing Long File Names (LFNs) through a Virtual FAT (VFAT)

➤ Placing most of the system configuration details in the Registry files

➤ Showing the user a Desktop with a Taskbar and Start button, rather than Program Manager, Program Groups, and Task Manager

➤ Including a more sophisticated and integrated Installation Wizard and Installation Shield for installing new software

➤ Improving the integration of networking and security within the Windows environment

➤ Improving system resource control with a larger memory heap

➤ Having Microsoft become directly involved in controlling the Windows 9x compatibility certification and approval of software applications development

Right-Click for Properties

A new Properties menu list, showing almost every aspect of a Windows 9x object, is always available by right-clicking the mouse. The right mouse button had been mostly useless in all the previous versions of Windows. A few pioneering companies (e.g., Borland) decided to use the right button to offer a shortcut to the main menu at the top of the screen. This was called a *properties floating menu*. The idea caught on, and Windows 95 compatibility required that all programs running under Windows 95 use a right-click of the mouse for properties. Mice today often have a third button, or middle button, that can be assigned various functions (e.g., the double-click). Mice may also have a mouse wheel for scrolling.

Note: CompTIA refers to clicking the right mouse button as alternative click(ing). This alternative click process has nothing to do with pressing the Alt key.

The Registry

Computers are different from other types of machines because they remember things. Settings, the color of a Desktop, or the arrangement of icons are now all remembered in the Windows *Registry*. Originally, the CONFIG.SYS and AUTOEXEC.BAT files did some of this remembering. Later, the INI files, including the Windows SYSTEM.INI and WIN.INI files, began storing configuration information. One of the problems that showed up with Windows 3.x was that there were too many INI files being splattered all over the hard drives. Aside from the number of files, all these critical settings files were text-based, making it too easy for people to modify them, even if they didn't know what they were doing.

One of the primary ways Windows moves away from text-based interfaces is the way that we access a command line. Windows 95 also made the basic changeover from a 16-bit operating system to a 32-bit OS. Many people tend to assume that this change to 32-bit operation was the most important change. Actually, the more important change was the incorporation of the Windows Registry. From Windows 95 all the way through to Windows NT and Windows 2000, the Registry is what holds all the versions of Windows together.

Windows 3.x used a combination of the SYSTEM.INI, WIN.INI, and REG.DAT files to keep track of device drivers, environment settings, and objects that were controlled by Windows. When Windows 95 came along, the decision was made to (theoretically) remove the two INI files and move as much as possible into a greatly expanded Registration database—changing the name to the Registry. Since then, the Windows Registry has become one of the most obscure and complicated aspects of low-level work with Windows. Practically no one really understands the Windows Registry, but you should know how to identify some of its parts.

The Registry combined most of the INI files into a consolidated set of binary files, preventing people from casually changing settings. Less knowledgeable users could no longer open a critical configuration file in Microsoft Word and then save it again in a different format, which would cause a catastrophic system crash.

The Windows Registry is an outgrowth of the Windows 3.x Registration database (REG.DAT). This original database is a little-known tool that managed the OLE and drag-and-drop features in Windows. OLE is a way to place (embed) a document (client) inside another document, using a kind of pointer to data (package) from an outside program's (server's) data. This kind of document is called a *compound document* because you can view or edit the data in the OLE connection (link) without knowing which application created it.

For example, the [Embedding] section in the WIN.INI file might contain the entry:

```
PBrush=Paintbrush Picture,C:\Programs\Access\MSPAINT.EXE,picture
```

This would indicate that a certain type of OLE picture object found in, say, a Microsoft Word document should find MSPAINT.EXE in the specified location. Furthermore, the line tells Windows that it should use Microsoft Paint to open the picture when the picture's OLE object is double-clicked.

When a program can embed a piece of itself as an embedded object, that program is said to be an *OLE server*. It's called a server because it provides functional services to the program trying to open the object—the *OLE client*. ActiveX controls and Desktop shortcuts both grew out of the original OLE technology.

The original Registration database maintained information about the pathname and file names of OLE servers, the file names and extensions of data files and their associated programs, the *class* name of the objects that the OLE servers could edit (e.g., a picture), and protocols used by the objects. The Windows 3.x Registration database was held in a binary file called REG.DAT, which could be edited only by using a registration information editor called REGEDIT.EXE.

Note: REGEDIT.EXE continued to be the preferred editor for Windows 95, 98, and ME. The preferred editor for Windows NT and 2000 is REGEDT32.EXE.

Microsoft claimed that OLE would increase the amount of interconnectivity among computer applications, which meant that compound documents would focus users more on the data and documents rather than worrying about how to open and use a particular program. To some extent, the World Wide Web's Hypertext Markup Language (HTML) superseded OLE, although not necessarily by using the same process. The technology behind OLE and Dynamic Data Exchange (DDE) is complex, but you should know what the acronyms stand for.

Another important fact about the Registry is that it contains references to file locations (pointers) being used by hardware and software. For instance, if a scanner requires a file like SCANNER.DLL in order to run, the Registry holds the location of that DLL file, along with the various configuration switches and options the file is working under. If an application uses a particular Windows *system file*, possibly COMDLG32.DLL, references to those file locations are also held in the Registry. These consolidated references are used by the Windows Update Manager to find older, or out-of-date, files.

The concept of using a pointer (vector) to another object, along with using an icon to represent the pointer, eventually led to the Windows *shortcut* (LNK) files. Shortcuts can be created in many ways, but the simplest way is to highlight a program file name, hold down the right mouse button (properties button), drag the file name onto the Desktop (or into another folder), and then release the mouse button. On the short menu dialog box that pops up, select Create Shortcut(s) Here.

Note: From the first release of Windows 1.0, certain letters in a graphical menu option have always represented the use of shortcut keys. Pressing the Alt key highlights the first option in any Windows menu. Pressing the underlined letter of an option drops down that main Options menu. With the Options menu showing, pressing a combination of the Alt key and the underlined letter of an option executes the specific choice without requiring an additional mouse click.

The Windows 9x Registry is made up of two files, each of which is a hidden, read-only, system file (+H +R +S attributes) in the WINDOWS folder. USER.DAT holds user-specific customization settings to the way Windows looks, such as the Desktop, video resolution, and so on. These user settings were formerly held in the WIN.INI file in Windows 3.x. The SYSTEM.DAT file, the largest of the three, stores all the hardware configurations, Windows internal settings, and application settings that were originally held in SYSTEM.INI.

REGEDIT.EXE is installed into the WINDOWS folder during setup. The two Registry files are also stored in the WINDOWS folder and have all their attributes set as hidden, read-only, and system. (ATTRIB.EXE and file attributes are discussed in Chapter 10.)

Although a common procedure for making a copy of SYSTEM.DAT includes turning off all the attributes in order for DOS to see the file, the Explorer or File Manager will happily copy or move hidden files with only a brief dialog box asking for confirmation. Be sure that you check a question about SYSTEM.DAT for any reference to which environment is being used.

Remember that the Registry files are binary files and cannot be edited directly with a simple text editor. Instead, REGEDIT.EXE (Registry Editor) runs from the command line or a custom icon. REGEDIT combines the two files in a window that looks much like the Explorer, listing the *HKeys* (handles) on the left-hand pane and the information within those keys on the right-hand pane.

HKeys

Windows Explorer lists folders in the left pane, using a + or – symbol to indicate any subfolders within (below) a given folder. The Registry looks the same, but calls each primary heading a *handle*, with *keys* as the underlying subdivisions. The Computer Management tool in Windows 2000 also looks like the Explorer or Registry, but refers to *nodes* at the folder level and *branches* as the subdivisions.

The HKey is Microsoft's language for a program handle to a key that contains configuration information. Looking at the various HKeys in REGEDIT is the same as looking at a drive in Windows Explorer. Each key is represented by a folder icon that can be expanded or collapsed just like folders and subfolders.

Note: The little + sign to the left of a folder is a one-click way to expand the folder.

The Windows 9x Registry contains six primary HKeys. Each HKey is like a primary folder located in the root directory of a drive, and they each have many levels of subkeys that descend like a directory tree. The six primary HKeys are:

➤ *HKEY_CLASSES_ROOT*—File extensions and applications used for OLE

➤ *HKEY_USERS*—Data stored in USER.DAT that keeps network information and user configuration options

➤ *HKEY_CURRENT_USER*—User information specific to the current Windows 95 user at the moment (if networking is disabled, this is a duplicate of HKEY_USERS)

➤ *HKEY_LOCAL_MACHINE*—The hardware and software configurations for a computer (multiple configurations can be stored for the same computer)

➤ *HKEY_CURRENT_CONFIG*—Current hardware profile (devices attached to the local machine)

➤ *HKEY_DYN_DATA*—Dynamic data in RAM having to do with how Windows 95 is running (shown by the System Monitor applet)

 Although we didn't see any questions asking for a list of all the main HKeys, there may be a reference to the Local Machine key as the location for all the device configurations. The odds are high that questions about the Registry keys will provide the correct names in the response or body of the text. You would be asked to choose or identify an HKey in terms of what it does, and we're fairly confident that you'll only have to know the Local Machine.

Most of the Registry is controlled by Windows during startup, within a work session, or is set up during installation. If problems occur during setup and some hardware device refuses to be recognized, editing the Local Machine key might help. However, the main problem is that removing software or changing a hardware device doesn't automatically change every one of its entries in the Registry.

Information about hardware and software is stored in many places within the Registry, and uninstaller programs have varying degrees of success in finding all occurrences and references.

Note: Always make a backup of the Registry, particularly the SYSTEM.DAT file, before you make any changes to the system. This includes running an uninstaller program, because an incorrect guess on the part of the program can render the system totally inoperable.

USER.DAT

As we've said, the Registry is composed of two files—SYSTEM.DAT and USER.DAT—both of which are binary and neither of which can be edited with Notepad, Edit, or any other ASCII editor. (The only way to edit the Registry is by using REGEDIT.EXE or a third-party program designed specifically for that purpose.)

Note: The data in SYSTEM.DAT can be exported (copied to another format) in an ASCII format, where it can be changed using an ASCII text editor. After the changes have been saved, another feature of REGEDIT.EXE is that it can import (reabsorb information from another format) the ASCII file, thereby changing SYSTEM.DAT. However, REGEDIT.EXE is still required in order to perform the export and import process.

Copying the two Registry files to another location is a way to back up the files, but in order for the files to actually function, they must be in their original locations with the file attributes properly set. The recommended way to back up the Registry is with the Emergency Recovery Utility, discussed under the "REGEDIT.EXE" section in this chapter.

USER.DAT contains specific environment configuration (e.g., the Desktop) information for the user.

The Structure of INI Files Revisited

According to the *Microsoft Windows 95 Resource Kit*, the Registry eliminates the need for AUTOEXEC.BAT, CONFIG.SYS, and INI files, unless they are needed by legacy applications. This is about as true as saying that Congress simplifies the government of the country by eliminating the need for citizens to govern themselves. Initialization files are used routinely in Windows 9x, and, as we've seen, both CONFIG.SYS and AUTOEXEC.BAT are alive and well. Yes, it's true that neither of the startup files are *as* necessary as before, and that INI files aren't the *only* way to configure Windows, but they still exist and are used regularly.

Most, but not all, of the information that was once in INI files is now stored somewhere in the Registry. In some cases, Windows itself creates new INI files (e.g., TELEPHON.INI) that didn't exist under Windows 3.x. Most INI files are stored in the WINDOWS folder.

 The important INI files used by Windows 3.x and Windows 9x include SYSTEM.INI, WIN.INI, PROGMAN.INI (Program Manager), and CONTROL.INI (Control Panel). PROGMAN.INI contains a listing of the Program Group files (*.GRP) used within Program Manager.

SYSTEM.INI and WIN.INI

Windows 3.x used the SYSTEM.INI and WIN.INI files to load various devices and to set the overall Windows environment. We've seen that Windows 9x still uses these two files and that devices in SYSTEM.INI take precedence over those in the Registry if there's a conflict with two of the same devices. Windows 9x allows you to change many of the Registry settings from within a Windows session, including the following:

➤ Memory-related options are set in the Performance tab of the System Information option (in the Control Panel System icon).

➤ Hardware device options or parameters are set in the Device Manager tab of the System Information option (in the Control Panel System icon).

➤ Network and resource-sharing parameters are set using the Network icon of Control Panel.

➤ Mouse and keyboard options and parameters are set from the Mouse and the Keyboard icons, respectively, in the Control Panel.

➤ Screen and display options are set either from the Display icon of the Control Panel or by right-clicking on the Desktop and selecting Properties.

REGEDIT.EXE

We've said that the REGEDIT.EXE editor is installed in the WINDOWS folder during setup; however, no icon or menu entry is created. Although some entries and subkeys in the Registry are created by the different versions of Windows, we're concerned here only with the generic Registry format and entries.

Working with the Registry requires a serious amount of caution because accidental changes can lead to a total reinstallation. Unlike in word processors, changes take place in the Registry as soon as the Enter key is pressed. Some important points to remember about changes in the Registry include the following:

➤ The Registry is changed directly by changes to the Control Panel and some other Windows applets.

➤ The 9x Registry is also changed directly by using REGEDIT.EXE or a third-party application specifically designed to edit the DAT files. (In Windows 2000 and NT, the preferred editor is a 32-bit editor called REGEDT32.EXE.)

➤ Some installation routines use INF (program information) files to write changes to the Registry automatically.

➤ Changes to the Registry take place immediately and are written to the SYSTEM.DAT and USER.DAT files without using a typical File|Save option.

➤ The *only* way to undo a change in the Registry is to either re-edit the line that was changed or to copy a previous version of the DAT file over the newly changed version.

Unless you know exactly what you're doing, you shouldn't edit the Registry. Use the Control Panel interface to make changes to the system. As always, before you install any new software or any new hardware device, you should make a safe backup of the existing SYSTEM.DAT file and USER.DAT file.

Bizarre and amazing changes to Windows can occur with the installation of any new component. Sometimes, mystical gremlins can knock out a piece of hardware for no apparent reason. Copying SYSTEM.DAT to another directory (e.g., REG_BACK) is simple to do from the Windows Explorer and can save you hours (if not days) of time recovering from a corrupted Registry.

To copy Registry files from a DOS command line, the hidden, system, and read-only attributes must be turned off. From within Windows Explorer, the files can be copied without adjusting the attributes. If you use the Explorer (or File Manager) to copy the SYSTEM.DAT file, you must be sure to set the view options to show hidden files. From the main menu bar in the Explorer, select View|Options|View tab and check Show All Files. From the main menu bar in File Manager, choose View|By File Type|Show Hidden|System Files.

On the Explorer View tab, you should not have the Hide MS-DOS Extensions For File Types That Are Registered checkbox selected. There are several files with the name SYSTEM.* and USER.* in the WINDOWS folder, but only SYSTEM.DAT and USER.DAT are the current Registry files.

Backing Up the Registry

Don't rely on the DA0 files as a backup of the Registry. If you do, it's easy to start the computer and create a bad SYSTEM.DAT file, which copies to the SYSTEM.DA0 file along with the bad information. If the computer locks up and is rebooted, the bad SYSTEM.DA0 can copy over the bad SYSTEM.DAT and cause the same problem, leaving two copies of the bad Registry file. Then, your only recourse is the SYSTEM.1ST file, which has only original configuration information of the first successful startup. SYSTEM.1ST is in the root folder of the boot disk and contains none of the changes that have been made since the original installation.

The Emergency Recovery Utility (ERU.EXE) can be used to back up the Registry, but usually not to a floppy disk. SYSTEM.DAT is often larger than 1MB and, except for the most minimally configured computer, won't fit on a single floppy. However, ERU.EXE can copy specified system files to a different drive or directory, so using an Iomega Zip or Jaz disk will work. You can also copy critical Registry files to a different directory on the hard drive and use a disk-spanning archive tool.

Copies of Registry Files

When Windows 9x is set up for the first time (from installation disks), a SYSTEM.NEW file is created as the first Registry. This file contains the hardware and software configuration information made during the detection phase of Setup. If everything works well and Windows starts successfully (without crashing), SYSTEM.NEW is renamed SYSTEM.DAT.

Once Windows is installed and working, the first successful Registry (SYSTEM.DAT) is renamed SYSTEM.DA0 and is held as a backup of the original Registry. The very first SYSTEM.DAT used when Windows 9x starts from the hard disk is also copied to SYSTEM.1ST in the root directory as another backup of the clean, first installation.

SYSTEM.1ST includes everything up to the first reboot of the system. If you replace SYSTEM.DAT with SYSTEM.1ST at any time and then reboot the computer, you get the "Starting Windows 9x for the first time" screen, and Windows goes through the hardware configuration process, initializing the Control Panel, Start menu, and all the other aspects of a first-time start. Windows then reboots and starts up normally.

Every time Windows starts successfully, it backs up SYSTEM.DAT to SYSTEM.DA0, and USER.DAT to USER.DA0 (overwriting any existing DA0 files). If something goes wrong, the .DA0 files are used automatically on restart to return the computer to the successful previous startup. This is essentially the same process as the Windows NT and 2000 Last Known Good hardware profile.

If Windows 9x is unable to start correctly, it tries to start again in Safe Mode. If the problem is something that Windows can recognize clearly enough to start the session in Safe Mode, the Registry files are *not* copied to the DA0 names. By manually copying the previously good DA0 files to DAT names, Windows can successfully start again. However, not all problems are recognized by Windows' recovery capabilities.

To be safe and to provide the most convenient and speedy recovery from inadvertent or random corruption of the Registry, keep the following points in mind:

➤ Always keep a backup of the latest successful Registry—SYSTEM.DAT and USER.DAT—somewhere other than in the WINDOWS folder.

➤ SYSTEM.1ST is a last-resort backup of the first configuration file created following a successful first-time installation on a given computer. If this file doesn't work, you're probably going to have to reinstall everything on the computer (including Windows and all the software that's been added since the last installation).

➤ SYSTEM.1ST is located in the root directory of the bootable partition.

➤ SYSTEM.DAT and USER.DAT are located in the WINDOWS subdirectory.

➤ SYSTEM.DA0 and USER.DA0 are also located in the WINDOWS subdirectory (by default).

Installing Windows 95, 98, and ME

Windows 9x provided two installation methods and several different versions. The two installation methods are the *upgrade* and *full version*. The upgrade installation materials (disks or CD-ROM) require that the computer already have a copy of DOS and Windows 3.x installed, but the full installation disks require that no previous copy of Windows exists on the installation hard drive. Both formats require a logical partition with more than 32MB of free space.

Although the Windows upgrade can be installed in a way that the computer can boot up into either Windows 3.x or Windows 9x, the documentation doesn't really explain how to maintain the full integrity of DOS files earlier than version 7.0 and all the existing Windows 3.x files. All the previous DOS and Windows 3.x files are ordinarily removed from the hard drive.

Note: Third-party books about Windows often provide far clearer documentation and understanding of how to install an upgrade that keeps the Windows 3.x system safe and that retains older DOS versions.

CD-ROM Device Drivers

Windows 9x often comes preinstalled on a hard drive, with the installation being done at the retail point of sale. Usually, disk images are copied to the hard drive, and the user has the option of making floppies from these images. Otherwise, Windows 9x is available on CD-ROM. Disk images are special files that can be used to create an exact copy of a floppy disk, including bootable floppies.

Modern machines usually have a BIOS-compatible CD-ROM drive, meaning that the motherboard BIOS will recognize a CD-ROM drive during the POST. On older machines, the CD-ROM drive requires a device driver. On a system on which Windows 9x is running smoothly, the CD-ROM device is handled by Windows' internal list of device drivers. Assuming that Windows 9x is a full operating system, many computer vendors don't include an external device driver for the CD-ROM drive. If the hard drive becomes irrevocably corrupted and must be reformatted, how will the user use the CD-ROM drive to install Windows from a CD-ROM?

The full installation version of Windows 9x includes a bootable 3½-inch disk for partitioning and formatting, but it often doesn't include the CD-ROM device drivers. It is good practice to maintain a separate DOS system disk with the CD-ROM device driver for the installed drive.

Installation Phases

With today's computers moving more and more toward unique configurations, it's almost impossible anymore to demonstrate a generic installation. For that reason, we'll present a Windows 95 installation with the caveat that the Windows 9x family installs the same way. Most installations nowadays are done by the vendor, using a standardized disk image. These installations include Windows and all the applications sold with the system. As an A+ technician, you'll most likely run a recovery from an original configuration CD-ROM.

Note: With the trend toward removing any installation and configuration control from individual users, purchasing an installation copy of the Windows operating system is becoming increasingly more difficult. The operating system and recovery disks are sometimes included with a new machine, but in many instances, the only way to buy a copy of Windows 98 is through the so-called gray market (OEM versions sold at flea markets and swap meets).

The four phases for installing Windows 9x are as follows:

1. The startup and information-gathering phase

2. The hardware detection phase

3. The copying and expanding files phase

4. The final system configuration phase

Windows takes over more of the decision-making process from the user and provides more direct control over how the software will be installed on a given computer. Again, the idea is to make using the computer as far removed from the technical configuration of that computer as possible. Many potential problems arising from an installation can be traced to the fact that the computer is still under the control of the user, and that not every computer is set up exactly as the Installation Shield expects to see it.

Startup and Information-Gathering Phase

When SETUP.EXE runs from a DOS prompt, the program searches all local drives for any previous version of Windows. If Setup was started from DOS, the program assumes that an existing copy of DOS is on the bootable hard drive. If a previous version of Windows is found, one of two things will happen, depending on whether this was an upgrade or a full installation version of Windows 9x. If it was an upgrade version, Setup pauses, then suggests running Setup from within Windows. If it was a full installation version, Setup quits, then displays an error message that a previous copy of Windows was found. The suggestion to run Setup from within Windows can be bypassed.

It may come in handy to know that Setup looks for WIN.COM and WINVER.EXE only to determine if a previous version of Windows exists on the drive. If you need to reinstall an upgrade version of Windows 95, it's less messy, and you can save a lot of time by just copying these two files to a C:\WINDOWS directory and then running the Windows 95 setup.

If you need to reinstall a Windows 9x system and you have only the full installation version CD, you can just delete or rename WIN.COM and run Setup. The system won't detect the presence of the previous Windows installation.

As Phase 1 continues, Setup runs SCANDISK.EXE (located on the installation disk) and looks at the hard drive to make sure that it's running correctly and that it meets the minimum requirements for installing Windows 9x (i.e., enough memory, a modern CPU, and enough disk space). If any of the setup requirements are missing, the installation quits.

The rest of Phase 1 checks for extended memory and runs an XMS memory manager if one isn't running. Setup installs HIMEM.SYS if no other extended memory manager is found. Setup then checks memory for any existing terminate and stay resident programs (TSRs) that are known to cause problems. If any are found, Setup pauses to warn you before it proceeds.

 Windows 9x requires extended memory. If no other memory management program is loaded, Setup installs HIMEM.SYS, and IO.SYS loads HIMEM every time the system starts.

From a DOS startup, Setup installs the minimum files required to run Windows 3.1 and starts the kernel using the **SHELL=SETUP.EXE** in the SYSTEM.INI file. Until this point, Setup is running in Real Mode, and nothing is showing on the monitor until the system starts the GUI.

Note: Windows 2000 does not support Real Mode. We discuss Windows NT and 2000 in Chapter 13.

After the GUI starts, the Installation Wizard begins prompting the user for which components will be installed and for various networking options. It asks for user information, registration information, and which directory to install Windows into. When all the questions have been answered, the Installation Wizard moves on to the next phase.

Hardware Detection Phase

At this point, PnP and the concept of VxDs become relevant. Setup checks the entire system for hardware and peripherals attached to the computer. It also checks the system resources for I/O addresses, IRQs, and DMAs. This is where Windows begins to build the first Registry and hardware profile.

 PnP is a standards specification that attempts to remove IRQ and DMA conflicts among hardware devices. PnP data must be built in to ROM BIOS and a BIOS chip on the device. Finally, the operating system must be able to read the BIOS data and work with it for configuration purposes.

PnP devices let Windows know what hardware devices are available and which resources they need in order to run. For non-PnP devices, Windows looks at I/O ports and specific memory addresses, compares them against a database of known devices, and makes a best guess. If the computer has PnP BIOS, Windows 9x queries the system board's CMOS for all installed devices and their configurations. This same hardware detection process is used from the Control Panel under the Add New Hardware option when any new hardware device is added to the computer.

Copying and Expanding Files Phase

A number of *archiving programs* have been developed to pack as many files as possible onto a relatively small floppy disk. These programs (e.g., PKZip, Extract, and LHArc) change the form of a file to reduce its size (compression). Microsoft uses EXTRACT.EXE to *expand* these stored programs back to their original sizes. The DOS **COPY** command is insufficient to install any version of Windows because the files are on the installation disks in archived form.

The file copying phase uses a list of files that has been created during the hardware detection phase, depending on which components need to be installed. Windows then copies all necessary files to the installation destination directory and extracts them to their full executable size. While the files are in their compressed format, DOS is unable to read or execute the programs. Various Setup DLL files are run after the files are copied, to create directories that might not exist and to install network capabilities.

Creating a Startup Disk

The Installation Wizard offers the user the option to make a startup disk during the Files Expansion phase of the installation. The disk can be made at this time, or the option can be bypassed. If the option is bypassed, a startup disk can be made at any time by using the Add/Remove Software applet in Control Panel. The startup disk requires a minimum of 1.2MB of storage.

Emergency Startup Disk

The so-called emergency startup disk is mainly designed for troubleshooting the Windows 9x program and system. Many users think that the disk is a way to start their computers in MS-DOS Mode and to access the regular features and configuration of their PCs. However, the disk assumes that Windows is available on the hard drive, but is not starting for some reason.

The files on the startup diskette include the bootable system files (COMMAND.COM, IO.SYS, and MSDOS.SYS) along with FDISK, FORMAT, EDIT, SYS.COM, and a few other files for low-level access to partitioning and reformatting. Note that the copies of IO.SYS and MSDOS.SYS are the startup files for Windows 9x and are not the same files that started DOS 6.x and earlier.

Note: If Windows has become corrupted, the startup disk does not contain any device drivers or CONFIG.SYS or AUTOEXEC.BAT files to get the computer up and running. The computer will start, leaving the user at a plain DOS command line and without any device drivers loaded (e.g., CD-ROM drive).

Final System Configuration Phase

At this point, Setup makes irrevocable changes to any preexisting Windows 3.x files and directories. Setup makes upgrades to files in the C:\WINDOWS and C:\WINDOWS\SYSTEM directories and installs DOS 7.x to the C:\WINDOWS\COMMAND directory. DOS 7.x replaces COMMAND.COM with a new version of COMMAND.COM.

Unless any files in the C:\DOS directory have been protected, Setup removes them and prepares the computer for Windows 9x. To allow booting from a previous version of DOS, Windows must be set up in its own directory, and the older system must remain intact.

Keeping an Older Operating System

Some people actually prefer to keep an older operating system on their machine. The best way to do this is with a multiple-boot partitioning system, but in some cases, this may not be the optimal choice. Because Windows has a tendency to insist on looking in the WINDOWS and WINDOWS\SYSTEM folders for files, it's usually best to rename a Windows 3.x C:\WINDOWS directory to something new (e.g., WIN3_1) and to install Windows 9x into the expected WINDOWS folder. Likewise, to protect a previous version of DOS, it's best to transfer copies of everything in the DOS directory to something like OLD_DOS to avoid the high probability of losing those files during Windows 9x installation.

Setup prompts the user to restart the computer to continue the installation from within Windows. Prior to restarting the computer, Setup does the following:

➤ Modifies the boot sector of the boot drive and replaces the previous version of IO.SYS with the new Windows 9x version

➤ Replaces the old MSDOS.SYS with the Windows 9x version

➤ Renames pre-existing versions of the (hidden) DOS system files as IO.DOS and MSDOS.DOS

➤ Updates MSDOS.SYS with device drivers, startup mode notations, and any pre-existing CONFIG.SYS settings, along with any new configuration information that Windows will require at startup

First Restart

Windows 9x keeps track of the start and restart events, both during installation and with each new session. During an installation and following a successful restart of the computer for the first time, Windows makes further updates to the configuration of the system through the following process:

1. WINIT.EXE processes three sections of the WINIT.INI file (arial.win, user32.tmp, and logo.sys) to create a combined VMM32.VXD with all the VxDs needed by the specific computer.

2. SYSTEM.DAT is renamed SYSTEM.DA0, and SYSTEM.NEW is renamed SYSTEM.DAT.

3. The Registry flag (indicator) is set to indicate that this is the first time Windows is being run following a new installation.

4. The Run Once module is run to configure printers, MIDI, and PCMCIA devices (on a new computer), and to run any new hardware manufacturer's custom setup program(s).

5. If the installation was done over a pre-existing Windows 3.x system, GRPCONV.EXE converts all Program Groups and Program Items from the previous version of Windows to Windows 9x format and renames the files to use Long File Names.

Installation Log Files

Windows uses a number of *log files* for tracking the state of applications and the way in which the applications load. These states are generated through *error codes*, and the log files contain messages written to the files by the error codes. A "good" or successful code can still be understood as an error code. During installation, even with custom choices and settings offered by the Installation Wizard, Windows still fails to install many of the additional utilities that come on the installation disks or CD-ROM.

The files in the root directory that Windows 9x Setup uses to track installation and successful configuration are:

➤ *SETUPLOG.TXT*—Setup sequence and pass/fail

➤ *DETLOG.TXT*—Hardware detection log file

➤ *NETLOG.TXT*—Networking setup log file

➤ *DETCRASH.LOG*—Hardware detection failure/crash log

➤ *BOOTLOG.TXT*—Success/fail boot sequence log

DETLOG.TXT keeps track of what hardware devices are found on the system. BOOTLOG.TXT keeps track of the first startup process and the success or failure of each step.

If the F8 Startup menu key is pressed, BOOTLOG.TXT can be changed to reflect the current startup, and the previous version is overwritten. To keep a copy of the original installation startup sequence, copy BOOTLOG.TXT to another name (e.g., FIRSBOOT.TXT).

Windows Setup tracks each phase of an installation and makes success or fail notations in SUWARN.BAT (SetUp WARNings batch file). Setup also makes notations in the AUTOEXEC.BAT prior to a successful complete installation. Much of the moment-by-moment installation process is tracked in SETUPLOG.TXT and DETCRASH.LOG in case the setup crashes. If the installation and setup are successful, DETCRASH.LOG is deleted.

The Windows 9x Setup can fail at three points:

➤ When insufficient, incorrect, or unavailable system resources are detected during SETUP.EXE in Real Mode

➤ When a crash occurs during the hardware detection phase, creating DETCRASH.LOG

➤ When a device stops working following hardware detection

Setup uses SETUPLOG.TXT to list information about the steps in the installation, including the sequence of the steps and the error information returned at the end of a step (whether it completed successfully or why not). In case of a failed setup, Windows uses SETUPLOG.TXT to bypass the steps that completed successfully and continues only with the steps that failed.

If the installation fails, the process is designed to continue from a restart of the computer. Rather than reformat the drive and reinstall from the beginning, restart the computer and let Windows Setup pick up where it left off, trying to correct the installation problem itself.

LOGVIEW.EXE

Windows 9x includes the SYSEDIT.EXE program that came with Windows 3.11. System Edit examines initial configuration files, but doesn't open the Windows 9x log files. Log files can be opened with any ASCII text editor (e.g., WordPad) for viewing and printing.

Log files are plain ASCII text (TXT) files that show when a program was last run and that report any problems encountered at the time. If the log files don't find any problems, they hold an exit status report. The LOGVIEW.EXE program utility is similar to SYSEDIT, but shows all the log files on the drive.

LOGVIEW.EXE is found in the OTHER\MISC\LOGVIEW folder on the Windows 9x installation CD-ROM and must be manually copied from the CD-ROM to a destination on the hard drive.

BOOTLOG.TXT

The BOOTLOG.TXT file is a hidden ASCII text file located in the root directory of the primary active drive. This file keeps a record of the entire startup process for the first time Windows is installed successfully. The F8 option for an interactive Startup menu (pressed when the "Starting Windows 9x" message displays at bootup) allows you to create a new BOOTLOG.TXT file at any time. Additionally, you can create a new file by using the /B switch with WIN.COM (i.e., **WIN /B**) from a DOS command prompt in MS-DOS Mode.

The details in the BOOTLOG.TXT file are written in sequence during the startup and generally break down to about five major sections. Although a line in the BOOTLOG.TXT file might indicate that something has failed, it doesn't necessarily mean that the startup process has aborted. For example, the line entry

```
loadfailed=
```

means that the specified VxD failed to load for some reason, probably because whatever the driver was referring to doesn't exist or couldn't be found.

 It's usually wise to make a copy of the BOOTLOG.TXT file before creating a new one, just to have a copy of a successful installation and startup.

Starting Windows 9x

Windows requires a minimum of 3MB of uncompressed space on the bootup partition (i.e., active, primary). Under DOS and Windows 3.x, the DOS system files were COMMAND.COM, MSDOS.SYS, and IO.SYS. The DOS command processor looked to the CONFIG.SYS file to load device drivers, and it also transferred control to AUTOEXEC.BAT to display recurring configuration commands at startup.

Windows 95 changed the basic system files, using the hidden IO.SYS to read configuration and device information from the MSDOS.SYS hidden file, a CONFIG.SYS file (if one was present), or both. IO.SYS must still be in the boot sector of the bootable partition; MSDOS.SYS is placed in the root directory, also hidden. COMMAND.COM is also carried forward in DOS 7.x, and installed in the C:\WINDOWS directory.

IO.SYS runs first from DOS 7.x (just as it did in DOS 6.x), but contains a series of commands for processing device drivers out of both the MSDOS.SYS and the CONFIG.SYS file. CONFIG.SYS and AUTOEXEC.BAT are still required by some applications, which won't start without finding one of these files. The Windows Emergency Recovery Utility (ERU) requires that a CONFIG.SYS and an AUTOEXEC.BAT file exist.

POST and Bootstrap

No matter which operating system you use, the motherboard's ROM BIOS runs the POST routine when the computer is first turned on. Everything that applies to a plain DOS computer applies to a Windows computer. The bootstrap loader (discussed in Chapter 11) looks to the boot sector of the primary, active partition (the boot partition) for instructions on how to start whatever operating system is installed on that partition.

 The boot sector and the Master Boot Record (MBR) are technically two different things. However, the exam tends to confuse the two and may ask you to treat the MBR as though it were another name for boot sector.

Windows looks in the boot sector, where it finds IO.SYS. Windows NT and OS/2 can be booted from the *boot track*, making it possible to boot them from a different partition than the primary, active one. However, note that Windows NT and 2000 still run the NT Loader that looks in the boot track. In Windows 9x, the "Starting Windows 9x..." message is displayed on the screen following the initial POST and parity check and is written into IO.SYS.

Pressing F8 between the "Starting Windows 9x..." message and the Windows logo splash screen interrupts the boot process and allows you to choose various options from a Startup menu.

Note: A splash screen is jargon for anything that appears on the screen prior to the actual program environment. This can often be a corporate logo, a shareware registration screen, or simply a notification screen that the program is still being prepared to run.

DOS

If you remember the DOS boot sequence, you'll recognize IO.SYS as one of the system files in the DOS startup trio. IO.SYS starts DOS in Real Mode. IO.SYS in Windows 9x does the same thing. It sets up the segment addressing in conventional memory and loads Real Mode device drivers into the first segment of memory (low memory). IO.SYS then reads MSDOS.SYS (or an existing CONFIG.SYS file).

Windows 9x uses a preliminary hardware profile from the hardware detection phase to attempt to start the computer (e.g., interrupts, BIOS serial and parallel ports, and CMOS or BIOS system board identification). After the computer is started for the first time, the Registry tells Windows which settings to use at startup. IO.SYS reads the MSDOS.SYS file to process specific devices, and it reads the Registry (SYSTEM.DAT) for device *settings*.

If a CONFIG.SYS file, an AUTOEXEC.BAT file, or both are supposed to run, IO.SYS loads the COMMAND.COM command interpreter and runs the two configuration files. Depending on which lines are found in these files, DOS runs other Real Mode commands and programs. Remember that whatever is loaded into the DOS environment at this point will descend to any DOS sessions run from within Windows.

Technically speaking, IO.SYS reads CONFIG.SYS, then MSDOS.SYS, and then passes control to MSDOS.SYS. After MSDOS.SYS, control passes to COMMAND.COM, which reads CONFIG.SYS *again* before passing control to AUTOEXEC.BAT.

Although CONFIG.SYS technically is read twice, we believe the exam expects CONFIG.SYS (if it exists) to process following COMMAND.COM. This is one of those ambiguous, imprecise questions where Microsoft says what happens, but the proper response may not be listed.

MSDOS.SYS

Whether or not CONFIG.SYS, AUTOEXEC.BAT, or both exist, IO.SYS reads the MSDOS.SYS file first and reads it again for VxDs and other configuration settings. MSDOS.SYS is a plain ASCII text file that can be edited by DOS's EDIT.COM or Microsoft's WordPad. The important point is that all attributes are set on the file, making it hidden, system, and read-only. Before you can edit MSDOS.SYS, you're expected to know what you're doing and how to change the file attributes (see Chapter 11).

The MSDOS.SYS file tells Windows about multiple booting options and startup menus, which mode to start in, and whether the Windows GUI is supposed to start at all following bootup. If you press and hold the Shift key, instead of the F8 key, before the Windows splash screen, MSDOS.SYS is bypassed and not read at all.

WIN.COM

If MSDOS.SYS is configured to start Windows, it runs WIN.COM and loads Windows. Windows then looks for WINSTART.BAT and runs it if the file is found. MSDOS.SYS also contains path locations for important Windows files, including where to find the Registry. To enable the F4 shortcut key option of running a previous version of DOS, the directive **BootMulti=** must have the value **1** (**BootMulti=1**) in the [Options] section of MSDOS.SYS.

Start Sequence

Remember that Windows 9x was an interim interface that was trying to stay compatible with 16-bit Windows 3.x and DOS Real Mode applications. Microsoft was also trying to induce programmers to write programs in the 32-bit Windows NT format. The resulting combination of 16-bit Windows, DOS, Windows NT, and 32-bit Windows 9x is confusing, which is why Microsoft changed the name of the operating system to Windows 2000. Following any Real Mode device drivers, Windows 9x loads any *static* VxDs required by Windows 3.1x programs.

Virtual device drivers were first introduced in Windows 3.1 by loading into memory and remaining there throughout the session, making them static (not moving). Windows 9x *dynamic* VxDs can be loaded into memory and then un-loaded when a program terminates, if the VxD is no longer needed.

Just as in Windows 3.1x, the executable Virtual Memory Manager (VMM) runs, but this time VMM32.VXD includes both a Real Mode loader and the VMM, as well as common, static VxDs from 16-bit format (in MRCI2.VXD).

VMM32.VXD is a combination file with many common VxD files bound up inside it. Typical VxD files are about 80KB, and typical VMM32.VXD files are about 650KB. The devices found inside this file were once loaded in the [386Enh] section of the SYSTEM.INI file. Windows 9x first checks the WINDOWS\SYSTEM\VMM32 directory for any 32-bit VxD files, rather than the VxDs bound in VMM32.VXD. If it finds any newer files, it loads them from that folder.

 The Windows 2000 Help System includes the Update Manager (dis-cussed in its own section later in this chapter) that can access Internet Web sites for updated DLL and VXD files.

Assuming Windows finds no later-version virtual device drivers in the VMM32 folder, VMM32.VXD loads static device drivers found in the **DEVICE=** line of the SYSTEM.INI file (which still comes with Windows 9x). The actual devices load from within VMM32 but show in the SYSTEM.INI file for back-ward compatibility.

The Registry contains entries for every VXD file and, through its processing, controls VMM32.VXD. The Registry also contains entries for every VxD that isn't directly associated with a piece of hardware. If two devices have a conflict at load time, the VxD in the SYSTEM.INI **DEVICE=** takes precedence over the one specified by the Registry. If the device can't be found, an error occurs.

As Windows starts up, the following three files are run in the sequence listed here (note the continued use of WIN.COM and SYSTEM.INI):

1. *WIN.COM*—Controls the initial environment checks and loads the core Windows 95 components.

2. *VMM32.VXD*—Creates the VM and installs all VxDs.

3. *SYSTEM.INI*—Is read for **DEVICE=** entries, which may differ from the Registry entries.

Final Steps to Loading Windows 9x

After device drivers have been loaded into memory and the virtual machine is up and running, Windows loads KERNEL32.DLL for the main Windows components and KRNL386.EXE, which loads Windows 3.x device drivers. GDI.EXE and GDI32.EXE load next, followed by USER.EXE and USER32.EXE. (Notice the continued path from Windows 3.1x as the same files append a "32" to their names.)

To ensure backward compatibility, Windows 9x loads in the same way that Windows 3.x loads. One of the primary differences is that Windows 9x runs DOS programming code under a *virtual* 8086 machine rather than a Real Mode machine. Keep in mind that Windows NT and 2000 ended all support for this Real Mode. When the installation is complete and Windows 9x starts from the hard disk, it goes back and checks to see if it has a matching internal 32-bit VxD for any static device drivers in memory. If it does, Windows comments out the original device's line in either CONFIG.SYS or AUTOEXEC.BAT.

When the startup process calls WIN.COM, the SYSTEM.INI file is read for Real Mode device drivers, and the SYSTEM.DAT file is read for the rest of the device configurations. In other words, Windows 9x reads both the Windows 3.x INI files and the Registry DAT files as it loads. Most of the devices and their configurations are installed from the SYSTEM.DAT file, but SYSTEM.INI is still read first.

Following the SYSTEM.INI and SYSTEM.DAT processing, WIN.INI is read for associated resources and environment values, such as fonts, wallpaper, associated file extensions, and so on. Once WIN.INI has been processed, the USER.DAT file is read.

If networking has been enabled, Windows reads the USER.DAT file after the WIN.INI file for Desktop configurations. Sometimes USER.DAT and networking are used on standalone machines to maintain consistencies throughout a corporate environment. At home, networking can be enabled to allow individual family members to have their own customized Desktop.

Finally, the **SHELL=** line in SYSTEM.INI is run to load EXPLORER.EXE, assuming that no other shell has been specified in a default installation.

Rudimentary security can be configured for the Windows 3.x Program Manager by making changes to the PROGMAN.INI file. These security measures (called *policies* at the time) have been enhanced with the Windows 9x Policy Editor, allowing for more complete security maintenance.

Loading Device Drivers

We've said that Windows 9x continues to use IO.SYS to begin the startup process and initiate Real Mode. (If the computer is started using a previous version of DOS, IO.SYS is renamed WINBOOT.SYS.) Even in DOS 6.x, IO.SYS had rudimentary capabilities built into it to handle some of the basic directives (command lines) of the CONFIG.SYS file. However, the program wasn't ready to assume full control until Windows 95.

The Windows 9x IO.SYS finally took over from CONFIG.SYS; it loads HIMEM.SYS, IFSHLP.SYS, SETVER.EXE, and DBLSPACE.BIN or DRVSPACE.BIN by default, if they exist (see Table 12.1). Additionally, the DOS 7.0 version includes defaults for all the old CONFIG.SYS directives, such as **FILES, BUFFERS, COUNTRY,** and **SETVER.**

Note: CONFIG.SYS ordinarily doesn't use a SHELL= directive because the default assumption of the system is that COMMAND.COM is used and found on the boot disk. This directive is used primarily to increase the DOS environment space, and in that case, the /p switch must be included, as noted in Table 12.1. We discuss the DOS environment in Chapter 10.

Because of market pressures to maintain backward compatibility, IO.SYS still checks for a CONFIG.SYS file just as the older version did. If the CONFIG.SYS file is found and if it contains a **DEVICE=** line with the same directive as one found within IO.SYS, the one in CONFIG.SYS takes over.

To change a **DEVICE** setting from the default within IO.SYS, create a CONFIG.SYS file and use the same **DEVICE=** directive, but with a different setting. For example, **FILES=100** would override the default **FILES** directive in IO.SYS and would change the default from 60 to 100 possible open files.

Table 12.1	The common device directives that moved from CONFIG.SYS to IO.SYS.
DEVICE=	**Description**
DOS=	HIGHIO.SYS does not load EMM386.EXE. (If this expanded memory manager is found in an existing CONFIG.SYS file, the **UMB** line is added.)
HIMEM.SYS	Real Mode memory manager to access extended memory; part of IO.SYS by default.
IFSHLP.SYS	Installable File System Helper that loads device drivers and allows the system to make file system connections to the DOS file management I/O from within Windows.
SETVER.EXE	To maintain backward compatibility with some older TSRs that won't run under newer versions of COMMAND.COM; optional and usually not necessary.
FILES=	60 (default); included for compatibility; specifies how many files can be open at any one time when running an MS-DOS session; not required by Windows 95.
BUFFERS=	30 (default); specifies the number of file buffers; used by IO.SYS calls from DOS and Windows 3.x programs.
STACKS=	9,256 (default); the number and size of the stack frames that the CPU uses during prioritization of incoming interrupts; used for backward compatibility; not required by Windows 95.
SHELL=	**C:\COMMAND.COM /p**; Indicates which command processor to use (e.g., NDOS or DRDOS); not the same as the **SHELL=** line in SYSTEM.INI. (If the directive is used, but the **/p** switch is not used, AUTOEXEC.BAT is not processed. The **/p** switch makes the command processor permanent in the environment.)
FCBS=	4 (default); a very old method of controlling open files (file control blocks); necessary only with DOS programs designed for DOS 2.x and earlier.

Here are some final thoughts to keep in mind regarding IO.SYS:

➤ IO.SYS cannot be edited (unlike MSDOS.SYS).

➤ Directive values in CONFIG.SYS must be set to the default or higher in IO.SYS to change their settings.

➤ EMM386.EXE can be loaded only in CONFIG.SYS for DOS, 16-bit Windows, and Windows 9x.

AUTOEXEC.BAT

Windows 9x specifically disables (with **REM**, or "remark") SMARTDRV, DBLBUFF.SYS, and MOUSE.SYS from any existing CONFIG.SYS, and it disables any incompatible TSRs in an existing AUTOEXEC.BAT file by using an internal "known conflicts" list. It removes **WIN** and **SHARE** commands from an existing AUTOEXEC.BAT file, if they exist, and updates the **PATH** line.

Note: Before making updates to an existing AUTOEXEC.BAT, Windows copies the file to AUTOEXEC.DOS.

Many of the older device drivers that were needed for DOS and Windows 3.x are handled by the loadable VxDs in 32-bit Windows. Microsoft says (in a technical white paper) that it will use 32-bit code wherever it significantly improves performance in Windows 9x without sacrificing application compatibility. It will also use 32-bit code in the event that programming would require more memory without significantly improving performance. To that extent, it's sometimes difficult to tell whether a given device would be better off using the Windows 9x 32-bit VxD or the 16-bit device driver loaded from within CONFIG.SYS.

Devices loaded from CONFIG.SYS often require command-line setting switches in the AUTOEXEC.BAT file. An AUTOEXEC.BAT file is usually required to set the path to something other than the Windows default search path (C:\WINDOWS; C:\WINDOWS\COMMAND). Likewise, an AUTOEXEC.BAT file is needed to change the Temporary (TEMP) directory to something other than C:\WINDOWS\TEMP.

Useful Extra Utilities

Oddly enough, Windows 9x doesn't always install some of the more useful utilities that come on the installation CD-ROM. Among these extra utilities are the Accessibility options for people with disabilities, the LOGVIEW program mentioned earlier, and the Emergency Recovery Utility (ERU.EXE), which can back up the Registry files. Although the Accessibility options are important for people who need them, they can be useful for just about anyone.

Not all the extra utilities are listed in the Windows Setup Wizard. For example, the Emergency Recovery Utility is in the OTHER\MISC\ERU folder and must be manually copied to the hard drive. Remember that you can click once on the folder icon, press Ctrl+C to copy, and then Ctrl+V to paste the entire folder into a new location—perhaps a new folder called Registry Backup, rather than the obscure ERU name.

To install additional Windows components from Control Panel:

1. Insert the installation CD-ROM into the drive bay.

2. Select Add/Remove Software.

3. Select the Windows Setup tab on the dialog box.

4. Check the new component's checkbox (leaving any previously installed checkboxes gray). If you uncheck something that already was installed (showing as gray), Setup assumes that you mean to remove it.

Tweak UI

Microsoft technical support has had access to a collection of small utility programs ever since Windows 95 was released. Over time, those tools made their way onto many Internet sites and became known as "power toys." This collection is called Tweak UI and provides a graphical interface for changing various settings without going directly into the Registry. Some of these changes, such as turning off the ubiquitous animation and tool tips, can't be accessed through the Control Panel.

Tweak UI was finally included on the Windows 98 installation CD-ROM; it's located in the \TOOLS\RESKIT\POWERTOY\ folder. Note that each version of Windows has its own specific version of the program utilities, so don't use the Windows 95 version on a Windows 98 system.

Tweak UI can be downloaded from the Microsoft Web site, but the tools have gradually become less and less powerful. Windows 2000 incorporates a few of the most innocuous features from the old Tweak UI in the Accessories area of the Start Menu. Too many less-knowledgeable users were crashing their system, so although the Windows 95 version of Tweak UI is harder to find, some of the extra features will work on a Windows 98 system. Additional tools and utilities have been developed, many of which can be found on the **www.annoyances.org** Web site.

Note that Tweak UI has a bug in the installation routine. Therefore, to install this software, right-click on the INF file and select Install. If you are prompted for the disk, point to the folder containing the files and click on OK.

Startup Menu (F8) and Safe Mode

If you press the F8 key between the time the POST has ended and the Windows splash screen appears, you can halt the processing of MSDOS.SYS and call up the Windows 9x Interactive Startup menu. This menu allows you to start in MS-DOS Mode, Safe Mode, or other options. Each of these choices offers different processes and results. The Startup menu offers the following choices:

➤ Normal

➤ Logged (BOOTLOG.TXT)

➤ Safe Mode

➤ Safe Mode with network support

➤ Step-by-step confirmation

➤ Command prompt only

➤ Safe Mode command prompt only

➤ Previous version of DOS

The message "Starting Windows 9x..." is written into IO.SYS, which means that if you make a bootable system disk and start the computer, you'll still see the message, even though you don't have the files available to start Windows. The text-based Startup menu is also contained within IO.SYS, although you won't necessarily have access to all the options on the menu. For example, selecting Option 3 from an emergency boot disk leaves you at the command prompt because the floppy disk doesn't contain WIN.COM or a path to the Windows subdirectory.

Normal and Logged

Normal (Option 1) starts Windows normally and brings the user to the Desktop. If any networking configuration data is installed, Windows connects to the network and provides a Logon dialog box from within Windows (depending on the type of network). Don't confuse *logged* (writing to log files) with *logging in* to a network. Normal and Logged (Option 2) are the same thing, except that Logged writes the steps and status of the startup to the BOOTLOG.TXT file in the root directory of the bootable drive.

 BOOTLOG.TXT is created following the first successful startup of Windows. The file contains lines for each step of the startup process and a notation regarding the step's successful or failed outcome. A new boot log is created only when you choose the option from the (F8) Startup menu.

Safe Mode (F5)

One of the critical concepts you need to know about 32-bit Windows is the use of VxDs (those first developed for Windows 3.1). In Safe Mode, Windows bypasses all network configurations, bypasses CONFIG.SYS and AUTOEXEC.BAT, and loads with only the most generic settings and minimal, static VxDs.

Pressing F5 at the "Starting Windows 9x..." message is the same as selecting Option 3 from the menu to bypass all configuration files and start the session in Safe Mode. Safe Mode installs the minimum Windows setup in VGA Graphics Mode, with no network connections.

 Safe Mode runs in VGA Mode and does not load any device drivers other than a keyboard driver, HIMEM.SYS, and the standard VGA device.

Safe Mode with Network Support (F6)

Safe Mode starts Windows without any network configuration or connections. Safe Mode with network support provides whatever networking connections are possible. Safe Mode is available in both choices mainly to help troubleshoot when Windows doesn't start correctly. Sometimes Windows will start in Safe Mode, but for some reason won't allow the network connection. Safe Mode is primarily a diagnostics tool, or the way in which Windows starts when a problem exists.

Step-by-Step Confirmation (Shift+F8)

Beginning with DOS 5, two keystrokes have been available to control the way in which the system starts up. You must be watchful and quick with your fingers, but if you use the keystrokes, you can bypass configurations or choose a line-by-line agreement for every configuration step. The following startup messages appear right after the initial BIOS startup messages:

➤ "Starting MS-DOS..." (DOS 5.0 and later)

➤ "Starting Windows 9x..." (DOS 7.x and Windows 9x)

Choosing the step-by-step confirmation option from the F8 Startup menu is the same as pressing Shift+F8 at the "Starting Windows 9x..." message in Windows 95. This combination of F8 and F5 and their shifted states can be confusing, but you should know the differences for the exam. Table 12.2 lists what happens if you press the keys as soon as you see the "Starting" messages for DOS or Windows.

 If you press and hold the Shift key from the time you see the first Windows splash screen until you see the Desktop and the Taskbar, Windows bypasses anything in the Startup folder.

Table 12.2   F8 and F5 "Starting" options in DOS and Windows.

DOS Keystroke	Result
F5	Bypasses CONFIG.SYS and AUTOEXEC.BAT configurations.
F8	Processes CONFIG.SYS and AUTOEXEC.BAT one line at a time,
Windows Keystroke	**Result**
F5	Starts Windows in Safe Mode, bypassing CONFIG.SYS and AUTOEXEC.BAT.
Shift+F5	Starts in Real (DOS) Mode.
F8	Calls up text-based Startup menu.
Shift+F8	Starts Windows and processes configurations one line at a time.

Command Prompt Only (Shift+F5)

If you want to start the computer in plain, real DOS 7.0, you can either modify MSDOS.SYS to always start with the command prompt, or choose Option 6 in the Startup menu. Certain commands (e.g., FDISK.EXE) can't be run from within Windows 9x, and this option gives you a plain DOS environment.

Note: Windows NT and Windows 2000 provide a Recovery Console tool as an optional installation, which allows you to start at a plain command prompt.

To start Windows 9x from the command prompt, type "WIN" and press Enter. When you exit a Windows session after starting from the command prompt, you return to the DOS prompt rather than the "It is now safe to shut off your machine" final exit screen.

The final shutdown screen is actually one of two graphics image files and can be changed. These files are located initially in your WINDOWS folder. LOGOW.SYS is the one that reads "Please wait while...," and LOGOS.SYS is the one that reads "It is now safe to...." Make backup copies of the files LOGOW.SYS and LOGOS.SYS, put them in a safe place, and then copy the two originals into a temporary folder. (The splash screen is called LOGO.SYS, and you can also choose to modify the way it looks.)

These files are standard bitmaps, so rename the extensions of these duplicates to .BMP. You can use any graphics editor to edit these files, such as Microsoft Paint, Photoshop, or Paint Shop Pro. The files are 256-color Windows bitmaps (RGB-encoded, but not RGB color), 320×400. Because the aspect ratio (width / height) of these files is not a standard 4:3 like most computer screens, the bitmaps will appear vertically elongated.

To make your new design conform to this aspect ratio, resize the bitmap to 534×400 while you're working on it. Make sure to resize them back to 320×400 when you're done. Save your changes, and rename the extensions of your new files back to .SYS. Last, copy the new files back into your WINDOWS folder.

Safe Mode Command Prompt Only

This option is like pressing the F5 key in DOS 5.0 and 6.0, which starts DOS without networking. The startup bypasses the CONFIG.SYS and AUTOEXEC.BAT files, and stops at the command prompt. It probably would have made more sense to call this option "Command Prompt with No Configurations."

Previous Version of DOS (F4)

This option on the Startup menu can also be run by pressing the F4 key when the "Starting…" message appears. The option is a bit misleading because a default installation of Windows 9x deletes any previous version of Windows 3.x and DOS.

> You'll need to remember that F8 and F4 are important Windows startup keys. F8 gets you the text-based Startup menu. F4 (may) get you a previous version of DOS.

The Installable File System (IFS) Manager

DOS has always had the 8.3 file name structure. Although the creative use of directory and subdirectory names can produce a lot of information about a file, Apple's method of using common English names has been easier for most users. Because of the way the DOS FAT works, the maximum limit for a file name, including all the directory information, is 64 characters. Windows 9x LFNs allow up to 255 characters and can include previously illegal characters, such as <space> and the + symbol.

Novell's NetWare NOS created something called the OS/2 name space feature, which was designed to resolve conflicts between DOS and Apple computers running on the same network. If an Apple user saved a file as "1997 Third Quart Annual Report" and a DOS user opened and saved that file again, the Apple user might see "1997thir.dqu" as the new file name. NetWare and the OS/2 name space helped resolve the abrupt cutting off (truncating) of anything after 11 characters.

Windows 9x uses something similar to the OS/2 name space in that the Installable File System Manager (IFS Manager) works to convert Long File Names to the 8.3 names required by the underlying 16-bit FAT. IFS Manager works the other way as well in that a request for a short file name goes out to retrieve the correct LFN in the directory listing. The IFS Manager is loaded through a helper file called IFSHLP.SYS (in the WINDOWS folder).

> File naming conventions are voluntary ways of naming files. File naming rules, on the other hand, are statements of what characters may or may not be used in a file name. The exam may confuse you by using the term "convention" to mean "rule."
>
> Remember that in DOS file names, the <space>, plus, asterisk, question mark, and slashes are not allowed. Even though Windows 9x LFNs allow some of these illegal characters, our feeling is that the exam will test your knowledge of allowable characters rather than whether a certain file name is possible under the extended capabilities of the Long File Name feature.

The Windows 9x IFS is a way to store additional file information about LFNs while allowing the DOS 16-bit FAT to control the location of the basic file clusters and sectors. Remember that part of a file system's job is to associate human names to a series of numbers that describe the cylinder, track, sectors, and clusters where data is physically stored. This new file system is made up of three parts:

➤ *IFS Manager*—Works out the problems and differences between different file system components.

➤ *File system drivers*—Provide access to low-level disk devices, CD-ROM file systems, and network devices.

➤ *Block I/O subsystem*—Deals directly with physical disks.

People sometimes refer to FAT32, 32-bit FAT, VFAT, or even HPFS when discussing the Windows 9x IFS. VFAT stands for Virtual FAT and is part of the Installable File System. VFAT was first introduced in Windows for Workgroups 3.11 and was tightened up in Windows 95. The IFSHELP.SYS driver reference in the Windows 3.x startup sequence refers to the prototype version of what went on to become the Windows 95 IFS Manager.

On the other hand, HPFS stands for *High Performance File System*, which was engineered into OS/2. Neither Windows 95 nor Windows NT uses nor currently supports the HPFS. NT uses the NT File System (NTFS). For simplicity, we refer to the underlying 16-bit FAT as the *base file system*, the Windows 95 modification as the IFS, and any other file systems by their own names. Windows 95 uses a 32-bit VFAT that works in conjunction with the 16-bit base FAT controlled by DOS 7.0. The "32" in FAT32 refers to this VFAT.

 NTFS is the Windows NT File System, but WINS is a Windows Internet Naming Service used for certain types of network protocols. Although we don't believe you'll see a question on the WINS, NTFS, or HPFS, you should make note of their names and abbreviations.

Network Redirectors

Usually, an application, operating system, or both use Interrupt 21 to access the disk and file system. Networking operating system *redirectors* (TSRs) and CD-ROM drivers keep an eye on Interrupt 21 and determine whether the file system request is for the base file system or for their own 32-bit systems. A redirector grabs a request for the base file system and redirects the request to a different file system. A redirector is like the executive secretary, watching the phone and directing calls either to the boss or to someone else in the company. (For more on redirectors, see Chapter 8.)

One problem with this idea is that you must load different device drivers for each system watching over that ever-popular IRQ 21. Different networks have their own redirector devices, and they often argue about who gets to take the file home to Mom and Dad. Aside from that, PCs have a terrible time connecting to more than two different networks at the same time.

The Windows 9x IFS Manager controls all the network redirectors as though they were different file systems. This allows an unlimited number of 32-bit redirectors to be used at the same time, as well as allowing the system to connect with any number of different networks. On any given machine, including standalone machines, the DOS file system is used as though it were just another network file system.

For any software to work with any hardware, instructions must be stored somewhere, either in a ROM BIOS chip on an expansion card or in a software program—a device driver. One way or another, the device driver must end up in memory somewhere. Although memory isn't a hardware device per se, extended memory still requires an XMS device driver (e.g., HIMEM.SYS). Likewise, expanded memory requires an EMS device driver (e.g., EMM386.EXE) in conjunction with and following the extended memory driver.

The limitations of the FAT and the large storage capacity of new hard drives and CDs put an increasing strain on the capabilities of the old 16-bit FAT to keep up. If DOS could be magically turned into a network operating system, many of those problems would just go away. The IFS Manager is that interim magic wand, acting somewhat like a network redirector by grabbing all the Interrupt 21 requests from applications that want to access the DOS file system. The DOS file system is still laying down bits of information in clusters, on sectors, in tracks, and on cylinders. However, instead of DOS making the decisions about names, IFS Manager is now doing that.

VFAT

Using LFNs and improving disk caching required a way to connect newer network operating systems to the old DOS file system on the same computer. Because the required FAT couldn't be eliminated, a second FAT had to be developed—a *Virtual FAT*. This new VFAT had to live side by side with the original, and that could work only if one of them was the boss. IFS Manager makes sure that VFAT is in charge.

When Windows starts up, the IFS waits for the system files to run all the Real Mode device drivers, and for the drivers to connect to the file system and hardware devices. Once DOS has the computer functioning, Windows steps in and takes control with VMM32. As we saw earlier, VMM32 uses its compiled library of internal VxDs to replace whatever Real Mode drivers it finds in memory.

The VxDs in VMM32 are designed specifically to communicate with the IFS Manager, so the DOS file system is *mounted* (connected) in the same sense that a network volume is mounted and recognized by a network operating system. This ability to communicate with the IFS is part of what it means to write a 32-bit application that's 100 percent Windows compatible.

Truncating to Short File Names

Windows 9x has an internal list of all the interrupts that DOS can use (a maximum of 71) and adds a few more. Among the extra interrupts is the way in which Long File Names can be recognized by the operating system. Because DOS itself can't recognize the long name, IFS Manager uses one of the extra interrupts to store the file name with an *alias* pointer (similar to a vector) and returns to tell DOS what to do with the file.

IFS Manager also takes what you enter as a Long File Name and splits it apart (parses it) so that part of it can be used as a corresponding short file name (regular DOS 8.3 name). The rest of the name is stored for later rebuilding, and the alias pointer is associated with all the pieces of the file name.

If you have a file called "1998 Fooferaugh + My list of stuff" and another file called "1998 Fooferaugh and Dave's stuff," IFS Manager truncates the two files to an 8.3 name. Theoretically, that would result in two files called 1998foof.era at the same time—*totally* illegal by DOS rules and the United Nations Resolution 439 on International Tom Foolery, as well as a breach of the 1927 Zambian nuclear arms treaty.

When IFS Manager finds two files that will truncate to the same name, it uses the first six characters (minus spaces) and adds a tilde (~) plus incremental numbers (beginning with 1). If any periods are in the Long File Name, IFS Manager uses the first three characters after the last period as the DOS extension. Otherwise, it uses the next three characters it finds. In our example, the files would be named 1998fo~1.era and 1998fo~2.era for the short DOS name.

Note: The default use of the tilde can be changed by editing the Registry.

Short Names and Aliases

A typical way for a file system to come calling on the disk is when a DOS VM is created to run a DOS application in Windows. Windows 3.x applications also make calls to the file system, and both use Interrupt 21. The file system works to find room on the disk, store a file name in the directory allocation table (DAT), and help the disk controller move the hardware around. The DAT is an index for the longer FAT.

Along with the short name in the FAT, the parsed LFN is given the pointer to hang on to. When anything calls the file system, IFS Manager goes back to DOS and presents the request. DOS hands IFS Manager the file location information, and IFS Manager looks at the associated alias number to find the rest of the file name. IFS Manager then shows the user the Long File Name.

By the time the proposed Windows 9x Long File Name reaches the file system, IFS Manager has parsed it and added a pointer number. Meanwhile, DOS hasn't a clue that anything unusual is happening and still thinks it's running the same as it did back in 1981. DOS dutifully lays down the file, stores what it was told to store in the DAT, and goes back to sleep. The file is stored in clusters all over the disk, and IFS Manager makes sure that anything and everything in Windows sees the file name that it's supposed to see.

Note: In certain circumstances, the VFAT and the 16-bit DOS FAT can become partly desynchronized. In this strange situation, Explorer (not the File Manager, though) can end up showing two files with exactly the same name in the same directory. This is rare, but it results from the fact that the names being presented in Explorer aren't the actual file names any more than the name being presented in any other Windows 9x application is the actual name.

The **DIR** command in a DOS window is stolen by IFS Manager and returns the DOS directory with the Long File Name set aside in the IFS name space (to the far right of the DIR listing). Restarting the computer in MS-DOS Mode shuts down the entire Windows environment and eliminates the IFS and IFS Manager, along with LFN support. A **DIR** command at a plain DOS prompt (e.g., Option 6 from the F8 Startup menu) shows only the short name of the file as it's actually registered in the DAT.

From a DOS command prompt within Windows, you can still use a long name (if you know it) by surrounding the long name with quotation marks. For example, if you type

CD "Program Files"

instead of

CD PROGRA~1

Windows IFS Manager puts you in the right folder. This also works for individual files on a command line. The second, or closing, quote isn't usually necessary.

Saving Long File Names

As you can see, the only thing keeping track of the LFNs is IFS Manager. If you decide to store all the files from a Windows computer on older networks, the Long File Names will be stored only if the OS/2 name space has been enabled. If name space isn't enabled, the LFNs are lost in the river of history. This same problem occurs if you store files on a floppy disk and copy them over to a 16-bit DOS or Windows machine.

There are two other places where LFNs can fail: in certain Internet transfers and under the old File Manager (WINFILE.EXE). Sometimes File Manager is easier to use than Explorer, but you can't see LFNs, and if you rename a file from within File Manager, the next time that you look at it under Explorer, it will have a DOS file name. The same goes for file transfers from a Windows machine to some other machine that doesn't support LFNs.

A little-known (and hardly referenced) utility that comes with the Windows CD-ROM is the LFNBK.EXE utility (for Long File Name backup). LFNBK.EXE is found in the ADMIN\APPTOOLS\LFNBACK folder, along with LFNBK.TXT, which describes the basic operations and switches. Perhaps the program is hard to notice because Microsoft says that it's for experienced users and shouldn't be relied on for day-to-day maintenance.

The most immediate problem with LFNs is that they're stored within Windows. In addition, part of that storage is the alias map that connects the physical location of the file to its corresponding IFS long name. Suppose that you decide to use a 16-bit defragmenting utility from the DOS prompt. Part of the defragmenting process involves moving file clusters around. Naturally, the utility is in constant communication with the file system's DAT, which keeps track of the clusters no matter where they end up. But who's telling all this to IFS Manager? No one.

Using a DOS-based file maintenance program can disassociate the short file name from the Long File Name, causing the LFN to be lost forever. Reformatting a hard drive and reinstalling Windows will not keep previous Long File Names associated with the short file names held by DOS. Keeping the original LFNs requires a complete backup of the existing Windows environment.

An interesting problem arises when Long File Names disappear from the system. Certain program instructions that are internal to Windows 9x program files make calls to other files by their specific LFNs. The files exist on the drive, but only in short-name form. Because Windows is looking for the exact file name of a program and is expecting IFS Manager to have that name, it can't find the file because it can only see the short name. At that point, Windows fails to run.

Reports and Utilities

One of the less obvious ways in which the various versions of Windows differ from each other is in an almost adversarial relationship between the computer user and the operating system. DOS was generally known as an *open system*, in that, aside from allowing developers access to all the programming aspects, whoever was using the computer could make just about any configuration changes he or she wanted. Windows 95 began making user access to system-level configuration and repair tools more difficult. Sometimes this was done by referencing the particular programs in thick books such as the *Windows Resource Kit*, sold separately from the operating system. Other times, as with the Registry and REGEDIT.EXE, the user had to know where the file was located and how to work with the results of running the file.

The old Windows 3.11 Program Manager introduced policies that allowed system administrators to prevent users from accessing certain parts of the underlying file system. Windows 95 increased this security with a Policy Editor feature, which allowed systems administrators and IT professionals an even more sophisticated way of locking less knowledgeable users out of the basic configuration features for the system. This trend continues, and one of the ways Windows ME differs from Windows 95 and 98 is that it is much more difficult to use diagnostic tools and utilities in Windows ME.

When we discuss Windows NT and Windows 2000 in the next chapter, we'll focus more on what you're allowed to do, as opposed to what a fully authorized systems administrator can do. Windows NT is where the first real separation between the corporate and home-user market took effect. Windows 2000 is an attempt to reintegrate the entire PC market through the use of a single name for all versions of the Windows operating system.

Hardware Diagnostics

We've talked about how DOS came with several program files that weren't essential to the operating system, but that provided tools and utilities for managing files and disks. Tweak UI was a set of utilities like this. We've also spoken about how third-party developers—both commercial and shareware—created a market of ancillary tools and utilities, and Norton Utilities is an example of commercial utilities. In DOS 5.0, Microsoft began licensing some of these third-party technologies, and for the first time, DOS wasn't developed wholly "in house," so to speak.

Windows 95 began focusing more attention on the tools and utilities needed by system administrators to properly maintain and support the increasingly complex operating system and system configurations. Diagnostics tools continued to be left either on the installation disk (rapidly becoming a CD-ROM, rather than many floppy disks) or as obscure files somewhere in the Windows subfolder. However, Windows 95 introduced a consolidated reporting capability for a basic presentation of the hardware connected to a given system. The feeling seems to have been that a report wouldn't damage the functionality of the system, but having access to tools and utilities could be trouble.

Borrowing from the Apple Macintosh, the My Computer icon made its first appearance on the Desktop. By right-clicking on this icon and going to a standardized Properties option, Windows 95 provided a way for the user (or more likely an administrator) to *explore* the various devices and peripherals attached to the motherboard, along with their basic settings. This metaphor of exploring, or *browsing* a system, began with the Windows Explorer and carries through in all subsequent versions of Windows. However, Microsoft frowned upon the use of the word "browsing" and has begun using different words to describe what it would like you to do.

Building on the detailed reporting capabilities of MSD.EXE (Microsoft Diagnostics), HWDIAG.EXE (Hardware Diagnostics) is a much more sophisticated diagnostics tool, running a thorough analysis of the specific hardware devices attached to the system. HWDIAG.EXE works in conjunction with PnP to report out such things as the manufacturer for a network card, the way the card is configured, and even the software version the card is using.

Note: HWDIAG.EXE and MSD.EXE are both hardware and configuration diagnostics tools. Neither program was installed by default in Windows 95, but remained on the installation disk during the basic setup routines.

Windows 95 introduced some important changes in how machines were configured and fixed. The Control Panel became much more sophisticated than the original applet in Windows 3.x, allowing for more control over the configuration of the machine at both the hardware and software level. Changes to the overall look and feel of the system continued to be implemented in the Control Panel, and CONTROL.EXE was still found in the C:\WINDOWS folder.

Windows 98

Windows 98 came in two basic versions: Windows 98 Original and Windows 98 Second Edition. Just as the version information in Windows 95 indicates that it's Windows 4.0.x, version information in Windows 98 indicates that it's Windows 4.1.x (e.g., 4.10.2222A). The Windows Explorer in Windows 95 was Explorer version 4.00.950. In Windows 98, it became Explorer 5.0.

Windows 98 Original standardized the varying modifications of Windows 95 OSR/1 and OSR/2 (A and B), and was very much like the mysterious Windows 95 OSR/D. Because Windows 98 was the next in a line of many improvements, it could easily be said that Windows 98 was an improved version of Windows 95. The basic differences were the inclusion of FAT32 (from OSR/2 of Windows 95), streamlined administration tools, and better remote connectivity. In the original release, Windows 98 included:

➤ Accessibility Utility, which was originally a barely documented feature in Windows 95, and which allows users with certain disabilities to tailor the system

➤ Backup, which was a set of utilities available from DOS 1.0. The Windows 95 utility uses a different file compression format based on the QIC 113 tape backup specification

➤ HyperTerminal, which was a 32-bit telephony API and unimodem subsystems for asynchronous connectivity

➤ Internet Explorer 5.0

➤ USB support in the evolving Pnp capabilities

➤ Outlook Express 5.0, which was a better email client than Exchange

➤ Net Meeting 3.0, a small application designed for audio/video conferencing on the Internet

➤ System Agent, a utility designed to automatically launch specific programs in scheduled system maintenance

➤ Windows Media support for MP3, WAV, AVI, and MPEG multimedia file formats with Windows Media Player 6.1

➤ Broadband Internet access support

Windows 98 Second Edition added updates that were included in Windows ME, which then went on to become part of Windows 2000. The Second Edition included:

➤ Improved USB support

➤ Pentium III 3D video support

➤ Internet connection sharing, which allowed multiple machines to share a single modem and ISP connection

➤ IEEE 1394 (FireWire) support, which was high bandwidth for digital cameras and new storage device connections

➤ Support for the latest advances in hardware features, such as multiple monitors, AGP video, and DVD drives

➤ Better IRQ sharing to handle the increasing number of devices installed on computer systems, such as printers, scanners, Webcams, Zip drives, and so on

Utilities

One of the primary changes in Window 98 was the Internet integration features of the Active Desktop. One of the installation options allowed for using features of a Web page on the Desktop. The Internet's popularity was making most users familiar with how a Web browser worked, and the Windows 98 Desktop included single-clicking on icons and programs (as opposed to double-clicking), and a bubble help descriptive feature for icons and programs. These small help notations, often called toolbar tips or mouse-overs, make Desktop objects more understandable when the mouse pointer hovers over the object. (This need for bubble help only goes to show that, if we'd been meant to see things in pictures, we would be speaking in hieroglyphs.)

Windows 98 introduced the concept of using the original file management and browsing tool (Explorer) as a Web browser. The Web browser made the idea of browsing the Internet a commonly understood metaphor, so the File Manager, limited to moving and changing files, became the Windows Explorer. In Windows 98, one of the installation options gave the Explorer a way to present the contents of a local hard drive in a Web browser format.

This browser format allowed for direct support of HTML (HTM) files and common Web features, such as one-click transfers from one file to another. Windows 98 tried to bring the Internet to every user, and Windows 98 shipped with a wide array of Internet-related tools and features. Explorer added support for dynamic HTML (DHTML), a way of making a typical HTML page (at a Web site) change according to different parameters. For example, a Web site might present different information to a user depending upon the user's address or the time of day. Several of the technologies are involved in dynamic page changes and include Common Gateway Interface (CGI), Java, JavaScript, and ActiveX.

Note: The technologies that brought about DHTML introduced a scripting language that permitted plain text commands to be formed into a sort of combination macro and batch programming language. Explorer support for scripting on the local machine's Desktop allows virus-like scripts to be run in ways that were previously impossible. This is how email messages could run a destructive script that acts much the way a virus does without ever running an executable (EXE or COM) program.

Additional administrative tools included a better Backup and System Recovery interface, specialized System Configuration and System Information utilities, an expanded Troubleshooting interface, and the Maintenance Wizard and Task Scheduler to help keep the machine running smoothly. New setup options made it easier to install Window 98 in an office environment, with the inclusion of several batch programs and new scripting (pseudo-programming) tools.

Help Desk

One of the biggest changes between Windows 95 and Windows 98 is the Help feature. The Help Desk takes all HLP files and administrative wizards and expands them through something that looks very much like a standard HTML window. Help, in Windows 98, provides four levels of tech support on the machine: Local Help, Microsoft's *Getting Started Online*, Web Help, and System Troubleshooting.

Local (home-based) help is a help system that loads into a special help *engine* that displays HTML files. Windows 98 assumes that everyone wants (or needs) to be connected to the Internet in an always-on connection. When you access a Web Help link, you're moved to the Windows 98 Support Online page, either through a broadband connection or by having Windows 98 automatically run your modem. After you've completed an online registration form, you're given access to the Support Online databases, as well as a *knowledgebase* (database of peoples' experiences) of troubleshooting wizards and *frequently asked questions (FAQs)*, as well as other resources.

The Troubleshooter simplifies how you specify which processes you want to activate during startup, using a view similar to the SYSEDIT System Editor. In this applet, you can edit the CONFIG.SYS, AUTOTEXEC.BAT, SYSTEM.INI, and WIN.INI files from directly within the troubleshooting tools. You're given a way to edit or disable individual lines in the various initialization files, but you can also access which area of Windows you're making changes to. For instance, the Startup tab presents the various configuration files and the lines within those files that affect the Windows Startup—the programs that automatically begin running after Windows finishes loading.

The Troubleshooter dialog box is similar to many other properties menus, where each tab offers a view of the settings within the configuration areas for that tab. There are tabs for the Control Panel, Device Manager, and other areas.

Windows Update Manager

Through the Help Desk, you can access the Update Manager to keep the Windows operating system current with the latest software drivers, patches, bug fixes, and incremental release updates. Under the supposition that most computers would eventually always be connected to the Internet in some fashion, accessing the Update Manager produces an automatic attempt to access the Internet and go directly to the Web site for Windows updates.

The Update Manager examines the Registry, working through all the software and hardware configurations, along with the associated files being used in those settings. The Update Manager then compares the files it finds on your hard drive with the information held in the update database on the Web site, downloading appropriate updated files into the locations pointed to in the Registry keys.

Once various files have been flagged (marked) for updating, the Web site provides links to various other locations on the site where these updated files can be found and downloaded. The Update Manager then helps install and/or uninstall various files. Following an Update Manager session, the program creates a history log (file) of the activities and file modifications that took place during the session. Through this history log, you can remove previous updates and return the machine to original configurations in the event it becomes necessary.

Maintenance Wizard

This wizard schedules routine tasks, such as ScanDisk, Defrag, or the Disk Cleanup utility. Prior to Windows 98, DOS users were versed at creating small batch files containing all the various programs, switches, and file locations involved in certain maintenance tasks. For instance, to copy any changed files from a directory to a floppy disk, a batch file would store the various switches used by XCOPY.EXE, along with whichever directories were to be examined. However, they were left in the hands of third-party developers to figure out how to time the batch files to the system clock.

Windows 3.x introduced various macro language (automated series of steps) events, and third-party developers soon began to create small programs making it easier (in theory) to use these macros. IBM created something called Rexx in OS/2, as something more than a batch language, but less than a full-blown programming language. Microsoft did something similar in the Excel, Word, and Access (database) macro programming languages and in Visual Basic.

In time, it became quite clear that the average user had no intention of, nor interest in, learning a complex programming language for anything. To bring the ease of automated task steps down to Earth, Microsoft introduced the concept of a wizard. Essentially, a *wizard* is a series of dialog boxes that prompt the user with various questions about what they hope to accomplish. Each dialog box is programmed with decision branches where, depending upon what the user types into a dialog line or which button the user clicks, the underlying program stores the necessary files and variables used to perform the automated task. The Maintenance Wizard stores not only the time of day, but also the number of times a particular maintenance task should be performed.

System Information Utility

This utility provides a single interface for several Windows 95 utilities, including the Device Manager and HWDIAG.EXE. Accessed through Start|Programs| Accessories|System Tools|System Information Utility, the Windows 98 version gives you not only detailed information about the hardware, software, and system configuration, but also provides a *configuration history* for each device. Much like the Update Manager history log, the configuration history keeps track of when and how each item in the system was changed.

The System Information utility also acts as a central control panel for several other troubleshooting and debugging tools. One of the tools included in System Information is a utility for making backup copies of the Registry. Remember that in Windows 95, this was the almost undocumented ERU.EXE.

Microsoft has historically tried to keep end users separate from developers, tech support people, and systems administration. Inevitably, the Internet has opened access to all sorts of specialized tools and utilities that people have developed to make supporting Windows easier. In time, these in-house, undocumented programs have made their way into the open market, taking on growing status within the tech support community. After a program has become a "must-have" utility for anyone involved with troubleshooting a system, Microsoft eventually comes around and formally puts it into a new release of its software, giving it a user interface, menus, a name, and some supporting help.

Registry Checker

As with many utilities installed with Windows 98, the Registry Checker (SCANREGW.EXE) was a separate, downloadable program that was originally available only from the Microsoft Web site (or various shareware sites). This utility examines the Registry for various signs of corruption, such as invalid entries or empty data blocks. If there are no errors, the program makes a backup copy of the system files (SYSTEM.DAT and USER.DAT) with all the working Registry settings.

If the Registry Checker detects a problem, it tries to use the previous backup to restore the Registry. If no backup is available, Registry Checker makes a best-guess attempt to repair the Registry, by examining the many separate locations that configuration information is held for any hardware device or software application. Although this is better than nothing, the Registry is so complicated that sometimes the attempted repair is worse than the original problem. The best insurance is to always maintain current backups of the Registry independently of all these utility backups.

System File Check (SFC)

Windows 95 tech support people were able to use a Registry Checker utility, available for download from the Microsoft site (if you knew about it), to analyze a corrupted Windows Registry and to attempt to fix it. Windows 98 incorporated the System File Check (SFC) to work in a similar fashion on overall system files.

This utility checks through the critical system files on a machine by taking a snapshot of each file whenever a program calls any of the files. DOS used something called a checksum to keep a database of how many bits a file should contain. Some of the original, simple virus checkers used a database made up of the file name, how many bits the file included, and the time and date of the original file. SFC checks these system files against a similar database each time a file is run.

If the SFC finds a difference between a current file and the description of that file in its database, it offers to either restore any file that has changed, or to update its database to reflect a new version of the file.

Version Conflict Manager

This utility tool tracks version numbers of important system files, providing reports and methods for updating older system files. This came from several attempted commercial programs that would immediately log on to the Web and download the files when you tried to access, upgrade, or install a program that wanted a particular version of a system file (e.g., WINSOCK.DLL).

Disk Cleanup

Somewhat similar to Defrag, Disk Cleanup "cleans up" the hard drive by removing or compressing files you don't need. The program runs through the files on a hard drive, flagging those that are out of date or that haven't been used in a long time, warning you when the drive is getting filled up. At that point, you can make decisions as to what you'd like to do with those files.

Windows ME

The year 2000 came and went, and the world didn't come to an end. With the release of Windows 95, Microsoft decided to stop using a version number in the name of the operating system, choosing instead to use a year reference. The underlying incremental releases still continued, and when enough changes had taken place, the next major release updated the year. As Windows 98 continued to change through updates and fixes, it too eventually required a full version release, becoming Windows Millennium Edition (ME). This was where things really started getting confusing.

Based on the logic of the names, one would think that Windows ME and 2000 are essentially the same thing. In fact, ME and 2000 are a point of divergence in Microsoft's wish to merge the home PC user with the commercial business user and Windows NT (see Chapter 13 for a discussion of NT). The release of Windows ME was based on a marketing assessment where Microsoft believed the home market was ready to abandon the original Windows finally and completely.

For the first time, Windows ME removed support for virtual machines running in Real Mode. If you remember, Real Mode is a reference to the original XT computers and to addressing real memory with direct addresses. The CONFIG.SYS and AUTOEXEC.BAT configuration files, having always been necessary for any hardware or software expecting to find a basic, 16-bit DOS machine, vanished. Because ME eliminated support for this type of virtual machine, all references to the configuration files disappeared.

Remember that Windows 95 automated the process of checking for real device drivers to see if it could replace or substitute those drivers with VxDs. If a VxD could do whatever the original driver was designed to do, a knowledgeable user could comment out the driver from the CONFIG.SYS file, reboot the machine, and see if the device still worked. Windows ME took on more responsibility for this process, going through any existing CONFIG.SYS file and assigning what it thought were the appropriate VxDs. Once the file was stripped of all its device drivers, ME went through the AUTOEXEC.BAT file and moved all configuration switches into the Registry.

Both the CONFIG.SYS and AUTOEXC.BAT files could continue to reside on the hard drive, and ME would leave them there in the event it found one of the pesky buggers during an update installation. However, after Windows ME was installed, it would modify the file names and their locations, keeping an eye on any new hardware installations. If an installation searched for either of the Real Mode configuration files, ME would intercept the search and hand off its own location to the installation routine. The device's installation routine commands were allowed to modify the older files, and ME would then wait for a reboot.

The next time the Windows ME machine started up, ME went through the changed configuration files, placing **SET** commands in the AUTOEXEC.BAT file and adjusting the installation according to the way Microsoft thinks things ought to be. In more than a few instances, Windows ME made the wrong choices and many programs, games, and devices that the home computer user wanted very much to use failed to run.

 There is very little on the low-level specifics of ME on the current A+ exam, although the exam seems to be continually evolving. The primary change in Windows ME was the elimination of Real Mode support. Other than that, Windows ME is essentially the same as Windows 98, with many of the configuration utilities being better protected from the casual user.

Practice Questions

Question 1

Windows maintains file names through which of the following? [Choose the three best answers]

- ❑ a. LFNs
- ❑ b. VFAT
- ❑ c. FAT32
- ❑ d. DAT

Answers b, c, and d are correct. Choice a, Windows Long File Names (LFNs), are not a maintenance process. After names have been created, Windows uses the Virtual FAT (VFAT), the underlying 32-bit file allocation table (FAT32), and the directory allocation table (DAT) to maintain the address locations for the data in the file's clusters.

Question 2

The Windows Registry is made up of which set of files?

- ○ a. USER.BAT, SYSTEM.BAT, SYSTEM.INI, WINDOWS.INI
- ○ b. SYSTEM.INI, WIN.INI, HKEY.DAT, REG32.DAT
- ○ c. USER.DAT, SYSTEM.DAT
- ○ d. SYSTEM.INI, WIN.INI

Answer c is correct. Although Windows 9x may still use the original initialization files from Windows 3.x, the SYSTEM.INI and WIN.INI files are not part of the Registry. Therefore, choices a, b, and d are all incorrect. A BAT file has a batch file extension, and the Registry files are in binary format.

Question 3

> Where will Windows look before finding a 32-bit virtual device driver to replace a static VxD?
>
> ○ a. SYSTEM.INI
>
> ○ b. WIN.INI
>
> ○ c. VMM32.DLL
>
> ○ d. KRNL328.EXE

Answer a is correct. Note the use of "before" in the question, along with a reference to a static device driver. The first place Windows 9x looks for these static VxDs is in the SYSTEM.INI file. Answer b is incorrect because the WIN.INI file maintains user configuration settings, not device driver settings. Answers c and d are incorrect because Windows doesn't look in either DLL or EXE files for device drivers.

Question 4

> The best way to back up the system registration files is with the _____ utility.
>
> ○ a. BACKUP.EXE
>
> ○ b. ERU.EXE
>
> ○ c. REGEDT32.EXE
>
> ○ d. LFNBK.EXE

Answer b is correct. ERU.EXE is the Emergency Recovery Utility program specifically designed to back up the Windows Registry, sometimes called the system registration files. Answer a is incorrect because the DOS Backup program is designed to back up entire file areas. Answer c is incorrect because it refers to the 32-bit version of REGEDIT.EXE, the preferred Registry Editor for Windows 2000 and NT. Answer d is incorrect because it refers to a utility for backing up Long File Names.

Question 5

FAT32 has the advantage over FAT16 due to which of the following main reasons? [Choose the two best answers]

- ❑ a. Files larger than 2GB
- ❑ b. Multiple 2GB partitions
- ❑ c. Variable cluster sizes
- ❑ d. The nonactive bootable file system

Answers a and c are correct. FAT16 is limited to a maximum file size of 2GB, either in one file or a single partition size. FAT32 uses larger, 32-bit addresses in the FAT to provide access to partitions larger than 2GB. FAT32 also provides adjustable cluster sizes, making storage of small files more efficient. Answer b is technically correct, but functionally incorrect, in that, although FAT32 can easily support many 2GB partitions, so can FAT16, NTFS, and HPFS file systems. There is no such term as the one referenced in answer d.

Question 6

Windows 95, 98, and ME all create a Real Mode VM during a DOS session.

- ○ a. True
- ○ b. False

Answer b, false, is correct. The primary distinction between Windows ME and all previous versions of Windows is that Windows ME terminated support for Real Mode. Windows 95 and Windows 98 both continued that support for backward compatibility reasons.

Need to Know More?

 Chellis, James, Charles Perkins, and Matthew Strebe. *MCSE Networking Essentials Study Guide, 3rd Edition*. San Francisco, CA: Sybex Network Press, 1996. ISBN 0-7821-2695-2. This book goes into more detail than you'll need for the certification exam but is a good place to start if you're considering a career as a network engineer.

 Derfler, Frank J. *PC Magazine Guide to Connectivity*. New York, NY: Ziff Davis, 1995. ISBN 1-56276-274-5. This book is easy to read and provides a good introduction to networking.

 Microsoft Windows 95 Resource Kit. Redmond, WA: Microsoft Press, 1995. ISBN 1-55615-678-2. This is the definitive resource for all Windows 95 questions. It assumes that you have a good working knowledge of Windows 95.

 Microsoft Windows 98 Resource Kit. Redmond, WA: Microsoft Press, 1998. ISBN 1-57231-644-6. This is the definitive resource for all Windows 98 questions. It assumes that you have a good working knowledge of Windows.

 Norton, Peter and John Mueller. *Complete Guide to Windows 95*. Indianapolis, IN: Sams Publishing, 1997. ISBN 0-672-30791-X. This very good introduction to Windows 95 explains the "why" as well as the "how."

 Tidrow, Rob. *Windows 95 Registry Troubleshooting*. Indianapolis, IN: New Riders, 1996. ISBN 1-56205-556-9. This book goes into more detail than you'll need for the certification exam, but if you really want to get into it, this is your source.

 Trulove, James. *LAN Wiring*. New York, NY: McGraw-Hill, 1997. ISBN 0-07-065302-X. This book addresses every aspect of physically wiring and testing a local area network (LAN). It is easy to read and provides a wealth of information that is rarely covered in books on networking.

Windows NT and Windows 2000

Terms you'll need to understand:

✓ Multitasking and the virtual machine (VM)

✓ Network server and local machines

✓ End user and network administrator

✓ Logging on to a network

✓ Load and initialize (a program)

✓ A network or machine event

Concepts you'll need to master:

✓ Modular programming and development

✓ Operating system layers surrounding a kernel

✓ Security, granting, and blocking access rights

✓ User and group accounts and profiles

✓ Loader programs (NT Loader)

✓ Booting from multiple operating systems

✓ Volume sets, mirroring, and RAID

✓ The Control Panel

We begin with Windows New Technology (NT) in terms of how it differs from previous versions of Windows. If you remember, Windows 3.x provided a multi-tasking environment for DOS and 16-bit Windows applications, but it was not an actual operating system. Rather, Windows 3.x was an interface that ran on top of DOS. Windows 3.x gave each DOS program its own session machine (process), and all Windows applications shared a single virtual machine, called the System Virtual Machine (System VM).

All applications shared this one VM, and they weren't isolated in any way, allowing one badly behaved program to bring down every other running program, including Windows itself, causing a full crash. Rather than sharing a single VM, Windows 9x runs a separate process for each application, thereby isolating each new VM from the others.

Multitasking

Windows 3.x used *cooperative* multitasking rather than *pre-emptive* multitasking. In cooperative multitasking, the CPU has no control over a given program, and that program can completely take over the CPU. If the program doesn't give back that control, too bad. A single program can "steal" the CPU, along with all the memory resources, and keep other programs from getting any attention. In pre-emptive multitasking, the operating system retains control of the CPU and manages how any given program can gain access to both the resources and central processor.

In pre-emptive multitasking, each Win32 program (32-bit program) is separate, so if one crashes, it won't affect any other VMs. For example (except in unusual circumstances), if a 16- or 32-bit program crashes within Windows 9x, the operating system can shut down that specific virtual machine, leaving the other processes running untouched.

Windows 9x retains control of the CPU, giving running programs access to the CPU under its own decision-making process. The operating system gives only *conditional* access to the CPU. At any given time, Windows 9x can *pre-empt* (prevent by acting first) a program, stepping in to take control and suspending the program's operations, along with the program's access to any resources, including the CPU. This prevents any individual program from hogging the processor. Windows 9x supports multithreaded multitasking as long as the program has been written with the appropriate programming threads.

The Origins of Windows NT

Keep in mind that although NT seems to have been built on the features and capabilities of Windows 95, we've seen that NT was actually a completely different operating system interface, originally developed in conjunction with IBM.

Remember, too, that OS/2 was the underlying operating system and NT was the user interface. When Microsoft and IBM split up, each company took some of the joint technology to begin work on its own independent version of the operating system and the interface.

Windows NT was designed from the ground up as a full, 32-bit operating system with networking and security built into the system. Because of the focus on networking, NT has always found greater acceptance in the business world, with NT being a direct competitor to Novell's NetWare network operating system and all its features.

Windows NT was the foundation for Windows 95, 98, and Millennium Edition (ME). Newer Pentium processors are designed to work in conjunction with more than one processor, and NT supports multiple CPUs. Windows 9x can work only with a single CPU. An operating system without a CPU is as pointless as a CPU without an operating system, so changes in chip technology have a natural impact on modifications to an operating system.

Note: Although there's no reason why you can't run Windows 9x on a multiprocessor system, what happens is that Windows 9x shuts down the additional processors, returning the system to a single-processor environment. NT actually runs the different processors.

Both IBM and Microsoft were trying to come up with a completely integrated network operating system that would bring together processors, operating systems, and hardware under one central umbrella. When we talk about *portability*, we mean that an operating system can be ported (carried over) to many different kinds of platforms using the broad diversity of hardware on the market.

NT Versions 3.1 and 4.0

NT 3.1 was Microsoft's first release of its own version of the OS, including much of the IBM original code. Windows NT was a sort of precursor to Windows 95. There doesn't seem to be a reason why there wasn't a 3.0 release, or, for that matter, a version 1.0 or 2.0. The NT 3.1 interface looked almost exactly like the 16-bit Windows 3.1 GUI, but when you opened up an object on the Desktop, the menus were all different. This made for a nicely confusing situation.

NT 3.x was an early example of how separating hardware device drivers from the underlying motherboard caused serious compatibility problems. Microsoft began including with NT a book with lists of all the specific devices that had been tested successfully for compatibility with NT. This hardware compatibility list was updated on the Internet, demonstrating the difference between the logical **AND** and **NOT** operators.

Excluding with **AND** vs. Including with **NOT**

A logical **AND** operator is used in an exclusionary statement because it assumes an exclusion of everything but the specific items stated. For example, if you ask for information about Illinois **AND** California, the result automatically excludes any other place in the world. A logical **NOT** operator is used with inclusion statements. If you ask for information about the United States, but **NOT** Illinois and California, the result includes all information about the United States and any individual states it contains except Illinois and California.

In a **NOT** statement, you don't have to know all the details of a body of information. All that information is included, except what you do *not* want included. In an **AND** statement, you must know the specific items of information you're looking for. It's always easier to include everything and exclude some things, than it is to exclude everything and rely on your all-knowing mind to come up with every instance where you'll allow something.

Windows NT 4.0 began the real divergence between Microsoft and IBM when OS/2 Warp made a momentary splash on the market and NT took a foothold in corporate America. Remember, too, that Microsoft had been trying to convince the home PC market of the benefits of a full 32-bit operating system. Windows 95 was the first serious attempt to move the general public into NT. When the move failed, mostly due to lack of support for many 16-bit applications and hardware, Microsoft tried to compromise and went back to build in support for those old DOS and Windows 3.x applications and software drivers.

Windows 98 and ME were a gradual but continuous development effort, designed to bring about a convergence between ongoing developments in the 32-bit NT operating system, the 16-bit home market, and those old device drivers. Windows 2000 (discussed in its own section later in this chapter) brought about that final convergence.

Version Convergence

Windows 95 came in both a full and upgrade version; which one you purchased was based on whether or not an existing 16-bit system would be converted (upgraded) to a 32-bit system. Windows 98 and ME began a trend where the operating system is no longer readily available to the retail customer, coming instead as a preinstalled configuration. Windows 2000 ships to commercial vendors in four distinct product lines:

➤ *Windows 2000 Professional*—Essentially the Windows NT Workstation version, packaged for the individual desktop machine

➤ *Windows 2000 Server*—An entry-level network server version, equal to Windows NT Server, with support for two-way symmetric processing (using two CPUs simultaneously) and designed for medium-sized deployments

➤ *Windows 2000 Advanced Server*—A mid-sized deployment with support for four CPUs in simultaneous processing and support for more physical memory

➤ *Windows 2000 Datacenter Server*—A large-scale deployment with support for 16 CPUs and 64GB of physical memory

So what about Windows NT 5.0? When you look at the underlying version of Windows 9x, you discover that Microsoft is calling it Windows 4.x, with the minor version numbers associated with Windows 95, 98, or ME. Oddly enough, this is the same number associated with NT, as in Windows NT version 4.0. This could be because Windows NT 3.x used the graphic interface from Windows 3.11, but NT 4.0 uses the graphic interface from Windows 95 and later.

Microsoft ran into a problem with names when it reached the final approach of joining Windows NT 4.x with the home market versions of Windows 9x. Not only that, but "new technology" in 1992 seems a bit more like "obsolete technology" in 2001, meaning that:

➤ Windows 2000 Professional is the same as Windows NT Workstation 5.0.

➤ Windows 2000 Server is the same as Windows NT Server 5.0.

➤ Windows 2000 Advanced Server is the same as Windows NT Server 5.0 Enterprise Edition.

The Windows 2000 Datacenter Server package has no counterpart in the NT line of products, indicating that Microsoft has redefined the series names. Datacenter Server is an extremely powerful version of the operating system and is designed for the online transaction-processing business (e.g., banking industry), large data warehousing situations, and science and engineering applications. Data warehousing is where a massive amount of information is gathered together from many different databases into one central location.

Regardless of the changed names, Windows 2000 seems to be the best of both worlds. The joined features bring together the ease of use Microsoft learned how to implement in the home market (Windows 9x), and the portability and scalability developed for the commercial networking market with Windows NT.

The Interface

Microsoft was in charge of developing the user interface for the new operating system, and its first effort was the original Windows GUI. Nothing changed in that plan, so Windows 3.x, Windows 9x, and Windows NT became a progression.

From the interface perspective, Windows NT looks very similar to Windows 98 and ME, and equally similar to Windows 2000. That's the interface, though, not the way the underlying operating system works. As we've often said, Windows 9x is still interfacing with 16-bit DOS and gradually taking on some of the 32-bit functions of Windows NT.

Internally, Windows NT is designed differently from DOS and uses a *modular* design. This isn't the same as saying that DOS used separate program files, but rather that NT uses separate *components*, with each component managing a separate conceptual function of the overall operating system. One of the problems with updating DOS was that the three basic system files all had to be modified to work with each other. Following any change to the system files, all the ancillary files had to be updated. Modular design is a way to upgrade separate parts of the operating system without the expense of having to upgrade the entire OS and its extensions at the same time.

Spaghetti Code

We know that a computer program is a series of very exact statements, where each statement leads to the next statement. A series of statements is often called a *routine*. No statement has to necessarily be the next line of code because a computer can read very fast and find the next statement wherever it's located in the program (like the Find feature in a word processor). When a statement tells the computer to go to another statement that isn't next in line, we could say the program is making a *call*. The program calls system functions and memory functions, but when it asks the computer to run another whole set of instructions before it returns to where the program left off, we say the main routine is calling a subroutine.

Originally, programming was done in a long line of sequential statements. Whenever anyone had to modify the program, they would insert a call to a subroutine and write the entire modification somewhere else in the program. Sometimes those subroutines had to be modified, in which case someone would insert another call to a new subroutine. Programs can often be hundreds of thousands, or even millions of lines long, and after a while, all the modifications calling other modifications became known as *spaghetti code,* referring to the total mess of tangled references.

Modular programming was introduced as a way to keep the related parts of a program all in one area. Main routines were kept separate from subroutines, and modifications were done in an organized fashion. The programs are still very long, but at least they tend to follow an orderly progression of references.

Each module in Windows NT is entirely independent of every other module, with none of them sharing any specific program code. The way the modules work together is with *system calls*. Not only is NT a modular program, but the operating system is divided into two larger divisions: the *Kernel Mode* and *User Mode*.

A Kernel

DOS was known as an *open* operating system because any knowledgeable person could access the fundamental system files. Some people refer to IO.SYS as the DOS kernel. When the underlying system files of an operating system—the files that speak directly with the BIOS—are placed out of bounds by the OS developers, we refer to that operating system as being based on a kernel. A kernel uses *metadrivers*, created by the OS developers, as a way to connect third-party device driver software to the operating system and motherboard. The prefix "meta" comes from Greek, meaning after or beyond. Windows NT and 2000 are differentiated from DOS, 16-bit Windows, and Windows 9x in that Microsoft terminated the use of an open OS and began using a kernel.

Kernel Mode

In Kernel Mode, certain critical components of the operating system give direct access to system hardware. We speak of the *privileges* of a given module, and Kernel Mode is more privileged than User Mode. When components of the OS are running in User Mode, they have no direct access to the system hardware. Therefore, we say they run in a less privileged mode. Applications and some of the NT subsystems run in User Mode.

The Hardware Abstraction Layer (HAL)

We can divide the Kernel Mode into two separate levels, or *layers*. At the lowest level is the *hardware abstraction layer (HAL)*—not to be confused with the fictional super-computer that Arthur C. Clarke wrote about. If you remember our networking discussion in Chapter 8, you'll remember we spoke about the OSI model and how different layers of the network operating system are designed with different purposes. The HAL takes a look at different kinds of hardware, disguising the actual (concrete) properties of each device and presenting an *abstraction* of that hardware (a symbolic reference) to the next layer.

The HAL presents a uniform, standardized interface to this next higher layer called the Windows NT Executive layer. To make matters even more confusing, the Executive layer also contains two layers. Let's take a moment to look at the various divisions of Windows NT:

➤ Kernel Mode is where the system is given direct access to hardware.

➤ User Mode is where applications and some of the NT subsystems run in a less privileged mode than Kernel Mode.

➤ The Kernel Mode is divided into two layers. The lower layer is the hardware abstraction layer (HAL), and the higher layer is the Executive layer.

➤ The Executive layer is divided into the *microkernel* layer and the *system services* layer.

The Executive Layer

The lowest level within the Executive layer is the microkernel, sometimes called simply the *kernel*. This could be considered the core component of Windows NT. The NT microkernel is responsible for scheduling all jobs going to the CPU and controls every processor in a multiprocessor system. While an IRQ controller is a set of instructions built into a hardware device, the NT microkernel is more like a command interpreter because it must reside in main memory. Because the microkernel is the fundamental control structure for the CPUs, it can never be removed from main memory in any type of *memory paging* (discussed in Chapter 4).

Just above the microkernel layer of the Executive layer is the *system services* layer. The system service modules are the components within the Executive layer that interface upward with the applications and subsystems in the User Mode. The system services layer is made up of a number of modules, including:

➤ The Process Manager

➤ The Object Manager

➤ The Security Reference Monitor

➤ The Local Procedure Call Monitor

➤ The Virtual Memory Manager

➤ The I/O Manager

User Mode

Aside from the Kernel Mode, Windows NT also uses the User Mode. This User Mode is then divided into additional modules, each of which interface with the system services in its own fashion. Two of the more important components of the User Mode are the Win32 subsystem and the Security subsystem.

NT applications run in the User Mode and have no direct access to either the microkernel (kernel) or the hardware abstraction layer. For example, a 16-bit virtual machine is itself an application process. If the DOS VM is running a database program, the combination is also considered to be an application. Unlike Windows 9x and DOS, you can see the many levels of underlying control NT is exerting to prevent that database application from ever having any access to the actual computer system.

An application connects to the operating system partly through the Win32 subsystem, which then interfaces with the Executive layer (running in Kernel Mode), which in turn places calls to either the system services or the HAL. Again, although this is complicated, it's not all that different from the way the networking OSI layers interact with each other.

NT Workstation and NT Server

We've mentioned client/server networking as a network where individual PCs act as clients to a central file server. The client machines are often referred to as *local* machines, and the file server (or servers) is often referred to as a remote server because it's often quite a distance away from the local machines. We've also said that Windows NT was designed from its inception to be a networking operating system that could run on many hardware platforms (portability). As a result, Windows NT comes in both a server version and a workstation version.

Both versions of NT share the same, *core operating system* code (within modules). NT, like the offshoot Windows 9x products, also uses a Registry. During startup, NT checks with the system registration to learn whether the system should be run as either a workstation client or an NT server. The workstation is designed specifically to run as a secure, multitasking desktop client.

NT Server has many additional administrative tools as well as disk-level enhancements because it was designed as a full network operating system. Aside from the administrative tools, Windows NT uses a distinct disk and file management structure called the New Technology File System (NTFS). We've seen how Windows 9x can use either a FAT16 (16-bit file allocation table) or a FAT32 (32-bit FAT) at the disk level. The NT File System, somewhat related to the OS/2 High Performance File System, is a completely redesigned networking file management system.

The NT Registry

Windows 9x uses the Registry to hold a consolidated configuration manifest for the overall system, and it requires the 16-bit binary REGEDIT.EXE program to make modifications in its Registry. Windows NT uses the 32-bit REGEDT32.EXE (note the traces of the old DOS eight-dot-three file name) to perform essentially the same thing on an NT machine.

The Windows NT Registry is broken into five separate subtrees, much like Windows 9x. Once again, we can see how Windows 9x borrowed from the development efforts coming from NT, with the NT Registry being:

➤ *HKEY_LOCAL_MACHINE*—Holds local hardware configurations, the Security Accounts Manager database, and software configurations.

➤ *HKEY_CLASSES_ROOT*—Holds file associations and application links that can be defined through the NT Explorer Options menu.

➤ *HKEY_CURRENT_CONFIG*—Holds the current hardware profile and configuration for the devices currently in use.

➤ *HKEY_CURRENT_USER*—Holds the current user profile for the person logged on to the machine (e.g., user preferences for Desktop and network privileges).

➤ *HKEY_USERS*—Holds every user profile for the machine, including the currently logged on user, along with a generic user profile that acts as a template for new, first-time users.

NT Networking

We set up a computer in a building somewhere, and then we install some kind of software on that machine. After we've configured a particular machine, we then *deploy* (spread out) a networking strategy. NT networking is based on *work groups* and *domains* (territories), with each grouping defined through the use of security.

In a work group deployment, each individual machine is considered an equal to every other machine, much like peer-to-peer networking. Each machine holds its own Security Account Manager (SAM) database (and Sam is not related to Hal!). With each computer using its own security administration, work groups are good in small situations where it's feasible for someone to go around to each local PC and adjust who has access to what.

In larger environments, often covering many buildings, managing network security becomes a problem. Some corporate campuses can have thousands of employees, and it would be nearly impossible for the few IT professionals to be constantly running to each PC when an employee needed different sharing access to network resources. This kind of environment calls for *distributed* applications, where central file servers hold various applications and distribute session copies to whoever needs that application at any given time.

Distributed applications are set up using the Windows NT domain structure. When NT is set up using domains, every participating computer in a domain uses a Central Domain SAM database. These domain SAMs are managed by

Windows NT file servers, where an individual network administrator can go into one machine and assign such things as resource sharing, login names, and passwords. When we speak of how an operating system can be used for a range of deployments going from small to large, we say Windows NT is *scalable*.

Security

When a machine has been set up and all the software has been installed, it's ready to be used by a person. In the case of a file server, the machine is ready to be used by other machines; however, even file servers have to be managed (administered) by a person. As we talk about NT security, we refer to an *end user* as the person doing day-to-day work on a local computer, and we refer to the *network administrator* as the person in charge of giving network access to end users.

Microsoft designed Windows NT to be used in government installations, as well as multinational corporate environments. One of the reasons the following discussion of security is so complicated is that NT has been designated a C-2 compliant operating system by the National Computer Security Council (NCSC). NCSC security levels are then specified in U.S. Department of Defense Trusted Computer Systems Evaluation Criteria, known as the Orange Book. C-2 allows NT to be used by the Department of Defense, along with other government agencies. That doesn't make the ensuing discussion any easier to understand, but we thought you'd like to know.

Logon

The first step anyone has to take in a networking environment is to *log on* to (with the *logon* procedure or **logon** command) the network. This means the network computers have to recognize a human being in order to understand what that person will or won't be allowed to do. The list of these privileges is called a user *account*, and the end user's account information defines which areas and resources on the network that person will have access to.

Networks use a logon name as the *user identification* (User ID). The typical way to ensure that a given person is who they say they are is for the end user to invent a user password. First-time users are given a User ID and an initial password by the network administrator. The User ID stays the same, but the password changes periodically.

The logon procedure in Windows NT begins by pressing the Control, Alt (alternate), and Delete keys all at once (Ctrl+Alt+Del). Originally, this was the way to restart a machine with a warm boot (see Chapter 11). In Windows 9x, the keystrokes were reassigned to the Task Manager, calling up TASKMAN.EXE in order to show every program running in memory at that moment. Pressing Ctrl+Alt+Del on an NT machine calls up an NT Logon Information dialog box, generally called WinLogon.

Making Up Passwords

Passwords are the only real protection you have in terms of keeping your identity secure on a network. In many corporate environments, your password allows you access to information that can have legal ramifications. Rather than making up something fairly logical as a password, such as your initials or birthday, a better password is a certain phrase you remember. For instance, you might like the phrase, "I'm a little teapot," so you can easily remember it. Why not make your password IALTP? This acronym makes no sense whatsoever on its own, but each letter stands for the words in a phrase you particularly like and can remember. This sort of password is extremely difficult to crack by an illegal user, yet very easy to remember (and type) as a phrase. If you like short phrases and your password must be longer, make a rule that you type your password twice in a row, as in IALTPIALTP.

Within the dialog box, you select the option indicating you want to log on to the network, then enter your User ID and password. When you've entered your information, NT begins the Local Security Authorization process, which runs the *logon authentication package*. Whether the logon is referring to a work group or a domain deployment, the authentication package compares what you entered against the SAM. Once again, a work group will have a local Security Account Management database on the machine you're using, whereas a domain will transmit the package to the Central Domain SAM database on a file server.

Note: In very large corporations, different User IDs can be assigned to seek out completely different sets of remote file servers.

If the information in the logon authentication package doesn't match the SAM, a dialog box pops up displaying a "Logon failure" warning. If the authentication package matches, NT creates a *logon session* and passes specific account information to the *Local Security Authority (LSA)*. The software making up the Local Security Authority creates a *security access token (SAT)*.

Finally, the logon process calls the Win32 subsystem in the User Mode module, and Win32 creates a *user process* and connects the security access token to that user process. After all this has been completed, the Win32 subsystem creates the end user's Desktop from the person's profile held in the HKEY_CURRENT_USER configuration area of the NT Registry. (This all sounds pretty complicated. Imagine the people who dreamed up all this stuff in the first place!)

The reason for so much complexity focuses on the two basic philosophies of network security. Peer-to-peer networks have generally tended to begin with the premise that individual people should control their own machines, relying on honor and character in giving every user full access to the entire network. Client/server networks tend to be based on a more skeptical perspective, taking total control over the network and allowing individual users specific privileges. NT, much like NetWare, begins with the assumption that no one has access to anything, and then it creates user profiles where specific access is granted, little by little.

The Local Security Authority (LSA)

Windows NT provides a way for every logon session to be stored, much like any history log (as with the Windows 98 Troubleshooting log). This *session log* can then be *audited*, which means that a network administrator can review the log for information about what was done by the end user. The LSA is the software interface between the end user, the User Mode, and the Kernel Mode.

Following a successful logon procedure, after the Local Security Authority has generated the security access token, this token has its own properties. The SAT contains the end user's *security identification* (*security ID*, or *SID*), the SID for any groups to which the end user belongs, and the various network privileges (user rights) assigned to that person.

The SID is a permanent account identifier, based on a hashing algorithm. Once the SID is generated, it stays the same even when the account name and/or password is changed. The only way to change the SID itself is to delete the user account and then re-create it.

The security access token (SAT) is only generated one time, following a successful logon procedure. Any rights or privileges the network administrator changes will not change the SID, but will take effect only after the end user has logged off the network and begins the logon process the next time.

The Security Reference Monitor

When the LSA has generated the authentication package, created the security access token, and opened a session, the Local Security Authority logs *audit messages* generated by the *Security Reference Monitor* module. Referring back to the "Kernel Mode" section, we've said that the Security Reference Monitor is part of the Executive layer. Remember, too, that the system services layer is just above the microkernel and that these two layers are held within Kernel Mode, just below the User Mode.

The Security Reference Monitor takes charge of verifying whether a request for access (an *access request*) to an object is allowed, and whether the requesting process has permission to perform an operation on the object. In other words, part of your account profile gives you certain user rights. These rights grant you and your machine permission to initiate certain processes, such as saving a file (process) to a disk (object) somewhere. When you and your machine request access to disk space on a file server, the Security Reference Monitor checks to see whether you have permission to access that disk.

Entities, Attributes, and Masks

An *entity* is a single thing. That thing exists in some fashion, and we human beings understand its existence by observing its attributes. An apple is an entity and it has many attributes. The apple's attributes include seeds, a core, leaves, red skin, sour or sweet taste, worms, and so on. A 2 is also an entity, but in this case the 2 is an *abstraction*. You can't point to a 2, but can only point to the influence of *two-ness* on other entities. For instance, two apples are not the same thing as the two-ness of the "pair" of apples. Pair-ness is an attribute of 2.

A concrete entity is something you can perceive directly with your senses. An abstract entity is something you can perceive only with your mind. A 2 has attributes in exactly the same way that an apple or a file has attributes. Some of the attributes of a 2 include the actual symbol we use to describe the two-ness of things (2 or II), its even-ness, and the fact that it contains a 1 and a 1. The 1 is also an entity, with attributes of singleness, oddness, unit, and individuality.

In an object-oriented computer world, we try to consolidate various associated attributes into a single entity. Then we call the entity an object. An entity is the same thing as an object. Because attributes are often abstract, the entities themselves are even more abstract (high-level or low-level abstractions). The computer world is being created in an ongoing way, and each programmer or developer sees sets of attributes in his or her own way. NT is a world of abstractions, and Microsoft has chosen to assign names to things based on what it considers to be similarities. In one world, a description is a list of attributes assigned to an entity. In the NT world, Microsoft changed the word "description" to the word "mask," and proclaimed it good. This would be the philosophy of Microsoftism, or a Microsoftian way of understanding reality.

The Security Reference Monitor generates the audit messages we just mentioned, and in order to come up with these particular messages, it looks in the *access-control list (ACL)*. The access control list is made up of *access masks*. These masks are just a complicated way of saying that each object has a list of which end users and groups can mess with (technical term) the object. Remember how we said NT's hardware abstraction layer disguises an actual piece of hardware? In a way, HAL is treating every piece of hardware like an object. Filled with an overblown sense of its own importance, NT chooses to call each entry on the access control list, an *access-control entry (ACE)*.

Note: There are three types of access masks: specific (specific to an object), standard (objects within a group), and generic (pointers to both specific and standard masks). A specific access mask can have up to 16 properties used to describe a specific object. A mask is nothing more than the list of things that describe an object. Your driver's license is a specific access mask for you, the specific object. In this case, your driver's license could have 16 places to put some descriptive information, like your hair color, your weight, or the color of your eyes.

If you go along with this for a minute, you can see how NT also creates a sort of end user object out of whoever is using an NT workstation. Part of the network operating system assigns attributes to the living, people-type objects, while another part of the operating system is busy assigning attributes to the hardware and file resource objects. Just like you would have an account profile that tells NT what you're allowed to do, every object has an access mask (description) that tells NT what groups of people can mess with that object.

In the NT world, an object could be a printer, a modem, a word processor application, a folder, or even a file within a folder. The network administrator builds an access mask for every object and lists those masks in the access control list, the ACL we were just talking about. The Security Reference Monitor is like a hall monitor in school, constantly interrupting the flow of requests and asking to see a pass. When the security access token shows its pass, the monitor checks its clipboard, looking at the ACL to see whether the next step is allowed. One thing is for sure: The world of computers isn't a free democracy!

Blocked access takes precedence over *granted* access. NT always finds that a user has been blocked before it checks to see whether the user has permission to access an object.

To sum it all up in the simplest possible terms and to make all of this exceptionally easy to remember, we could say that the SRM from the LSA looks at the SAT for the SID. If the SAT compared to the ACL's ACE doesn't match, the SRM and ACL deny the SAT's SID access. See? Nothing could be simpler. Oh, and don't forget the User Mode working alongside the Kernel Mode, talking through the Executive layer with the Win32 subsystem in order to get the microkernel to fool around with the system services. And just think, you don't even have to try to install an NT system.

User Accounts

We've mentioned user accounts and profiles, saying that a profile is a way for the network to understand end users and what kind of privileges they have. An *account* is basically another way of talking about a *user profile*. If you were to open a savings account, you would put specific money into your account, and the bank would assign you an account number. At the same time, the bank could look at how you seem similar to other people and create a profile of all people like you. The bank could try to tailor different kinds of accounts to every individual person in the world, or it could tailor its services to a lesser number of profiles.

The Windows NT Administrator account is a default account, meaning that it's been set up within the operating system and will always be there. Every installation of NT will have someone in charge of managing the networking events, and that person takes ownership of the Administrator account. The Administrator account cannot be removed, and it grants permissions to that person (or group of people) to make changes within the operating system itself.

Windows NT comes with a second type of default account called the guest account. It's not at all unusual for a corporation to have many file servers and applications, all designed to produce whatever work the company does. In all that specific technology, there will usually be a generic word processor and spreadsheet application. The files being created each day for those two applications are stored on various disks with more or less security and privacy. But what happens when a visiting person wants to borrow a computer to type a memo to his or her secretary back at the home office?

The guest account provides a way for someone who isn't an end user with a user account assigned to them to use network resources in a very restricted fashion. The network administrator has control over all accounts and all resources, and can set the default rights to the guest account.

Managing User Accounts

The Windows Explorer is a dulled-down version of the Windows NT Explorer. In Windows 9x, the Explorer is mostly used for file maintenance tasks, such as copying, moving, deleting, and creating folders and subfolders. The NT Explorer is used for folder and file maintenance, but also to view and set object permissions and to configure *auditing* on files and folders. Beyond the basic file maintenance found in the NT Explorer, workstations configured as work groups use the *User Manager* utility to manage user accounts.

User IDs (account names) can be up to 20 characters in length, where both letters and numbers, along with certain special characters (e.g., asterisks, dashes, underlines, and so forth), can be used. Each user account can optionally be assigned a password up to 14 characters in length, but there is a limitation on the minimum number of characters that must be used. The password may be blank, but the account *policy* must be configured to allow blank passwords. Passwords can use the same characters as the User ID names.

Remember that User ID names can be up to 20 characters long, and must be unique for each domain on a network. The names are not case sensitive and can include letters (both uppercase and lowercase), numbers, and certain special characters.

NT can also be configured to keep password lists with a history of up to 24 previous passwords. This is done to prevent end users from using the same passwords each time the system goes through a change-password cycle. The required change for passwords helps to protect against a system invasion where over-familiarity with a password has made that password pointless. The network administrator often requires a password change once a month.

 Passwords can be up to 14 characters long, but the use of a password can be set to required or optional by an administrator. Unlike User ID names, passwords are case sensitive, meaning that if you created a capital letter in some position, you must type a capital letter in that same position the next time you use the password. Passwords can also be a combination of letters, numbers, and certain special characters.

Groups

Windows NT, like the Novell operating system, provides a way to assign rights and permissions to many end users at the same time. You can imagine what it would be like if you were setting up an NT network in a corporation with 5,000 employees and you had to create a user account for each person, and then assign rights and access to individual folders and files every time. To aid in this process, many end users can be assigned to a single group.

One example would be where a project group in the real world is in charge of developing and writing a business course. Each person has his or her own user account, so a management person would have access to things that a temporary employee would not. By creating a project group in NT, anyone involved in that particular project automatically takes on the rights and permissions allowed while that particular project is under way.

Policies vs. Profiles

Beginning with Windows for Workgroups 3.11, various levels of networking were built into the system. In WFW 3.11, this networking was simple peer-to-peer. NT is a much more sophisticated, fully developed network operating system. In the old days, part of managing a network was to set certain *policies*, or general rules as to how people could interact with the overall network. The term "policies" has fallen into disuse, being replaced by the concept of group rights, domain management, and systems administration templates.

Windows 3.x introduced an almost undocumented feature whereby the PROGMAN.INI file could be opened (in a text editor) and a [Restrictions] heading could be inserted at a blank line. These restrictions included **NoRun=**, **NoClose=**, **NoSaveSettings=**, **NoFileMenu=**, and **EditLevel=**. Depending on the numeric values (0 through 4) entered after the equal sign, an administrator could prevent users from running certain programs, saving modified settings, or even accessing the main menu's File option.

Windows 95 began making the restrictions more sophisticated, introducing the optional Policy Editor with the first release of OSR/A. This time the restrictions broadened to include restricted access to the Control Panel, customization limits for the Desktop, and restrictions on network access configuration changes. An example would be the administrator setting the policy for the MS-DOS environment where certain types of programs could not be run at all.

Policies are an exclusionary authorization process, meaning that out of all possible ways an end user might get into trouble, certain global areas can be excluded. Profiles are more like an inclusive authorization process, meaning that the systems administrator has to figure out ahead of time what an end user may need to accomplish. Given that work environments are constantly adapting to meet changing conditions, an inclusive process tends to carry with it a much greater burden (overhead) on the corporate network administrators as they run around adding rights and permissions they hadn't thought of previously.

NT establishes certain groups at the time it's installed, giving those groups certain default permissions. These templates are the changeover point where policies began turning into profiles. The default groups are: Administrators, Backup Operators, Power Users, Users, and Guests. Each of these groups has certain default rights and permissions.

NT Workstation uses local groups, as opposed to NT Server's use of both local and global groups. A *local group* is specific to a local machine (your own PC), whereas a *global group* can be set up across an entire domain. Any end user assigned to a global group can go to any machine on the network and log on under that group name, gaining access to all the resources assigned to the global group anywhere in the domain.

In addition to the default groups available on NT Workstation, NT Server also includes the Administrators group, but provides for additional groups based on Operators rights. These rights are assigned in terms of Account, Backup, Print, and Server operators. Once again, each group is given certain rights and permissions, with the Administrators having all rights and permissions. Also remember that group rights take precedence over individual rights, so someone who has many rights in their own user account, could lose some of those rights when they log on to the network as part of a group.

Starting Windows NT

Windows NT is a portable operating system, meaning, as we've said, that it can be installed on systems using an Alpha CPU or an Intel CPU, among others. Because of this, the way NT starts up is different for each platform. We'll focus on the Intel environment, given that it's the most typical environment for an A+ technician to be working with. If you understand the way NT starts up, you'll have a much better understanding of how Windows 2000 does almost exactly the same thing.

The startup process has 17 steps. The first step, as it is for any other computer, is the POST. At the end of the POST, the BIOS hands off to the bootstrap loader, which looks for something in the boot sector of a disk.

NT, like any other operating system, looks in the boot sector of a disk for the Master Boot Record (MBR). Instructions in the MBR tell the operating system to look for the active partition and to load the NT boot sector from that partition. In DOS, the location of the boot sector was restricted to an active, primary partition. OS/2 didn't have this restriction and could load from a so-called nonbootable partition. NT must find its system files on an active, primary partition.

After the information in the boot sector goes into memory, it loads the NT *boot loader* (NTLDR) into memory. The boot loader (or simply the NT Loader) switches the processor into 32-bit mode and starts a *mini file system* to support either a FAT or NTFS volume. At that point, the system reads a BOOT.INI file, displaying the available operating system selections to the end user. A specific configuration line in the INI file defines how long the options list stays displayed.

 The BOOT.INI file displays a list of any other operating systems available on the disk.

Following the BOOT.INI file and display, the NT Loader then runs NTDETECT.COM to detect and prepare a list (profile) of the currently installed hardware. This list of hardware is passed back to the NT Loader, which then asks whether or not you want to invoke the Last Known Good hardware profile. This assumes NT has been run before, and pressing the spacebar during this message accepts that last hardware profile.

Assuming you've chosen to use the previously known-to-be good hardware profile, NT Loader then brings the NT kernel (NTOSKRNL.EXE) into memory and passes the hardware profile to the kernel. At this point, the kernel loads, *but does not initialize*, all the hardware device drivers associated with the hardware profile. The kernel then attempts to take control of the hardware devices, turning the monitor's screen blue only when it has successfully accomplished that control.

Note: Loading a program into memory is not the same as running that program. We say that NT loads a program or device driver, but the initializing step is separate and begins running that program.

Following the NT blue screen, when all device drivers have been initialized and their companion devices are under control, the kernel loads and initializes a second group of drivers. (This is step 11, by the way, for anyone who's counting.)

Windows NT then runs the Session Manager (SMSS.EXE), which starts the high-level subsystems and services. When the SMSS is successfully in place, NT runs a boot-time Check Disk (not anything at all like the old DOS CHKDSK.EXE, but much like ScanDisk) on every partition, to verify partition integrity.

NT then sets up a swap file, giving it a different (and cooler) name. This swap file is called the *paging file* and is used pretty much the way that any other swap file is used for virtual memory disk swapping (paging). After the paging file has been set up, NT runs the Win32 subsystem to set up the User Mode and control user input at the keyboard and monitor.

Win32 starts WINLOGON.EXE, which runs the Local Security Authority (LSASS.EXE) that pops up the Logon dialog box. This is the same as the Local Security Authority in Window 2000, and at this point, even though a logon process can begin, the startup process is still continuing with system services loading in the background.

Note: When we talk about multitasking, one event is in the foreground, taking the computer's focus and interacting directly with the user. Other events are in the background, running on the system out of sight from the user and behind the window on the screen.

Once an end user has successfully logged on, the startup is considered to be "good," and the HKEY_LOCAL_MACHINE\System\LastKnownGood Registry subkey is updated to point to the particular key containing the hardware configuration that was just used to start NT.

Each time NT has a successful startup, the hardware profile and associated pass/fail error codes are recorded in a particular file. LastKnownGood accesses this file in the event of a crash on startup, and allows you to choose whether you want to use that last profile. This safety feature was carried over to Windows 9x, and we've seen how the Registry makes an automatic copy of itself, along with a first-time startup file, each time a successful startup takes place.

NT File System (NTFS)

Windows NT was designed to work with not only different hardware platforms, but with different file management systems. Novell's NetWare (operating system) was the clear market leader in the field, allowing IBM-type PCs to work alongside Macintosh machines on the same network. Because Apple computers use a completely different way of storing files, NetWare had almost no competition in its ability to work with both systems.

As we've said, the two file systems most commonly supported by NT nowadays are the FAT and NTFS. Once again, the file allocation table systems came out of the original DOS environment. We saw previously how the original decision to create a 16-bit file allocation system created all the convoluted development efforts in Windows 9x. Most of these efforts were spent reconciling the operating system with multigigabyte disks, far larger drives than anyone ever envisioned.

Windows NT continues to format all floppy disks using a FAT16 format, still the most widely used system in the world. FAT16 can be accessed by DOS, all versions of Windows, and OS/2. The file names in FAT16 retain the 8.3 format of a name and an extension, meaning that Windows 9x and NT Long File Names are truncated.

Another problem with FAT16 is that individual files have no security protection. The only attributes available are the archive, hidden, system, and read-only (AHSR) attributes. Network operating systems usually include additional attributes for assigning file access rights to individual users. However, the biggest problem with FAT16 is that file sizes are limited to 2GB.

In Windows NT and Windows 2000, only partitions formatted as NTFS volumes provide the local file security of network file attributes. FAT16 and FAT32 file systems do not provide this security.

NTFS is a completely different way of managing files. A FAT is essentially a simple (flat file) database. Each entry contains the cluster addresses for a file, and the entire volume is contained within a single table. NTFS works more like a relational database.

FAT systems maintain a primary table and a single copy of that table. In some cases, the copy of the FAT can actually be useful following a system failure. NTFS, on the other hand, maintains a *transaction log* for file management operations. In a catastrophic system failure, NT can use this transaction log to rebuild the cluster addresses of almost every file on the volume. The specific differences between NTFS and FAT include:

➤ Local security at the volume, folder, and file level.

➤ Support for Long File Names up to 255 characters in length.

➤ Support for files up to 16 exabytes (EB) in size (16 billion billion, or 16 quin-tillion, bytes). That would be 16 to the 18th power, or a 16 with 18 zeros after it; 1 megabyte is a million bytes, and 1 exabyte is a billion gigabytes.

➤ Automatic generation of the DOS 8.3 format file names for compatibility.

➤ Support for case-sensitive file names for compatibility with the Portable Operating System Interface for Unix (POSIX) used in many government installations.

Note: POSIX is a particular type of file management system.

NTFS uses 2MB of space on any disk where the system is installed, making it more appropriate for larger drives. Given the size of today's drives, this space overhead is no longer an issue; however, it can't be used on a floppy disk or small drives. Additionally, NTFS is currently available in only Windows NT and Windows 2000.

Relational vs. Flat File Databases

A so-called flat file database is where every record contains the fields and data used to capture information. Searching for data is done by looking at every record in a single file. Relational databases break up the database into many smaller files for faster processing of very large amounts of data. In a relational database, fields are not necessarily locked to every other field in a record of information. For example, one database might contain a person's name, address, and phone number. Another database might contain all the cars the person owns. The two databases are linked together through the related information of the phone number.

Transaction logs track each activity in and out of a relational database to re-create each of the small databases making up the overall system in the event of a problem. This activity can be anything associated in any way with any access to the many databases within the overall relational database system. Some of these activities include querying a file, reading or writing data to a record, storing the results of a query, and so forth.

NT Disk Administration

One of the important modules we mentioned in the system services layer was the I/O Manager. This module controls the disk subsystem, along with all input and output requests made through NT. Remember that we said the system services are part of the NT Executive layer (along with the microkernel), and that the Executive layer acts as an interface between the high-level (User Mode) and low-level (Kernel Mode) components of the operating system.

The I/O Manager uses a series of layered software drivers that communicate with each other through the Executive layer. For example, for the file system driver to communicate with a disk drive, an I/O request is routed through the I/O Manager. The I/O Manager communicates the request to the disk controller and the controller's device driver. Because each driver is kept separate and contained, NT (theoretically) makes it easier to replace devices or to update drivers without having to completely reinstall the system.

The disk subsystem's Disk Administrator utility is a graphical systems management tool that you can get to through the Administrative Tools menu. Disk Administrator has two views within the graphical presentation: the partition view and the volume view. (Refer to the "Logical Formatting and Partitions: FDISK" section of Chapter 10 for a discussion of the difference between a partition and a logical drive [also called a volume]).

NT Partitions

Windows NT creates a small *boot partition* at the front of the disk, and this boot partition contains the boot loader that tells the operating system where to find the NT system files. The system files are installed on a *system partition*, and this system partition is the volume that contains the required files needed to load NT. The system partition must be on a disk that the bootstrap loader can find directly through the BIOS. The boot partition can be on the same disk as the system partition, but it doesn't have to be.

In Windows NT, there can be a maximum of four primary partitions (as opposed to three in DOS). In both NT and DOS (or Windows 9x), there can only be one extended partition per disk. Remember that an extended partition is then subdivided into formatted, logical drives (volumes).

The Disk Administrator Tool

Both NT Server and NT Workstation have the Disk Administrator utility. Both versions allow you to:

➤ Create or delete partitions.

➤ Create or delete, format, extend, and label volumes.

➤ Create or delete striped sets.

➤ Assign drive identification letters.

➤ Save and restore drive configurations.

The NT Server version of Disk Administrator also allows you to establish or break *disk mirroring* (or duplexing) and to create, delete, or regenerate striped sets with parity. We discuss volume sets and striped sets, along with mirroring and duplexing, in the next two sections.

Note: The Disk Administrator is accessible only to members of the Administrator user group.

Volume Sets

One of the important ways NT differs from Windows 9x in its use of disk space is that several partitions can be joined together in a single, logical area called a *volume set.* These partitions can be on a single physical disk or can be located on several physical disks running off of different controllers. Another interesting thing about a volume set is that it can include different types of disks. A volume set can have a maximum of 32 different partitions joined together in this fashion.

When data is written to the volume set, the process takes place in a sequential fashion. When the first partition in the volume set fills up, the data is written to the next partition, and so on down the line. Neither the system partition nor the boot partition can be part of a volume set.

 Volume sets combine free space in partitions on 1 to 32 disks, writing data in sequential order.

Striped Sets

Striped sets can be configured either with or without parity. A *striped set* is somewhat like a volume set because data is written across different physical disks. The partitions on each disk are equal in size, giving rise to the term "stripes." Much like random access read/writes take place on different platters of a hard drive, striped sets allow for something akin to random access read/writes to whole sets of disks.

Striped sets can be set up on anywhere from 2 to 32 physical disks. One of the problems with striped sets is that if any of the disks in the set fails, all data on that particular physical disk will be lost. This kind of setup is called *no fault tolerance* because the system has no tolerance at all for any faulty machinery.

 Boot partitions can be mirrored or duplexed, but not striped. System partitions cannot be used in a striped set. Striped sets provide better read/write efficiency by writing to whichever disk is idle at the moment.

Striped sets *with parity* can be set up on anywhere from 3 to 32 partitions and work in a fashion vaguely similar to the parity circuits used to test main memory (see Chapter 4). In this configuration, one of the partition stripes in the disk array (group, or set) is set up as a parity check. If any of the disks in the set fails, that data can be reconstructed using the parity information in the parity stripe. NT generates an error message, but it continues to function until the systems administrator has a convenient time to replace the failed disk. This requires shutting down the network, so a convenient time would be when network use is very low.

Note: One of the problems with maintaining a parity stripe on a single partition is that a bottleneck forms at that parity stripe when many other disks are writing their data recovery information to the single stripe.

Disk Mirroring and Duplexing

With volume sets and striped sets, many physical disks are set up to act as a virtual, single entity. Different data is written to any of the partitions within the two types of sets. Disk *mirroring*, on the other hand, is where two partitions are mirrors of each other. Each partition contains an exact copy (not actually reversed like a real mirror) of every piece of data on the other, mirrored partition (also called a mirrored set). We call it disk mirroring because these two partitions are almost always on two separate disks.

The advantage of disk mirroring is that if one physical disk fails, no reconstruction is necessary. The network continues operating using the data from the mirrored (constantly-updated backup) copy of whatever information was on the failed disk. NT generates an error message, and once again, the failed disk drive can be replaced at a more convenient time for the systems administrator.

Disk duplexing is almost the same as mirroring, except each disk is connected to a different drive controller. One of the problems with both mirroring and duplexing is that any amount of data requires twice the physical resources. In other words, rather than having room for two files on two disks, this data redundancy means having one file on two disks, with an exact copy on each disk. On the other hand, this means less chance of losing any data.

Mirrored sets are set up on two physical drives using a single controller as with an IDE or SCSI controller. If the two drives use separate controllers, this is called duplexing or disk duplexing. Mirroring is also known as RAID 1, and it is available only in the NT Server version of Windows NT.

RAID

The word "redundant" means an unnecessary repetition. A *Redundant Array of Inexpensive Disks (RAID)* is essentially where a network file server uses extra disks to keep multiple copies of data. In these situations, the data itself is more valuable than the cost of the disks, so making repeated copies of the same data isn't actually unnecessary. Still, that's what the computer people called it, using the word "redundant." The concept of RAID data protection has been around long enough that there are now six different levels of protection (0 through 5). Each level indicates a higher degree of protection.

RAID Level 0 (RAID 0) is the no fault tolerance process of using 64KB block storage areas in a striped set. Once again, the striped set means multiple partitions all of the same size. Both Windows NT Workstation and NT Server use RAID 0 in most instances. Even though the data protection is limited, read/write access is more efficient.

 Striped partitions are partitions of equal size on one or more physical disks, joined into a logical area called a set. Striped sets provide no fault tolerance and can be set up using anywhere from 2 to 32 partitions on 1 or more physical disks.

RAID 1 is the most common form of RAID at the moment and is often used in disk mirroring and disk duplexing. Level 1 provides positive fault tolerance, but at the cost of a 50 percent reduction in resources. This is that double disk problem we just spoke about, where two disks are used to store one set of data. RAID 1 is only available on NT Server machines.

RAID 2 is similar to striped sets, but the data is moved at a bit level, rather than in 64KB blocks. One of the disks in RAID 2 is set aside for data recovery. This method of data protection is currently unavailable through Windows NT.

RAID 3 is disk striping with parity, with data being moved at the bit level rather than the block level. RAID 4 is disk striping at the block level, with one disk reserved for parity recovery. RAID 5 is also block-level disk striping, but the parity information is evenly spread across all the disks in the array, as opposed to being on only one disk. This removes the typical single-stripe bottleneck of parity writing.

 Windows NT supports RAID Levels 1 and 5 on the Server version, along with RAID 0 on both the Server and Workstation versions.

Troubleshooting Tools

From the perspective of the A+ exam, CompTIA assumes you won't be involved in an NT installation beyond the point of following a list of basic instructions from a systems administrator. You'll most likely be presented with a scenario in which an NT machine has successfully started and you've been called in to find out the nature of a problem involving day-to-day operations. This is where you'll need to know some of the basic tools and utilities.

Floppy Disks

Two important hardware tools you'll want to understand are a *bootable floppy disk* and a so-called *emergency repair disk*. The bootable floppy disk is far too small to hold the entire Windows NT operating system, but it can hold the key files necessary to begin a startup process. If NT will boot from a floppy disk, you'll at least have a general idea of the most likely next step. If all the workstations in an environment have been set up the same way, the bootable floppy disk can use a generic hardware profile to start all the machines.

If the bootable floppy disk can't start the machine, another tool you can try is the emergency repair disk. The programs on this disk can be used to repair some of the problems associated with Windows NT system partitioning and to restore the NT configuration. This repair disk cannot be used to start an NT session because it isn't a bootable disk.

The emergency repair disk also differs from a bootable floppy disk in that each repair disk is inextricably linked to the specific machine that was used to create it. If the network has 300 computers and they've all been set up the same way, you can have a single, generic bootable disk, but you'll need 300 emergency repair disks.

Note: Corporate network administrators rarely use an emergency repair disk, given how many disks it would entail. Instead, if a corporate machine has a serious startup problem, the administrator will wipe the entire system clean from the machine and create a new installation, often from a disk image.

Disk Images

One of the lost advantages of DOS and 16-bit Windows is that software installed on one of these machines was folder-specific as opposed to sector-specific. What this means is that any files, excepting the two DOS system files, could be copied from one machine to another, or from one location on the disk to another, without affecting how the operating system or applications would run. Certain **SET=** changes and INI file lines might have to be updated, but if you installed Windows 3.x on a machine, you could do a complete system backup using the XCOPY.EXE program.

Windows 95 introduced sector-specific installations where the location of certain system files was tracked not only through folder locations, but right down to specific sectors on the hard drive. When a file is copied from a hard drive to a floppy disk and then back to the hard drive, that file is assigned a track, sector, and cluster by the FAT in accordance with whatever free space is available. If the Windows Registry expects to find the start of a file on an exact disk sector, the copy procedure causes a fatal crash in the system.

A disk image is created using special software, and the image is an exact photograph of a partition or even an entire hard drive. The image is so exact that it includes the track, sector, and cluster information. Writing a disk image to a CD-ROM or network drive allows you to wipe a hard drive clean and then write the image back to the hard drive or to a new hard drive with all the original address locations intact.

The Event Viewer

An A+ technician is generally a first-tier tech support person and will rarely have an Administrator password or be involved in a large-scale network installation. A typical problem-solving situation might involve working with a network administrator to uncover what events took place prior to a problem, and how those events took place. First-tier support handles the basic detective work in terms of describing the "crime scene." After the specifics of the problem have been isolated, you will most likely hand the problem off to a network administrator for final resolution.

That being said, one of the important troubleshooting utilities you should know about is the Event Viewer. Like many of the later versions of Windows, NT provides the Event Viewer tool in a graphic format, bringing together a consolidated set of underlying files gathered into a single presentation area. These files are log files, and although the tools may be fairly easy to use, interpreting the results of an Event Viewer session isn't always so simple. No special permissions are necessary to view the System and Application logs; however, only a member of the Administrator group can view the Security log.

Access to the Event Viewer takes place through the Administrative Tools menu. The viewer brings up the System, Application, and Security log files. The System log file holds event information generated by the operating system itself. The Application log contains both system and user information, such as which user tried to open a spreadsheet and what happened at that time.

The information in the Security log file is generated by the audit policy and audit messages managed through the Security Reference Monitor. Security events include such things as failed passwords, failed ID names, inappropriate access attempts, or any other breach of system security as defined by the network administrators.

The Event Viewer logs the following information with each event: the system date, the system time, the application or component that logged the event, the category of event, an event number, the User ID (who was logged on during the event), and the computer name where the event took place (assigned during installation).

Typically, the Event log presents lines and symbols indicating that an application was started successfully, an exclamation point indicating a warning of a possible problem, and so on. The log files are very extensive, and if something crashes, the log files can often describe what happened. After NT has successfully started, the Event Viewer is one of the first places you'll go to find out what problem has taken place. Note that NT must have successfully started in the first place.

The Task Manager

All the way back in 16-bit Windows, Microsoft provided the TASKMAN.EXE program as a way of viewing what programs were running in memory. Windows 3.x offered the Switch To option to call up the Task Manager from a pull-down menu in the upper left-hand corner of any window. Additionally, information pertaining to the available Windows resources was on the Help|About menu of any Windows-compliant program.

Windows 9x removed the pull-down Switch To option, changing the entire concept into the new Taskbar. Access to the Task Manager became less obvious, but the information became more detailed. In Windows 9x, the Task Manager is accessed through the Ctrl+Alt+Del keystroke combination. System resources information was moved to the Performance tab of the My Computer properties dialog box.

In Windows NT, you can access the Task Manager by right-clicking on the Taskbar and then selecting the Task Manager option from the Properties menu. The Ctrl+Alt+Del keystrokes in NT begin a logon procedure. However, once you're logged onto the NT machine, Ctrl+Alt+Del offers several choices, one of which is the Task Manger. The NT Task Manager combines a detailed report of every program running in memory, system performance in terms of resources and available memory, and a recent usage history. The recent history tracks what processes are taking place and which resources are being assigned, along with a real-time graphic representation of a resource monitor showing how the overall system is working.

Performance Monitor

The Task Manager reports on the overall status of the machine. Performance Monitor is similar, except that it can be set to monitor specific aspects of the machine either in a moving graphic or a tab format. A few of the many things you can assign to the Performance Monitor include the CPU, the percent of processor time, the percent of user time, memory, available bytes, page faults per second, logical disk usage, the percent of free space, average disk cue length, and so on.

Many of these low-level performance details are obscure and are probably something you'll never use. You should know about the utility, though, because it's another way to get into the underlying set of events taking place on the machine. In its graphic-charting form, the items you've chosen to monitor show as a real-time change line in a small window.

The Network Management Monitoring Agent

We've said that Windows 9x was an attempt to bring all the alleged benefits of large-scale networking to a consolidated market of both business and home users. Net Watcher first appeared in Windows 95 and was designed to allow a network administrator to monitor the network in terms of usage load and traffic. NT includes the Network Monitor in only the Server version of the operating system.

The monitoring agent can track how the network is functioning at any given time and report out many statistics. Network Monitor is essentially the same product as the NT Systems Management Server (SMS), but the NT Server version has several of its functions disabled. To that extent, SMS is really only the fully functional monitoring agent.

The Network Monitor initially displays in a window divided into four areas. These areas show a real-time graph representing network use, total network statistics, session statistics, and station statistics. The full SMS management tool adds such features as: Find Routers, Resolve Address From Names, tracking local traffic, and more.

NT Error Messages

At this point, you've probably sensed that Windows NT is a somewhat complex operating system. We've heard stories of people who've actually taken seminars lasting weeks in order to understand only a few of the intricacies of the system. Naturally, we fully expect you to have a complete and thorough understanding of everything involved with NT in 25 or 30 pages. No, we're kidding again. All we can do is to give you a broad overview of the most likely way in which an A+ technician will come in contact with NT. You probably won't deal with NT Server, but will spend most of your time working with the Workstation version.

Someone once told us about a young man who wanted to become one of the world's great writers. When he was asked to define what he meant by great, he said, "I want to write stuff that the whole world will read; stuff that people will react to on a truly emotional level; stuff that will make them scream, cry, and howl in pain and anger!" He now works as an operating systems developer, writing error messages.

NTDetect

Of the thousands of error messages generated during Windows NT operations, certain messages are fairly common for workstations, and we'd like to at least reference them at this point. The first error message we'll mention is "NTDetect Failed."

As we've said, NTDETECT.COM is responsible for the hardware detection phase of the startup process. The file is located in the root folder of the boot drive, and if it becomes corrupted or is missing, you can try booting from a bootable floppy. If this solves the problem, copy NTDETECT.COM from the floppy to the root folder on the hard drive. Another possibility would be to boot the system from an NT setup disk, then repair the problem with an emergency repair disk.

Missing Kernel

Another common error message is "The kernel file is missing from the disk." One way to solve this problem is to strike the machine repeatedly with a five-pound sledgehammer. This is not a recommended procedure for the corporate environment. A better strategy would be to understand that the NT Loader (NTLDR.COM) file is missing or has become corrupted. Like NTDETECT.COM, this file is in the root folder of the boot drive and can be copied over from a bootable floppy disk or an emergency repair disk.

Missing BOOT.INI

Sometimes NT is feeling so poorly that it can't even give you an error message telling you what's wrong. An example of this is where the machine starts Windows NT but does not display the operating system selection menu. This is the menu we mentioned previously where you're asked if you want to use the Last Known Good hardware profile, and in this problem scenario, neither the menu display nor the waiting time takes place.

A likely cause of this kind of error is that the BOOT.INI file is missing from the root folder of the boot drive. You might recall that after the NT Loader has finished loading, the system reads the BOOT.INI file in order to display the available operating system selections. To recover from this, allow the system to start and then log on to Windows and copy the .INI file from the bootable floppy to the root folder of the bootable disk.

Note: If NT or Windows 2000 can't find a BOOT.INI file, the system will load from the first partition on the first disk it finds, looking in the winnt folder for its files.

Missing Files

Another common type of error message comes up as "Windows NT could not start because the following file is missing or corrupt," with a listing of some particularly obscure file name. Below the allegedly missing file is the statement "Please reinstall a copy of the above file." For some strange reason, people seem to make the assumption that when NT says a file is missing, a file must be missing. After all, the machine is a self-aware consciousness, right?

Many television shows have been written about the hilarious and zany antics of a group of happy-go-lucky network administrators joyfully copying file after file into some unknown folder, only to have the same error message come up time and time again. Each time, the name of the file changes, but NT doesn't seem to care. One of the critical lines in the BOOT.INI file is the line pointing to the location of the system partition. You would think that NT could figure out where to find its own files, wouldn't you? This is a classic instance of an error message that gives you all kinds of interesting information, none of which has any bearing on the actual problem.

Try to boot the machine from the bootable floppy, and if that works, replace the BOOT.INI file on the bootable hard drive. If the same error message keeps coming up, try using an NT setup disk or an emergency repair disk to resolve the problem.

Windows 2000

We've talked about the gradual transition from 16-bit DOS machines to 32-bit Windows NT machines, and how along the way, Windows 95, 98, and ME were all attempts to reconcile backward compatibility issues. The Windows 98 graphic interface is very similar to Windows NT, with many of the underlying modules making their first integrated appearance in Windows 98. Windows 2000 is where the underlying operations take a final step over the line of making Windows 2000 and Windows NT almost the same thing. Perhaps the biggest differences between Windows 9x and Windows 2000 are the security issues that come into Windows 2000 from NT.

In the same way that Windows 9x tried to use software intelligence (wizards) to help users make configuration and setup choices, Windows 2000 applied those wizards to help an NT user set up networking, work groups, and domains. It's almost as though Microsoft kept an internal, corporate split, using two different project groups to develop the GUI and the operating system, like in its original joint effort with IBM.

We've also mentioned that Microsoft has always tended to believe that understanding how a computer works shouldn't be necessary when simply using a computer. Although this philosophy is all well and good for end users, less and less information is available to the tech support community on how to repair current operating system problems. This applies to Windows 2000, where there is very little information on the underlying structure.

Starting Windows 2000

We can make a statement that Windows 2000 is essentially the same as Windows NT, but where you'll see the truth of that statement is in the loading process. We won't go into the detail we did with Windows 95 because computers have become so dependent upon their own local configurations that it's almost impossible to describe a generic boot process.

As with NT, the basic landmarks in a boot process include the prebooting events of the POST and the boot process itself. Following these two steps, there's a distinction between the *load* events and *initialization* events. This is Microsoftian for getting something into memory (loading), after which it's connected to a piece of hardware or software and made to start running (initialized). Finally, there's the logon procedure, which, like NT, continues forward while the services load in the background. The short version of loading Windows 2000 Professional is as follows:

1. *NTLDR.COM*—Acts as a bootstrap loader for the basic operating system. This begins the NT hardware detection phase, switches the CPU into 32-bit mode, and loads a mini file system that can work with either a FAT or NTFS file management system.

2. *BOOT.INI*—Contains a pointer listing any other operating systems available, along with a configuration statement as to how long the options list will display.

3. *NTDETECT.COM*—Identifies current hardware components installed on the machine and prepares a list of that configuration. This is where the spacebar option takes place, allowing different hardware profiles to be loaded.

4. *NTOSKRNL.EXE*—Loads the operating system kernel and creates the current Registry hardware key. Along with the kernel, the file loads (not initializes) device drivers and loads (not initializes) the Session Manager.

5. *HAL.DLL*—A dynamic link library that generates the hardware abstraction layer, interfacing between the operating system and the specific hardware.

6. *SYSTEM*—Opens the Registry and reads the operating system configuration, initializing the device drivers loaded previously by NTOSKRNL.EXE, and then loads any additional device drivers found in the Registry.

7. *SMSS.EXE*—Initializes the Session Manager, executes any boot-time command files (like the old AUTOEXEC.BAT), and then loads basic services and sets up the so-called page file (swap file). The program creates links to the file system that can be used by DOS commands and then starts the Win32 I/O subsystem and begins the logon process.

8. *WINLOGON.EXE*—The specific program file that generates the logon process and starts the Local Security Authority (LSA).

9. *LSASS.EXE*—The program file for the LSA, it provides all the security checking done by the system.

Note: Although we've listed the primary files in this startup process, Windows 2000 (like NT) uses countless other DLL files, device drivers, helper files, and system files to load and run the system.

Multiple Boot Options

Back when IBM was developing OS/2 (which looked a whole lot like DOS), the company developed a little program that would allow a machine to have more than one operating system and that would give the user a menu to choose which OS to boot from. The IBM Boot Manager was one of those rare moments of elegance where the program was designed to do one single thing and do it perfectly. You'll still find that program packaged with PowerQuest's PartitionMagic, but we should remember that Microsoft's Windows NT was originally part of the OS/2 joint development effort.

Windows NT and 2000 both provide a paused screen during the startup process, partly to ask you if you want to use the same hardware profile that worked the last time (LastKnownGood), but also to offer you a menu of any other available operating system you might want to boot from. This internalization of a multiple boot process began showing up in DOS 5.0, where you could boot to different configurations. At that time, you were still restricted to DOS as the operating system, but NT 3.x introduced an internalized multiple OS option.

Note: A situation where the last known hardware profile might not be the appropriate selection could arise when a laptop computer connects through a docking station.

One of the optional files used during a Windows 2000 startup is BOOTSECT.DOS. This file allows you to start the machine with MS-DOS, Windows 95, or Windows 98. Keep in mind that a DOS or Windows 9x partition must be a primary partition, and it must be marked as Active in order to boot the machine. One of the installation problems with Windows NT is that the NT Loader must be in the very first tracks and sectors of a physical disk. This can conflict with the IBM Boot Manager, which uses a 2MB partition at the very front of the disk, then hides all the other bootable partitions. Boot Manager unhides a partition (depending on your OS selection) and marks that partition as Active. It seems strange that NT and the Boot Manager would struggle for the same bit of disk real estate, but there you have it.

We've also spoken about how prior to the Universal Serial Bus (USB), a number of devices started using the fast parallel port to connect a SCSI device. One of the most successful of these devices was the Iomega removable disk drive system—the Zip and Jaz drives. Many people wanted to use one of these removable drives as a bootable disk, where the size of the disks (greater than 100MB) would allow for all the system files. If you remember, an NT bootable disk can hold only the very few files used at the very beginning of the startup.

How do you make a removable drive bootable if the system sees it as a secondary disk drive? Windows 2000/NT provides the NTBOOTDD.SYS file (in the root directory of the boot partition) for just that purpose. Iomega also provides certain utility files for the same purpose. Note that NTBOOTDD.SYS will run only following the NTDETECT.COM hardware detection phase.

Safe Mode

Windows 2000 is very much like NT. For both, you can return to the Last Known Good Registry by pressing the spacebar at the paused operating system selection menu. Windows 2000 uses either an emergency repair disk or bootable floppy disk in the same way that NT does. Another option is to load Windows 2000 in Safe Mode (just like Windows 9x), where only the minimal default device drivers are loaded.

If dual-boot is installed on the local machine, meaning that more than one operating system is available during the BOOT.INI pause, then when the boot loader prompts for an operating system, pressing the spacebar will start Windows 2000 normally.

When the boot loader prompts for an operating system, pressing F8 will present an options menu screen from which you can start Windows 2000 in Safe Mode. If Windows 2000 is the only operating system installed on the local machine, hold down any of the arrow keys as the computer starts, and an options screen will be presented. From this screen, choose the Safe Mode option, or any of the other typical Windows 9x Safe Mode start options.

We'll remind you here that in Windows 98, pressing and holding the Control key (Ctrl) during the startup process brings up the boot menu. The F8 Safe Mode key is still available, but although a two-second delay at the "Starting Windows 95…" gave you time to press the key, that delay has been removed from the "Starting Windows 98…" startup point.

Note: In the event that you require the startup boot menu on a regular basis, you can use the MSCONFIG.EXE program to access the Advanced option and to reconfigure Windows 98 to always show this boot menu at startup.

Active Directory

Perhaps one of the most important differences between Windows 2000 and Windows NT is that Windows 2000 includes the new Active Directory feature. Active Directory is a component of the Windows Open Services Architecture (WOSA), and provides what is called Directory Service to all the objects on a network, across the entire network. The Directory Service gathers up information on every object, such as users, computers, printers, hardware, and all the policies and permissions, and presents this information in a single, hierarchical view. A hierarchical view has headings with subheadings going down in levels. This is similar to the outlining you had to learn in school, where you start with a book of information that is divided into chapters, which is divided into topics and then into ideas, and you eventually end up with a specific paragraph of details.

Date warehouses use a concept called *drilling down* into information, and this too, uses the principle of outlining. The Windows Explorer works with drive letters at the top of the hierarchy, and below each drive is a root directory folder containing many subfolders, going all the way down to the last leaf on the last twig of the last branch—a file. The Registry uses handles (HKeys) to contain many subkeys, all of which end up with a specific configuration line. The Computer Management tools work with nodes and branches to arrive eventually at a specific event for a specific device.

We should mention here that in a very large network, each domain doesn't necessarily have to be running the same network operating system. In fact, one of the biggest problems Novell had to work out in the historic development of networks was that a single business location could easily have many IBM-type PCs running alongside Macintosh computers. Active Directory is one of the latest developments growing out of a long line of methods for joining together different operating systems.

Windows NT presents each domain to the systems administrators as the top level of the network hierarchy. This is all well and good, but you can easily have hundreds of domains in a network. That would be like opening up the Explorer and discovering that you had 100 separate drives to work with. In addition to the drives, the administrators would have to configure each "drive" (domain) separately, going in and adding all the resources to that domain, along with all the rights and profiles.

Novell and Microsoft eventually figured out a better way to do this, and Windows 2000 consolidates all the old NT domains into a single, higher-level called the Active Directory. In addition to the Directory Service hierarchical (outline) presentation, Active Directory gathers together and consolidates the security and authentication services across the network. These two features combine to make it easier for anyone on a Windows 2000 network to get to resources, while at the same time making it much easier for network administrators to control that access.

The Directory Service is actually integrated into the Domain Name System (DNS) concept we mentioned in Chapter 8. As we discussed, a DNS entry is a way of making a numeric IP address more user-friendly by providing a descriptive name to the underlying address. Active Directory does somewhat the same thing by taking the complicated resource names of objects on the network and turning them into something an average human being can understand. For example, an NT network might provide a printer somewhere and list it with a long line of symbols, characters, slashes, and colons. Windows 2000 can use Active Directory to call that printer "Bob's printer in the Raleigh, North Carolina branch office." The users don't need to know what the underlying name for that printer is anymore.

Although the principle is similar to the DNS concept, Active Directory goes even further than merely cross-referencing names and building in security for each network object. Within an Active Directory database, access requests for a network object are handled with Lightweight Directory Access Protocol (LDAP) queries. DNS is essentially a very simple listing of an IP address and the cross-referenced name. Active Directory is more like a full-scale database.

With a complete database made up of many fields (categories of details), Active Directory can produce varying amounts of information about an object on the network. Some of these queries (questions) can return (answer) to a network administrator such information as a user name, contact information, administrative contact information, access permissions, ownership information, and object attributes.

When you go to an Internet search engine, you type in a query, and the system goes out and gathers all the IP addresses of Web sites where it finds something related to your question. Before the search engine presents you with your results, it converts the IP addresses to domain names by using DNS entries. But that's not what you see, right? The final presentation is a top-level (hierarchical) link with a descriptive title, together with a short description of what that titled link is all about. When you click on that link, you're taken to the site location, where you can begin to drill down into the site by clicking other links.

Note: A DNS server doesn't require the Active Directory feature, but Active Directory can work only in conjunction with DNS servers. For that reason, Active Directory can run only on one of the Windows 2000 Server versions.

Windows 2000 Diagnostics and Troubleshooting

Following the NT philosophy of merging diagnostics tools into the graphical interface, Windows 2000 doesn't use an MS-DOS command-line mode for troubleshooting. In Windows 9x, if Safe Mode failed, you could always go to the underlying DOS prompt and rummage around in the system to run various utilities. Windows 2000 and NT don't rely on specific files as utility programs, relying instead on groups of associated files combined into a tool with its own interface, menus, and presentation. In most cases, you can't even find the underlying files used in an administrative tool.

System Configuration Utility

This utility became available in Windows 2000, and you can find it through the following navigation route: Start|Programs|Accessories|System Tools|System Information. From the System Information option, you first select Tools and then the System Configuration Utility.

Note: Another way to get to the System Configuration Utility tool is by going to the Start menu, choosing the Run option, typing "MSCONFIG" in the Open line, and then pressing Enter.

The MSCONFIG.EXE program first became available in Windows 98, where it was located under the same menu navigation route as Windows 2000, with the exception of choosing Diagnostic Startup as the last step.

The Windows 2000 System Configuration Utility presents a graphical interface with a number of tabs across the top area, just like any properties dialog box. Each tab is associated with a particular type of configuration, or an area within Windows where you can adjust specific settings. For example, the Startup window has been available as far back as Windows 3.0. By dragging a program icon or file name into the Startup window (or onto the Startup icon), you were able to change the underlying configuration of Windows without having to know the configuration details.

Windows 9x carried forward the idea of a Startup "group" where you could change the underlying Registry by dragging an icon or a program file name from the Explorer onto the Start menu or onto the Desktop. The problems began when you had programs running during the Windows Startup that you didn't want to have running.

Windows 9x provides a Startup folder under the [*drive*]:\Windows\Start Menu directory where you can go into either the Programs or Shortcuts subfolder. Within the Program folder, one of the subfolders is called Startup, and this is where you'll find *some* of the references to what Windows will load during the starting process. Unfortunately, this isn't the only place where Windows autoloads programs. In Windows 9x, you can run REGEDIT to examine the following location: HKEY_LOCAL_MACHINE/Software/Microsoft/Windows/Current Version/Run or Run Service.

This is where you'll find *more* references to programs that will start with Windows, such as System Agent, NetMeeting, the active movie check, and so on. Startup programs may show up in the system Registry in four primary locations (in Windows 9x):

➤ HKEY_LOCAL_MACHINE\SOFTWARE\Microsoft\Windows\ CurrentVersion\Run

➤ HKEY_LOCAL_MACHINE\SOFTWARE\Microsoft\Windows\ CurrentVersion\RunServices

➤ HKEY_USERS\.DEFAULT\SOFTWARE\Microsoft\Windows\ CurrentVersion\RUN

➤ HKEY_CURRENT_USER\SOFTWARE\Microsoft\Windows\ CurrentVersion\RUN

You can see why the integrated System Configuration Utility in Windows 2000 is the first place to look for something as simple as a program you don't want to run during the Startup process. Additional tabs in the tool include General, System.ini, Win.ini, Static VxDs, Startup, Environment, and International. (Note the Static VxDs tab, showing the virtual device drivers we discussed in Chapter 12.) Each tab shows the current way Windows 2000 will start, and each tab has areas where specific configuration settings can be adjusted.

Note: In Windows 98, the MSCONFIG.EXE System Configuration Utility tabs were General, Config.sys, Autoexec.bat, System.ini, Win.ini, and Startup.

In Chapter 12, we mentioned Tweak UI (where the UI stands for user interface) and said that this is a set of more powerful tools used by in-house Microsoft tech support people. These tools worked in a similar fashion to the System Configuration Utility that came with Windows 98. The tool was an optional installation, and it was not installed by default. If you chose to install it, it became available from Start|Settings|Control Panel, where you could double-click on the Tweak UI icon.

Note: In Windows 2000, the power tools went back into hiding, but a much more simplified UI option became available in a default installation.

The Windows 2000 Desktop is very similar to the Windows 9x Desktop, with a Start button that opens up a path to Programs, Accessories, and System Tools.

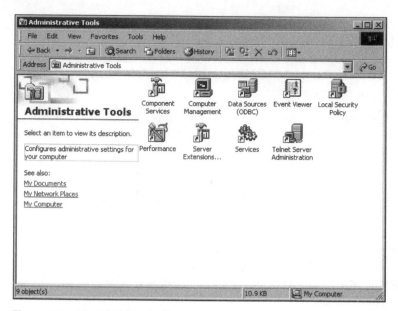

Figure 13.1   The Administrative Tools folder.

From the System Tools option, you can then choose either the Administrative Tools option, which opens up the Control Panel series of tools, or the System Information option specifically. Figure 13.1 shows the Administrative Tools folder containing the various utility tools, including the Computer Management tool that opens up into the System Information area.

Figure 13.2 is the local Computer Management window, which looks remarkably like the Windows Explorer or the Windows Registry. The left panel is arranged in nodes and branches, and the right panel contains the specific lines of information pertaining to whichever local management tool you've highlighted. Note that the System Information section is only one of several tools. You can also see the System Tools section, Performance Logs And Alerts section, Shared Folders section, Device Manager section, and Local Users And Groups section.

Each node has its branches, just like the Explorer and the Registry. For example, the System Information tool has a System Summary branch, which tells you all about the overall condition of the computer. You can run reports from these information tools, giving a detailed report of such things as available memory, percent of resources being used, and so on.

My Computer and Control Panel

Many court cases have proven that the Microsoft Windows Desktop bears little or no resemblance to the Apple Computer Macintosh Desktop. Any similarity of an icon representing the hardware attached to a specific computer is purely

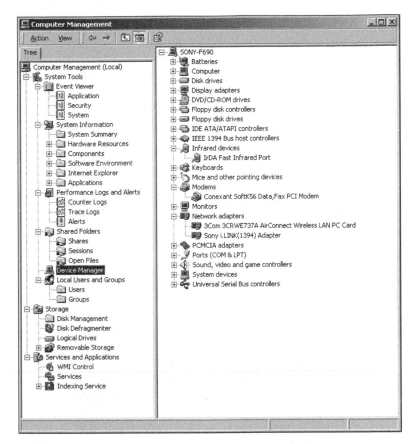

Figure 13.2   The administrative Computer Management tools window.

coincidental. Coincidentally, Windows uses an icon called My Computer (by default) to represent the computer you're working with. Double-clicking on the My Computer icon opens up a window listing all the accessible drives, along with a Control Panel icon and an Available Printers icon.

Right-clicking for the Properties menu on the My Computer icon opens a dialog box with several tabs, including the Device Manager. Whether you choose a pathway from the Start button or the My Computer icon, one way or another you'll have access to these system reporting tools.

The Control Panel applet (tool) has been available since the first release of Windows, way back when. The only thing that's changed is how you get to the Control Panel and what new and interesting ways it offers for you to get into trouble…or rather, for troubleshooting. Part of the evolving security in Windows pertains to preventing an untrained user from accessing critical system components and whacking (technical term) the machine.

Windows 98 offered exceptional troubleshooting and diagnostics tools; however, those tools were readily accessible and made it too easy for end users to cause problems. One of the main differences in Windows ME, was that many of the configuration tools were hidden away from casual access. Windows NT and Windows 2000 can be set up to block access to some of the more critical configuration tools.

One of the management icons in the Control Panel is the System icon. Double-clicking on System gives you access to the specific device configurations for any device associated with the machine. The Windows 2000 Computer Management tool brings in the NT Event Manager and Local Security Policy tools, along with such things as Performance, Services, Server Extensions, and other areas focusing on networking and dial-up connectivity.

The Device Manager

Beginning with Windows 95, the Device Manager was one of the tabs on the Properties dialog box arising out of the My Computer icon. As we've said, the Device Manager could also be accessed by navigating from the Start menu to Settings|Control Panel and then double-clicking the System icon.

The Device Manager is a graphic representation of all the hardware devices attached to the local machine. Aside from the various drives and controllers, monitors, and ports, one of the nodes in the Device Manager is the System Devices node. This is where low-level motherboard devices are listed, along with their configurations. (We discuss the Device Manager again in Chapter 14.)

Networking (My Network Places)

Another of the critical troubleshooting icons located in the Control Panel is the Network And Dial-up Connections icon. We'll follow a specific troubleshooting procedure in the next chapter, but we also want to mention this icon here. As you know, a local machine (your PC) can gain access to a network only when it has some way to physically connect to the wires and computers making up that network. The connection is generally accomplished with a network interface card (NIC) plugged into an expansion slot on the motherboard.

Network cards come in many varieties and brands. However, each network card must not only be physically installed in a machine, but it must also be configured. We've said that a NIC has a specific address stored in ROM on the card, and that address must be initialized on the network. In order to make the card "visible" to the local machine, both the hardware and the operating system have to be reconfigured. This configuration process takes place in both the Device Manager and the Network icon in the Control Panel.

Interactive Partitioning

One of the interesting changes introduced with Windows NT and 2000, is the Storage section under the Computer Management tool (where System Information is also found). This graphic presentation of the physical disks attached to the system goes one step farther than simply presenting the partitioning information for the disks. Borrowing a good idea from PowerQuest, you can now manage partition chores, such as resizing or deleting, directly in the windows. On the one hand, this makes partitioning a drive a lot more intuitive, but on the other hand, it could lead to the total loss of any information on the system. This is another area where access rights can be assigned to allow or block the feature.

Note: Some of these system tools make their first appearance in Windows 2000 and are unavailable in Windows NT. We would expect that future versions of Windows will be released on the Windows 20xx banner.

System Agent

The System Agent was first available in Windows 98. You could begin at the Start menu and navigate a route through Programs and Accessories until you got to the last option, which was Maintenance Wizard. This tool provided a way to schedule tasks (date, time, and frequency), such as ScanDisk and defragmenting a drive. The same routing path held true in Windows 2000, except that the tool name was changed to Schedule Tasks.

The Recovery Console

We remember that when OS/2 Warp was first released on the market, we asked how we could get to the "real" computer system, the black text-based screen with a DOS prompt. We were told we couldn't get there anymore, and that OS/2 was always in a graphic mode. It turned out that we could open an editor into the CONFIG.SYS file, which was a vastly expanded version of the old DOS file and contained all sorts of configuration options (much like the Registry).

Windows 2000 appears to be similar to OS/2 because it no longer provides an MS-DOS Mode command-line interface. You can run individual commands in the CMD.EXE line, but when the program or command terminates, you're returned to the Windows Desktop. We said that it appears to be this way, but in fact, Recovery Console is one of the utilities installed during a Windows 2000 setup.

Recovery Console gives you a way to run a nontransient command environment where almost all of the DOS commands continue to live on. Some of the more useful commands are **XCOPY, MOVE, CD, DEL**, and the good old **DIR** command. In many cases, a graphic environment requires so many mouse clicks that you can do the same thing a whole lot faster with a basic knowledge of DOS. In some instances, you can't do certain things in Windows.

The Recovery Console is one of the low-level troubleshooting utilities that comes with Windows 2000, but it may have its access blocked by a network administrator. On your own PC where you're given Administrator rights by default, you can still get to the old DOS-looking environment. See—there was a reason we talked at length about DOS in Chapter 10.

Practice Questions

Question 1

> Which of the following two modules are contained in the Windows NT Kernel Mode?
>
> ○ a. The Executive assistant and Security Options layer
>
> ○ b. The hardware abstraction layer and Executive layer
>
> ○ c. The User Applications layer and hardware abstraction layer
>
> ○ d. The Executive layer and Local Security Authority layer

Answer b is correct. The Kernel Mode is divided into two layers. The lower layer is the hardware abstraction layer (HAL), and the higher layer is the Executive layer. Answer a is incorrect as there is no Executive Assistant or Security Options layer. Answer c is incorrect because it confuses a User Applications layer with the User Mode and the Applications layer. Answer d is incorrect because the Local Security Authority is part of the Security Reference Monitor module within the Executive layer.

Question 2

> A Windows 2000 network can be divided into _____, _____, and _____.
>
> ○ a. computers, stars, base topologies
>
> ○ b. groups, profiles, accounts
>
> ○ c. users, groups, domains
>
> ○ d. domains, directories, profiles

Answer c is correct. NT and 2000 networks are commonly divided into individual users, groups of objects, and large domains of groups. Answer a is incorrect in the use of base topologies, and because star topologies are architecture types rather than network divisions. Answer b is incorrect because profiles and accounts are associated with both groups and users. Answer d is incorrect because networks aren't commonly divided into directories and profiles.

Question 3

> Which two tools or utilities would you use to troubleshoot a Windows NT
> computer that failed to successfully boot?
>
> ❑ a. A bootable system disk
>
> ❑ b. The emergency repair utility
>
> ❑ c. A systems information disk
>
> ❑ d. An emergency repair disk

Answers a and d are correct. NT and Windows 2000 both provide an opportunity to create a bootable system disk and an emergency repair disk. The emergency repair disk is customized to a specific machine, but both disks can be tried
with a machine that fails to boot. Answer b is incorrect because it refers to the
ERU.EXE utility in Windows 9x that is used to back up a Registry. Answer c is
incorrect because there is no such disk.

Question 4

> What is the requirement for an employee to gain access to a printer in the
> Accounting domain?
>
> ○ a. An access code
>
> ○ b. A user identification
>
> ○ c. A group password
>
> ○ d. A guest account

Answer b is correct. The question refers to requirements and an Accounting domain, implying that some sort of password is required. NT and 2000 networks
require a User ID (identification). Answer a is incorrect because an access code is
usually applied to an entryway of some sort and is much too broad a term to be
applied to the operating system. Answer c is incorrect because groups are not
provided with passwords. Answer d is incorrect because a guest account is almost
always assigned extremely limited rights and would rarely allow access to Accounting department information.

Question 5

WINLOGON.EXE is the program file that runs the _____ procedure and begins the _____.

○ a. logon, Local Security Authority

○ b. Windows splash screen, logon process

○ c. Session Manager, security logon process

○ d. logon, device loading process.

Answer a is correct. The WINLOGON program initiates the logon procedure, which then starts the Local Security Authority (LSA). Answer b is incorrect because no program runs the splash screen; the splash screen is called by a program. Answer c is incorrect because the Session Manager is part of the basic NT operating system and loads near the beginning. Answer d is incorrect because devices are loaded and initialized in several places prior to the logon process.

Question 6

Which of the following cannot be done in the Recovery Console?

○ a. Run an XCOPY procedure.

○ b. Access the Registry HKeys.

○ c. Examine partition information.

○ d. Format a system disk.

Answer b is correct. The Recovery Console allows all DOS command-line operations that do not require a graphical interface. The Registry Editor is a graphic editing environment run through REGEDT32.EXE and, as such, requires that you are in a Windows GUI environment. Answer a is incorrect because XCOPY is a commonly used file-copying utility program found only in DOS. Answer c is incorrect because FDISK is capable of reporting on partitions without necessarily repartitioning a disk. Answer d is incorrect because formatting a floppy disk is a common option for a command-line interface.

Need to Know More?

Honeycutt, Jerry. *Introducing Microsoft Windows 2000 Professional.* Redmond, WA: Microsoft Press, 1999. ISBN 0-7356-0662-5. This provides a good comparison of Windows 2000 to other Windows operating systems but tends to be sales oriented.

Matthews, Martin S. *Windows 2000: A Beginner's Guide.* Berkley, CA: Osborne/McGraw-Hill, 2000. ISBN 0072123249. This is the one must-have book for anybody new to Windows 2000 in a network environment. It simply covers it all.

Pearce, Eric. *Windows NT in a Nutshell.* Sebastol, CA: O'Reilly & Associates, 1997. ISBN 1-56592-251-4. This is a very good "how to" book for day-to-day operation of Windows NT.

Reeves, Scott, Kalinda Reeves, Stephen Weese, and Christopher S. Geyer. *A+ Exam Prep, 3rd Edition.* Scottsdale, AZ: The Coriolis Group, 2001. ISBN 1-57610-699-3. This is a good reference that concentrates on providing exam-required information.

Troubleshooting

Terms you'll need to understand:

✓ Boot, startup, and connectivity

✓ POST and beep codes

✓ Switching out components and hot swapping

✓ Windows services

✓ Cleaning out files

✓ PING utility

✓ Virus and stealth viruses

Concepts you'll need to master:

✓ CMOS settings and machine passwords

✓ CMOS checksum validation

✓ Drive jumpers and master and slave settings

✓ Reporting out device information

✓ Windows menu options and icon navigation routes

✓ Recovery Console

✓ User and password configuration

In many cases, your first contact with a problem PC will be when the person using it says, "I don't know what the problem is. Everything was working just fine yesterday, and now it [*fill in the exam question*]." Typically, the system won't boot up, or the operating environment won't start. Another common situation is where the PC is an unknown system requiring some sort of identification, repair, or optimization. Often, a written problem description will be taped to the box. In instances in which no information at all is attached to the computer, don't worry; as you'll see in this chapter, a computer can be made to report almost everything about itself.

In the following discussion, we break out troubleshooting problems into three broad categories:

➤ *Boot and hardware problems*—Refer to hardware and booting events taking place between the time the power is switched on and when the operating system takes control.

➤ *Startup problems*—Refer to events surrounding a failure to load the operating system.

➤ *Connectivity problems*—Assume that a machine has booted up and an operating system is present, but the machine can't connect to an existing network.

This chapter is a reminder chapter and presents a broad overview of the types of problems you'll need to be familiar with for the A+ exam, and the diagnostics tools you'll need to use to fix them.

Boot Problems

During the initialization process, a machine can't display anything to the monitor, and you can't enter anything from the keyboard. We discussed the power-on self test (POST) in Chapter 11 and included a listing of the error indicators in the "Beep Codes" section. If the machine can't get past the initialization, the most likely problems involve either a bad power supply or a failed motherboard.

Sometimes, a machine has actually booted up okay, but the monitor is turned off or broken. In some instances, the monitor's image controls have been changed, dimming the image to point where you can't see it. Check the brightness controls and monitor indicator lights, but in a worst case, you might have to try a different monitor. When we refer to the process of using a piece of equipment we know to be good, we speak of *switching out* the problem piece of equipment. After the machine has passed the initialization stage and before ROM BIOS hands off to the operating system, the most common area where you'll encounter problems is with the CMOS.

CMOS Problems

A machine can have a hardware password stored in the CMOS, in which case it will prompt the user for that password upon completion of the POST. Some PCs offer separate passwords for the machine and general access to the operating system. The default option in the CMOS Password setting is to disable the password completely (with a None or Disabled selection). If the machine password is disabled, the POST automatically hands off to the operating system.

If the user forgets the password, the recommended way to recover the system is to remove the CMOS battery long enough for the loss of power to clear the chip, or to reconfigure a jumper on the motherboard to clear the chip. These steps clear all CMOS settings and require reconfiguring the CMOS when the battery is replaced. In the field, some technicians have been known to short-circuit the CMOS jumper to clear the chip. However, although this could be the only available option on the exam, the procedure is not recommended.

Another important setting in CMOS is the order in which the machine checks its drives for an operating system. Keep in mind that a *default* setting is the value that will be set if no manual configuration change takes place, or when a cleared CMOS receives power for the first time. The default in most PCs is that the system will search first in drive A: and then drive C:. Other settings include completely disabling the checking of drive A:, checking for a bootable CD-ROM, or checking for a bootable SCSI drive.

Note: In the event that drive C: becomes disabled, the operating system can often be booted from drive A:. If the CMOS has disabled the checking of drive A:, there will be no way at all to access the hard drive. If a CMOS password is enabled, the only way to change the CMOS is to remove the battery (or reset the jumper on those motherboards that provide a jumper).

CMOS Error Messages

If no operating system is found, CMOS returns an error message to the screen and pauses the system. The two typical messages about a missing operating system are "Bad or missing command interpreter" or "Non-system disk or disk error." These errors will show on any DOS or Windows machine, and they indicate that you should try to reinstall the system files. On Windows 9x machines, you can try the SYS.COM utility. On a Windows NT or 2000 system, try using a bootable disk and an emergency repair disk.

Remember that CMOS errors can often be generated after someone has changed the settings for the computer. This situation can lead to anything from an inability to boot the machine, to a simple pause at the POST screen. Some errors might allow the machine to continue booting after pressing a function key (often F1).

CMOS settings are stored in a sort of file, and checksum validation works with CMOS memory much the way it works with files. *Checksum validation* means that a number is read when the file is created and stored, and that number can be appended to (added on to) the file and stored for later checking. When the file is read, the same process runs and should generate the same number. If the new number doesn't match the stored number, a *checksum error* occurs. The settings file has a stored checksum, and when the CPU reads the CMOS internal file, the numbers should match.

There are many CMOS errors, but some of the important ones to know include:

➤ *CMOS display type mismatch*—This error indicates that the video settings don't apply to the actual monitor installed on the system. The first step is to re-enter CMOS and verify that the correct monitor has been selected.

➤ *CMOS memory size mismatch*—This error will appear on many machines when more memory has been added. Autodetection will usually reconfigure the CMOS with a pause during the POST to make sure that what CMOS saw matches reality.

➤ *CMOS device mismatch error*—Displays and hard disks are considered devices, and any one of the attached devices can generate this error. Most likely, the wrong device is listed in CMOS for the physical device attached to the machine.

➤ *CMOS checksum failure*—A checksum failure indicates that corruption exists in the CMOS memory. This can often happen with a bad battery or a loose connection to the battery. If changing and checking the battery doesn't solve the problem, it might be a motherboard going bad. Checksum errors may also indicate a virus.

Hardware Problems

One of the most common problems uncovered during the boot process is where a piece of hardware isn't recognized by the system. A bad keyboard will generate a beep code and often, a message to the monitor. Keyboards are inexpensive enough that if you can't switch out the keyboard, replacing it should solve the problem.

If the machine seems to be running okay, you'll probably hear the cooling fan making some amount of noise, and some indicator lights should be showing on the faceplate. A bad monitor doesn't have a cooling fan, so without sophisticated testing equipment, the only way to test a video connection is to switch out the monitor.

Master/Slave Jumpers

Another problem is where a new drive of some kind has been added to one of the controllers on the motherboard. For example, you might have a hard drive attached to one IDE controller and then attach a second drive to the same controller. If you weren't paying attention to jumpers, you might discover that the system doesn't recognize the second hard drive.

Most drives have a configuration setting for Primary Only, Primary Second Available, and Second (or terminology to that effect). The typical default setting for a new drive is to make it the Primary Only (master) drive. If the original hard drive is configured as a Primary Only drive, then when you add a second drive, the controller won't even see it because it's being told there's only one drive on the controller interface. Additionally, even if the first drive was configured to see a second drive, the new drive is probably set to Primary Only.

 The default IRQ for a primary IDE fixed disk controller is IRQ 14. The secondary controller takes IRQ 15 by default. Note that jumpering an additional drive on the same controller isn't generally an IRQ problem, but rather a jumper switch problem.

Jumper settings are the first thing to check when a new drive isn't being recognized. Make sure you've opened up access to the new drive by changing the first drive's jumper switches. You'll also have to set the jumpers on the second drive to make it a secondary drive (or slave). The second thing to look for is a bad power supply at the cable connections. When all else fails, switch out the new drive with a drive that you know is good, and verify that any power connectors are working and in good condition.

Note: A good place to have electronic testing equipment is where you're having possible troubles with power connectors and cables. If nothing else, a multimeter can verify that a connection is providing a complete circuit between one location and another.

Circuitry Failures

It's not often that you'll come across a machine where the entire motherboard has been fried (technical term). It happens, though, and in those instances, it might be more cost-effective to buy a new computer. You should already know that integrated circuits are delicate and can be short-circuited with a blast of static electricity (electrostatic discharge [ESD]). Another way to fry a motherboard is when a bad power supply sends a high voltage discharge through the electronics of the entire system, melting many of the components.

Lightning is another source of high voltage, and when lightning discharges to a nearby ground point, it's called a *proximity strike*. If a powerful storm is moving through the area, it's a very good idea to disconnect all computers from the building's wiring structure. Not only should you disconnect the power cords, but you should remember that any modems are connected to the building's telephone wiring.

In Chapter 8, we touched on *hot swapping*, one of the features of USB. You also know that a computer constantly polls a keyboard, waiting for any activity coming from that keyboard. Because of the constant interplay between the motherboard and the various devices attached to that motherboard, it's never a good idea to unplug a device or plug in a new device while the power is on. The Universal Serial Bus is one of the first technologies that safely allows you to add and remove devices without turning off the main power supply.

Some computer reference manuals indicate that you don't need to turn off the machine to attach or detach a device. Laptop computers often use portable floppy drives or detachable CD-ROM drives. Desktop machines can run into trouble with keyboards, scanners, removable storage devices, and even a mouse. Anything that attaches to the motherboard can cause an electronic pulse to run through the motherboard and its components.

Although you would think the reference manual would tell you the truth about the machine, it's a rare instance where the machine will recognize a new device without a cold boot (machine reset). It may be possible to attach a new device with the machine running, but you can get into real trouble when you detach a device in this manner. Unless you're working with a USB device, the recommended method is still to turn off the machine before you plug in or unplug any piece of hardware.

Startup Problems

Assuming the hardware and initialization processes have all completed successfully, the next category of problems involves the operating system. Windows 9x and 2000 attempt to use a previous version of the Registry files if the system crashes during startup. In some instances, this is helpful, but in other instances, all that happens is that the previously useful Registry files become corrupted.

The typical strategy for fixing a Windows machine with a startup problem is to begin with the last, working Registry files. In Windows 2000, you'll also have a Last Known Good hardware profile to work with. If the problem can't be solved, you'll have to try an emergency boot disk or an emergency repair tool of some kind. If the machine manages to get to the point where it starts but it's limping, Windows 9x and 2000 all offer Safe Mode.

Windows 9x

With so many versions of Windows, we can't do more than run through what we've already discussed at greater length in the chapters devoted to each version. Safe Mode is probably the most accessible diagnostics area you'll be working with, so knowing how to arrive at Safe Mode is something to remember.

Windows 95 introduced Safe Mode as a way to get the system up and running with only the most essential components. In Windows 9x and 2000, if something fails during the startup, Windows automatically tries to start in Safe Mode. In other instances, you may have to bring up Safe Mode manually. With a Windows 95 machine, the way to do this is by pressing the F8 function key when the "Starting Windows 95…" message appears on the screen. You have two seconds to do so.

Windows 98 and ME removed the two-second delay, but when the "Starting Windows 98…" message flashes past, F8 still works. The way to bring up Safe Mode in Windows 98 is to hold down the Ctrl key during the startup process.

Safe Mode provides a limited operating environment, but it gives you access to the various diagnostics tools and utilities within the operating system. REGEDIT is the Windows 9x Registry Editor, and SYSEDIT opens the critical INI files, AUTOEXEC.BAT, and CONFIG.SYS. Finally, LOGVIEW opens the various log files where crash information may be stored, including BOOTLOG.TXT.

Windows NT and 2000

Correcting boot problems in Windows 2000 is similar to correcting them on a Windows 9x machine because Windows attempts to use the Last Known Good Registry files and to call up Safe Mode. Like Windows 9x, the next step is to try an emergency boot disk, but Windows 2000 also provides a way to create an emergency repair disk. Remember that if many machines are set up with similar configurations, an emergency boot disk can support all of those machines. On the other hand, the emergency repair disk is specific to each machine.

 To call up Safe Mode on a Windows 2000 machine, press and hold any of the arrow keys during the startup process.

Diagnostics Tools

We've discussed various diagnostics tools and utilities in previous chapters, but we'll pass over them one last time so they're fresh in your mind. Certain tools have either disappeared or have been modified as Windows has developed, including MSD.EXE. Microsoft Diagnostics was a command-line program that would generate a report of the configuration files used on the machine. MSD was superseded by Hardware Diagnostics.

Hardware Diagnostics (HWDIAG.EXE)

Windows 95 offered HWDIAG.EXE as a reporting and diagnostics utility, but it wasn't installed by default on a new machine. The program was available on the installation disks and ran in a graphical environment. Hardware Diagnostics generated a detailed report of every device attached to the machine, as long as Windows could recognize the device. This file is no longer included with Windows 98.

Another way to generate a report of the many devices listed is from the Device Manager, located using the Properties menu of the My Computer icon. You can print either a System Summary Report or an All Devices And Summary Report. Although the HWDIAG.EXE program seems to have vanished, the detailed report printed using the Device Manager is sophisticated enough to read manufacturer information, version numbers, and so forth.

If you choose to print any reports to a file, you should be aware that if the default printer is a typical laser printer, the file will be created using the Printer Control Language (PCL) format the printer uses. It's always a good idea to set up (during installation) the *generic printer* and configure its port setting to print to a file. If you print with this printer, configured in this fashion, you'll always be asked for a file name and destination.

Note: You can always set up a generic printer with the Add Printer option under the Printers icon of the Control Panel.

Windows 95 Emergency Recovery Utility (ERU.EXE)

We've discussed the way that Windows attempts to use a previously existing version of the system registration files, and how sometimes a corrupted hardware profile can cause those previous files to become corrupted. Windows 95 provided the Emergency Recovery Utility (ERU.EXE) as a way to back up and restore the system registration files. You cannot mix and match Registry files, and the system will fail to start if Windows 95 Registry files are restored into a Windows 98 system.

Windows 98 Registry Checker (SCANREGW.EXE)

The ERU.EXE backup program was changed to the Registry Checker in Windows 98 and ME. Not only can SCANREGW.EXE be used to back up and restore the Registry files, but the Registry Checker attempts to go through corrupted system files and make a best guess as to how to fix them. Registry Checker also comes in a DOS version (SCANREG.EXE) and is used during the installation procedure.

The last known good Registry is not the same as the LastKnownGood hardware profile Windows NT and 2000 choose when you press the spacebar during a boot process. Windows 2000 also has the ERU tool, along with the emergency repair disk. You should know that in order to use the Emergency Recovery Utility, Windows 2000 requires an emergency repair disk and a repair folder located somewhere on the computer's hard disk.

Control Panel

Windows 9x gathers together most of the diagnostics and repair utilities in the Control Panel. You can navigate to the Control Panel several ways. The first way is to double-click on the My Computer icon on the Windows Desktop. This results in a program window with icons for all the available drives, a Printers icon, and a Control Panel icon.

Another way to reach the Control Panel in all versions of Windows is to begin with the Start button and navigate through Start|Settings|Control Panel. In a Windows 9x machine, the main icons to know are the System icon, the Printers icon, the Network icon, and the Passwords icon.

Administrative Tools

Windows 2000 has several other icons, and a machine set up as a networking machine will have options that are different than a standalone machine's options. To reach the Windows 2000 utility tools, double-click on My Computer, open the Control Panel, and double-click on Administrative Tools.

Another way is to navigate through Start|Settings|Control Panel|Administrative Tools and to look at the various selections under Administrative Tools. Two of the main icons to know are Component Services and Event Viewer (refer back to Figure 13.1 in Chapter 13).

System Reports and My Computer

You can troubleshoot a failed system from within the operating system environment, viewing many of the logs and reports at the computer. Generally, you'll be better off if you print out reports of the various event logs, diagnostics tools, and configuration viewers. We've mentioned that the Device Manager in Windows 9x is a thorough reporting utility for the many hardware devices attached to the machine. Device Manager reports also provide sections on memory usage, IRQ, and DMA usage.

Windows 2000 provides several tools from the Start|Programs|Accessories|System Tools menu. At the System Tools option, you can access Backup, Disk Cleanup, Disk Defragmenter, Schedule Tasks, and System Information. The

System Information Print option is very similar to the old HWDIAG.EXE, with very detailed reports on all devices.

Make a note of these menu navigation routes because you'll likely be asked to recognize them during the exam.

When you right-click on the My Computer icon in a Windows 2000 environment, the Properties menu selection brings up a dialog box with the following tabs: General, Network Identification, Hardware, User Profiles, and Advanced.

Note: Remember that double-clicking on the My Computer icon brings up a program window with the drives and the Control Panel icon.

The Advanced tab has a Performance button where you can set environment variables, along with Startup and Recovery options. The Startup and Recovery options include a series of checkboxes that tell the computer what to do when it crashes.

The Hardware options tab offers choices to get to the Hardware Wizard and the Device Manager. The Windows 2000 Device Manager offers another two choices, one of which is Driver Signing To Ensure That All Drivers Are Digitally Signed By Microsoft To Validate Drivers. The other is Hardware Profiles, where you can create the different profiles offered at the BOOT.INI pause screen. Once again, hardware profiles might include a docking station, a Desktop profile, and so forth.

Windows 2000 Recovery Console

When you've tried a bootable disk and an emergency repair disk, and you've tried to get into Safe Mode on a Windows 2000 machine, one of your last options before reinstalling the machine is to try the Recovery Console. The Recovery Console requires an Administrator password and allows you to attempt to repair the boot sector and to create a new boot floppy or emergency repair disk.

In Chapter 13, we said that you can run a transient command-line window by navigating through the Start menu to Run. At the Run window, type "CMD" (to run CMD.EXE), and press Enter. Whatever program you run eventually terminates, and you're returned to the Widows Desktop. Recovery Console provides a DOS-like command-line interface used for repairing Master Boot Records (MBRs), disk partitioning, and disk formatting.

Recovery Console is started from the Windows 2000 setup disks (either CD or floppy) where, after booting from a setup disk, you follow the instructions to "Repair a Windows 2000 installation using the Recovery Console." If you have multiple partitions with different operating systems, you are asked to choose which drive you want to log on to by picking a number and then pressing Enter. You must then enter the Administrator password and press Enter, after which you are presented with a C:\WINNT prompt.

Some of the familiar DOS commands available at the Recovery Console include: **ATTRIB, CD, CHKDSK, COPY, DIR, DEL, FORMAT, MD, RD,** and **REN.** You can also type "HELP" and get a complete list of commands, just like at the DOS prompt, or you can use **COMMAND /?** for the typical short form of the command.

The Report and Fix program options include: **DISABLE** or **ENABLE,** to allow or disallow device drivers; **Partition** (DISKPART.EXE), to add or delete a disk partition; **FIXBOOT** and **FIXMBR,** to correct problems with the boot record and MBR; and **LISTSVC,** to list the device drivers and services available on the computer.

Cleaning Out Temporary Files

One of the biggest problems with modern iterations of Windows and the Internet is the number of temporary files accumulated on the hard drive. In Windows 9x, the way you removed those files was to use the Explorer's saved search criteria to create shortcuts for ~*.* and *.TMP files. You could also create Desktop shortcuts for ScanDisk and Defrag. Windows 2000 offers a utility called Disk Cleanup.

To reach the cleanup utility, choose Start|Programs|Accessories|System Tools|Disk Cleanup. One of the options under Disk Cleanup is Select Drive, which reads the drive you select and produces a menu. The menu options are checkboxes asking you which types of files you want to delete. Among the types you can select are downloaded program files, temporary Internet files, offline Web pages, Recycle Bin, temporary files, temporary offline files, offline files, or catalog files for the Content Indexer.

Note: The Content Indexer is similar to the Windows 9x Find Fast utility, which would index an entire hard drive and provide speedier searches through the index rather than searching the drive directly.

Other option tabs in the Disk Cleanup utility include Windows Components and Installed Programs. The Windows Components menu allows you to remove optional components you don't use. You're presented with a list of checkboxes, and you then tell Disk Cleanup what you want it to get rid of. The Installed Programs menu is much the same as the Windows Components menu and lists all the installed programs on the PC, along with how much space they take. To help you decide what you'd like to remove, the lists can be sorted in several ways, such as by frequency of use, date last used, and names and sizes.

Connectivity Problems

Up until this point, we've mostly discussed troubleshooting procedures for either a standalone machine or a network machine. However, one of the biggest headaches to deal with is when a machine has started successfully but won't connect to a network. In this scenario, the two possible causes are the network interface card (NIC) itself, or the way that the NIC is interfacing with the operating system.

You can use the Device Manager to go in and look at the type of card Windows thinks is installed in the machine. However, the only way to know for sure what type of card is installed is to open the machine and actually look at the card. Older cards had no way of telling you whether they were working or not, so unless the card has LED indicators, you'll have to first switch out the card in order to prove whether or not it's working. Keep in mind that when you install another card, you'll have to reconfigure most of the network settings.

Windows 9x introduced a Network Neighborhood icon on the Desktop, which became My Network Places in Windows 2000. Double-clicking on the Network icon opens up much of the configuration information, but the more thorough way to check the network configuration is through the Control Panel.

The Windows 2000 Control Panel includes a Network and Dial-up Connections icon, which includes a Make New Connection option. There can be more than one connection, and assuming networking has already been set up and there is an active connection, the Windows Taskbar displays a small icon that looks like two computers talking with each other.

Double-clicking the icon on the Taskbar brings up a status and activity dialog box that shows the connection status, duration, and speed of a good connection. A second box shows connection activity in terms of real-time packets sent and received. Right-clicking on the icon brings up a Properties menu of options, such as configuring the network and NICs, and includes a second button that allows you to disable a specific network connection.

Network Card Configuration Problems

Assuming you've been lucky and the NIC has onboard LEDs to indicate that the card is in good working condition, the second aspect of connectivity is how the card is configured within Windows. We're only going to touch lightly on the entire concept of installing a NIC and configuring connections, but you should know how to get to the places where you might be asked to find out any existing information.

Begin with the Start|Settings|Network And Dial-up Connections menus. You're given a choice of all available connections or networks that have been set up for that computer. When you highlight any of the available networks, you'll be given a screen with icons representing each network and a Make New Connections Wizard.

Double-click on any of the existing network connections to produce a window that tells you the connection, status duration speed, activity, and properties. The Properties option opens the Network Configure window, where you can add or configure a new protocol, NIC, or client. Note that these options are the same as when you double-click on the icon on the Taskbar, which we mentioned a moment ago.

Another way to get to the same place is to right-click on My Network Places (Windows 98 and 2000) or Network Neighborhood (Windows 95). The Properties option takes you to the Network And Dial-up Connections window, where you can examine the configurations for the local machine's network installation.

Note: Remember that one of the tools available in Windows 2000 is the Performance Monitor (discussed in Chapter 13), which can be set to monitor specific aspects of the machine either in a moving graphic or a tab format. Another tool is the Net Watcher that first appeared in Windows 95, which became the Network Monitor in Windows NT and 2000 Server.

Services Icon

According to Microsoft, services are those programs or routines that provide support for other programs, particularly at low or hardware levels. Network services are a specialized software-based functionality provided by network servers (such as Directory Service), which is like a phone book used for locating users and resources.

One of the icons in the Windows NT and 2000 Control Panel is the Services icon. There are a great many services, but some examples include Alerter (notifies selected users of computers of administrative alerts); Dynamic Host Configuration Protocol (DHCP) Client; Domain Name System (DNS) Client (resolves and caches domain names); Event Log; Network Connections; Plug and Play; Print Spooler; Telephony; and the Utility Manager (accessibility tools to start and/or set up accessibility features).

Connection Validation

PING is an acronym for Packet INternet Groper, which is a protocol for testing whether a particular computer is connected to the Internet—or any Transmission Control Protocol/Internet Protocol (TCP/IP) network—by sending a packet to its IP address and waiting for a response. The name actually comes from the submarine's active SONAR where a sound is sent out and surrounding objects are revealed.

PING is a Unix protocol used to test whether a computer is connected to another computer through a network. To use the PING utility, you must know the specific IP address of that computer.

Access Denied

Another common problem with networked computers is that end users who attempt to use one of the network resources can be denied access. The resources could be a file folder, a printer, an Internet connection, or even their own computers. Typically, the cause is either a password problem, or an administrative authorization situation.

Before you can even begin to work with passwords and access rights, you must have an Administrator password. Although A+ technicians will most likely not have administrative rights, CompTIA indicates they will be asking questions about administrative areas.

Assuming that you have the Administrator password, navigate through the Start|Settings|Control Panel menu to the Users And Passwords icon. Double-click on the icon to bring up a dialog box with two tabs: User and Advanced. The User tab lists all the users available on the local machine. When you highlight any one of the listed users, you're presented with a list of checkboxes. One of the checkboxes states that the User Must Enter A User Name And Password To Use This Computer. If this box is checked, when you go to any user, you will see three buttons: Look At Properties, Remove, or Add A User.

Note: On many new machines, Windows 2000 is preinstalled, and the purchaser is given a default Administrator User ID and password. In a home environment, the machine can be reconfigured to start up without a user name or password.

Below the three buttons is an option to change the password for that highlighted user. The Look At Properties button provides two additional tabs: General (information about the user) and Group Memberships. The Group Memberships tab provides choices for the level of access that user will be granted.

PROTOCOL.INI

We've discussed the SYSEDIT.EXE system files editor, saying that this was a utility program used in Windows 3.x and Windows 9x to call up the essential INI files. We've also referenced the startup configuration tab in the Systems Tools accessories. One of the lesser known .INI files called up in the system editor for Windows for Workgroups 3.11 and Windows 9x is PROTOCOL.INI, the Real Mode networking configuration file.

Information stored in this file is overwritten by information stored in the Registry, so although you can edit the PROTOCOL.INI file from SYSEDIT, the information won't necessarily stay there. Information in the files is created through the setup INF files for any installed networking components. The best way to edit this file is through the Network icon in the Windows 9x Control Panel, used in conjunction with the setup software for the network hardware.

PROTOCOL.INI contains information about the I/O address, DMA access, IRQs, and separate sections for each network adapter and network protocol. If a network card develops a memory access conflict with a video controller, using a combination of error messages and the protocol information may sometimes help you to adjust one of the conflicting devices.

Viruses

A computer virus is a set of instructions (a program) that tells the PC to execute a series of actions without the owner's consent or knowledge. A virus can operate only by running the instructions held within a program. Even the modern macro and scripting viruses are a series of instructions. The difference between a program virus and a macro virus is that a macro virus uses an application—such as Microsoft Word, Microsoft Excel, or Netscape—rather than the operating system as the command interpreter.

Note: Some versions of Windows and DOS offered the Microsoft Anti-Virus (MSAV) utilities as a primitive defense against viruses. Third-party virus protection programs are far better choices because they constantly upgrade their virus databases. Often, these third-party virus-fixing updates can be downloaded from an Internet site. McAfee and Symantec's Norton AntiVirus are two popular virus-fighting tools.

A virus program usually waits for an event to take place, then executes its instructions. That event might be a specific date and time on the system clock, or a set of keystrokes. A virus also works by attaching itself to a particular program. When the program is run, the virus executes. Each virus program has its own program code, called a *signature*.

Note: Many email messages are clogging the Internet, warning of deadly email viruses. Opening and reading a text email message provides no opportunity to execute a binary program. Only the attachments that come with email messages are potential virus carriers.

Types of Viruses

A virus is classified according to how the virus is transmitted and how it infects the computer. No matter which kind of virus is involved, it can't be spread by coughing on a machine or by placing a PC too close to another PC (or a VCR). Another common myth (with no basis in reality) is that viruses can enter a PC through some sort of sub-band channel of a modem connection.

The main categories of viruses are as follows:

➤ *Boot sector*—Overwrites the disk's original boot sector with its own code. Every time the PC boots up, the virus is executed.

➤ *Master boot sector*—Overwrites the master boot sector's partition table on the hard disk. These viruses are difficult to detect because many disk examination tools don't allow you to see the partition sector (head 0, track 0, sector 0) of a hard disk.

➤ *Macro viruses*—Written in the macro language of applications, such as a word processor or spreadsheet. Macro viruses infect files (not the boot sector or partition table) and can reside in memory when the specific application's document is accessed. Usually, the virus is triggered by an autorun feature in the application that runs a macro, much like an AUTOEXEC.BAT file. Otherwise, the virus runs by user actions, such as certain keystrokes or menu choices.

➤ *Scripted viruses*—Uses JavaScript, ActiveX controls, or other such scripting languages to introduce instructions to the machine through the operating system. Scripted viruses use Internet functionality as the command processor and can be written as plain text commands that will run from email messages, graphics files, or any other area where the virus programmer hides them.

Macro viruses can be stored in files with any extension. Most modern applications can recognize their own files by information stored in the header of the file. A Microsoft Word document might have the default .DOC extension or an .XYZ extension. Regardless of the extension, it's still a Word document and is capable of running macros. Macro viruses are spread through file transfers and email. However, they can be executed only by the program that interprets the macro commands. Once again, until email programs include some sort of macro capability, plain email messages can't contain viruses.

How Viruses Work

Viruses of different types work in different ways. Some viruses keep the same code and attach to programs or load into memory. Newer viruses are aware of antivirus programs, so they make an effort to change their code while continuing to do their damage.

Functional characteristics of viruses include the following:

➤ *Memory-resident viruses*—Load themselves in memory, take control of the operating system, and attach themselves to executable files (e.g., EXE, COM, and SYS). These viruses often change the file attribute information and the file size, time, and date information.

Note: Viruses can't attach to BAT files because these files are text-based lists of commands. A virus may, however, be attached to a program file called by a batch file.

➤ *Nonresident file viruses*—Infect other programs when an infected program is run. They don't remain in memory, so they don't infect the system. These viruses often change the file attribute information and the file size, time, and date information. Like memory-resident viruses, nonresident viruses attach themselves to executable files.

➤ *Multipartite viruses*—Combine the characteristics of memory-resident, non-resident file, and boot sector viruses.

Remember that COMMAND.COM is a program. If a virus attaches itself to the main command interpreter, executing any of the DOS internal commands (e.g., **DIR**, **DEL**, or **MD)** will cause the virus to execute. Inserting a disk infected with a boot sector virus in drive A: and running a simple **DIR** command often causes the virus to be copied to the hard drive's boot sector.

➤ *Polymorphic viruses*—Modify their appearance and change their *signatures* (their program code) periodically (for example, by changing the order of program execution). This allows the virus to escape signature-scanning detection methods.

➤ *Stealth viruses*—Hide their presence. All viruses try to conceal themselves in some way, but stealth viruses make a greater effort to do so. This type of virus can infect a program by adding bytes to the infected file. It then subtracts the same number of bytes from the directory entry of the infected file, making it appear as if no change has taken place.

It seems that the exam capitalizes on the bizarre and complex names and acronyms used in the PC world. If you know only that polymorphic and multipartite are weird names that you don't hear much at all, you'll have a tool for deciphering any questions that throw these terms at you. Keep in mind that the most deadly viruses tend to affect the boot sector, Master Boot Record, and partition table.

Two common types of stealth viruses are the Trojan and the Worm virus. A Trojan is a destructive program disguised as a game or other useful program. Users download a program that looks like it will meet some particular need, but when they run it, the virus enters their system. In many cases, the program containing the virus actually does what the victim had hoped it would do. A *Worm*, coming from the Write Once, Read Many (WORM) acronym, propagates across computers by duplicating itself in memory, then duplicating itself again and again. The Worm writes itself to the infected machine one time and then copies itself again and again, eventually filling up an entire disk. Some Worms can even transfer themselves to other machines through links between the two machines' memory.

Practice Questions

Question 1

> Exchanging a portable floppy drive is best done when it is connected to which of the following interface connectors?
>
> ○ a. PS/2
>
> ○ b. DB9
>
> ○ c. USB
>
> ○ d. DB25

Answer c is correct. The question makes no mention of the machine's power status, and exchanging any hardware components is best done either with the power turned off or with a USB device. Answers a and b are incorrect because a floppy drive uses neither a PS/2 mouse connector nor a DB9 serial port. Answer d is incorrect because the DB25 interface connector is almost always used as a printer connection or a SCSI pass-through for removable hard drives, scanners, and so forth.

Question 2

> Which of the following are indications that a virus has possibly infected the computer? [Choose the two best answers]
>
> ❑ a. CMOS memory size mismatch error
>
> ❑ b. CMOS checksum error
>
> ❑ c. Insufficient space on drive D: error
>
> ❑ d. GUI image failure error

Answers b and c are correct. A checksum failure indicates that a file has changed between the time it was read into memory and written back to disk, a common first indicator of a virus. Another common indicator is when files begin to unexpectedly fill up a disk. Answer a is incorrect because this is an indication that physical memory has been changed by the addition or removal of memory modules. The error listed in answer d doesn't exist.

Question 3

> Which menu would you choose in order to connect a user to a different
> printer on a network?
>
> ○ a. Start|Programs|Accessories|System Tools
>
> ○ b. Start|Settings|Accessories|Printers
>
> ○ c. Start|Programs|Settings|Control Panel
>
> ○ d. Start|Settings|Control Panel

Answer d is correct. Although the faster way to access this menu would be through
the Start|Settings|Printers option, you can also get to the Printers icon through
the Control Panel under the Start|Settings menu route. Answer a is incorrect
because printers are not configured or added from the System Tools menu. Answer b is incorrect because the Settings menu does not include an Accessories
option. Answer c is incorrect because the Programs menu does not include a
Settings menu.

Question 4

> Of the following options, which would fail to uncover a bindings problem
> with the network card on a local machine? [Choose the two best answers]
>
> ❑ a. Selecting Start|Settings|Control Panel|System
>
> ❑ b. Right-clicking on the Network Neighborhood icon in Windows
>   2000
>
> ❑ c. Double-clicking on the My Computer icon
>
> ❑ d. Selecting Start|Programs|Accessories|System Tools|Connection
>   Manager

Answers b and d are correct. Answer b is correct because Windows 2000 does not
have a Network Neighborhood icon (it uses a My Network Places icon instead).
Answer d is correct because no version of Windows has a Connection Manager
menu option. Answer a is incorrect because the System icon in the Control Panel
provides access to the Device Manager, where you can do some initial detective
work about a network card. Answer c is incorrect because double-clicking on the
My Computer icon is another way to access the Control Panel and network configuration information.

Question 5

An employee has called with a problem where he or she cannot print to the Customer Service line printer. What are actions you would take to see where the problem might lie? [Choose the two best answers]

- ❑ a. Select Start|Settings|Control Panel|Network And Dial-up Connections.
- ❑ b. Click on the Local Area Connection icon.
- ❑ c. Right-click on the NIC LED icon in the System Tray.
- ❑ d. Edit the PROTOCOL.INI file through SYSEDIT.COM.

Answers a and b are correct. The Network And Dial-up Connections option of the Windows 2000 Control Panel offers a connections status report under the Local Area Connection icon. The responses to this question are tricky in that response b is the next step after going to the menu listed in response a. Answer c is incorrect because although the Taskbar may have a Connections icon showing, there is no NIC LED icon, and the System Tray is not used for this purpose. Answer d is incorrect because the PROTOCOL.INI file is a listing of any Real Mode networking hardware configurations and does not show any status problems with network cards.

Question 6

Which of the following utility programs is used to check the structural integrity of the system registration files?

- ○ a. Emergency Recovery Utility
- ○ b. Emergency Registry Recover
- ○ c. Registry Checker
- ○ d. Registry File Monitor

Answer c is correct. The Registry Checker (SCANREGW.EXE) can back up the system registration files and also do a simple structural test of the Registry. Answer a is incorrect because the Emergency Recovery Utility provides only backup and restore capability. Answer b and d are incorrect because the utilities listed in those options don't exist.

Need to Know More?

Aspinwall, Jim. *IRQ, DMA and I/O*. New York, NY: MIS Press, 1995. ISBN 1-55828-456-7. Sooner or later, you are going to get confused about DMAs, IRQs, and I/O addresses. This book will straighten things out.

Bigelow, Stephen. *Troubleshooting and Repairing Computer Printers*. New York, NY: TAB Books, 1996. ISBN 0-07-005732-X. Printers are in a world of their own, and this book presents that world.

Freedman, Alan. *Computer Desktop Encyclopedia, 2nd Edition*. AMACOM, 1999. ISBN 0-814-479-855. This is great for a fast look-up or refresher.

Messmer, Hans-Peter. *The Indispensable PC Hardware Book, 3rd Edition*. Reading, MA: Addison-Wesley Publishing Company, 2000. ISBN 0-201-403-994. This is a comprehensive, up-to-date reference book that covers far more than you will need to know for the exam.

Minasi, Mark. *The Complete PC Upgrade and Maintenance Guide, 11th Edition*. San Francisco, CA: Sybex Network Press, 2000. ISBN 0-782-128-009. This is considered one of the best reference books available. In fact, Minasi's book was instrumental in the formulation of the first A+ exam.

Muller, Scott. *Upgrading and Repairing PCs, 12th Edition*. Indianapolis, IN: Que, 2000. ISBN 0-7897-2303-4. This is one of our favorites. If you are only going to have one reference book, give this one serious consideration.

Reeves, Scott, Kalinda Reeves, Stephen Weese, and Christopher S. Geyer. *A+ Exam Prep, 3rd Edition*. Scottsdale, AZ: The Coriolis Group, 2001. ISBN 1-57610-699-3. This is a good reference that concentrates on providing exam-required information.

Rosch, Winn. *Hardware Bible, 5th Edition*. Indianapolis, IN: Sams Publishing, 1999. ISBN 0-789-717-433. This is a well-organized reference book that covers software issues as well as hardware.

Sample Test

Question 1

Your primary controller is connected to a disk, with one active partition and one extended partition formatted as one logical drive. You connect a second disk drive to the secondary controller and create two partitions. Which drive letter will be assigned to the first of the new partitions?

○ a. C

○ b. D

○ c. E

○ d. F

Question 2

How many devices can be attached to a SCSI chain?

○ a. 5

○ b. 6

○ c. 7

○ d. 8

Question 3

If you use IRQ 2 in an AT system, which IRQ cannot be used?

○ a. IRQ 13

○ b. IRQ 5

○ c. IRQ 9

○ d. IRQ 8

Question 4

You are upgrading Windows 3.1 to Windows 95. What should you do with regard to SMARTDRV?

○ a. Expand its size to speed loading.

○ b. Disable SMARTDRV.

○ c. Change the settings for SMARTDRV to Protected Mode.

○ d. Activate the write-through option for SMARTDRV.

Question 5

A user complains that he has connected his Windows 2000 workstation to the network, but cannot find any other devices on the network. What would be the best thing to do first?

○ a. Remove the NIC and start over.

○ b. Replace the patch cable with a known good cable.

○ c. Check the card link status light.

○ d. Reload the drivers for the NIC.

Question 6

What function key stops the automatic loading of Windows 95 and provides you with a menu of options for loading?

○ a. F1

○ b. F8

○ c. F9

○ d. F3

Question 7

Which of the following would aid system cooling?

- ○ a. Removing the expansion covers in the back of the system case for increased airflow
- ○ b. Attaching covers to any open expansion slots on the back of the system unit
- ○ c. Placing the system unit against a cool inside wall
- ○ d. Opening windows to increase airflow in the room

Question 8

Which is the common default IRQ used for LPT2?

- ○ a. IRQ 5
- ○ b. IRQ 9
- ○ c. IRQ 7
- ○ d. IRQ 14

Question 9

When a piece of paper comes out of a laser printer almost completely black, the primary corona wire has failed to properly charge which of the following things?

- ○ a. The separation pad
- ○ b. The heating roller
- ○ c. The EP drum
- ○ d. The paper

Question 10

A friend has just upgraded her personal computer to Windows 2000 and complains about needing to log on with a user name and password. What could you do to help?

○ a. Nothing. Windows 2000 security requires a user name and password.

○ b. Disable networking if it is a standalone computer.

○ c. Log on as Administrator and uncheck the password requirement Users Must Enter A Username And Password To Use This Computer box in the Users And Passwords dialog box.

○ d. Change the password to blank.

Question 11

A user of a Windows 98 peer-to-peer networked computer has loaded one of his favorite DOS-based programs but cannot print from it to the network printer. What is the most likely reason?

○ a. The DOS print drivers are not loaded.

○ b. DOS program support has not been enabled.

○ c. The printer is not supported in DOS.

○ d. The printer port has not been captured for DOS applications.

Question 12

The thermal fuse fails in a laser printer. What is the most probable cause?

○ a. The fuser overheated.

○ b. The corona wire shorted.

○ c. The drum overcharged.

○ d. The laser diode needs changing.

Question 13

How would you deactivate the infrared port on a laptop computer running Windows 2000?

- ○ a. Go to My Computer|Control Panel|Add/Remove Hardware, select IrDA, and select Remove.
- ○ b. Go to the Device Manager, expand the Infrared Devices node, select IrDA, and select Disable.
- ○ c. The infrared port is a system board component and must be deactivated on the system board.
- ○ d. Infrared ports are autosensing and do not need to be deactivated.

Question 14

The print from a dot matrix printer is erratic, with some characters only partially printed. What needs to be done?

- ○ a. The ribbon needs to be replaced.
- ○ b. The print head needs to be aligned.
- ○ c. A lighter weight paper needs to be used.
- ○ d. The tractor feed needs adjusting.

Question 15

HIMEM.SYS is reported missing or corrupted as Windows 98 loads. What will happen?

- ○ a. Nothing. Windows 98 does not require HIMEM.SYS.
- ○ b. Windows 98 will load in Safe Mode.
- ○ c. Windows 98 will fail to load.
- ○ d. Windows 98 will load, but will have access to only the first 1MB of RAM memory.

Question 16

Windows 98 recognizes a new modem as a standard modem and does not identify the type and manufacturer. Why?

○ a. Windows 98 does not have a driver for this modem.

○ b. The modem is not PnP.

○ c. The SYSTEM.DAT does not have a listing.

○ d. The modem is not seated correctly.

Question 17

Windows Safe Mode loads which of the following display drivers?

○ a. SVGA

○ b. VGA

○ c. EGA

○ d. CGA

Question 18

How would you start a Windows 2000 computer in Safe Mode if no other operating systems were present?

○ a. Press an arrow key immediately following the POST, and select Safe Mode.

○ b. Hold down the Ctrl key during the logon screen.

○ c. Press F6 during the POST.

○ d. Select Start|Run, type "CMD" to enter Command Mode, and then type "Safe".

Question 19

> A consultant recommends you enable RAID Level 4 on your NT server for reliability. How would you do this?
>
> ○ a. Go to the Disk Administrator utility to remove the existing partitions, and then select Tools|RAID|Level 4|Initialize.
>
> ○ b. Delete all partitions using the Recovery Console, and then reinitialize the drives as a RAID array.
>
> ○ c. RAID Level 4 is not supported in NT Server.
>
> ○ d. Enable block striping with parity blocks in the Disk Administrator.

Question 20

> **ATTRIB C:*.SYS /S /-H** will cause which of the following to occur?
>
> ○ a. Archive all SYS files on drive C:.
>
> ○ b. Hide all SYS files in the root directory.
>
> ○ c. Unhide all SYS files in the root directory.
>
> ○ d. Unhide all SYS files on drive C:.

Question 21

> The CONFIG.SYS file contains the line **LASTDRIVE=F**. The system uses a CD-ROM, one primary partition, and three logical DOS drives. A loaded CD-ROM disk will do which of the following?
>
> ○ a. Install a program.
>
> ○ b. Become the G: drive.
>
> ○ c. Become the F: drive.
>
> ○ d. Do nothing at all.

Question 22

To bypass the execution of a line in a configuration file, which two of the following choices are used?

❑ a. **REM**

❑ b. :

❑ c. ;

❑ d. *//*

Question 23

What device would best protect a PC against erratic power and blackouts?

○ a. A line conditioner

○ b. A surge protector

○ c. The UPS

○ d. The ATA

Question 24

Which files are required by Windows 98 to load? [Choose the two best answers]

❑ a. IO.SYS

❑ b. AUTOEXEC.BAT

❑ c. MSDOS.SYS

❑ d. CONFIG.SYS

Question 25

What is the default interrupt and address for COM1?

○ a. IRQ 4 and 27F8h

○ b. IRQ 5 and 03F8h

○ c. IRQ 4 and 03F8h

○ d. IRQ 3 and 02E8h

Question 26

What does the small "h" following an address indicate?

○ a. The address should be read in hexadecimal.

○ b. The address uses a high-order bit.

○ c. The address is a default address.

○ d. The address uses hard coding.

Question 27

Which of the following resolutions apply to a standard VGA monitor? [Choose the two best answers]

❑ a. 640 pixels

❑ b. 480 pixels

❑ c. 600 pixels

❑ d. 800 pixels

Question 28

What is a monitor called when it draws every other line on the screen, then returns and draws skipped lines?

○ a. Interfaced

○ b. Noninterfaced

○ c. Interlaced

○ d. Noninterlaced

Question 29

A cable in a 10BaseT Ethernet network breaks. What is the most likely result?

○ a. The entire network crashes.

○ b. Only the PC attached to that cable loses connectivity.

○ c. The network operating system forces a system shutdown.

○ b. Nothing.

Question 30

What is the default networking protocol used on the Internet?

○ a. IPX/SPX

○ b. DNS

○ c. TCP/IP

○ d. MIME

Question 31

Which of the following types of files are executable? [Choose the three best answers]

❑ a. EXE

❑ b. BAT

❑ c. INI

❑ d. COM

Question 32

How can you verify what services are running under Windows 2000?

○ a. Go to My Computer|Control Panel|Administrative Tools|Computer Management, and select the Services icon.

○ b. Go to My Computer|Control Panel|Administrative Tools|Computer Management, and select the Event Viewer.

○ c. Hold down the Ctrl, Alt, and Del keys, and select Task Manager.

○ d. Go to Start|Settings|Control Panel, and select the System icon.

Question 33

Which command will list all files in the directory where the third character of the extension is the underscore (_)?

○ a. **DIR *._**

○ b. **DIR *.*_**

○ c. **DIR *.?_**

○ d. **DIR *.??_**

Question 34

The Windows REGEDIT.EXE program is used to edit which of the following files? [Choose the two best answers]

❑ a. USER.DAT

❑ b. CLASSES.DAT

❑ c. MSDOS.SYS

❑ d. SYSTEM.DAT

Question 35

Which file is used to control the boot process in Windows NT and Windows 2000?

○ a. NTOSKRNL.EXE

○ b. NTLDR.COM

○ c. SMSS.EXE

○ d. NTBOOTDD.SYS

Question 36

Which of the following cannot be changed by a polymorphic virus?

○ a. The boot sector

○ b. The Master Boot Record

○ c. The master cylinder

○ d. The partition table

Question 37

How many DMA controllers and DMA channels are on an ATX system board?

○ a. 2 controllers and 8 DMA channels

○ b. 1 controller and 16 DMA channels

○ c. 1 controller and 4 DMA channels

○ d. 2 controllers and 16 DMA channels

Question 38

What is the preferred editor for changing the Registry entries in Windows NT and Windows 2000?

○ a. REGEDT32.EXE

○ b. REGEDIT.EXE

○ c. SYSEDIT.EXE

○ d. NTEDIT32.EXE

Question 39

Which commands can be run from the Recovery Console? [Choose the two best answers]

❏ a. **FIXBOOT**

❏ b. **FIXREG**

❏ c. **FIXDSK**

❏ d. **FIXMBR**

Question 40

A user has set a password in CMOS and then forgotten it. What would you do to gain access to the system?

○ a. Use one of the password-breaking programs available on the Internet.

○ b. Remove battery power to CMOS to clear it, reconnect the battery, and then reconfigure the CMOS.

○ c. Go to Start|Settings|Control Panel|Users And Passwords, and check the No Password Required option.

○ d. Run the FIXBIOS.EXE program to reinstall the master password.

Question 41

There is no beep code at system startup. What is the most likely problem?

○ a. The speaker is disconnected.

○ b. There is no beep code for a normal system start.

○ c. The system clock is not working.

○ d. A memory module failed the POST.

Question 42

What is the best cleaning solution to use on a dirty system case?

○ a. Alcohol

○ b. Carbosol

○ c. Mild soap and water

○ d. Diluted muratic acid

Question 43

Which of the following are not used to connect a CPU to a motherboard? [Choose the two best answers]

❑ a. Socket 7

❑ b. Socket B

❑ c. Slot 1

❑ d. Slot 4

Question 44

Which electrical component commonly found in computers can hold an electrical charge even when disconnected from power?

○ a. A resistor

○ b. A capacitor

○ c. A diode

○ d. A transistor

Question 45

A good fuse will give what kind of reading when tested with a standard multimeter?

○ a. High DC volts value

○ b. Low ohm value

○ c. High ohm value

○ d. High capacitance value

Question 46

To reduce possible ESD damage while repairing a PC, what is the most effective way to ground yourself?

○ a. With a copper strap attached to the workbench

○ b. With a copper strap attached to the PC

○ c. By touching the chassis while replacing components

○ d. None of the above

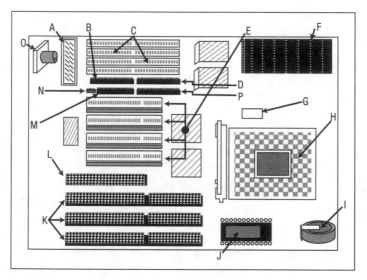

Exhibit 15.1 Use this motherboard diagram to answer questions 47 through 51.

Question 47

What are the two items that the letters "D" and "P" point to?

○ a. IDE controllers

○ b. ISA bus slots

○ c. L-2 cache chips

○ d. SIMM banks

Question 48

What is the item that the letter "H" points to?

○ a. Modem

○ b. Battery

○ c. CPU

○ d. Parallel interface

Question 49

What are the three items the letter "K" points to?

○ a. PCI slots

○ b. 8-bit ISA slots

○ c. Memory banks

○ d. 16-bit ISA slots

Question 50

What is the letter "C" labeling?

○ a. PCI bus

○ b. SIMM slots

○ c. ZIF socket

○ d. BIOS chip

Question 51

What does the letter "A" point to?

○ a. AT keyboard connector

○ b. Orientation chip

○ c. Power connector

○ d. LPT connector

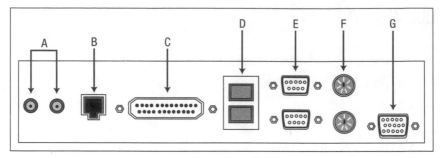

Exhibit 15.2 Use this chassis back panel diagram to answer questions 52 through 54.

Question 52

A parallel printer cable connects to which item (designated by a letter)?

○ a. C

○ b. D

○ c. E

○ d. F

Question 53

What items does the letter "E" point to?

○ a. Video interface connectors

○ b. USB interface connectors

○ c. Serial interface connectors

○ d. PS/2 interface connectors

Question 54

A USB port is shown in the diagram by which letter?

○ a. B

○ b. C

○ c. D

○ d. E

Question 55

How would you change the drive letter assigned to the CD-ROM in a Windows 2000 system?

○ a. Change the load order in the SYSTEM.INI file so that the proper drive letter is assigned.

○ b. Change the drive assignment in CMOS.

○ c. Use REGEDIT.EXE to open the Registry. Highlight the HKEY_LOCAL_MACHINE, and select the CD-ROM subkey.

○ d. Select the CD-ROM drive properties on the Device Manager|Settings tab. Set the Start Drive Letter and End Drive Letter.

Question 56

A user wants to change his default printer on an NT workstation. How would you do this?

○ a. Go to Start|Programs|Accessories|Printer Tools, and select the Print First checkbox.

○ b. Select the properties for the printer that the user wants in the Printer window, and choose Set As Default.

○ c. Configure the existing default printer as Secondary, and set the desired printer as Primary.

○ d. Provide the desired printer with a lower IP address.

Question 57

What is the best and simplest solution for resolving Ethernet congestion?

○ a. Add another hub to the network.

○ b. Segment the network with a router.

○ c. Segment the network with a bridge.

○ d. Set up a secondary IP network token.

Question 58

What are the first two files called when Windows NT and 2000 begin to boot?

❑ a. NTSYS.DLL

❑ b. NTOSKRNL.EXE

❑ c. WINNT.SYS

❑ d. NTDETECT.COM

Question 59

When a PC is powered on, the POST routine completes with one beep. What does this mean?

○ a. The system is testing the PC speaker.

○ b. The system has a nonsystem disk in drive A:.

○ c. The system has completed the POST with no errors.

○ d. The system CMOS has a bad battery.

Question 60

Windows 98 can use all of the following files during boot-up, except which one?

○ a. WIN.COM

○ b. MSDOS.SYS

○ c. PROGMAN.INI

○ d. LOGO.SYS

Question 61

When you save a file to a disk, where is the information about which sectors and clusters the file is using placed?

○ a. PAT

○ b. FAT

○ c. MBR

○ d. HPFS

Question 62

The Windows ME default installation process removes which file reference from a CONFIG.SYS file?

○ a. EMM386.EXE

○ b. MSCDEX.SYS

○ c. SMARTDRV.EXE

○ d. MSDOS.SYS

Question 63

Which device can be connected to the computer and recognized while the computer is running?

○ a. A keyboard

○ b. A monitor

○ c. A serial joystick

○ d. A USB mouse

Question 64

Which type of connectors do the AMD Athlon and Duron processors use? [Choose the two best answers]

❑ a. Socket 1

❑ b. Slot A

❑ c. Socket 370

❑ d. Socket A

Question 65

IRQ 14 is the default IRQ assigned to which of the following?

○ a. Secondary disk controller

○ b. Primary disk controller

○ c. Master slave disk controller

○ d. XT drive controller

Question 66

A cable has a 25-pin male connector at one end and a Centronics 36-pin male connector at the other end. A common use for this cable is best described by which of the following choices?

- ○ a. A parallel printer connection
- ○ b. A modem connection
- ○ c. A serial printer connection
- ○ d. A SCSI device connection

Question 67

Which of the following keys are displayed by the **REGEDIT** command? [Choose the three best answers]

- ❑ a. HKEY_USERS
- ❑ b. HKEY_CLASSES_ROOT
- ❑ c. HKEY_LOCAL_SECURITY
- ❑ d. HKEY_CURRENT_CONFIG

Question 68

The number 5 in the 10Base5 standard refers to which of the following?

- ○ a. The maximum length of the cable in hundreds of meters
- ○ b. The width of the cable in centimeters
- ○ c. The width of the center conductor in millimeters
- ○ d. The maximum number of connections per meter

Question 69

A user is assigned proper user permissions in Windows 2000 but still cannot access a shared resource. Why?

○ a. The user is a member of a group that does not have access to the resource.

○ b. User permissions are not activated.

○ c. The resource is already in use.

○ d. The resource ACL has not been set to Active.

Question 70

Which of the following connectors are not used in a typical networking situation? [Choose the two best answers]

❑ a. Mini DIN

❑ b. RJ-11

❑ c. RJ-45

❑ d. DB15

Answer Key

1. c	19. c	37. a	55. d
2. c	20. d	38. a	56. b
3. c	21. d	39. a, d	57. c
4. b	22. a, c	40. b	58. b, d
5. c	23. c	41. a	59. c
6. b	24. a, c	42. c	60. c
7. b	25. c	43. b, d	61. b
8. a	26. a	44. b	62. a
9. c	27. a, b	45. b	63. d
10. c	28. c	46. d	64. b, d
11. d	29. b	47. a	65. b
12. a	30. c	48. c	66. a
13. b	31. a, b, d	49. d	67. a, b, d
14. a	32. a	50. b	68. a
15. c	33. d	51. c	69. a
16. a	34. a, d	52. a	70. b, d
17. b	35. b	53. c	
18. a	36. c	54. c	

Question 1

Answer c is correct. Drives A: and B: are automatically installed on a PC. The primary controller has one fixed disk with drive C: as the active partition and drive D: as the extended partition. The second disk will start with the letter E, regardless of how many logical drives are installed on that disk. The one active partition is bootable because it is active. For that reason, it becomes drive C:. The one extended partition is formatted as one logical drive; therefore, the entire extended partition on the first disk is a logical drive D:. The C and D letters are being used, so any new disk (or change in the extended partition) will begin with E, the next available letter. In this scenario, **LASTDRIVE=** does not need to be changed because the system recognizes five drive letters by default.

Question 2

Answer c is correct. This is a tricky question because the question specifically uses the word "devices." The automatic host adapter for a SCSI card takes up one of eight possible ID numbers. That leaves room for up to seven devices to be daisy-chained to the SCSI controller, each with a unique ID number. Answers a and b are technically correct, but the implication of the question itself is that you're being tested on the limits of a SCSI chain. For that reason, answers a and b are incorrect in this context. Answer d is incorrect because the host adapter takes up the eighth ID number.

Question 3

Answer c is correct. The AT BIOS cascades IRQ 9 to IRQ 2. If the system is using IRQ 2, then it must also be using IRQ 9, and you cannot use IRQ 9 for anything else. IRQ 13 is a red herring; it is typically set aside for a math coprocessor. IRQ 5 is the default line assigned to LPT2, and IRQ 8 is the default line set aside for the system clock.

Question 4

Answer b is correct. Windows 95 doesn't use SMARTDRV. If you don't remove or comment out the SMARTDRV line from your CONFIG.SYS file, SETUP.EXE does it for you. Answer a is incorrect because you can't expand the SMARTDRV program; you can increase only the size of the cache. Answer c is incorrect because whether SMARTDRV runs in Real Mode or Protected Mode is irrelevant to an upgrade installation. The installation process will halt and ask you to disable the program. Answer d is incorrect because SMARTDRV has no "write-through" option.

Question 5

Answer c is correct. A link status light on the NIC would indicate that the physical connection to the network is okay and that the card is functioning. Absence of a link status light could point to a physical problem with the card or cable, or a missing driver. Answer a is incorrect because without a network interface card, the user will never connect to a network. Although physically reinstalling the card might be useful, this is not what you would do first, given that response c offers you the link status LED. Answer b is incorrect because although the next step in the process would be to replace the patch cord, the question asks "What would be the best thing to do *first*?". Answer d is incorrect because reloading drivers is a much more complex process than simply checking the link status light.

Question 6

Answer b is correct. The F8 key, pressed between the time the "Starting Windows 95…" message and the Microsoft Windows 95 logo appear, interrupts the load process and produces the text-based Start menu. Pressing the F1 key, the F9 key, or the F3 key at this point will do nothing to interrupt the startup process. Although you can still use the F8 key in Windows 98, the way to arrive at Safe Mode is to hold down the Ctrl key while Windows 98 is starting.

Question 7

Answer b is correct. The expansion slot covers are part of the engineering design to allow for optimal airflow within the case of any PC that uses expansion slots and covers. Answer a is incorrect because removing unused slot covers causes cooling air to flow out of the case and generally increases the temperature inside the case. Answers c and d might provide minimal aid in cooling the overall environment, but they are incorrect in the context of the "system cooling" referred to in the question.

Question 8

Answer a is correct. LPT2 uses IRQ 5. Answer b is incorrect because IRQ 9 is generally redirected to IRQ 2. Answer c is incorrect because LPT1 is assigned to IRQ 7 by default. Answer d is incorrect because IRQ 14 is normally assigned to the primary disk controller. (See the "IRQs, DMA, and I/O Ports" section of Chapter 5 for a complete listing of the default IRQ assignments.)

Question 9

Answer c is correct. The primary corona wire is used to place a negative charge on the electrophotographic (EP) drum. This removes toner from those areas that will not produce an image. The secondary corona wire places a charge on the paper to attract toner to the correct locations. If the paper fails to charge, no toner will stick to the paper for fusing. If the drum fails to charge correctly, the entire drum will take on toner and transfer it to the whole piece of paper. The separation pad, answer a, prevents more than one sheet of paper from entering the printer at any given time. Answer b is incorrect because the fusing assembly contains the heating roller and is used to fuse the image toner particles to the paper. Answer d is incorrect because if the paper is completely black, something failed to move an image to the paper. The transfer corona wire, not the primary corona wire, charges the paper.

Question 10

Answer c is correct. Windows 2000 provides a checkbox in the Users And Passwords dialog box so that the user name and password function can be bypassed in standalone situations where security is not an issue. Answer a is incorrect because although Windows 2000 is designed as a network operating system, it does not *require* a user name and password. Answer b is incorrect because Windows 2000 passwords are a separate issue from networking capabilities. Disabling networking does nothing to resolve the password problem. Answer d is incorrect because configuring a blank password will not remove the initial logon dialog box, which is the original complaint.

Question 11

Answer d is correct. Windows 98 asks if the printer will be used for DOS applications during setup. If you respond yes, all of the settings are made automatically. However, if the printer was not configured for DOS initially, you must go back to the Printer|Properties|Detail dialog box and select Capture Printer Port to enable DOS printing. Answer a is incorrect because although applications use printer drivers and DOS has a printer device driver, nothing uses "print drivers." Answer b is incorrect because the program is apparently working and the complaint is only that the user cannot print. Answer c is incorrect because it is Windows printer support that is the issue, not DOS printer support. The program is running in a virtual DOS machine and Windows 98 is controlling the surrounding peripherals, including the printer.

Question 12

Answer a is correct. The fuser step of the printing process involves high amounts of heat to melt the toner and to fuse it to the paper. For safety, a thermal fuse is inserted in the circuit to prevent possible fire hazards. Answer b is incorrect because a short circuit at the corona wire would shut down the printer or cause a fire. The corona wire does not have a thermal fuse. Answer c is incorrect because the EP drum does not use heat, and answer d is incorrect because the laser printer contains no such thing as a laser diode.

Question 13

Answer b is correct. Selecting a device from the Device Manager display and choosing Disable will deactivate the device driver instructions for any device showing in the listing. The question refers to deactivating a device, not removing a device. Answer a is incorrect because the device should be deactivated, not removed. (If it is removed, the system will try to add it back again when the system next starts.) Answer c is incorrect because activation and deactivation are almost always Windows choices, not system board events. Answer d is incorrect because although autodetection is a feature in Windows, autosensing is not.

Question 14

Answer a is correct. The clue is that some characters are only partially printing. The immediate diagnostic test would be to replace the existing ink ribbon. Print head alignment is not a common cause of partial character printing. The weight of the paper has no direct connection to the print quality. The tractor feed could cause misalignment of characters, but would be unlikely to cause partial printing.

Question 15

Answer c is correct. Windows 98 requires HIMEM.SYS and a minimum of 4MB of extended memory. HIMEM.SYS is a memory manager that allows access to all memory above the first 1MB of conventional memory. If HIMEM.SYS is missing or fails, Windows cannot access anything more than 1MB of memory and will fail to load. Answer b is incorrect because in order to reach Safe Mode, Windows must have been able to access extended memory in the first place. Answers a and d are incorrect because Windows cannot load at all without HIMEM.SYS.

Question 16

Answer a is correct. If Windows 9x can access the device and understand that the device is a modem, it attempts to find an internal device driver for the specific modem. Windows will use PnP BIOS to read the manufacturer's name and the model of the modem, if available. However, whether or not the device is PnP, Windows understands it is a modem. If an internal device driver is not named, Windows assigns a generic device driver and calls it a standard modem. After the name and settings are assigned, they are written to the SYSTEM.DAT file. Answer b is incorrect because although the modem is not PnP, Windows still recognizes it enough to assign resources and a device name. Answers c and d are incorrect because the device must be listed and correctly seated if it shows up in the Device Manager.

Question 17

Answer b is correct. The Windows Safe Mode installs a keyboard driver and a standard VGA display driver, and bypasses network connections without loading network drivers. Safe Mode is a diagnostic mode designed to reduce configuration problems to their absolute minimum. EGA and CGA graphics modes are obsolete standards, so answers c and d are incorrect. Answer a is incorrect because SVGA graphic mode has numerous configuration options, making it an inappropriate mode for troubleshooting possible display problems.

Question 18

Answer a is correct. If the Windows 2000 computer is not set up for dual booting, pressing any of the arrow keys after POST will bring you to a menu where you can select Safe Mode booting. Answer b is incorrect because Safe Mode does not initialize network connections, and a logon screen is part of networking. Answer c is incorrect because you do not have access to the keyboard during the POST. Answer d is incorrect because neither DOS nor Windows has a **SAFE** command.

Question 19

Answer c is correct. A Windows NT file server must be running the Windows NT Server version of the operating system, which supports RAID Levels 0, 1, and 5. Level 4 is not supported in Windows NT Server. Answer a is an option made up entirely of nonexistent terms and features. Answer b is incorrect because Recovery Console is a Windows 2000 feature. Answer d is incorrect because although disk mirroring and striping is done through the Disk Administrator, the system will still be unable to support RAID Level 4.

Question 20

Answer d is correct. The /S switch tells **ATTRIB** to operate on all subdirectories. The C:*.SYS tells **ATTRIB** to operate on all SYS files on drive C:, beginning at the root directory. The -H switch tells **ATTRIB** to turn the hidden attribute off or to unhide the file. Answer a is incorrect because the archive attribute is set with the /+A switch. Answer b is incorrect because the /-H switch uses the minus sign, not the plus sign (hide). Answer c is incorrect because the /S switch extends the reach of the command beyond the root directory.

Question 21

Answer d is correct. If no CONFIG.SYS file existed, or if an existing file did not contain a **LASTDRIVE=** statement, DOS would be able to read only the default maximum of five drives. In this question, CONFIG.SYS exists and contains a **LASTDRIVE=F** statement telling DOS to recognize a maximum of six drives. The system has the default drive A: and drive B:; a drive C: primary partition; and drives D:, E:, and F: as three additional logical DOS drives. The CD-ROM would become the seventh drive with drive G: assigned to it by default. To make seven drives visible, the **LASTDRIVE=F** statement would have to be modified to **LASTDRIVE=G**. Unless the modification were made, an additional CD-ROM drive would fail to be recognized, and none of the events in answers a, b, and c would take place.

Question 22

Answers a and c are correct. **REM** (an abbreviation of remark) is used in DOS to bypass a line (comment out or remark out) in batch files and configuration files. Windows uses the semicolon (;) to bypass lines in an INI file. Answer b is incorrect because the colon is used to signify drive letters. Answer d is incorrect because paired forward slashes are commonly used as a directory statement in networking operating systems.

Question 23

Answer c is correct. An uninterruptible power supply (UPS) contains a battery backup to provide power to the PC during power interruptions and blackouts.

The UPS also provides line conditioning, meaning that erratic power events are stabilized before reaching the computer. Answer a is incorrect because a line conditioner will protect against erratic power, but not blackouts. Answer b is incorrect because a surge protector provides no protection from a blackout. The ATA referenced in answer d is the AT Attachment bus specification associated with an IDE controller, and it has nothing to do with protecting a computer.

Question 24

Answers a and c are correct. Only IO.SYS and MSDOS.SYS are required by Windows 98. CONFIG.SYS and AUTOEXEC.BAT can be used to install Real Mode device drivers and applications, but the two files are not required to load any version of Windows.

Question 25

Answer c is correct. COM1 uses IRQ 4 and address 03F8h for the default installation. (COM1 is odd and uses even IRQs.) Answers a and b are not COM addresses. Answer d is the default address for COM4. COM ports 1 and 3 use IRQ 4, whereas COM ports 2 and 4 use IRQ 3.

Question 26

Answer a is correct. A common indicator that a number or address is a hexadecimal unit is either a lowercase or an uppercase h before or after the unit.

Question 27

Answers a and b are correct. A standard VGA monitor has a resolution of 640×480. Although an SVGA monitor can be configured to a 640×480 resolution, 600×800 is a more common configuration. (As a reminder, *pixels (picture units)* is a designation for graphic resolution in displayed images such as monitors or graphics. *Dots per inch (dpi)* is a designation for printed or scanned resolutions.)

Question 28

Answer c is correct. Monitors are either interlaced or noninterlaced, not interfaced or noninterfaced. When the electron gun at the back of a CRT monitor draws every odd line then returns and draws every even line, it is interlaced (like lacing up shoes). If the electron gun draws every line in a single pass (not skipping lines), the monitor is a noninterlaced monitor.

Question 29

Answer b is correct. 10BaseT is a twisted-pair wiring configuration. Twisted pair allows each PC to connect to a hub directly. If the wire breaks, only the specific PC connected by that wire will be affected. The overall network connection is designed in such a way that each PC has its own connection, and the wiring integrity is not dependent on a functional connection between all the PCs.

Question 30

Answer c is correct. The Internet is a Unix-based network using Transmission Control Protocol/Internet Protocol (TCP/IP) networking protocols. Internet Packet Exchange/Sequenced Packet Exchange (IPX/SPX) is typically used in a local area network (LAN) running NetWare. DNS is a service that converts host names to IP addresses. Multipurpose Internet Mail Extensions (MIME) is an email protocol.

Question 31

Answers a, b, and d are correct. Files with a suffix (extension) of .BAT, .EXE, and .COM are all considered executable. Although Windows considers PIF files to be executable, files ending in .INI are Windows configuration files and cannot be executed (run) from a command line.

Question 32

Answer a is correct. Windows 2000 provides many services that help other programs run. The status of these services is listed under the Services icon in Computer Management. The action in answer b would be used to view each event associated with a specific situation taking place on the computer to find out why something failed to work properly. The action in answer c would be used to find out what programs were currently in memory. Answer d is incorrect because the System icon is used to check the devices installed on the system and to check the percentage of Windows resources remaining.

Question 33

Answer d is correct. The ? wild card is used to represent a single, unknown character. The question indicates a three-character extension, so **DIR** *.??_ is correct. **DIR** *._ will find all files with only the underscore character following the period.

DIR *.*_ will find any file with any extension. DIR *.?_ will find any file with a two-character extension ending with an underscore.

Question 34

Answers a and d are correct. The REGEDIT.EXE program is used to edit the USER.DAT and SYSTEM.DAT files making up the Windows 9x Registry. Answer b is incorrect because although CLASSES.DAT may be a file that exists somewhere, it is not one related to the Registry. Answer c is incorrect because MSDOS.SYS is a text-based system file and can be edited with any text editor.

Question 35

Answer b is correct. The Window NT Loader file (NTLDR.COM) controls the boot process for Windows NT and Windows 2000. NT Loader then loads NTOSKRNL.EXE, the operating system kernel. SMSS.EXE is the Windows NT or Windows 2000 Session Manager. NTBOOTDD.SYS is a special file used to make NT bootable from a removable hard drive.

Question 36

Answer c is correct. A polymorphic virus or any other type of virus cannot make changes to the master cylinder, because a cylinder is a single track located in the same place on every platter making up a hard drive. A virus is a set of program instructions and, as such, can make programming changes anywhere on a system where other program or instruction data can be stored. The boot sector, Master Boot Record, and partition table all contain data. Although a cylinder is made up of tracks and each track contains sectors and clusters, a virus program (in this context) can affect only one of those sectors or clusters, not the whole cylinder.

Question 37

Answer a is correct. XT motherboards contained one DMA controller with four channels. The AT system board added a second controller and four more channels, making a total of two DMA controllers with eight channels (four channels per controller). The ATX (as well as the LPX and NLX) form factor is an outgrowth of the AT motherboard, continuing the use of two controllers and eight channels.

Question 38

Answer a is correct. REGEDT32.EXE is the 32-bit version of REGEDIT.EXE and is the preferred editor for Windows 2000 and Windows NT. REGEDIT.EXE was the Registry Editor included in Windows 9x, and was originally designed to edit the Windows 3.x REG.DAT file. SYSEDIT.EXE is a utility program that opens the main DOS configuration files and Windows INI files. Answer d refers to some fictitious file, unrelated to the Windows Registry.

Question 39

Answers a and d are correct. The Windows 2000 Recovery Console allows the **FIXBOOT** and **FIXMBR** commands, along with a number of other DOS-like commands. The fictitious red herrings referred to in answers b and c do not exist in the Recovery Console.

Question 40

Answer b is correct. The CMOS chip cannot be accessed by any program that requires an operating system to be loaded, because operating systems work only after a PC has been configured. As such, answers a, c, and d are incorrect because they all refer to a program or a program option. There is no generic, master password for CMOS, and the password is contained within the chip itself. The only way to clear the password is to clear the CMOS by removing all power to the chip.

Question 41

Answer a is correct. Beep codes are always generated by the POST. Regardless of the number of beeps generated, there will always be at least one. If no beeps are heard, the most likely problem is that the speaker is disconnected or broken.

Question 42

Answer c is correct. Mild soapy water is noncorrosive and provides the best cleaning solution for plastic, vinyl, or metal cases. Alcohol is used mainly where no residue should be left, such as certain internal metal or plastic parts. Carbosol is a fictional term, and muratic acid (diluted or otherwise) is a form of hydrochloric acid used to clean concrete.

Question 43

Answers b and d are correct. Note that this is a tricky question because it asks you to choose what does *not* do something. If you aren't paying attention you can easily choose the wrong answers based on what you know *will* work. Neither Socket B nor Slot 4 is associated with microprocessors and their packaging, making them the correct choices for this question. Socket 7 is a flat design used to install a CPU on the motherboard. Slot 1 is a vertical design, using a small circuit board with a single edge connector and a special processor slot on the motherboard.

Question 44

Answer b is correct. Capacitors store electricity for later release. Resistors, diodes, and transistors are other electronic components often found on a motherboard, but all three of these components require a constant flow of electricity in order to function.

Question 45

Answer b is correct. A fuse is a breakable part of a circuit line. Ohms are used to measure resistance. If the circuit enters a condition beyond a specified tolerance, the fuse breaks, and the circuit line is interrupted. If the fuse is unbroken, it appears as a normal part of the circuit line and has no more resistance than any other part of the circuit line. A high ohm value would mean there is a great deal of resistance in the circuit coming from somewhere else on the circuit. A low ohm reading at the fuse would indicate that current is flowing through the fuse with no interruption, and that the fuse is good.

Question 46

Answer d is correct. Ground straps must have a resistor placed in the line to avoid electrocuting the technician in the event of a short. All the other answers offer ways to ground yourself, but none of the options offers protection against an electrostatic discharge. The question asks for the most effective way to reduce ESD damage, and none of the listed options interferes with an electrical discharge.

Question 47

Answer a is correct. A good approach to this question is to first eliminate what you know to be incorrect answers. ISA bus slots are usually long and divided, and are typically located near the edge of a motherboard, as in the case of K. Level 2 (L-2) processor cache chips are located very close to the CPU and are very small, as in the case of G. SIMM banks are typically the same size, much smaller than ISA slots, and narrower than PCI slots, as in the case of C. When you've eliminated most of the expansion slots, the remaining connectors in the area close to D and P are probably interface controllers. IDE controllers are usually paired, one above the other (not side by side).

Question 48

Answer c is correct. Typically, the CPU is the largest chip on a motherboard and, up through the Pentium Pro, is usually large and square. An internal modem is a separate expansion card and not part of the motherboard. The CMOS battery, offered as answer b, is almost always round or cylindrical and either clips or is soldered onto the motherboard. H points to something square. Parallel port interfaces are small, narrow connectors, longer than floppy controllers but smaller than memory banks. Most modern PCs have only one parallel interface.

Question 49

Answer d is correct. Although the diagram does not show 16 connector points, the general shape of an expansion slot is fairly accurate. 16-bit slots are longer than 8-bit slots, and ISA slots (if they exist) usually were offered as three 16-bit connectors and one 8-bit connector. The 8-bit ISA slot is pointed to by L and the three 16-bit slots are pointed to by K. Four PCI slots are pointed to by E; PCI slots tend to be in the middle of the motherboard. The memory banks are pointed to by C.

Question 50

Answer b is correct. The SIMM (or DIMM) memory banks are usually closer to the outer edge of the motherboard, narrow, and observably smaller than ISA and PCI slots. The letter E points to a PCI bus, which is often closer to the center of a motherboard. A Zero Insertion Force (ZIF) socket is a CPU socket and will always have some kind of handle (like a paper cutter) connected to the socket. This handle is pictured on the left side of the square CPU socket pointed to by H. The BIOS chip, pointed to by J, is usually preinstalled on a motherboard and is smaller than the CPU socket. This motherboard is using socket technology, as opposed to slot technology, to mount the CPU.

Question 51

Answer c is correct. The main power supply almost always connects to the computer near the edge of the motherboard with a large pin-connector. The AT keyboard connector (not interface) must be at the edge of the motherboard in order for the keyboard to plug into it. "Orientation chip" is a fictitious term, and "LPT" is a DOS device name, not a connector. When differentiating between answers a and c, remember that the keyboard connector should look round and small, but the power supply connector should look large and rectangular and be a one-of-a-kind connector.

Question 52

Answer a is correct. Most modern PCs have only one printer port, and that connector is a DB25 female connector. When there are two serial ports, one is almost always a 9-pin connector and the other a DB25 male connector. This panel shows only one 25-pin connector, so C is pointing to the parallel port. D points to the USB connectors, E points to a pair of 9-pin serial ports, and F points to a pair of 6-pin PS/2 connectors.

Question 53

Answer c is correct. The video connector is a 15-pin connector, and you can count on the fact that there will be only one video connector on an exam exhibit. If you know that the parallel port is a DB25 connector, and if you remember that PS/2 connectors are round, the choices reduce to either answer b or answer c. USB connectors are square and about the size of a PS/2 connector. E is pointing to a 9-pin cable connector, making it a serial port interface.

Question 54

Answer c is correct. USB ports are square and typically come as a vertical pair, as pointed to by D. Network connectors (if they're built in) are almost always RJ-45 connectors with the recognizable clip-slot at the bottom (like a modular phone jack). B points to a network connector. C is the parallel port, and E is a 9-pin serial port.

Question 55

Answer d is correct. Drive letters are assigned by the operating system during the boot process. Answer b is incorrect because CMOS controls only the order in which the system will look at drives. Windows 2000 provides a way to reassign drive letters from within the operating system by selecting the device (in this case, a CD-ROM drive) in the Device Manager and then choosing the appropriate start and end drive letters. Answer a is incorrect because SYSTEM.INI has no control over assigning drive letters. Answer c is incorrect because the Registry contains configuration settings for the hardware device, not drive letter assignments.

Question 56

Answer b is correct. Setting the default printer for a Windows NT workstation is done in the same way as in Windows 2000 and Windows 9x. Right-click on the printer in the Printers folder, and select Set As Default. Answer a presents a fictitious menu path, and there is no Print First checkbox in Windows. Answer c is incorrect because changing a printer involves making a printer the default, not the primary or secondary printer. Answer d is incorrect because although a network printer may have an IP address, the relative priority of a network resource has nothing at all to do with the many-digit IP address number, and the IP address has no bearing on whether a printer is the default printer.

Question 57

Answer c is correct. A bridge was specifically designed to reduce network traffic congestion by segmenting an existing network. Routers move traffic between networks, and hubs provide a way to add additional resources to a network (increasing possible congestion). Answer d, "Set up a secondary IP network token," is purely fictitious. A token, in a token ring network, uses an Internet Protocol (IP) address to correctly transfer data packets.

Question 58

Answers b and d are correct. NTDETECT.COM identifies hardware for the hardware abstraction level (HAL), and NTOSKRNL.EXE loads the core operating system. The files referred to in answers a and c may exist somewhere, but they have nothing to do with loading Windows NT or Windows 2000 (or any other version of Windows, for that matter).

Question 59

Answer c is correct. If a POST routine completes with one beep, it means that the system has completed the POST with no errors. There is no provision on a computer to self-test the PC speaker (how would the computer hear it?). Answer b is incorrect because it refers to a CMOS error generated by a disk in the floppy disk drive. Answer d is incorrect because the POST is a low-level hardware validation routine, and beep codes tell you only if the fundamental connections have been made with the basic system components. A bad CMOS battery may cause the loss of all configuration settings, but it has nothing to do with the POST.

Question 60

Answer c is correct. Windows 3.x used the Program Manager as its primary shell interface. Program Groups and Program Items were maintained partly through the PROGMAN.INI file. Although an upgrade installation from a Windows 3.x machine can make a one-time conversion of the GRP files referenced in the PROGMAN.INI file, the question asks about files Windows uses for booting. WIN.COM is the small loader program used to start Windows. MSDOS.SYS is one of the DOS system files, used to boot the operating system. LOGO.SYS is the graphic file that produces the Windows splash screen.

Question 61

Answer b is correct. The FAT is the file allocation table used for storing addresses of file clusters on a disk. The partition allocation table (PAT) stores information about the location of each partition on a disk and is not used for file storage information. The Master Boot Record (MBR) is used to store information pointing the system toward the location of an operating system. The High Performance File System (HPFS) is a file management system used by OS/2.

Question 62

Answer a is correct. EMM386.EXE is an expanded memory manager, and Windows 95, 98, and ME do not use an expanded memory manager. Following Windows 3.x, all versions of Windows require the HIMEM.SYS extended memory manager, and they will load the file from either a CONFIG.SYS file or from MSDOS.SYS. Windows ME will automatically place a **REM** and a space before any line in a CONFIG.SYS file containing EMM386.EXE and SMARTDRV.EXE references. Smart Drive is a DOS file caching program, and it is not used by Windows ME. MSDOS.SYS is a system file, and no references to it are ever used in CONFIG.SYS. MSCDEX.SYS is the generic Microsoft CD-ROM drive device driver and may be a required reference in a CONFIG.SYS file on machines where the BIOS cannot recognize a drive.

Question 63

Answer d is correct. USB devices are designed to be safely attached or detached from a running computer (hot swapping) and, at the same time, recognized by the operating system. Monitors, serial devices, and keyboards are checked at the POST and can actually damage the system board if disconnected or connected during operation.

Question 64

Answers b and d are correct. Athlon and Duron processors were produced in both the Slot A and Socket A configuration. They are not pin compatible with Intel-designed Slot 1, Slot 2, Socket 7, Socket 8, or Socket 370 architectures. There may have been a Socket 1 at some point in time, but if there was, it has long since disappeared. Athlon and Duron processors are modern processors.

Question 65

Answer b is correct. IRQ 14 is assigned to the primary disk controller. IRQ 15 is assigned to the secondary disk controller. There is no such thing as the master slave disk controller. IRQ 2 was originally assigned to the XT drive controller, but now contains cascaded instructions from IRQ 9.

Question 66

Answer a is correct. The clues here are both the 25-pin male connector and the Centronics connector. Because there can be serial cables with DB25 female con-nectors, the Centronics connector indicates that in this case, the question is re-ferring to a parallel printer cable. If the cable had a DB25 female connector on one end and a 9-pin serial connector at the other, it could be a modem connec-tion. The 36-pin male Centronics specifies that this is not a serial printer con-nection, and the DB25 connector specifies that it is not a SCSI cable. SCSI cables often use 50-pin ribbon cables.

Question 67

Answers a, b, and d are correct. HKEY_USERS, HKEY_CLASSES_ROOT, and HKEY_CURRENT_CONFIG are three of the six keys displayed in **REGEDIT**. There is no HKEY_LOCAL_SECURITY key.

Question 68

Answer a is correct. Originally, the last digit in network wiring referred to the maximum length of a cable in hundreds of meters. 10Base5 refers to a cable with a maximum length of 500 meters. 10Base2 is a thinner cable, with a maximum length of 200 meters. When 10BaseT wiring was introduced, the last character changed to reflect the type of wiring. T refers to twisted pair.

Question 69

Answer a is correct. Even though a user may be given individual rights, restrictions on a group that the user belongs to will supersede the assigned rights if they conflict. User permissions are not a feature that needs to be activated or deactivated, and neither does the resource ACL have such a feature. Networks provide shared access to resources, making answer c incorrect. The user may have to wait until the resource is free, but in this context, the question refers to permissions and rights, not queues and hardware problems.

Question 70

Answers b and d are correct. Mini DINs are used in Apple Computer networks and RJ-45, or, more properly, "modular data connectors," are extensively used in 10BaseT networks. RJ-11 is a modular telephone connector, and DB15s are often used for monitors.

Acronym Glossary

AC (alternating current)
Changes from a positive voltage to a negative voltage during one cycle. The most common example is household electricity, which is 110 volts at 60 hertz in the United States.

ADC (Analog-to-Digital Converter)
An electronic device, usually packaged in a chip, that converts analog signals, such as speech, to a digital bit stream.

AGP (Accelerated Graphics Port)
Provides the video controller card with a dedicated path to the CPU. Found on newer PCs.

AM (Amplitude Modulation)
A type of radio transmission.

AMD (Advanced Micro Devices)
A corporation specializing in micro-processor chip manufacturing.

ANSI (American National Standards Institute)
One of several organizations that develop standards for the information technology industry.

AOL (America Online)
An international private networking system that provides online services to paying subscribers.

API (application program interface)
Provides a set of uniform building blocks that many programmers can use when building an application. (See MAPI.)

ASCII (American Standard Code for Information Interchange)
Specifies a 7-bit pattern used for communication between computers and peripherals.

ASPI (Advanced SCSI Programming Interface)
A protocol for a program or device to interface with the SCSI bus. (See SCSI.)

AT (advanced technology)
IBM's name for its 80286 PC form factor, which it introduced in 1984.

AT&T (American Telephone and Telegraph)

One of the world's largest communications providers, which was originally Bell Telephone Co. (1878).

ATA (advanced technology attachment)

The ANSI standard for Integrated Drive Electronics (IDE) drives.

ATAPI (ATA Packet Interface)

A specification for attaching additional drives to an ATA connector. The ANSI standard for Enhanced IDE (EIDE) drives.

ATX (Advanced Technology eXtensions)

A system board form factor that incorporates an Accelerated Graphics Port (AGP). It is designed for the Pentium II and is mounted vertically.

Basic (Beginner's All-Purpose Symbolic Instruction Code)

A popular programming language developed in the 1960s at Dartmouth College.

BBS (bulletin board service)

Online access locations where users post information and where other users can read or download information.

BDOS (basic disk operating system)

One of the original system files in Control Program for Microcomputers (CP/M). The other is BIOS (which is not the same thing as the ROM BIOS chip on a motherboard).

BIOS (basic input/output system)

A set of detailed instructions for PC startup that usually are stored in ROM on the system board.

BNC (bayonet nut connector)

A type of connecting hardware used with network cables and interface cards.

CAD (computer-aided design)

Drawing programs used in engineering and architectural settings.

CAV (Constant Angular Velocity)

One of the ways in which an optical disk maintains a correct speed by using a small data buffer.

CCD (charge-coupled device)

A semiconductor that is sensitive to light and is used for imaging in scanners, video cameras, and digital still cameras.

CCP (console command processor)

The original command interpreter used in Control Program for Microcomputers (CP/M).

CD (compact disk)

A plastic disk measuring 4.75 inches in diameter that is capable of storing a large amount of digital information.

CDC (Control Data Corporation)

One of the original developers of the Integrated Drive Electronics (IDE) specification.

CD-RW (compact disk, read-write)

A compact disk that can be written to and read from. Technically, the RW does not stand for rewritable.

CGA (Color Graphics Adapter)

An IBM video standard that provides low-resolution text and graphics.

CGI (Common Gateway Interface)

An Internet scripting language.

CLV (Constant Linear Velocity)

One of the ways in which an optical disk maintains a correct speed by adjusting spindle motor speed.

CMA (common monochrome adapter)
IBM's original PC monitor, also known as monochrome display adapter (MDA).

CMOS (complementary metal oxide semiconductor)
The type of chip commonly used to store the BIOS for a PC. It is usually backed up with a small battery for times when the PC power is off.

CMY (cyan, magenta, and yellow)
The three primary colors of reflective light used in paint, ink, and other indirect sources of color. CMY is used in LCD color monitors.

COBOL (Common Business Oriented Language)
A high-level programming language commonly used on mainframe and minicomputers.

CompTIA (Computing Technology Industry Association)
A nonprofit organization made up of more than 6,000 member companies that developed the A+ certification program.

CP/M (Control Program for Microcomputers)
The first operating system developed for microcomputers.

CPU (central processing unit)
The main chip where instructions are executed.

CRC (cyclic redundancy check)
A method used to verify data.

CRT (cathode ray tube)
The picture tube of a monitor.

CSMA/CD (Carrier Sense Multiple Access/Collision Detection)
An access method used in Ethernet networks.

DAC (Digital-to-Analog Converter)
An electronic device that converts digital signals to analog.

DASD (direct access storage device)
The technical name given by the IBM PC Institute for a disk drive subsystem.

DAT (digital audio tape)
Used in small cassettes for storing backup information. (Also used to refer to a directory allocation table.)

DC (direct current)
Electricity that flows in only one direction. The power supply in a PC converts alternating current from the wall socket to direct current at voltages needed by PC components.

DDE (Dynamic Data Exchange)
A message protocol within Windows that allows applications to exchange data automatically.

DDR (double data rate)
Usually associated with DDR SDRAM (Synchronous DRAM).

DEC (Digital Equipment Corporation)
One of the original corporations involved with the development of PCs.

DHTML (dynamic Hypertext Markup Language)
Like HTML except that information can be changed, based upon data gathered at a Web site. For example, user location can be captured to change the contents of a Web page.

DIMM (dual inline memory module)
A popular form factor for random access memory (RAM) in which each side of the edge connector has separate connections.

DIN (Deutsche Institut für Normung)
The German Standards Institute, which developed standards for many of the connectors used in PCs.

DIP (dual inline package)
A common rectangular chip housing with leads on both of its long sides.

DMA (direct memory access)
Specialized circuitry, often including a dedicated microprocessor, that allows data transfer between memory locations without using the CPU.

DMF (Distributed Media Format)
Microsoft's proprietary 1.7MB formatting method for distribution disks.

DNS (Domain Name System)
A DNS server works to convert readable host names to numeric IP addresses.

DOS (disk operating system)
The most widely used single-user operating system in the world.

dpi (dots per inch)
Written in lowercase. A measure of resolution mostly applied to printers and scanners.

DRAM (dynamic random access memory)
The most common type of computer memory.

DS (double-sided)
Description of a storage method used with disks. (See HD.)

DS/DL (double-sided, double layer)
A storage format for DVDs.

DS/SL (double-sided, single layer)
A storage format for DVDs.

DSL (digital subscriber line)
A high-speed Internet connection system.

DVD (digital versatile disk)
An optical storage disk much like a compact disk (CD) using a different method for storing. DVDs have storage capacities approaching 10GB.

DVD-R (digital versatile disk-recordable)
An optical storage disk that can be written to by the consumer.

EB (exabyte)
1,024 petabytes or 1 million terabytes.

ECC (error correction code)
This code tests for memory errors, which it corrects on the fly.

ECP (electronic control package)
The circuitry used by a laser printer to communicate with its CPU and control panel. (Not to be confused with the Extended Capabilities Port for parallel interfaces.)

ECP (Extended Capabilities Port, or IEEE 1284)
The standard for enhanced parallel ports that are compatible with the Centronics parallel port.

EDO (Extended Data Output)
A type of memory that approaches the speed of Synchronous RAM (SRAM) by overlapping internal operations.

EEMS (Enhanced Expanded Memory Specification)

An enhancement of the Expanded Memory Specification. EEMS was developed by AST, Inc. together with Ashton-Tate Corporation.

EEPROM (electrically erasable programmable read-only memory)

Holds data without power. It can be erased and overwritten from within the computer or externally with an electrical charge.

EGA (Enhanced Graphics Adapter)

A medium-resolution IBM text and graphics standard. It was superseded by today's VGA standard.

EIDE (Enhanced Integrated Drive Electronics)

An extension of the IDE interface that is compatible with more devices and offers increased transfer rates.

EISA (Extended Industry Standard Architecture)

Expands the 16-bit ISA bus to 32 bits and provides bus mastering.

ELD (electroluminescent display)

A type of video display used in notebook computers.

EMI (electromagnetic interference)

An adverse effect caused by electromagnetic waves emanating from an electrical device.

EMS (Expanded Memory Specification)

The expanded memory specification developed by Lotus, Intel, and Microsoft prior to the development of extended memory (XMS).

EP (electrophotographic)

The EP drum in a laser printer that is sensitive to light.

EPP (Enhanced Parallel Port, or IEEE 1284)

A high-speed ECP capable of bidirectional speeds approaching 2MB per second.

EPROM (erasable programmable read-only memory)

A type of ROM that can be erased and reprogrammed.

ESD (electrostatic discharge)

Electrical current moving from an electrically charged object to an approaching conductive object.

ESDI (Enhanced Small Device Interface)

An interface specification for hard drive controllers. (See IDE.)

FAT (file allocation table)

The part of DOS that keeps track of where data is stored on a disk.

FC-PGA (flip chip pin grid array)

A configuration of CPU connector pins where the chip is turned upside down.

FCB (file control block)

Used in the CP/M file management system.

FDDI (Fiber Distributed Data Interface)

Used in fiber optics for transmission of large bursts of high-speed data.

FH (Firmware Hub)

(See GMCH.)

FIFO (first in, first out)

Applied to buffering, usually in a modem buffer.

FM (frequency modulation)

A type of radio transmission.

FORTRAN (*for*mula *trans*lator)
Designed by John Backus for IBM in the late 1950s. FORTRAN is the oldest high-level programming language.

FPM (Fast Page Mode)
A type of RAM using addressing pages.

FPU (floating-point unit)
Commonly called a math coprocessor. It was available as an optional chip for Intel CPUs up to and including the 80386. The unit was internally integrated in the 80486 and Pentium processors.

FTM (flat technology monitor)
A monitor with a flat face in front (not the same as a flat panel display used in notebooks).

GB (gigabyte)
1,024 megabytes or 1 million kilobytes.

GIF (graphics interchange format)
A file format for bitmap graphics made popular by CompuServe (online service). Often used in Web page designs.

GMCH (Graphics and Memory Controller Hub)
Part of the 800 series chip set hub architecture, along with the I/O Controller Hub (IOCH) and the Firmware Hub (FH).

GUI (graphical user interface)
Implemented with Windows. It incorporates icons, pull-down menus, and the use of a mouse.

HAL (hardware abstraction layer)
One of the foundation layers of Windows NT and Windows 2000.

HAZMAT (Hazardous Material)
Chemical compounds that can cause public health dangers. (See MSD.)

HD (high density)
Description of data density on a floppy disk (e.g., DS, HD).

HDTV (high-definition television)
A standard for displaying high-resolution television images.

HMA (High Memory Area)
Area of the memory map above the 640KB conventional mark and below the 1,024KB threshold.

HPFS (High Performance File System)
The preferred file management system for OS/2.

HTML (Hypertext Markup Language)
A standard for defining and linking documents on the World Wide Web.

Hz (hertz)
A unit measuring cycles per second. (MHz is millions (mega) of cycles per second.)

IBM (International Business Machines)
The corporation that developed the first personal computer (PC).

IC (integrated circuit)
An arrangement of circuit traces and electronic components often placed on a so-called integrated circuit card or board.

IDE (Integrated Drive Electronics)
A popular hardware interface used to connect hard drives to a PC.

IEEE (Institute of Electrical and Electronic Engineers)
An organization with an overall membership of more than 300,000

members that is highly involved in setting standards.

IFS (Installable File System)
Windows file management component. (IFS can also mean the Image Formation System in a laser printer.)

InterNIC (Internet Network Information Center)
A committee funded by the National Science Foundation to provide specifications for the Internet.

I/O (input/output)
An acronym used to reference any place where data is moving into or out of something.

IOCH (I/O Controller Hub)
(See GMCH.)

IP (Internet Protocol)
An IP address is a series of numbers and periods, and the address is used by many networks. The protocol is the set of rules for that addressing.

IR (infrared)
A frequency of electromagnetic energy in the light spectrum.

IRQ (interrupt request)
A hardware interrupt generated by a device that requires service from the CPU. The request is transmitted through one of 8 to 16 physical lines on the system board, with one device typically allowed per line.

ISA (Industry Standard Architecture)
An expansion bus commonly used on PCs. It provides a data path of 8 to 16 bits and is sometimes referred to as an AT bus because of its use in the first IBM AT computers.

ISDN (Integrated Services Digital Network)
A specification for digital transmission of data over analog phone lines.

ISO (International Organization for Standardization)
An umbrella group for many of the international standards committees, such as ANSI.

ISP (Internet service provider)
Usually a business involved in providing Internet connections and Web hosting.

JPEG (Joint Photographic Experts Group)
A compression format used for graphic image files, resulting in a common .JPG extension.

KB (kilobyte)
1,024 bytes.

LAN (local area network)
Standard acronym for most networks. (See WAN.)

LBA (logical block addressing)
Used to overcome early BIOS and IDE controller limitations in recognizing hard drives larger than 512MB.

LCD (liquid crystal display)
A type of computer display panel using liquid crystals to pass or block light.

LDAP (Lightweight Directory Access Protocol)
A query language used by Windows NT and Windows 2000 to manage access requests.

LED (light-emitting diode)
A small electrical device that generates light when current passes through it.

LIM (Lotus/Intel/Microsoft)
Three companies that jointly developed a standard for memory management greater than 640KB.

LPX (Low Profile Extensions)
An AT system board form factor used in small desktop cases.

LSA (Local Security Authority)
A module in Windows NT and Windows 2000 acting as the interface between User Mode and Kernel Mode.

MAPI (Messaging Application Programming Interface)
Built into Windows as a way for different email programs to work together.

MB (megabyte)
1,024 kilobytes or 1 million bytes.

MB/s (megabytes per second)
A data transfer rate of 1 million bytes per second.

Mbps (megabits per second)
A data transfer rate of 1 million bits per second.

MBR (Master Boot Record)
The first sector on a bootable partition.

MCA (Micro Channel Architecture)
A 32-bit expansion bus developed by IBM. The bus requires specially designed cards that are not interchangeable with other popular bus designs.

MDA (monochrome display adapter)
The first IBM standard for monochrome video displays for text.

MDRAM (Multibank dynamic random access memory)
A type of video RAM that uses many 32KB dynamic RAM (DRAM) chips to form an interleaved array of graphics memory banks.

MICR (Magnetic Ink Character Recognition)
Used in some scanners to capture magnetic pattern information.

MIME (Multipurpose Internet Mail Extensions)
A specification used to translate binary files to the text-based email messaging protocol used by the Internet.

MIPS (million instructions per second)
A unit of measure to gauge the speed of a CPU.

MMDS (Multi-channel Multipoint Distribution System)
A form of broadband Internet connection using line-of-sight transmission towers.

MMU (memory management unit)
A component of a microprocessor (CPU).

MMX (MultiMedia eXtensions)
An expanded CPU instruction set optimized for multimedia applications.

Modem (MOdulator-DEModulator)
A device for sending data over telephone lines.

MPEG (Motion Picture Experts Group)
Pronounced m-peg. A type of video compression.

MSCDEX (Microsoft CD-ROM Extensions)
The MSCDEX.EXE generic software driver for CD-ROM drives.

MSD Sheet (Material Safety Data)
Usually written as MSDS. A required description of each and every hazardous material used in a business

location. (Not to be confused with MSD.EXE, the Microsoft Diagnostics program utility.)

NCSC (National Computer Security Council)

A government agency that defines levels of security for computer systems. Windows NT is C-2 compliant.

NIC (network interface card)

Provides the physical connection of a PC to the cable of a local area network.

NLX (InteLex form factor)

A trademark of the InteLex Corporation. The NLX was a form factor designed to follow the LPX motherboard form factor. NLX is a standard supported by Intel and IBM.

NOS (network operating system)

An operating system used to connect many computers together.

NRZI (Non-Return-to-Zero-Inverted)

A signaling process using voltage changes to generate binary numbers in a USB cable.

NT (New Technology)

Windows NT is a multitasking operating system that became Windows 2000.

NTFS (New Technology File System)

The preferred file system used by Windows NT.

NTSC (National Television Standards Committee)

The committee responsible for setting video standards in the United States. NTSC signals are composite signals used with television and VCRs and are different than RGB signals on a computer monitor.

OEM (original equipment manufacturer)

An OEM version of Windows means that it was created specially for the original maker of the computer, to be sold by that vendor as part of a package.

OS/2 (Operating System 2, second generation)

IBM's single-user, multitasking operating system for PCs.

OSI (Open Systems Interconnection)

The OSI model describes the way various parts of a network communicate with each other.

PAL (Phase Alternating Line)

The predominant television specification used in Europe.

PARC (Palo Alto Research Center)

The Xerox development center where laser printers, the mouse, and the GUI were developed.

PAT (partition allocation table)

The first sector on a fixed disk, containing partition information for that disk.

PB (petabyte)

1,024 terabytes, 1 million gigabytes, or 1 billion megabytes. 2 petabytes would hold the contents of all U.S. academic research libraries.

PCB (printed circuit board)

A board where electrical paths are etched on the board as opposed to connected with wires.

PCI (Peripheral Component Interconnect)

A popular expansion bus that provides a high-speed data path between the CPU and peripherals.

PCL (Printer Control Language)
Formatting commands used by a
printer during the print process.

PCMCIA (Personal Computer Memory Card Industry Association)
A nonprofit industry association that
standardized the 16-bit socket,
allowing portable computers to use
credit card–sized expansion cards.

PDP (Plasma Display Panel)
A type of video display sometimes used
in notebook computers (also referred
to as a gas plasma panel).

PGA (pin grid array)
An arrangement of connection pins on
a microprocessor. When the pins are in
a set of staggered rows, they are called a
staggered pin grid array (SPGA).

PIC (program interrupt controller)
An improvement added to the second
series Pentium chips.

PIF (Program Information File)
A proprietary format file used by
Windows to store configuration
settings for a Real Mode virtual
machine session.

PnP (Plug and Play)
An Intel standard that allows components to be automatically configured
when added to a PC. The standard
requires support from the BIOS, the
expansion card, and the operating
system.

POSIX (Portable Operating System Interface for Unix)
An operating system used in many
government offices.

POST (power-on self test)
A series of built-in tests that are
performed at system startup.

PROM (programmable read-only memory)
This ROM requires a special machine
to write instructions to a chip one time
only, and the chip cannot be changed.
(See EPROM.)

QDOS (quick and dirty operating system)
The original version of the disk
operating system (DOS).

QIC (quarter-inch cartridge)
A format used in tape backup
machines.

RADAR (Radio Detecting/Detection and Ranging)
Radio waves generated by a source to
bounce back from an object for the
purpose of revealing the object's shape.

RAID (Redundant Array of Inexpensive Disks)
Used in networking as a form of data
protection. There are six levels of
RAID (0 through 5).

RAM (random access memory)
The computer's main workspace. Data
stored in RAM can be accessed
directly without having to read
information stored before or after the
desired data.

RAMDAC (Random Access Memory Digital-to-Analog Converter)
A component used with graphics cards
and video subsystems to convert binary
information to analog images.

RDRAM (Rambus dynamic random access memory)
A special type of DRAM memory chip
developed by the Rambus corporation.

Rexx (Restructured Extended Executor)
A batch language developed for OS/2, with many more powerful commands than those in DOS.

RGB (red, green, and blue)
The three primary colors of light used in color monitors.

RIMM (Rambus inline memory module)
A memory module composed of Rambus memory chips on a printed circuit board.

RLE (run-length encoding)
A compression format used for graphic image files, commonly used to compress Windows logo files. These files have an .RLE extension.

ROM (read-only memory)
A memory chip that permanently stores instructions and data.

rpm (revolutions per minute)
The speed at which a disk revolves around a spindle.

SAA (System Application Architecture)
A user interface standard developed by IBM.

SAM (Security Accounts Manager)
A security module in Windows NT and Windows 2000.

SASI (Shugart Associates Systems Interface)
Developed by Alan Shugart as part of the original floppy disk drive system.

SAT (security access token)
A token created for each user on a Windows NT or Windows 2000 network. The SAT carries identification information across the network.

SCSI (Small Computer System Interface)
A hardware interface that allows the connection of up to seven devices.

SDRAM (Synchronous dynamic random access memory)
SDRAM is a DRAM chip with an internal synchronizing clock designed to reduce interrupt requests to the CPU.

SEC (Single Edge Connector)
A chip packaging design where chips (often memory chips) are placed on a printed circuit board with a single, edge connector.

SECAM (SEquential Couleur Avec Memoire)
A French video standard adopted by the Eastern bloc countries of the former Soviet Union.

SEP (Single Edge Processor)
A type of packaging for a microprocessor with a Single Edge Connector.

SGRAM (Synchronous Graphic Random Access Memory)
A type of video memory that uses an internal clock to synchronize graphics memory to the motherboard clock.

SID (security identifier)
The security ID is part of the security access token in Windows NT and Windows 2000.

SIMM (single inline memory module)
A narrow printed circuit board that holds memory chips. The connector is integrated into the edge of the board so that it can easily be added to sockets on the system board. This module uses dynamic RAM (DRAM) chips on one side of the board.

SMI (System Management Interrupts)
Used for power conservation and management.

SONAR (Sound Navigation and Ranging)
Sound signals generated by a source to bounce back from an object for the purpose of revealing the object's shape.

SONET (Synchronous Optical NETwork)
A protocol used for fiber optics cable data transfers.

SPGA (staggered pin grid array)
Microprocessor connection pin configuration. (See PGA.)

SPI (SCSI Parallel Interface)
Pronounced "spy." A subdivision of the SCSI-3 specification.

SPP (Standard Parallel Port)
The original parallel port controller. Assigned the LPT or PRN device abbreviation name.

SQL (Structured Query Language)
A query language used to request information from a database.

SRAM (Synchronous random access memory)
A memory chip with an internal clock that synchronizes the memory to the motherboard clock. Requires power to hold content, but does not need refreshing like other types of RAM. Because of this, it is very fast. (Sometimes referred to as Synchronous RAM.)

SS (single-sided)
Description of a storage method used with floppy disks. (See DS.)

SS/DL (single-sided, double layer)
A storage format for DVDs.

SS/SL (single-sided, single layer)
A storage format for DVDs.

SSFDC (Solid State Floppy Disk Card)
The original name for the SmartMedia flash memory card.

ST (Seagate Technology, Inc.)
The ST-506/412 interface was the accepted standard for all PC hard disks and stood as the basis for the ESDI and IDE hard drive controller interfaces.

STP (Shielded Twisted Pair)
A type of shielded twisted-pair wire used in networking and telephony.

SVGA (Super Video Graphics Array)
The SVGA video standard provides a higher resolution than VGA, providing 16 million colors and resolutions up to 1600×1200 pixels.

TB (terabytes)
1,024 gigabytes, 1 million megabytes, or 1 billion kilobytes. 10 terabytes would hold a printout of the entire U.S. Library of Congress. Estimates indicate that the human mind can hold approximately 15 terabytes of information.

TCP/IP (Transmission Control Protocol/ Internet Protocol)
Formerly named Transmission Control *Program*, the Transmission Control Protocol coordinates packet information for the many IP packets and addresses in an online transmission.

TIFF (tagged image file format)
A compression format used for bitmap image files, resulting in a .TIF extension that can be read by both PCs and Macintosh systems.

TSR (terminate and stay resident program)

A type of program that stays in memory (resident) even when it has stopped running (terminate). A TSR can be called up using a hot key and runs in its own DOS window.

UART (Universal Asynchronous Receiver Transmitter)

A semiconductor device that transmits and receives data through the serial port.

UDMA (Ultra DMA)

The way direct memory access (DMA) was sped up in the Ultra ATA specification. Also called UDMA/33. (See ATA.)

ULSI (Ultra Large-Scale Integration)

A type of manufacturing for microprocessor chips.

UMB (upper memory blocks)

An area of the first megabyte of memory.

UPS (uninterruptible power supply)

Provides backup power when the main power fails or moves to an unacceptable level.

URL (Uniform Resource Locator)

An Internet address, typically presented as a domain name.

USB (Universal Serial Bus)

A new standard that allows 127 devices to be daisy-chained to a cable running at 1.5MB per second.

UTP (Unshielded Twisted Pair)

A type of twisted-pair wire used in networking where there is no special shielding against electromagnetic interference.

UV (ultraviolet)

A frequency of light in the long wave spectrum.

VCR (video cassette recorder)

A device used to record NTSC signals from television inputs.

VDT (Video Display Terminal)

Any video device used to display video information.

VESA (Video Electronics Standard Association)

An organization composed of PC vendors that is dedicated to improving video and multimedia standards.

VFAT (Virtual file allocation table)

A 32-bit file system used in Windows for Workgroups and Windows 95. The VFAT is faster than the DOS FAT and provides for Long File Names.

VGA (Video Graphics Array)

The IBM video standard that has become the minimum standard for PC displays. It provides 16 colors at 640×480 resolution.

VHD (Very High Density)

Found in SCSI connectors, it provides high data transfer rates.

VID (voltage identification)

The voltage ID pins that work with a voltage regulator module (VRM) to control voltages on a microprocessor.

VL-Bus (VESA Local-Bus)

A type of VESA bus interface.

VLSI (very large-scale integration)

A type of manufacturing for microprocessor chips.

VM (virtual machine)
Windows uses software to create a representation or emulation of a Real Mode 8086 PC.

VMM (Virtual Memory Manager)
Responsible for managing the swap file that is used to increase the amount of available memory a system can use. This is done by creating 4KB pages in the swap file that it can use to swap out addresses in RAM to disk, so that there is more available RAM for currently running instructions/applications.

VMM (Virtual Machine Manager)
The Windows software that manages the Real Mode virtual machines (VMs).

VRAM (video random access memory)
Differs from common RAM in that it uses two ports (dual-ported) to simultaneously refresh the video screen and to receive data for the next screen.

VRM (voltage regulator module)
An electronic component that can provide varying levels of voltage to another component.

VxD (virtual device driver)
Runs in the most privileged CPU mode and allows low-level interaction with hardware and internal Windows functions.

WAN (wide area network)
Typically used for very large networks, often where multiple geographic locations are included. (See LAN.)

Web (World Wide Web)
A subdivision of the Internet that uses HTML formatting.

WORM (Write Once, Read Many)
Usually a compact disk that can be written to one time and then read from many times. WORM is sometimes associated with a worm virus.

WRAM (windows random access memory)
Windows RAM bears no relation to Microsoft Windows and is a type of dual-ported video memory with large block addressing.

WYSIWYG (What You See Is What You Get)
Refers to the ability to display text and graphics on a monitor using the same fonts and size relationships that will be printed in the final document.

XGA (eXtended Graphics Array)
The first IBM video adapter to use video random access memory (VRAM).

XMS (Extended Memory Specification)
Any physical memory beyond the first 1MB of conventional memory.

XT (eXtended Technology)
The first IBM PC with a hard drive. It used the same 8088 processor and 8-bit expansion bus as the original PC.

ZIF (Zero Insertion Force)
A socket that uses a lever to grasp the pins of a chip after it is inserted. This eliminated bent pins and became very popular for mounting CPUs.

Index